# ACCOUNTING FOR RISK, HEDGING, AND COMPLEX CONTRACTS

With the exponential growth in financial derivatives, accounting standards setters have had to keep pace and devise new ways of accounting for transactions involving these instruments, especially hedging activities. This book addresses the essential elements of these developments. The early chapters provide a basic foundation by discussing the concepts of risk, risk types and measurement, and risk management. This is followed by an introduction to the nature and valuation of free standing options, swaps, forward and futures as well as of embedded derivatives. Discussion and illustrations of the cash flow hedge and fair value hedge accounting treatments are offered in both single-currency and multiple-currency environments, including hedging net investment in foreign operations. A final chapter is devoted to the disclosure of financial instruments and hedging activities. The combination of these topics makes the book an essential, self-contained source for upper level students looking to develop an understanding of accounting for today's financial realities.

**A. Rashad Abdel-khalik** is a Professor of Accountancy and Director at the V.K. Zimmerman Center for International Education and Research in Accounting.

# ACCOUNTING FOR RISK, HEDGING, AND COMPLEX CONTRACTS

A. Rashad Abdel-khalik



Routledge
Taylor & Francis Group
NEW YORK AND LONDON

First published 2014
by Routledge
711 Third Avenue, New York, NY 10017

Simultaneously published in the UK
by Routledge
2 Park Square, Milton Park, Abingdon, Oxon OX14 4RN

*Routledge is an imprint of the Taylor & Francis Group, an informa business*



Typeset in Stone Serif by Swales & Willis, Exeter, Devon
Printed and bound



Library of Congress Cataloging in Publication Data

ISBN 13: 978–0–415–80893–4 (hbk)
ISBN 13: 978–0–203–13753–6 (ebk)





SFI Certified Sourcing
www.sfiprogram.org
SFI-00453

Printed and Bound in the United States of America by Edwards Brothers Malloy, Inc.

To the memories of my parents, Mohamed and Gamilah, and
E. J. Demaris, Nicholas Dopuch and Leon E. Hay, American educators
who had significant influence on my life

# BRIEF CONTENTS

# DETAILED CONTENTS

# LIST OF ILLUSTRATIONS

## Exhibits

## Figures

## Tables

# PREFACE

Those of you who have read the standard on financial instruments and understood it have not read it properly.

Sir David Tweedy, Former Chairman, International Accounting Standards Board

I think that given you are breaking new ground; you are putting forward thoughts and ideas for debate.

Anonymous

Derivatives and hedging represent one of the more complex and nuanced topical areas within both US GAAP and IFRS.

*IFRS and US GAAP: similarities and differences*. PwC October 2011

Starting in the early 1990s, concern about matters related to the economics of information, risk and uncertainty in financial reporting has overtaken almost all the efforts devoted to financial reporting and the standard setting process. Awareness of these issues is not new, however. Informed accountants and interested financial analysts have known all along that every number on the balance sheet is an estimate from a distribution of values and no single number can adequately describe an asset or a liability. The unprecedented development of complex financial instruments, financial derivatives and complex contracts since early 2000 has brought this awareness to the forefront. The resulting equally complex accounting rules have undoubtedly created a final resting place for any view of accounting as a cut and dried subject matter.

Viewing the development in accounting, it is fair to note that accounting standards and thought have come of age; analysis of contracts and exposure to risk has led to establishing a new accounting model. After decades of debate and argumentation, accounting standard setters and academics have come to agree that (a) reporting current values would be informative and that (b) the elements of compound contracts should be sorted out and accounted for in accordance with their economic substance.

This shift in focus and analysis is not the result of a master plan. It is, rather, an outcome of intensive engagement by standard setters in responding to significant shifts in the sectors that run the economic engine in our society; it is the financial sector accompanied by the astronomical growth in the volume and transactions involving financial derivative instruments. Typically, the historical cost of these derivatives is negligible, if any at all, but they create rights and obligations as the conditions underlying their formation change. In this setting, only current value could describe the rights and obligations of counterparties to a contract. These instruments have been growing at an exponential rate since December 21, 2000 when Congress and the Clinton administration pre-empted the States' anti-bucket shop laws[1] following the 1999 repeal of critical terms of the 1933 Glass-Steagall Act, thereby allowing commercial banks to also undertake investment banking.[2] Both actions have handed banks and financial institutions a significant unguarded free playing field. According to a survey by the International Swap Dealers Association (ISDA), the volume (notional amounts) of trade in over-the-counter financial derivatives in 2011 has exceeded $540 trillion and, according to the Bank for International Settlements, *the notional (face) amount of over-the-counter financial derivatives has grown from about $20 trillion in 2000 to over $638.9 trillion at the end of June 2012.*[3] Unfortunately for the public and public interest, all of these trades are carried out in "dark" markets—no transparency of any kind and it has never been made clear how markets could operate efficiently without information! What does this mean for accountants? It signifies the absence of observable prices creating the need to develop knowledge and expertise on how to estimate the fair values of these derivatives for the purposes of preparing and auditing financial reports.[4] Additionally, the structure of the contracts of these derivatives and their wide-spread use created the need to develop a special set of accounting rules that are both new and alien—this is the new accounting.

During the same period of time, claims were made regarding the flight of capital out of the U.S. financial markets to the London Stock Exchange which reportedly had less arduous listing and reporting requirements than the exchanges in the USA. Adding these developments to the high rate of growth in global commerce has led both the U.S. Financial Accounting Standards Board (FASB) and the International Accounting Standards Board (IASB) to recognize the necessity of cooperation and collaboration for the development and convergence of accounting standards. The efforts on both sides have led to very similar structures and content of Generally Accepted Accounting Principles (GAAP) of the USA and international GAAP (IFRS for International Financial Reporting Standards) with respect to accounting for financial instruments and hedging. Furthermore, contrary to folk tales, both systems are detailed, complex and approach accounting to contracts and transactions in an equally convoluted manner. Indeed, the assertion that one system is more rule-based than the other does not appear to be founded in reality because, in my judgment, both systems are essentially rule-based and laborious.

It is also worth noting that the thought processes of accounting standards, setters and regulators have come a long way over the past few decades. In the early 1970s, for example, the American Institute of Certified Public Accountants (AICPA) objected to two research monographs authored by Maurice Moonitz and Robert Sprouse (and published by the Research Division of the AICPA) that had espoused the then new-on-the-scene views such as discounting long-term receivables and reporting their present values. Thirty years later we find accounting standards and guidance aim at incorporating the economic substance of complex transactions and making use of the necessary economic tools such as option valuation models, Macaulay's *Duration*, risk transfer and risk sharing and judgment about what constitutes thin or broad (liquid) markets so as to decide on which path to take in estimating fair values.

These developments have created a new accounting model that continues to be missed by many financial accounting courses and textbooks. For example, typical financial reporting presentations never entertain the notion that the enterprise could earn or lose profits by trading on its inventory while it is still in stock. It is true that we need to teach our students about inventory cost flow assumptions, but when the value or cash flow related to inventory is hedged and the hedge meets certain criteria, the book value of inventories may be written up or down in keeping with the *changes* in market values. Furthermore, the new accounting considers management actions while holding inventory: the management could hedge the funds that are forecasted to be collected for the inventory when sold, could hedge the fair value of inventory as an asset, or could hedge the cash flow risk of replacing the inventory. It is also important to emphasize that these actions involve using instruments such as options, futures, forward and swap contracts among others and very often result in recognizing unrealized gains and losses that are, unfortunately, not always separately identified on the income statement. All of these actions entail material consequences to reported profits, cash flow and the financial position of the enterprise and, because of the conflicting interests and incentives, it would be quite risky for the accountant and the auditor to rely on management's assertions without full knowledge and understanding of the complexities involved. To account for these instruments and transactions, the accountant must know the makeup of these contracts, how they are valued and how well they succeed in hedging the designated risk. So far, accounting standards require evaluating the success (effectiveness) of the hedging relationship and its linkage to the adopted Enterprise Risk Management system and philosophy in deciding on the appropriate accounting method.[5] These developments unambiguously reveal that the traditional accounting model no longer fits a world dominated by complex contracts.

## The Ever-changing Accounting Standards

Accounting has always responded to changes and movements in the economy and the business environment. As the economies of Western countries have shifted from manufacturing to financial services, the focus has also shifted from manufacturing cost accounting to accounting for contracts and, as always, accounting adaptation follows changes on the ground with lags that depend on several factors including the complexity of the issues being considered. The establishment of the European Union (EU) has further intensified the need for high-quality and more harmonious accounting standards which led to the EU's acceptance and adoption of IFRS.[6] Having a block of European countries adopting one set of accounting standards, while the USA continues to have its own set of GAAP created problems and friction simply because multinational companies had to comply with different accounting standards if their business crosses the Atlantic or the Pacific Oceans. Compliance cost has increased with the significant growth in the globalization of commerce and services. The IASB and the FASB have decided that the environment is right for reconciliation and rapprochement to unify or at least reduce the differences between the two sets of accounting standards. On February 27, 2006, the FASB and the IASB issued a Memorandum of Understanding which outlines a Road Map for convergence of U.S. GAAP and IFRS. Since then both organizations have been working feverishly to reconcile differences between the two sets of rules leading to numerous significant changes in both systems. However, the two boards have agreed to reconcile differences between standards in four areas only and more recently, in 2012, the FASB decided not to rush to full conversion. With the difficult economic circumstances created by the 2007 economic crisis, the urge to converge has come to a standstill.

There are differences between U.S. GAAP and IFRS in connection with the topics covered in this book. However, a few observations should be of interest to the readers. First, those differences have been narrowed significantly in recent years. In fact, the FASB has issued a proposal noting the intent to adopt a classification of marketable securities and investment very similar, though not identical, to that of IFRS.[7] Second, the FASB has issued (in June 2012) a proposal for an Accounting Standards Update to require disclosure of liquidity risk and interest rate risk which would provide information very similar, but not identical, to IFRS 7.[8] Third, the frameworks of hedge accounting of the two systems are essentially the same; there has been a continuous cross-fertilization of ideas and policies between the two boards. Indeed, in comparing U.S. GAAP and IFRS, *PwC* reported that the topics of hedge accounting and financial instruments have the least differences of all areas between U.S. GAAP and IFRS.[9] Finally, the IASB issued, in September 2012, a proposed modification to IFRS 9 and, in the meantime, the FASB has circulated proposals to reduce the differences and approach the accounting treatment of IFRS 9.

It is arguable, however, that the normal state of accounting standards is one of constant change; there have always been revisions and updates in response to changing business and economic conditions as well as for correctness and improvement. There is no reason to expect this state of influx to suddenly stop; in the years to come, accounting standards will continue to undergo changes perhaps at an uncomfortable pace. For this reason, this book provides a foundation of concepts forming the bases for understanding the instruments, the contracts and related problems in order to facilitate adaptation to changes in accounting standards whenever they occur. In addition, this book introduces enough material to gain functioning knowledge (under accounting standards as of midyear 2013) of hedge accounting and accounting for derivative instruments in single currency and in multiple currency environments.

Guided by the perceived need in both university and public accounting education, this book covers the following areas:

- *Concepts*: Risk definitions, types, measurement and management.
- *Instruments*: Basic types of financial derivatives and their valuation—options, swaps, forwards, futures and credit default swaps.
- *Embedded derivatives*: when terms and conditions contained (embedded) within a contract have the same attributes as a free standing derivative.
- *Hedge accounting (single currency)*. Cash flow hedge and fair value hedge elaborated with illustrations.
- *Hedge accounting (multiple currencies)*: A primer on currency and types of currency risk exposures: transaction, operating and translation. Hedging currency risk exposure of net assets in foreign operations forms a third hedge accounting component with the other two components being *cash flow hedge* and *fair value hedge*.
- *Disclosure* of risk and hedging.

This book should be helpful to anyone seeking basic knowledge about risk, financial derivatives and the special accounting treatments of hedging contracts and transactions. This audience would include (a) students at the senior or master's level who are studying to earn degrees in accounting, finance or business, (b) public accountants and practitioners who graduated from universities before this material was part of the standards or introduced into the curriculum, and (c) bankers, financial analysts and other practitioners of finance and accounting. The reader must be aware, however, that the technical materials in this book are not for quick or light reading.

## Learning Resources

In addition to this book, there are numerous resources that could inform and teach interested individuals. Of great benefit to me were the publications by accounting firms, including several regular series: *Heads Up* by Deloitte; *Financial Reporting Development* by Ernst & Young; *Defining Issues* by

KPMG; and both *Data Line* and *In Brief* by PwC. These resources also refer to other relevant publications by regulators, especially the SEC, the FASB and the IASB. Additionally, there is a rich website established and maintained by Robert E. Jensen.[10] This website is an excellent resource for consulting on numerous issues related to financial instruments and hedge accounting.

## Acknowledgments

I am grateful to my students who persevered throughout my development of the course on Risk Reporting that I had introduced at the University of Illinois. I am especially indebted to my former students Salvadore Carmona, Po-Chang Chen, Raluca Chiorean, Jana D. Lin, Charles Martin, and Jundong Wang, and to my colleagues Michael Donohoe and Paul W. Polinski, Jr, for providing feedback on some chapters.

I am also grateful to Rachel Hutchings and Tania Lown-Hecht for their excellent editorial support.

A. Rashad Abdel-khalik
Champaign, Illinois
December 2012

## Suggestions for Instructors

1. It might take more than one semester to cover all the material in this book.
2. The instructor should exercise judgment on rearranging the material for a one-semester course.
3. The boxed materials in Chapter Five may be required for students who are not familiar with valuation models of options, swaps and forward contracts.

## Notes

1 Bucket shops were arrangements engaged in a form of gambling that allowed people to place bets on the stock market and other securities. See, for example, Frank Partnoy (2003) and Robert E. Jensen, History of Fraud in America, http://www.trinity.edu/rjensen/FraudAmericanHistory.htm.

2 The Glass-Steagall Act is referred to here as the Banking Act of 1933 (48 Stat. 162) which prohibited commercial banks from engaging in the investment banking business.

3 http://www.bis.org/statistics/otcder/dt1920a.pdf. These numbers refer to the notional amounts, not to settlement values. Settlement values are approximated by the fair values of these derivatives, which are estimated to be between 3.5% and 4.5% of notional amounts. The fair value of these derivatives (the amounts actually due) is estimated to be about US$25 trillion. See also, www.isda.org

4 Using accounting standards jargon, this estimation could be Fair Value Level 2 or Level 3 both of which require knowledge of the valuation models, cash flow patterns, and uncertainty. Even the giant JP Morgan Chase discloses that 13% of all their financial assets are estimated using Level 3, which is based completely on management assumptions, judgment, and choice of models.

5 Both the FASB and the IASB are discussing the possibility of departing from the current quantitative measures of hedge effectiveness to a more lax qualitative approach that allows the management to state whether or not a hedge is "reasonably" effective. No decisions about changing the quantitative measures

of effectiveness have been made as of November 2012, the time of concluding the writing of this book. Nevertheless, I often wonder why give the management all the cards in view of the fact that their self interest may not be consistent with the interests of shareholders.

6 The adoption process is not that simple. Members of the European Union must adopt the accounting standards that the EU Commission has issued as a Directive. The EU Commission decided to adopt IFRS with modifications resulting in carving out some important segments of specific standards in response to certain pressures from constituents and regulators. However, on the whole, it is reasonable to state that the EU countries are using IFRS for consolidated (group) financial statements.

7 The Appendix to Chapter Seven is a reproduction (with permission) of the summary provided by Deloitte & Touche in its series of *Heads Up* authored by Magnus Orrell and Jason Nye.

8 If accepted, these updates will put into effect the Securities and Exchange Commission's (SEC) long-standing ruling on disclosure of liquidity risk and interest rate risk.

9 PricewaterhouseCoopers, 2011, *IFRS and US GAAP: similarities and differences*, p. 7.

10 http://www.cs.trinity.edu/rjensen/000overview/mp3/133intro.htm.

# PART I

# FOUNDATIONS

## CHAPTER 1

# DEFINITIONS OF RISK AND RISK APPETITE

## 1.1 Risk and Open Systems

Not long ago, the Biologist Karl Ludwig von Bertalanffy introduced the concept of open systems.[1] At that time, no one could have imagined that this concept would extend to all activities, including those of business entities. The open system concept states that no system, person, organization, or object is completely self-contained; every system is open to "its environment"; it can affect the environment and the environment can affect it. Thus, any organization or system is impacted by elements over which the organization or the system has no control. It follows that the impact of the environment on the organization would be unpredictable, which led von Bertalanffy to conclude that uncertainty is a fact of life for every organization or system, which echoed the words of Frank Knight as he writes:

> It is a world of change in which we live, and a world of uncertainty. We live only by knowing something about the future; while the problems of life, or of conduct at least, arise from the fact that we know so little.
>
> (Knight, 1921, p. 199)

Almost a century after Knight published his book, these words remain germane. However, until very recently, the concept and impact of risk was not fully recognized in the field of accounting at large. Indeed, the standards and practice of auditing have been ahead of financial reporting in incorporating risk as both a cause and effect of certain actions. Nowadays, concerns about risk seem to have overtaken the discipline of financial reporting. It is now an essential part of accounting as a discipline to know more about risk, instruments of risk, risk orientation, measurement and reporting of risk exposures, and the extent to which the business enterprise manages and succeeds in mitigating risk.

This chapter discusses definitions of risk and specific aspects of uncertainty—volatility and exposure to loss. It provides summaries of decision makers' disposition toward risk-taking and introduces the reader to two prominent theories of decision making under uncertainty.

However, it seems that confusion between uncertainty and risk is a persistent phenomenon. This chapter clarifies some issues related to the relationship between the two concepts, but it seems that we end up where Frank Knight took us almost a century ago: risk is the uncertainty for which outcomes and probabilities are known objectively or subjectively; it is measurable uncertainty.[2]

## 1.2 Risk and Uncertainty

In common speech, risk is defined as exposure to the chance of injury or loss or as a hazard or dangerous chance. One often hears the expression "it is not worth taking the risk."[3] This appears to be the sense in which Benjamin Graham viewed financial analysis in his well-known book, *The Intelligent Investor* (1973, 1986). He notes that risk is

> a loss of value which either is realized through actual sale, or is caused by a significant deterioration in the company's position—or, more frequently perhaps, is the result of the payment of an excessive price in relation to the intrinsic [true] worth of the security.

Others define risk in terms of expected loss: the probability of a bad event happening multiplied by the economic value of the consequences that will occur if the identified bad event does take place.[4]

To summarize the notions that different authors have espoused, risk can be defined by reference to the joint space of outcomes and probabilities. As Exhibit 1.1 shows, it is possible to construct four combinations of probabilities, outcomes, knowledge or lack of knowledge.

1. *Case A* is the condition in which possible outcomes and the probability of occurrence of each outcome is known. This case is Frank Knight's definition of risk.
2. *Case B* is the combination that Frank Knight defines as "uncertainty." It is the condition in which outcomes could be enumerated, but the probabilities of occurrences of these outcomes are not known.
3. *Case C* is the situation in which outcomes are not identified. It is therefore not feasible to specify a probability distribution.
4. *Case D* is a state of indifference or complete ignorance as defined by Bayes (Jaynes, 2003). It is the condition in which neither the outcomes nor the probabilities of occurrences are known.

### Exhibit 1.1 Combinations of Probability, Outcome and Knowledge

| | | *Outcomes* | |
|---|---|---|---|
| | | *Known* | *Unknown* |
| Probabilities | Known | (A): Risk | (C): Not Feasible |
| | Unknown | (B): Uncertainty | (D): Ignorance |

Many authors interpret Knight's conception of risk and uncertainty as comparing the two situations of Case A and Case B: (A) "risk" describes situations with known outcomes and known or estimable probability of occurrence of each; (B) "uncertainty" describes situations in which the possible set of outcomes is known but the probabilities of occurrences cannot be assigned to these outcomes either objectively or subjectively. But Knight added to the confusion between *risk* and *uncertainty* by additionally noting that "measureable uncertainties do not introduce into business any uncertainty whatsoever" (1921, p. 232).[5] Today, almost 90 years later, the distinction between risk and uncertainty continues to engender debate.

More recently, Holton (2004) notes that uncertainty about the potential outcomes that matter must be present as a pre-condition for the existence of risk. He provides the example of a person jumping off a high-flying airplane. If that person is equipped with a parachute, he/she would still be uncertain about making a safe landing after jumping. This uncertainty arises because there is a chance, no matter how small, that the parachute might not function properly. In contrast, there is no uncertainty in the landing outcome of a person jumping without a parachute from an airplane while flying at a high altitude. In this case, there is no risk in the sense of a probabilistic outcome, but there would be a loss of life with certainty.

Holton describes risk as the uncertainty that matters. Some authors consider this definition more encompassing than Knight's distinction between risk and uncertainty. For example, human beings are constantly faced with the risk of being inflicted with cancer from consuming the chemical products inputted into the foods we eat, the water we drink, the air we breathe and the clothes we wear. In this type of environment, the probability of having cancer—the outcome that matters—is unknown, but it is not zero.[6]

Risk transferring and sharing are methods of risk reduction. The most common form of risk sharing is insurance. Insurance against risk has existed for centuries in one form or another,[7] but it was not until the 1950s that the explicit consideration of risk in investment decision making began to take shape. It was the publications of Kenneth Arrow (1951) and Harry Markowitz (1952) that sparked the interest of academia and of finance practitioners in the role of risk in making choices (Arrow, 1951; Markowitz, 1952). As the concept of risk gained prominence, some authors referred back to Frank Knight's characterization of risk, while others have defined it by how it is measured—as the volatility of prices or returns. One could argue that the continuation of the confusion between risk as a concept and risk as an empirical metric may have been reinforced by Markowitz' four conditions:

1. Investors try to avoid volatile investments.
2. Investors will take on more volatility (i.e., risk) only if they are rewarded for it.
3. Volatility is induced either by general market conditions (systematic risk) or by unique characteristics of the particular business enterprise (idiosyncratic risk).
4. Because volatility involves gains and losses, the unique components of risk that are attributed to any particular enterprise would be randomized as the number of investments increases.

As a consequence of these propositions, if someone invests in relatively volatile investments or projects, she/he should expect to earn, on average, a high enough return to compensate her/him for taking on the risk depicted by the observed high volatility. In general, people want to be compensated for investing in risky projects by earning a commensurate risk premium. By the same logic, people would be willing to pay someone to take the burden of risk away from them, as is the case in insurance.[8]

The question that must be asked is whether using volatility and risk interchangeably is an acceptable generalization. To illustrate the relevance of this issue, consider the view of volatility and risk in health sciences, for example. In this context, the risk that matters is the probability of falling ill or of failing to respond to treatment. This type of risk is not necessarily a function of volatility or variability of exposure to contaminants—having a high variability among individuals' responses to exposure to hazardous chemicals does not in itself mean exposure to risk because the range of variability might be at a level of toxicity so low that it would have no impact on health—i.e., high volatility, but low risk. On the other hand, the variability of response to hazardous chemicals could be very low, but at a high level of toxicity—i.e., low volatility, but high risk. Therefore, in this context, variability and uncertainty are factors to consider in the assessment, evaluation and measurement of the risk that matters. It is evident that this simple comparison between the environments of business and health reveals two different views of the connection between risk and volatility.

To summarize, consideration of the issues raised above might lead us to agree on four propositions:

1. Risk is exposure to loss or harm and is context specific.
2. In business transactions, risk is the probability of exposure to loss (which is parallel to, but is not the same as, the probability of exposure to illness in the health sciences).
3. Higher volatility of the financial variables of interest (sales, rates of return, equity indices, etc.) implies greater exposure to loss for a given level of probability, or higher probability of loss for a given loss level.
4. Therefore, volatility in the business environment is an indicator of risk exposure and it is possible to use variability as a proxy for risk but, in the meantime, it is preferable to refrain from overgeneralization of this proxy to other contexts or environments.

## 1.3 Risk Taking Types of Decision Makers: Three Schools of Thought

In 1967 Kogan and Wallach suggested that risk-taking propensity is a function of either personality trait (intrinsic) or situational (extrinsic) factors. Since then researchers appear to have populated three different camps:

1. *The Intrinsic School Camp*: This approach is held by personality psychologists and classical economists.
2. *The Extrinsic School Camp*: This camp argues that personality traits are secondary and individuals' risk disposition is determined mainly by external situational stimuli. Experimental psychologists and behavioral economists fall in this camp.
3. *The Pragmatic School*: This school of thought considers risk disposition to be a function of both intrinsic and extrinsic factors that interact in a more dynamic way to formulate an individual's risk-taking propensity.

### 1.3.1 The Intrinsic School

Various authors have studied several dimensions of decision makers' personalities and their relationships to risk-taking. Zuckerman and Kuhlman (2000) summarize the research findings of their work and that of other colleagues to show that the propensity toward risk-taking is a function of the decision maker's psychological makeup, such as impulsive sensation seeking, aggressiveness, and sociability. Other studies have considered the biological and behavioral makeup of decision makers such as impulsivity, cognitive ability, genetics, or risky behavior in general (Barsky, Juster,

Kimball, and Shapiro, 1997; Zuckerman and Kuhlman, 2000; Dohmen, Falk, Huffman, and Sunde, 2007; Zyphur, Narayanan, Arvey, and Alexander, 2009).

Traditionally, economists could be considered to fall in this camp. While they assume complete rationality of decision makers, they also posit the theory of utility maximization; namely, people are assumed to behave in a manner that would maximize their expected utility.[9] Expected Utility Theory postulates that decisions are dependent on the final utility of the outcome of decision making and that the outcome is not to be affected by the situation or the context of the decision. Furthermore, the theory assumes that individual decision maker's disposition toward risk is stable within the individual and is not affected by differences in situations, by framing of decision problems, or by the context in which the decision is made.

The classical theory of decision making prevailed for decades until some scholars began to question the validity of assuming complete rationality and utility optimization as a goal. In addition, economists have assumed that utility maximization cannot be standardized for various individuals because, intrinsically, decision makers have different dispositions toward risk-taking. In particular, decision makers could be in one of three types:

- Type 1: *Risk Proclivity* (*Risk Lovers*)—this class of decision makers describe individuals who seek risk for the thrill of it, even when the expected benefits from the decisions they make could be lower than the cost they incur.
- Type 2: *Risk Neutral*—these are the individuals who are indifferent between risky and safe situations if these situations have the same expected outcome for a given cost or effort.
- Type 3: *Risk Averse*—these are the individuals who would prefer safe over risky situations even if these situations have the same expected benefits for a given cost.

The illustration in Exhibit 1.2 provides a simple example for basic differences among the three categories.

## Exhibit 1.2 An Example of the Classification of Decision Makers' Attitudes toward Risk

A fair coin is one that is perfectly symmetrical and has no physical imperfections so that, when tossed repeatedly, the coin lands heads-up (H) one-half of the time, and tails-up (T) the other half of the time. Now, assume a person is playing a game that offers the following payoff:

Pay $39.00 for a ticket to participate in a coin toss game. The outcome of the game has two options:

| | | *Decision Making Options* | |
|---|---|---|---|
| *Outcome* | *Probability* | *Option A* | *Option B* |
| Head | 0.50 | Gain = $80 | Gain = $40 |
| Tail | 0.50 | Gain = 0 | Gain = $40 |
| Expected Value | | $40 | $40 |

The expected value of each option is calculated as the (probability) weighted sum of different outcomes. That is:

Expected value of Option A = (0.50 × \$80) + (0.50 × 0) = \$40.00
Expected value of Option B = (0.50 × \$40) + (0.50 × \$40) = \$40.00

1. A *risk lover* would prefer Option A as compared to Option B.
2. A *risk-neutral* decision maker would be indifferent between the two options.
3. A *risk-averse* person would prefer Option B over Option A.

### 1.3.2 The Extrinsic (Situational) School

The challenge to EUT appeared first in what has become known as Allais Paradox after the French economist/physicist Maurice Allais (1953) showed that in simple probabilistic choices people do not behave as predicted by EUT. However, no coherent alternative was provided until 1979 when Kahneman and Tversky introduced Prospect Theory which states that disposition toward risk-taking depends on the situation; risk-taking attitude when the situation is a *gain* is different from the risk-taking disposition when the situation is a *loss*. Each decision, therefore, has two possible outcomes having two different domains with respect to a point of reference:

1. The gain domain when decision makers become risk averse because of trying to preserve the gains they made by avoiding taking on (what they view as) situations bearing excessive risk that could expose them to losses.
2. The loss domain when decision makers become risk seekers by taking on excessively risky projects in the hope of realizing abnormal gains that would reverse the losses they have incurred.

In the words of Tversky and Kahneman (1991) "losses and disadvantages have greater impact on preferences than gains and advantages." This impact is reflected in the weights a decision maker assigns to weighting gains versus losses such that this behavior makes them risk averse in the domain of gains and risk seeking in the domain of losses. While it appears counterintuitive, this behavior has been observed repeatedly in experimental and real-life settings and has led to formulating the concept of *loss aversion* stipulating that risk-takers fear losses more than they desire making gains.

This behavior is illustrated in Figure 1.1, where the *x*-axis is for gains (+) and losses (–) and the *y*-axis is for value (utility).

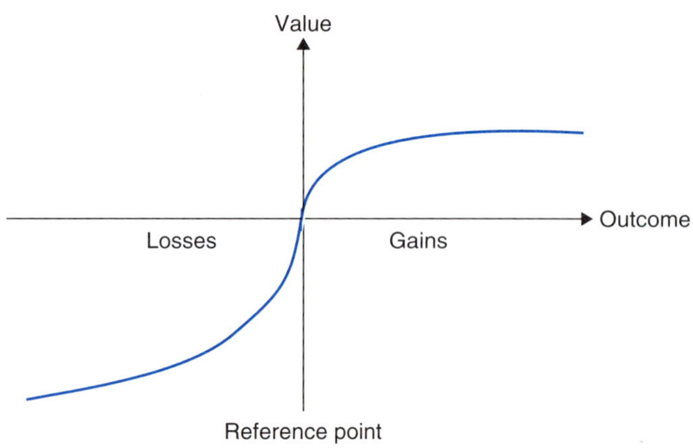


**Figure 1.1** Prospect Theory Payoff Function

### 1.3.3 Comparing the Two Theories

Both Expected Utility Theory in the intrinsic camp and Prospect Theory in the situational camp make use of the concept of utility, but in totally different contexts. Expected Utility Theory assumes that the expected utility of the final outcome derives the decision-making process irrespective of the situation or the environment in which decisions are made. Expected Utility Theory is a normative theory that assumes that the objective function of each decision maker is utility maximization.

In contrast, Prospect Theory is a descriptive (positive) theory describing behavior in the real world although much of the evidence is generated in the laboratory. The theory assumes a context-specific decision-making under uncertainty defined with respect to a point of reference which delineates situations of gain and situations of losses. Therefore, human behavior and disposition toward risk-taking is, according to this school of thought, unstable and varies depending on which domain the decision maker is facing. An individual decision maker could be risk averse (with respect to a prospect that is realizing gains) and risk seeking (with respect to a prospect that is realizing losses) at the same time. Therefore, Prospect Theory is contextual and situational rather than intrinsic.

The personality traits that affect decision making under uncertainty are traits that have been acquired and are used by individual decision makers to edit and simplify the situation. These acquired traits are referred to as heuristics such as anchoring and adjustments, representativeness, and priority. These heuristics are not manifestations of intrinsic characteristics of the decision maker; they are acquired traits and come to the forefront only as a means of simplifying the complexity of the decision context.

While Prospect Theory was developed based on observing individual decision-making in the laboratory and field studies, subsequent research (e.g., Bowman, 1982) finds evidence to suggest that firms appear to follow a similar pattern in the loss domain. Bowman examined the behavior of the mean and variance of ROE (Return on Equity = Net Income/Equity) for a sample of U.S. firms and concluded that *troubled firms are risk seeking*. The justification for this behavior appears to be the same as that of Prospect Theory: troubled firms take more risk and adopt gambling strategies in the hope that they will achieve a large payoff and offset the losses they have suffered.

### 1.3.4 The Pragmatic School

The main premise of this school is that neither intrinsic human traits nor the situation of the decision being made adequately explain the decision-making process; instead, both types are essential for understanding human decision-making under uncertainty. Early advocates of this school of thought include George Katona (1951) and Herbert Simon (1959) who have led the movement to modify Expected Utility Theory by integrating the psychological concepts of decision-making with decision makers' environments or external factors. Most notable are Simon's concepts of *bounded rationality* and *satisficing*. He argued that individual decision makers do not maximize expected utility because a complete enumeration of alternatives and their consequences is not feasible. Even if we did understand the alternatives and consequences, we could not possibly process them quickly enough due to information overload and fatigue. Because of these limitations to human decision-making ability, Simon suggested that decision makers do *satisfice* rather than maximize. *Satisficing* in this context means that decision makers may aim at utility maximization with added constraints that incorporate their cognitive abilities and levels of aspiration. He writes:

> Broadening the definition of rationality to encompass goal conflict and uncertainty made it hard to ignore the distinction between the objective environment in which the economic actor "really" lives and the subjective environment that he perceives and to which he responds. When this distinction is made, we can no longer predict his behavior—even if he behaves rationally—from the characteristics of the objective environment; we also need to know something about his perceptual and cognitive processes.
>
> (Simon, 1959, p. 256)

It was not until the mid-1970s when the literature commenced a series of studies to study the determinants of risk-taking appetite. These studies were conducted in at least seven countries by different authors to determine how households allocate their portfolios between risky and safe investments (for example, Cohn et al., 1975; Friend and Blume, 1975; Donkers and van Söest, 1999; Donkers, Bas, Melenberg, and van Söest, 2001; Guiso and Paiella, 2005, Dohmen et al., 2007). The collective findings of these studies are that risk-taking appetite decreases with age, increases in income, wealth and education and that women are more risk averse than men.

In a different strand of literature, Sitkin and Pablo (1992) suggest that individual risk traits interact with decision situations and jointly form the individual's disposition toward risk-taking.

In some cases, business enterprises refer to the risk-taking appetite of the management as the risk appetite of the entity. For example, *Barclays PLC* defines risk appetite as

> the level of risk that Barclays is prepared to sustain whilst pursuing its business strategy, recognising a range of possible outcomes as business plans are implemented. Barclays' framework combines a top-down view of its capacity to take risk with a bottom-up view of the business risk profile associated with each business area's medium term plans. The appetite is ultimately approved by the Board. The Risk Appetite framework consists of two elements: "Financial Volatility" and "Mandate & Scale." Taken as a whole, the Risk Appetite framework provides a basis for the allocation of risk capacity across Barclays Group.
>
> (Barclays plc Annual Report 2010, p. 69)

## 1.4 Internal Controls and Risk-Seeking Behavior

Prospect Theory has been developed and imputed from observing human behavior in experiments and simplified decision setting, but several cases of high profiles and high cost provide support. These cases are:

1. **Daiwa Bank in New York City (1989–1995)**

Toshihide Iguchi, a profitable trader with the Daiwa Bank branch in the USA, had a reversal of fortune and accumulated over $1.1 billion, which was the result of risk-seeking behavior after reaching a loss level of $575 million. Believing in his ability to recover the losses, Iguchi decided to take a temporary cover-up measure by selling bonds that the bank was holding in custodial accounts. However, instead of making profits, Iguchi added to his losses and the more losses he accumulated, the more aggressive his trading strategies became. His total losses added up to over $1.1 billion. He then wrote a 30-page confession letter to the management, but the management of the bank acted in ways that led the Federal Reserve Bank to prohibit Daiwa Bank from continuing its operations in the United States.

2. **Barings Bank (1992–1995) in Singapore**

In 1992, the Singaporean branch of Barings Bank, then the oldest bank in the United Kingdom, hired a young trader by the name of Nick Leeson (Bank of England, 2005). Initially, the bank's management was cautious about giving Leeson broad authorization, but that attitude changed when his first efforts brought in unexpected profits to the bank. Leeson was dealing with currency, mostly the Japanese Yen and betting on the Nikie spread, but his trades began to lose money when currency prices moved against his expectations which was exacerbated by the aftermath of the 1995 Great Hanshin Earthquake of Kobe. He was able to exploit weaknesses in the internal control and accounting systems of the bank and found a way to hide the reversal of fortune from others at the bank as well as from external auditors and the regulators. Instead of disclosing his problems to the management and seeking resolution, he kept on trading currency and increasing the depth of his bets in the hope of recovering large enough profits to offset the accumulated losses and reverse direction. His risk-taking escalated to the point of accumulating over one billion dollars in losses, which was more than the bank's capital.[10] The bank went into bankruptcy, and was sold to ING Group of the Netherlands for a single British pound.

3. **Allied Irish Banks (1993–2002)—Baltimore, USA**

In 1993, at about the same time that risk-seeking behavior was going on at Barings Bank, Allfirst Bank, the Baltimore-based subsidiary of Allied Irish Banks, hired a young currency trader by the name of John Rusnak (Fuerbringer (with Kilborn), 2002). In 1997, Rusnak was betting on the Japanese Yen in a hopeful anticipation of its appreciation against the U.S. Dollar, but the reversal in currency directions from that prediction led Rusnak to accumulate massive losses. As with Nick Leeson, Rusnak kept increasing his trading volume in the hope of making profits and reversing the losses, which he also kept hidden away from the management and the auditors by exploiting the weaknesses of internal control and accounting systems at Allfirst Bank. By 1997, Rusnak's trading strategies sustained substantial losses and when the massive losses were uncovered in 2002, Rusnak's "betting" on currency increased (in terms of notional amounts) as high as $7.5 billion dollars. When the dust settled, Allied Irish Banks' net losses from these transactions exceeded $750 million and the bank closed its operations in the USA. Also, like Leeson, Rusnak did not personally benefit or profit greatly from the trade other than succeeding in keeping his job until the problem was uncovered.

4. **Kidder, Peabody & Co. Inc. (1991–1994)—New York City**

Joseph Jett was hired in 1991 and moved up the ladder to become the head of government bond trading. He traded on STRIPS, RECONS[11] and government bonds and initially accumulated losses of over $100 million. To cover the losses, he fabricated $350 million profits and attached them to his trading on STRIPS and RECON derivative securities. In the specific situations cited in the case, there were no purchases or sales, but Kidder's internal recordkeeping created the opportunity to book nonexistent profits by treating STRIPS and RECONS exchanges with the Federal Reserve Bank as a buy on one side of the exchange and a sale on the other. Unlike Leeson and Rusnak, Jett benefitted from his fake success; the SEC litigation records show his income had increased from $75,000 in 1991 to $9.3 million in 1993.[12]

Jett was tried but not convicted of securities fraud or violation of the securities law simply because the administrative judge at the Securities and Exchange Commission ruled that STRIPS and RECONS are "not" securities in the sense intended by securities laws. However, Jett was ordered to disgorge $8.2 million of ill-taken bonus and pay a $200,000 penalty.

5. **Société Générale (2008)—Paris, France**
SocGén is a French-based money center bank headquartered in Paris. SocGén was established in 1864 and was incorporated in 1971. In 2008 it operated more than 2,300 retail branches in France and 3,800 branches worldwide. In 2000, SocGén hired Jerome Kerviel as trader responsible for hedging using plain vanilla futures. Contracting to buy and sell stock index futures with different maturities, Kerviel was able to realize gain of small Basis Points which resulted in huge profits due to the large trading volume. Upon making large gains on unauthorized trades, Kerviel purposely traded on losing transactions in an effort to offset the gains he realized so that his superiors would not find out that he acted without authorization. In addition, he carried out one side of the hedging transactions and covered it up by falsifying offsetting fictitious transactions without disclosing the identities of counterparties. He continued to increase the volume and frequency of trades to cover losing positions only to get deeper into losses. Several events took place before being uncovered in 2007:

- His superiors warned him of potential problems 74 times.
- Net losses from his trades added up to over $3.00 billion.
- His total trading volume reached $73 billion.
- To unwind his open trade positions, the bank lost over €5.00 billion or a total of $7.2 billion.

Kerviel was sentenced to five years in jail and ordered to pay restitution in an amount equal to the actual loss the bank has sustained in unwinding his trades, which amounts to €4.9 billion.[13]

All of these cases share common elements that are discussed throughout this book. The most conspicuous element is the weak accounting and internal control systems. Yet, the most salient element is the connection between the behavior of the actors in these cases and theories of decision making. Clearly, in each case, the trader was exhibiting the type of risk-seeking behavior that Kahneman and Tversky discovered in the laboratory. When faced with losses, each of these traders escalated their actions, trying to recover the losses by seeking larger bets, and ended up losing even more.

## 1.5 A Summary and Transition

This chapter addresses the basics of:

1. The debate between scholars on the distinction between risk and uncertainty.
2. The definition of risk as making a choice between two generic concepts: (a) exposure to loss (financial) or harm (psychological or physical), and (b) the variability of outcomes.
3. The role of the decision maker's attitude toward risk and the notion of risk appetite.
4. A brief view of two decision-making theories and three schools of thought.
5. Providing examples of risk-seeking behavior in real life.
6. Irrespective of which definition of risk one adopts, the propensity to take risk is attributed to (a) personality traits, (b) expected benefits or expected utility of outcomes, and (c) the weights a decision maker places on losses versus gains. These traits are also considered to be determinants of individual decision makers' risk disposition toward neutrality, aversion, or proclivity.

Chapter Two provides an overview of a subset of the *types of risk* facing a business enterprise. These are the risks that could be managed, insured or hedged.

## Notes

1 The English-language publications started in 1950 (von Bertalanffy, 1950a, 1950b).
2 As an example of this confusion, the National Research Council (NRC, 1994) states that "uncertainty forces decision makers to judge how *probable* it is that risks will be overestimated or underestimated for every member of the exposed population, whereas variability forces them to cope with the *certainty* that different individuals will be subjected to risks both above and below any reference point one chooses" (Ref. 24, p. 237).
3 An online Dictionary (http://dictionary.reference.com/browse/risk) provides a discussion of the origin of the word "risk." It notes that the word "risk" is of obscure origin and may have evolved from French word "risqué" that was first introduced into the French language in 1655. While the origin of this term is unknown, it is perhaps useful to add that the word "Rizq" in the Arabic language goes back to the rise of Islam in the seventh century and connotes "taking a chance on earning a living." The connection to, and evolution from Arabic to French or vice versa, is unclear.
4 http://www.rmartin.com/risk_defined.html.
5 Some authors allege that Knight has added to the confusion by also noting that "measureable uncertainties do not introduce into business any uncertainty whatsoever" (Knight, 1921, p. 232).
6 The Environmental Protection Agency has identified 189 hazardous air pollutants (Committee on Risk Assessment of Hazardous Air Pollutants, 1994, p. 14).
7 History shows that the first insurance was part of Hammurabi Code in ancient Babylonia, about 4,500 years ago, in which King Hammurabi legalized the caravan-trade practice of forgiving a debtor's loans in the event of a personal catastrophe such as death, disability, loss of property, or if the caravan carrying commercial goods does not arrive to its destination safely. For additional discussion of the history of risk, see Peter Bernstein (1996).
8 An interesting and short summary of the evolution of risk may be found in Braddock (2010).
9 In the context of modern business conditions, the concept of utility goes beyond intrinsic satisfaction; it relates to expected tangible benefits of profits or wealth.
10 Typically, a bank's capital is less than 8% of total assets.
11 "STRIPS" are the zero coupon securities created from the interest payments and principal piece of a stripped bond, and these STRIPS are traded in the secondary market for U.S. Treasury securities. An arbitrage opportunity may be created for traders when the value of the component parts is greater or less than the value of the bond as a whole. RECONS are reconstituted STRIPS.
12 The escalation of falsification of profits is illustrated in a table provided by the SEC.

Employment History

| *Date* | *Event* |
|---|---|
| July 1991 | Hired at $75,000 as Vice President |
| 1991 Total Reported Profit (7/91–12/91) | $787,000 |
| December 1991 | $5,000 bonus |
| June 1992 | Raise to $150,000 |
| October 1992 | Promoted to Senior Vice President |
| 1992 Total Reported Profit | $32,481,000 |
| December 1992 | $2.1 million bonus |
| February 1993 | Promoted to head of Gov't Desk |
| 1993 Total Reported Profit | $150,654,000 |
| December 1993 | $9.3 million bonus |
| December 1993 | Named Kidder's Man of the Year |
| 1994 Total Reported Profit (1/94–3/94) | $80,100,000 |
| April 1994 | Fired |

*Source*: http://www.sec.gov/litigation/aljdec/id127cff.htm

13 The financial press estimated that it will take Kerviel an estimated 177,000 years to pay off the financial judgement against him. In 2012, Kerviel appealed his sentence claiming that the loss was part of an internal plot. *Financial Times*, June 19, 2012, p. 22.

CHAPTER 2

# TYPES OF RISK

## 2.1 Open Systems and Different Risk Exposures

Business enterprises operate as independent legal entities that aim at creating values and increasing owners' wealth. A business entity uses the funds the owners provide to purchase inputs, and process or combine them in certain ways to produce output (a product different from the individual components of inputs) that it can sell to others. These stages—financing, acquisition of inputs, processing and disposing of output—require the entity's interaction with people and organizations outside its boundaries. In general, we can define these boundaries as the conceptual space determined by the extent to which an organization has control over resources, obligations to satisfy, and rights to exercise.

All components that exist outside the entity's boundaries are collectively referred to in the organization behavior literature as the "organization's environment" and the entity is referred to as an "open system." The biologist Karl Ludwig von Bertalanffy is credited with popularizing the concept of open systems to describe all living organisms (von Bertalanffy, 1950b). Not long after von Bertalanffy, the concept of open system was extended beyond biological organisms to describe any group, entity, or structure; whether the entity is physical such as the automobile or the thermostat, or conceptual, such as an organization (Katz and Kahn, 1966).

The open systems concept has its own terminology: the acquisition of all inputs (e.g. labor, financing, or raw materials) is referred to as *importation* of energy from the environment; the production that an organization undertakes to combine and transform inputs into new products and services is referred to as *throughput*; and the sale and distribution of final products and services is known as *output or exporting energy* (Katz and Kahn, 1966, pp. 23–30). In each of these three stages, the organization faces a variety of risks resulting from events that vary in frequency and severity of impact.

If management cannot discriminate between these events in terms of severity of impact, it may allocate its risk mitigation resources in accordance with the frequency of risk exposure instead of the severity of impact. This is basically the theme of *The Black Swan* (Taleb, 2010), which is shared by The Federal Reserve Bank of San Francisco (Lopez, 2002) and the Deloitte publication *Disarming the Value Killers* (Deloitte Development, LLC, 2005) among many others.

Because the implications of open systems apply to all entities, strategic risk can be uniquely defined in terms of open systems properties *as the portfolio of the organization's exposure to adverse conditions in transacting with its environment*. Strategic risk assumes greater relevance in any of the following situations:

1. Scarcity of skilled labor in the pool of work force available to the entity.
2. Competitive and costly financing choices.
3. Making ineffective production plans and decisions.
4. Inefficient allocation of capital.
5. Competitive pressures in the raw materials and supply chain markets.
6. Competitive pressures in the markets for output.
7. Failure in planning and evaluating the firm's ability to take risk.
8. Failure of control systems to detect problems with high impact.
9. Management's inability to distinguish between low cost and low impact events (such as minor accounting errors) that could occur very frequently, and the high cost events that may occur infrequently (fraud at Enron, WorldCom and Tyco; the stock market crash of 1987 and of 2008; or destruction such as that caused by Hurricane Katrina).

While much attention in the literature and actual policy making targets the first seven items, little attention is given to the high impact/low frequency events. Figure 2.1 is an attempt to interrelate the different subsystems of risk drivers that are discussed in the remainder of this chapter. Identifying, diagnosing and prioritizing these risk drivers are essential features for proper design and execution of effective risk-mitigation policies and processes. The components of the flow chart in Figure 2.1 are not entirely hypothetical; the example of Bank of America in Exhibit 2.1 illustrates how the Bank's management views strategic risk, which is in conformity with the above definition.

## Exhibit 2.1 Strategic Risk Management at Bank of America

Strategic risk is the risk that adverse business decisions, ineffective or inappropriate business plans, or the failure to respond to changes in the competitive environment, business cycles, customer preferences, product obsolescence, execution and/or other intrinsic risks of business will impact our ability to meet our objectives. We use our planning process to help manage strategic risk. A key component of the planning process aligns strategies, goals, tactics and resources throughout the enterprise. The process begins with the creation of a corporate-wide business plan which incorporates an assessment of the strategic risks. This business plan establishes the corporate strategic direction. The planning process then cascades through the lines of business, creating business line plans aligned with the Corporation's strategic direction. At each level, tactics and metrics are identified to measure success in achieving goals and assure adherence to the plans. As part of this process, the lines of business continuously evaluate the impact of changing market and business conditions, and the overall risk in meeting objectives. [...] Corporate Audit monitors and independently reviews and evaluates the plans and measurement processes.

One of the key tools we use to manage strategic risk is economic capital allocation. Through the economic capital allocation process, we effectively manage each line of business's ability to take on risk. To incorporate approval of economic capital allocation, the business reviews and approves business plans. It monitors economic capital usage through financial and risk reporting. It incorporates economic capital allocation plans for the lines of business into the Corporation's operating plan; this plan is approved by the Board on an annual basis.

(Source: Form 10-K, 2009, p. 49. Available at http://www.sec.gov/Archives/edgar/data/70858/000119312509041126/d10k.htm)

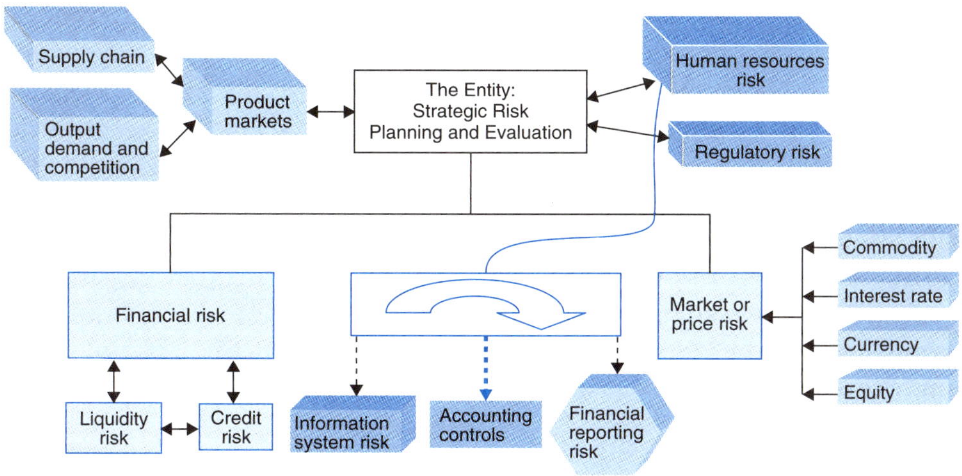


**Figure 2.1** Linkage of Different Risk Exposures

## 2.2 Qualitative Classification of Risk

Risk can be categorized along two qualitative dimensions: (a) insurability, and (b) diversifiability.

### 2.2.1 Insurability

From the point of view of (traditional) insurance, risk is partitioned into two types:

1. pure risk; and
2. speculative risk.

Pure risk consists of the risk of loss due to hazards that (a) are not under the control of the insured, and (b) have loss as the only outcome. This includes, for example, automobile accidents, fire hazard, health problems, death, and loss of property. All other types of risks are the risks for which the outcome is either a loss or a gain and are considered speculative. Because of the potential of gainful outcome, speculative risk is uninsurable.

Exposure to unexpected loss is, by nature, stochastic and unknown. Damage caused by fire in a particular building might happen, but it is not certain. Without insurance, individuals bear the cost of pure risk. If each house in a given neighborhood has, for example, a 1 in 1000 chance of catching (accidental) fire, and the residents do not know which house will actually have the unlucky event, the homeowner will bear the total cost of repair or replacement. Severe damage could cost the owner the entire house as total loss. The problem is that under normal conditions no one can tell in advance which house will suffer loss and damage due to fire, flood, or tornado. Under the Bayesian principle of maximum ignorance, one can assume that every house in the neighborhood has the same likelihood of suffering damage due to these causes. Risk sharing is a possible way of reducing this burden. For example, it would be to homeowners' benefit to form a community box (an account) to which each household contributes a small sum of money for the purpose of responding to fires or floods, and to compensate owners of damaged property. The concept of a community box or a neighborhood association to perform these functions does exist in rural areas where volunteer fire fighters operate fire stations and members of the community participates in bearing risk. This practice is a predecessor to what we now know as insurance, except for the fact that insurance companies are intermediaries that are able to use historical patterns and analysis to generate statistical tables describing probabilities of losses under different conditions. These activities are governed by some principles, the main one being the *Principle of Indemnity* specifically stipulating that no one can gain from insurance.[1]

Insurance as a risk-sharing or a risk-transfer mechanism simply means that the insured pays the insurer a price (a premium) to take the risk which the insured does not wish to bear. Accounting for insurance contracts from the viewpoint of the insurer (the insurance company) has its own unique features and complexity.

### 2.2.2 Diversifiability

The concept of risk came to focus in the financial literature on investment when portfolio theory was conceived. Until the publication of the first article by Markowitz, investment choices were made based on charting trends of financial ratios and prices (Markowitz, 1952). This was the tradition of Graham and Dodd, that began in 1949, and which many analysts and investment advisors continue to use, even if they only use it to supplement modern theories of investment.[2] However, the success of the chartists' strategies did not lead to a good understanding of the underlying causes of the differences in market rates of return. Without articulation of risk, it was difficult to understand why a given investment earns a higher or lower rate of return than a seemingly similar investment. Profitability was, and continues to be, a key determinant of market value and expected return. However, consideration of profitability levels alone does not adequately capture the process of valuation because, as Markowitz has convincingly showed, *risk* (or volatility) is another major determinant.

Markowitz' work precipitated the development of a vast literature and took information and financial economics in new and challenging directions. The theory has two large implications: the first is that investors can invest in more risky assets if they are rewarded for taking the risk by earning a corresponding risk premium, such that total expected return will be commensurate with the level of risk taken. If an investment has an average degree of risk, as average as the entire market, this investment should be expected to earn an average market risk premium. Similarly, if the degree of risk of an investment is higher than average (market) risk, such an investment should be expected to earn a risk premium higher than average. The reverse is also true.[3]

Additionally, Markowitz (1952) and Sharpe (1964) among others have identified the sources of risk as (1) general macroeconomic factors, and (2) unique, entity-specific factors. The component of risk that could be attributed to general market-wide factors is known as "systematic risk," while the component of risk that is unique to the entity's own activities and characteristics is known as the firm-specific, nonsystematic or idiosyncratic risk.

The second implication lies in showing the effect of combining different investments on the level of risk. When several investments are grouped (forming a portfolio), the nonsystematic or idiosyncratic components of risk are randomized—i.e., washed away—leaving only systematic risk for the investor to bear. In addition, the systematic risk component of a portfolio is a weighted average of the systematic risk measures of all the investments included in the portfolio, with the weights determined by the relative size of capital allocated to each investment.

This theme is observed throughout the development of the literature. While much of the research has shown that only systematic risk matters for a portfolio of investments because idiosyncratic risk can be randomized by diversification, recent research in finance is revisiting this issue and is reevaluating the extent to which nonsystematic (firm-specific) or idiosyncratic risk is priced, and thus is not fully diversifiable.

A further refinement of the notion of systematic risk involves expanding the number of factors that can be considered economy-wide determinants of systematic risk. Through intensive data search, Fama and French (1993) have identified a three-factor model which includes the (average) market portfolio return and two additional factors: relative size and relative book to market values. Fama and French offer these three factors as indices to measure macro/general sources of risk to which every business firm is exposed. The three-factor model is extensively used in empirical work and Fama and French maintain a website updating these indices and make them available to anyone interested in the three-factor model.[4]

## 2.3 Functional Classification of Risk

For our purposes we consider three categories:

1. Operational risk and accounting controls.
2. Accounting risk exposure.
3. Market price risk.

### 2.3.1 Operational Risk and Accounting Controls[5]

In its consultative document of 2001, the Basel Committee on Banking Supervision (the Bank for International Settlements) defined operational risk as "the risk of loss resulting from inadequate or failed internal processes, people and systems or from external events. This definition includes legal risk, but excludes strategic and reputational risk." This definition is still in use today. The Basel Accord definition has several elements:

1. Employees' actions.
2. Internal processes such as accounting and internal controls.
3. Information systems technology and security.
4. Other factors.

Employees' actions are on the top of the list of potential causes of exposing the enterprise to operational risk because the first threat to the business entity often comes from its employees. These threats can come in different forms that go beyond shirking; the most costly threats are incidents of embezzlement and theft. A *Wall Street Journal* article (December 11, 2008) notes that the proximity of employees to the workplace gives some of them an advantage in embezzlement and in committing fraud: "Employers are hot targets for theft because workers know their systems, controls and weaknesses, and they can bide their time waiting for the right opportunity."

It is estimated that business establishments in the USA lost over $119 billion in 2011 due to employees' theft and embezzlement (Hayes, 2011). This fact alone renders the selection and training of employees an essential ingredient for dealing with operational risk. These estimates do not include the theft of intellectual property such as research and development and creation of new technology and products. If this estimate included theft of intellectual property, employees' theft would have increased more than sixfold.[6]

The case of Enron is a recent massive and intricate case of fraud perpetrated at all levels of management. Enron's revenues grew from $13.3 billion in 1996 to $100.8 billion in 2000, which was $5.3 million per each one of its 19,000 employees. Some of that revenue was the result of incorrect accounting for derivatives, recording losses as assets, recording liabilities as profits, and allocating its debt to unconsolidated special purpose entities. The Federal Bureau of Investigation (FBI) (2012) summarizes this case as follows:

## Information Log (The FBI Report on Enron)

**WHITE-COLLAR CASE: Enron**

As a result of its deceptive accounting practices—including the creation of earnings, the manufacture of cash flow, and the concealment of debt—officers of Enron Corporation misled the investing public regarding its reported financial condition. In addition, investment banks and other business partners aided Enron in perpetrating the fraud through the creation of financial structures and other devices that facilitated the deceptive accounting practices.[7]

There are several mechanisms that could deal with expropriation of the entity's resources. The first line of defense is to establish a strong system of internal accounting and auditing controls. In the early 1970s, Congress discovered that over 400 U.S. corporations had given bribes to foreign officials to obtain business contracts abroad, which is illegal in the USA and under U.S. law. As a result, the 1977 Foreign Corrupt Practices Act (FCPA) requires U.S. business enterprises to establish effective systems of internal controls to provide reasonable assurance of the legitimacy of management actions. However, over time, compliance with this section of the FCPA was not enforced and corporations did not invest to enhance their internal control systems.

The collapse of Enron and WorldCom in early 2000 elevated the debate about corporate governance in general and about internal accounting controls in particular. In 2002, Congress enacted what we now know as the Sarbanes-Oxley Act (2002), which requires the development of mechanisms to ensure the effectiveness of corporate internal controls. According to section 404 of the Act, the management of all publicly held enterprises that file annual reports with the Securities and Exchange Commission must state their responsibility for establishing and maintaining effective internal control structure and procedures to assure the reliability of financial reports. In addition, two attestation reports (certification) are mandated. In the first, corporate executives must attest to the effectiveness of the internal control systems of their enterprises. In the second, external auditors of these corporations are required to attest to the veracity of management's assurance.

The emphasis on the role of internal accounting and controls was given another boost when the Basel Committee on Banking Supervision of the Bank for International Settlements (BIS) issued *Basel Accord II* in 2007 in which operational risk was identified as one of three important types of risks.[8] One highlight of the *Basel Accord* document is its emphasis on internal controls (Basel Committee on Banking Supervision, 2011). In the buildup to the Basel Accord, BIS issued a document entitled *"Framework for Internal Control Systems in Banking Supervision"* (1998). Principle 4 of the *Framework* sets the scope of internal control as follows:

> An effective internal control system requires that the material risks that could adversely affect the achievement of the bank's goals are being recognized and continually assessed. This assessment should cover all risk facing the bank and the consolidated banking organization (that is, credit risk, country and transfer risk, market risk, interest rate risk, liquidity risk, operational risk, legal risk and reputational risk). Internal controls may need to be revised to appropriately address any new or previously uncontrolled risks.
>
> (Basel Committee on Banking Supervision, 2011, p. 3).

This description of the scope of the internal control function encompasses much more than the simple conception of internal control merely as "segregation of duties." Although the *Basel Accord* is aimed at the banking industry and large banks in most countries have adopted it, its concepts and principles apply equally well to other industries. In fact, a weak internal control system is the most common unique feature of almost every corporate failure case.

When internal controls fail, external audits are expected to assist in the discovery of fraud. This approach is generally effective unless management creates ways to circumvent this process as, for example, in the case of *HealthSouth*.

## Accounting Log: *HealthSouth* Internal Control Debacle

While the disastrous fraud of *HealthSouth* was not of the same complexity or scale as Enron or WorldCom, *HealthSouth* had 60,000 employees in 2000 compared to Enron's 19,000 employees. The case of *HealthSouth* shows that massive fraud can take place by one simple violation of accounting controls that can confound external audits.[9] Richard Scrushy, the co-founder, was CEO from the foundation of the company in 1984 until March 2003. Scrushy's goal was to see stock prices on a continuously rising trajectory because he believed that achieving his goal would be attainable if *HealthSouth* met or beat analysts' earnings forecasts. The company offered outpatient healthcare in 26 states and began to open branches overseas. Revenues grew quickly to about $4.5 billion in 2003. When generating profits from legitimate business slowed down, Scrushy and a succession of Chief Financial Officers turned to the art of showing profits by manipulating accounting numbers in such a way that it would not be detectable by external auditors. In this case, fraud was at the highest level of the organization and internal control systems were seriously compromised. The senior management counted on its knowledge that the company's external auditors do not consider entries of less than $5,000.00 to be material and thus did not audit them. The top management spared no effort in creating thousands of entries in amounts falling short of the $5,000.00 magic number until these false entries added up to $2.7 billion in fraudulent profits. Shortly after Enron, the SEC followed by the FBI began investigating *HealthSouth* and the stock price dropped from a high of $30.00 to 14¢ per share as of 2012. *HealthSouth* is still operating with stockholders' equity of negative $72 million.[10]

### 2.3.2 Accounting Reporting Risk Exposures

In this book, *accounting reporting risk is defined as the risk of exposure to loss due to misreporting and misrepresentation of information in financial statements.* Misreporting can arise for several reasons many of which are related to the wide discretion the management applies in areas such as the following:

- Estimation and judgment.
- Making unguided accounting choices.
- Applying accounting standards incorrectly.
- Committing fraud.
- Invoking assumptions to approximate fair values in the absence of observable prices.
- Determining asset impairment.

### *2.3.2.1 Accounting Reporting Risk:* Estimation and Judgment

An argument can be advanced to show that every asset on the balance sheet is an estimate, though each estimate has a different degree of subjectivity. Accounts and notes receivable, for example, are reported at the expected "net realizable" value, which is essentially a *prediction* of what the management anticipates to collect. It is the nominal initial amount adjusted for two items:

1. The balances that are considered impaired and are very likely uncollectible.
2. The balances whose collectability is in doubt.

Neither of these two items is based on objectively verifiable information, especially the latter one for which reserves or provisions have to be established. Here the management of the enterprise applies judgment based on a number of assumptions. The end result of this process is that the amounts reported for accounts and notes receivable are the management's prediction of what the entity is expecting to collect. This is the same process that banks follow in estimating loan or credit card balances, expected losses, and loan loss reserves. In many cases, the estimates are based on subjective evaluation of aging accounts and on the bank's tracking the nonpayment history of the accounts. In other cases, banks and large commercial enterprises use statistical models of default prediction. Some of these models incorporate individual specific information on purchasing habits and payment history. The precision of these models notwithstanding, the ultimate product is estimation or prediction of collectible amounts. The possible inaccuracy resulting from management assumptions and estimates is emphasized by the Federal Deposit Insurance Agency (FDIC) as quoted in Exhibit 2.2.

## Exhibit 2.2 The Federal Deposit Insurance Corporation Statement on the Use of Estimation in Financial Statements

**Use of Estimates**

Management makes estimates and assumptions that affect the amounts reported in the financial statements and accompanying notes. *Actual results could differ from these estimates. Where it is possible that changes in estimates will cause a material change in the financial statements in the near term, we have disclosed the nature and extent of such changes in estimates*. The more significant estimates include the assessments receivable and associated revenue; the allowance for loss on receivables from resolutions (including loss-share agreements); the estimated losses

> for anticipated failures, litigation, and representations and warranties; guarantee obligations for the Temporary Liquidity Guarantee Program and debt of limited liability companies; valuation of trust preferred securities; and the postretirement benefit obligation.
>
> (FDIC, 2009; emphasis added)

Similar reporting risk concerns arise with respect to inventory valuation. The management of the business enterprise decides on the choice of the valuation method, but unless inventory is hedged and the hedge is effective, the valuation is generally dominated by the lower-of-cost-or-market rule,[11] although neither the cost nor the market value numbers are objectively verifiable: market is net realizable value and cost may include allocation of overhead that is determined by some guides internal to the organization. As an illustration, the following disclosure by EADS N. V. (EADS, 2010, p. 23) highlights the areas that call for exercising judgment.[12]

> **Inventories**—Inventories are measured at the lower of acquisition cost (generally the average cost) or manufacturing cost and net realisable value. Manufacturing costs comprise all costs that are directly attributable to the manufacturing process, such as direct material and labor, and production related overheads (based on normal operating capacity and normal consumption of material, labor and other production costs), including depreciation charges. Net realisable value is the estimated selling price in the ordinary course of the business less applicable variable selling expenses.

EADS N. V. is not unique in this setting; it is similar to the situation in many other manufacturing enterprises. This quote points out the discretion the management has over reported values. For example, under the lower-of-cost-or-market rule, the reported values could be influenced by different assumptions for each of the cost bases of valuation:

- *Average Acquisition Cost*—management judgment and assumptions determine the choice of the pool of products and the period over which average cost is calculated. If management uses smaller pools of assets held in the inventory for the purpose of valuation, it will have greater flexibility in determining the ultimate numbers it will report. The reported numbers could also differ depending on the length of time management chooses to include in its data collection. These choices depend on management's objectives which may or may not be aligned with shareholders' interest.
- *Manufacturing Cost*—measurement of inventories under this option is loaded with judgment and estimation because the cost of manufacturing includes allocated overhead and indirect costs, allowing the management to choose allocation bases and methods. Similarly, deciding what is "normal operations" and "normal capacity" in determining the basis of indirect cost allocation is another management choice.
- *Net Realizable Value*—this measure is based on estimating both selling prices and related transaction cost. Estimating both numbers depends on the liquidity of the markets for the particular commodities in the inventories, the choice of vendors, and the availability of competitive information. The aggregate effect of these assumptions introduces measurement noise in the inventory value estimates reported to external users. This is relevant information because errors in judgment will result in shifting cost of goods sold and earnings across time.

## Accounting Log: Valuation of Inventories under IFRS

Under U.S. GAAP, writing down the inventories to net realizable (fair) value may not be reversed; under IFRS, management is permitted to revalue the inventories upward in cases where market declines do not persist. In the latter case, revaluation is permitted only to the maximum of the original cost level. The second difference is that using the LIFO method of inventory valuation is prohibited under IFRS.[13]

The situation is no different with respect to depreciation accruals. In general, depreciation expense is not based on wear and tear resulting from using the asset and obsolescence of technology. Depreciation is often referred to as a "systematic allocation of cost" but it is only systematic to the extent that it is "arithmetic" calculation with a certain pattern. Usually, the management elects each of the following:

- The period over which the asset will be depreciated.
- Estimates of the salvage value.
- The pattern of depreciation.

All are based on criteria consistent with management objectives, mostly to show a smooth pattern of profits.

There is no shortage of examples, but consider the actions of airlines in searching for a way to boost profits (or reduce losses). The productive life of a jet airplane depends heavily on maintenance and the frequency of takeoff and landing. Until 1998, most major airlines calculated depreciation charges based on an average life of 20 years and an estimated residual value of generally 5% of the cost of the airplanes. In 1998 Continental Airlines, Inc. led the charge to change this policy by extending the depreciable lives of certain newer generation aircraft to 30 years and increased the estimated residual values of those aircraft from 10% to 15% of cost. These types of changes in estimates are often carried out with the goal of affecting earnings rather than attaining a more accurate description of the wear and tear of the asset. In October 21, 2005, American Airlines disclosed the change in depreciation policy that increases reported earnings (before income tax) by $108 million. The footnote in the 2005 Form 10-K of American Airlines states:[14]

> Effective January 1, 2005, in order to more accurately reflect the expected useful life of its aircraft, the Company changed its estimate of the depreciable lives of its Boeing 737–800, Boeing 757–200 and McDonnell Douglas MD-80 aircraft from 25 to 30 years. As a result of this change, Depreciation and Amortization Expense was reduced by approximately $108 million for the year ended December 31, 2005.[15]

### *2.3.2.2 Accounting Reporting Risk:* Unguided Accounting Choices

Financial reporting risk also arises when standards allow the management to select an accounting treatment consistent with "*management intent.*" Under both U.S. GAAP (ASC topic 320) and IFRS, *management intent* is used as the primary criterion for the choice of accounting for marketable securities and hedge accounting. In the U.S. GAAP, this criterion for choice of the classification of marketable securities is spelled out in Paragraph 7 of FAS 115 (1993, p. 6; now ASC 320), which states that:

> Investments in debt securities shall be classified as *held-to-maturity* and measured at amortized cost in the statement of financial position only if the reporting enterprise has the *positive intent and ability* to hold those securities to maturity.

Under current U.S. GAAP (as of August 2012) marketable securities are classified into three categories:

1. *Held-to-Maturity* (amortized cost): This category is restricted to those debt securities for which an enterprise has a *positive intent and ability* to hold to maturity. Market forces and prepayment risk would have no effect on this classification because these securities are not used for near-term profit making or for asset/liability management.

   Held-to-maturity (HTM) securities are measured and valued at amortized historical cost. HTM securities are to be downward revalued at fair value only in the event of impairment that is considered "other than temporary" with the write down being charged to earnings.
2. *Trading* (FV-NI, fair value through net income): These are the debt and equity securities that are bought and held for short periods principally with the intent of market and profit making. Trading securities are measured at current market values with the changes in fair values flowing through the income statement. That is, the *anticipated, unrealized gains and losses are recognized and accounted for precisely as realized gains and losses.*[16]
3. *Available-for-Sale* (FVOCI, fair value through other comprehensive income): These securities are defined by exclusion; they are neither HTM nor *trading* securities. As with trading securities, the available-for-sale securities (AFS) are measured at current market values, but unlike trading securities, the changes in market values are deferred (parked) in other comprehensive income (OCI) and are reclassified to earnings under one of three conditions: (i) if estimating fair value is not feasible; (ii) if there is an impairment in fair value that is judged to be "other than temporary"; and (iii) when these securities are sold.

The primary criterion the standards require for placing securities in one of these categories is management "intent," knowing full well that "intent" cannot be verified. The notion of "intent" has significance in law more than in accounting, especially when dealing with actions of individuals. In this respect, the legal definition of intent is "the state of one's mind at the time one carries out an action."[17] Accounting standards do not offer a definition of intent that could draw boundaries for management choices. The three restrictive conditions required by U.S. GAAP (ASC 320) are:

1. To declare the intent at acquisition date.
2. Not to engage in selling HTM securities, except under the conditions specified in the standard.[18]
3. Restrictions on transfer between categories.

## Accounting Log: Proposed Changes in Accounting Standards

The IASB and the FASB have recently (January 2012) reached an agreement on proposed changes in accounting standards for possible adoption in 2015. The agreement relates to the classification of financial instruments and includes the following:

Classification of financial instruments will be in three categories:

1. Amortized Cost
2. FV-NI: Fair valuation with the changes flow through earnings (or P&L, for Profit & Loss statement).
3. FVOCI: Fair valuation with the changes in fair values reported in Other Comprehensive Income (equity account).

The choice of classification of financial instruments will depend on three factors:

a) *Cash flow characteristics of the instrument*: whether or not the cash flow includes principal plus interest only and whether there is any contingency that leads to modification and variability in the cash flow.

- If the cash flow includes any amounts or modification to the principal plus interest (compensation for time value of money), the instrument would be classified as FV-NI.
- If the cash flow includes only the principal plus interest, the financial instrument may be classified differently from FV-NI, depending on the business model.

b) *Replacing "management intent" by the "business model" or "business strategy."*

- Eligibility of the Amortized Cost Classification: If the instrument passes the Principal + Interest cash flow characteristic, it was not initially acquired for sale, and the business model calls for holding the instrument up to the contractual settlement to collect the contractual cash flow.
- If the business model is to hold the asset for a purpose that encompasses both (i) holding the financial asset to collect contractual cash flows, and (ii) selling the financial assets (i.e., both AFS and HTM), the financial instrument is eligible for the FVOCI classification.

c) *Whether the financial instrument is debt or equity*. Equity instruments are classified as FV-NI.

The above noted classification is not yet a standard in the U.S. GAAP, but it is a standard in IFRS. It is IFRS No. 9, which is set to be effective in 2015. The anticipation is that the FASB will adopt the above noted classification and substantially converge to IFRS No. 9.

*Source*: FASB (2012).

Using the notion of management "intent" and the restriction of movement of marketable securities from one classification has given companies like *Fannie Mae* and *Freddie Mac* opportunities to distort reported earnings. Both of these companies came under public scrutiny because of their quasi-government-owned status. Two extensive reports were issued by the Office of Federal Housing Enterprise Oversight (OFHEO, 2003, 2006).

Some specific (abusive) transactions by *Freddie Mac* are cited in the OFHEO Report of 2003:

> Management created an essentially fictional transaction with a securities firm to move approximately $30 billion of mortgage assets from a *trading account* to an *available for sale* account. Other than to reduce potential earnings volatility, the transaction had no other meaningful purpose (p. iii).
>
> [...]
>
> Freddie Mac could identify *held-to-maturity* PCs (Participation Certificates) in its portfolio with mark-to-market losses and move them to a *trading account*, where a loss could be immediately recognized as income. The maneuver planned by management was to execute forward sales of mortgage-backed securities in November and December 2000 to lock-in the market value of PCs with embedded losses. On January 1, 2001, management would move the PCs to the *trading account* and recognize a loss to offset gains on the derivatives portfolio (p. 28).
>
> [...]
>
> Indeed, the economic aspects of the deal were negative when one considers the operational hazards created by the transaction. (p. 36).

The impact of manipulating the classification of marketable securities on earnings was not minor: Table 2.1 shows the effect of switching earnings across periods. By exploiting the absence of guidance in making accounting choice, *Freddie Mac* has actually reported lower earnings by $4.5 billion. The main guiding force for the management was to smooth earnings over time so as to maximize executives' income-based bonuses.

Uncovering other types of manipulation in 2000–2005, including the misclassification of marketable securities, at *Fannie Mae* led to *Standard & Poor*'s downgrading its credit rating and to OFHEO tightening regulatory control, requiring changes in corporate governance, and to directing the company to cease practicing inappropriate accounting. Subsequently, the SEC ordered *Fannie Mae* to pay $400 million in civil penalties, and to replace its top management.

**Table 2.1** Restatement of Earnings at Freddie Mac

| *Year* | *Net income as reported (US$ billion)* | *Restated net income (US$ billion)* | *Restated NI minus Reported NI (US$ billion)* |
|---|---|---|---|
| 2000 | 2.55 | 3.67 | 1.12 |
| 2001 | 4.15 | 3.15 | (0.99) |
| 2002 | 5.76 | 10.09 | 4.33 |

### *2.3.2.3 Accounting Reporting Risk:* Incorrect Application of Accounting Standards

Accounting information risk could also arise from improper use of accounting standards. When these events are uncovered, public enterprises are required to correct them and "restate" financial statements. The act of restating and re-filing financial statements with the SEC is a confirmation of misreporting, whether or not the misreporting was intentional it is an admission that financial statements contain material errors. The consequences could be severe, as in the case of WorldCom, which capitalized expenses related to establishing telephone services instead of expensing them. Though it seems simple, the effect of overstating earnings and misleading investors took the company into a downward spiral culminating in bankruptcy. The cost of this failure was very high to the employees who lost their jobs and retirement savings invested in the company's stock, to shareholders who lost their investments, and to the managers, some of whom ended up in jail.

Restating financial statements to correct errors is not limited to a given country or region, but there was a period of time in which the number and frequency of restatements in the USA surged to a record high. At the request of Congress, the United States Government Accountability Office (GAO) prepared two reports in 2002 and 2006 (GAO-06-678 Financial Restatements) in which it noted that the number of restatements had increased to 1,390 during the period between July 2002 and September 2005, resulting in significant losses to investors:

> The market capitalization of the companies—those we were able to analyze from among the listed companies that we identified as announcing restatements of previously reported information between July 2002 and September 2005—decreased an estimated $36 billion when adjusted for overall market movements (nearly $18 billion unadjusted) in the days around the initial restatement announcement.
>
> (GAO, July 2006, p. 5)

Thirty-seven percent of the restatements related to incorrect accounting for expenses. Qwest Communications International was one of the restating companies about which the GAO Report (ibid., p. 172) states that the company:

> (1) had incorrectly applied accounting policies with respect to certain optical capacity asset sale transactions in 1999, 2000, and 2001; (2) further adjustments were required to account for certain sales of equipment in 2000 and 2001 that the company had previously determined had been recorded in error; and (3) that in a limited number of transactions, it did not properly account for certain expenses incurred for services from telecommunications providers in 2000 and 2001.

As a result, the restated and reported income numbers are:

| | *2001* | *2000* |
|---|---|---|
| Restated earnings (US$ billion) | (5.6) | (1.04) |
| Reported earnings (US$ billion) | (4.0) | (0.8) |

Shortly after disclosing the need to restate financial statements, Qwest's stock price dropped from a high of $35.00 to $11.00.

In other cases, the misreporting came about by improper recognition of assets or liabilities as, for example, the understatement of liabilities at Aurora Corporation. This case is detailed in the first GAO Report on financial restatement (2002), which states the reasons for reporting errors in the first place:

Through its investigation, the independent auditor determined that liabilities that existed for certain trade promotion and marketing activities and other expenses (primarily sales returns and allowances, distribution and consumer marketing) were not properly recognized as liabilities and that certain assets were overstated (primarily accounts receivable, inventories, and fixed assets).

(GAO, 2002)

The chart in Figure 2.2 is reproduced from the 2002 GAO Report and shows the decline of share prices of Aurora from a high of $15.00 to a low of about $3.00 in a few months, with a sharp drop in February 2000 when it became public knowledge that the company's financial statements were in error.

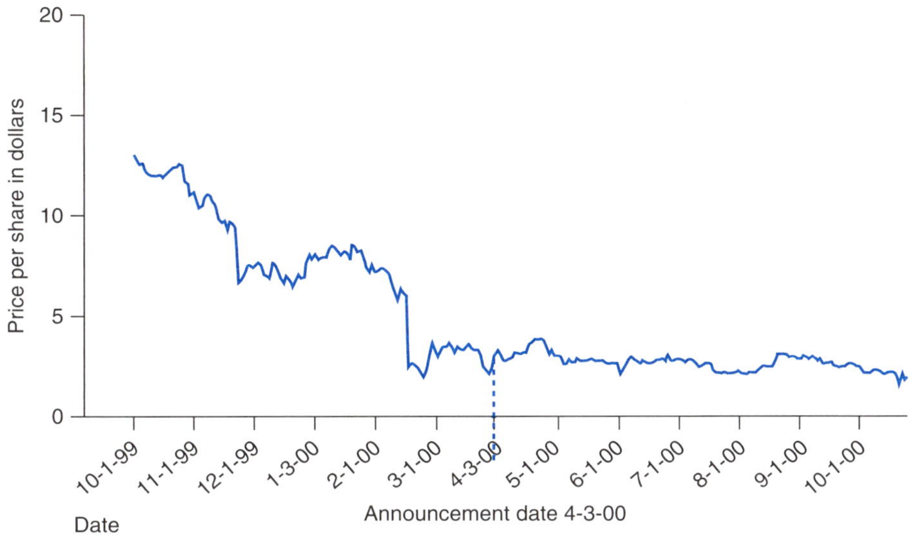


**Figure 2.2** The Impact of Restatement of Financial Statements on Stock Prices of Aurora Company

## *2.3.2.4 Accounting Reporting Risk:* Assumption Underlying Fair Value Estimation

In the tradition of the relatively old accounting theory book of Paton and Littleton (1940), accounting practice has incorporated the distinction between *costing* and *valuation*. For many decades, the accounting profession and standard setters have followed the philosophy of Paton and Littleton who argued that assets are deferred costs and accounting does not report values. This tradition has been eroding gradually ever since the publication of the *Trueblood Report*, which established the foundations for what became the *Conceptual Framework*[19] that defines assets as a store of future benefits, and liabilities as a store of future sacrifices. The "store" is measured by the present value of the future cash flow the asset is *expected* to generate or the present value of future cash flow the entity is expected to transfer to settle the obligation. These definitions are assumed to be in harmony with the objectives of financial statements as stated in the *Conceptual Framework*: to assist investors and creditors in predicting future cash flow with respect to *timing, amounts and uncertainty*, three essential elements in valuation of assets or claims to assets. These elements are easier to assess for financial assets and liabilities than for non-financial assets due to (a) divisibility, and (b) having relatively more liquid markets.

Accounting standards regarding fair values have evolved through May 25, 2011, when the FASB and the IASB reconciled their differences and agreed on one standard (as of this day, the new ASC 820 is the same as the new IFRS 13). Fair value is defined as:

> *The price that would be received to sell an asset or paid to transfer a liability in an orderly transaction between market participants at the measurement date.*

Implementing this definition will depend on the liquidity and availability of active markets, which led to making distinction between three levels:

- *Level 1*—Quoted prices in active markets that are unadjusted and are accessible at the measurement date for identical, unrestricted assets or liabilities.
- *Level 2*—Using several indirect market inputs. Quoted prices for identical assets and liabilities in markets that are not active, quoted prices for similar assets and liabilities in active markets or financial instruments for which significant inputs are observable, either directly or indirectly.
- *Level 3*—Prices or valuations that require inputs that are both significant to the fair value measurement and unobservable.

The final joint standard agreed upon by the FASB and the IASB (in May 2011) makes six important observations:

1. Fair value is equal to exit price: what the entity could sell the asset for or could transfer to pay the liability.
2. The unit of measure of fair value is the individual asset or liability without aggregation or consideration of premiums or discounts resulting from the size of the position (i.e., blockage is not permitted). This is clearly the case for *Level 1*, but the standard allows for incorporating control discount or premium in estimating the fair value in *Level 2* or *Level 3* because this adjustment is viewed "as a characteristic of the asset being measured." For example, investment in private ventures might require *Level 3* estimation. In this case, if the investor has control over the private venture by virtue of owning a large number of shares, this fact alters the features of all other shares. Blockage adjustment, therefore, is a feature applicable to *Level 2* or *Level 3*, but not to *Level 1*.
3. Valuation is to be based on the assumptions of market participants, not those of the entity.
4. There is a distinction between the fair values of a financial and non-financial asset. The former is to be evaluated on a standalone basis, while the latter is to be based on best and most advantageous value in use by market participants. While the value of a non-financial asset to the user of the asset is likely to be based on the synergy between the asset in question and other assets, this entity-specific factor is not relevant in estimating fair value because "the best and most advantageous use" should be based on assumptions external to the entity—assumptions made by buyers and sellers in the marketplace.
5. Whether the non-financial asset is held for sale or for use, the concept of fair value is based on a hypothetical sale transaction in one of the following two situations by reference to external markets, not to the entity:

    i. *Principal Markets*: These are the markets with highest volume and trading. Absent other evidence, it is presumed to be the market in which the entity transacts.
    ii. *Highest and Best Use*: The use that will generate the maximum amount to be received for sale of the asset or the least amount to be transferred to settle the liability.

6. When prices are quoted as a "range" such as in the bid/ask spread, the fair value would be a price falling within this range. The management must make judgment as to which price is "most representative." (We will see in Chapter Three that bid/ask spread is one measure of risk.)

While the new fair value standard has shifted the focus from "value in use specific to the entity" to adopt the concept of "market participants," making an extensive use of assumptions and judgment will continue to be problematic primarily when it comes to *Level 3* type valuation, and to some extent *Level 2*. Essentially, in this case, the management has to make assumptions about every aspect of the valuation—the pattern of future cash flow, the amounts, the timing, the uncertainty, and the model to be applied. While *Level 1* is referred to as "mark-to-market," *Level 2 and Level 3* are often referred to as "mark-to-model," implying the admission of possible biasedness.[20]

For example, 13% of all fair-valued assets in JP Morgan Chase are based on *Level 3* and the management clearly discloses some of the issues and concerns related to the invoked assumptions and judgment:[21]

> For instruments classified within level 3 of the hierarchy, judgments used to estimate fair value may be significant. In arriving at an estimate of fair value for an instrument within level 3, management must first determine the appropriate model to use. Second, due to the lack of observability of significant inputs, management must assess all relevant empirical data in deriving valuation inputs—including, but not limited to, yield curves, interest rates, volatilities, equity or debt prices, foreign exchange rates and credit curves. In addition to market information, models also incorporate transaction details, such as maturity. Finally, management judgment must be applied to assess the appropriate level of valuation adjustments to reflect counterparty credit quality, the Firm's creditworthiness, constraints on liquidity and unobservable parameters, where relevant. The judgments made are typically affected by the type of product and its specific contractual terms, and the level of liquidity for the product or within the market as a whole.
>
> (Form 10-K, 2010, p. 152)

Similarly, IBM highlights the assumptions made (Form 10-K, 2010, p. 77):

> The company considers certain market valuation adjustments to the "base valuations"
>
> - Counterparty credit risk adjustments are applied to financial instruments, taking into account the actual credit risk of a counterparty as observed in the credit default swap market to determine the true fair value of such an instrument.
> - Credit risk adjustments are applied to reflect the company's own credit risk when valuing all liabilities measured at fair value. The methodology is consistent with that applied in developing counterparty credit risk adjustments, but incorporates the company's own credit risk as observed in the credit default swap market.

While the standard has shifted the focus from the entity-specific valuation to market-based, it is never clear how the management would be able to capture and incorporate "the assumptions that market participants" use in setting prices. Time will tell, but it is entirely possible that all these assumptions will simply be what the management of the reporting entity wants to make of them.

### 2.3.2.5 *Accounting Reporting Risk:* Judgment on Asset Impairment

When buying a house you might want to pay 20% of the price as a deposit, then borrow 80% on a 15- or 30-year mortgage. The house you just purchased is used as collateral (security) for the mortgage. But after the 2007 financial crisis, the housing market collapsed and the house for which you borrowed $300,000 as a mortgage (80% of the house price), may have dropped in value to below $180,000. Suddenly you owe more than the value of the house. The expression developed for that situation is that the "mortgage is upside-down." Even if you did not borrow a mortgage and your house drops in value from $400,000 to $250,000, then your property is upside-down because it cost you more than the price you could achieve by selling it.

In accounting, the term "asset impairment" is similar to the common speech expression of "upside-down" which is the subject of ASC 360. The main purpose of following asset impairment in accounting is actually deep rooted in the postulate of "Conservatism." Namely, recognize anticipated loss, but not anticipated profits; impairment standards require writing down an asset to its depressed value, but not writing up (it should be noted that IFRS allows writing up an asset that was impaired only up to the level of capturing the previously recognized impairment).

In general, standards define impairment in reference to an asset or asset group using the following two definitions (ASC 360-10-20):

1. Impairment is the condition that exists when the carrying amount of a long-lived asset (asset group) exceeds its fair value.
2. An asset group is the unit of accounting for a long-lived asset or assets to be held and used, which represents the lowest level for which identifiable cash flows are largely independent of the cash flows of other groups of assets and liabilities.

The scope of the standard covers long-lived assets held for use or for disposal (ASC 360-10-35). The concept of impairment is not a complex one. It is simply an expanded version of the lower-of-cost-or-market rule if the excess of the carrying value over market (fair) value is deemed not recoverable.

#### To Impair or Not to Impair

Before undertaking an elaborate process to estimate the impairment amounts, the U.S. GAAP provides a "bellwether" to decide whether to proceed with the process or not. This check is carried out for an asset or group of assets. This early indicator is as follows:

Undiscounted net cash inflow > Carrying amount → Do not do the impairment test.
Undiscounted net cash inflow < Carrying amount → Proceed with the impairment test.

#### Impairment Test

If the decision is made to proceed, then the next step is to proceed with the Recoverability Test, which has four elements:

1. When to apply the recoverability test?
2. How to measure the impairment?

3. When to recognize the impairment?
4. Where and how to report the impairment?

We will consider each of these in turn.

1. *Timing the Measurement of Impairment*: The management must exercise judgment in making the decision that the drop in value is not recoverable. ASC 360-10-35-21 provides examples of events that lead the management to properly time making this decision. These are:

a. A significant decrease in the market price.
b. A significant adverse change in legal or functional use of the asset.
c. A cost overrun higher than the level of expected cash inflow for the asset.
d. It is more likely than not (a probability greater than 50%) that a long-lived asset will be used or transferred out of the enterprise by sale or disposal at a time significantly before the end of its estimated productive life.

2. *Measurement of Impairment*: The size of impairment is measured by comparing the fair market value against a benchmark. Both measures (the fair value and the benchmark) require making numerous assumptions and judgment, which give the management room for committing errors.

It is very likely that impairment will be tested for each asset group because testing for each individual asset will be costly. The asset group includes the smallest number or collection of assets for which an independent series of future cash flow could be identified. It is also expected that active markets do not exist for these asset groups since they are unique to the enterprises that use them or hold them for sale (this is less true for financial assets) and the management will turn to other methods to determine fair value. Estimating fair value by the discounted future cash flows is one of those methods.

The management therefore is in a position to select the asset group, the remaining productive life of the asset group, determining the amounts and pattern of future net cash flow, and the discount rate (although it is expected that the risk-free discount rate be used). The U.S. GAAP addressed one of the factors: the productive life of the asset group would be the productive life of the primary asset in the group. The management is left with identifying the dominant asset in the asset group. Furthermore, the management must do the following.

i. "Incorporate the entity's own assumptions about its use of the asset (asset group) and shall consider all available evidence" (ASC 360-10-35-30).
ii. The projected cash flows must "be based on the existing service potential of the asset (asset group) at the date it is tested ... which includes the remaining useful life, cash-flow generating capacity, and for tangible assets, physical output capacity" (ASC 360-10-35-33).
iii. For assets under development, "the expected service potential of an asset (group) when development is substantially complete" (ASC 360-10-35-34).

On the other side of the impairment test is the benchmark, which is the carrying (book) value. The benchmark of comparing the fair value of a long-lived asset is the carrying (or book) value. It should be noted that this benchmark is the acquisition cost net of depreciation (or amortization for intangibles). An overstatement of depreciation in prior years will lower earning and the carrying book value and, conversely, understatement of depreciation or amortization in prior years will result in reporting higher earnings and higher book value. Therefore, the benchmark (carrying value) used in estimating the significance of the deviation between fair value and the benchmark is influenced by the preceding depreciation policy and charges. Therefore, to ascertain the credibility of the benchmark reference point, the management must review prior depreciation charges and adjust the book value of over-or-understatement of accumulated depreciation charges.

3. *Recognition of Impairment*: Impairment is a loss. The estimated impairment of a long-lived asset held for sale or use must be recognized in earnings (income from continuing operations before income taxes).

4. *Disclosure*: Two important pieces of information must be disclosed:

i. The Asset: Long-lived assets held for sale or for potential disposal are to be classified in a separate category on the balance sheet.
ii. The Loss: A description of the impaired asset whose change in value gave rise to the impairment loss; the amount of impairment; and the method the enterprise used to discount cash flow to estimate the present value.

### 2.3.3 Market (Price) Risk

As a consequence of being an "open system," the entity is exposed to the risk of unexpected changes in market prices of inputs and output. This risk is a subset of strategic risk as defined in this book. In general, market risk is the exposure to loss due to one of the following:

1. *Commodity Price Risk*: Changes in the prices of raw materials used for production or prices of finished products.
2. *Currency Risk*: Changes in currency exchange rates.
3. *Interest Rate Risk*: Changes in the price of money.
4. *Equity Risk*: Changes in Equity Indexes.

For any of these prices, changes might be either anticipated or unexpected. Each type requires a different approach to managing the resulting risk exposure. For expected changes, management could make appropriate plans and make decisions with corrective actions; it could buy insurance, or it could establish provisions and reserve balances. In contrast, *unexpected changes are surprises for which the management is not able to plan, manage, or insure the outcome*. In this case, hedging using financial derivatives appears to have low transaction cost as compared to other means and has emerged over the past 30 years as the primary method for mitigating the risk arising from unexpected price changes.[22] These differences in mitigating risk create dilemmas for accountants because they must devise appropriate accounting methods to reflect management's success or failure in managing the risks facing their enterprises.

#### *2.3.3.1 Commodity Price Risk*

A major concern for the management of a business enterprise is the exposure to potential loss due to adverse unexpected movement in the prices of the raw materials that the entity acquires from others, as well as exposure to unexpected changes in the prices of the products that it sells to others (noted as Market Risk in Figure 2.1). Unexpected increases in the prices of raw materials will increase the cost of production and will reduce profits. Similarly, unexpected decreases in the prices of output will reduce current and future revenues. Either type of commodity price change will result in squeezing profit margins and reducing reported earnings. Exposure to loss due to adverse (unfavorable) unexpected commodity price movements—either rising input prices or declining output prices—is known as *commodity price risk*. Accounting for hedging commodity price risk is covered in Chapters Seven and Eight for single currency and in Chapters Ten and Eleven for multiple currencies.

### 2.3.3.2 Currency Exchange Rate Risk

Money is a medium of exchange and every country or region (e.g., the Eurozone) has its own currency. According to the CIA World Fact Book, there are 178 currencies in the world[23] even after 17 European countries consolidated their currencies to form the Eurozone.

Currencies are convertible into other currencies at prices known as currency exchange rates. A currency exchange rate is the price of one currency expressed in units of another currency. For example, exchange rates between the Chinese renminbi (CNY or ¥) and five other major currencies for the two months of August 2006 and June 2010 are presented in Table 2.2.

**Table 2.2** Exchange Rates between the Chinese Renminbi and Five other Currencies

| | *CNY/USD* | *CNY/EUR* | *CNY/100JPY* | *CNY/HKD* | *CNY/GBP* |
|---|---|---|---|---|---|
| August 2006 | 7.9585 | 10.2137 | 6.7894 | 1.02334 | 15.1619 |
| June 2010 | 6.7909 | 8.2710 | 7.6686 | 0.87239 | 10.2135 |
| June 2012 | 6.36489 | 8.0643 | 7.94826 | 0.82026 | 9.99356 |

Key: CNY = the Chinese renminbi (¥); EUR = the euro (€); JPY = the Japanese yen (¥); HKD = Hong Kong dollar ($); GBP = Great British pound (£)

#### Currency Transaction Risk

Increasing the scope and depth of transactions across boundaries increased enterprises' exposure to loss due to movements in currency exchange rates. To understand one aspect of the impact of changing exchange rates, consider two situations for two different entities:

- On 10 August 2006, a business enterprise in France purchased textiles from China in the amount of CNY10,000. Given that the exchange rate of renminbi into euros is CNY10.2137 for one euro at the time of the transaction, the cost to the French entity in euros would be €979.07. The management of the French enterprise paid the price at acquisition time because it did not wish to be subjected to the risk of adverse movement in the exchange rate between renminbi and the euro.
- Another business enterprise in Italy purchased equipment from China also on 10 August 2006 in the amount of CNY10,000 on credit (a note payable for the Italian entity, which is a note receivable for the Chinese business firm). Assume (for simplification) that the note does not bear an explicit interest rate. That entity is subject to currency risk because of the possibility of changing currency exchange rates before settlement. In June 2010, the Italian entity paid off the note payable at the then prevailing exchange rate on the date of settlement, the payment amounted to €1,209.04.

Although the French and Italian enterprises in this illustration purchased products from China at the same time and for the same transaction price, the Italian enterprise paid €229.97 more than did the French entity. The reason for this difference is the change in currency exchange rate CNY/EUR during that interval from CNY10.2137/€.1.00 to become CNY8.2710/€1.00.

Because the movement in exchange rates from August 2006 to June 2010 meant that a smaller number of renminbi is required for each one euro, it is said that the Chinese currency has *appreciated* in relationship to the euro. An equivalent statement would be that the euro has *depreciated* in relationship to the Chinese renminbi. From the point of view of the Italian entity, this change in currency exchange rate is an unexpected adverse movement. Because the Italian entity waited and postponed settling the Note Payable after purchase, the entity was exposed to the possibility of having to pay more in euros to settle the debt; but the entity was also exposed to the possibility of saving money if the exchange rate changed in the opposite direction. The risk exposure in this case is called "transaction currency risk," because a specific transaction initiated the potential of currency loss. *Transaction currency exposure may then be stated as the potential of incurring losses due to adverse changes in the currency exchange rates between the time of the transaction and the time of settlement.*

### Currency Translation Risk

Exposure to currency risk goes beyond transaction exposure. Many multinational corporations build plants and have operations on foreign soil where the currency of the region is different from the currency of the parent company. In this case, the value of the foreign-located assets that a multinational company owns will change as the exchange rate between the currency of the parent and the currency of the foreign region fluctuates. The potential of reducing the values of the foreign-located assets due to exposure to currency fluctuations is a different type of currency risk from the transaction risk discussed above.

The parent company should report consolidated financial statements, which will be stated in the parent company's reporting (generally home) currency. If the parent company is located in the United Kingdom, the reporting currency is likely to be the British pound. If the parent company is located in Canada, it is very likely that its reporting currency is the Canadian dollar. If either the UK or the Canadian multinational has a subsidiary in Germany and that subsidiary performs most of its activities in euros, then preparing consolidated financial statements will require converting the financial statements of the German subsidiary from the euro to British Sterling for the British Company or to the Canadian dollars for the Canadian company. In the absence of any accounting standards requiring the use of a specific exchange rate, there are several approaches:

- The exchange rate at the time the asset was acquired or the liability was created—i.e., historical rate.
- The currency exchange rate on the date of closing the books and preparing financial statements—i.e., current rate.
- Some average exchange rate.
- One exchange rate for each *type* of asset and a different rate for liabilities.

There must be reasonable foundations for the choice of one rate over the others. The rationale and the choice of the exchange rate used are stated in ASC 830 (FAS 52) in the USA and IAS 21 in IFRS. Currency translation is the subject of a segment of Chapter Eleven. However, it is of interest to note that currency translation risk is often referred to as accounting risk because it is the result of an accounting transformation, not of real transactions.

### Operating Risk

The impact of changes in currency exchange rates on the economic activities of the enterprise impacts both the current reporting periods and future operations. Currency operating risk is the likelihood of foreign currency-denominated operations facing declining revenues or facing a cost increase during future periods because of current changes in currency exchange rates. Financial economists refer to the sum of transaction risk and operating risk as "currency economic risk."

The three types of currency risk are presented in Exhibit 2.3.

## Exhibit 2.3 Currency Risk Exposure

| *Type of Currency Risk* | *Conditions* | *Combination* |
|---|---|---|
| Transaction Risk | When currency exchange rates might change between the time of a transaction and the time of settlement. | Economic Risk (Transaction Risk + Operating Risk) |
| Operating Risk | This is the extent to which unexpected changes in currency exchange rates will adversely affect future operations—reducing revenues or increasing cost—when income statement in future periods is translated into the parent currency. | |
| Translation (Accounting) Risk | Net assets invested in a foreign country whose functional currency is not that of the parent company may be exposed to loss in value when converted (translated) to the parent currency. | |

### *2.3.3.3 Interest Rate Risk*

Liquid assets and liabilities of a business enterprise (a bank, for example) consist of a combination of the following:

- Short-term financial instruments due within one year.
- Long-term financial instruments due over a horizon longer than a year.
- Fixed-interest-rate instruments that pay at predetermined coupon rates.
- Floating-rate financial instruments that pay interest rates that are indexed to some market index or rate such as LIBOR (London interbank offered rate) or Euribor (European interbank overnight rate) for interest-bearing instruments or equity index for equity instruments.
- Zero-coupon rate where the market price is discounted to account for the present value of imputed interest.

Exhibit 2.4 presents the combination of these five features.

## Exhibit 2.4 The 2x2 Combinations of Fixed-Rate and Floating-Rate Instruments

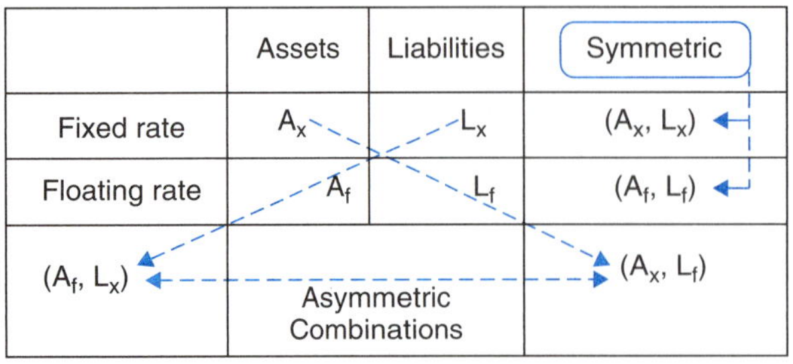


$L_x$ = fixed-rate obligations $L_f$ = floating-rate obligations
$A_x$ = fixed-rate assets $A_f$ = floating-rate assets

The impact of changes in interest rates on financial statements can be examined using the information in Exhibit 2.4. The four cells could be categorized into four combinations: two combinations have symmetric interest rate structures, and two combinations have asymmetric interest rate structures. Each of the four groups is discussed below.

### *Symmetric Scenario A*: Floating-rate Assets and Floating-rate Liabilities ($L_f$, $A_f$)

When both assets and liabilities have floating (variable) interest rates, they will generate similar cash flow patterns and the impact of changes in interest rates on the cash flow will not be difficult to construct. In this combination, as interest rates increase, the cash inflow from interest-earning assets will increase and, at the same time, the cash outflow for interest payment on floating-rate liabilities will also increase. The reverse is true for the impact of a decrease in interest rates—there will be a decline in both the cash inflow from the earned interest income on floating-rate financial assets, and the cash outflow for paying interest on floating-rate liabilities. The cash inflow and outflow will be fully matched if floating-rate financial assets and floating-rate financial liabilities are equal in amounts and duration.[24]

To illustrate the cash flow (and earnings) impact, consider the impact of changing interest rates on cash flow related to interest income/expense for three different scenarios:

- Scenario 1: floating-rate assets = floating-rate liabilities.
- Scenario 2: floating-rate assets < floating-rate liabilities.
- Scenario 3: floating-rate assets > floating-rate liabilities.

Table 2.4 presents the results of upward and downward interest rate movements in each scenario. For equal floating-rate assets and liabilities in Scenario 1, any increase or decrease in interest rate will not affect the cash flow or interest income/expense. In Scenario 2 where floating-rate liabilities are greater than floating-rate assets, the entity will experience increase in net cash outflow as interest rate increases, and increase in net cash inflow as interest rate declines. The reverse impact is true for Scenario 3 where floating-rate assets are higher than floating-rate liabilities.[25]

In summary, assuming that floating-rate financial assets and floating-rate financial liabilities have the same maturity and face values, a change in market interest rate will not affect the financial conditions of the business entity. There will be an effect only if the assets and liabilities have different face amounts or different durations. The scenarios presented in Table 2.3 consider the differences in the amounts of assets and liabilities, but do not address the difference in duration which is deferred until Chapter Three. A qualitative description of Table 2.3 is in Exhibit 2.5.

**Table 2.3** Impact of Interest Rate Changes on Cash Flow for Floating-Rate Assets and Floating-Rate Liabilities

| | | *Scenario B* | | *Scenario C* | | *Scenario D* | |
|---|---|---|---|---|---|---|---|
| | | *Asset* | *Liability* | *Asset* | *Liability* | *Asset* | *Liability* |
| *Row* | *Amount (m = 1,000)* | $20 M | $20 M | $12 M | $20 M | $15 M | $ 10 M |
| A | *Interest Charged = LIBOR* | +1% | +2% | +1% | +2% | +1% | +2% |
| B | *Base LIBOR = 3%* | $ 800 | $1,000 | $ 480 | $1,000 | $ 600 | $ 500 |
| C | *LIBOR ↑ 0.5%* | 900 | 1,100 | 540 | 1,100 | 675 | 550 |
| D | *Change in Interest (Row C – Row B)* | 100 | 100 | 60 | 100 | 75 | 50 |
| E | *Net Effect (Column Asset – Column Liability)* | = 0 | | = (40) | | = 25 | |
| F | *LIBOR ↓ 0.5%* | 700 | 900 | 420 | 900 | 525 | 450 |
| G | *Change in Interest (Row F – Row B)* | (100) | (100) | (60) | (100) | (75) | (50) |
| H | *Net Effect (Asset – Liabilities )* | = 0 | | = 40 | | = (25) | |

## Exhibit 2.5 Impact of Changes in Market Interest Rate on Cash Flows of Floating-Rate Assets and Floating-Rate Liabilities

| ↓ *Floating-rates financial instruments on the firm's balance sheet* | *Cash Flow Impact Due to Change in Interest Rates* | |
|---|---|---|
| | Increase in Interest Rate | Decrease in Interest Rate |
| Assets > Liabilities | ***Favorable impact*** | Adverse impact |
| Assets = Liabilities | *Immunized* | *Immunized* |
| Assets < Liabilities | Adverse impact | ***Favorable impact*** |

### *Symmetric Scenario B*: Fixed-Rate Assets and Fixed-Rate Liabilities ($L_x A_x$)[26]

In this case, changes in interest rate do not result in changes in cash flows because the cash outflow payable for interest on liabilities and the cash inflow receivable from investment are contractually fixed. For a 10% coupon financial instrument, for example, the amount the entity pays as interest is only a function of the face amount of the instrument and is invariant to market yield, the interest rate in the marketplace. That is, an increase or a decrease in market interest rates will not change the amount of cash outflow that the enterprise pays for interest on its fixed-rate debt, or the amount of cash inflow the enterprise collects from its fixed-rate investments.

But the change in the relationship between the coupon rate and market interest rate cannot be ignored because this change has other effects. More specifically, investors have no incentive, at any time, to invest in an asset that provides a yield lower than the market rate. Similarly, bond issuers (borrowers) have no incentive to make interest payments at a coupon rate higher than market rate (provided the appropriate adjustment is made for credit risk). Therefore, in the hypothetical example noted above, the 10% rate this bond issuer pays must be equal to the market rate of interest *at the time of issuing* and selling that bond in the marketplace.[27] When the market rate changes, this relationship between the coupon and the market rates also changes even though the cash flow related to the instruments remains unchanged.

Further interest in accounting for fair value hedge (see Chapters Seven and Eight) requires having a review of how a fixed-income instrument (such as a bond) is valued and how this value responds to changes in market interest rates. Consider the following contract for an example:

- The term to maturity of the bond is $T$.
- Face value of the bond is $F$.
- The coupon interest rate *per annum* on the bond is fixed at $cr$.
- The market yield (for the same risk class as that of the issuer entity) is $y$.

How much should the bond issuer expect to collect from selling this bond in an arms-length exchange transaction?

We should reiterate that the value of a bullet bond (a bond without optionality of recall, redemption or conversion) is the present value of all future cash flow associated with this bond. Using the conditions noted above, the market value of a (plain vanilla) bond should be equal to:

$$MV = \{\textstyle\sum_{n=1}^{T} F * cr/(1+y)^n\} + \{F\,(1+y)^T\}.$$

The first term on the right-hand side is the present value of coupon interest payments, and the second term is the present value of the settlement amount—the amount to be paid at maturity. Given this valuation relationship, the answer to the above question will therefore depend on the relationship between the coupon rate, $cr$, and the market yield, $y$. Exhibit 2.6 and Figure 2.3 show the impact of this relationship on the market value of the bond:

## Exhibit 2.6 The Impact of Change in Market Interest Rate on the Values of Fixed-Rate Instruments

| | *Implication* | *Market Value vs. Face Value* |
|---|---|---|
| Market Yield = Coupon ($y = cr$) | No change in market yield means no change in value | Market Value = Face Value ($MV = F$) |
| Market Yield < Coupon ($y < cr$) | Drop in the market yield, means an increase in market value | Market Value < Face Value ($MV > F$) |
| Market Yield > Coupon ($y > cr$) | A rise in the market yield, means a decrease in market value | Market Value < Face Value ($MV = F$) |

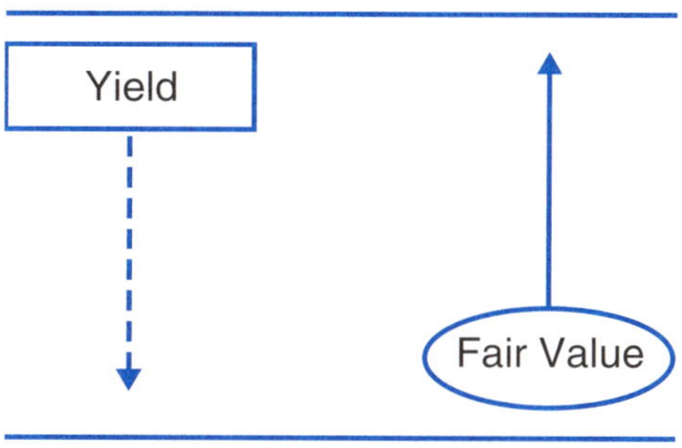


**Figure 2.3** Impact of Changing Market Interest Rate on the Market Value of a Fixed-Rate Instrument (Bond)

**Examples:**

*Case A1*: Assume the following conditions:

- The term of the bond is $T = 5$ years.
- Face value of the bond is $F = \$10{,}000$.
- The coupon interest rate on the bond is fixed at $cr = 10\%$ *per annum*.
- The market yield (for the same risk class) is $y = 10\%$.
- Interest payments are made once a year at year end.

Given this information, the market value of the bond should be

$$MV = \{\Sigma_{n=1}^{T} F * cr/(1+y)^n\} + \{F/(1+y)^T\}$$

$$MV = \{\Sigma_{n=1}^{5} 10{,}000 * 0.10/(1+0.10)^n\} + \{10{,}000/(1+0.10)^5\}$$
$$= \$10{,}000.00$$

Under these conditions, a new bond will have to be sold at face value without discount or premium, and a seasoned bond having the same terms will also trade at face value (assuming no change in credit risk).

*Case A2*: Assume the following conditions:

- Term of the bond is $T = 5$ years.
- Face value of the bond is $F = \$10,000$.
- The coupon interest rate on the bond is fixed at $cr = 10\%$ per annum.
- The market yield (for the same risk class) is $y = 9\%$.
- Interest payments are made once a year at year end.

Under these conditions, a new bond will have to be sold at a premium because it pays interest higher than the market yield.

$$MV = \{\Sigma_{n=1}^{T} F * cr/(1 + y)^{n} \} + \{F /(1 + y)^{T} \}$$

$$MV = \{\Sigma_{n=1}^{5} 10{,}000 * 0.10/(1 + 0.09)^{n}\} + \{10{,}000/(1 + 0.09)^{5}\}$$
$$= \$10{,}389.00$$

The bond should sell at a premium of $388.90.

*Case A3*: Assume the following conditions hold:

- Term of the bond is $T = 5$ years
- Face value of the bond is $F = \$10,000$
- The coupon interest rate on the bond is fixed at $cr = 10\%$ per annum.
- The market yield (for the same risk class) is $y = 11\%$.
- Interest payments are made once a year at year end.

Under these conditions, a new bond will have to be sold at a discount.

$$MV = \{\Sigma_{n=1}^{T} F * cr/(1 + y)^{n} \} + \{F/(1 + y)^{T} \}$$
$$MV = \{\Sigma_{n=1}^{5} 10{,}000 * 0.10/(1+ 0.11)^{n} \} + \{10{,}000/(1 + 0.11)^{5}\}$$
$$= \$9{,}630.30$$

The bond will be sold at a discount (of face value) equal to $369.70

To facilitate comparison, Table 2.4 presents the three cases of differing market yield and coupon rates (please note that numbers in the calculations above differ slightly from those in the table because of rounding). In these cases, it is clear that *the market value of the fixed-income instrument (the bond) moves opposite to the movement in market interest rate.* An increase in market value of the fixed-income instrument (as a result of decline in market interest rate) is a gain to the investor and a loss to the borrower (issuer of the bond). Conversely, a decrease in market value of this instrument (bond) resulting from an increase in market yield (market interest rates) is a loss to the investor and a gain to the borrower.

A general description of this behavior is in Exhibit 2.7.

**Table 2.4** Market Value (Present Value) of a Fixed-Rate Instrument for Scenarios of Different Market Yield

| *Period* | *Cash inflow* | *Cash outflow* | *Present value at 10% Market yield* | *Present Value at 9% Market yield* | *Present Value at 11% Market Yield* |
|---|---|---|---|---|---|
| 0 | *$10,000* | 0 | — | — | — |
| 1 | | $1,000 | $909.1 | $917.4 | $900.9 |
| 2 | | $1,000 | $826.5 | $841.7 | $811.6 |
| 3 | | $1,000 | $751.3 | $772.2 | $731.2 |
| 4 | | $1,000 | $683.0 | $708.4 | $658.7 |
| 5 (a) | | $1,000 | $620.9 | $649.9 | $593.4 |
| 5(b) | | $10,000 | $6,209.2 | $6,499.3 | $5,934.5 |
| Total | | — | $10,000 | $10,388.9 | $9,630.3 |

*Note*: 5(a) is for Coupon and 5(b) is for Principal. When market yield increases, the market value of the fixed-rate instrument declines, and when the market yield declines, the market value of the fixed-rate instrument increases.

## Exhibit 2.7 Impact of Change in Market Yield on the Fair Value of Fixed-Rate Financial Instruments

| *Fixed-rate financial instruments on a given firm's balance sheet* ↓ | *Impact on net fair value changes as a result of change in interest rate* | |
|---|---|---|
| | *Increase* | *Decrease* |
| Assets ($A_x$) > Liabilities ($L_x$) | Adverse impact | Favorable impact |
| Assets ($A_x$) = Liabilities ($L_x$) | Immunized | Immunized |
| Assets ($A_x$) < Liabilities ($L_x$) | Favorable impact | Adverse impact |

## Accounting Log

A change in an interest rate that would have adverse effects on the fair value of assets or liabilities is classified in accounting as "fair value risk." If an entity manages this risk by hedging, it would be classified as a "fair value hedge," for which there is a special accounting treatment as will be discussed in Chapter Seven and Chapter Eight.

### *Asymmetric Scenarios*: Mixed Interest Rate Cases

The two mixed interest rate cases are ($L_x$, $A_f$) for fixed-interest-rate liabilities and floating interest rate assets, and ($L_f$, $A_x$) for floating interest rate liabilities and fixed-interest-rate assets. In each combination, there is an asset/liability cash flow mismatch that results in exposure to different types of interest rate risk. Such risk cannot be managed by immunization (natural hedging) and will be managed mostly by hedging. An entity that has either combination has a mixed exposure to interest rate risk of different types.[28]

The entity with ($A_f$, $L_x$) would have both of the following exposures:

- A cash flow risk exposure on the assets side.
- A fair value risk exposure on the liabilities side.

The entity with ($A_x$, $L_f$) will have both of the following exposures:

- Fair value risk exposure on the assets side.
- Cash flow risk exposure on the liabilities side.

## Accounting Log

The accounting for hedging that will be discussed later classifies $L_x$ and $A_x$ exposure to interest rate risk in the same pool of fair value risk and fair value hedging. Similarly, hedge accounting classifies $L_f$ and $A_f$ in the same category of cash flow risk and cash flow hedging. Elaboration on these concepts and the accounting treatment is covered in future chapters.

### *2.3.3.4 Equity Risk*

Recent accounting standards distinguish between equities and liabilities based on transfer of assets and residual claims:

- A liability is an obligation to transfer cash or other assets to an external entity.
- Equity is an investment or an instrument for which the investor is a residual claimant.

From the standpoint of a given enterprise, a financial instrument could be a liability, equity, or a combination of both. The first two types are typically fundamental instruments such as stocks and bonds, while the last type exists in hybrid securities such as convertible bonds and some types of preferred stock. As we will see in Chapter Nine, redeemable preferred stock could be a hybrid of equity and debt if distribution of preferred dividends is at the discretion of the management, but mandatorily redeemable preferred stock is debt. Similarly, a convertible bond is a hybrid of debt (the base or host contract) and equity if the conversion requires issuing a fixed number of common shares to satisfy the option. More details about hybrid securities are presented in Chapter Nine.

Depending on the objective of the analysis, an equity investment could be considered in terms of a single type of asset or instrument as well as in terms of a portfolio that could be as large as net assets (assets less liabilities), including the equity components of a hybrid instruments.

Investing in equity is exposed to the risk of loss of value due to market dynamics or due to idiosyncratic (asset-specific or firm-specific) factors. Exposure to idiosyncratic risk is usually eliminated by diversification, but the investor is always exposed to the loss of value due to uncontrollable market conditions. Exposure to equity risk under this definition is limited to systematic (market) risk component and does not exclude or subsume other types of risk. For example, if an enterprise in country A invests in a foreign company domiciled in country B by acquiring a percentage of its shares when that acquisition does not give the acquirer control or significant influence over company in country B, the acquiring enterprise may treat this investment as available-for-sale, which should be valued at fair value through OCI (equity account). This available-for-sale investment is exposed to (at least) three types of risk:

1. *Currency risk*: the risk of loss due to changes in currency exchange rates between Country A and Country B.
2. *Country risk*: the risk of loss due to political, regional and governmental actions and regulations.
3. *Equity risk*: probable loss of value due to market volatility, which is also referred to as *volatility risk*. In other cases, equity risk is treated as "tail risk," which is the risk of loss beyond a specified decline in value such as, for example, the expected loss beyond three standard deviations of value distributions.[29]

Equity risk premium is a slight modification of equity risk because it is the exposure to the risk level associated with returns in excess of the risk-free rate. In the following chapters, we will see that mitigating these different types of risk requires different risk management strategies, including hedging.

### 2.3.4 Credit Risk

When an enterprise obtains financing through loans, the lender might be an institution such as a bank (private lending) or it might be public investors in the marketplace (as in the case of issuing publicly traded bonds). In both cases, lenders consider the borrower's ability to meet debt obligations; the ability to pay the periodic payment and the principal amount at the end of the loan term. Credit risk, therefore, is the risk of loss in the event that the borrower is not able (or willing) to make debt payments according to the terms of the contract.

We encounter an evaluation of credit risk in our daily routines when we apply for credit cards or when we purchase products on credit. The lender or the enterprise that sells on credit seeks information about the borrower (the buyer) before concluding the transaction. This information is aimed at assessing the borrower's ability and willingness to pay. Credit rating and history signal the borrower's creditworthiness, which is a major factor in the determination of the terms of the loan: amount, duration, interest rate, frequency of payment. A high score on creditworthiness is, therefore, a low credit risk—i.e., the event of nonpayment on schedule according to the terms of the contract is highly unlikely. As the borrower's creditworthiness worsens, the probability of default increases.

It should be noted that borrowers may default on their loans either because of inability or unwillingness to pay.[30] If we use the ability to pay as a criterion, we define *credit risk as the probability that the debtor (the borrower) may not make the scheduled debt payments for interest and/or principal in accordance with the terms of the loan contract.*It must be noted that the probability of default is closely tied to liquidity risk because if lenders cannot collect the funds others owe them, they might not have sufficient liquidity to finance their own operations.

Lenders have a way of mitigating credit risk at the start. They can set conditions to restrict the borrower (the issuer of the bond or debt instrument) from taking on excessive risk, divesting of assets, entering into binding agreements that could alter anticipated cash flow and profitability (e.g., merger) and other reasonably well-specified conditions. Those conditions are known as debt covenants that are established as terms for extending and maintaining credit facility. The specific covenants are either negotiated terms as in the case of bank or syndicated loans or stipulated by the indenture of a public offering. Different companies emphasize different covenants to appeal to different investors. Chapter Four provides more discussion of debt covenants as a way of managing credit risk.

Subsequent to issuing the bond or concluding debt contracting, investors (the lenders) are left on the receiving end. If the borrower's credit risk increases, investors' exposure to risk will depend on whether the instrument carries a floating rate or a fixed rate. Investors would be exposed to possible loss in cash flow (cash flow risk) for floating-rate debt instruments, and would be exposed to loss in value (fair value risk) for fixed-rate debt instruments. Mitigating each of these two risk exposures requires different strategies of asset/liability management and hedging.

Measurement of credit risk could be guided by different tools. There are statistical models that estimate the probability of default or bankruptcy. In addition, credit rating agencies such as Moody's, Standard & Poor's, Fitch and Morningstar provide rating scales for creditworthiness of different financial instruments and different borrowers. Discussion of these measures is a subject in Chapter Three.

## Information Log: Counterparty Credit Risk

Credit risk is often thought of as the "lending" risk where only one party to a contract, the borrower, has not completed its contractual obligations. This is the case, for example, in non-contingent credit sale; after delivery of the product and assuming the seller has not granted the buyer the right of return or any other kind of warranty, the seller would have completed its role in the transaction and expects the buyer to do the same over time. In this case, the seller would be exposed to loss without any recourse if the buyer defaulted. This is also the case of issuers of (plain-vanilla) bonds and lenders, as well as of selling commodities on credit without the option to return or exchange the sold items. In making a bank loan, for example, the bank would have fulfilled its obligations by transferring the funds to the borrower, while the borrower is expected to fulfill its contractual obligations at future dates by repaying the principal and interest on time. Therefore, the borrower in this case does not bear any risk, but the bank bears credit risk in the event that the borrower fails to meet its obligations.

Counterparty credit risk extends beyond unilateral credit risk exposure noted above; it is the risk that both parties may default on fulfilling their obligations (Gregory, 2012). To provide a simple illustration, consider two different buyers purchasing two automobiles from a given dealer:

- In the first case, the dealer extends credit to the buyer, ABC, to purchase the car, but does not provide any type of warranty. By delivering the car to ABC, the dealer would have fulfilled its obligation, while ABC is expected to fulfill its obligation to the dealer by paying interest and an amortized part of the principal periodically for the period stipulated in the contract. Therefore, in this contractual relationship only the dealer is exposed to default risk if the buyer does not make the payments according to schedule.

- In the second case, the dealer extends credit to the buyer, LMN, to purchase the car as well as offering a seven-year warranty. In this case, both the dealer and the buyer have not fulfilled their obligations upon completing the sale contract. While the buyer may default on the loan, the dealer also might not provide the warrantied service. This is a case of counterparty risk in which the expected loss for the dealer is the loss arising from the buyer's default net of the gain the dealer may accrue by not providing the warrantied service.

While this simple illustration provides the intuition for the concept, counterparty risk is more prevalent in the derivative market because, in most of these instruments, the obligations of each party to a contract are not completely alleviated before final settlement. For example, a farmer enters into a forward contract with a wheat wholesaler. The farmer is obligated to deliver a specified quantity of wheat for a pre-determined price at a specified future date; the wholesaler has the obligation to take the wheat and pay the specified price. In this contractual arrangement, both the dealer and the farmer have obligations to each other and each party is exposed to the risk of default by the counterparty.

A brief discussion of the disclosure of counterparty risk is presented in Chapter 12.

## 2.3.5 Liquidity Risk

> [Liquidity risk] *is the risk that an entity may not have sufficient liquidity to perform its operations and meet its obligations without incurring unacceptable losses. An alternative definition of liquidity risk is the probability that an entity may not be able to convert its assets into cash without incurring significant losses or high transaction cost.*
>
> (Lopez, 2008)

Under this definition, commodity price risk, interest rate risk, currency risk, safeguarding the enterprise resources and almost all the risks presented above have bearing on liquidity risk. Liquidity risk is emphasized for financial intermediaries because if a large bank faces a liquidity problem, the impact will be felt in many other sectors in the economy. Liquidity risk is a significant matter for other industries as well because an enterprise facing liquidity problems will become high credit risk which may exacerbate the problem because extending credit to companies in these situations will be costly. The case of downgrading the credit ratings of General Motors and Ford Motor Company on May 5, 2004 was caused primarily by liquidity risk that these two companies were facing. In less than two months after the downgrading, the bond spread of both companies jumped by about 400 Basis Points (Acharya, Schaefer, and Zhang, 2007).

In order to bring liquidity risk home to an accounting audience, consider the distinction made in accounting between earnings (or profits) and the net cash flow generated from operations. Earnings are measured as the excess of revenues over related cost. If revenues are generated by selling only on credit, the seller's liquidity will depend on whether the resulting accounts receivable are collectible. Any level of uncollectible accounts receivable means that the seller will not be able to convert all of its accounts receivable into cash. The higher the percentage of uncollectible accounts receivable, the smaller the amount the seller can collect. Thus, the seller faces the risk of not having the liquidity it needs to operate its business and to pay its obligations—i.e., the greater the liquidity risk.

Liquidity risk can be managed, but not hedged as will become clear in the following chapters. By appropriate configuration of assets and obligations and enhancing the quality of granted credit, the enterprise could manage its own credit risk. Liquidity risk takes on greater importance in financial institutions such as banks; inability to meet depositors' demands for taking their deposits out of the bank will create a run on the bank that could easily lead to bankruptcy.

## 2.4 Summary of Key Points

This chapter provides an overview of the types of risk relevant for understanding management hedging activities which we need to know before we venture into hedge accounting.

1. Strategic risk is viewed as an overarching concept that includes the entity's exposure to market risk, credit risk, liquidity risk, operational risk (as defined by Basel Accord) among other elements in the entity's environment.
2. The role of internal information governance and the impact on financial and risk reporting that extend beyond the risk-seeking behavior of managers described in the preceding chapter are emphasized. This segment includes an introduction to management's use of accounting standards and processes to create reporting risk to investors as was the case with Freddie Mac and Fannie Mae among others.
3. An introduction to interest rate risk exposure emphasizes the effect of the terms of the financial contract on the type of risk exposure an enterprise faces. Fixed interest rate contracts create exposure to loss in value, while floating interest rate instruments create exposure to cash flow volatility. These risk exposures could be managed by managing assets and liabilities to have similar contractual arrangements and amounts. However, additional risk exposure arises when assets and liabilities have dissimilar mix of fixed-rate and floating-rate instruments. More on the measurement of interest rate risk is in Chapter Three.
4. Liquidity risk and credit risk exposures are presented briefly but more on the nature and measurement of these risks is in Chapter Three.
5. Exposure to currency risk is defined in terms of three different types of risks: (i) the risk of loss upon the settlement of foreign currency denominated contracts of transactions that occurred previously when exchange rates were different; (ii) operating risk as the risk of potential loss of future revenues or increase in cost of future operations due to adverse currency movement; and (iii) translation risk as the risk of reporting losses on net investment in foreign operations. This segment provides only identification and a brief explanation of the different types of currency risk exposures, but further detailed discussion of these risks is in Chapters Ten and Eleven.
6. Familiarity with these risks is essential for understanding the hedging and hedge accounting activities that are the subject matter of this book.

## Notes

1 Further discussion of insurance is in Chapter Four.

2 The first book was published in 1949. Several editions follow with the latest having a Foreword by Warren Buffet (Graham & Dodd, 2008).

3 In insurance, one pays a premium to transfer the risk to others, but in investment one must earn a premium to accept taking risk.
4 http://mba.tuck.dartmouth.edu/pages/faculty/ken.french/data_library.html
5 The conception of strategic risk in the Basel Accord (BIS) risk is not the same as the one presented in this document. In this book, strategic risk is assumed to be all-encompassing whereas the Basel Accord focuses on banks. For operational risk, see Basel Committee on Banking Supervision (June 2011).
6 The Dictionary's definition of fraud is the "use of deception for unlawful gain or unjust advantage." The U.S. GAO defines financial reporting fraud "as an instance in which a company intentionally misstates its financial statements or intentionally misapplies an accounting pronouncement" (2006, p. 1).
7 The report continues to state: "By the end of 2009, 34 individuals had been charged in the investigation. Of these individuals, 22 have pled guilty or been convicted, including former Enron Chief Executive Officer (CEO) Jeffrey Skilling, former Chairman and CEO Kenneth Lay (conviction later vacated due to his death), and former Chief Financial Officer Andrew Fastow. Skilling was sentenced to 24 years and four months in prison, the largest term handed down in connection with the case. Fastow was sentenced to six years in prison for his role in the accounting scandal. The cases were handled by the Enron Task Force, which consisted of members of the DOJ, FBI, and IRS. The Securities and Exchange Commission provided considerable assistance in this investigation."
8 The three types of risk are market risk, credit risk and operational risk.
9 A lesson learned from *HealthSouth* is that external auditors should never allow the management to know the pattern with which they conduct audits and should change that pattern frequently.
10 *HealthSouth* Form 10-Q, March 31, 2011. http://investor.healthsouth.com/secfiling.cfm?filingID=785161-1-32.
11 In Chapters 7 and 8 on fair value hedge accounting it will be noted that if the inventory is hedged and the hedge is effective, accounting standards require that the carrying value of inventories should be adjusted by changes in market values from the inception of the hedge if the hedge is effective and the management elects to use hedge accounting.
12 EADS, N.V., Financial Statements, 2010. Available at http://applications.eads.com/eads/investor-relations/int/annual-report2010/data/FS_EV_050511_PDFi.pdf.
13 In any of these cases, only valuation at market applies if inventories are hedged and the hedge is effective.
14 This change is a "change in estimate" and would be effective contemporaneously and prospectively.
15 http://sec.edgar-online.com/american-airlines-inc/10-k-annual-report/2006/02/24/section13.aspx
16 This author rejects the reasoning by standard setters for aggregating realized and unrealized gains and losses without differentiation to inform external uses of financial statements as to their relative proportions. This problem becomes more acute in accounting for derivatives because financial derivative instruments are always valued at fair value and the changes in fair value are recognized in earnings unless the derivatives are designated for effective cash flow hedging relationships.
17 http://www.thefreedictionary.com/intent
18 These acceptable cases are:

"Par. 8. The following changes in circumstances, however, may cause the enterprise to change its intent to hold a certain security to maturity without calling into question its intent to hold other debt securities to maturity in the future. Thus, the sale or transfer of an HTM security due to one of the following changes in circumstances shall not be considered to be inconsistent with its original classification:

a. Evidence of a significant deterioration in the issuer's creditworthiness.
b. A change in tax law that eliminates or reduces the tax-exempt status of interest on the debt security (but not a change in tax law that revises the marginal tax rates applicable to interest income).
c. A major business combination or major disposition (such as sale of a segment) that necessitates the sale or transfer of held-to-maturity securities to maintain the enterprise's existing interest rate risk position or credit risk policy.

d. A change in statutory or regulatory requirements significantly modifying either what constitutes a permissible investment or the maximum level of investments in certain kinds of securities, thereby causing an enterprise to dispose of a held-to-maturity security.
e. A significant increase by the regulator in the industry's capital requirements that causes the enterprise to downsize by selling held-to-maturity securities.
f. A significant increase in the risk weights of debt securities used for regulatory risk-based capital purposes."

19 *The Trueblood Report* is the name given to a publication by the American Institute of Certified Public Accountants in 1973, which was the Report of the Study Group on the Objectives of Financial Statements headed by Robert M. Trueblood who was the head of Deloitte Haskins & Sells and the chair of the committee authoring the monograph entitled *Objectives of Financial Statements*. Prior to the creation of the FASB, the *Trueblood Report* stated that the basic objective of financial statements is to provide information useful for making economic decisions.
20 In reality, Level 3 is "mark to management."
21 http://www.sec.gov/Archives/edgar/data/19617/000095012311019773/y86143e10vk.htm
22 This subject is presented later in the book. However, for the uninitiated, hedging simply means taking a course of action, such as writing a contract, whose unexpected payoff moves opposite to the behavior of price changes which the management does not wish for the entity to absorb.
23 See also: http://fx.sauder.ubc.ca/currency_table.html
24 For the time being, duration and maturity are assumed to be the same. However, as discussed in Chapter Three, the term "duration" is used in the sense of Macaulay's definition: the total weighted average time for recovery of the interest payments and principal in relation to the current market price of a fixed-rate instrument (i.e., fixed-rate bond). For example, a bond with time to maturity of five years and coupon rate of five years will have duration of 4.25 years. For a floating-rate bond, however, duration is either zero or the time it takes for the next rate adjustment.
25 The difference between interest rate-sensitive assets and interest rate-sensitive liabilities is called *Gap* and is elaborated in the measurement of interest rate risk in Chapter Three.
26 This section is similar to the preceding section in that the information provided might not be new to many readers. However, reviewing it is essential for understanding the upcoming discussion of hedge accounting.
27 This is true under the assumption that the bond issue does not have any optionality such as being callable or convertible and does not have warrants, attached or detachable.
28 A natural hedge is a situation in which the entity holds both: (a) assets with given amounts, patterns, and currency denomination of cash inflows, and (b) liabilities with similar amounts, patterns, and currency denomination of cash inflows.
29 But there are scholars who suggest distributions with fatter tails that have higher probability of loss with three standard deviations than normal distribution.
30 Creditworthiness reflects both the ability and willingness to make debt payments on time. However, only the ability to pay is of concern to us in making financial analysis. Willingness to pay is a matter of character and legal jurisdiction and is not a subject of interest in this book.

# CHAPTER 3

# MEASUREMENT OF RISK

## 3.1 Risk and Ambiguity

Models can be developed to show how risks "should" be measured, but without quantification and experiential learning, normative models will only provide insights for policy making. Not all risks are measurable even after they are identified. For example, there is no good way to measure the exposure to human resource risk or to reputation risk. Nevertheless, many known qualitative indicators can provide guidance for managing these risks.

Quantitative measurement bases have been developed for several critical risks that impact businesses. Researchers constantly subject these measurements to refinement and improvement as technology evolves. Empirically, developing high-quality descriptive measures to assist in decision-making requires access to longitudinal historical observations and the absence of such historical information limits the scope of the information accessible by decision makers. A one-time occurrence may generate an observation of a single outcome. When the absence of information is due to the inability to observe the occurrence of events of interest, decision makers may appeal to the *Principle of Indifference* developed by the mathematician Reverend Bayes. This principle suggests that, in absence of information, all movements have equal probability of occurrence. The *Principle of Indifference* is also known as the *Case of Maximum Ignorance*, suggesting that one needs more information than a single observation in order to be able to generate more refined measures of risk.

## 3.2 Measurement of Risk with Limited Observations

### 3.2.1 Using Two Observations

#### *3.2.1.1 Boundaries: Maximum & Minimum*

If one data point is insufficient for developing a viable measure of risk, will two observations suffice? While the answer will depend on the context and nature of these two observations, two observations could inform decision makers of the degree of risk exposure in many situations. To illustrate, assume a person is searching for work in the field of accounting and comes across different advertisement for a position as an assistant controller. Samples of four advertisements in the job market section of "classified ads" are shown in Exhibit 3.1.

What these four cases have in common is the fact that there is a vacant position for an assistant controller, but they differ in the amount of relevant information they provide. The first case

## Exhibit 3.1 Advertisements for an Employment Position

| *Announcement by* ↓ | *Beginning Date* | *Offered Compensation* | *Uncertainty about Compensation* |
|---|---|---|---|
| Entity A | July, 20xx | Depends on qualifications and experience | Very high |
| Entity B | June 10, 20xx | $100,000 | None |
| Entity C | August 15, 20xx | Between $100,000 and $140,000, depending on qualifications and experience | ?? |
| Entity D | September 1, 20xx | Between $80,000 and $160,000, depending on qualifications and experience | ?? |

(advertisement by Entity A) is the most ambiguous one about compensation because the jobseeker would not have any idea about the level of compensation the employer is offering and would view this situation as high risk. This ambiguity is resolved in the second case (advertisement by Entity B) because it states a specific dollar amount for the salary level the Entity would be offering. The third and fourth cases, advertisements by Entities C and D, provide boundaries for compensation by stating the minimum and maximum compensation levels these entities would be willing to pay. Each one of the two advertisements by Entity C and Entity D adds more information than either A or B because they provide ranges of compensation, but both of them offer other uncertainty conditions.

In both of these two cases (C and D), the midpoint between the maximum and the minimum is $120,000, which is the average. If both advertisements were to state only the midpoint between the two extremes, the differentiating features between them would be masked and the advertisements would not be as informative. For example, if an advertisement states, "on average, the salary will be $120,000.00," job applicants would not know the floor or the ceiling of the proposed compensation. While Entities C and D will pay on average more than Entity B, the salary also might fall at any point inside the range. Therefore, there is more uncertainty about the level of pay of either Entity C or Entity D compared to case B. But there is also an issue with using the different range. The range in Case C is $40,000; the range in Case D is twice as much. Case D therefore has higher uncertainty because at the lower tail, the actual income Entity D is offering is less than the lower tail of the income offer by Entity C. The wider the range, the higher the uncertainty about the point of landing. Although this information is limited, the range provides a primary measure of uncertainty. The most common cases in this respect are discussed next.

### *3.2.1.2 Boundaries: The Bid/Ask Spread*

## Accounting Log: Relevance to Accounting

In estimating the fair value of an asset, the standards recognize the possibility of observing bid/ask spreads but not the final transaction prices. In this event, the standards permit the management to exercise judgment in determining the point on the spread range that represents the fair value.

The above illustrations are hypothetical but suggest using the range as a measure of risk as is the case with using the bid/ask spread in financial markets. The bid/ask spread, also called offer/ask spread, is the difference between the bid price (the highest price that prospective buyers offer for a product) and the asked price (the lowest price that sellers of this exact product declare to be acceptable to them). In the absence of an intermediary such as a dealer, the bid/ask spread arises because of disagreement between buyers and sellers on the value of the asset or security being traded. This disagreement may be attributed to each party having access to different information about the asset or security and the expectations about its future cash flow generating capacity. However, when an intermediary is involved, the bid/ask spread represents two components: (i) market conditions of supply and demand, and (ii) the dealer's commission.

The bid/ask spread is common in currency markets (as discussed in Chapter Ten), in market analysis and decision-making, in evaluation of information asymmetry between buyers and sellers, and in measures of liquidity risk. As noted earlier, liquidity risk is the risk that an entity may face in liquidating its assets on a timely basis, at low cost and at prices that would generate sufficient liquidity to meet its obligation and to pay for its operations. A wide bid/ask spread produces small volumes of trade because buyers and sellers cannot easily agree on a price. Therefore, *the wider the bid/ask spread, the greater the liquidity risk of the seller.*

While the liquidity of the seller might be an outcome of the range of the bid/ask spread, the liquidity of the market could be the driver of that spread. This connection can be highlighted by comparing differences between *broad* and *thin* markets. In thin markets, the number of traders and the volumes of trade are low, there are relatively fewer offers, and the competition between buyers is less intense than in broad markets. As a result, there is little incentive for buyers to search for and acquire information about the object of trade. The less informed the buyers or the sellers, the more the disparity between their evaluation of the value of the product or the security being traded and the wider the bid/ask spread.

Unlike thin markets, broad markets are characterized by a large number of traders, a large volume of trade, and greater frequency of trading. In active markets with high volumes of trade and large number of traders, buyers and sellers have incentives to search for information about the object of trade which could be a product (a known grade of wheat), a bond, a stock, or another asset. The more informed the buyers and the sellers are, the narrower the spread between the bid and the asking prices. As a result, broad markets are characterized by relatively low information asymmetry and the sellers' exposure to liquidity risk is lower than in thin markets.

In general, using bid/ask spread as a measure of risk is a special application of using "range"; as a measure of risk, spread is appealing for its simplicity and the absence of estimation. Estimation requires assumptions that may be influenced by other incentives. These features led law professor R. A. Booth (1999) to note, "[t]he single most reliable measure of risk is the spread."

### *3.2.1.3 Boundaries: Yield Spread and Basis Spread*

When borrowing a mortgage loan, the homeowner might be offered a loan with either a fixed rate of interest or a variable (floating) rate of interest. The variable rate will typically consist of a specified markup of Basis Points added to a reference rate or an index, such as prime rate or LIBOR (London Interbank Offer Rate), Treasury yield, or the yield on AAA-rated bond (low-risk securities). The size of the spread depends on the creditworthiness (credit score) of the borrower—the lower the credit scores, the greater the spread, and the higher the mortgage rate charged to the customer. Similarly, customers with high credit scores (low risk) will be eligible for lower spreads and lower mortgage rates. Thus, the magnitude of the spread is a measure of the bank's assessment of the riskiness of the borrower. For a low-risk client, the mark up would be low, say 100 Basis Points or 1%, while a spread of 300 Basis Points (i.e., 3%) above the benchmark would indicate a relatively higher risk (lower creditworthiness) client.

In general, spread is the difference between two rates or two prices, one of which might be a reference benchmark. However, there are at least 30 different definitions of yield spread. A simple definition is that "yield spread is the difference between yields to maturity of two bonds."[1] Or, "The difference in yield between different security issues, usually securities of different credit quality."[2] There is also confusion between default risk (quality) and maturity in defining yield spread.

Spread as the difference between two rates applies to numerous situations where the spread would have a meaning. Straight corporate bonds (these are the bonds without any optionality such as call or conversion features), have a "maturity" spread, which is the excess of the yield on a bond of certain term to maturity over the yield of a bond with shorter maturity. For example, on September 2, 2011, the yield on AAA-rated corporate bonds was 1.19% for a 5-year maturity, 2.55% for a 10-year maturity, and 4.42% for a 20-year maturity. The longer the bond's term to maturity, the greater the exposures of bondholders to borrowers' default risk and the more that investors will demand compensation, or premium, for taking that additional risk.[3]

Examples of spreads representing the different types of risk to which lenders may be exposed are as follows:

- *Default Risk*—the risk that the bond issuer is likely to default on scheduled payments of coupon and/or principal.
- *Liquidity Risk*—the possibility of trading assets in thin markets or not having a readily available method of trade.
- *Inflation Risk*—the increase in nominal interest rate due to inflation.
- *Swap Spread*—the difference between the fixed interest rate and the yield of Treasury securities having the same maturity as the term of the swap.

### 3.2.2 Risk Measures Using Three Observations

With respect to financial accounting and reporting, triangular distribution has not been applied directly. Occasionally one might find examples using triangular distribution (Abdel-khalik and Keller, 1979) or using it without calling it as such. For example, in discussing impairment of fair value, ASC 360-10-55-26 describes an estimate of expected cash flow under risk and uses three-point information from which the mean of the distribution can be estimated.[4] To estimate the present value of forecasted cash flow to measure impairment of financial instruments (i.e., *Level 3*), one must make assumptions about the probability of realization of each level of cash flow and use the resulting distribution in estimating the expected value. The illustration provided by the FASB is presented in the *Accounting Log* below.

#### Accounting Log: Accounting use of the Triangular Distribution in Fair Value Estimation

Triangular distribution is a probability distribution with three observations only. In this segment, it is worth noting that the FASB made use of elements of this distribution, although it was not labeled as such in the illustration provided for estimating the present value information required to implement ASC 360 on impairment.

In ASC 360-10-55-26, the Board presents two cases illustrating estimation of fair (expected) value of expected future cash flow using three probability points: 20%, 50%, and 70% (the standard presented the last probability number as the Upper 30%). These three points may be described differently:

*b* (most optimistic) → 30%
*m* (most likely) → 50%
*w* (worst or minimum) → 20%

In Case A presented in ASC 360-10-55-27 there are two possibilities (which we call states of nature): the asset may be sold in 2 years (a probability of 60%) or it may be sold in 10 years (probability of 40%). The data presented in Case A are shown in Table 3.1.

**Table 3.1** Probabilities of Different States of a Triangular Distribution (ASC 360-10-55-27)

| | *Predicted Cash flow* | *Probability* | *Expected Value* | *Likelihood of Occurrence* |
|---|---|---|---|---|
| State of Nature 1 | \$38 | 20% | *w* = \$7.60 | |
| Sale in 2 years | \$41 | 50% | *m* = \$20.50 | |
| | \$43 | 30% | *b* = \$12.90 | |
| | Expected Value = 7.60 + 20.50 + 12.90 = \$41.00 | | | 60% |
| State of Nature 2 | \$37 | 20% | *w* = \$7.40 | |
| | \$49 | 50% | *m* = \$24.50 | |
| Sale in 10 years | \$56 | 30% | *b* = \$16.80 | 40% |
| | Expected Value = 7.40 + 24.50 +16.80 = \$48.70 | | | |
| Expected Fair Value of Asset | 0.60 × \$41.00 + 0.40 × \$48.70 = \$44.1 | | | |

This illustration is provided by the FASB as an example of estimating the fair value of an asset that is expected to generate different cash flow in different years under different conditions. In this illustration, if the book value of the asset is materially below the expected value of \$4.1, and this difference is "more likely than not" permanent, then a judgment would be made that the asset is impaired. The difference between the book value and the estimated fair value would be charged to earnings as a loss.

It must be noted that all the input information required for this analysis comes from the assumptions and judgment made by the management.

The situation is different in business applications and management accounting. The application is particularly popular in connection with project management using PERT (Program Evaluation and Review Technique) and CPM (Critical Path Method) which were developed by the U.S. Navy in 1956 in the process of managing the project of building Polaris submarines (van Drop and Kotz, 2002;

Punmia and Khandelwal, 2006). PERT and CPM are used extensively in multiple business applications, even in areas such as geological studies (see the U.S. Geological survey study by Klett, Charpentier, and Schmoker (2000)). Both of these techniques are based on the properties of the triangular distribution.

In a typical PERT setting, the project management team estimates three points: *b*, *m* and *w* with the following properties:

- *b* = best-case scenario, or most optimistic estimate. This is an estimate of the shortest time in which the activity could be completed.
- *m* = the most likely estimate. This is the most likely time estimated for completing the project.
- *w* = worst-case scenario or the pessimistic estimate of how much time it could take to complete the project.

For the geological survey of undiscovered oil fields (referenced above), the three points used are located on a scale from 0 to 100 and are called fractiles—these are F100, F50, and F0. The U.S. Geological Survey reports that three fractiles represent the:

> [N]umber of undiscovered fields and the coproduct ratios. A triangular distribution is uniquely determined by these fractiles and it is not necessary to specify a mode for the distribution. The number of undiscovered fields and the average coproduct ratios have distributions that represent the uncertainty of a single value and the triangular distributions show the assessor's uncertainty of that value.
>
> (Source: http://energy.cr.usgs.gov/WEcont/chaps/OP.pdf, 2000, p. OP8)

Two assumptions are necessary to estimate the first two moments (i.e., the mean and the standard deviation) of a triangular distribution: (a) the estimates of three points: *b*, *m*, and *w* are independent, and (b) the distance between the best and worst estimates cover six standard deviations.

Given these assumptions and based on the properties of the triangular distribution,[5] the first two moments are estimated as follows:

Mean: $\mu = (b + 4m + w)/6$

Standard Deviation: $\hat{\sigma} = (w - b)/6$

The standard deviation is the measure of variability or risk and it is proxy for the standard deviation calculated under the assumption of a normal distribution.[6] The relative volatility measure is the coefficient of variation measured by $\hat{\sigma}/\mu$.

In business or information systems applications, triangular distribution is often used in estimating the Critical Path for the time to complete a project in PERT. For the measurement of risk, however, the standard deviation $\hat{\sigma}$ is the statistical moment of interest because it measures the uncertainty of the distribution.

### An Example

Figure 3.1 presents the expected distribution of cash flow under three competing projects. The likelihood of occurrence is on the *y* -axis, and amounts of cash flow are on the *x* -axis. The differences between the features of these distributions can be summarized in a few points:

- The area under the curve of each distribution is one.
- Profiles 1 and 2 have close means but very different standard deviations resulting in different coefficient of variations.

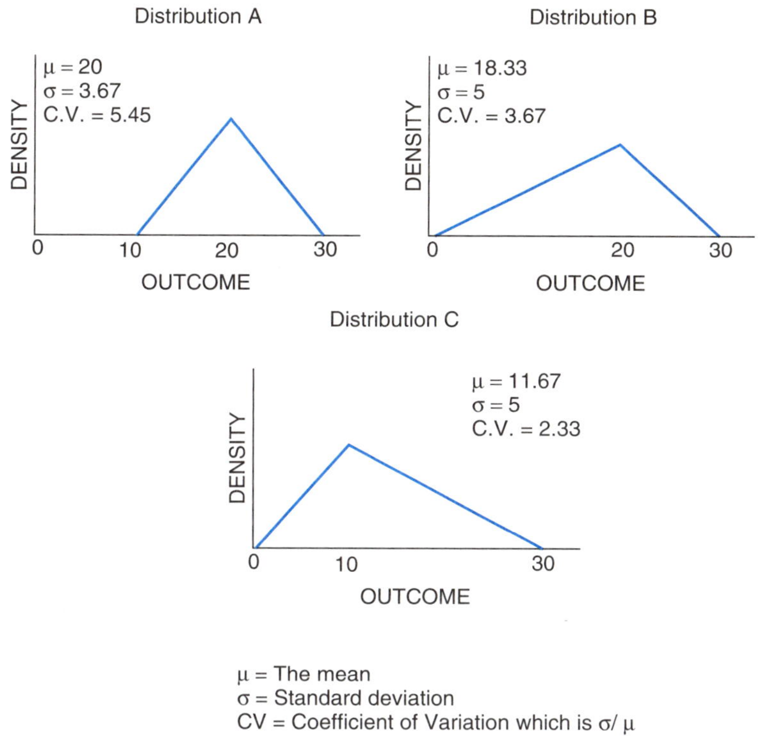


**Figure 3.1** Three Different Triangular Distributions

- Profiles 2 and 3 have the same standard deviations but very different means and coefficient of variation measures.

These properties also assist in understanding the use of triangular distributions in PERT in project management and costing. A typical PERT begins by drawing a chart connecting all the stages needed to complete the project. Some of these stages are sequential and others are concurrent.

Three estimates are made for the time-to-completion of each stage: *b* (shortest possible), *m* (most likely), and *w* (worst possible). The mean and standard deviation of the time that each stage would take to complete is estimated by using these three-point estimates to calculate the mean and the standard deviation of each stage. The stages are then connected to show the different possible paths to complete the project. The Critical Path has the longest mean-time-to-completion and it could delay completion of the project if it does not receive special attention and possibly additional resource allocation. However, given the three examples of triangular distribution above (Figure 3.1), using the means of these distributions could be misleading because of differences in risk (approximated by standard deviations). In making policy recommendations, we should consider the variability (the risk) as well as the means of the distributions.

### 3.2.3 Measurement of Risk for Multiple Observations

The triangular distribution discussed in the previous section has two parameters that are estimated from three-point observations. When the number of observations increases, the triangular shape of the distribution takes on a smoother and a more symmetric pattern providing a good approximation of the *Beta* distribution.[7] However, according to the Central Limit Theorem, the distribution of averages coming from any shape tends to follow the (Gaussian) normal probability distribution.

The (Gaussian) normal distribution is characterized by:

- A symmetric bell-shaped curve for which the mean = the mode= the median.
- The area under the curve is equal to one (as with any probability distribution).
- The mean divides the area under the curve into two halves.
- The distribution is determined by two parameters: the mean and the standard deviation. For the population , including all $N$ observations of the variable $x$ (which could be any variable of interest in the study such as prices, quantities, changes in currency rates, interest rate, or number of computers exported, etc.),

$\mu$ = the mean of the population.
$= \sum_{i=1}^{i=N} x_i / N$
$\sigma^2$ = the variance of the population about the mean
$= \sum_{i=1}^{i=N} (x_i - \mu)^2 / N$
$\sigma = \sqrt{\sigma^2}$ is the standard deviation of the population measuring the dispersion about the mean.

However, these two parameters are almost never observed for the population as a whole and are typically estimated by sampling. Under the assumption that sampling is random, a sample of $n$ observations (notice that $N$ is for the population and $n$ is for the sample) consisting $x_1, x_2, \ldots x_n$ can be used to estimate the mean and variance of the population as follows:

$\bar{x}$ = the mean of the sample that is calculated as

$= \sum_{i=1}^{i=n} x_i / n$

$s^2 = \sum_{i=1}^{i=n} x_i\ (x_i - \bar{x})^2 / n - 1$ is the variance of the sample
$s = \sqrt{s^2}$ is the standard deviation of the sample describing the dispersion of observations about the mean.

$\bar{x}$ and $s$ are unbiased estimates of the population means and standard deviation. This simply means if we take several random samples ($r_1, r_2, r_3 \ldots K$) from the same population and calculate $\bar{x}_1, \bar{x}_2, \bar{x}_3, \ldots \bar{x}_K$ and $s_1, s_2, s_3, \ldots s_K$ for the mean and standard deviation of each sample in the $K$ samples, then

a. The sampling distribution is approximated by a normal distribution.
b. The best estimate of the population mean would be equal to the average of all sample means:

$$\mu = E(\bar{x}) = \bar{x}_1 + \bar{x}_2 + \bar{x}_3 + \ldots \bar{x}_K / K$$

c. The best estimate of population variance[8] is the average of the variances of all samples,

$$\sigma^2 = E(s^2) = s_1^2 + s_2^2 + s_3^2 + \ldots s_K^2 / K$$

These results are known as the Central Limit Theorem, which is the basis for much of applied statistical analysis. Every observation, $x$, in the population can be normalized in standardized units of the estimated standard deviation as $Z = (x_1 - \mu)/\sigma$. The distribution of $Z$ is the "standard normal distribution." The standard normal curve has a mean ($\mu$) = 0 and $\sigma$ (standard deviation) = 1.

But because neither $\mu$ nor $\sigma$ is observable, $Z$ can be approximated from sample observations as

$$t = (x - \bar{x}) / s$$

Unlike the *Z*-distribution, the *t*-distribution depends on the degrees of freedom and, in the limit, as degrees of freedom approach infinity (i.e., become very large) the *t*-distribution approaches the *Z*-distribution.

The standard normal distribution has some useful features. The $x$ -axis is measured in units of the standard deviation of the sample. Because of the symmetrical nature of the distribution, the area under the curve is partitioned evenly about the mean—50% above the mean and 50% below the mean. On each side of the mean, 34% of the area under the curve falls within one standard deviation; 47.6% falls within two standard deviations; and 49.8% is within three standard deviations.

Figure 3.2 shows the shape of the *standardized* normal distribution (*Z*), also called probability density function, in which all observations are standardized by the estimated standard deviation and are transformed into *Z* units of standard deviation. We will make use of the standard normal distribution in multiple subjects in this book, including *Value-at-risk* discussed next.

In setting the stage for introducing the *value-at-risk* measures, we could benefit by noting that hypothesis testing (in statistical analysis) depends on: (a) specifying a confidence level, (b) an error tolerance, and (c) whether the test is one-sided or two-sided. Suppose we wanted to test the hypothesis that A = B with a 90% confidence. That means we are leaving 10% tolerable error. Because A may be greater or less than B, this test is a two-tailed test suggesting that the 90% confidence level is at the center of the distribution, leaving 5% at each tail. It turns out that moving away from the mean by 1.645 standard deviations on each side of the mean will give us 90% under the distribution as confidence level and 5% at each tail as the error (often referred to as the $\alpha$ probability). Figure 3.2 displays the different probabilities areas under the curve for different units of standard deviation.

### 3.2.3.1 *Illustrations*[9]

#### Confidence Interval for Two-Tail Test

Assume the following information came to your attention:

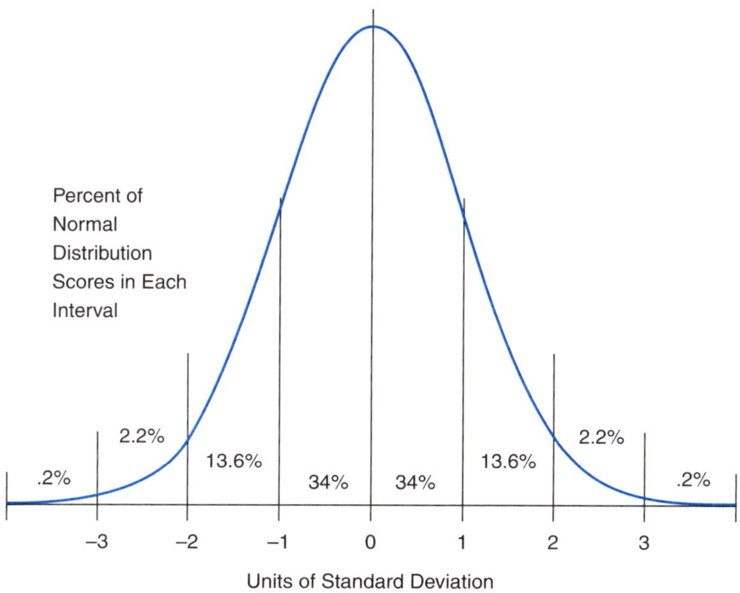


**Figure 3.2** The Standard Normal Z (Units of Standard Deviation) Probability Distribution

In 2010, the USDA National Agriculture Statistics reported detailed information about Florida orange production yield and prices.[10] For the Valencia variety, the average price per box was \$9.832372. Assume that the standard deviation of the price per box was 0.851 for the 100-day harvest season. In 2010, owners of the orchards wanted to forecast their revenues for 2011. With 90% confidence, what is the range of price per box (for the entire harvest season) the growers should use in making this calculation?

- The 90% confidence interval is equal to

  The mean ± 1.645 (Standard Deviation)
  = \$9.832372 ± 1.645 * \$0.851

- \$8.43277 < Forecasted Price Range < \$11.232267
- This confidence interval could be described in one of two ways:
  - With 90% confidence, the price will not fall below \$8.43277 and will not get higher than \$11.232267 within the harvest season of 100 days.
  - There is a 10% probability that the price would not go below \$8.43277 or above \$11.232267 within the next three days.

### Confidence Interval for One-Tail Test

Assume instead that the owners are interested in estimating the *lowest* possible price with 95% confidence. To make this estimation, we ignore the probability of error at the upper tail and include the entire 50% upside in the confidence interval. At the lower tail, the 1.645 standard deviation from the mean has 45% in the confidence region and 5% in the tail as the probability of error. The upper 50% plus the lower 45% provides the 95% confidence. Therefore, the lower tail confidence level is

\$ 8.43277 = \$9.832372 – 1.645 * \$0.851

Notice that \$8.43243 is the lower bound for the two-tail test at the 90% confidence level, and it is the lower bound for the one-tail test at the 95% confidence level.

## 3.3 Value-at-Risk

As part of this broad interest in risk reporting, the U.S. SEC issued Financial Reporting Release No. 48 in 1997 (FRR 48), which required registered companies with publicly traded securities to disclose *value-at-risk* (*VaR*) if it is considered material (SEC, 1997). Although this disclosure is generally placed in the section of Management Discussion & Analysis of the annual report, the auditor must review the information (See Chapter Twelve; MD&A is introduced as a disclosure of strategic risk). If the entity elects to place the information in the footnotes to financial statements, the auditor must audit the estimation process, including the bases for the assumptions made. To perform a credible review, accountants must know the basics of what *VaR* is and how it is measured. IFRS 7 also requires disclosure of *VaR* if material as one measure of market risk.

### 3.3.1 Meaning and Estimation of *VaR*

There are different stories about the early history of *VaR*; Glyn Holton (2002) traces it back to a study by Leavens in 1945 and the creation of RiskMetrics.[11]

There are four important components of estimating *VaR*:

1. The maximum amount one expects to lose.
2. The expectation formed for a given period of time.
3. A specific confidence probability level associated with this expectation.
4. The assumption of normal business conditions.

Thus, the elements of measures of basic *VaR* are:

a. *A Monetary Amount (or a rate of return)*: Managers are concerned with the exposure to downside risk and expected losses of different portfolios. *VaR* was developed to estimate how much the value of an asset or of a portfolio is expected to fall below a specified value level for a given level of confidence. Usually the mean (average) or the expected value of the distribution is taken as a benchmark.
b. *Probability*: The decision maker must estimate the likelihood that the estimated specific drop in value will occur. This is the degree of the manager's confidence in the estimate. We can quantify this estimate using some general assumptions based on the properties of the normal probability distribution, as we will detail below. Generally speaking, choosing a confidence interval must be consistent with the management's goals and strategies and must be based on supporting evidence.
c. *Time Horizon*: The time horizon over which decision makers need to know the change in value is also relevant because different periods will entail different distribution moments and different exposures.[12]
d. *Business Conditions*: All of the three factors above—the estimated amount of loss exposure, the degree of confidence, and time horizon—are considered under the assumption of ordinary business conditions. They are not estimated under the assumption of financial distress conditions or emergency measures.

There are several methods of estimating *VaR*. The variance/covariance method begins by generating a distribution of values (or rates of return, depending on the variable of interest) based on either historical data or simulation of "what if" scenarios. The underlying distribution is often assumed to be the normal distribution. This assumption is justified by the Central Limit Theorem (noted above), which states that in the limit, the means of all samples and subsamples are normally distributed. The concern in the measurement of *VaR* is about the lower tail—i.e., when the value or rate of return decline sharply below an acceptable level. Therefore, the increase in value above the mean—i.e., the probability of upside risk is exactly 50%—is accepted in full in the measurement of *VaR* because the management welcomes any increase in asset values or profitability.

Similar to hypothesis testing, the question of relevance in *VaR* analysis may be asked in one of two different ways:

1. What is the probability the value of a specified asset will decline to a particular level?
2. What would be the value of the particular asset or portfolio under consideration for a given probability of occurrence?

The two versions of the question have different motivations: the first attempts to estimate the expected loss given a certain confidence level; the second tries to estimate the probability of loss given a predetermined loss tolerance.

*VaR* estimation assumes that prices and returns are normally distributed and the first two moments provide all needed information. The $Z$ -values (standardized units of standard deviation in a Standard normal distribution) corresponding to three most commonly used probability levels are as follows:

| *Probability of confidence level* | *Probability of values falling below the accepted level* | *Corresponding Z-value connoting the number of units of standard deviations away from the mean* |
|---|---|---|
| 0.99 | 0.01 | 2.33 |
| 0.975 | 0.025 | 1.965 |
| 0.95 | 0.05 | 1.645 |

### 3.3.1.1 *Basic Measures of VaR*

*VaR* provides an answer to the question, "How far will the value of an asset or portfolio, the rate of return, the currency exchange rate, or any other 'value' of an item of interest drop below the expected value (the mean) within a specific number of days?" Any measure developed will have to be positioned in a world of uncertainty where one could seek some confidence level, but not certainty. That is, the one-day *VaR* is:

The expected value of the portfolio or the asset

minus

The value to which the portfolio or the asset will drop in one day if conditions remain normal within a specified confidence level.

Assume that the asset in question is "a portfolio" whose prices or rates of return are normally distributed and for which the standardized units of standard deviation, $Z$, can be used to measure the distance from the mean. For a 95% confidence level, the lowest value to which the portfolio is expected to drop is

$$L_{VaR} = \bar{x} - Z_{0.95} * \text{Standard Deviation for the period}$$

Expressed differently, there is a 5% chance that the value of the portfolio could fall below $L_{VaR}$.

### 3.3.1.2 *Graphing* VaR

Figure 3.3 presents a histogram of the history of simulated price movements of a hypothetical stock. A smooth curve over this histogram will be the usual normal distribution. The location of *VaR* is shown on the graph as the distance between the mean and lowest expected value with 95%

confidence. To illustrate, assume the stock price of a hypothetical stock has a mean of $28.00 and a standard deviation of $3.22. Figure 3.3 shows the distribution of prices over a two-year period. *VaR* with 95% confidence is calculated and shown in this figure.

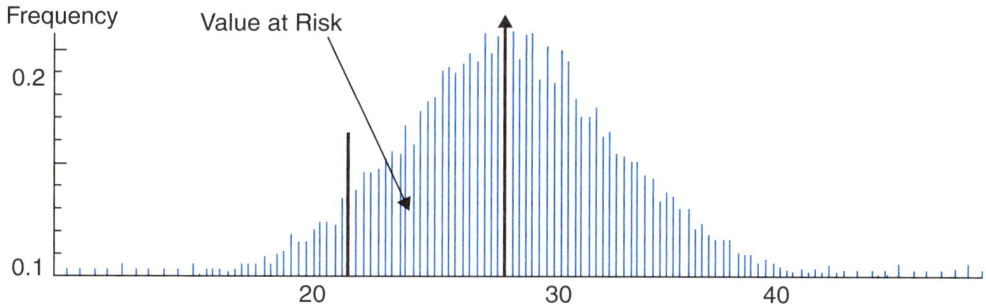


Assume:
Mean = 28
$\sigma$ =3.22
$VaR_{0.95} = 1.645 \times 3.22 = 5.297$
[With 95% confidence, the maximum loss in one week under normal operating conditions]
$L_{VaR}$ = Mean – $VaR_{0.95}$
= 28 – 5.3 = 22.703

**Figure 3.3** Measurement of *VaR* for Prices of a Hypothetical Stock

### Examples

Assume that your company has a portfolio of stocks for which you are able to collect the following information. The investment value is $1 million; average rate of return 6%; standard deviation of the rate of return is 1.2%. You need to calculate and interpret *VaR* for different levels of confidence. This information is in Table 3.2.

**Table 3.2** *VaR* Calculation for Portfolio *ZK7*

| | *95% Confidence* | *99% Confidence* |
|---|---|---|
| *VaR* (Return) | 1.645 * 0.012 = 0.01974. | 2.33 * 0.012 = 0.02796 |
| *VaR* (Dollar Amount) | 0.01974 x 1,000,000<br>= $19,740<br>There is a 95% chance that the value of the portfolio will drop by $19,740. | 0.02796 x 1,000,000<br>= $27,960<br>There is a 95% chance that the value of the portfolio will drop by $27,960. |
| Lowest Value | $1,000,000 – $19,740<br>= $980,260 | $1,000,000 – $27,960<br>= $972,040 |
| Interpretation | (a) There is a 95% chance that the value of the portfolio will drop to $980,260.<br>(b) There is a 5% chance that the value of the portfolio will drop below $980,260. | (a) There is a 95% chance that the value of the portfolio will drop to $972,040.<br>(b) There is a 5% chance that the value of the portfolio will drop below $972,040. |

For another example, consider the case of the Valencia orange producers discussed in the previous section; assume that the owner is expecting a harvest of 100,000 boxes. At a price of \$9.832372 per box (Florida Department of Agriculture and Consumer Services, 2011), her expected sales revenues would be \$983,237.20. She wants to sell this produce to makers of frozen orange juice. But the Brazilian growers began dumping (selling below cost) their orange harvest in U.S. markets and this dumping is threatening the attainability of the \$9.832372 price per box. The orange grower wants to know the maximum amount she could lose in nine days under normal circumstances with some reasonable assurance. She will then use this amount as a benchmark: If her future losses do not surpass this estimate, then she could conclude that the Brazilian dumping of oranges did not affect her business adversely.

In the language of financial economics, the orange grower wants to know the nine-day *VaR*. She also knows that no one could be certain and asked for a reasonable estimate, which is translated in the risk language to be 95% confidence level. To estimate *VaR*, we first have to estimate the one-day standard deviation. From the history of price movements, the standard deviation for the 100-day harvest season was \$0.851. The daily standard deviation may then be estimated as

$$= 0.851/\sqrt{100}$$
$$= 0.0851 \text{ per box.}$$

The nine-day standard deviation is $\sqrt{9} * 0.0851 = 0.2553$.

The lowest price per box for which this producer's crop may be sold within nine days is likely to be

$$= \$9.832372 - (1.645 * 0.2553)$$
$$= \$9.4124 \text{ per box.}$$
$$VaR = \$0.41997 \text{ per box}$$

The *VaR* is therefore what the grower could expect to lose within three days with 95% confidence, which is \$41,997.20 for the entire crop of 100,000 boxes.

### 3.3.2 The Effect of Diversification on *VaR*

The assumption underlying *VaR* is that the value (or the return) of an asset, say asset A, is distributed as a (Gaussian) normal distribution with a mean of $\mu_A$ and a standard deviation of $\sigma_A$ such that the (standardized) standard deviation from the mean is:

$$Z_A = (X_{iA} - \mu_A)/\sigma_A,$$

where $X_{iA}$ is the $i$th observation of the value of $A$, $Z_A$ is the standardized normal deviation from the mean, $\mu_A$ is the population mean, and $\sigma_A$ is the population standard deviation. Typically, the true parameters are unknown and must be estimated by sampling. For a sample obtained from the population $A$, the estimated mean is $\bar{A}$ and the estimated standard deviation is ${}_A\hat{\sigma}$. Also, assume there is a sample of another asset, Asset $B$, with estimated values of $\bar{B}$ and estimated standard deviation ${}_B\hat{\sigma}$.

The 95% confidence *VaR* for each asset is as follows:

$$VaR_{0.95,A} = 1.645 * {}_A\hat{\sigma} \text{ for asset } A,$$
and
$$VaR_{0.95,B} = 1.645 * {}_B\hat{\sigma} \text{ for asset } B.$$

If the assets $A$ and $B$ are added up together in a portfolio, then the value of the portfolio will also follow a normal distribution because the sum of two normal distributions is normal. The mean or expected value of the portfolio is $\bar{P} = \bar{A} + \bar{B}$, but the standard deviation of the portfolio is not the sum of the standard deviations of the two assets for two reasons: (a) the *standard deviations are not additive*, and (b) *these two assets may be correlated*. Also, assume that the enterprise invests ${}_{A}w$ proportion of its investment capital in $A$ and the proportion ${}_{B}w$ in $B$ (${}_{B}w = 1 - {}_{A}w$). Because variances are additive, the variance of the portfolio of assets $A$ and $B$ together will be

$${}_{A+B}\hat{\sigma}^2 = {}_{A}w^2\ {}_{A}\hat{\sigma}^2 + {}_{B}w^2\ {}_{B}\hat{\sigma}^2 + {}_{A}w * {}_{B}w * 2\ cov(A,B)$$

And the standard deviation is the square root of the variance

$${}_{A+B}\hat{\sigma} = \sqrt{{}_{A+B}\hat{\sigma}^2}$$

where ${}_{A}w$ is the proportion of the portfolio invested in asset $A$; ${}_{B}w$ is the proportion of the portfolio invested in asset $B$; ${}_{A}\hat{\sigma}^2$ is the variance of asset $A$; ${}_{B}\hat{\sigma}^2$ is the variance of asset $B$; $cov(A,B)$ is the covariance of the values of asset $A$ and asset $B$. The covariance is a measure of the extent to which these values move together (positive covariance), opposite of one another (negative covariance) or do not move together at all (covariance of zero).

The *VaR* for the portfolio of $A$ and $B$ with 95% confidence is then calculated as:

$$VaR_{0.95,\,A+B} = 1.645 * {}_{A+B}\hat{\sigma}$$

The above measures could be applied for valuation in dollars, for total dollar return or for the rates of return. If it is for rates of return, it is the convention to report and present volatility of rates over one year. In this case, if the horizon of *VaR* is different from one year, then for a five-month period of example the appropriate estimation of *VaR* would include adjustment for the time period of five months out of 12.

$$VaR_{0.95,\,A+B} = 1.645 * {}_{A+B}\hat{\sigma} * \sqrt{5/12}$$

The effect of diversification on *VaR* will be the excess of the sum of *VaR* values for the individual assets over the value of *VaR* for the portfolio. That is,

$$\text{Diversification Effect} = [VaR_{0.95,\,A} + VaR_{0.95,\,B}] - VaR_{0.95,\,A+B}$$

A detailed example of *VaR* for a portfolio of two stocks is presented in Exhibit 3.2.

## Exhibit 3.2 An Illustration for Measuring Effect of Diversification on *VaR*

An investor purchased the following stocks:

10,000 shares of GE at $20.00

and 10,000 shares of Pfizer at $18.00

Over the past year, the prices of GE shares ranged between a low of $15.00 and a high of $30.00. Pfizer share prices ranged between $14.00 and $29.00. The volatility measures of return on these stocks were 30% and 20%, respectively (usually, volatility is annualized).

The expected prices over the next year are $24.00 for GE and $19.00 for Pfizer.

To calculate *VaR* for each stock, we need the following steps:

- Decision on *VaR* horizon: 10 days
- Assuming the trading days in a year are 250, the daily standard deviations are calculated as follows:

  for GE $= 0.30/\sqrt{250} = 0.01897$

  for Pfizer $= 0.20/\sqrt{250} = 0.01265$

- Calculate the 10-day standard deviations for each stock:

  $\hat{\sigma}_{GE} = 0.01897 * \sqrt{10} = 0.06$
  $\hat{\sigma}_{Pf} = 0.01265 * \sqrt{10} = 0.04$

- Find the 10-day 95% confidence *VaR* (in %):

  GE $= 1.645 * 0.06 = 0.0987$
  Pfizer $= 1.645 * 0.04 = 0.0658$

- Find the 10-day 95% confidence *VaR* (in $):

  GE $= \$200{,}000 \times 0.0987 = \$19{,}740$
  Pfizer $= \$180{,}000 \times 0.0658 = \$11{,}844$

- Find the 10-day 99% confidence *VaR* (in $):

  GE $= \$200{,}000 \times 2.33 \times 0.06 = \$27{,}960$
  Pfizer $= \$180{,}000 \times 2.33 \times 0.04 = \$16{,}776$

- Estimate relative weights of each stock in the portfolio:

  $w_{GE} = \$200{,}000/380{,}000 = 0.526$
  $w_{Pf} = \$180{,}000/380{,}000 = 0.474$

Assuming the correlation between GE and Pfizer stock to be 0.60, calculate the covariance.

Since the correlation is equal to the covariance divided by the product of the two standard deviations and the correlation of (*GE, Pf*) $= \dfrac{Cov(GE,Pf)}{\hat{\sigma}(GE) * \hat{\sigma}(GE)} = 0.60$, then the covariance is $Cov\,(GE, Pf) = 0.6 \times 0.3 \times 0.2 = 0.036$.

- Calculate the variance for the portfolio of GE plus Pfizer.

  $= (w_{GE})^2\,(\hat{\sigma}_{GE})^2 + (w_{Pf})^2\,(\hat{\sigma}_{Pf})^2 + 2 * w_{GE} * w_{Pf} * Cov(GE, Pf)$
  $= (0.526)^2\,(0.30)^2 + (0.474)^2 * (0.20)^2 + 2 * (0.526)\,(0.474)\,(0.036)$
  $= 0.05184$

and

The annual standard deviation of the portfolio is
$\hat{\sigma}_p = \sqrt{0.05184} = 0.22768$

- The standard deviation of the portfolio for 10-days is

  $\sqrt{(0.05184/250) * 10}$
  $= 0.0143944 \times 3.162$
  $= 0.04554$

- Estimate the 10-day *VaR* of the portfolio as:

  For 95% confidence = 1.645 * 0.04554 = 0.07491
  For 99% confidence = 2.33 * 0.04554 = 0.10611

- Calculate the 10-day *VaR* (in $):

  For 95% confidence = 0.07491 * 380,000 = $28,466
  For 99% confidence: = 0.10611 * 380,000 = $40,321

- Measure the diversification effect:

  For the 95% confidence = (19,740 + 11,844) – 28,466 = $3,118
  For the 99% confidence = (27,960 + 16,776) – 40,321 = $4,415

## Information Log

The diversification effect could be extended to more assets. For example, estimating *VaR* for a three-stock portfolio

Consider a portfolio of three assets A, B, and C. To calculate *VaR* for the new portfolio, assume the following:

${}_Aw$ = Proportion of funds invested in A.
${}_A\hat{\sigma}$= Standard deviation of A.
${}_Bw$ = Proportion of funds invested in B.
${}_B\hat{s}$ = Standard deviation of B.
${}_Cw$ = Proportion of funds invested in C.
${}_C\hat{\sigma}$ = Standard deviation of C.
*cov(A, B)* = Covariance of A and B.
*cov(A, C)* = Covariance of A and C.
*cov(B, C)* = Covariance of B and C.

The variance of the portfolio is

$${}_{A+B+C}\hat{\sigma}^2 = {}_Aw^2 * {}_A\hat{\sigma}^2 + {}_Bw^2 * {}_B\hat{\sigma}^2 + {}_Cw^2 * {}_C\hat{\sigma}^2 + {}_Aw * {}_Bw * 2cov(A, B) + {}_Aw * {}_Cw * 2cov(A, C) + {}_Bw * {}_Cw * 2cov(B, C)$$

and the standard deviation is

$${}_{A+B+C}\hat{\sigma} = ({}_{A+B+C}\hat{\sigma}^2)^{1/2}$$

so that

$$VaR_{0.95,\ A+B+C} = 1.645 * {}_{A+B+C}\hat{\sigma}$$

and the diversification effect is

$$[VaR_{0.95,\ A} + VaR_{0.95,\ B} + VaR_{0.95,\ C}] - VaR_{0.95,\ A+B+C}$$

### 3.3.3 Limitations of *VaR*

The primary advantage of *VaR* is the simplicity of interpretation and the relatively straightforward process of estimation. However, *VaR* has several drawbacks:

1. It is a static measure that does not incorporate any dynamic feature of change.
2. It assumes a normal distribution, while actual distribution may or may not be approximated by normal.
3. It assumes the past is a good predictor of the future.
4. The estimated *VaR* measures are sensitive to the assumptions made.

In spite of these and other limitations, *VaR* is used extensively for analysis and planning in financial markets. For example, JPMorgan Chase reports in its 2010 Annual Report the extent to which its asset diversification reduces *VaR*:

> The Firm's average IB (investment banking) and other *VaR* diversification benefit was $59 million or 37% of the sum for 2010, compared with $82 million or 28% of the sum for 2009. The Firm experienced an increase in the diversification benefit in 2010 as positions changed and correlations decreased.

### 3.3.4 Illustrations of *VaR* in Annual Reports

Exhibit 3.3 presents brief excerpts from Form 10-K of *The Coca-Cola Company* and *Dell, Inc.* Exhibit 3.4 presents an example of *VaR* diversification reported by the European Aeronautic Defence and Space Company (*EADS, N.V.*, the producer of AirBus) using IFRS. The disclosures by JPMorgan Chase are presented in Chapter Twelve.

## Exhibit 3.3 *VaR* Disclosure Examples, The Coca-Cola Company and Dell, Inc.

**The Coca-Cola Company**

Form 10-K (Securities and Exchange Commission File No. 1-2217, April 21, 2010), p. 65

*Value-at-Risk*

We monitor our exposure to financial market risks using several objective measurement systems, including value-at-risk models. Our value-at-risk calculations use a historical simulation model to estimate potential future losses in the fair value of our derivatives and other financial instruments that could occur as a result of adverse movements in foreign currency and interest rates. We have not considered the potential impact of favorable movements in foreign currency and interest rates on our calculations. We examined historical weekly returns over the previous 10 years to calculate our value-at-risk. The average value-at-risk represents the simple average of quarterly amounts over the past year. As a result of our foreign currency value-at-risk calculations, we estimate with 95 percent confidence that the fair values of our foreign currency derivatives, over a one-week period, would decline by not more than approximately $34 million, $44 million and $20 million, respectively, using 2009, 2008 or 2007 average fair values, and by not more than approximately $34 million and $30 million, respectively, using December 31, 2009, and 2008 fair values. According to our interest rate value-at-risk calculations, we estimate with 95 percent confidence that any increase in our net interest expense due to an adverse move in our 2009 average or in our December 31, 2009, interest rates over a one-week period would not have a material impact on our consolidated financial statements. Our December 31, 2008 and 2007 estimates were also not material to our consolidated financial statements.

(Source: http://investing.businessweek.com/research/stocks/financials/drawFiling.asp?docKey=136-000104746910001476-1PFCKABMTRA5RALS1H2O2MV0O9&docFormat=HTM&formType=10-K (p. 65))

**Dell, Inc.**

Form 10-K Securities and Exchange Commission file number: 0-17017, p. 37.

Based on our foreign currency cash flow hedge instruments outstanding at January 29, 2010, and January 30, 2009, we estimate a maximum potential one-day loss in fair value of approximately $86 million and $393 million, respectively, using a Value-at-Risk ("VAR") model. By using market implied rates and incorporating volatility and correlation among the currencies of a portfolio, the VAR model simulates 3,000 randomly generated market prices and calculates the difference between the fifth percentile and the average as the Value-at-Risk. In Fiscal 2009, both higher volatility and correlation increased the VAR significantly. Forecasted transactions, firm commitments, fair value hedge instruments, and accounts receivable and payable denominated in foreign currencies were excluded from the model. The VAR model is a risk estimation tool, and as such, is not intended to represent actual losses in fair value that will be incurred. Additionally, as we utilize foreign currency instruments for hedging forecasted and firmly committed transactions, a loss in fair value for those instruments is generally offset by increases in the value of the underlying exposure.

(Source: http://i.dell.com/sites/content/corporate/financials/en/Documents/fy10-year-in-review/FY10_Form10K_Final.pdf (p. 37))

## Exhibit 3.4 Corporate Reporting *VaR* Diversification Effect

EADS, 2010 Annual Report, pp. 71–72

http://www.eads.com/eads/int/en/investor-relations/key-financial-information/annual-report/2010.html

Note 2.5 / 34 to Consolidated Financial Statements under IFRS

**Sensitivities of Market Risks**—The approach used ... the value-at-risk ("VaR"). The VaR of a portfolio is the estimated potential loss that will not be exceeded on the portfolio over a specified period of time (holding period) from an adverse market movement with a specified confidence level. The VaR used by EADS is based upon a 95 percent confidence level and assumes a 5-day holding period.

[...]

Although VaR is an important tool for measuring market risk, the assumptions on which the model is based give rise to some limitations, including the following:

A five-day holding period ... may not be the case in situations in which there is severe market illiquidity for a prolonged period.

A 95 percent confidence ... there is a five percent statistical probability that losses could exceed the calculated VaR.

[...]

A summary of the VaR of EADS' financial instruments portfolio at 31 December 2010 and 31 December 2009 is as follows (in € million):

| | *Total VaR* | *Equity price VaR* | *Currency VaR* | *Interest rate VaR* |
|---|---|---|---|---|
| **31 December 2010** | | | | |
| FX hedges for forecast transactions or firm commitments | 1,203 | 0 | 1,230 | 160 |
| Financing liabilities, cash, cash equivalents, securities and related hedges | 102 | 85 | 53 | 25 |
| Finance lease receivables and liabilities, foreign currency trade payables and receivables | 49 | 0 | 9 | 48 |
| Diversification effect | (186) | 0 | (106) | (41) |
| **All financial instruments** | **1,168** | **85** | **1,186** | **192** |

## Exhibit 3.5 Comparison of *VaR* Disclosure by Four Companies (2009 & 2010)

| **Company** | *Coca-Cola* | **Dell** | **EADS** | **JP Morgan Chase** |
|---|---|---|---|---|
| *VaR Horizon* | One Week | One Day | Five Days | One Day |
| *VaR Confidence* | 95% | 95% | 95% | 95% |
| *VaR Amounts* | *For FX:* $34 million | *For FX:* $86 million | *For FX:* 1,203 million | For Investment Banking only: $114 million |
| *% of Diversification Effects* | Not reported | Not Reported | 15% | 38% |

FX risk stands for foreign currency risk

### 3.3.5 Comparison of *VaR* Disclosures

Different firms present different amounts of detail about *VaR*. Exhibit 3.5 presents the disclosures by four companies: Coca-Cola, Dell, EADS, and JPMorgan Chase. It shows the different time horizons for estimating *VaR* and different disclosure of the beneficial effects of diversification. For example, EADS and JPMorgan Chase disclose the diversification effects, while Coca-Cola and Dell do not.

### 3.3.6 *Quasi* Value-at-Risk in Accounting

Business firms extend credit in many forms, but the two common forms are selling products and services on credit, and providing business loans. For credit sales, the business firm delivers the products and transfers the risk of ownership and control over the products to the buyers. The firm anticipates collecting the proceeds from the sale at an agreed upon future date. This type of transaction creates accounts and notes receivable, which are forms of loans or financial instruments—i.e., as if the seller provided a loan to the buyer and the buyer turned around and used that money to purchase products from the seller. In that sense, accounts and notes receivable are similar to bank loans. These two types of assets, therefore, face similar issues: the borrower must repay these loans at some future dates and the lender (whether a bank or a seller) has to be concerned about the borrower's (a) ability, and (b) willingness to pay.

It is in the creditor's self-interest to assess the risk of nonpayment *a priori* and to monitor and evaluate this risk continuously until repayment is complete. Having extended credit to specific borrowers in the first place implies that the creditors (lenders) had evaluated the debtors' (buyers, borrowers) creditworthiness and were satisfied with the level of credit risk the evaluation showed. But creditworthiness is subject to change over time and creditors must reevaluate the debtors' abilities to repay the debt. The need for reevaluation increases if creditors observe interruption in the regularity of the cash flow received from the debtors (in the form of interest payment or installment).

To safeguard assets and plan for contingencies, business practice has evolved over the years to generate some processes to anticipate the collectability of debt. Experience and history have shown an association between the pattern of interruption in the cash inflows and a lender's ultimate inability to recover the amounts due. As an example of this association, let us say 20% of borrowers who miss one payment will miss a second payment. Of the borrowers who miss two payments, only 10% will end up being totally illiquid and unable to pay. Financial institutions and sellers thus use the correlation between the duration (aging) of default on payments and loss, in full or in part, of the loan or the accounts receivable balances to evaluate the amounts of the account balances that they do not expect to collect. This process is called "aging."

Historically, *aging of accounts receivable or loans has been a way of subjectively estimating the likelihood of default.* According to accounting standards on contingencies, these loans and receivables are to be grouped according to the probability of loss into three categories: (i) assets having *remote* or no probability of loss; (ii) assets having *low probability* of loss; and (iii) assets having *high probability* of loss. These general guides have now been expanded to offer tests for asset impairment. Because an asset's value is the present value of future benefits, with benefits represented as collectible cash flow, assets in the first category continue to satisfy this definition and remain recognized as such on the balance sheet. At the other extreme are the assets in category (iii) that have a high probability of being lost—i.e., no potential cash inflow is likely to be received from those accounts. As a result, these accounts do not meet the definition of an asset and their present values are near zero. There would be no justification to keep them on the balance sheet and GAAP requires that these accounts be written off.

The second category of assets facing probable loss, category (ii), is connected with the estimation of *VaR*. Historically, GAAP has required that creditors, whether they are banks that extend loans to others or merchants that sell products and services on credit, recognize the possibility of the partial loss of these balances and set up "provisions," "reserves," or allowances if the likelihood of default increases. This reserve is typically called "allowance for bad debt," or "loan loss reserve."

Given the above description,*loan loss reserve and allowance for bad debt are the maximum amounts expected under GAAP to be lost under normal operating conditions with a certain degree of confidence, albeit subjective and not quantitatively measured.* Note the similarity of this definition to the formal definition of *VaR* presented above. Allowance for bad debt and loan loss provisions are essentially primitive measures of *VaR* and are what is referred to here as *Quasi-VaR*.

The difference between *Quasi - VaR* and the modern estimation of *VaR* lies in the underlying assumptions and measurement processes. Unlike the new processes of estimating *VaR*, estimating allowances for bad debt or loan loss reserve incorporates more subjectivity in estimating the likelihood of loss and does not make explicit assumptions about the underlying distribution. This subjective estimate, however, is guided by judgement rather than quantitative simulation of historical patterns, aging of receivables and loans, and an analysis of changes in the credit risk of borrowers and their history of default on making payments on time.

### 3.3.7 Earnings at Risk

Earnings at risk (*EaR*) is a measure of how much earnings will change as a result of a given adverse movement in prices, interest rates or currency exchange rates within a certain period of time and at a specific confidence level. Compared to the measurement of *VaR*, *EaR* measures only the change in *VaR* that will affect earnings and is often measured on a daily basis (*DEaR*). *DEaR* is also used internally by organizations to manage risk.[13] This is the context in which JPMorgan Chase presents *EaR* for the IB portfolio (reported in Chapter Twelve on Disclosure).[14]

## 3.4 Interest-Rate-Gap and Duration-Gap as Measures of Interest Rate Risk

**Accounting Log: Relevance to Accounting**

Because *interest-rate-gap* and *duration* are summary measures of liquidity risk exposure, IFRS 7 requires that enterprises present information which would in effect allow users to calculate interest-rate-gap and duration. Up to this time (July 2012), U.S. GAAP (ASC 825-10-50-23) has encouraged but not required enterprises to produce interest-rate-gap and duration information. But this state will change; on June 27, 2012, the FASB issued an Exposure Draft for a proposed Standard Update that, if adopted, will require enterprises to disclose the relevant information about interest-rate-gap and to disclose duration measures. The proposed Standard Update will also require disclosing information about the resources available to the enterprise from which to draw liquidity and the extent of the enterprise cash obligations at various dates in the future.

This proposed Standard Update is discussed in more detail in Chapter Twelve.

### 3.4.1 Interest-Rate-Gap Measures[15]

As defined earlier, interest rate risk is the risk of loss due to adverse changes in market (or benchmark) interest rates. This loss can be stated in terms of the value of debt (for fixed-rate instruments), or in terms of net cash inflow for variable, floating-rate instruments—i.e., increase in the cash outflow or decrease in the cash flow. It should be noted that financial instruments that generate cash inflow for one company are obligations of cash outflow for others. Therefore, the gain of one party to the contract of the financial instrument is a loss to the counterparty.

Changes in interest rates have different consequences depending on whether the financial instrument has a fixed or a floating rate:

- For fixed-rate financial instruments, the cash flow related to these instruments is unaffected by changes in market interest rates. However, the market (fair) values of these instruments must change when market interest rates change so that the relationship between the interest payment (at the given fixed coupon rate) and market price would be equal to current market yield. Accordingly, a rise in market interest rates should result in reducing the market values of the fixed-rate instruments, and vice versa.
- For floating-rate financial instruments, changes in market interest rates will change the cash flow associated with these instruments. An increase in market interest rates will result in increasing cash inflow from interest income generated by investments in floating-rate financial instruments, and a corresponding increase in the cash outflow for interest payment by debtholders. Similarly, a decline in interest rates will reduce the cash inflow for investors and the cash outflow for debtholders. In either case, the change in market interest rate does not alter the fair value of floating-rate instruments.[16]

The impact of changing market interest rates on cash flows will naturally affect a firm's liquidity position, and possibly its credit risk. The liquidity of the business firm will be adversely affected if the resulting increase in cash outflows exceeds the increase in cash inflows. A similar impact will take place if the decrease in cash inflows is greater than the decrease in cash outflows. These differences take place when floating-rate obligations are not equal to floating-rate assets; balancing these differences is one of the concerns of the "asset-liability" management programs, especially in financial institutions.

The potential problems that can arise from mismatching financial assets and financial liabilities give rise to liquidity risk—the possibility of having insufficient liquidity to meet scheduled obligations and finance normal operations without incurring additional cost. Interest-rate-gap is one of the measures that assist in capturing and managing this risk.

To show the definition and measurement of interest rate interest-rate-gap, assume that

$RSA = dollar amount for interest-rate-sensitive assets.
$RSL = dollar amount of interest-rate-sensitive liabilities.

Then, interest-rate-gap is measured as the difference:

$$\text{Interest-rate-gap} = \$RSA - \$RSL$$

But not all $RSA or all $RSL are of the same maturity (or duration[17]). Therefore, it is necessary to group each type according to time to maturity (or duration). Consequently, a proper definition of interest-rate-gap would make use of the relevant time bucket, denoted T:

$$\text{Interest-rate-gap}_T = \$RSA_T - \$RSL_T$$

where the subscript "T" refers to a particular class or bucket of rate-sensitive assets and rate-sensitive liabilities of the same maturity group. For the entire enterprise, interest-rate-gap is the total of $RSA minus the total of $RSL over a period of time (a month, a quarter, a year) for: (i) instruments that will mature during that period, (ii) floating-rate instruments, and (iii) full or partial payment of principal that will become due during the period.

Interest-rate-gap is used to calculate the potential impact on interest income for a given 100 Basis Points (0.1%) change in interest rate. For an enterprise to avoid exposure to interest rate risk, interest-rate-gap should be zero.

The interest-rate-gap ratio (*IRGR*) is:

*IRGR* = Rate-Sensitive Assets/Rate-Sensitive Liabilities

There is no benchmark for what constitutes a good interest-rate-gap ratio, but business practice convention tends towards having an interest-rate-gap ratio higher than one. Exhibit 3.6, Panel A shows the different directional impact of change in interest rate under different relationships of $RSA to $RSL.

## Exhibit 3.6 Panel A: The Directional Impact of Change in *Interest-Rate-Gap* on Cash Flow

| **Panel A:** *Relationship of interest rate sensitive assets and interest rate sensitive liabilities Change in Market Interest Rate (i.e., LIBOR)* | *Increase* | *Decrease* |
|---|---|---|
| IR-Sensitive Assets > IR-Sensitive Liabilities | Favorable | Unfavorable |
| IR-Sensitive Assets = IR-Sensitive Liabilities | Neutral | Neutral |
| IR-Sensitive Assets < IR-Sensitive Liabilities | Unfavorable | Favorable |

**Panel B:** Examples

| *Positive Interest-Rate-Gap* | *Negative Interest-Rate-Gap* |
|---|---|
| • $30 million in rate sensitive assets (i.e. floating rate investments).<br>• $20 million of rate sensitive liabilities (floating rate instruments).<br>Then, *Interest-Rate-Gap* = $10 million.<br><br>A change in interest rate:<br><br>• If interest rate increases 1%,<br>• Net Interest Income increases by ($10 Million X 1%) = $100,000.<br><br>• If interest rate decreases by 1%,<br>• Net Interest Income declines by ($10 Million X -1%) = –$100,000. | • $30 million in rate sensitive assets (i.e. floating rate investments).<br>• $50 million of rate sensitive liabilities (floating rate instruments).<br>Then, *Interest-Rate-Gap* = – $20 million.<br><br>A change in interest rate:<br><br>• If interest rate increases 1%,<br>• Net Interest Income decreases by (–$20 Million X 1%) = –$200,000.<br><br>• If interest rate decreases by1%,<br>• Net Interest Income increases by (–$20 Million X –1%) = $200,000. |

Furthermore, Panel B of Exhibit 3.6 shows the relevance of interest-rate-gap in estimating the impact of a change in market interest rate on income (and cash flow before taxes). To evaluate the impact of change in interest rate on *net worth or firm value*, we need to estimate the cumulative income effects over the duration of financial instruments. An example of interest-rate-gap and its use is shown in Exhibit 3.7.

## Exhibit 3.7 An Illustration of Using Interest-Rate-Gap

**Δ Interest-Rate-Gap Scenario**

Balance Sheet 31 December, 20x4 (in million dollars)

| *Assets* | | *Liabilities & O.E.* | |
|---|---|---|---|
| Rate-sensitive (yield = 8%) | 1,000 | Rate-sensitive (cost = 4%) | 1,500 |
| Fixed-rate coupon-paying bond at 10% (yield = 11%) | 800 | Fixed-rate (cost = 9%) | 400 |
| Others | 300 | Others (O.E.) | 200 |
| | ===== | | ===== |
| Total | 2,100 | | 2,100 |

Without change, Net Interest Income (NII) is as follows:

$$\begin{aligned}\text{NII} &= (\$1{,}000 \times 0.08 + \$800 \times 0.10) - (\$1{,}500 \times 0.04 + \$400 \times 0.09)\\ &= \$160 - \$96\\ &= \$64 \text{ million}\end{aligned}$$

After increase in yield ($y$) by 1%

1. Change in NII = interest-rate-gap × $\Delta y$
   = –$500 × 1% = –$5 million
2. Change in fair value loss on fixed-rate assets

   - Assuming an increase in yield from 10% to 11% and term to maturity is 3 years, the present value of $80 a year for three years plus $800 at end of three years is:

     $$\begin{aligned}&80/1.11 + 80/(1.11)^2 + 80/(1.11)^3 + 800/(1.11)^3\\ &= \$72.08 + \$64.93 + \$58.50 + \$585\\ &= \$780.50\end{aligned}$$

   - The loss in FV of fixed-rate asset due to increase in yield = 780.5 – 800 = (19.5) loss

3. Change in the fair value of fixed-rate liabilities due to increase in yield:
   Increase in yield from 9% to 11% and assuming term to maturity is 3 years, then, present value of $36 every year plus $400 at end of three years is equal to:

   $$\begin{aligned}&36/1.11 + 36/(1.11)^2 + 36/(1.11)^3 + 400/(1.11)^3\\ &= \$380.42\end{aligned}$$

   Therefore, the fair value gain on fixed-rate liability = 400 – 380.42 = $19.58 (gain)

4. The net impact of increase in yield on fair value of fixed-rate instruments

= \$5 + (\$0.08)
= \$5.08

The total effect on realized and unrealized earnings arising from 1% increase in yield is

NII + NFV gain (loss)
= \$5 + \$0.08 = \$5.08

↓ ↓

Realized Unrealized

The accounting disposition of the unrealized gains will depend on whether or not the assets and/or liabilities are hedged (Chapter Seven).

Assumptions:

- The rate-sensitive assets are not classified as held-to-maturity because (under current accounting standards) held-to-maturity securities are valued at acquisition cost, not fair value.
- The change in fair value of any portion of RSA that is classified as available-for-sale (AFS) will be posted to other comprehensive income, not earnings.
- We have assumed that RSA and RSL have approximately similar duration (discussed next).
- We have assumed that the change in yield coincided with a parallel shift in the yield curve.

In general,

- Δ Net Interest Income (ΔNII) = Interest-Rate-Gap × $\Delta y$.
- A decline in RSL or an increase in RSA leads to larger interest-rate-gap and higher impact on NII.
- There is no measure for optimal interest-rate-gap, but the enterprise exposure to interest rate risk is at its lowest point when interest-rate-gap is zero.

### 3.4.2 Duration Measures

It is important to note at the outset that the duration of a financial instrument may or may not be the same as its maturity. The first known measure of duration is provided by Fredrick Macaulay in 1938. Macaulay's duration is the period of time that it will take for the time-weighted present values of cash inflows to equal the market price of the financial instrument (e.g., a bond). Macaulay's duration uses the bond's internal rate of return to discount cash flow, while "exact duration" uses the zero-coupon rate to discount cash flow. It is measured as a quotient of two numbers: the numerator is the time-weighted present value of cash flow and the denominator is the present value (market price) of the cash flow for the remaining time to maturity. The discount rate used is the spot market rate of a zero-coupon bond. To show Macaulay's model, assume:

$F$ = face value of the instrument (bond).
$C$ = the fixed coupon rate.
$T$ = time to maturity.
$y$ = yield (on a zero-coupon bond of same maturity).
$t$ = the index used to connote the period 1, 2, 3, … $T$.

Calculate the time-weighted present value of cash flow:

$$TWCF_{t=0} = [\Sigma_{t=1}^{T} t * \{F * C/(1+y)^{t}\} + \{T * F/(1+y)^{T}\}]$$

Then, calculate the present value of the instrument (or use the market price if it is reliably available),

$$PV_{t=0} = \{\Sigma_{t=1}^{T} F * C/(1+y)^{t}\} + \{F/(1+y)^{T}\}$$

(notice that $PV_{t=0}$ is equal to market price, assuming no market friction).

Using these two measures, duration is measured as:

$$D_{t=0} = TWCF_{t=0} / PV_{t=0}$$

### 3.4.2.1 An Example

Assume a 3-year bond.
Face value is 10,000.
Coupon rate is 5% and interest is paid annually.
The zero-coupon bond rate is 10%.

To measure duration (or simply D) requires making the following calculations:

| *Year* | *Payment* | *PV at market yield* | *t = Cash flow time* | *t * PV* |
|---|---|---|---|---|
| 1 | \$500 | \$455 | 1 | \$455 |
| 2 | \$500 | \$413 | 2 | \$826 |
| 3 | \$500 | \$376 | 3 | \$1,128 |
| 3 | \$10,000 | \$7,513 | 3 | \$22,539 |
| Sum | | \$8,757 (≈ market price) | | \$24,948 |

Using this information, Macaulay's duration is 2.85 years (D = 24,948/8,757).

Next, assume the *market interest rate increases* by 1%, the change in the value of this bond will be:

$$-D * 1\% * PV = -2.85 \times 0.01 \times \$8,757 \approx -\$249.6$$

Alternatively, a *decline in market interest rate* by 1% will increase the value of the bond by:

$$-D * (-0.01) * (8,757) = -2.85 \times -0.01 \times 8,757 \approx \$249.6$$

This same approach could be used to evaluate the effect of changes in interest rates on net worth. That is calculated as:

{Duration of assets – Duration of liabilities} * Change in interest rate.

The result of applying Macaulay's duration:

- The duration of a zero-coupon bond is equal to its time to maturity.
- The duration of a coupon bearing bond is less than its time to maturity.

#### 3.4.2.2 Modified Duration

In 1966 Larry Fisher introduced the measure of *modified duration* (*ModD*) as an extension of Macaulay duration, which is measured as:

$$ModD = D/(1 + y/k),$$

where $D$ is Macaulay duration as measured above, $y$ is the yield of a zero-coupon bond having the same maturity, and $k$ is the frequency of coupon payment ($k = 2$ for semi-annual, for example). *ModD* measures the sensitivity of the price of a fixed-rate instrument to changes in the yield.

Using the information in the above example, $D = 2.85$; $y = 10\%$; and $k = 1$. Therefore,

$$ModD = 2.85/(1.10) = 2.59.$$

This *ModD* implies that the price of the fixed-rate instrument would change by 2.59% for every unit change in the yield. The higher the duration measure, the more sensitive is the value of the bond or fixed-rate instrument to changes in the yield.

### 3.4.3 Same Present Values for Assets with Different Durations

If two instruments have equal present values, it is tempting to consider them equal on other dimensions including riskiness. But that view might change in consideration of risk. Knowledge of duration measures of different instruments should help in developing a profile that captures both present value and risk. In Exhibit 3.8, the example offered by the FASB[18] is extended to show that bonds having essentially the same present values could differ significantly in their response to shocks in the yield rate because of their differing duration and exposure to risk. The Exhibit presents a comparison of three bonds: Coupon-paying bond, zero-coupon bond, and amortizing bond. Their similarities and differences are as follows:

*Similarities of the three bonds:*

- Same maturity—five years.
- Earning interest at the same "coupon" rate—9% per annum.
- Comparable market prices.

*Differences between the three bonds:*

- *Cash flow*: The zero-coupon bond does not pay out any cash until retirement when the accumulated principal and interest are paid off at once. The coupon-paying bond pays an annual interest income and redeems the face value at retirement. The amortizing bond makes equal payments of principal plus accrued interest over the five-year maturity.

- *Fixed vs. Floating*: the duration of a floating-rate bond is the period extending up to the reset date, which could be as long as a quarter for quarterly reset periods or six months for a biannual reset. Such a short horizon for a 30-year maturity, for example, is not significant and it is often simpler to assume zero duration for floating-rate bonds.

## Exhibit 3.8 A Comparison of Duration and *Modified Duration* for 9% Fixed-Rate Bonds Having Different Cash Flow Patterns

| | | *9% Coupon Bond* | | *Zero-Coupon Bond* | | *Amortizing Bond* | |
|---|---|---|---|---|---|---|---|
| *Yield (Spot)* | *Period* | *Cash Flow* | *Period x P.V.* | *Cash-Flow* | *Period x P.V. cash flow* | *P.V.* | *Period x P.V.* |
| — | 0 | (100,000) | | (100,000) | | | |
| 0.06 | 1 | 9,000 | 8,490 | 0 | 0 | 24,254 | 24,254 |
| 0.07 | 2 | 9,000 | 15,722 | 0 | 0 | 22,455 | 44,508 |
| 0.075 | 3 | 9,000 | 21,735 | 0 | 0 | 20,695 | 62,085 |
| 0.08 | 4 | 9,000 | 26,460 | 0 | 0 | 18,897 | 75,582 |
| 0.09 | 5 | 109,000 | 354,210 | 153,862 | 500,000 | 16,709 | 83,543 |
| | Sum | 45,000 | 426,617 | | 500,000 | 103,010 | 289,972 |
| | | Duration | 426,617 / 101,051 = 4.22 | | 500,000 / 100,000 = 5 | | 289,972 / 103,010 = 2.815 |
| | | Yield to Maturity | = 8.75 | | = 9.0% | | =7.87% |

*Source*: See the FASB discussion on *Duration* and *Modified Duration* in its Summary of Types of Derivative Instruments (FASB 1999).

*Assumptions:*

- All three bonds face the same spot (zero-coupon) curve.
- There is no difference or change in credit risk.

The data in Exhibit 3.8 show the following information:

- Using same yield curve, the present values (i.e., market prices) of the three bonds are as follows: \$101,051 for the coupon-paying bond, \$100,000 for the zero-coupon bond, and \$103,010 for the amortizing bond.

- Macaulay duration measures are: 4.22 years for the coupon-paying bond, 5 years for the zero-coupon bond, and 2.815 for the amortizing bond.
- The yields to maturity of these instruments are: 8.73 for the coupon-paying bond, 9% for the zero-coupon bond, and 7.87 for the amortizing bond.
- The three bonds respond to given changes in interest rate very differently. Using the market yield for the zero-coupon bond, the *ModD* measures are 3.87% for the coupon-paying bond, 4.58% for the zero-coupon bond, and 2.61% for the amortizing bond.

#### 3.4.3.1 The Relevant Issue

The fact that these three bonds have almost equal present values does not make them equal in risk, in their response to changes in interest rate, or other cash flow features. (See Chapter Twelve for a discussion of the new proposed Accounting Standards Update on liquidity risk disclosures).

*If* we adopt hedge accounting, the hedging relationship must be highly effective.[19] It means that we will need a different derivative instrument to provide an effective hedge for each of these three bonds because each derivative instrument must be expected to respond to changes in interest rate in a way that would offset the impact on the hedged item. It must match the particular bond duration and sensitivity to shocks in interest rates. An item required in hedge documentation is to show (both *ex-ante* and *ex-post*) that the hedged risk and the risk of the hedge instrument match. If these risks do not match the enterprise would not qualify for adopting hedge accounting.

**Information Log: Limitations**

- Duration as discussed above is an appropriate measure for straight bonds; these are the bonds that do not offer optionality of conversion, callability, puttability or other types of embedded derivatives because any optionality feature alters the cash flow pattern of the bond.
- Duration and modified duration measures assume that the change in yield is a result of parallel shift of the yield curve. This means that these duration measures ignore bond convexity, which is the second derivative of the bond market value to changes in yield. Even with this assumption, duration and modified duration provide good approximations for the effect of change in yield on fair values of fixed-rate instruments for short horizons.
- Duration measures ignore changes in credit risk.

## 3.5 Other Liquidity Risk Measures

One of the oldest measures of liquidity is the *acid test ratio* or *quick ratio*. It is a measure of the availability of sufficient amounts of liquid assets to allow a business entity to meet its short-term cash outflow commitments. The acid test ratio is measured as

$$\frac{\textit{Current Assets} - \textit{Inventories}}{\textit{Current Liabilities}}$$

While there are no standard benchmarks, the general rule of thumb is that an enterprise's quick ratio should not be lower than one, although higher ratios suggest better liquidity and reveal the business entity's ability to pay its short-term obligations. Different industries have different benchmarks for the acid test ratio, but (except for financial institutions) the general formulation is not usually industry specific. Adapting the acid test ratio to specific industries does not alter its nature as an indicator of the short-term ability to pay. For example, in the banking industry, *Basel Accord II* (December 2003) distinguishes between high- and low-quality assets in terms of liquidity. A high-quality asset is one whose cash-generating capacity, either as a security for secured borrowing or by sale, is expected to remain intact during periods of financial distress. The *Accord* requires that banks maintain a level of stock of high-quality liquid assets to fill funding interest-rate-gaps between cash inflows and cash outflows during periods of financial distress.

Another risk metric useful in the banking industry is the *liquidity leverage ratio*. This metric is measured as:

$$\frac{\textit{High Quality Liquid Assets}}{\textit{Net Cash Outflow over a 30 day Period}}$$

As with the generic acid test ratio, the liquidity leverage ratio has a recommended minimum threshold of 100%.

The *Basel Accord* provides other indicators of liquidity risk that are less structured by highlighting sources of red flags for liquidity, which include:

- Contractual maturity mismatch of cash inflows and cash outflows.
- Concentration of funding, which measures the extent to which funding is concentrated by specific counterparties, financial instruments, or currencies.
- Available unencumbered assets, the assets that are "free" and can be used as collateral for secured borrowing if needed.
- Other market-related monitoring tools.

### 3.5.1 Fixed Charge Ratio

Lease payments and interest on debt are recurrent payments that borrowers must make on time to avoid defaulting. Therefore, the enterprise must assess the extent to which cash inflow provides a safety margin after the enterprise covers those fixed commitments. This is measured by the fixed charge ratio and is traditionally calculated as:

$$= \frac{\textit{Net Income before interest and taxes} + \textit{Lease payments}}{\textit{Interest} + \textit{Lease payments}}$$

Entities are required to relate cash inflow to the fixed charge in the short run; however, except as a proxy for cash flow, "net income" may not be a good indicator of cash flow from operations. Accrual, terms of credit, sales turnover, and many other factors that could be industry specific create different relationships between cash flow and earnings. The fixed charge ratio would provide a better indicator if operating *cash flow* is used in the numerator instead of income.

A *fixed charge ratio* of one does not provide any safety margin; the safety margin improves as the ratio increases above one. As an example, Fitch Ratings has announced an improvement in its rating of Colonial Properties Trust due to positive signs including improvement in the company's fixed charge ratio from 1.5 to 1.6 in 2010 and further improvement to the level of 2.0 in the first quarter of 2011.[20]

## 3.6 Measurement of Credit Risk

As defined in Chapter Two, credit risk is the default risk, or the risk that counterparties (debtors) may default on payments or will go bankrupt, which will have a spillover effect on the liquidity of creditors.[21] Traditional financial measures of credit risk and liquidity risk have some commonalities because a business entity with bad liquidity constraints will have higher probability of defaulting on servicing its debt obligations when they become due. However, liquidity measures such as those discussed above have implications for short-term credit risk and other measures are needed for evaluating long-term credit risk.

An overall measure of the credit risk of an entity can be developed from two main sources:

1. Factors related to operations, which provide measures of the business entity's ability to generate net cash flow.
2. Factors related to the financial conditions that provide indicators of the business entity's liquidity in relationship to its obligations.

Different tools are used to assess each of these types. These tools include financial accounting ratios and various models of default risk.

### 3.6.1 Using Financial Analysis Ratios

Business enterprises have long used accounting information to assess credit risk. Specific financial ratios work as risk indicators and continue to be highly relevant. These ratios include measures of *leverage*. In traditional financial analysis, the extent to which a business firm finances its activities by borrowing reflects the probability of default. The capacity of the business firm to carry and service debt is often measured in relationship to the business firm's equity and total assets—leverage ratios that are measured differently:

1. Total Debt/Owners' Equity
2. Long-term Debt/Owners' Equity
3. Long-term Debt/(Long-term Debt + Owners' Equity)
4. Total Debt/Total Assets

A low leverage ratio (however measured) provides greater safety to creditors because a larger proportion of the asset pool and cash inflows would be uncommitted and free to service a relatively smaller amount of debt. If the debt is considered an option on the firm's owner's equity with a strike value equal to its book value, in a low leverage situation, the option would be deep in the money because, in these cases, the value of uncommitted assets (equal to owners' equity) is greater than the strike price. Conversely, a high leverage ratio indicates a smaller uncommitted asset pool and thereby narrows the safety margin (and the assumed option could be out of the money). Accordingly, when faced with financial difficulties, those firms with low leverage ratios are more likely to be able to meet the required debt service while funding their normal operations.

Generally, high leverage ratios indicate higher cash flow demands on the borrowers. Therefore, the debt burden could create more credit risk for entities in cyclical business where the cash generated from operations is not flowing in steadily, but the cash demanded to service the debt has a steady outflow. With this type of cash flow mismatch, high leverage ratios can indicate higher credit risk.

Some analysts set heuristics and rules about the acceptable levels of leverage ratios. However, it would be misleading to offer one level of leverage as "optimal" or "normal" because the default diagnosticity of these ratios depends on other factors, such as the type of industry in which the firm operates. For example, a company operating in the heavy machinery industry sector will, by the very nature of its operations, have a lower debt to equity ratio than a bank does. Banks have the highest leverage ratios of any industry because the majority of a bank's assets are financed by debt in the form of short-term and long-term deposits. Bank regulators such as the Federal Deposit Insurance Corporation (FDIC) and the Federal Reserve Bank specify the maximum leverage acceptable to regulatory agencies to consider a bank "solvent." This maximum acceptable leverage ratio implies a minimum capital requirement a bank should maintain in order to remain solvent. Thus, keeping a minimum capital equal to 8% of total assets implies a total debt to equity ratio of 12.5. At that level, banks are considered solvent. However, this level of leverage would not be acceptable for any other industry. Similarly, the insurance industry has its own measures of solvency.

To show the influence of the type of industry, Exhibit 3.9 presents two measures of leverage for five companies in different industries. Of the five companies, the highest leverage ratios are for Bank of America followed by IBM. Because banks generate a large proportion of their financing from depositors' funds, several leverage ratios are calculated for banks. The Assets/Equity ratio is the ratio of total debt plus deposits to equity. To compare banks with others, different gearing ratios are calculated. These are basically measures of the debt that the bank has raised in a traditional credit financing and does not include unsolicited depositors' funds. As shown in the table, the gearing ratio (the ratio of borrowed debt to equity) of Bank of America is 1.84, but the leverage ratio is 10.2.

## Exhibit 3.9 Two Measures of Financial Leverage for Five Corporations

| *Company* | *AT&T* | *IBM* | *Microsoft* | *McDonald* | *Bank of America* |
|---|---|---|---|---|---|
| Total Debt / Equity | 0.66 | 1.55 | 0.17 | 0.95 | 1.84 Gearing Ratio*<br>10.20 Assets/Equity |
| Long-term Debt / Equity | 0.56 | 1.24 | 0.17 | 0.80 | 1.66 |

* Gearing ratio is equal to borrowed debt divided by equity.

## Accounting Log

This log considers some relevant issues in connection with these ratios in light of the information risk concerns discussed in Chapter Two. These concerns relate to the choice of measurement and valuation basis. For example, what measurement bases (amortized cost, fair value, etc.) are used to measure assets? How about different methods of inventory valuation or management classification of marketable securities that lead to a mix of valuation based on historical cost or fair value? Are there omitted assets such as the economic value of Research & Development projects, brand names, or executory contracts? Do the values presented for plant, property and equipment provide fair representation or approximation of fair values? Are all liabilities recognized on the balance sheet? How about contingencies?

In other words, it is of import *not* to assume that reported numbers provide a complete and accurate picture of the underlying economics of the enterprise.

## 3.6.2 Multivariate Analysis of Default Risk Using Financial Ratios

William H. Beaver (1966) was the first known author to use financial ratios to predict failure (a stage beyond default). However, he used univariate analysis to look at the behavior of one ratio at a time. Subsequently, Edward Altman (1968) combined those financial ratios in a multivariate discriminant analysis model, which showed that the results of one ratio depend on the impact of other ratios.[22]

In a discriminant analysis, the dependent variable (*DepV*) is a binary indicator for the bankrupt (*DepV* = 0) and non-bankrupt (*DepV* = 1) state. Altman's analysis yielded the following relationship:

$$\begin{aligned} DepV = & \ 1.2 \text{ Working Capital/Total Assets} \\ & + 1.4 \text{ Retained Earnings/Total Assets} \\ & + 3.3 \text{ Earnings before Interest and Taxes/Total Assets} \\ & + 0.60 \text{ Market Value of Equity/ Book Value of Liabilities} \\ & + 1.00 \text{ Sales/Total Assets.} \end{aligned}$$

Altman used the letter $Z$ (unrelated to the $Z$-value of a normal distribution) to refer to the predicted value of the dependent variable and identified three zones:[23]

$Z > 2.99$ => Safe Zone, the risk of default is remote.
$1.8 < Z < 2.99$ => Grey Zone, moderate risk of default.
$Z < 1.80$ => Distress Zone, default is likely.

### 3.6.2.1 *Moody's "Financial Statements Mode" of Estimating Risk of Default*

Moody is one of the large credit rating agencies (the others are Fitch Ratings, Morningstar, and Standard & Poor's). Moody's uses several approaches and models to estimate credit risk.[24] In its use of financial statement ratios, the company notes that "[t]he Financial Statement Only mode is best suited for users who desire a stable estimate of a firm's default risk for certain applications." The model includes financial statement variables that capture a firm's long-run performance. There are seven broad categories that Moody's ratings use in the Financial Statements Only (FSO) mode (Dwyer and Zhao, 2009):[25]

1. *Profitability ratios*: ROA and change in ROA—*High profitability reduces the probability of default.*
2. *Leverage*: LTD/(LTD + Equity); retained earnings/current liabilities—*High leverage increases the probability of default, where LTD is equal to long-term debt.*

3. *Debt coverage*: cash flow/interest expense—*Low debt coverage increases the probability of default.*
4. *Growth variables*: growth in sales—*Rapid change, either as growth or decline, tends to increase a firm's default probability.*
5. *Liquidity*: cash plus marketable securities/total assets—*High liquidity reduces the probability of default.*
6. *Activity ratios*: inventory/sales; change in accounts receivable turnover; current liabilities/sales—*A low inventory turnover tends to increase the probability of default.*
7. *Size*: total assets—*Large firms do not have as frequent default events as smaller firms.*

The estimated model for use in predicting default is not publicly known, but appears to be a linear combination of these variables. The weights assigned to these ratios are the coefficients estimated by the statistical model used—probit, logistic or Cox-proportional hazard.[26]

### 3.6.3 Merton's and *KMV* Models

The main model of Moody's ratings appears to be the *KMV*™ model for estimating the probability of default; the model was developed by Kealhofer, McQuown, and Vasicek (Kealhofer, 2003a, 2003b) based on the Merton model (1974) of estimating *distance to default* (see also Dwyer and Zhao, 2009). It appears that among all default prediction models developed in the literature, the Merton model had the greatest impact on the various approaches used in predicting default. The model calculates the distance to default as a function of the standardized distance between the adjusted fair value of assets and the book value of liabilities. Adjusted assets are estimated as the total value of the enterprise liabilities plus equity after taking asset growth into consideration. The book values of liabilities are used in the model under the assumption that these are also the settlement values.[27] The Merton model is based on option pricing because the total settlement (book) value of liabilities is like a strike price of a call option (held by debtholders) on the firm's total assets. The enterprise is considered far from default by the extent to which the adjusted fair (market) value of assets exceeds the settlement value of liabilities (i.e., the degree of being in the money). The enterprise reaches the default point when the book value of liabilities (the strike price) equals the fair (market) value of assets (i.e., the option is at the money). The critical measure is the distance to default, which is an indication of how deep the option is in the money. The model assumes that the values of assets and liabilities follow log normal distribution. A simplification of the Merton model may appear as follows:

$$DD = [\ln A + \text{growth drift} - \ln L]/\text{volatility of A},$$

where *DD* is *Distance to Default*; *ln* is for natural logarithm; *A* is for market value of assets; *L* is for book value of liabilities; and volatility is the standard deviation of assets. Volatility is typically measured as the standard deviation for one year, so if we estimate *DD* for a period shorter than one year, both the numerator and denominator should be adjusted to measure *DD* for that time as a fraction of one year.

To view the distance to default more intuitively, *DD* is the number of standard deviations away from the mean at the point in which the adjusted fair value of assets (adjusted by a growth factor) and the book value of liabilities are equal. In that sense, *DD* follows a standardized normal distribution of the type shown in Figure 3.2.

For a simple example, assume:

$MVA$ (market value of the assets) = \$40,000
$\mu$ (annual growth drift of assets) = 0.02
$BL$ (book value of liabilities) = \$25,000
$\sigma_{mva}$ (volatility of assets) = 30%
$M$ (Time horizon for DD in months) = 3 months
$T$ (Fraction of Horizon to year, 3/12) = 0.25

$$\begin{aligned} DD &= [(ln\ MVA + \mu - 0.25 \times 0.5\ (\sigma_{mva})^2 - ln\ BL] \ / \ [\sigma_{mva} \times \sqrt{0.25}] \\ &= [ln\ 40{,}000 + .02 - 0.5(0.09) \times 0.25) - ln\ 25{,}000] \ / \ 0.30 \times \sqrt{0.25} \\ &= [10.5966 + 0.000225 - 10.127] \ / \ 0.15 \\ &\approx 3.19 \end{aligned}$$

This means that the distant to default is 3.19 standard deviations away from the mean. The area under the tail of the distribution beyond three standard deviations is the probability of default, which in this example would be 0.07%. If the balance of liabilities increases to \$30,000, this probability of default will increase to about 3%.

Because $ln \frac{MVA}{BL} = ln\ MVA - lnBL$, the distance to default of the Merton model could be restated as follows:

$$DD = \{ln(MVA/BL) + (\mu - 0.5\sigma^2_{mva})T\}/\sigma_{mva} {*} \sqrt{T}$$

where all variables are defined above.

Leaving the details of the model for specialized books in this area, the intuition of the Merton model lies in the method of using three important features of the enterprise's financial profile:[28]

1. *Leverage*: The market value of equity over the book value of debt, which is in effect the inverse of leverage.
2. *Profitability of the firm*: This is measured by the rate of return on the firm's assets.
3. *Volatility* of the firm's assets.

The Merton model was extended and commercialized by Kealhofer, McQuown and Vasicek who developed what is now known as the *KMV*™ default prediction model that was acquired by Moody's in 2003 for its use in estimating and predicting the probability of default and for scoring credit rating. The model refers to the probability of default as *estimated default frequency* or EDF. EDF is measured daily for more than 35,000 publicly traded firms worldwide and is made available to the public *ex-post* for publicly traded and sovereign companies. As noted above, the genesis of EDF is the distance to default of Merton model.

## 3.6.4 Morningstar's Comparison of Models

All default prediction models utilize leverage as a primary determinant. In fact, the main variable in both Merton and its variants such as the *KMV*™ model is $ln \frac{MVA}{BL}$ which is the inverse of the conventional measure of leverage. The development of these models has gone through three stages:

1. Employing univariate analysis of financial ratios, means and trends to classify firms into bankrupt or going concern (Beaver, 1966).
2. Using multivariate forms of linear statistical models (e.g., discriminant analysis) that implicitly assume that the variables follow multivariate normal distribution (e.g., Altman, 1968).
3. Applying the Merton model, the basis for the *KMV*™ model and for many other variants published by others.

Several studies compare the predictive accuracy of different default prediction models. Of particular interest are the comparisons by Martin Bemmann (2005) and Warren Miller (2009). In this study, I use the predictive accuracy of three models provided by Warren Miller of Morningstar, Inc. (2009). These models are:

1. A naive prediction model that uses a single variable of leverage measured as Total Debt/Total Assets.
2. Altman *Z* -Score discriminant analysis model.
3. The Merton model of distance to default.

The results are graphed in Figure 3.4, which is reproduced from Miller (p. 5). Miller finds that Merton model outperforms the other two models with the naive model being the last. However, he notes: "Curiously, the *Z*-Score's ordinal utility [i.e., predictive accuracy] is nearly equal to the other two models when ranking relatively safe companies, but performs worse in situations where the probability of bankruptcy is high" (Miller, 2009, p. 9).

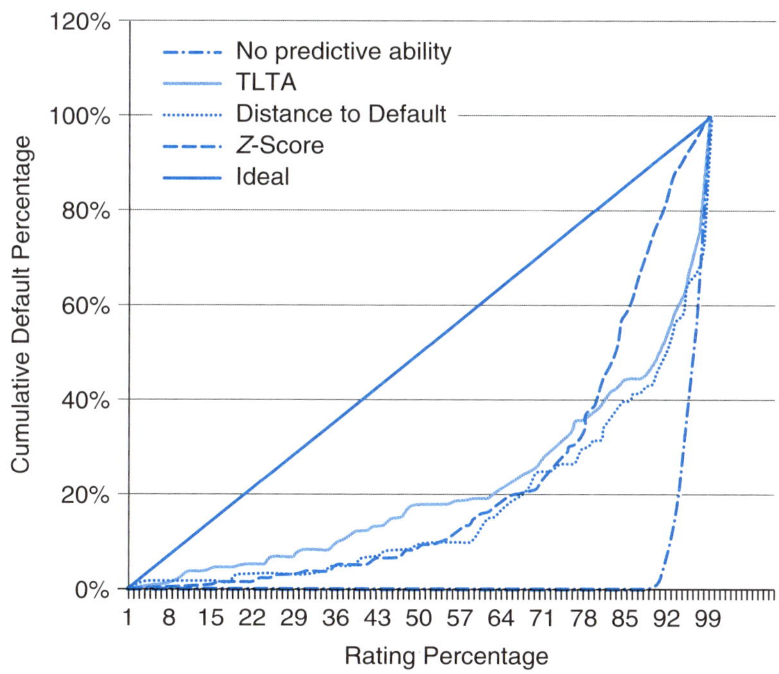


**Figure 3.4** Comparison of Models as reported in Miller (2009)

Source: Reproduced with the permission of Warren Miller, the author of "Comparing Models of Corporate Bankruptcy Prediction: Distance to Default vs. Z-Score", Warren Miller of Morningstar (July 1, 2009). Available at SSRN: http://ssrn.com/abstract=1461704.

### 3.6.5 Credit Scoring

Predicting the probability of default is an important step in evaluating credit risk, but it is not the final step. Credit risk evaluation is summarized in a credit rating score reflecting, among other things, the probability of default, liquidity of markets, and restrictiveness of debt covenants. Any enterprise that borrows money has credit rating scores for the enterprise as a whole and for each of its debt instruments. Different debt instruments of a given enterprise can have different credit ratings based on the terms of these debt contracts. Some are secured by collaterals, some are senior, and others are subordinated.

Credit rating scores matter because they have implications for the enterprise's ability to access capital markets and financing. A lower credit rating almost guarantees a higher cost of financing because lenders (e.g., bondholders and banks) will require risk premiums commensurate with the risk exposure indicated by the credit rating. Similarly, a high rating will reduce the cost of financing significantly so that the risk premium and default spread will be low. For example, on September 2, 2011, the yield on a 10-year, AAA corporate bonds was 2.55%, which increased to 3.22% for the AA-rated corporate bond and to 3.3% for the A-rated corporate bonds.

Although five large companies in the USA are known to issue those ratings, the rating methodologies differ in details but not in the main characteristics and determinants. In fact, the elements that John Moody introduced in 1909 for rating railroad companies remain the general guiding foundation. At that time he suggested the use of *financial strength, default frequency, loss severity, and transition risk*. Ever since then, the credit rating industry has grown and the rating process involves more than estimating the probability of default; all credit rating methodologies consider dimensions of profitability, leverage, management quality, diversification, growth, and liquidity. For example, in September 2011, the Morningstar credit rating of McDonald's Corporation was AA- and, in discussing the rating, Morningstar makes the following observation concerning the accounting measures of leverage and profitability:[29]

> Our credit rating for McDonald's includes important assumptions regarding operating leases, which Morningstar's credit rating methodology treats as debt-like obligations for the purpose of calculating our forward-looking Cash Flow Cushion estimate and common credit-relevant ratios like debt/EBITDA. Accordingly, we have capitalized $11.4 billion in lease obligations. We estimate cash lease payments of $9.1 billion over the next five years, a sum substantially higher than the minimum operating lease obligations articulated in the company's filings, but consistent with our own rent expense calculations. Our operating lease forecast constitutes 54% of our estimate of total contractual obligations over the next five years.

However, default risk is so critical that almost all methodologies take estimating the probability of default as the starting point. Although each company promotes its model as a "better model," the publicly available literature shows that all have two common characteristics:

1. Heavy reliance on financial statements ratios to predict solvency, profitability, and ability to pay.
2. Adaptation of variants of Merton model (1974) of estimating distance to default.[30]

Morningstar, for example, uses the Merton model and 26 financial ratios plus a ratio called "cash cushion." The financial statement ratios cover profitability, liquidity, leverage, and growth. Similar to Moody's and Morningstar, Standard & Poor's rating criteria make heavy use of financial ratios and consider a wide range of factors including the firm's diversification, seniority of debt issues, and whether the debt has security (i.e., collateral).

Public knowledge of credit rating methodologies became of more serious interest after the financial crisis began in 2007. The public found that investment banks had inflated the credit ratings of the sub-prime mortgage-backed securities and credit default swaps, which allowed high-risk companies to have access to capital markets at low financing costs and use the funds they raised to make more high-risk loans and investments.[31]

In a recent book by the International Finance Corporation of the World Bank, Roggi, Garvey, and Damodaran (2012) provide a tabulation of the default spread associated with each of Moody's and Standard & Poor's ratings. Segments of the authors provided are reproduced in Exhibit 3.10 to show how default risk increases from a low of 0.45% to a high of 7.75%.

## Exhibit 3.10 Correspondence of Default Spread and Credit Rating Scores

| *Rating Moody's/S&P* | *Default Spread on Ten-Year Bond* |
|---|---|
| Aaa/AAA | 0.45% |
| Aa1/AA+ | 0.50% |
| ... | |
| Aa3/AA– | 0.60% |
| ... | |
| A3/A– | 1.05% |
| ... | |
| Baa2/BBB | 1.75% |
| ... | |
| Ba1/BB+ | 3.50% |
| ... | |
| B1/B+ | 5.00% |
| ... | |
| B3/B– | 6.25% |
| Caa/CCC+ | 7.75% |

*(Source: Roggi, et al. 2012, p. 24)*

## 3.7 Summary of Key Points

Measurement of risk follows from the definition of risk in Chapter One—risk is volatility or measurable uncertainty. Based on this view, this chapter considers two approaches: (i) a generic approach based on the available data distributions, and (ii) a functional approach based on risks of different functions discussed in Chapter Two.

### 3.7.1 Generic Measures of Risk

- *Extreme Cases*: When there are no observations, every outcome is equally likely (Bayes) and when there is one observation, it serves as the centroid and all other outcomes are distributed about it. When there is a maximum and a minimum, bid/ask spread, or yield spread, the range or the width between the two observations is the best (simplest) measure of risk. Even in this case and in the absence of other information, different outcomes between the two end points are assumed to have equal probability of occurrence.
- *With Three Observations*: Three outcomes having different probabilities of occurrence add much more information about risk. Mathematical statisticians have shown that this type of distribution (triangular distribution) is an approximation of a specific probability distribution called *Beta Distribution*. In its simplest form, the risk measurement one obtains from triangular distribution is the range divided by six. This distribution has wide use (starting with the Navy in 1950 development of the Polaris submarine) in Program Evaluation and Review Technique (PERT) and Critical Path Method (CPM).
- *With Multiple Observations*: With increased number of observations, the occurrences of most events tend (in the limit) toward a normal distribution. The properties of normal distributions are well studied: a bell-shaped symmetric curve having 99.9% of observation fall within six standard deviations. The standard deviation (square root of the variance) is the measure of risk that underlies much of the functional risk measures. Under the Central Limit Theorem, the distributions of means (averages) obtained from any form of distribution tend to follow normal distribution.
- *Value-at-risk* (*VaR*): A measure of the maximum amount expected to be lost within a specified period of time and a probability of confidence under normal operating conditions. Normal distribution is commonly assumed to underlie the data for which *VaR* is estimated. *VaR* decreases with diversification. It is proposed that the allowance for bad debt or loan loss reserve that accountants have been estimating for years is a *quasi* measure of *VaR*.

### 3.7.2 Functional Measures of Risk

- *Interest Rate Risk*: Interest-rate-gap and duration are the two measures emphasized. Interest-rate-gap is the difference between interest-rate-sensitive assets and interest-rate-sensitive liabilities. The impact on income and cash flow will depend on the size of interest-rate-gap. An enterprise will bear downside risk if (a) Gap is positive, and market interest rates decline, or (b) Gap is negative and market interest rate increases. Macaulay's duration is the period of time it will take for the time-weighted present values of cash inflows to equal the market price of the bond. Modified duration measures the sensitivity of the price of a fixed-rate instrument to changes in interest rate.
- *Other Liquidity Risk Measures*: Financial ratios such as liquid asset ratio and fixed charge ratio.
- *Credit Risk*: Sometimes called "default" risk because it is a measure of the ability and willingness of debtors (counterparties) to pay. Basic ingredients are financial ratios that always include a measure of leverage. More quantitatively developed methods include statistical analysis that combines financial ratios and default prediction models that are based on Merton's model of distance to default.

## Notes

1 Shaughnessy Financial: Glossary. Available at: http://www.shaughnessyfinancial.com/glossary.php?show=y
2 Alder Financial: Glossary. Available at: http://alderfinancial.com/Financial%20Glossary.htm
3 The yield curve or the *term structure of interest rates* is a graph presenting yield rates (or zero-coupon rates) for different maturities and different risk classes.
4 It is a popularized form of *Beta* distribution. Next to normal distribution, it is claimed that triangular distribution is the second most widely used distribution.
5 Statistical distributions have shown that the moments of a triangular distribution are a reasonable approximation of *Beta* probability distribution. (See Punmia and Khandelwal, 2006; van Drop and Kotz, 2002.)
6 It is worth noting, though, that the measure of risk using triangular distribution is simply the range scaled by a constant.
7 Brighton Webs Ltd: Statistics for Energy and the Environment, Beta Distribution. http://www.brighton-webs.co.uk/distributions/beta.htm
8 Notices that variances are additive, but standard deviations are not.
9 This is a repeat for most people who recall their prior exposure to statistics, but it is a prelude to Value-at-risk measurement.
10 Orange prices are actually quoted to six decimal places. See Florida Department of Agriculture and Consumer Services (March 2011).
11 RiskMetrics Products are at http://www.msci.com/products/riskmetrics.html.
12 The two moments of interest here are the mean and the standard deviation.
13 See also use of Earnings at Risk at Du Pont: Montante (2000).
14 In general, *VaR* = Fair Value * DEaR *.
15 This section ignores Macaulay's duration that will be discussed next.
16 Except for accrued interest and assuming no optionalities that will alter this general feature.
17 The term duration is not the same as time to maturity in many cases as will be discussed later.
18 In an educational piece entitled, *Types of Derivative Instruments*, FASB 1999.
19 Effectiveness is discussed in detail in Chapter Six. For the moment equate effectiveness with the degree of success in offsetting the hedged risk.
20 Fitch Ratings defines fixed charge ratio as "recurring operating EBITDA including Fitch's estimate of recurring cash distributions from partially-owned entities less recurring capital expenditures less straight line rent adjustments, divided by interest expense, capitalized interest and preferred dividends." See: Fitch Ratings (August, 2011).
21 See Chapter Twelve for a summary of the new proposed Accounting Standards Update related to liquidity and credit risk.
22 Discriminant analysis is a statistical technique that finds the coefficients that maximize the difference between the two group means (centroids). For a large sample, conclusions based on the results of discriminant analysis are generally similar to those obtained by estimating logistic regression or Probit regression.
23 It is important not to confuse Altman *Z* -score of predicting bankruptcy and the *Z* -score of standardized normal distribution. Altman could have called his predicted variable the *X* -score, for example.
24 Moody's disclosed some of their use of statistical models that include probit, logistic, and Cox-proportional hazard models. Interested readers should consult books on limited dependent variables and survival models.
25 See also http://www.moodyskmv.com/products/files/RiskCalc_v3_1_Model.pdf.

26 These models are like regression analysis except that (a) the dependent variable is a dichotomous, binary variable; (b) the method used for estimation is the maximum likelihood instead of minimizing least squares as in the Ordinary Least Squares regression; and (c) Cox-proportional hazard assumes a non-linear relationship.

27 Introducing the fair value option and hedge accounting changed that condition since the values of some of the debt components will be the fair values not the settlement values.

28 If not known, the market value and volatility of assets could be estimated by using Black-Scholes option pricing model for European style options.

29 http://www.morningstar.ca/globalhome/industry/news.asp?articleid=325610

30 Moody's KMV™ model discussed in the previous section is built on Merton's model. Also Morningstar's methodology appears to use the model in a similar way (Morningstar®, 2009; Standard & Poor's, 2012).

31 Competition among credit rating companies in the USA makes the general framework of their methodologies public. Recently, The National Securities Commission (CNV) of Argentina issued a resolution ordering the rating agencies to publish reports on its methodology (M24 digital.com, 2011). In the USA, the SEC and Congress are discussing rating agencies' independence and methodologies, but no action has been taken (see McDermott and Emry, 2009).

## CHAPTER 4

# BASICS OF RISK MANAGEMENT

## 4.1 Enterprise Risk Management (ERM)

"Risk management will be an area of focus for finance professionals and companies moving forward."[1] This is the conclusion of the Financial Executive Research Foundation's 2011 annual risk survey. The survey also revealed that 66% of respondents indicated that their companies have a risk management program in place.

## 4.2 Definition of ERM

The introduction to decision-making theories and cases presented above highlights the significant differences among decision makers' attitudes toward risk. Consequently, businesses need a structure for risk management to mitigate their enterprise's exposure to loss. These types of structures are called "enterprise risk management" or simply ERM.[2] The first known complete ERM structure was initially recommended by the Committee of Sponsored Organizations (COSO) of the Treadway Commission, formed in 1985.[3] In 1993, the committee issued a report on internal controls in which the first ERM was formulated. In 2004, COSO issued a report specifically devoted to ERM: *Enterprise Risk Management—Integrated Framework*, which has become known by the acronym "the COSO Report." COSO revised the report in 2010; many regard the new report (COSO 2) as a slight improvement over the first report. Since then, ERM has become an integral part of the organizational structure of large business entities in the USA and abroad, as well as in the subsystems of business entities such as information technology. In practice, the internal audit function has assumed the responsibility for assurance about the quality of ERM.

The COSO Report defines ERM as:

> a process, effected by an entity's board of directors, management and other personnel, applied in strategy setting and across the enterprise, designed to identify potential events that may affect the entity, and manage risk to be within its risk appetite, to provide reasonable assurance regarding the achievement of entity objectives.

A somewhat more refined definition is provided in a United Nations report: "*An organization-wide process of structured, integrated and systematic identification, analysis, evaluation, treatment and monitoring of risks towards the achievement of organizational objectives*" (Terzi and Posta, 2010, p. 4).

The COSO report was preceded by the 1977 Foreign Corrupt Practices Act (FCPA), which legislated penalties for corporations and corporate officers for paying bribes to obtain business contracts abroad.[4] The FCPA emphasized the need for effective internal controls. Nevertheless, corporate fraud and corruption continued and even escalated, which led to enacting the Sarbanes-Oxley Act (SOX) in 2002. The Act emphasizes the need for establishing processes to ensure that management effectively manages risk and to inform the public of methods and degrees of success in controlling risk. Under the auspices of SOX, the Public Company Accounting Oversight Board (PCAOB) was born.

## 4.3 The COSO Cube

The ERM framework is defined by three components that are presented in what is known as the COSO Cube, which has the following elements:

| | *Structure* | *Elements* |
|---|---|---|
| a) | *Organizational* | The levels of the entity, division, business-unit, and subsidiary. |
| b) | *Functional* | Strategic, operations, reporting, and compliance. |
| c) | *Structural* | Internal environment, objective setting, event identification, risk assessment, risk response, control activities, information and communication, and monitoring |

A similar movement took place in other parts of the world. In the U.K., the two influential reports are the Internal Control Guidance (known as the Cadbury Report, 1992)[5] and Turnbull Report (1999; see Page and Spira, 2004). The Turnbull Report was developed for The Institute of Chartered Accountants in England and Wales; it established that corporate directors were responsible for setting up a sound system of internal control, reviewing its effectiveness and reporting their findings to shareholders. Shortly after the Cadbury Report was released, the U.K. government established the Financial Service Authority (FSA) to regulate all financial services, including the creation of risk-based supervision systems. The London Stock Exchange adopted this requirement and put it in place at least two years prior to the enactment of the Sarbanes-Oxley Act in the USA in 2002.

In Canada, the Toronto Stock Exchange commissioned the Dey Report and issued it in 1994 (Stymiest and Mackinlay, 1999). It required companies to report on the adequacy of internal control systems. Subsequently, the Canadian Institute of Chartered Accountants issued the CoCo Report (Guidance on Control) in 1995. This report requires that the evaluation of internal controls should include risk assessment and risk management.

In Australia and New Zealand, the Risk Management Standard was issued in 1995. It advocated formalizing what we now call the ERM system. In Germany, the KonTraG was enacted into law in 1998; it includes a clause requiring management to establish a system for risk management and internal controls.

These initiatives have been developed through the work of private organizations. Regulatory efforts have also been active in attempting to improve internal control systems and the assessment and control of risk. In the USA, the PCAOB took over setting auditing standards and oversight of the profession. In 2004, the PCAOB issued Standard No. 2, which required public companies to establish all control points within the organization immediately and to revamp their internal control systems effectively. Standard No. 2 was controversial because it was too demanding and costly to implement. In 2007, it was replaced by Standard No. 5 (2007), which had the same goals but was less cumbersome. The PCAOB and the SEC continually update and amend the regulations to enhance corporate risk management and reporting.[6]

In 2005, the European Commission set up a "European Group of Auditors' Oversight Bodies" (EGAOB).[7] The Group aims to ensure effective coordination between the newly constituted public oversight systems of external (statutory) auditors and audit firms within the European Union. It may also provide technical input in the preparation of possible measures to implement the Commission's Directive, such as the endorsement of the International Standards on Auditing, or the assessment of the quality of developing countries' public oversight systems.

## 4.3.1 An Example of Implementing a COSO-Like System

The Intercontinental Hotel Group, plc reported a framework for its risk management that includes six stages, shown in Exhibit 4.1. These stages are:

1. Identification and prioritizing risk.
2. Quantification and measurement of risk.
3. Developing a response plan and solutions.
4. Implementing and testing the proposed solutions.
5. Reporting on corporate governance and culture.
6. Reviewing the risk process.

### Exhibit 4.1 Risk Management at Intercontinental Hotel Group, plc.

**Corporate risk management**

Intercontinental Hotel Group's (IHG) Risk Management function has recently reviewed how to manage corporate risk and the major risks to IHG. It seeks to develop a framework to improve risk management capability further, represented diagrammatically below:

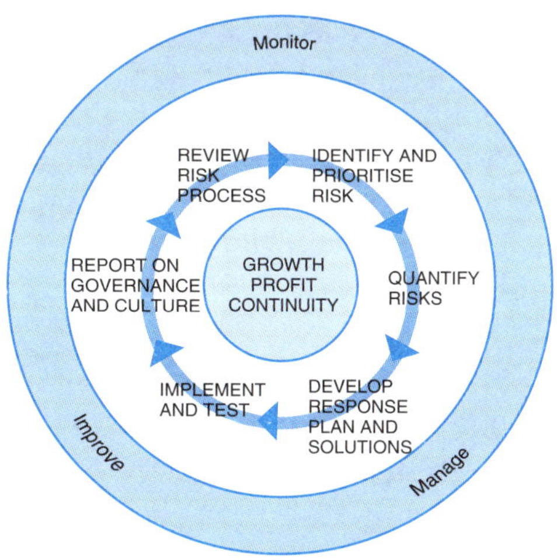

Each year, the senior IHG management runs risk identification workshops. The output is a 'Group Risk Register', divided into areas of accountability for each member of the Executive Committee.

The Executive Committee uses the findings to identify the major areas of risk for IHG and to assign accountability for cross-functional leadership between them. The Executive Committee prioritises and co-ordinates efforts to optimise the management of major risks to IHG.

(Source: http://www.ihgplc.com/files/reports/ar2008/index.asp?pageid=32)

## 4.4 Event Severity and Likelihood

In its Form 10-K of 2011, General Electric (GE) states:[8] "Risks identified through our risk management processes are prioritized, depending on the probability and severity of the risk" (p. 36).

While this statement from GE considers the micro-level, in his book, *The Black Swan*, Nassim Taleb (2007) argued that the problem facing the financial sector is its failure to predict severe-impact, low-frequency events. This is the same problem that the survey of Deloitte (2005) had revealed to be a critical issue in the evaluation and management of risk. The proposed Probability/Impact matrix below is a simple decision aid. It emphasizes the value of evaluating the tradeoff between frequency of occurrence and severity of impact.

Two real-life illustrations show the attention to frequency of occurrence and severity:

- The above noted statement by GE.
- Similarly, in its discussion of risk, Barclays Group, plc notes that "management estimates the potential earnings volatility from different businesses under various scenarios, represented by severity levels:
    - expected loss: the average losses based on measurements over many years
    - 1 in 7 (moderate) loss: the worst level of losses out of a random sample of 7 years
    - 1 in 25 (severe) loss; the worst level of losses out of a random sample of 25 years."

Figure 4.1 presents a simple form of a 3 × 3 classification of the probability of occurrence and severity of outcome into: high, moderate, and low. In this 3 × 3 table, the elements along the diagonal, which are high-high, moderate-moderate, and low-low, are typically attention attractors. The manager pays attention to high-impact events that appear highly frequently and, to a lesser extent, moderate-impact events that appear frequently enough to cause concern. But management might not focus on low-severity/low-frequency events and might even delegate the responsibility for those events to someone else at a lower echelon of the organizational hierarchy. Accordingly, the elements along the diagonal are likely to receive more serious managerial consideration in terms of actions or delegation so that the type of risk management will be commensurate with frequency and impact.

A different story emerges for the elements of the matrix above the diagonal in Figure 4.1; Cell 1 could consist of highly influential events simply because of the anticipated severity of impact, yet the event is less frequent. Although this cell requires making a conscious effort for prediction, assessment and evaluation, it receives less attention because it occurs infrequently (e.g., the financial crisis of 2007). This is followed in terms of significance by Cell 2 of high impact/moderate frequency and moderate impact/high frequency. In general, the elements above the diagonal of the probability/impact matrix require setting up contingencies for different scenarios.

| | | Probability of Occurrence | | |
|---|---|---|---|---|
| | | High | Moderate | Low |
| IMPACT | High | 3 | 2 | 1 |
| | Moderate | 4 | 3 | 2 |
| | Low | 5 | 4 | 3 |

**Figure 4.1** Probability/Impact Matrix

## 4.5 Approaches to Managing Risk

There is no risk-free setting; risk and uncertainty are elements of all scenarios. However, different types of risk (such as those presented in Chapter Two) require different methods of management, mitigation, and control. The goal of a good management control system is managing risk and reducing the negative impact on an organization's activities so that it can achieve its goals. This chapter addresses some alternative ways to manage and mitigate risk, while others are beyond the scope of this book. The choice of a particular method depends on the management's risk appetite and the event or task. In any scenario, risk may be avoided, managed, insured, or hedged.

The following section will discuss the rudiments of the following approaches:

1. Risk avoidance
2. Self-insurance
3. Second party insurance (for insurable risk only)
4. Diversification
5. Hedging
6. Asset/liability management
7. Factoring (liquidity risk)
8. Securitization
9. Writing restrictive covenants

Some of these approaches are consistent with the themes presented by Jose Lopez of the Federal Reserve as well as by GE Corporations as shown in Exhibit 4.2.

## Exhibit 4.2 Examples of Concern about Consideration of both Severity of Impact and Probability of Event Occurrence

**Panel A: A Financial Economist's Viewpoint of Methods of Managing Risk:**
In broad terms, risk management is the process of mitigating the risks faced by a bank, either by *hedging* financial transactions, purchasing *insurance*, or even *avoiding* specific transactions. With respect to operational risk, several steps can be taken to mitigate such losses. For example, damages due to natural disaster can be insured against. Establishing redundant backup facilities can mitigate losses arising from business disruptions due to electrical or telecommunications failures. Losses due to internal reasons, such as employee fraud or product flaws, are harder to identify and insure against, but they can be mitigated with *strong internal auditing* procedures. [Emphasis added]

Jose Lopez, Federal Reserve Bank of San Francisco
(Source: http://www.frbsf.org/publications/economics/letter/2002/el2002-02.html)

**Panel B: Approaches to Managing Risk at General Electric**
Risks identified through our risk management processes are prioritized and, depending on the probability and severity of the risk, escalated to the Chief Risk Officer (CRO). The CRO, in coordination with the CRC, assigns responsibility for the risks to the business or functional leader most suited to manage the risk. Assigned owners are required to continually monitor, evaluate and report on risks for which they bear responsibility. Enterprise risk leaders within each business and corporate function are responsible to present to the CRO and CRC risk assessments and key risks at least annually. We have general response strategies for managing risks, which categorize risks according to whether the company will avoid, transfer, reduce or accept the risk. These response strategies are tailored to ensure that risks are within acceptable GE Board general guidelines.

Depending on the nature of the risk involved and the particular business or function affected, we use a wide variety of risk mitigation strategies, including delegation of authorities, standardized processes and strategic planning reviews, operating reviews, insurance, and hedging. As a matter of policy, we generally hedge the risk of fluctuations in foreign currency exchange rates, interest rates and commodity prices. Our service businesses employ a comprehensive tollgate process leading up to and through the execution of a contractual service agreement to mitigate legal, financial and operational risks. Furthermore, we centrally manage some risks by purchasing insurance, the amount of which is determined by balancing the level of risk retained or assumed with the cost of transferring risk to others. We manage the risk of fluctuations in economic activity and customer demand by monitoring industry dynamics and responding accordingly, including by adjusting capacity, implementing cost reductions and engaging in mergers, acquisitions and dispositions.

(Source: Form 10-K, General Electric, 2010, p. 35. Available at: http://ir.10kwizard.com/filing.php?ipage=8092464&rid=23&attach=ON&doc=1&source=329&welc_next=1&fg=24)

### 4.5.1 Risk Avoidance

One way of managing risk is to avoid undertaking the activity that might create the type of risk exposure the decision maker wants to avoid. For example, some individuals are averse to airplane travel. They avoid the risk of flying by driving or taking public transportation. Similarly, the management of a business enterprise that does not wish to bear currency risk can avoid entering into contracts with foreign currency denominations. In other situations, risk avoidance is the only way to manage specific risk exposure. For example, federal and local airport regulations do not permit airlines to have airport ground crews working outside the terminal to prepare planes either for departure or arrival when there is lightning.

In general, however, risk avoidance is not a feasible option for managing risk, businesses must take risks to achieve benefits and to make profits.

### 4.5.2 Self-Insuring

If an entity has a plan in place to bear all the risk of loss due to specified uncertain events such as fire, the enterprise is said to be self-insured. To cover losses, the management can set aside reserves and provisions to allow for the cost of restoring the damaged property. For example, a large state university with a great number of widely dispersed buildings might find that self-insuring against fire hazard is less costly than paying a high annual insurance premium to an insurance company for providing coverage. In these circumstances, it might be necessary to estimate and hold in reserve an amount of contingency fund to allow for adequate cost recovery. An institution usually makes that choice on the basis of a careful cost-benefit analysis, perhaps with the assistance of actuaries.

However, it is generally not a good policy to self-insure against potentially costly events. In other cases, self-insurance might be the rational choice. For example, self-insurance is effective when the available insurance for specific events is highly costly, when insurance is not available, or when the potential loss is too small to be a concern and there is an alternative effective risk management reduction in place.

### 4.5.3 Second Party Insurance

Insurance is a method for transferring risk; for a fee, the insured transfers the risk of loss due to the occurrence of an event specified in the contract. However, not all risks can be insured.

#### *4.5.3.1 Insurable Risk*

As noted in Chapter Two on Types of Risk, the insurance industry classifies risk into two categories:

1. Pure or hazard risk.
2. Speculative risk.

Speculative risk is the risk that has uncertain outcomes that can be either loss or profit. In contrast, pure risk is the risk of hazard that can only result in a loss (resulting in a gain is not in the outcome set), such as the risk of loss due to fire, flood, wind, earthquake, hurricanes, health, unemployment, or job-related injury. In an insurance contract, the insured seeks recovery of losses caused by the insured risk.[9] The insured stands to recover only the loss or the value of the damage (depends on the contract) and must not gain from insurance.[10] To be classified as insurable risk, it must meet several conditions:

- The insurer can charge a high enough premium to cover (a) the expected cost of claims, (b) own cost of operation, and (c) normal profits.
- The outcome of the insurable event must be either: (a) a loss to the insured, or (b) no loss. It cannot be an event in which the insured can generate gains.
- An insurable loss is one that may be realized due to *uncertain and involuntary events*; these are events that are not controllable by the insured (or its affiliates) and are not the result of the insured actions. For example, loss from accidental fire is insurable, but loss from self-started fire is not.
- A sufficiently large number of insured persons or entities demand this particular insurance. By pooling risks of a large number of individual exposures, *risk transfer* becomes also a *risk sharing* so that the total funds collected from charging the insurance premium would cover all claims from the relatively small number of entities that realized losses from the insured events. If only a small number of entities elect to have a particular type of insurance, the insurance enterprise is said to face *adverse selection* because it is highly likely that only those anticipating loss from the insured event would apply for insurance—and no effective pooling of risk would be possible.
- The loss must be determinable. This is usually feasible for events with frequent recurrence. But there are events, especially rare occurrences, for which there is no recorded history of the extent of damages or losses. For example, hurricane Katrina of 2005 and the financial crisis of 2007 do not happen with a frequency that could help insurers estimate the cost of the damage or loss. In cases like these, the amount of losses is so large and indeterminable that insurers cannot estimate the required premium and thus cannot cover it.

#### 4.5.3.2 Principles of Insurance

There are several principles that every insurance practice must follow. Four major principles are discussed here.

1. *Principle of Indemnity*

The insured may not gain from insurance and may not collect more than the actual loss in the event of damage caused by an insured peril. Actual loss is equal to the market value or amount of cash equivalent that preserves the equity of the insured to its level prior to the occurrence of the damaging event. In general, estimating fair value is necessary for the determination of recovery amounts, but there are some special cases that differ such as:

- Valued policies such as insuring rare paintings. The fair value of a unique painting is not determinable unless it is put up for auction. In these cases, the owner seeks to insure the rare painting at an individually stated value.
- Replacement cost insurance, such as insuring a structure for the cost of replacing it with an exact replica. That cost will depend on market conditions for materials and labor, both of which can change over time.
- Life insurance contracts—the benefits of a life insurance policy are determined by an agreement between the insured and the insurance enterprise based either on income or on expense expectations.

2. *The Principle of Insurable Interest*

For insurance contracts to have legitimacy, the insured must have an economic interest that demonstrates the right to loss recovery. It is not acceptable for someone to seek insurance for events in which they have no economic interest. For example, one could seek life insurance for a relative, but not for a stranger. Life insurance on mortgage borrowers is another example; mortgage lenders may require the borrower to purchase life insurance with the lender being the beneficiary and the insurance benefit being the loan balance. Here, the mortgage lender has a legitimate insurable interest and has the right to be indemnified should the borrower be unable to repay the loan.

The entity or person seeking insurance must demonstrate the existence of an insurable interest at the time of incurring the loss. In life insurance contracts, the insurable interest must exist at the inception of the contract.

3. *Principle of Subrogation*

An insurer that indemnifies the insured for loss caused by the insured event is entitled to loss recovery from any liable third party who is responsible for causing the loss. For example, if A and B have an auto collision where B is at fault, A's insurance company will cover the loss for A, then seek recovery from B or from his/her insurance company. In this case, the insurer takes on the role of the insured, A, to collect from a third party, B. Because of the principle of indemnity, the insured cannot collect recovery of damage claims for the same loss twice (subrogation does not exist in life insurance or in health insurance in general).

4. *Principle of Utmost Good Faith*

Insurance contracts require a high standard of honesty and transparency; both the insured and the insurer must make truthful representation and disclosure of all facts that could materially affect the contract. Innocent misrepresentation or concealment of material facts is not an acceptable defense.

### 4.5.3.3 Consequences of the Four Insurance Principles

As a consequence of the above stated principles (among others not included here):

1. Ambiguities and uncertainties in an insurance contract should be construed and interpreted against the insurer (the concept of *Adhesion*).
2. Only one party to the contract makes promises and warranties to the other party (the concept of *Unilateral*).
3. The insured must perform acts to minimize the loss and assist in recovery (the *Conditional* Concept). For example, assume that an enterprise has a fire insurance policy on a factory. If a gas tank in that factory explodes, the management of the insured entity must act immediately to cut off the flow of gas into and out of the tank, evacuate workers, and call the fire department. Acts to the contrary will violate the Conditional Concept because the insured would not have taken the necessary steps to reduce the level of actual damage.
4. The values exchanged by both parties are not equal (the *Aleatory* Concept); the insurance premium is less than the expected benefits.

## 4.5.4 Diversification

### *4.5.4.1 Systematic and Nonsystematic Components*

The common advice, "Do not keep all your eggs in one basket" is the folklore expression of diversification that can translate to: "Do not put all your resources in one investment." This is basically the concept of *diversification*. The financial economics literature has evolved over the past five decades (since Markowitz, 1952) to give this expression more elaborate meaning. For a group of ventures, investments or objects considered together, the genesis of the benefits of diversification in business arise from two principles:

1. The causes of volatility could be attributed to factors that are (a) of a common and general nature that are applicable to every member of the group, or (b) of a specific nature unique to each individual member.
2. Because of the common causal factors, there is a correlation between the behavior of the members of the group that will always exist (given all else is held constant).

The correlation between members of the group (portfolio) will almost always be present because of sharing the effects of the common factors. This portion of the volatility of the portfolio attributable to this correlation is, therefore, systematic and could not be diversified away.

After removing the systematic component of volatility from the total volatility, the remaining portion is due to the unique factors of individual members of the group or portfolio. Because these unique factors behave on their own without commonalities, they are therefore nonsystematic or idiosyncratic. The randomness inherent in these unique factors means that each member of the group or portfolio will behave differently and unpredictably. The various unique or idiosyncratic movements of different members "could be" offsetting one another. The offsetting task will increase as the number of members of the group or portfolio increases. Therefore, the more diversified the membership of the portfolio or the group, the more likely that the various idiosyncratic effects will cancel each other out.

As a result:

- For an individual asset, investment or project, the volatility of any indicator such as sales, profits, or rates of return arises from both the common factors that impact all others as well, and idiosyncratic factors unique to the individual project or portfolio.
- For a group of assets, investments or projects, the impact of common factors on volatility remains, but the impact of idiosyncratic factors is diversified.
- The larger the membership of the portfolio or the group of projects, the more the benefits of diversification will be realized.

Markowitz (1954), Sharp (1964) and others have introduced these concepts in the analysis of rates of return on individual security versus a portfolio of securities. The two known simple models are the capital asset pricing model (CAPM) and the market model. The CAPM takes the following forms:

1. For expected return: $E(R_j) = R_f + \beta_j E(R_m - R_f)$
2. For realized return: $r_j = R_f + \beta_j (r_m - R_f) + e$

Where: $E(R_j)$ = expected rate of return on stock *j*
$R_f$ = the risk-free rate
$R_m$ = expected rate of return on the market portfolio
$E(R_m - R_f)$ = expected market risk premium
$\beta_j$ = systematic risk parameter for the rate of return on stock *j*
$r_j$ = realized rate of return on stock *j*
$r_m$ = realized rate of return on the market portfolio
$e_j$ = unexpected rate of return on stock *j*

In the CAPM form, the expected volatility of the rate of return of stock *j* is equal to the expected volatility of the market portfolio because both are expected to be affected by the same common factors. However, the expected rate of return of stock *j* is equal to the expected market return modified by the sensitivity of stock *j* to the market, which is measured by $\beta$ (beta).

For $\beta = 1$, the expected return of *j* will be the same as the market.
For $\beta > 1$, the expected return of *j* will be higher than the market.
For $\beta < 1$, the expected return of *j* will be lower than the market.

In this form, the expected volatility of the return of stock *j* is fully explained by the volatility of the market portfolio.

However, reality deviates from expectations. In equation (2), the realized rate of return on stock *j* is equal to the market realized rate of return adjusted by the sensitivity coefficient, $\beta$, and an unexpected deviation as measured by *e*.

In this model, the volatility of the rate of return of stock *j* consists of two components: the systematic component due to common market factors and the idiosyncratic component due to the unique factors of enterprise *j*. The partition of the volatility of *j* would be as shown below:

| | | | |
|---|---|---|---|
| A) *Rates of Return* | $r_j = R_f +$ | $\beta_j (r_m - R_f) +$ | $e$ |
| B) Variation | Total Variation | Explained Variation | Unexplained Variation |
| | | ↓ | ↓ |
| C) *Type of Risk* | | Systematic Risk | Non-Systematic Risk |
| | | ↓ | ↓ |
| D) *Diversification* | | Non-Diversifiable | Diversifiable |

The CAPM (and market model) have, therefore, succeeded in (a) disaggregating total risk into two components by reference to the main sets of causal factors and (b) showing which component is diversifiable.

### 4.5.4.2 *The Impact of Asset Correlation on Risk Reduction*

The breakdown of total variation into systematic and non systematic components depends, in part, on the correlation between the rates of return of assets and the rates of return on market factors. In the following segment, the role of correlation is examined in a direct way. Total volatilities of two assets are measured individually and as a portfolio with varying degrees of correlation between the two assets.

1. *Investing in a single asset*

Assume that an investor wishes to invest in a single asset, say asset $i$, such as buying stock in The Boeing Corporation. This investor also has different (*a priori*) probability expectation for earning different rates of return under different conditions (these conditions are generically referred to as *states of nature*), $c$, where $c = 1, 2, \ldots C$. The probability of occurrence of each condition or state is $p_c$ where

$$0 \le p_c \le 1.$$

The best estimate of return the investor could expect to earn from investing in this one asset is the probability-weighted average, which is estimated by the expected return given by:

$$E(r_i) = \Sigma_{c=1}^{C} p_c * r_{ic}$$

The variance and standard deviation of return on this investment are given by:

$$s_i^2 = \Sigma_{c=1}^{C} [p_c (r_{ic} - E(r_i)]^2$$

$$s_i = \sqrt{s_i^2}$$

where:

$E(r_i)$ = expected (average) return on investment $i$.
$c$ = condition or state of nature, $c = 1, 2, \ldots C$.
$p_c$ = probability of condition or state $c$ occurring, $0 \le p_c \le 1$.
$r_{ic}$ = the rate of return on investment in condition $c$.
= the variance of return on investment $i$.
$s_i$ = the standard deviation of return on investment $i$.

A numerical example of the single investment case with three conditions of economic growth is provided in Table 4.1.

2. *Investing in Two Assets*

Let us assume that our investor decides to invest a proportion, $w$, of his investment fund in asset $i$, and the remainder, $1 - w$, in asset $j$. The expected return for a portfolio consisting of these two investments is

$$E(r_p) = w\,E(r_i) + (1 - w)\,E(r_j)$$

**Table 4.1** An Illustration of Rates of Return for the Investment Asset *i* Given Three States of Nature

| *Economic Growth Rate* | *Probability* | *Return on Stock i* | *Probability x Return* |
|---|---|---|---|
| Low | 0.30 | 0.05 | 0.015 |
| Medium | 0.40 | 0.10 | 0.04 |
| Hugh | 0.30 | 0.20 | 0.26 |
| $\Sigma$ | 1.00 | | 0.115 |

For this illustration,

$E(r) = 0.30*0.05 + 0.40*0.10 + 0.30*0.20$
$= 0.115$

$s_i^2(r) = (0.30)^2 * (0.05 - 0.115)^2 + (0.4)^2 * (0.10 - 0.155)^2 + (0.30)^2 * (0.20 - 0.115)^2$
$= 0.00107$

$s_i(r) = (0.00107)^{1/2}$
$= 0.0327$

To calculate the variance of the portfolio, we need to know the relationship between the return on stock *i* and the return on stock *j*. There are three possibilities: (a) return on investment *i* and return on investment *j* move independent of one another; (b) they are not independent; they are either positively correlated or negatively correlated.

a. When both investments are independent, the variance and standard deviation are estimated as follows:

$$s_p^2 = w^2 * s_i^2 + (1 - w)^2 * s_j^2$$

$$s_p = \sqrt{s_p^2}$$

b. When the two investments are not independent, then we need to estimate the extent to which the returns on *i* and *j* move together or opposite of one another; that is, we estimate the covariance, $cov\ (r_i, r_j)$. The sign of this covariance will inform us as to whether these two investments move in the same or in the opposite direction. In either case, the portfolio variance and standard deviation would be:

$$s_p^2(r) = w^2 * s_i^2 + (1 - w)^2 * s_j^2 + 2 * w * (1 - w) * cov\ (r_i, r_j)$$

$$s_p = \sqrt{s_p^2}$$

It is important to recall that variances are additive, but standard deviations are not. Furthermore, it is useful to know the relationship between the covariance and the correlation coefficient.

$$\text{Correlation} = \rho_{ij} = cov(i,j)/s_i * s_j$$

$$\text{Covariance} = cov\ (r_i, r_j) = \rho_{ij} * s_i * s_j$$

That is, the covariance of the return on the two assets $i$ and $j$ is the product of the correlation ($\rho_{ij}$) between the two rates of return multiplied by the product of their standard deviations.

For our example, assume that the second investment, $j$, faces the same conditions or states of nature as those noted above for investment $i$, but the rates of return are different from those stated for investment $i$. Given the rates of return on $j$ (not reported here) for each state $c$ and calculating the expected return, variance, and standard deviation as we did for investment $i$ in Table 4.1, we obtain the following for investment $j$ (and compared with stock $i$) as follows:

$$E(r_j) = \Sigma_{c=1}^{c} p_c * r_{jc} = 0.16 \quad \text{(for stock } i = 0.115)$$

$$s_j^2 = \Sigma_{c=1}^{c} [p_c * (r_{jc} - E(r_j)]^2 = 0.0018 \quad \text{(for stock } i = 0.00107)$$

$$s_j = \sqrt{s_j^2} = 0.0424 \quad \text{(for stock } i = 0.0327)$$

Additionally, assume that our investor decides to invest 40% of his wealth in stock $i$ and 60% in stock $j$. If the correlation between the rates of return of the two investments is zero (i.e., the convariance is 0), then the expected return, variance, and standard for portfolio of $i$ and $j$ would be as follows:

$$E(r_p) = 0.40 * 0.115 + 0.60 * 0.16 = 0.142$$

$$s^2 (r_p) = (0.4)^2 * 0.00107 + (0.6)^2 * 0.0018 = 0.0008192$$

$$s (r_p) = (0.0008192)^{1/2} = 0.0286$$

Assume instead that the rates of return of the two assets are not independent. They change in the same direction, but not by the same magnitude; the correlation ($\rho_{ij}$) between the rates of return of $i$ and $j$ is 0.50, so the expected return, variance, and standard deviation would be estimated as follows:

$$E(r_p) = 0.40 * 0.115 + 0.60 * 0.16 = 0.142$$

$$s^2 (r_p) = (0.4)^2 * 0.00107 + (0.6)^2 * 0.0018 + 2 * 0.40 * 0.0327 * 0.60 * 0.0424 * 0.5$$

$$= 0.001152$$

$$s (r_p) = 0.0339$$

Assume instead that the correlation between stock $i$ and stock $j$ is negative, say –0.50. Using the same approach the variance of the portfolio will be 0.000486 and the standard deviation will be 0.02205. The excess of the sum of individual variances over the portfolio variance is the effect of diversification.

Table 4.2 shows descriptive statistics for the individual stocks and the portfolios under different assumptions about the correlation between the two stocks.

### 4.5.4.3 On Diversification of Different Activities

Theoretically, most types of risk that we discussed in Chapter Two can be controlled by diversification. Faced with risks in the markets for output, for example, an enterprise might reduce exposure to loss of market share by merging with, or acquiring an interest in a competitor, diversifying its

**Table 4.2** Comparison of Individual Stocks and Portfolios Assuming Different Correlations

| *Asset* | *Mean* | *Variance* | *Standard Deviation* |
|---|---|---|---|
| Stock *i* | 0.115 | 0.00107 | 0.0327 |
| Stock *j* | 0.16 | 0.00180 | 0.0424 |
| Portfolio (proportions of invested funds in $i$ = 40% & $j$ = 60%). | | | |
| Correlation = 0 | 0.142 | 0.000812 | 0.0286 |
| Correlation = 0.50 | 0.142 | 0.001152 | 0.0339 |
| Correlation = –0.50 | 0.142 | 0.000486 | 0.02205 |

channels of distribution, expanding the territories and regions in which it markets its products, or by diversifying its product lines. Regulators and accounting standard setters recognize that investors will need to be informed if the enterprise customer base is not diversified. As a result, accounting standards require enterprises to disclose information about any single customer purchasing at least 10% of the enterprise's sales. Similarly, standards require that enterprises identify any segment or region that has at least 10% of sales.

Similar applications and benefits apply to input markets. Diversifying the supply chain is essential for managing risk; relying on few suppliers would place the operations of the enterprise in jeopardy if, for example, the supplier's employees go on strike and shut down the operation.

To illustrate, consider the case of Eicher Ltd in India. In a recent disclosure, the CEO of Eicher Ltd, the third largest auto maker in India, raised concerns about limits on production caused by inadequate input supply: "There are some constraints we are facing from the supply side, we are talking to our suppliers to rectify that. We were held back a little due to the suppliers' capacity," Lal told Reuters (Basu, 2010).

Diversification of inputs may also be achieved by designing and planning input substitutions; e.g., using metal alloy instead of steel inputs to cope with shortages or unusual price rises, or using natural gas or ethanol to run engines instead of using gasoline.

Reliance on one supplier could also lead the management to engage in economically unwise activities. This was, for example, the case with Cisco Systems, Inc. in 2001. One supplier provided a component of Cisco's products and, fearing shortage, Cisco's management decided to order more units than it needed so that the company would have the product ready on the shelf as production schedules demand. This action among others (including missing the forecast for demand) ended up costing the company about two billion dollars (Berinato, 2001).

Diversification of funding sources also diversifies liquidity risk and reduces dependence on a single market. A salient example is the case of Sony. Until 1961, Japanese companies did not venture outside Japan to raise capital and the dependence on capital markets in Japan alone made some companies vulnerable to the mandates of domestic financial institutions. When these institutions made it difficult for Sony to raise capital at a lower cost than the cost of capital in Japan, Akio Morita, the then chairman and cofounder of Sony Corporation, surprised the community by listing Sony's shares on the New York Stock Exchange through the issuance of American Depositary Receipts (ADR). This action opened the door for other Japanese companies to challenge the tradition of restricting capital sources only to Japanese markets.

Diversifying the product line is also a method of reducing exposure to multiple types of risk. General Electric Company (GE) offers a good example of diversification. GE has interests in appliances, including health care equipment, aviation (jet airplane engines), customer appliances, electrical distribution and power systems; healthcare products for medical imaging and diagnosis; lighting products; technology for the oil and gas industries, railroad tracks and locomotives; electronic services including hardware and software; broadcasting and entertainment (it owns 80% of Universal Studios jointly with Vivendi of France and owned NBC until the sale of 51% share to Comcast in 2010); consumer and commercial finance and insurance; water treatment systems; and other product lines in finance and insurance.[11] In addition, GE operates in over 100 countries and thereby diversifies its exposure to country risk. GE products and markets have diverse demand, seasonality, regions, technology, and currencies. This diversity should provide the company stability even in the presence of interruptions in some industries or regions. In spite of the risk reduction afforded GE by the multiple natural hedges resulting from diversification, GE's management allegedly uses aggressive accounting methods and estimation to smooth earnings (Henry, 2009).

## 4.6 Alliances and Interlocking Ownership (*Keiretsu* & *Chaebol*)

Merger and acquisition, or even adding new product lines, is typically a costly endeavor. To achieve similar objectives at lower costs, corporations developed more economical corporate structures and arrangements to diversify operations and markets and retain flexibility. Corporate alliances are some of these alternate corporate structures. Alliances provide flexibility in maintaining or renegotiating relationships. They also diversify sources of capital, input suppliers, and output market. Alliances can be limited to sharing markets and services as in the case of airline alliances such as Oneworld and Star Alliance.[12] For example, American Airlines (USA) and Qantas (Australia) are members of the Oneworld alliance. Under the terms of agreement, American Airlines would give its passengers some advantage for flying Qantas or Japan Airlines. Similarly, these companies would give its passengers advantage for flying American Airlines or other members of the Alliance. The least of these advantages is the ability to earn and use frequent flyer miles across members of the alliance. This type of arrangement reduces the need for American Airlines to compete in Australian markets and for Qantas to compete in the American markets (although the ability to enter these markets is restricted by regulators). Forming alliances is advantageous especially in view of domestic regulations that place restrictions on carriers from other countries and limit access to worldwide markets. Members of the alliance agree to share certain services and set up a transfer pricing mechanism to ensure reciprocal and equitable treatment of member companies.

Corporate alliances can be structured more formally than the airline industry's alliance. In Japan, for example, the popularized form of corporate alliance is through structures of interlocking corporate group membership known as *Keiretsu*. The corporate groups of Mitsubishi, Mitsui, Sumitomo, Fuyo, and Fuji are large *Keiretsu* organizations. These groups typically include a bank, an insurance company, a trading company, and several industrial companies. A typical *Keiretsu* has interlocking directorates, reciprocal ownership (generally limited to a maximum percentage of capital per each member company), joint appointment of executives, and coordination of activities and investments. The member bank is typically the main supplier of liquidity to other members of the *Keiretsu* in the forms of short-term and medium-term loans and standby lines of credit. This arrangement gives the bank's CEO the strongest power and influence in the group. Membership of a *Keiretsu* assures member companies of stable input supply, harmonization of technology, and reliable distribution channels.

In South Korea, a *Keiretsu*-like alliance is called *Chaebol*, which is a group of family-controlled companies. In all three types of alliances—the free form as in the case of the airlines, the *Keiretsu* as in Japan, or the *Chaebol* as in South Korea—member companies achieve diversification in different markets—input, technology, coordination and output—at a relatively low cost.

## 4.7 Hedging

### 4.7.1 Definition of Hedging

*Encyclopedia Britannica* defines hedging as

> [A] method of reducing the risk of loss caused by price fluctuation. It consists of the purchase or sale of equal quantities of the same or very similar commodities, approximately simultaneously, in two different markets, with the expectation that a future change in price in one market will be offset by an opposite change in the other market.

The elements of this definition include:

- The aim of reducing risk of loss.
- The concern for price fluctuations.
- Basing actions on expectations.
- The need to have a negative correlation (opposite price movements).

Hedging differs from speculation in a fundamental way. The objective of hedging is to mitigate and reduce risk; the goal of speculation is to make profits by taking risk.

Hedging can be achieved by natural means such as vertical combination of complementary products, borrowing and investing in same foreign currency, or by financial means that require strategic investment in financial instruments.

### 4.7.2 Natural Hedging

Successful hedging means taking a position that is highly negatively correlated with the risk being hedged. Sometimes these positions arise in the normal course of business, such as when a business enterprise invests in two different assets or business units with negatively correlated cash flow streams. When a business firm enters into transactions or undertakes activities, it expects a particular future cash flow pattern. However, the future realization of this expectation is uncertain and the management of a business enterprise would be concerned about the volatility that could expose the firm to losses. To hedge its position, the management might enter into other transactions or activities that it expects to produce opposite cash flow patterns. For example, the cash flow of an ice cream shop is volatile due to the seasonality of the demand for the product. Investing in skiing equipment can generate cash flow during the winter season when the demand for ice cream is lowest. This investment would be considered a diversification offering a natural hedge.

Similarly, a U.S. exporter sells merchandise on three-month credit to a buyer in Europe and the transaction is denominated in euros. At the end of three months, the exchange rate between the euro and the U.S. dollar is not likely to be the same as it was at the time of sale. An appreciation of the euro (e.g., changing from \$1.30 to \$1.35 for one euro) means more U.S. dollars coming to the U.S. exporter. The reverse is true: depreciation in the euro means fewer dollars coming to the U.S. seller. To have a "cover" for the possible loss if the euro depreciates in value (i.e., the U.S. dollar appreciates against the euro), the exporter purchases equipment from Europe on credit for a three-month term. The resulting accounts payable is denominated in euros, as was the accounts receivable. If the U.S. dollar appreciates, the exporter will collect fewer dollars when collecting the receivable, but will also pay fewer dollars to settle the payable. Similarly, if the U.S. dollar depreciates, the exporter will collect more dollars from cashing the receivables, but will also pay more dollars to settle the payable. Holding a receivable and simultaneously owing a payable of equal amounts, same term to maturity and currency denomination, the net impact of changes in currency exchange rate will be nil.

For another intuitive example of natural hedging, consider two business enterprises with different products and business models: an airline and a petroleum company. The airline's cost of jet fuel moves in the same direction as the price of oil (petroleum); as oil prices rise, the cost of fuel to the airline increases, and vice versa. The demand for airline services is not perfectly inelastic and the airline company cannot easily pass this increase in cost to the consumer in the form of higher ticket prices. Comparing these two companies, it is clear that the cost of fuel to the airline company is revenues for the oil company. Increasing fuel prices squeezes the airline's profits, but increases the oil company's profits. The reverse is true for declines in oil prices.

If we draw a picture of the payoff profile of each company (with the $x$ -axis being the change in oil prices, and the $y$ -axis the change in profits), these profiles will take the forms shown in Figure 4.2. The combination of these two profiles reflects a zero-sum outcome—the gains of one are the losses of the other. Thus, it would be natural for these two companies to merge into one. By merging, both companies would be engaged in natural "hedging" because the oil company would be protected against loss arising from oil price declines and the airline company would be protected against losses arising from oil price increases. This type of merger, where one company is a supplier of the products used by the other, is known as vertical integration. It should be noted that, while a merger of the type described above is a form of natural hedging, we account for it as a business combination, not as a hedge.[13]

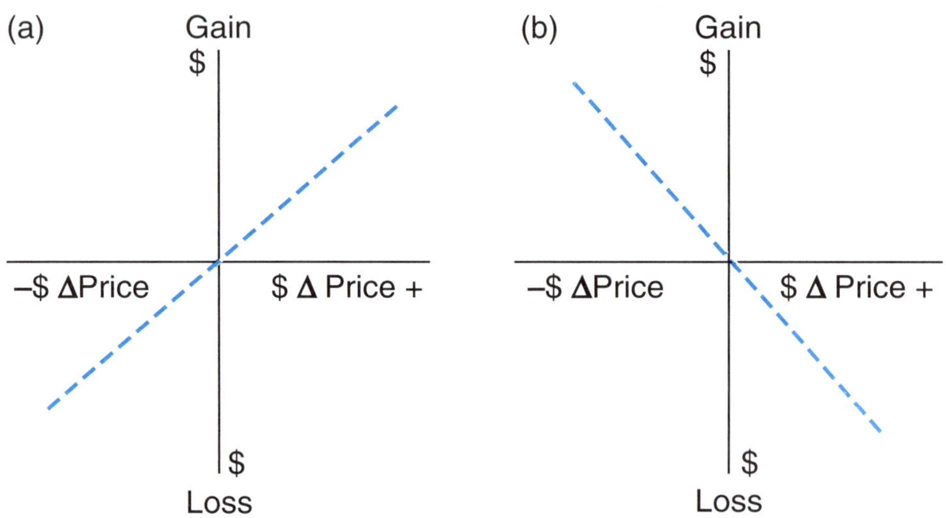


**Figure 4.2** (a) Risk (Payoff) Profile of the Oil Company in Face of Changing Oil Prices; (b) Risk (Payoff) Profile of the Airline Company in Face of Changing Oil Prices

Natural hedging is not limited to any particular industry or activity. For example, McDonalds Corporation reports, "In addition [to financial hedging], where practical, the Company's restaurants purchase goods and services in local currencies resulting in natural hedges."[14] Cox and Lin (2007) provide an example of natural hedge in the insurance industry by combining life insurance and annuity liabilities. The values of these instruments move in opposite directions in response to a change in the underlying mortality. Natural hedging utilizes this feature to stabilize aggregate cash flow.

Three features separate natural hedges from other types of hedging:

1. A natural hedge does not involve financial instruments or financial derivatives.
2. Natural hedges focus on the negative correlation between streams of cash flows: if one increases, the other declines, and vice versa.
3. There is no specialized hedge accounting for natural hedges. In fact, natural hedging is not recognized as such in accounting. Instead, the accounting treatment of a natural hedge is generally based on the nature of the transactions in accordance with GAAP. The accounting treatment for such transactions will be the same whether or not the activity is entered into for the purpose of achieving a hedge.

### 4.7.3 Financial Hedging

Trying to achieve a natural hedge by merging companies with complementary cash flow and economic benefits is costly and does not provide flexibility to enter and exit the combined relationship as conditions change. Derivative financial instruments provide an alternative approach which can allow an enterprise to hedge exposure to risk at a relatively low cost, provided that the enterprise goes about it strategically.[15] This approach means an enterprise facing a particular risk can enter into a derivative contract with the potential payoff behaving in the opposite direction of the risk being faced. This type of contract can be terminated, liquidated, or extended to fit the enterprise's needs.

However, the enterprise must retain certain types of risk in order to make profits; there is no compensation above the risk-free rate levels if the enterprise does not take some types of business risk. Therefore, the goal of hedging is not to eliminate exposure to all risks. Even if the management of an enterprise wishes to do so, hedging all risk exposures is not a feasible option. As we will see later (Chapter Eight), hedging substitutes one risk for another.[16]

In general, hedgeable risks have the following features:

- They are not part of the core business.
- They are caused by external conditions not controllable by the enterprise.
- They can have large negative impact on the enterprise.
- They have large enough markets to allow risk transfer among various participants.

The ideal hedge is one that (a) provides hedge for downside risk; (b) offers offsetting payoffs; (c) provides flexibility; and (d) can also be done and undone at low cost. These characteristics are captured by the profiles shown in Panel A of Figure 4.3, which describes the downside risk for a petroleum company, as an example. As petroleum prices decline, the profits of a petroleum producer also decline. To hedge this risk exposure, the company can invest in a financial instrument that increases in value as petroleum prices decline. In Panel B of Figure 4.3, we observe the risk profile of a consumer of petroleum products such as an airline. The company would be exposed to downside risk as petroleum prices increase (the cross-dashed line). It can hedge this exposure by investing in a financial instrument that generates gains as petroleum prices increase. The basic instruments used for these types of hedges are presented in Chapter Five.

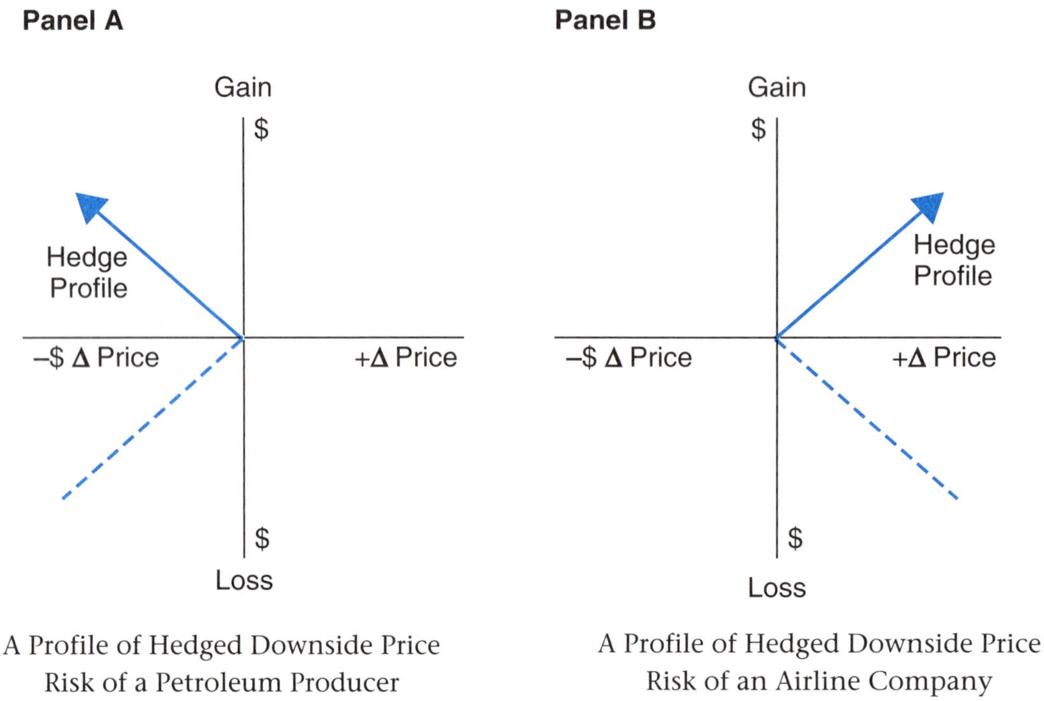


**Figure 4.3** Hedging Profiles of Different Downside Risks

## 4.7.4 Factors to Consider in Hedging

1. *Hedging Is Not Costless.* While many derivative financial instruments do not require significant investment of funds, undertaking hedging programs costs money. Furthermore, the relatively small initial investment in derivative instruments can add up quickly to large amounts and may not be recouped. For example, for many years, the government of Mexico hedged oil prices. In 2010, the government hedging program was so successful that the realized gains from the hedge were about $1.20 billion dollars and the administrative cost was $120 million. If prices moved in the opposite direction, that administrative cost might not have been recovered.

2. *Hedging Entails Substitution of Risk.* Hedging to reduce one type of risk exposes the enterprise to another risk. For example, fair value hedge of interest rate risk of an asset entails entering into a swap contract to pay fixed and receive floating; the result is to hedge fair value but take on cash flow risk. Similarly, an enterprise that has an asset that earns interest income indexed to Treasury Rates is facing cash flow risk. To hedge exposure to this risk, the enterprise enters into an interest rate swap agreement to pay floating and receive fixed. This enterprise is hedging cash flow risk but is taking on other risks, namely fair value risk and counterparty credit risk.

3. *Evaluating Cost and Benefits*. Undertaking a hedge program must be justified on the basis of cost/benefit analysis. Management must analyze the cost and risk of hedging versus the cost and risk of not hedging. For example, U.S. Airways abandoned hedging oil prices when it turned out that this type of hedging was costly to the airline.

4. *Hedging is not insurance*: As noted earlier, insurance is a contract between an insured (a person or an entity) and an insurer, typically a financial institution. In exchange for a fee, the insured receives a promise from the insurer to cover specific losses under pre-specified conditions. Insurance contracts have characteristics that are not consistent with hedging:

a. Insurance is a risk-sharing process that requires pooling of a large number of insured individuals or cases, while hedging is a risk transfer between two contractual parties.
b. Insurance provides compensation for losses only (indemnification), while in hedging, there is no assurance that losses will necessarily be covered, but the hedger has the opportunity to gain.
c. Furthermore, insurance operates under the principle of full disclosure (utmost faith), but hedging involves strategies that operate under the conditions of asymmetric informational advantages, rather than information sharing.
d. Finally, the concept of subrogation does not apply in hedging. Neither party in a hedging relationship can seek compensation for losses from a third party that is responsible for causing the loss.

## Exhibit 4.3 Hedging Fuel Cost at Airlines

The cost of operating airlines increases with the increase in fuel cost and several airlines have been carrying on large hedging programs. There are no hedge instruments specifically for jet fuel because of the absence of specialized markets, but the cost of jet fuel moves in tandem with oil prices and airline companies achieve the same goal by hedging oil prices.

Southwest Airlines Co. is the most successful airline in hedging oil prices. According to a Forbes article,[17] "hedging alone saved Southwest Airlines over $3.5 billion and made up almost 83% of the company's total profits between 1998–2008." This is true in spite of the fact that Southwest reported its first quarterly loss in 2008 because of hedging (Hinton, 2008).

Alaska Air Group earned about $380 million in a year. However, the CFO, Brandon Pederson noted that hedging "premiums aren't cheap. ... the costs have totaled the company around $200 million" (Bergman, 2011).

This phenomenon seems to be contagious:

- Singapore Airlines (SIA) tends to hedge within a range regardless of changes in oil price.
- Hedging fuel prices at Air New Zealand reportedly reduced its fuel hedges to 65 per cent in the first quarter of financial year 2009 (July–September).
- Similarly, Japan Airlines Corp trimmed its hedges to 75 per cent for March 2008–April 2009.
- Jet Airways Ltd, India's top private carrier, shelved hedging plans due to high crude prices. Air India ... is unhedged currently (*Business Times*, 2012).

## Exhibit 4.4 Hedging at Public Utilities

Public utilities hedge risk exposure to commodity prices. For example:

- Kansas Gas Service hedges prices of natural gas. The company starts the hedge program in the summer to hedge price volatility in the following winter. Interestingly, the cost of hedging is charged to customers as a line item of components of price the company charges customers. In order to permit this charge, the company seeks the approval of the Public Corporation (Service) Commission.

  Every early spring, Kansas Gas Service develops its Hedge Program for the coming winter. It obtains hedging instruments during the summer. Beginning in April and continuing through October, Kansas Gas Service customers pay a gas *hedge charge* to recover gas hedging costs to protect next winter's natural gas prices. Natural gas billing statements display "Gas Hedge" as a separate line item. Hedge "settlements," which return any hedge benefits during the months of November through March, will be included in the cost of gas factor (and not separately displayed).[18]
- Another example of hedging by public utilities is the case of Dominion Resource, the large power producer and distributor on the east coast of the USA. In its 10-K Form of 2010, the company notes:

  > Dominion manages electric and capacity price volatility of its merchant fleet by hedging a substantial portion of its expected near-term sales with derivative instruments and also entering into long-term power sales agreements. However, earnings have been adversely impacted due to a sustained decline in commodity prices. Variability also results from changes in the cost of fuel consumed, labor and benefits and the timing, duration and costs of scheduled and unscheduled outages.[19]

  Dominion Resources has a relatively large hedging program that includes, in addition to hedging commodity prices as noted above, hedging interest rate risk, investment risk, and credit risk.

## Exhibit 4.5 Hedging Oil Revenues by the Government of Mexico

Mexico is set to earn an $8 billion windfall from financial contracts it bought last summer as insurance against low oil prices this year …

… Mexico, the world's sixth-largest oil exporter, has already started to hedge a small portion of its oil revenues for next year after it successfully locked in an average price of $70 a barrel for all its oil exports in 2009.

(Source: Javier Blas (September 8, 2009) "Mexico's big gamble on oil pays off," *Financial Times*, London. Available at http://www.ft.com/cms/s/0/a9d4cb3a-9c0e-11de-b214-00144feabdc0.html#axzz1aGCHii5O)

## 4.8 Asset/Liability Management

A direct approach to managing liquidity risk is to manage the assets and liabilities such that cash demands will match cash inflows. In a bank, for example, this can be achieved by balancing the choice of interest-rate-sensitive assets and interest-rate-sensitive liabilities to maintain a level of *GAP* about unity. However, the bank must also balance the "tenor" of cash flows. In addition, the mix of instruments and duration of assets should diversify the bank's exposure to cash inflow volatility as well as its exposure to the credit risk of borrowers and investors in bank assets. Similarly, the bank's exposure to liquidity risk can be influenced by the composition of deposits. If all deposits were to be demand deposits (i.e., checking), the bank could face sudden withdrawals of large amounts and would have to maintain a higher proportion of the deposits as compensating balances. The exposure to liquidity demands by bank depositors would be different if maturity of the deposits varied between demand, medium term, and long term. Other retail and business accounts should diversify exposure such that cash outflow needs would not cluster to form bottle necks.

The same philosophy applies to enterprises in other industries. Good risk management should maintain portfolios of assets and liabilities that would balance cash inflow patterns with cash outflow needs in terms of amounts, timing, and uncertainty. Three excerpts demonstrate business enterprises' concern for managing liquidity risk. Exhibit 4.6 for Deutsche Bank and JPMorgan Chase and Exhibit 4.7 for Landsvirkjun, an Icelandic power company, show these concerns.

### Exhibit 4.6 Managing Liquidity Risk

**At Deustche Bank:**

The bank identifies, measures, and manages the liquidity risk position … at least weekly via a Liquidity Scorecard. The liquidity risk management approach starts at the intraday level (operational liquidity).

- Managing the daily payments queue.
- Forecasting cash flows.
- Evaluating access to secured and unsecured funding sources.
- Analyzing maturity profiles of all assets and liabilities and our issuance strategy.
- Providing daily liquidity risk information to global and regional management.

(Source: https://annualreport.deutsche-bank.com/2011/ar/servicepages/downloads/files/dbfy2011_entire.pdf (p.115))

**At JPMorgan Chase:**[20]

The Asset-Liability Committee reviews and approves the Firm's liquidity policy and contingency funding plan. Corporate Treasury formulates and is responsible for executing the Firm's liquidity policy and contingency funding plan as well as measuring, monitoring, reporting and managing the Firm's liquidity risk profile.

[…]

The Firm employs a variety of metrics to monitor and manage liquidity. One set of analyses used by the Firm relates to the timing of liquidity sources versus liquidity uses (e.g., funding gap analysis and parent holding company funding, which is discussed below). A second set of analyses focuses on ratios of funding and liquid collateral (e.g., measurements of the Firm's reliance on short-term unsecured funding as a percentage of total liabilities, as well as analyses of the relationship of short-term unsecured funding to highly-liquid assets, the deposits-to-loans ratio and other balance sheet measures).

## Exhibit 4.7 Liquidity Risk Management at Landsvirkjun (Iceland)

**Liquidity risk strategy**

- Liquidity risk consists of the risk of losses should the Company not be able to keep its obligations at maturity date.
- Analyzing the flow of revenues and expenses and the maturity dates of financial assets and liabilities monitors the Company's liquidity balance.
- Insuring sufficient access to cash at each time.
- Preparing for contingencies by signing a contingent credit facility with the Ministry of Finance and the Central Bank of Iceland.
- According to the agreement, the Central Bank has, according to the agreement, the obligation to provide the Company with foreign currency.

(Source: 2009 Annual Report of Landsvirkjun available at http://www.landsvirkjun.com/media/enska/finances/Annual_report_2009.pdf (p. 52))

### 4.8.1 Factoring

To generate more liquidity, business enterprises can sell their accounts and notes receivable to financial institutions at a discount from settlement value. This sale, called factoring, can be with or without recourse, depending on whether or not the financial institution can claim any uncollectible accounts from the enterprise that sold them the receivables in the event of customers' default. Factoring without recourse means that sale of receivables is unconditional and the enterprise does not bear any risk of collectability. In contrast, factoring with recourse does not relieve the seller from the risk of loss. The magnitude of the discount from settlement value depends on who bears the risk. Without recourse, the financial institution will require compensation for bearing all credit risk and the discount off settlement value will therefore be greater than it would be in the case of factoring with recourse. Furthermore, without recourse, the transaction is a sale and factored receivables are replaced by cash on the balance sheet. With recourse, the transaction is treated as a loan from the bank. Factoring enhances the liquidity of the enterprise irrespective of the recourse status. This flow of this process is presented in Figure 4.4.

### 4.8.2 Securitization

Consider a bank (originator) that has made 10,000 mortgage contracts. The borrowers are individuals and families from different income and credit risk classes. Because of differences in borrow-

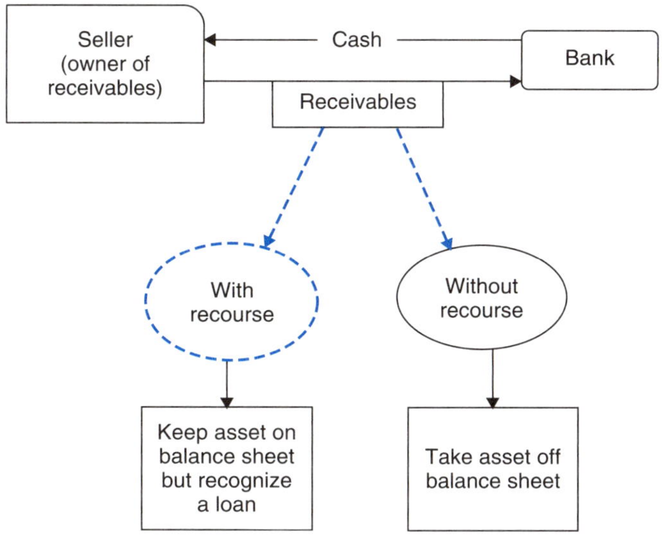


**Figure 4.4** The Process of Factoring Receivables Under Two Different Options

ers' credit scores, the interest rate charged to customers is negatively correlated with their credit scores.

For all these mortgages, the bank is exposed to the following risks:

- The risk of default on payment of interest.
- The risk of default on repayment of the principal.
- The risk of changing interest rate in the marketplace that would have adverse effects on the bank.
- Liquidity risk as more cash is tied up in relatively illiquid financial assets.
- Increasing own credit risk with the increased exposure to liquidity risk because banks may find it more difficult to pay off their obligations and operating costs if they are facing a liquidity problem.

The bank's operating needs may require converting these mortgages into cash—i.e., monetizing the mortgage portfolio. These mortgages are not short-term receivables and the originator bank cannot simply factor them by selling them to another financial institution. Instead, the bank creates four tranches (groups) of these mortgages based on the riskiness category of each using, for example, the credit risk scores of the borrowers.

Assume that the pool of borrowers falls into four risk classes (tranches):

| *Tranche (group)* | *Credit scores* | *Credit quality* | *Number of mortgages* |
|---|---|---|---|
| A | Rating ≥ 750 | High | 1,000 |
| B | 680 < Rating < 750 | Good | 4,000 |
| C | 620 ≤ Rating ≤ 680 | Average | 2,500 |
| D | ≥ 620 | Low | 2,500 |

Each of these tranches consists of mortgages originated by this bank, but they are made to different individuals who will be paying monthly interest plus amortization of principal over 30 years. The bank's management can sell the series of cash flows embedded in each tranche as a portfolio. Other banks would not purchase 30-year mortgages and would worry about exposure to credit risk of individual borrowers, but the originator bank could establish an entity specifically devoted to packaging these mortgages into securities and passing them to other investors. As an entity dedicated to this purpose, it is referred to as "special purpose entity" or "special purpose vehicle" (SPE or SPV). The main purpose of SPE is to isolate the transferred asset from the transferor (mortgage originator) and its creditors. But the newly established SPE (SPV) has no other activities and would have to resell these mortgages to someone else either directly or through another entity. Under U.S. GAAP, for a securitization agreement to be considered a sale (i.e., without recourse) the transferor must surrender control over the assets transferred. Control is considered to be surrendered only if *all* of the following three conditions are met:

1. The assets have been legally isolated.
2. The transferee (the person or entity that receives the transferred asset) has the ability to pledge or exchange the assets.
3. The transferor otherwise no longer maintains effective control over the assets.

Typically, the SPE is owned by the transferor (who is also the originator). It receives the financial assets (mortgages in this case) from the transferor and passes them to a "trust" representing the interests of the targeted investors. The trust entity packages the mortgages (or financial assets) and issues certificates for (1) sale of the repackaged transferred assets to external investors (such as financial institutions, pension funds, and hedge funds) and (2) for sale of the retained interest to the transferor (originator). The trust essentially acts as (a) a buyer that receives the transferred financial assets from the agent of the loan originator (the SPE), and (b) as a seller that issues certificates of ownership to investors and collects the funds from sale of these securities. The trust pays the originator (the bank) for the purchase of the transferred assets and manages the two-way cash flow: (i) the collection of the monthly mortgage payment from mortgage holders, and (ii) the payments to the new investors (holders of the certificates) to service the issued securities (certificates, or bonds).

The investments made by buyers of the issued certificates and future interest payments are backed by the streams of cash flow collected from the borrowers of the original mortgages included in each tranche; this is why these bonds are called Mortgage-Backed-Securities (MBS) or Asset-Backed-Securities (ABS). The funds that the Trust collects from selling MBS are used to pay the transferor (the originating bank). The SPE, therefore, acts only as a conduit to ensure that the transferor has transferred control over the assets and that these assets are passed on to the "Trust." The bank can then use the funds collected from selling the MBS to make new loans.

The above described structured finance process is only one of numerous arrangements that could be established for what is known as "securitization." Securitization is defined below and is graphed in Figure 4.5.

> Securitization is a process by which financial (other than cash) and illiquid assets are monetized. The process involves (i) the transfer of control over these assets from the originator to a special conduit (SPE or SPV); (ii) the SPE then transfers these assets to a "Trust" entity that packages these mortgages into pools of similar risk classes and establishes a price for each particular risk level; (iii) each pool is converted into debt or equity securities (certificates) to be sold to investors in the marketplace; (iv) the collected funds from the sale are used to pay the originator for the purchase of original mortgages or loans; and (v) the originator can then use these funds to make new mortgages or other loans.

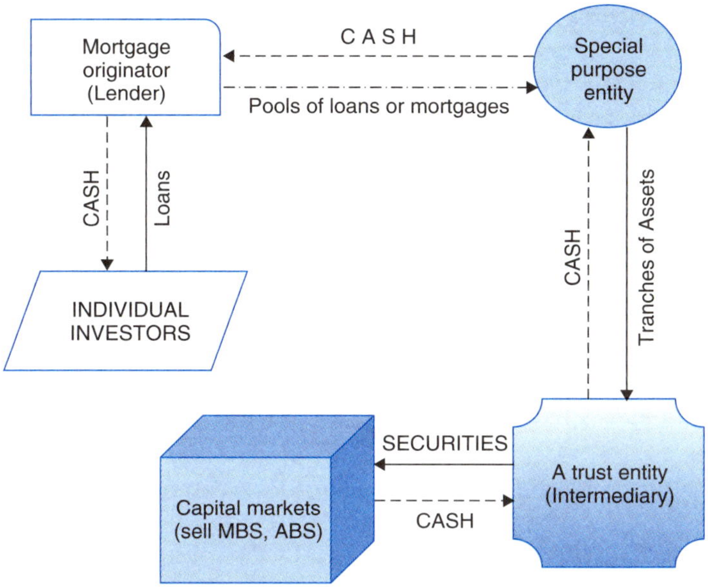


**Figure 4.5** The Basic Process of Securitization (Transfer of Financial Assets)

The SPV or SPE undertakes a "filtering" process that includes four steps.

1. Group the transferred financial assets into categories or tranches based on the riskiness of their cash flows. This classification ranges from highest quality (lowest risk exposure) to the lowest quality (high risk).
2. Transfer these portfolios to another entity to prepare for sale. This entity might be called a "Trust."
3. Prepare for severing the originator's interest in the cash flow received from the mortgage holders whose mortgages will be packaged into mortgage-backed securities.
4. The stage is now set to issue the specially designed securities and sell them to investors that are unrelated to the originator. The Trust has responsibility to investors in these asset-backed securities but only by the extent of the cash flow streams generated by the assets used as collateral.

The originator of the loans (the transferor) keeps the retained segment of the mortgages or loans that are not used as assets to support the issuance of debt instruments. In addition, the originator of the loans or mortgages also retains mortgage or loan service rights, which are intangible assets for the entity that should be valued at present value and recognized on the financial statements.

## Information Log

Mortgage loans are used in the above discussion to facilitate understanding the process of securitization. However, securitization is being done for many other assets such as mortgage loans, residential, commercial, and home equity; automobile loans and leases; high yield securities; insurance, and health care receivables among others.

#### 4.8.1.1 *Similarities and Differences between Factoring and Securitization*

Securitization and factoring receivables have the same goal which is reducing liquidity risk by converting financial assets into cash. That is where the similarities end. The major differences between factoring and securitization are outlined as follows:

1. Factoring is typically a negotiated agreement between the holder of the financial asset (receivables) and a bank; it is a bilateral contract. This is not the case with securitization because it is more like a public offering that involves raising funds from a larger number of self-interested investors.
2. Factoring is typically a sale of short-term receivables to a financial institution, whereas securitization converts illiquid assets of longer duration into cash.
3. Securitization is a transfer and sale of assets without recourse. Factoring can be done with or without recourse.
4. Converting illiquid assets to liquid assets by converting longer duration cash flows into shorter duration cash flows.

## 4.9 Managing Credit Risk

To ensure borrowers pay debt obligations on time, lenders monitor the activities and performance of the borrower to limit their ability to take on excessive risk that may lead to their default. One mechanism that lenders use is contracting with borrowers on acceptable boundaries for financial actions and performance. These conditions are known as debt covenants. They are established as conditions of granting credit. Lenders have the right to alter the terms of the covenants if the borrowers change of conditions warrant.

At the same time, bondholders (the investors) also have concerns about the borrower's (the issuer of the bond) credit risk. The concern of investors here extends beyond default to include volatility in the market value of their investments, which will drop with any increase in the borrower's credit risk. However, unlike bilateral loan contracts with banks, bondholders because they cannot recontract with the issuer (the borrower). Investors use the market as an institution to deal with credit risk. They can unload bonds or turn to investing in *credit derivatives*, which are financial instruments that derive their values from the credit risk of the bond or debt.

Derivatives are discussed in the following chapters, but this segment briefly discusses debt covenants.

### 4.9.1 Debt Covenants

A debt covenant is any contractual relationship between lenders and borrowers in a negotiated agreement that can place restrictions on the borrower's activities as well as set boundaries for expected level of performance. In explicitly stating debt covenants, lenders have three main objectives:

1. To reduce the borrower's tendency to take on excessive risk.
2. To limit competing demands for the borrower's cash flow.
3. To ascertain the borrower's ability to remain solvent.

To ensure adherence to the covenants, the lender places restrictions that make covenant violation costly. This cost could be a simple penalty, an increase in the loan interest rate, or an acceleration of the repayment of the debt.

Debt covenants therefore establish a mechanism by which the lender can monitor and influence the credit risk of the borrower. Monitoring might be passive in the sense of standing as an observer of specified indicators and taking action only when these indicators are violated. Usually these types of covenants are referred to as *maintenance* or affirmative covenants (Nini, Smith, and Sufi, 2011). For example, requiring the borrower to maintain a specific leverage ratio (debt to equity) or working capital ratio (current assets/current liabilities) is a maintenance type of covenant. Contractually, violating maintenance covenants gives the lender the right to seek accelerating the payment of the loan or increase the cost of debt. In practice, however, violation of maintenance covenants does not generally threaten the survival of the borrowing enterprise and lenders use these rights to renegotiate the terms of the loan agreement. Some covenants could contain a clause to show how the interest rate on the loan is reset as a function of maintenance covenant violation. In general, however, violation of these covenants leads to increased control and monitoring power of the lender.

On the other hand, covenant-driven monitoring can entail the active involvement of the lender in the borrower's business activities. For example, the covenants that place restrictions on the levels of capital expenditures or dividend payout require continuous monitoring by the lender. Similarly, covenants requiring that the borrower hedge certain risks also require the lender's active and direct involvement. These types of covenants are typically referred to as *incurrence* covenants. The penalties for violation of incurrence covenants are more severe than penalties for violating maintenance covenants because such violations involve actions by the management of the borrower that might not be reversible.

These covenants can be categorized as action-related or financial.[21]

### 4.9.1.1 Action-related covenants

- Restrictions on asset sales.
- Restriction on asset transfer.
- Purchasing insurance.
- Requirement to provide evidence of compliance with covenants.
- Requirement to pay taxes and comply with regulations.
- Allowing the payment of dividends only under certain conditions.
- Limiting levels of capital expenditures.
- Providing evidence of compliance with laws.

### 4.9.1.2 Financial-related Covenants

- Degree of leverage
  - Upper bound on leverage measured as total debt/equity, or long-term debt/equity.
  - A limit on borrowing by stating the upper limit for funded (borrowed) debt/tangible net worth.
  - Limits on liabilities/tangible net worth.
  - Upper limit on some specific measure of debt to EBTDA (earnings before taxes, depreciation, and amortization).

- Maintaining certain profitability level.
    - Set a minimum threshold for:
        - EBDTA
        - EBDTA/total debt
        - Fixed charge coverage
        - EBDTA/fixed charges
        - Cash flow/fixed charges
- Maintaining liquidity
    - Set a minimum threshold for:
        - Working capital
        - Current ratio (current assets/current liabilities)
        - Acid test ratio (liquid assets/current liabilities)
        - Restrict cash dividend payout.

## Exhibit 4.8 Disclosure of Debt Covenants of Seagate Technology Holdings as Reported in 10-Q (2009)

*Restrictions Imposed by Debt Covenants—Restrictions imposed by our amended credit facility and the indenture governing our 10% senior secured second-priority notes due 2014 may limit our ability to finance future operations or capital needs or engage in other business activities that may be in our interest.*

Our amended credit facility and the indenture governing our 10% senior secured second-priority notes due 2014 impose, and the terms of any future debt may impose, operating and other restrictions on us. Our amended credit facility and the indenture may also limit, among other things, our ability to:

- Incur additional indebtedness and issue certain preferred stock;
- Create liens;
- Pay dividends or make distributions in respect of our capital stock;
- Redeem or repurchase capital stock or debt;
- Make certain investments or other restricted payments;
- Sell assets;
- Issue or sell capital stock of subsidiaries;
- Enter into transactions with affiliates;
- Engage to any material extent in business other than current liabilities; and
- Effect a consolidation or merger.

However, these limitations are subject to a number of important qualifications and exceptions, including exceptions under our amended credit facility that permit us to pay dividends up to $45 million, in the aggregate, during the period beginning on April 4, 2009 and ending on January 1, 2010 (inclusive), and $300 million, in the aggregate, during any period of four consecutive quarters thereafter.

Our amended credit facility also requires us to maintain compliance with specified financial covenants. Specifically, our amended credit facility contains three financial covenants:

1. a covenant to maintain minimum cash, cash equivalents and marketable securities;
2. a fixed charge coverage ratio; and
3. a net leverage ratio.

Our ability to comply with these covenants may be affected by events beyond our control. Our recently amended credit agreement governing our credit facility provides for the relaxation of certain financial covenants through the quarter ending on January 1, 2010, and, based on our current outlook, we expect to stay in compliance with these covenants. However, after January 1, 2010, the financial metrics we are required to maintain under these covenants will revert back to their previous levels. If our business deteriorates or if business conditions worsen, we may need to further re-negotiate these covenants, obtain waivers and/or raise additional funds in order to remain in compliance.

A breach of any of the covenants described above or our inability to comply with the required financial ratios could result in a default under our amended credit facility. If a condition of default occurs, and we are not able to obtain a waiver from the lenders holding a majority of the commitments under our amended credit facility, the administrative agent of the amended credit facility may, and at the request of lenders holding a majority of the commitments shall, declare all of our outstanding obligations under the amended credit facility, together with accrued interest and other fees, to be immediately due and payable, and may terminate the lenders' commitments thereunder, cease making further loans and institute foreclosure proceedings against our assets. If our outstanding indebtedness were to be accelerated, we cannot assure you that our assets would be sufficient to repay in full that debt and any potential future indebtedness, which would cause the market price of our common shares to decline significantly. We could also be forced into bankruptcy or liquidation.

(Source: 10-Q, May 2009, Seagate Technology Holdings, pp. 96–97. Available at http://files.shareholder.com/downloads/SEA/2068719678x0xS1193125-09-100353/1137789/filing.pdf)

## Exhibit 4.9 Cases of Debt Covenant Violations

**At The Gap, Inc.**

In a statement issued [on December 18, 2001], Gap said Grant's [an online investment newsletter] miscalculated the level of EBITDA needed to maintain its covenant at the end of the fourth quarter by overstating the expected year-end debt levels. Grant's Investor reported that the company's $1.3 billion credit agreement requires a debt-to-EBITDA ratio of no more than 3.0, noting, "A covenant violation seems a high-probability outcome." However, Gap did not agree with the assessment of Grant's Investor and noted that the covenant-required EBITDA is in the range of $730 million to $770 million, not $1.084 billion as Grant's Investor reported.[22]

**At McClatchy**

On February 6, 2009, Reuters reported that the newspaper publisher McClatchy might violate its debt covenant due to a drop in revenues. "Given our expectation for revenue and EBITDA declines in 2009, we believe McClatchy is likely to violate its 7 times total leverage covenant in the December 2009 quarter, and we are uncertain at this time that lenders would grant additional temporary relief."[23]

**At Liberty Media**

Liberty Media plans to turn its Liberty Interactive (NASDAQ: LINTA) division into a new company. A group of investors owning more than $250 million in Liberty Media debt securities filed a legal complaint last July alleging that the spinoff would separate assets of the new company from Liberty Media debt to the extent of violating bond covenants. The resulting default could make $4.7 billion of Liberty Media's debt payable immediately. But the court ruled that the planned spinoff does not violate company debt covenants.[24]

**At ClearChannel**

On February 20, 2009, the blog *Zero Hedge* reported that S&P has downgraded the credit rating of Clear Channel because the company drew the last $1.6 billion line of credit facility amid the possibility of significant decline in sales and EBITDA. The *Zero Hedge* blog quoted the following from the announcement of S&P:[25]

> The ratings downgrade and continued CreditWatch listing reflects our deepening concerns about the company's ability to maintain compliance with financial covenants amid the worsening recession, especially in light of extremely weak recent results reported by peer radio and outdoor companies. Under our baseline scenario, including our assumptions regarding possible covenant add-backs under Clear Channel's credit agreement, we estimate that the company could violate covenants in the second half of 2009, or sooner if EBITDA declines are greater than our expectations. This scenario contemplates EBITDA declines in the 40% area over the next several quarters, with declines moderating toward the second half of the year. Our downside scenario contemplates EBITDA declines in the 40% to 50% range over the near term. Under our baseline scenario, EBITDA coverage of net interest could decline to less than 1x. For this reason, if the company were able to obtain an amendment from bank lenders, we believe it would need to use cash balances to meet any potential upfront fees and increases in interest rate spreads.

## 4.10 Summary of Key Points

1. Enterprise Risk Management (ERM) refers to any system of identifying, measuring, monitoring, controlling, and mitigating risk.
2. The ultimate goal of ERM is to reduce the adverse impact of events and to improve the processes governing input, processing, and output.
3. ERM should provide monitoring and response to low-frequency, high- or severe-impact events. It is argued in the literature that, although the tendency is to focus on more frequent, recurrent events, the low-frequency events might have severe impact that will have serious consequences.
4. Diversification and various combinations of grouping activities by acquisition, mergers, or membership in alliances are effective means of mitigating risk exposures. Different forms of

diversification could be influenced by the strategic goal of the enterprise such as the objective of ensuring the supply of inputs or the market for outputs (vertical integration), or diversification of credit risk to reduce the negative effects of concentration on few players. In Japan and Korea, diversification is accomplished by unique inter-organizational linkages.

5. Specific types of risk require self-tailored approaches to risk management. Mitigating the adverse impact of (external) market price movements might be effectively accomplished by hedging—taking positions having counter movements. Hedging could be accomplished by strategic management of assets and liabilities so that the cash inflows would exceed cash outflow, or by financial derivatives. This is the subject of the remainder of this book. Examples of significant involvement in hedging include hedging oil prices by airlines, hedging natural gas prices by public utilities, and hedging oil revenues by oil-producing countries or states.
6. Managing credit risk begins by setting up and administering a system of evaluating creditworthiness of counterparties and placing boundaries on counterparties' actions by stipulating appropriate credit limits and debt covenants. Adoption of any form of ERM must incorporate guides for credit approvals, collections, and diversification of customer base and counterparties.
7. Credit risk also spills over to liquidity risk as collectability of loans and receivables influences the liquidity of assets and availability of cash. In some cases, enterprises might ensure this inflow of funds by factoring or securitizing some of these assets. This chapter also outlines the similarities and differences between factoring and securitization.
8. Interest rate risk and currency risk are significant components of ERM because of their impact on firm performance and on liquidity risk.
9. The significance of developing and maintaining a high-quality ERM lies in the fact that the majority of business risk components (e.g., price risk, interest rate risk, currency risk) are not insurable.

## Notes

1 Financial Executives International (June 26/2012) "FEI Audit Fee Survey: Companies' Audit Fees and Hours Slightly Increase in 2011." Available at: http://www.financialexecutives.org/KenticoCMS/News---Publications/Press-Room/2012-press-releases/FEI-Audit-Fee-Survey--Companies-Audit-Fees-and--H.aspx.

2 The context in which the acronym ERM is used must be made clear because, in Europe, ERM is also used for "Exchange Rate Mechanism" as well as "Environmental Resources Management," and in medical contexts, ERM connotes Emergency Risk Management.

3 The Treadway Commission was formed in 1985 as a voluntary group of academic and professional organizations to study ways of controlling corporate fraud. The sponsored organizations are the American Accounting Association, the American Institute of Certified Public Accountants, the Financial Executives Institute, IMA, the Association for Accountants and Financial Professionals in Business, and the Institute of Internal Auditors. Available at: http://www.coso.org/documents/COSO_ERM_ExecutiveSummary.pdf.

4 This type of activity is not limited to any nation or region. See Schubert and Miller (December, 2008) "At Siemens, Bribery Was Just a Line Item," *The New York Times*. They report that "Siemens, one of the world's biggest companies, last week ended up paying $1.6 billion in the largest fine for bribery in modern corporate history." See article at http://www.nytimes.com/2008/12/21/business/worldbusiness/21siemens.html?_r=2&th=&emc=th&pagewanted=print.

5 *The Financial Aspects of Corporate Governance.* (1 December 1992). Report of the Committee on the Financial Aspects of Corporate Governance. Professional Publishing Ltd. London. Available at: http://www.ecgi.org/codes/documents/cadbury.pdf.

6 *An Audit of Internal Control Over Financial Reporting That Is Integrated with An Audit of Financial Statements.* Auditing Standard No. 2 (2004) & Auditing Standard No. 5 (2007): PCAOB. Available at: http://pcaobus.org/Standards/Auditing/Pages/Auditing_Standard_5.aspx.
7 European Commission—The European Single Market (2005) *The European Group of Auditors' Oversight Bodies (EGAOB).* Available at: http://ec.europa.eu/internal_market/auditing/egaob/index_en.htm
8 http://www.sec.gov/Archives/edgar/data/40545/000119312511047479/d10k.htm.
9 Life insurance is in a category called "value insurance."
10 This concept is difficult to state strictly with respect to life insurance; while the beneficiary of the policy collects death benefits, they are not considered profit-making since no one could assign a value to life.
11 See http://www.sec.gov/Archives/edgar/data/40545/000119312511047479/d10k.htm.
12 Oneworld Alliance, for example, includes American Airlines (USA), Japan Airlines (Japan), British Airways (U.K. and Europe), Qantas (Australia), Lan (Chile), Mexicana (Mexico), Cathay Pacific (Hong Kong), Finair (Finland, Europe), Iberia (Spain), Royal Jordanian (Jordan), Malév (Hungary), and S7 Airline (Russia).
13 An airline acquiring an oil production entity was considered a hypothetical illustration until Delta Airline acquired an oil refinery in New York for $130 million. Muwad, Jad (April 30, 2012). "Delta Buys Refinery to Get Control of Fuel Costs," *The New York Times*. Available at: http://www.nytimes.com/2012/05/01/business/delta-air-lines-to-buy-refinery.html?_r=1.
14 *McDonalds Corporation*, Form 10-K. Available at: http://www.sec.gov/Archives/edgar/data/63908/000119312511046701/d10k.htm (p. 23).
15 In 1898, butter began trading at Chicago Butter and Egg Board, the predecessor of the Chicago Mercantile Exchange. The Board started out with 48 members who traded eggs and butter in the form of "time contracts," which allowed for the delivery of butter at an agreed-upon future date. These time contracts were very informal. After haggling over prices, quality, and other matters, traders would agree upon the transaction terms. See http://library.thinkquest.org/26495/stocki/A%20Short%20History%20of%20Butter%20at%20the%20Chicago%20Mercantile%20Exchange.htm.

It continued to expand and grow and became listed in 2000 under the name of Chicago Mercantile Exchange (CME). CME traded futures and options on futures for a large number of agricultural products and livestock. Merger with the Chicago Board of Trade, New York Mercantile Exchange (NYMEX) and COMEX led to the creation of the Chicago Mercantile Exchange Group, which is a powerhouse in trading financial derivatives for agricultural products, livestock, and metals. It handles over 2.5 billion trades a year. See http://en.wikipedia.org/wiki/Chicago_Mercantile_Exchange.
16 As will be pointed out in later sections (Chapter Seven and Chapter Eight), when an enterprise hedges fair value, it takes on cash flow risk, and when an enterprise hedges cash flow, it takes on fair value risk. This important feature is often ignored in the literature as well as in accounting standards.
17 Trefis Team (6/30/2011). "Southwest Airlines Flies To $14 Unless Hedging Losses Eat Profits." Forbes, at: http://www.forbes.com/sites/greatspeculations/2011/06/30/southwest-airlines-flies-to-14-unless-hedging-losses-eat-profits/.
18 Source: Kansas Gas Service (undated) "Natural Gas Hedge Program." Available at: https://www.kansasgasservice.com/en/CustomerCare/RateInformationTariffs/NaturalGasHedge.aspx.
19 Source: Form 10-K Annual Report, 2010, p. 9. Available at: https://www.dom.com/investors/pdf/2010_10k.pdf
20 JP Morgan Chase 10-K Form, 2010, p. 110. Available at: http://www.sec.gov/Archives/edgar/data/19617/000095012311019773/y86143e10vk.htm.
21 For a useful classification of covenants, see Paglia, J. "An Overview of Covenants in Large Commercial Bank loans," *RMA Journal*, September 2007, pp. 74–78.
22 http://money.cnn.com/2001/12/18/companies/gap/
23 http://www.reuters.com/article/2009/02/06/mcclatchy-rating-sandp-idUSN0646639220090206
24 http://www.bizjournals.com/denver/news/2011/04/29/court-liberty-media-spinoff-doesnt.html
25 http://www.zerohedge.com/article/clear-channel-downgraded-covenant-compliance-concerns-0

# PART II

# INSTRUMENTS

CHAPTER 5

# AN INTRODUCTION TO DERIVATIVE FINANCIAL INSTRUMENTS (FREESTANDING DERIVATIVES)[1]

## 5.1 Fundamental and Derivative Financial Instruments

### 5.1.1 Fundamental Securities

Financing activities have, for a long time, depended on three fundamental types of securities:

1. *Equity Securities* consisting mainly of equity shares:

   a. Common shares are securities that represent ownership rights to unspecified cash flow (dividends) and control (voting power) proportionate to the capital investment the shareholders have made. These two types of rights place common shareholders at the end of the chain in establishing claims to the enterprise assets if the enterprise were to face financial difficulties; common stock shareholders are therefore referred to as the residual claimants.
   b. Preferred shares are securities that grant their shareholders some of the rights granted to common stock shareholders but with privileges. Preferred stockholders may have preference over common stock shareholders in distributing dividends. There are several types of preference privileges, however, as will be discussed in Chapter Nine. Because of these preferences, preferred stock shareholders usually do not have voting rights.

2. *Debt Securities* (bonds)

A business enterprise could obtain financing by issuing bonds and by borrowing funds from the public. A bond is a security (a certificate) that provides the holder with the right to redeem the borrowed funds after a specified period of time (maturity) and to receive compensation for allowing the borrower to use the funds during that period. This compensation could be in the form of a fixed coupon paid periodically (typically twice a year), compensation to be paid at maturity date (zero-coupon bond), or as part of installments (amortizing bond).

In a typical bond indenture, the interest rate (compensation) that borrowers pay lenders for using their funds depends on several factors related to money supply and demand in the economy, the creditworthiness of the issuing enterprise, and bond maturity because default risk increases with longer maturities. In the bond contract, the interest rate is stated either as a fixed rate of interest or as being indexed to a benchmark interest rate (such as LIBOR or Treasury Rates).[2] Bonds have preference in liquidation over preferred and common stock and that preference will depend on the bond seniority or subordination. Because of (a) guaranteed income, (b) repayment of principal, and (iii) preference over shareholders in liquidation, the rights of bondholders (of bonds without optionalities) are limited to cash rights. They do not participate in the management of the enterprise, i.e., they do not have voting rights.[3]

Bonds represent rights (assets) to bondholders, and obligations (liabilities) on the issuer (the borrower).

3. *Hybrid Securities*

These are securities that have a debt-like feature and an equity-like feature. In most of these securities, debt is the main or host component, such as in the case of convertible bonds, callable bonds, or redeemable preferred stock. There are also hybrid securities with equity as the main component such as convertible preferred stock.

Because hybrid securities assume a major role in accounting for derivatives and hedging, they are the focus of Chapter Nine in this text.

#### *5.1.1.1 A Generalization of Valuation*

Valuation of equity and debt securities depends on the cash flow streams that these securities are expected to generate. The anticipated cash flow stream to holders of equity securities is uncertain, but is generally contractually predetermined for debt securities. The value of a hybrid security is the present value of a combination of two cash flow streams: a predetermined component for the debt-like feature and an uncertain component for the equity-like feature.

### 5.1.2 Derivative Instruments

A derivative instrument is a contract whose value is derived from the change in a specific price of another security or contract or from the occurrence of a specific event. To illustrate, consider a farmer whose income is generated from planting, harvesting, and selling corn. To reduce uncertainty, the farmer could, for example, have one or two types of protection contracts:

1. An insurance contract (contract 1) to compensate the farmer for crop loss so that the farm's income would be maintained near expectation. This contract is a traditional insurance policy that does not pay any compensation if there is no crop loss.
2. A contract (contract 2) which would pay the farmer a specified amount of money if the temperature goes above 98°F, for example, for six consecutive days, and the farmer would pay the counterparty a specified amount of money if the temperature remains at 45–50°F for six consecutive days.

While contract 1 derives its value from the actual occurrence of crop loss, contract 2 derives its value from the change in temperature even if the farmer does not suffer any crop damage or loss. In contrast, crop loss is irrelevant for contract 2. If, for example, the temperature falls within the boundaries of the contract terms [50°F–98°F] the farmer will not receive (or make) any payment from (or to) the counterparty even if there is crop loss.

We referred to the two contracts as "protection contracts" only for simplification, but contract 1 is an insurance contract in the traditional sense, while contract 2 is not. A requirement for a contract to qualify as an insurance policy is that it should provide indemnity only—compensation for loss attributable to the insured risk (See Chapter Four). This feature is consistent with contract

1 only; it does not fit contract 2 because this contract would pay the policy-holder irrespective of loss or damage. Accordingly, the value of contract 1 is based on fundamentals, while the value of contract 2 is contingent on an index that may or may not relate to the fundamentals. Contract 2 is the type of financial instrument known as weather derivatives.[4]

This chapter presents the essential features of five basic types of freestanding financial derivatives: (1) options and warrants; (2) swaps; (3) forward contracts; (4) futures; and (5) credit default swaps.

## 5.2 Options

### 5.2.1 Types of Options

An option is a contract that gives its holder the right, but not the obligation, to elect undertaking a specific transaction in accordance with the terms of the agreement. The seller (writer) has the obligation to perform (deliver or purchase) the asset for which the option is written. There are two common forms of options ("call" and "put") distinguished by whether the holder of the contract has the right to buy or has the right to sell.

a. *Call options* are contracts that give the holder the right to buy an asset at some predetermined price within a specified period of time (American-style option) or at a specified date (European-style option). In exchange for collecting a premium, the option writer (also called issuer or seller) has the obligation to perform (deliver the asset) should the option holder decide to exercise the agreed upon contractual rights.[5]
b. *Put options* are contracts that give the holder the right to "put" the asset up for sale at a predetermined price within a specified period of time (American-style option) or at a specified date (European-style option). As with the call option, the put option writer (issuer or seller) has the obligation to perform (purchase the asset) if the holder of the option decides to exercise the right to *put* the asset up for sale.
c. *American vs. European styles*: When the holder of the option, be it a call or a put, has the right to exercise the option at any time before expiration date, the option is called an *American Option*. If the contract does not allow the holder to exercise the option before expiry, the contract is called a *European Option*.

### 5.2.2 Basic Features

A plain vanilla option, whether it is American-style or European-style, embodies only the very basic features of an option contract. These features are:

1. Two contracting parties: a holder (buyer of an option contract) and a seller (writer of an option contract).
2. The holder of the option pays a premium to acquire the rights granted by the contract.[6]
3. The seller of the option collects the premium in exchange for having the obligation to deliver.
4. The contract has a predetermined expiration date.
5. Contract terms are (generally) not changeable prior to expiration.

## Information Log: Some Other Types of Options

**Caps and Floors:**

A *cap* (i.e., a ceiling) is a *call* option that gives the buyer, who is also a debtholder, the right to be compensated for an increase in a specified benchmark interest rate past a specified strike rate. For example, an entity that has floating-rate debt could limit its exposure to increases in the benchmark interest rate; for an upfront premium, the company could purchase a cap in which the writer (seller of the option) would be obligated to pay the entity the excess of the market rate over the agreed upon benchmark rate. Assume the entity's floating rate on its debt is LIBOR plus 50 basis points. If LIBOR increases, the cost of servicing the debt will also increase. In purchasing a cap, the entity might agree with the dealer that LIBOR on the date of the contract, say 3%, would be the benchmark or strike rate. If LIBOR increases above a strike rate, say 3%, the writer of the cap option will pay the excess of the market rate over the 3% times the notional amount. A cap is settled sequentially over time; each settlement horizon is called a *caplet*. A cap is, therefore, a collection of caplets; each is like a European-style call option. Each caplet is valued as a European option by a suitable model such as Black-Scholes, Binomial (to be presented later in this chapter), or any of various other stochastic models. The value of a cap at any point in time is the sum of the values of all its caplets.

*Floors* are the analogue of caps for hedging against the fall of interest rates. While caps are like call options with boundaries, floors are like put options with boundaries. An entity could protect the level of earnings on floating-rate investments by purchasing floors; if interest rates fall below an agreed upon strike rate, the counterparty is obligated to pay the shortfall to the holder. A floor consists of *floorlets* that are sequentially settled and each floor contract could be viewed as a series of sequential European put options. Chapter Eight provides an illustration of accounting for hedging interest rates using floors. The value of a floor is the sum of all values of its floorlets.

An entity would have a *collar* if it owns both a cap and a floor.

**Some Exotic Options**

| | |
|---|---|
| *Bermudan*: | A contract that may be exercised at a set number of times or dates, usually equally spaced out, for example on "the first day of the month." |
| *Quanto*: | A contract that has an underlying in one currency but is settled in another currency. |
| *Asian*: | A contract whose payoff is determined by the history of the underlying price, such as the average price over some pre-set period of time. |
| *Lookback*: | The holder of a call (put) option has the right to buy (sell) the underlying instrument at its lowest (highest) price over some prior period. |
| *Russian*: | A lookback option without an end to the period into which the owner can look back. |
| *Barrier*: | A contract stipulating that the underlying security's price must pass a certain level or "barrier" before it can be exercised. If the barrier is to activate the right of the holder, the option is called a knock-in option. If the barrier is to suspend the rights of the holder the contract is called a knock-out option. |

The option contract might specify whether the contract is cash-settled or is to be settled by physical delivery. A contract is cash-settled if the counterparties exchange the difference between the current market price and the strike price; it is also called "net settled." Physical delivery requires settlement by actual delivery of the asset specified in the contract.

## Accounting Log

The distinction between net settlement and settlement by physical delivery of the subject asset is crucial for accounting purposes. Chapter Six will note that net settlement (or equivalent) is an essential requirement that must be satisfied in order to qualify for adopting hedge accounting.

Options may be traded on an organized exchange, may be traded over-the-counter, or may not be traded at all. For example, equity-related options are traded on organized exchanges such as the Chicago Board of Options Exchange (www.cboe.com) or on the CME Group mercantile exchange for options related to commodities and minerals. Generally, the exchange-traded options have standardized features and terms,[7] and are settled through a central organization known as the Options Clearing Corporation. Interest rate options and cross currency options are traded over-the-counter. Finally, employees' stock options are not traded because they are not transferrable.

### 5.2.3 Market Price versus Strike Price

At any point in time, the current (spot) market price of the subject asset could differ from the option exercise (strike) price.[8] The difference between market price and strike or exercise price is called the *intrinsic value*. For a call option, the intrinsic value is the *max* $(0, S–X)$, where $S$ is the current (spot) market price and $X$ is the specified strike price, while the intrinsic value of a put option is the *max* $(0, X–S)$.

When the intrinsic value of a *call option* is positive $(S - X > 0)$, the option is said to be *in-the-money* because the holder will realize gains upon exercising the option. If the call and put options were issued *at-the-money* (i.e., strike price equals market price), when a call option is *in-the-money*, the put option on that asset would be *out-of-the-money* and the holder of the put option would have no incentive to sell the asset in question at a price below the strike price.[9]

The reverse is also true. When the spot market price of the asset to be exchanged is below strike price $(X - S > 0)$, there is no incentive for the holder of the call option to exercise, but there would be incentive for the holder of the put option to exercise the option and earn profits equal to the excess of the strike price over the market price. In this case, the call option is said to be *out-of-the-money* and the put option is *in-the-money*.

Theoretically, when the option is at-the-money, the option holder would have three choices:

1. To let the option expire unexercised and do nothing.
2. To exercise the option.
3. To let the option expire and purchase (for a call option holder) or sell (for a put option holder) the asset in the marketplace.

In general, even when the option is at-the-money, the option holder might exercise it by physical delivery if buying or selling the asset in the marketplace has a higher transaction cost.

The different relationships of spot and strike prices for stock options are presented in Exhibit 5.1 for call and put options.

## Exhibit 5.1 Spot vs. Strike Prices of Options

| Spot Price vs. Strike Price | *Call Option* | | *Put Option* | |
|---|---|---|---|---|
| | *Sign* | *Meaning* | *Sign* | *Meaning* |
| Stock Price > Strike | Positive | In the Money | 0 | Out of the money |
| Stock Price = Strike | 0 | *At the Money* | *0* | *At the Money* |
| Stock Price < Strike | 0 | Out of the Money | Positive | In the Money |

### 5.2.4 Payoff Functions of Call and Put Options

An option is typically issued *at-the-money* (i.e., zero *intrinsic value*) and may be sold at a small premium (equal to time value of option). The premium is a revenue for the writer (seller) of the option, and is a sunk cost for the holder (the buyer). As the price of the subject asset increases, the premium of a call option increases by the increase in the *intrinsic value less the decline in time value of option* and the option would be *in-the-money* —more valuable to the holder.[10] As the price of the subject asset decreases, the premium of a put option increases by the increase in the *intrinsic value less the decline in time value of option* and the option would be *in-the-money* —more valuable to the holder. In either case, changes in option values affect wealth transfer from the writer of the option to the buyer of the option. But in a macroeconomic sense, it is a zero-sum game because the gain of the holder is the loss of the seller and no other goods are produced or consumed.

These relationships are graphed in Figure 5.1 for a call option and Figure 5.2 for a put option. In both cases, the change in the price of the subject asset is on the *x*-axis, while the gains (the positive region) or losses (the negative region) are on the *y*-axis.

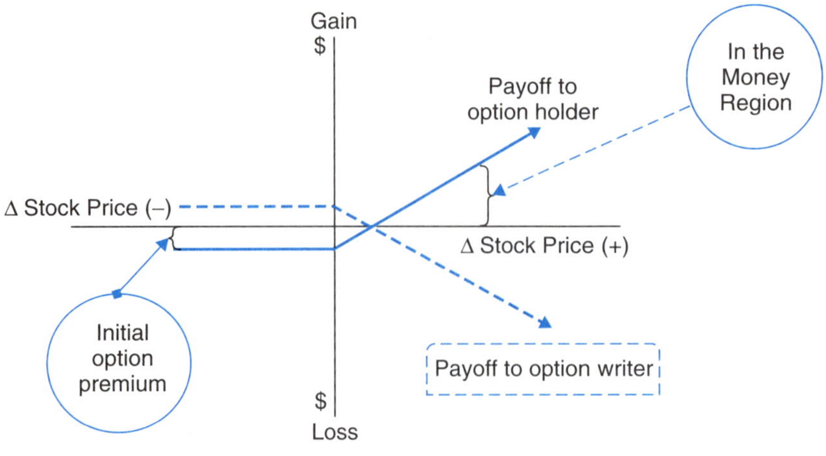


**Figure 5.1** Payoff of a Call Option for a Hypothetical Stock

For the call option in Figure 5.1, the solid lines show the payoff to the holder of the option, while the dashed line shows the payoff to the writer of the option. The premium revenue to the writer is a cost (negative) for the holder. The *intrinsic value* of the call option increases as the price of the subject asset rises. This is the value the holder of the option would realize from the writer at the time of exercise; the cash inflow to the holder is a cash outflow to the writer. The payoff of the put option is shown in Figure 5.2; the payoff to the holder of the option is the excess of the strike price over the spot market price and this is exactly the same as the cost to the writer of the option.

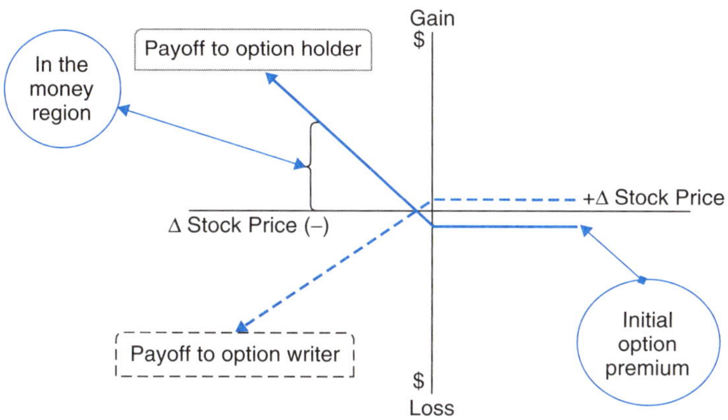


**Figure 5.2** Payoff of a Put Option for a Hypothetical Stock

## 5.2.5 Option Premium and Other Values

In a financial instrument, the *intrinsic value* of an option is the present value of net cash flow that accrues to the holder. Because the underlying (say, the stock price for stock options) is volatile, calculating the present value of net cash flows requires using models a bit more complex than a simple discounting model. The two most accessible models are the Black-Scholes model and the Cox-Ross-Rubenstein Binomial model.

The premium (market price) of an option might be equal to or higher than its *intrinsic value* because of the *time value of options*—the value that investors are willing to pay for the likelihood that the option will be in-the-money before expiration. To reiterate the basic concepts, the following definitions show the relationship between these two values.

- *Intrinsic Value*: For a call option, the excess of the market price of the asset for which the option is written over the strike price for the option. For the put option, it is the excess of the strike price over the market price. The intrinsic value is always non-negative.
- *Time Value of Option*: The excess of the option premium or market price of the option over its intrinsic value. Two main factors determine the time value of options: (1) time to expiration and (2) volatility (uncertainty) of the value of the subject asset. Because of volatility, there is always anticipation and hope that the price of the subject asset will change in such a way that the option will be in-the-money and the intrinsic value will increase. That anticipation diminishes at an increasing rate[11] as time to expiration approaches maturity (this behavior is shown in the example provided below). As with intrinsic value, the time value of option is non-negative.
- *Option Premium*: The option premium = *Intrinsic Value* + *Time Value of Option.*

## Accounting Log

In general, accounting standards treat time value of options differently from intrinsic value. Specifically, an entity could decide whether to include the time value of option in hedge effectiveness or to exclude it and charge the changes in time value of options to earnings as a finance item. ASC 815-20-25-82 shows the elements of the time value of options that the management may elect to include or exclude from hedge effectiveness. (This also applies to the time value of forwards and futures.)

However, as of the time of writing of this book, both the FASB and the IASB are debating whether the time value of options (and forward contracts) is to be posted to earnings, parked in OCI, or treated differently for hedge accounting.

### 5.2.6 Valuation of Options

The general rule of valuation is to estimate the present value of expected future net cash flows. Other than complexity, valuation of options is not an exception to this general valuation rule. In particular, the value of an option is the expected present value of anticipated future net cash inflows to the holder (the buyer) of the contract. But calculation of that present value of options requires estimating the probabilities of upward and downward price movements of the subject asset. Specific option valuation models are developed to take into consideration the volatility of the underlying (price). Two of these commonly used models are the basic form of Black-Scholes model and the Cox-Ross-Rubinstein (Binomial) model.

#### *5.2.6.1 Black-Scholes Model*

This model assumes that price changes follow a log normal distribution and makes use of five specific variables:

1. Current (spot) asset market price.
2. Option strike or exercise price.
3. Volatility of the underlying—asset price.
4. Discount rates—risk-free interest rate.
5. Time to expiration.

In this model, the premium (price) of a call option is the excess of expected present value of the asset to be received upon exercising the option over expected present value of cash to be paid out in the form of exercise price. Similarly, the premium (price) or value of a put option is the excess of expected present value of the cash to be received by selling the asset to a counterparty at the time of exercise, over the present value of the cash to be paid out for the strike price. In this context, the term "expected" means "probability weighted" and the term "present value" means discounted future cash flow. Exhibit 5.2 presents the basic form of Black-Scholes model and provides numerical examples.

## Exhibit 5.2 Determination of Option Premium Based on the Black-Scholes Model

**The Black-Scholes Model:**

To describe the Black-Scholes model and provide an example, the following terms need to be defined:

| | |
|---|---|
| $t$ | = time to expiration. |
| $\sigma$ | = volatility of the price of the underlying asset. |
| $C$ | = call option premium. |
| $P$ | = put option premium. |
| $S$ | = the current (spot) market price of the subject asset. |
| $d_1$ | = the number of standard deviations for stock price realization |
| | $= [\ln(S/X) + [r + (\sigma^2/2)] * t]/\ \sigma(t)^{1/2}$ |
| $N(d_1)$ | = the cumulative normal distribution of the value of the asset. |
| $S[N(d_1)]$ | = the expected value of the asset to be received. |
| $d_2$ | $= d_1 - \sigma(t)^{1/2}$ |
| $N(d_2)$ | = the cumulative normal probability of exercising the option. |
| $X$ | = exercise or strike price. |
| $r$ | = risk-free rate of interest. |
| $Xe^{-rt}\,[N(d_2)]$ | = the expected present value of the cash to be paid out. |

Using these terms, Black-Scholes option pricing model expresses the difference between expected present values of the cash expected to be received and the cash expected to be paid out, as shown in the following figure.

*The premium for a call option,* $C = S[N(d_1)] - Xe^{-rt}[N(d_2)]$

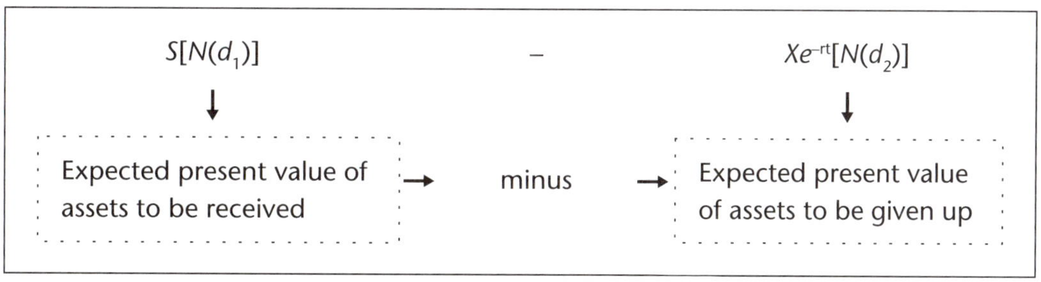


*The premium for a put option,* $P = [Xe^{-rt}\,[N(d_2)] - S[N(d_1)]$

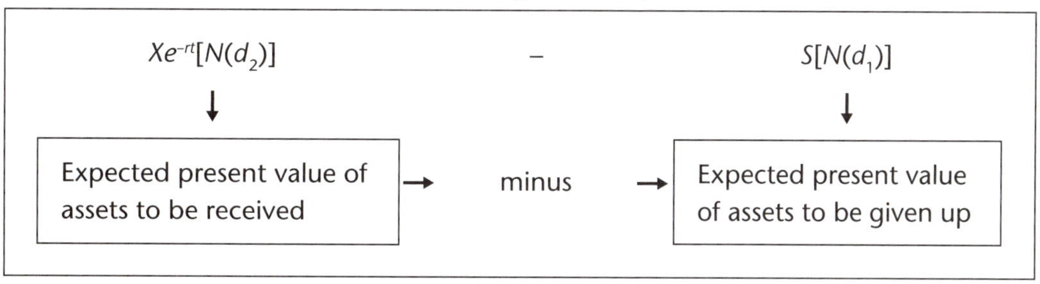

### 5.2.6.2 An Illustration

Table 5.1 presents information about a (hypothetical) stock option for an entity called AZIZA, Inc. In this table, the time value of option is the excess of the option premium over its intrinsic value. As time to expiration approaches maturity, the time value of option decreases to its final point of zero.

**Table 5.1** The Behavior of Changes in Option Values to the Holder of a *Call* Stock Option of AZIZA, Inc.

| *Date* | *Time to Expiration (Days)* | *Stock Price* | *Intrinsic Value of Option* | *Premium of Stock Option* | *Time Value of Stock Option* |
|---|---|---|---|---|---|
| October 20x0 | 810 | $14.00 | 0.00 | $2.74 | $2.74 |
| June 20x1 | 720 | $16.00 | 2.0 | 3.39 | 1.39 |
| October 20x1 | 630 | $16.50 | 2.50 | 4.10 | 1.60 |
| December 20x1 | 540 | $17.20 | 3.20 | 4.48 | 1.28 |
| March 20x2 | 450 | $17.90 | 3.90 | 4.85 | 0.95 |
| **July 20x2** | **360** | **$18.20** | **4.20** | **4.91** | **0.71** |
| October 20x2 | 270 | $18.50 | 4.50 | 4.97 | 0.47 |
| **December 20x2** | **180** | **$19.00** | **5.00** | **5.23** | **0.23** |
| March 20x2 | 90 | $19.00 | 5.00 | 5.09 | 0.09 |
| July 20x2 | 0 | $19.00 | 5.00 | 5.00 | 0.00 |

Assumptions:
Volatility 30%
Strike Price (October 20x0) = $14.00
Maturity 810 days
Risk Free Interest Rate = 2% per annum

Note that the *option premium* is the sum of the *intrinsic value* and *time value of option*. In the limit, the time value of option declines to zero at expiry and the option premium at that time would be equal to the intrinsic value. This behavior is visually presented in Figure 5.3. As shown, the option premium is the sum of the intrinsic value and the time value of option.

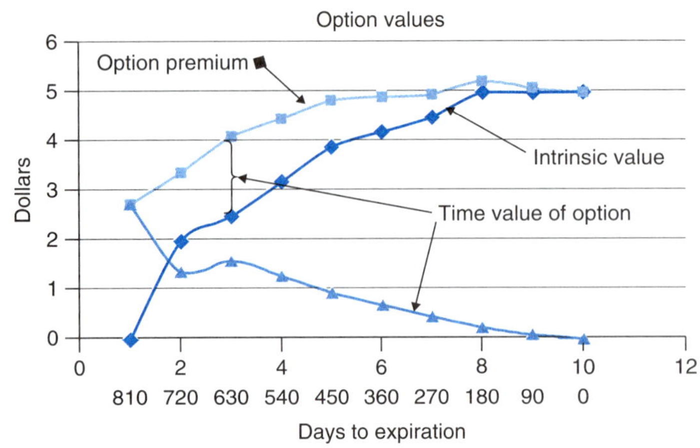


**Figure 5.3** The Behavior of Option Values to the Holder of AZIZA, Inc. Stock Option

The European option does not allow exercising the option before expiry, while the American option does. However, before expiration, the option contract is worth more if traded than if exercised because the time value of options could not be realized by exercising the option.

To show how the Black-Scholes model is used to arrive at the values of the premium, let us take two cases: Case 1 with 360 days remaining to maturity, and Case 2 with 180 days remaining to maturity.

| Panel A: Premium of call option when time to expiry is 360 days. | | |
|---|---|---|
| Variable | The first case with 360 days ($t$ = one year) to expiration: | The first case with 360 days to expiration: |
| $d_1$ | $[\ln(S/X) + (r + (\sigma^2)/2) * t]/\sigma * \sqrt{t}$ (Number of standard deviation of stock price from strike price given growth rate, volatility and time.) | $\ln(18.20/14) + (0.02 + (0.30)^2/2) * 1/0.30 * \sqrt{1}$ = 1.091 |
| $N(d_1)$ | CDF ($d_1$) from the standard normal distribution table | = 0.8622 |
| $d_2$ | $= d_1 - \sigma * \sqrt{t}$ | $= 1.091 - 0.30 * \sqrt{1}$ = 0.791 |
| $N(d_2)$ | CDF ($d_2$) from the standard normal distribution table | = 0.786 |
| PV($X$) | $= Xe^{-rt}$ (Present value of strike price) | $= \$14e^{-0.02*1}$ = \$13.723 |
| E(PV($X$)) | $Xe^{-rt}$ $[N(d_2)]$ (Expected present value of strike price) | = \$13.723 * 0.786 = \$10.7863 |
| E($S$) | $S$ $[N(d_1)]$ (Expected Value of Stock Price) | \$18.20 * 0.8622 = \$15.692 |
| $C$ | $= S[N(d_1)] - Xe^{-rt}[N(d_2)]$ Option Premium = Expected Value of Stock Price – Expected Value of Strike Price) | = \$15.692 – \$10.7863 = \$4.9057 (As in Table T5-1) |

| Panel B: Premium of call option when time to expiry is 180 days. | | |
|---|---|---|
| Variable | The first case with 180 days ($t$ = 0.50 of one year) to expiration: | The second case with 180 days to expiration calculation: |
| $d_1$ | $[\ln(S/X) + (r + (\sigma^2)/2) * t]/\sigma * \sqrt{t}$ (Number of standard deviation of stock price from strike price given growth rate, volatility and time.) | $\ln(19/14) + (0.02 + (0.30)^2/2) * (0.50)/0.30 * (0.5)^{1/2} = 1.59$ |

| | | |
|---|---|---|
| $N(d_1)$ | CDF $(d_1)$ from the standard normal distribution table | $= 0.9441$ |
| $d_2$ | $= d_1 - \sigma * \sqrt{t}$ | $= 1.59 - 0.3 *(0.5)^{1/2} = 1.37786$ |
| $N(d_2)$ | CDF $(d_2)$ from the standard normal distribution table | $= 0.915765$ |
| PV(X) | $= Xe^{-rt}$ (Present value of strike price) | $= 14e^{-0.02*(0.50)}$ $= 13.861$ |
| E(PV(X)) | $Xe^{-rt} * N(d_2)$ (Expected present value of strike price) | \$13.86 * 0.915765 = \$12.6925 |
| E(S) | $S[N(d_1)]$ (Expected value of stock price) | \$19 * 0.9441 = \$17.9397 |
| *C* | $= S[N(d_1)] - Xe^{-rt} * N(d_2)$ Option premium = expected value of stock price – expected value of strike price) | 17.9397 – 12.6925 = \$5.2454 (As in Table 5.1 with rounding errors) |

### 5.2.6.3 Cox-Ross-Rubinstein Binomial Model

The Binomial model as developed by Cox, Ross, and Rubinstein (1976) makes the assumption that the price of the subject asset (say a stock) is expected to move up or down at any point in time. (The Trinomial model assumes no change (flat) as a third state, but we do not include this model here.) For example, at time $t = t_0$, the price of the stock of XYZ, Inc. is $S_0$. It could increase in period one to $S_{1u}$ or decline to $S_{1d}$. At state $S_{1u}$ the price could be expected to increase in period 2 to $S_{2uu}$, or could decline to $S_{2ud}$. Similarly, at state $S_{1d}$, the price could be expected to move up to $S_{2du}$, or down to $S_{2dd}$. The process continues for every period and each node splits into two branches. When it is all done, the chart of the process looks like a lattice or a tree and the model is also known as the lattice model or the binomial tree model.[12] This two-period movement could be charted as shown in Figure 5.4 with the following definitions:

$S_0$ = the stock price at time $t = 0$.
$S_{1u}$ = the expected price in period $t = 1$ if the price were to *increase* in value.
$S_{1d}$ = the expected price in period $t = 1$ if the price were to *decrease* in value.
$S_{2uu}$ = the expected price in period $t = 2$ if the increased price in the first period $S_{1u}$ were to be followed by a price increase in the second period.
$S_{2ud}$ = the expected price in period $t = 2$ if the first period price increase $S_{1u}$ were to be followed by a decrease in the second period.
$S_{2du}$ = the expected price in period $t = 2$ if the first period decreased price $S_{1d}$ were to increase in the second period.
$S_{2dd}$ = the expected price in period $t = 2$ if the first period decreased price $S_{1d}$ were to be followed by a decrease in the second period.

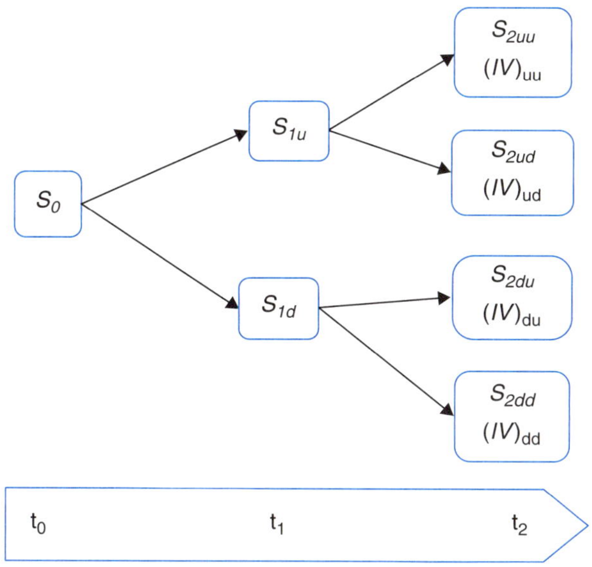


**Figure 5.4** A Two-Period Binomial Model

The upward and downward price movements depend on the volatility of asset (the stock in a case of stock option) prices. Assuming continuous compounding, these values are estimated as follows:[13]

$u = e^{\sigma\sqrt{t}}$ for the upward movement,

$d = e^{-\sigma\sqrt{t}} = 1/u$ for the downward movement.

where "$e$" is Euler's exponential, $\sigma$ is the annual volatility (typically presented in percentage terms) of the asset and $t$ is the time horizon to be used such as $t_0 \rightarrow t_1$ for the first period and $t_1 \rightarrow t_2$ for the second period.

Given these estimated values for $u$ and $d$, the asset prices at the end of first period would be estimated as follows:

$S_{1u} = S_0 * u$ for the up movement, and

$S_{1d} = S_0 * d$ for the down a movement.

This process continues until the terminal period. At the terminal period, the intrinsic values of the option will be calculated for each condition. For example, in the two-period situation above, there will be four probable intrinsic values as the difference between the predicted stock price and the strike price ($X$). These values are:

a. $IV_{uu} = S_{uu} - X$ = Intrinsic value if the price moves upward twice.
b. $IV_{ud} = S_{ud} - X$ = Intrinsic value if the price moves upward in period 1 and downward in period 2.

c. $IV_{du} = S_{du} - X$ = Intrinsic value if the price moves downward in period 1 and upward in period 2.
d. $IV_{dd} = S_{dd} - X$ = Intrinsic value if the price moves downward twice.

These intrinsic values are predictions, conditional on the path of the changes in the asset price (assuming a stationary level of volatility in this case). This conditionality can be expressed in probabilistic terms for the probability of upward movement and for the probability of downward movement. These probabilities are calculated by reference to a "normal" growth in asset prices. The "normal" growth represents the asset value at the end of a given period if the initial value of the asset was invested at the risk-free rate. The future value, *Fv*, of an initial investment of $1.00 continuously compounded at the risk-free rate, *r*, for a time period *t* is calculated as follows:

$$Fv_1 = Fv_{t_0} \rightarrow_{t_1} = e^{r * t_1}$$

Using this new information, we calculate the probabilities of price movements as follows:

1. The probability of the asset price increasing:

$$p_u = (Fv_1 - d)/(u - d)$$

2. The probability of the asset price decreasing:

$$p_d = (d - Fv_1)/(u - d)$$

$$= 1 - p_u$$

In our example,

a. $IV_{uu}$ has a probability of occurrence in period $2_{puu}$
b. $IV_{ud}$ has a $p_{ud}$ probability of occurrence in period 2

and the expected intrinsic value for this branch is:

$$\mathrm{E}(IV_u) = p_{uu} * IV_{uu} + p_{ud} * IV_{ud}$$

Similarly,

c. $IV_{du}$ has a $p_{du}$ probability of occurrence in period 2
d. $IV_{dd}$ has a $p_{dd}$ probability of occurrence in period 2

and the expected intrinsic value for this branch is:

$$\mathrm{E}(IV_d) = p_{du} * IV_{du} + p_{dd} * IV_{dd}$$

Each of these expected values is discounted from time t = 2 to time 1 using the risk free discount rate.

The process is followed to discount the expected intrinsic values to time t = 0 as shown in Exhibit 5.3 and Figure 5.5 that provide a numerical example for a two-period Binomial model valuation.

## Exhibit 5.3 An Illustration of Valuation of a Call Option Using the Two-Period Binomial Model

To illustrate, consider a call option with the following features:

- Market price at time $t = t_0$ is \$16.00.
- Exercise price is \$14.00.
- Time to expiration is 1 year.
- Annual volatility is 30%.
- Annual risk-free rate is 4% p.a.
- Interest is paid semi-annually.

The results of using these assumptions in a Binomial valuation model are detailed below and are summarized in Figure 5.5 (the option premium or values are in parentheses).

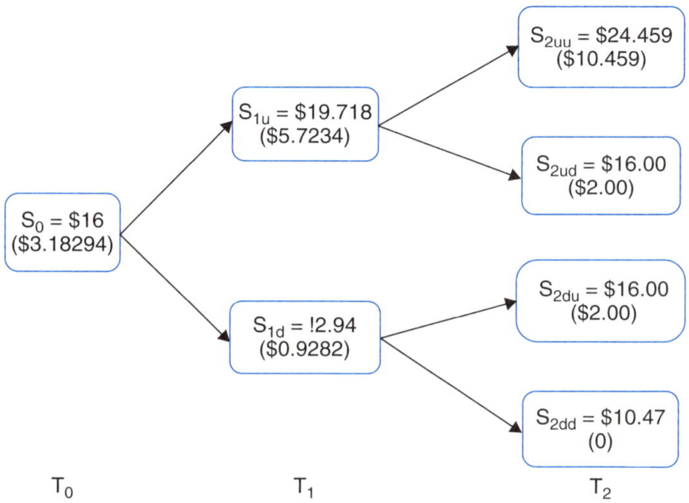


**Figure 5.5** A Two-Period Binomial Tree

Steps toward calculating the values in Figure 5.5.

For simplification, assume that t0 = January 1; t1 = July 1; and t2 = December 31.

Step A. Calculate the prices on the upward and downward movement. The upward movement is continuously compounded at the volatility rate of $\sigma$ of the underlying asset for the six-month period ($t = 0.5$ of a year) resulting:

$$S_0 \times u = \$16.00 \times e^{-0.30\sqrt{0.50}}$$

$$= \$16.00 \times 1.236$$

$= \$19.781$ for the up price movement from January to July.

and:

$$d = \$16.00 \times e^{-0.30\sqrt{0.50}}$$

$$= \$16.00 \times 0.808865$$

$= \$12.94184$ for the down price movent from January to July.

B. Calculate the riskless future investment value of the price of \$16.00 at the risk free rate of 2% per year for a period of six month from January to July:

$$\begin{aligned} FV(1) &= \$16.00 \times e^{0.02^{*}.50} \\ &= \$16.00 \times 1.01005 \\ &= \$16.1608 \end{aligned}$$

C. Calculate the probability of each movement

$P_u$ = (\$16.1608 – \$12.94184) / (\$19.781 – \$12.94184)
= 0.4707 for the probability of increasing prices.
$P_d$ = 1 – 0.4707 = 0.5293 for the probability of decreasing prices.

Note:

If the assumptions about volatility and interest rates do not change, then for every period of six month we will have

- The upward movement will be 1.2363 for every dollar.
- The downward movement will be 0.808865 for every dollar.
- The probability of up movement is 0.4707
- The probability of down movement is 0.5293

D. For the second period from July through December after the first up movement, the price might move up or down

- The price at the up movement is \$19.781 × 1.2363 = \$24.459.
- The price at the down movement is \$19.7881 × 0.808865 = \$16.00

E. For the second period from July through December after the first down movement, the price might move up or down

- The price at the up movement is \$12.9418 × 1.2363 = \$16.00
- The price at the down movement is \$12.9418 × 0.808865 = \$10.4682

Note: The time value of option at expiry date is zero. Therefore, the difference between the expected price at each node end and the strike price at that time is the intrinsic value only. Furthermore, these would be the expected option values at each.

F. Calculation of intrinsic values

- For the *up-up movement*, with a probability of 0.4707, the intrinsic value at maturity is \$24.459 - \$14.00 = \$10.459 at December 31.
- For the *up-down movement*, with a probability of 0.529045, the intrinsic value at maturity is \$16.00 – \$14.00 = \$2.00 at December 31.

→ Therefore, the expected value of the option at the end of the second period under this condition would be
\$10.459 × 0.4707 + \$2.00 × 0.5293 = \$5.9816.

→ At the beginning of the second period, which is July 1, the expected option value would be the present value of \$5.9816 discounted at the risk free rate for six months.
The present value would be \$5.9816 × $e^{-0.02*0.50}$ = \$5.7234

→ Thus, when the expected price is \$19.781, the expected intrinsic value is \$5.7234 and time value of option is (\$19.781 – \$14.00) – \$5.7234 = \$0.0576

G. Calculation of intrinsic and time values

- For the down-up movement, with a probability of 0.4707, the intrinsic (option) value at maturity is $2.00
- For the down-down movement, with a probability of 0.5293, the intrinsic value at maturity is zero.
  - ➔ Therefore, the expected intrinsic value at the end of the second period (December 31) would be
    $2.00 × 0.4707 + 0 = $0.9414.
  - ➔ At the beginning of the second period (July 1), the expected value would be the present value of
    $0.94191 discounted at the risk free rate for six months, which would be
    $0.9414 × $e^{-0.02*0.50}$ = $0.9282
  - ➔ But because the intrinsic value of the option at that time is zero, the $0.9282 would be the time value of option on July 1, the beginning of the second period.

H. Calculation of intrinsic and time values at initiation, January 1.

- For the up movement, the intrinsic value plus the time value of option at the end of the first period is
  $19.781 – $14.00 = $5.781 with a probability of 0.4707
- For the down movement, the expected time value of option is $0.93254 with a probability of 0.5293,
  - ➔ Therefore, the expected intrinsic plus time value of option at the end of the first period (July 1) would be
    ($5.781 × 0.4707) = $2.721 + (0.932 × 0.5293) = $3.2144.
  - ➔ The present value of the of the option at initiation of the contract (January 1) is
    $3.2213 × $e^{-0.02*0.50}$ = $3.18242.

**Conclusion**: For the expected price changes and for riskless investment, one should be willing to pay $3.2213 as an option premium for this call option.

### 5.2.7 Options Greeks

The behavior of the premium of an option with respect to its determinants is examined by evaluating the first or second (mathematical) derivative of the option premium with respect to the market price of the subject asset (e.g., equity stock for stock options), volatility, interest rate, and time to expiration. Each of these measures is given a Greek symbol (plus *vega*), hence the name "Options Greeks," which is sometimes described as The Greek Suite and is presented in Exhibit 5.4. The relevance to accounting follows the exhibit.

## Exhibit 5.4 The Options Greeks

A basic plain vanilla option valuation using Black-Scholes model has five variables:

1. *S*: The price of the subject asset for which the option is written such as the price of a par ticular stock in the case of stock options.

2. $\sigma$: The (expected future) volatility of the price in (1) above.
3. $r$: *Risk*-free interest rate.
4. $T$: Time to expiration, i.e., maturity, of option.
5. $X$: Strike price.

These five factors determine the premium (price) of the option, which is denoted by C for a call option and by $P$ for a put option. The option is on buying or selling an asset (e.g., stock). Each of these variables affects the premium of the option in a specific way, using a call option, the Greeks are as follows:

- Delta = $\Delta C/\Delta S = \delta$, reflects the sensitivity of the call premium to the change in the asset price.
- Lambda = $\%\Delta C/\%\Delta S = \lambda$, the percentage change in the option premium relative to percentage change in the price of the asset.
- Gamma = $\Delta\delta/\Delta S^2 = \Delta^2 C/\Delta S^2 = \Gamma$, is the sensitivity of Delta to price changes.
- Vega = $\Delta C/\Delta\sigma = v$, the extent to which the option premium changes as a result of the change in the asset price volatility.[14]
- Theta = $\Delta C/\Delta T = \Theta$, is the time decay in the value of the option premium.
- Rho = $\Delta C/\Delta r = \rho$, is the change in option premium in response to change in the risk-free rate of interest.

These indicators are important in establishing hedging strategies. However, Delta has an important role in hedge accounting as will become clear in discussing Hedge Effectiveness in Chapter Six.

### 5.2.7.1 Relevance of Options Greek in Accounting

Accounting for hedging is contingent on the degree of success in hedging the designated risk. Success is referred to as "effectiveness," which is measured by relating the changes in the value of the derivative instrument to the change in the value of the item being hedged. Elaboration on these criteria is in Chapter Six. However, before measuring hedge effectiveness, a decision has to be made about the measurement of the change in derivative values.

a. *For Options*: Does the change in value used to measure hedge effectiveness include or exclude the time value of options?
b. *For a Forward Contract*: Does the change in the value of the forward used to measure hedge effectiveness include or exclude "forward points?"

The Greeks are developed for options, and accounting standards recognize their usefulness in testing hedge effectiveness; ASC 815-20-25-82 states:

> In defining how hedge effectiveness will be assessed, …
>
> c. An entity may exclude any of the following components of the change in an option's time value from the assessment of hedge effectiveness:
>
> 1. The portion of the change in time value attributable to the passage of time (*theta*).
> 2. The portion of the change in time value attributable to changes due to volatility (*vega*).
> 3. The portion of the change in time value attributable to changes due to interest rates (*rho*).

## Exhibit 5.5 An Example of Privately Written Option Contracts

Cotton options for consumers

**Your need**

You are a consumer (buyer) of cotton and would like to have protection against rising cotton prices but you also want the opportunity to benefit if cotton prices fall.

**Solution**

A cotton option allows you to remain at a floating commodity reference price, but you are protected should commodity prices rise above the agreed maximum price (call strike price) in return for paying a premium.

**How it works**

After credit approval, you enter into a cotton option with the Bank. You will specify the call strike price, the transaction amount and the exercise date/s. We will determine the premium.

**Possible outcomes on the pricing date**

- If the commodity reference price is higher than the call strike price, we must pay the difference between the call strike price and the commodity reference price.
- If the commodity reference price is equal to or below the call strike price, you and the Bank will have no further obligations to each other with respect to the cotton option. You can buy physical cotton at a price that is equal to or more favorable than the call strike price.

**Benefits**

- You receive protection against any rise in the commodity reference price above the agreed call strike price and have the potential to benefit if prices fall.
- You can determine the call strike price, transaction amount and exercise date/s.
- The transactions are cash-settled so there is no need to physically deliver cotton to the Bank.
- There are no complex exchange-traded brokerage and margin calls.

**Points to consider**

- You have to pay a premium to the Bank as an upfront payment.
- You are not covered for the basis risk, which is the risk arising from entering into a hedge transaction that is not identical with the risk being covered.
- The cotton option may expire worthless, resulting in the premium being an additional cost to you.

(Source: http://www.commbank.com.au/business/agribusiness/commodities-risk-management/cotton/consumer-options.aspx)

## 5.3 Warrants

### 5.3.1 Nature of Warrants

A warrant is a financial instrument that conveys the right to purchase (a *call* warrant) or the right to sell (a *put* warrant) equity shares of a particular company according to predetermined conditions. Issuing warrants is intended to motivate investors to provide funds to the issuing enterprise and to allow the enterprise to raise funds at a relatively low cost.

Who issues warrants?

1. *Own Company*: Warrants could be issued by an enterprise granting the holders the right to purchase common equity shares of the same enterprise or of one of its subsidiaries. These warrants are exercised when the issuer calls for "subscription." Subscription warrants are issued as part of bond or stock public offering. In addition to providing a "sweetener" to investors, opening subscriptions for exercising warrants is another way of raising capital.

   These warrants can take one of two forms:

   - *Detachable*: These warrants are usually issued in connection with other (host) instruments such as bonds or stocks and could be physically detached from the host instrument and traded separately.
   - *Non-detachable*: This type of warrant is embedded (combined) with a host instrument in one security, a bond or a preferred common stock. Non-detachable warrants cannot be detached or traded separately. Non-detachable warrants will be discussed in Chapter 9 on Embedded Derivatives.

     Exhibit 5.8 provides an example for sale of warrants by General Motors and an example of a subscription invitation by Transense Technologies, PLC.

2. *Financial Institutions*: Banks or other financial institutions can issue warrants to buy or sell (for their own accounts, not as agents) common shares of another company. These warrants can be one of two types:

   - *Covered warrants*: This is one type of warrants issued by financial institutions when the issuer is in possession of the shares that warrant holders could acquire upon exercising warrants.
   - *Naked Warrants*: When the warrants' issuer does not own the shares that the holders could acquire when the call warrants are exercised.

3. *A Third Party*: Stockholders can issue warrants to sell their own stocks.

#### Information Log

*Harmless* or *Wedding Warrants*: when an outstanding bond (or preferred stock) is called for redemption, the investor, who also holds a warrant, surrenders the bond (or preferred stock) and exercises the warrant to buy another bond (or preferred stock) with similar terms as the surrendered one.

Detachable warrants are securities with contractual features similar to options that provide the right to purchase securities (*call warrant*) or the right to sell a security (*put warrant*). But they are also derivatives because they generate their values from the variability of changes in the underlying price of the security that warrants the right to purchase. The writer or issuer of a warrant has the obligation to perform should the holder decide to exercise the warrant when it is submitted in response to a subscription invitation by the issuer. Exercising warrants depends on the type of right the warrant conveys. Warrant contracts that give the holder the right to purchase an asset (a stock, a bond, or a commodity) are more like call options, and warrants that give the holder the right to sell an asset are more like put options. Like options, warrants provide the holder the opportunity to gain from exposure to the volatility of the underlying asset price while avoiding exposure to losses—i.e., as with options, the holder of the warrant bears only the upside risk and cannot lose more than the initial premium paid.

Although warrants are option-like securities, they differ from options in some key features. Exhibit 5.6 outlines the similarities and differences.

## Exhibit 5.6 Options and Warrants: Similarities and Differences

| *Similarities* | *Differences* |
|---|---|
| • Have an exercise price.<br>• Pre-specified expiry date.<br>• Could be in-the-money, at-the-money, or out-of-the-money.<br>• Both derive their values from the price volatility of the underlying asset.<br>• Both are valued by using any of the option valuation models—e.g., Black-Scholes or the Binomial model. | • Options are standardized in form, trading and settlement.*<br>• Warrants are self-tailored with the terms being set by the issuer.<br>• Warrants are issued for longer terms than options.<br>• Warrants are securities, but options are (executory) contracts.<br>• Exercising a warrant means issuing a new stock (or bond, depending on the type of warrant), while exercising options does not entail new issuance.<br>• The valuation of warrants is subject to a dilution factor due to issuing new shares.<br>• Warrants are traded on stock exchanges but options are traded on specialized exchanges. |

* There are forms of customized options.

See Exhibit 5.7.

## Exhibit 5.7 Flexible (Unstandardized) Options

While most books in finance and accounting talk about exchange-traded options as "standardized" derivative contracts, strictly speaking that is not always the case. Not all options are standardized. At least two classes of flexible options could be cited:

1. Caps, Floors, and Collars: As discussed in the Information Log on exotic options, these are negotiated interest rate options that are viewed as sequential European-style options. The terms, duration and frequency of settlements are generally customized to the contracting parties' needs. Caps and floors could have as long a maturity as ten years. Caps, Floors, and Collars are traded over the counter.
2. FLEX Options (FLEX®): Although most books in finance and accounting talk about options as "standardized" derivative contracts, strictly speaking that is not true. The Chicago Board of Options Exchange introduced FLEX Options in 1993. FLEX Options are negotiated (customized) contracts that can be denominated in any amount and have maturity dates that could extend to a 15-year period.

   FLEX Options are the only listed options that allow users to select option contract terms. Users may specify any of the following terms:

   1. The **underlying Index** (e.g., S&P 100, S&P 500, Nasdaq 100, Russell 2000 or Dow Jones Industrial Average Indices).
   2. **Option Type** – Call or Put.
   3. **Expiration Date** – Up to 15 years from creation. The expiration date specified must be a business day.
   4. **Strike Price** – May be specified as an index level, as a percentage, a numerical deviation from a closing index level or an intra-day value level, or any other readily understood method for deriving an index level, rounded to the nearest hundredth of an index point (e.g., 1440.27).
   5. **Exercise Style** – American or European, AM or PM, except as follows: If the expiration specified falls on the third Friday of the month (or the first preceding business day if the third Friday is a holiday), only European-style exercise is permitted.
   6. **Settlement Value** – Settlement may be based on either the opening settlement value or closing settlement value (see "Creating a FLEX Options" section for details). Exercise (assignment) will result in the delivery (payment) of cash on the business day following expiration.

   (Source: https://www.cboe.com/Institutional/IndexFlex.aspx)

In this sense, FLEX Options are more like forward contracts in flexibility and customization, but differ from forward contracts in several respects:

a. *Scope: FLEX®* contracts are written in equity indexes such as the S&P 100, S&P 500, Nasdaq 100, Russell 2000 or the Dow Jones Industrial Average Indices.
b. *Trading: FLEX®* Options are currently traded on the Internet (since 2007 after reaching an agreement in 2006 with Stockholm-based Cinnober Financial Technology to use Cinnober electronic trading technology) while continuing to utilize over-the-counter (OTC) platform.
c. *Margins: Index FLEX® Options* are generally subject to the same customer margin rules that apply to conventional listed index options, and are eligible for portfolio margining accounts.
d. *Credit Risk Exposure:* Exposure to counterparty credit risk is minimal because *FLEX®* contracts are option contracts with CBOE and are guaranteed by the Options Clearing Corporations.
e. *Price Discovery:* It is an auction-style—the customer submits a request for quote (RFQ) to the Exchange which it in turn disseminates to traders on the system, and then communicates the response back to the customer.

(Source: https://www.cboe.com/Institutional/IndexFlex.aspx)

**Accounting Implications**
Two of the important implications are:

1. Prices of FLEX Options are more transparent than the values of forwards. Therefore, estimating the fair value of a portfolio or a position in FLEX Options would be more reliable (would possibly be using Level 1 or Level 2 of the Fair Value Measurement hierarchy instead of Level 3).
2. Using Equity Index and settling net accounting for a hedging relationship using FLEX Options requires more special care.

## Exhibit 5.8 Two Examples of Selling Warrants

**1. General Motors**

Shortly after General Motors filed for bankruptcy ..., General Motors Corporation changed its name to Motors Liquidation Company and NewCo changed its name to General Motors Company. As a result of the sale transaction and the subsequent name changes, bondholders of former General Motors Corporation became bondholders of Motors Liquidation Company, whose primary assets were the stock and warrants in General Motors Company received in the sale transaction.

In Form 8-K that GM filed prior to issuing the warrants, the proposed settlement states:

**U.S. Treasury 363 Sale Proposal**

[...]

***Warrants***

*Old GM Warrant 1*

- Old GM to receive warrants to acquire newly issued shares of New GM equal to 7.5% of New GM common equity outstanding at closing, exercisable at any time prior to the seventh anniversary of issuance, with an exercise price set at the share price that would equate to an aggregate equity value of $15 billion based on the shares outstanding at closing, fully diluted for the issuance of such warrants

*Old GM Warrant 2*

- Old GM to receive warrants to acquire newly issued shares of New GM equal to 7.5% of New GM common equity outstanding at closing, exercisable at any time prior to the tenth anniversary of issuance, with an exercise price set at the share price that would equate to an aggregate equity value of $30 billion based on the shares outstanding at closing, fully diluted for the issuance of such warrants

*New VEBA Warrant*

- New VEBA [Voluntary Employees Beneficiary Association] to receive warrants to acquire newly issued shares of New GM equal to 2.5% of New GM common equity outstanding at December 31, 2009, exercisable at any time prior to December 31,

2015, with an exercise price set at the share price that would equate to an aggregate equity value of $75 billion based on the shares outstanding at issuance of the warrants, fully diluted for the issuance of such warrants.

(Source: SEC Form 8-K, May 28, 2009. Available at: http://www.sec.gov/Archives/edgar/data/40730/000119312509119940/d8k.htm)

2. An Example of Warrant Subscription at London Stock Exchange

| | |
|---|---|
| **Company** | Transense Technologies PLC |
| **TIDM** | TRT |
| **Headline** | Proposed Fundraising |
| **Released** | 07:00 21-Nov-2011 |
| **Number** | 4175S07 |

RNS Number: 4175S
Transense Technologies PLC
21 November 2011

**Transense Technologies plc (the "Company")**
The Company is pleased to announce a proposed Fundraising to raise up to approximately £2.54 million (before expenses) by way of an Offer made to Eligible Warrantholders.

**Key Points**

- Warrants are exercisable at 4.5 pence but with an entitlement to one Bonus Share for every two Warrants exercised during the Offer Period. The Bonus Share will be issued free of payment.
- The Company has already received irrevocable commitments from certain Warrantholders to subscribe under the Offer for 15,243,769 Subscription Shares resulting in gross proceeds to the Company of £685,970.
- The net proceeds of the Fundraising will be used to further develop the Company's strategy, and in particular to accelerate the pace at which it addresses the opportunities arising within the IntelliSAW division, and for general working capital purposes.
- The Offer is conditional in all respects on Shareholders passing the Shareholder Resolutions at the General Meeting and the Warrantholders passing the Warrantholder Resolution at the Warrantholder Meeting.
- A circular will be sent tomorrow to Shareholders and Warrantholders setting out the details of the proposed Fundraising, which is being put to Shareholders in a General Meeting and to Warrantholders in a Warrantholder Meeting, both convened for 15 December 2011.
- If the Offer is not fully subscribed or the Offer does not proceed, the authorities being sought from Shareholders and Warrantholders at the Meetings to implement the Offer may at the discretion of the Board be used to effect a placing of new Ordinary Shares to new and existing shareholders for up to an aggregate of £2.54 million on terms overall no more favourable than those being offered to Warrantholders under the Offer. The decision as to whether or not to proceed with a Placing has yet to be taken by the Directors and any Placing will not be underwritten.

(Source: http://www.londonstockexchange.com/exchange/news/market-news/market-news-detail.html?announcementId=11039365)

### 5.3.2 Valuation of Warrants

Warrants are valued using one of the option valuation models. However, warrants and options differ in one key feature: exercising a stock option does not require the company to issue new shares, but exercising warrants through the company's own subscription plans often requires issuing new shares. Holders of stock warrants will exercise the warrants only if they are in-the-money. This means that a warrantholder pays an exercise price below the market value of the underlying stock, yet the new shareholders will have the same voting and cash rights as all other equity holders (of the same class of stock), which dilutes the rights of other shareholders.

The Chief Accountant of the SEC has made it clear that the Binomial model is preferred over the Black-Scholes model for the valuation of warrants due to the flexibility in accommodating various specialized features. Exhibit 5.9 is a news report of the Chief Accountant's speech.

## Exhibit 5.9 A News Report about the SEC's Preference for the Binomial Option Valuation Model

**SEC Frowns on Black-Scholes**
By Susan Kelly | April 1, 2011

The Securities and Exchange Commission is cracking down on companies that use the Black-Scholes formula to value complicated warrants in an effort to get them to switch to more sophisticated methods.

The problem comes when companies rely on Black-Scholes to value warrants that can be exercised early or have provisions like a down round feature that protects investors in case the company goes out to raise additional funds, says Tony Alfonso, president of BDO Valuation Advisors.

[...]

"Where the SEC has come out is cautioning folks that you cannot use Black-Scholes for that," he [Alfonso] says. "You have to use an open-form model, either a lattice model, binomial, or a Monte Carlo simulation."

Companies that use Black-Scholes for valuing such warrants may find themselves on the receiving end of a comment letter from SEC staff, Alfonso says.

A slide from a speech last December by Wayne Carnall, ... "There may be multiple embedded features or the features of the bifurcated derivatives may be so complex that a Black-Scholes valuation does not consider all of the terms of the instrument. Therefore, the fair value may not be appropriately captured by simple models."

The slide goes on to note, "The staff frequently finds that errors in this area are the result of companies not carefully considering and evaluating the accounting implications of provisions of their agreement at the time they are negotiating them or when the transaction is completed."

[...]

Alfonso says there's no one answer as to how the value of a warrant or other instrument produced by the lattice model or another more sophisticated method will compare with the valuation using Black-Scholes. "I've seen a 100% change in value and I've seen some examples where the change in value was nominal," he says. "The reason we can't answer that definitively is that all these warrant terms are different, there's not really a homogenous deal."

(Source: http://www.treasuryandrisk.com/2011/04/01/sec-frowns-on-blackscholes)

### 5.3.3 Examples of Annual Report Disclosures of Warrants

Exhibit 5.10 presents a valuation of detachable warrants issued with preferred stock offerings by MidSouth Bank.

## Exhibit 5.10 Valuation of Detachable Warrants—MidSouth Bank

***Detachable Warrants Issued with Preferred Stock***

As part of the original offering of Series 2009A Preferred Stock, for every five shares of Series 2009A Preferred Stock purchased, a stockholder receives one detachable warrant which provides the stockholder the ability to purchase one share of common stock. The purchase price for the common stock shares from these warrants is equal to 75% of the fully converted book value of the Bank's common stock as of the previous quarter-end date. For each recipient, the warrants received are required to be exercised by March 31, 2016. At that time the warrants will expire. During 2011, there were 965 warrants exercised. During 2010, there were 121,901 warrants issued and 1,380 warrants exercised. During 2009, there were 83,038 warrants issued. There were 202,594, 203,559 and 83,038 warrants outstanding as of December 31, 2011, 2010 and 2009, respectively. As of December 31, 2011, 2010 and 2009, each Series 2009A detachable warrant had a fair value of $0.03 per share, $0.06 per share and $0.07 per share, respectively. The fair value of the detachable warrants that were issued in tandem with the Series 2009A Preferred Stock was determined to be approximately $30,000, $61,000 and $29,000 at December 31, 2011, 2010 and 2009, respectively.

In addition, as part of the offering of Series 2011-A Preferred Stock, for every five shares of Series 2011-A Preferred Stock purchased, the stockholder received one detachable warrant which provided the stockholder the ability to purchase one share of common stock. The purchase price for the common stock shares from these warrants is equal to 85% of the fully converted book value of the Bank's common stock as of the previous quarter-end date (unaudited). The exercise price cannot, however, exceed $11.00 per share or be less than $2.75 per share. The exercise price for these warrants as of December 31, 2011 was $3.55 per share based on a fully converted book value of $4.18 as of December 31, 2011. For each recipient, the warrants received are required to be exercised by May 31, 2017. At that time the warrants will expire. A total of 48,469 warrants were issued with the Series 2011-A Preferred Stock, and through December 31, 2011, none of those warrants have been exercised. As of December 31, 2011 and 2010, each Series 2011-A detachable warrant had a fair value of $0.04 per share for both dates. The fair value of the detachable warrants that were issued in tandem with the Series 2011-A Preferred Stock was determined to be approximately $9,000 at December 31, 2011.

The fair value of both series of the detachable warrants as of December 31, 2011 was estimated using the Black-Scholes warrant pricing model and the following assumptions:

| | *Series 2009A Warrants* | *Series 2011-A Warrants* |
|---|---|---|
| Risk-free interest rate | 1.09% | 1.09% |
| Expected life of warrants | 4.25 years | 5.42 years |
| Expected dividend yield | 0.00% | 0.00% |
| Expected volatility | 15% | 15% |

As of December 31, 2011, each Series 2009A detachable warrant had a fair value of $0.03 per share. The fair value of the Series 2009A Preferred Stock and the fair value of the detachable warrants were summed, and the carrying amounts for the Series 2009A Preferred Stock and the detachable warrants were calculated based on an allocation of the two fair value components. The aggregate fair value result for both the Series 2009A Preferred Stock outstanding and the related detachable warrants was calculated to be $5,114,000, with 0.6% of this aggregate total allocated to the detachable warrants and 99.4% allocated to the Series 2009A Preferred Stock. As a result of this allocation, the detachable warrants had a fair value of $31,000, and the Series 2009A Preferred Stock had a fair value of $5,083,000 as of December 31, 2011.

As of December 31, 2011, each Series 2011-A detachable warrant had a fair value of $0.04 per share. The fair value of the Series 2011-A Preferred Stock and the fair value of the detachable warrants were summed, and the carrying amounts for the Series 2011-A Preferred Stock and the detachable warrants were calculated based on an allocation of the two fair value components. The aggregate fair value result for both the Series 2011-A Preferred Stock and the related detachable warrants was calculated to be $1,333,000, with 0.7% of this aggregate total allocated to the detachable warrants and 99.3% allocated to the Series 2011-A Preferred Stock. As a result of this allocation, the detachable warrants had a fair value of $9,000, and the Series 2011-A Preferred Stock had a fair value of $1,324,000 as of December 31, 2011.

(Source: Form 10-K 2011, pp. F50–F51. Available at: http://www.midsouthbanking.com/wp-content/uploads/2012/11/MSB2011-10K.pdf)

## 5.4 Swap Contracts

A swap contract entails an exchange of two different streams of cash flows between two parties; it is a specialized type of promissory note in which each party to the contract promises delivery of goods or cash flow to the counterparty in exchange for other goods or cash from the counterparty. In one sense, swap agreements are not new; they are a complex form of bartering that has existed for hundreds of years and continues to be practiced in many parts of the world. However, the modern forms of swaps differ in complexity, features, risk, transferability, and impact on society.

In the current economic environment, swap contracts are used extensively for both hedging and speculation, especially in currency and interest rate markets. The practitioners of finance and financial economists continue to invent and develop swap contracts of increasing complexity, and accountants are left with the task of finding ways to account for them in order to reflect the enterprise activities in mitigating risk. Because swap contracts are traded over-the-counter, and because of the unusually powerful lobby of financial institutions, there is no disclosure or transparency of any kind—transactions, volume or prices.[15] While it is difficult to understand how markets could function efficiently without information, accountants face a different dilemma in that they have to establish fair values for swap contracts. It is clear that Level 1 of the Fair Value Hierarchy could not be implemented and the best that anyone could do is to use Level 2, if not go all the way down to Level 3 where management assumptions dominate the process. The outcome differences are not easy to comprehend because the volume of over-the-counter derivatives (mostly swap contracts) is in the hundreds of trillions of dollars.[16]

To show the extent to which financial institutions are involved in interest rate swaps, Table 5.2 presents some selected examples from JPMorgan Chase (USA), Barclays (UK), and General Electric (USA).[17]

**Table 5.2** Reported Statistics on Derivatives Activities for Three Companies

| | *JP Morgan Chase(a)* | *Barclays, PLC (b)* | *GE (c)* |
|---|---|---|---|
| Total notional amount of financial derivatives of which $63 Trillion are Interest Rate Contracts | $78 Trillion | | |
| The derivatives receivable before netting. | $1,520 Billion | £1,100 Billion | $11.4 Billion |
| The derivatives receivable after netting. | $80 Billion | N/A | $7.5 Billion |
| The derivatives payable before netting. | $1,481 Billion | £1,006 Billion | $6.7 Billion |
| The derivatives payable after netting. | $69 Billion | N/A | $2.8 Billion |
| Derivatives Impact on Net Income | $1,069 Billion | £808 Billion N/A | |

Sources:
(a) 2011 Form 10-K (p. 190) http://sec.gov/Archives/edgar/data/19617/000001961712000163/corp10k2011.htm
(b) 2011 Annual Report. http://www.annualreports.com/HostedData/AnnualReports/PDF/barc2011.pdf
(c) 2010 Form 10-K

The unimaginable size of the market has come into existence only in recent decades[1].

1 Modern development of swap contracts started with an unintentional move by the World Bank and IBM. In 1981 the World Bank and IBM swapped Swiss Francs for U.S. Dollars to fit the financing needs of each at low cost. The idea of swap contracts has evolved ever since but gained significant momentum by the repeal of the Bucket Shop law on December 21, 2000 which allowed companies to essentially speculate without regulatory constraints or oversight.

## 5.4.1 Interest Rate Swaps

### *5.4.1.1 Fixed-for-Floating Swaps*

The simplest type of swap is a contract in which one party promises: (1) to pay a counterparty an amount of cash equal to a specified fixed interest rate times a specified principal (notional) amount, and (2) to receive from the counterparty an amount of cash equal to a specified benchmark rate of interest times the same principal (notional) amount. This description portrays cash flow in both directions, but typically what happens is to settle net by exchanging the difference in cash flow periodically. The benchmark rate is market determined and is, therefore, time dependent or floating. This type of contract is known as a plain vanilla swap or "fixed-for-floating" interest rate swap. The two sides of the swap or exchange of interest are known as the "fixed-rate leg" and the "floating-rate leg." A simple example is shown in Figure 5.6.

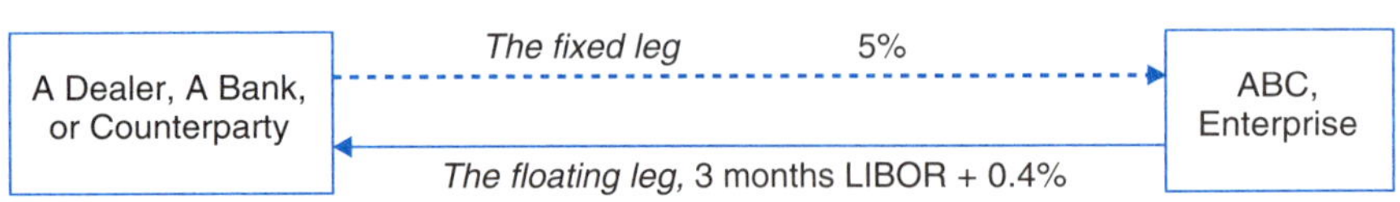


**Figure 5.6** Basic Plain Vanilla Interest Rate Swap

In this example, ABC, Inc. agrees with a dealer (counterparty) to swap interest payments: ABC, Inc. receives 5% fixed-rate and pays LIBOR + 0.4% variable rate. In this example, the benchmark rate is LIBOR. The notional amount is $100 million.[19] The terms of the swap are as follows: (a) three-year duration; (b) settling net every three months; and (c) resetting the floating rate of interest at each settlement. The notional amount is not exchanged (except for some currency swaps); it is the basis upon which the amounts of interest payments are calculated. The notional amount could be the number of dollars, bushels, tons or other relevant indicators that, jointly with the specified interest rate, determine the dollar amount of interest of each leg.

There are a few critical elements of this type of contract:

- The enterprise, ABC, Inc., may enter into this contract for trading and profit-making purposes. As such, it will be an investment like "trading securities" and would be accounted for in a similar manner—i.e., valued at fair value with the changes flow through earnings.
- The enterprise may enter into this contract for hedging purposes.
  - The hedge might not qualify for hedge accounting (in conformance with the qualification criteria explicated in Chapter Six). In this case, the hedge would be called an "economic hedge" and has the same accounting treatment as trading securities.
  - The hedge might qualify for hedge accounting (in conformance with the qualification criteria explicated in Chapter Six). In this case, a decision has to be made on the "type" of hedge as to whether it is a hedge of the risk of change in value or the risk of exposure to cash flow volatility and to account for it accordingly (see Chapters Seven through Eleven).

As detailed in the segment below on valuation of swap contracts, the rates of an interest rate swap are typically set such that the present value of the swap contract at inception is zero. That is, the present value of payments for the fixed leg equals the present value of payments for the floating leg at the start of the agreement.

### *5.4.1.2 Benefits of Interest Rate Swaps*

Other than profit making from trading derivatives, this type of contract came to being for several reasons ranging from improving liquidity to reducing financing cost.[20] These reasons vary in their economic substance and performance consequences. In this respect, the next section presents a discussion of two relevant factors.

### *5.4.1.3 Reducing Exposure to Unwanted Risk*

As discussed in Chapter Two, exposure to interest rate risk involves the following:

1. Uncertainty about future cash flow payments or receipts for variable-rate financial instrument. This uncertainty is reflected in probable volatility of cash flows related to that instrument—variability of cash outflow for debtors and of cash inflow for investors.
2. For fixed-interest rate debt, debtors bear an opportunity cost by sacrificing the possibility of paying lower interest when interest rates in the marketplace decline. Conversely, investors in

fixed-rate debt incur opportunity costs by not earning higher interest income when the interest rate in the marketplace increases. Because the cash flow required to service the fixed-rate financial instrument does not change when market rates change, this opportunity cost is reflected in changing the fair value of the debt. As discussed in Chapter Three, fair value increases with the decline in market rates, and decreases with the increase in market rates.

Volatility of cash flows is not limited to interest-bearing instruments. Changes in commodity prices of anticipated purchase or sale of products (e.g., corn, oil, gold, copper, coffee, etc.) are externally determined price "indexes" and the entity does not control them. Similarly, if lease contract payments are pegged to some index, they expose the lessor and the lessees to volatility of future cash flow as lease payments change with changes in the index.

This same implication applies to fixed-price commitments that are firmed up. For example, a fixed-price purchase contract agreed upon between a supplier and a wholesaler obligates both parties to honor the contractual commitment irrespective of price changes in the marketplace. If subsequent to signing the agreement, market prices increase, there is an opportunity loss to the supplier and gain to the buyer, and vice versa. This type of contract is an executory contract for which accounting standards do not allow recording values. However, either or both of the contracting parties may elect to hedge the anticipated loss that might arise from price changes. In this case, the hedge and the executory contract will be subject to the special standards of hedge accounting as is discussed in Chapter Seven.

## Accounting Log

It will be noted in Chapter Six that identifying the specific risk being managed is essential for purposes of determining the appropriate accounting. Hedge accounting requires documentation to show that the derivative instrument contract entered into for hedging purposes must be explicitly related to the risk being hedged. Under current accounting standards (as of December 2012), this documentation must be done both prospectively (i.e., *ex-ante*) and retrospectively (i.e., *ex-post*) at least quarterly (every reporting period). There are few exceptions to this general statement when using what is called the short-cut method or critical terms match.

### *5.4.1.4 Reducing Financing Cost: Qualified Spread Differential*

When two parties face different borrowing costs, the spread between fixed and floating rates can be significant. This differential is referred to as QSD (qualified spread differential) and both parties can reduce their financing costs if they would agree to share this QSD.

To illustrate, assume that two different companies have different credit risk ratings and, as a consequence, face different borrowing costs even though they may be operating in the same capital market. Company XYZ Unlimited, Inc. has higher creditworthiness (lower credit risk) than ABC, Inc., and could therefore obtain financing at a borrowing cost lower than ABC, Inc. Assume further that the cost of obtaining external funding available to these two companies is as shown in Table 5.3.

**Table 5.3** Borrowing Rates Available to XYZ Unlimited, Inc. and ABC, Inc.

| | *Variable Rate* | *Fixed Rate* |
|---|---|---|
| XYZ Unlimited, Inc. | LIBOR + 0.2% | 9% |
| ABC, Inc. | LIBOR + 0.9% | 10.70% |
| Qualified Spread | (0.70%) | (1.70%) |

If both firms borrow funds using floating-rate instruments, ABC, Inc. would pay 0.7% or 70 basis points higher than XYZ Unlimited, Inc. Alternatively, if both firms borrow debt at fixed rate, ABC, Inc. would pay 1.70% or 170 basis points higher than XYZ Unlimited, Inc. The fixed-rate option, therefore, is more costly to ABC, Inc. The net difference between the floating-rate and fixed-rate options is called Qualified Spread Differential (QSD) and, in this case, it is

QSD = (1.7%) – (0.7%) = 1.00%

The management of both firms might know this information and could be willing to discuss sharing QSD. This means that one enterprise borrows from capital markets at the fixed rate available to it, while the other party borrows also from the market at the floating rate available to it, then both parties make arrangements to exchange (swap) interest payments. To know which party should borrow at what rate from capital markets, let us compare the total cost for each combination of a fixed rate for one firm and a floating for the other.

Given the above information, there are two possible paths from which the management of the two companies could choose. For Path A: XYZ Unlimited, Inc. borrows from capital markets at fixed rate, while ABC, Inc. borrows from capital markets at a floating rate. For Path B: XYZ Unlimited, Inc. borrows at a floating rate, while ABC, Inc. borrows at a fixed rate. These two paths are presented in Exhibit 5.11.

## Exhibit 5.11 The Two Possible Paths if One Firm Borrows at Fixed Interest Rate and the Other Borrows at Floating Interest Rates

| | Variable (Floating) Rate | Fixed Rate |
|---|---|---|
| XYZ Unlimited, Inc. | LIBOR + 0.2% | 9% |
| ABC, Inc. | LIBOR + 0.9 | 10.70% |
| Qualified Spread | (0.70%) | (1.70%) |

Taking Path A, the two entities' combined cost is = LIBOR + 9.9%

Taking Path B, the two entities' combined cost is = LIBOR + 10.9%

Path A

Path B

If the two enterprises act as if they were a "community," taking Path A is less costly than taking Path B by annual rate of 1.0%, which is the QSD. But Path B, although more costly, is consistent with the expectations of both managements. In particular, the management of XYZ Unlimited, Inc. predicts an inverted yield curve, suggesting the likelihood of future decline in market interest rate (i.e., lower LIBOR). Based on this prediction, the management of XYZ Unlimited, Inc. prefers to borrow at a floating rate that is indexed to LIBOR. In contrast, the management of ABC, Inc. based its estimation of the behavior of interest rates on a yield curve constructed under different assumptions and projected a normal (upward sloping) yield curve, suggesting a future increase in LIBOR. To avoid making higher interest payments in the future should their expectations materialize, ABC, Inc. prefers to borrow at a fixed interest rate.

To obtain financing at the lower cost and in the meantime have cash flow commitments consistent with their expectations, managements of the entities agree to take two steps:

1. XYZ Unlimited, Inc. borrows from capital markets at the 9% fixed rate available to it, and ABC, Inc. borrows from capital markets at the rate of LIBOR +0.90 that is available to it.
2. XYZ Unlimited, Inc. and ABC, Inc. enter into a bilateral agreement in which they agree to swap interest payments as follows: XYZ Unlimited, Inc. would pay ABC at LIBOR and receive 9.3%, while ABC, Inc. would pay XYZ Unlimited, Inc. 9.3% and receive LIBOR.

These two steps are presented in Figure 5.7. XYZ Unlimited, Inc. has therefore succeeded in converting a fixed-rate commitment into a floating rate of LIBOR – 0.30%.

[(9.00% – 9.30%) + LIBOR] = LIBOR – 0.30%

Compared with the floating rate available to XYX Unlimited, Inc. in the marketplace, the cost of funds is 0.5% below its open-market rate equals

[(LIBOR + 0.2%]) – [LIBOR – 0.3%]) = 0.50%

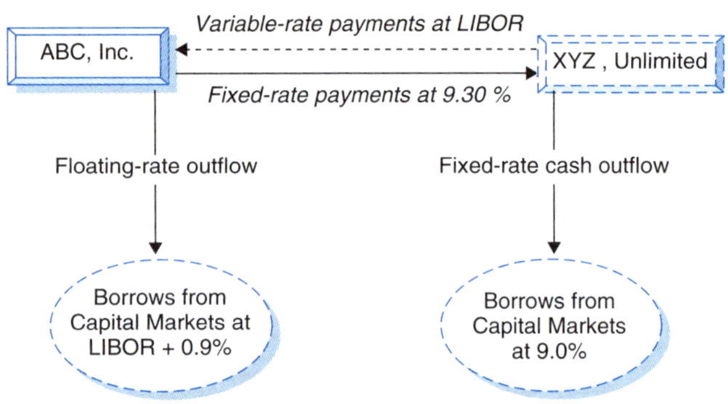


**Figure 5.7** Interest Rate Swap to Hedge Two Different Types of Debt

A Summary of the Debt and Swap Contracts showing the Net Borrowing Cost

| *Companys name* | | *XYZ Unlimited, Inc.* | *ABC, Inc.* |
|---|---|---|---|
| Borrowing cost from capital market (cash outflow for interest payments on the debt) | | 9.0% | LIBOR + 0.9% |
| Swap Contract | Receive (Cash inflow) | 9.3% | LIBOR |
| | Pay (Cash outflow) | LIBOR | 9.3% |
| Net cash outflow for interest payments | | LIBOR – 0.3% | 10.2% |

*A follow up note*: equal sharing of the qualified differential advantage in the manner described above is economically advantageous to both counterparties. However, interest rate swaps do not always achieve this outcome because, in reality, both parties contract with a dealer, not with one another.

By entering into the swap contract, XYZ Unlimited, Inc. is able to obtain funding at a floating rate of 0.50% below what is available to it in the marketplace.

For ABC, Inc. the management is able to convert a floating rate into a fixed rate, which is consistent with its strategy and expectations. The company also saves on the cost of debt because the net cost for ABC, Inc. is:

- + LIBOR to receive from XYZ for the swap contract.
- –9.3% to pay to XYZ for the swap contract.
- –(LIBOR + 0.9%) to pay to market for borrowing at the floating rate available to XYZ.
- Equals –10.20% is the net cost of financing.

Notice that the 10.20% is 0.50% lower than the fixed rate available to it from capital markets.

Three additional factors will determine the dollar amounts of interest payments that will exchange hands in accordance with the swap contract.

1. The *notional* amount upon which the interest is calculated may or may not be the same as the amount of the loans that either XYZ Unlimited, Inc. or ABC, Inc. has actually borrowed from capital markets.
2. The level of the *benchmark* rate (LIBOR) varies with macroeconomic conditions and with the supply of, and demand for funds.
3. The *mode of settlement* could be physical delivery or net. In reality, these types of plain vanilla swap contracts are typically net settled by exchanging the net difference between contractual interest rates of the swap.

## Accounting Log

While an interest rate swap contract is a single document between two parties, we will find out later that the swap contract creates two different rights and obligations for the two counterparties. As a result, each party to the contract applies different accounting treatment. Under both IFRS and U.S. GAAP, the enterprise ABC, Inc. will account for the swap as a "Cash Flow Hedge," while XYZ Unlimited, Inc. will account for it as a "fair value hedge," provided that each entity satisfies specific criteria (see Chapters Six, Seven and Eight).

### *5.4.1.5 Determining Initial Value of Plain Vanilla Swap Contracts*

As a general rule, the valuation of interest rate swaps follows the basic principle of valuation: the value of a swap contract is the present value of the expected net cash flow. In a single-currency interest rate swap, the cash flow exchanged between parties entails exchanging interest payments only; the principal, *notional or face amount is not exchanged*.[21] However, for simplification, it is convenient to think of the periodic net settlement of a swap contract as if it is a zero-coupon bond.[22]

A zero-coupon bond is a bond or a financial instrument that does not make periodic or other type of payments until maturity when the principal and the compounded interest are redeemed at once. A zero-coupon bond could be quoted at a discount off its face value and the full face value is redeemed at retirement. This is the case, for example, of the U.S. Treasury Bills. Alternatively, a zero-coupon bond could be quoted at the present value of face value plus the compounded interest up to the time of the quote. The zero-coupon curve is a market-wide representation of the yield charged in the marketplace for zero-coupon bonds. There is a zero-coupon curve for different levels of risk—e.g., Treasury Bills, AAA bond rating, A bond rating, etc.

Because a zero-coupon bond represents a reinvestment of the interest on the bond, the yield to maturity implicit in a zero-coupon bond is different for different durations. The zero-coupon yield curve for Treasury Bills is used as a risk-free rate benchmark. Risk adjustments are added to this term structure to obtain the zero-coupon curve for different grades of risky assets.

The variable rates on interest rate swaps are reset periodically—e.g., every quarter. However, in introducing the concept we will assume that the swap floating rates are reset once a year. Periodic swap payments can then be viewed as a series of payments of zero-coupon bonds. For a three-year interest rate swap, for example, the rates to be used for discounting future cash flow payments would be as follows:

- First-year cash flow (the amount of interest of the swap leg) is like a zero-coupon bond with one-year duration. Its value would be the expected cash flow at year end discounted at the rate of a one-year zero-coupon bond.
- Second-year cash flow (the amount of interest of the swap leg) would be like a zero-coupon bond with two-year duration. Its value would be the expected cash flow at the end of two years discounted at the compounded second-year rate.
- Third-year cash flow (the amount of interest of the swap leg) would be like a zero-coupon with three-year duration. Its value would be the expected cash flow at the end of two years discounted at the compounded third-year rate.

The data on the zero-coupon yield curve for several classes of risk are publicly available from many public agencies and private sources. For example, Figure 5.8 shows the quarterly U.S. zero-coupon bond rate for the ten-year period that ended April 2011. The data were compiled by *Reuters* and published by the *European Central Bank*. Figure 5.9 provides similar data obtained from Bloomberg for one year ended November 2011. It should be noted that for the year of 2011, it appears we had an inverted zero-coupon curve.

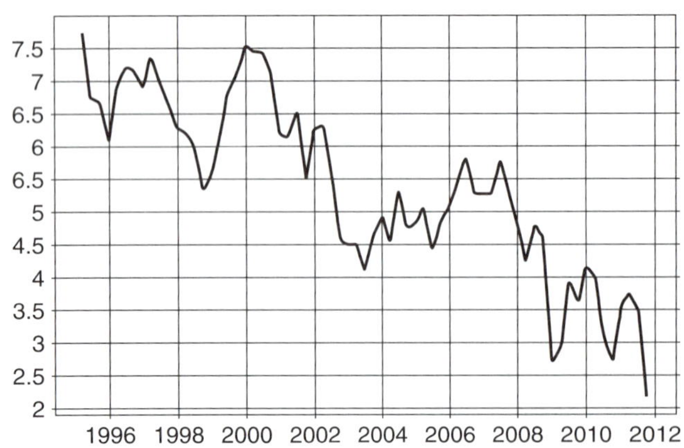


**Figure 5.8** U.S. Zero-Coupon 10-Year Yield Curve (European Central Bank)

(Source: http://sdw.ecb.europa.eu/quickview.do?SERIES_KEY=143.FM.Q.US.USD.RT.BZ.USD10YZ_R.YLDE)

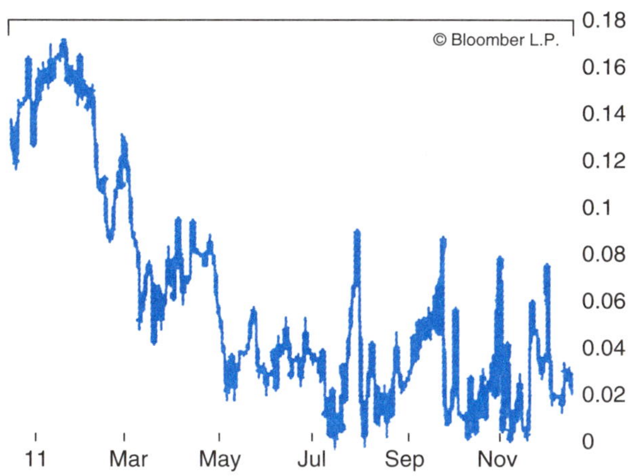


**Figure 5.9** Zero-Coupon Rates of the U.S. Treasury Month by Month for 2011

(Source: http://www.bloomberg.com/apps/quote?ticker=F08203M:IND)

### *5.4.1.6 An Illustration*

A numerical illustration highlights the process of deriving floating and fixed interest rates of swap contract. The illustration is for a case called BB Enterprises which is illustrated in Figure 5.10. On January 1, 20x1, the balance sheet of BB Enterprises has debt in the form of outstanding bonds reported at a book value of $1,000. Assume that the book value is also the face value and the fair value of the bond on that date. The bond pays a fixed annual coupon rate of 7.9%, has a five-year maturity, and (for simplicity) pays the coupon interest once a year.

On January 1, the management concluded that the market interest rate (LIBOR) is highly likely to drop below its current level and if the company has financing flexibility, it could obtain the same financing at a lower interest cost. If the management does not act on this expectation, the opportunity cost will be reflected in higher fair values of the debt. Because increasing the value of debt is a loss to the company, the management decides to find a way to avoid incurring this potential loss.

Refinancing is a costly option due to transaction cost and to being locked in a specific contract for a long time. A low-cost action to restructure the financing of the company is to enter into an interest rate swap agreement with a counterparty (a swap dealer, for example) to receive fixed and pay floating. The fixed-rate interest amounts received from the dealer would be paid to bondholders and the net cost to BB Enterprises would be the floating rate paid to the dealer. This process allows BB Enterprises to convert funding cost from a fixed rate to a variable rate.

The terms of the swap contract between BB Enterprises and the swap dealer are as follows:

- The notional (principal) amount is $1,000 (the two parties know that the principal is *not* exchanged).
- The term of the swap contract is five years.
- For the floating-rate leg, the rate would be LIBOR.
- For the fixed-rate leg, the interest rate would be 7.8%.[23]
- The floating rate is reset once a year.
- The two parties will settle net at year-end by exchanging the difference between the cash flow of the agreed upon fixed rate of interest and the cash flow based on LIBOR.

BB Enterprises now has two financial contracts: the contract of the debt indenture, and the contract for exchanging interest at different rates. This process is illustrated in Figure 5.10.

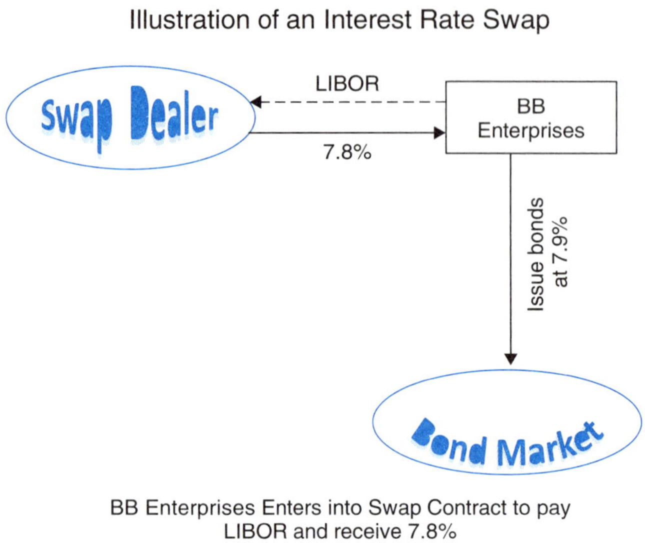


**Figure 5.10** BB Enterprises, Inc. Swap Contract to Hedge Fixed-Rate Debt

## Generating Required Interest Rates

In this segment, we will see how the two parties in the above example, BB Enterprises and the dealer develop the terms of their contract. First, the two parties must agree on the rates for the floating leg of the swap.[24] The floating rate for any period, $t \rightarrow t + 1$ is determined from the zero-coupon yield curve as follows:

$$fR_{t \rightarrow t+1} = [(1 + zR_{t+1})^{t+1} / (1 + zR_t)^t] - 1 \quad \text{(Eq. 5.1)}$$

where

$t$ = the time period, $t = 1, 2, \ldots, T$.
$zR_t$ = the zero-coupon rate for the same risk class at time $t$.
$fR_t$ = the forward-rate at time $t$.
$fR_{t+1}$ = the forward-rate at time $t + 1$.

Panel A of Exhibit 5.12 presents the details of this process for the five-year period.

The second step is to estimate the cash flow that will be generated by the floating-rate leg in each period. The cash flow for period $t \rightarrow t + 1$ is equal to

$$\$fR_{t \rightarrow t+1} = fR_{t \rightarrow t+1} * NP \quad \text{(Eq. 5.2)}$$

where $NP$ is the notional or principal value of the instrument.

Third, we calculate the present value of the cash flow of the floating leg as determined from Equation 5.2. The cash flow is discounted at the compounded zero coupon rate of each period. Panel B of Exhibit 5.12 shows this calculation.

## Exhibit 5.12 Deriving the Floating Rate for the Term of the Swap Using Data of the Illustration of BB Enterprises

### Panel A: Calculation of Forward Rates

| | | | *Zero-Coupon Rate[a] per Period* | | | | |
|---|---|---|---|---|---|---|---|
| | | | $t = 1$ | $t = 2$ | $t = 3$ | $t = 4$ | $t = 5$ |
| Zero-Coupon Rate[a] | | | 0.05 | 0.06 | 0.07 | 0.075 | 0.08 |
| Forward Rates | $fR_{t \to t+1}$ | Calculation of forward rates | | | | | |
| | 5% | $fR_{(0,1)} = 0.05$ | | | | | |
| | 7% | $fR_{(1,2)} = [(1+0.06)^2/(1+0.05)] - 1$ | | | | | |
| | 9% | $fR_{(2,3)} = [(1+0.07)^3/(1+0.06^2] - 1$ | | | | | |
| | 9% | $fR_{(3,4)} = [(1+0.075)^4/(1+0.07)^3] - 1$ | | | | | |
| | 10% | $fR_{(4,5)} = [(1+0.08)^5/(1+0.075)^4] - 1$ | | | | | |

[a] The zero-coupon rate is obtained from the zero-spot curve available in the marketplace for interest rates of zero-coupon bonds of different duration and same risk sector.

$fR_{t \to t+1}$ = is the forward rate for period $t + 1$ measured as $[(1 + zR_{t+1})^{t+1}/(1 + zR_t)^t] - 1$
$zR$ = zero-coupon bond rate.
$t$ = time period of interest accrual (a year, for example).
$T$ = maturity (time to expiration).

### Panel B: Verification of the Imputed Forward Rates

The face value (Notional Principal) times the forward rate should be equal to the market value (fair or present value) of the bond.

$$PV_{fR} = \frac{\$50}{1.05} + \frac{\$70}{(1.06)^2} + \frac{\$90}{(1.07)^3} + \frac{\$90}{(1.075)^4} + \frac{\$100}{(1.08)^5} + \frac{1000}{(1.08)^5} = \$1000$$

where

$PV_{fR}$ = Present value of the cash flow generated by the floating leg.

Fourth, we need to find the fixed rate of interest that would generate periodic cash flow having a present value equal to the present value of the floating-leg cash flow. This is accomplished by solving for $xR$ in the following equation:

$$PV_{fR} = \Sigma_{t=1}^{T}[xR\ */(1 + zR)^t] + NP/(1 + {}_{Z}R)^T \qquad \text{(Eq. 5.3)}$$

where $NP$ stands for Notional Principal.

This calculation is shown in Exhibit 5.13. The fixed rate of interest that would generate a cash flow having the same present value as that of the floating-rate leg is 7.807%.

In Exhibit 5.13, the equation to solve for the fixed rate of interest has the following known components:

- The discount factor based on the discount rate used for each period, which is the inverse of the zero-coupon rate.
- The settlement amount at the terminal period.
- The present value of the stream of cash flow, which is the fair market value.

The only unknown is the periodic amount of cash flow. Since the cash flow in each period for a fixed-rate bond is the product of the fixed interest rate and the face value of the bond, the only real unknown is the fixed rate of interest, *xR*.

The imputed value of *xR* is the fixed rate of return that will generate a constant amount of cash flow for interest payments of the fixed-leg of the swap. The goal of this process so far is to obtain a present value for the fixed leg equal to that of the floating leg of the swap so that the fair value of the swap contract at inception would be zero.[25]

$$\begin{array}{rl} & \text{Present Value of the Fixed-Leg } (PV_{fixed}) \\ - & \text{Present Value of the Floating-Leg } (PV_{floating}) \\ \hline = & \text{Present Value of the Swap Contract } (PV_{swap}) \end{array} \qquad \text{(Eq. 5.4)}$$

## Exhibit 5.13 Deriving the Fixed Rate for the Fixed Leg

$$PV = \frac{xR * NP}{(1+zR_1)} + \frac{xR * NP}{(1+zR_2)^2} + \frac{xR * NP}{(1+zR_3)^3} + \frac{xR * NP}{(1+zR_4)^4} + \frac{xR * NP}{(1+zR_5)^5} + \frac{Notional}{(1+zR_5)^5}$$

$$\$1{,}000 = (xR * \$1{,}000)\left[\frac{1}{1.05} + \frac{1}{(1.06)^2} + \frac{1}{(1.07)^3} + \frac{1}{(1.075)^4} + \frac{1}{(\$1.08)^5}\right] + \frac{\$1{,}000}{(1.08)^5}$$

- The present value of redeeming the Notional Principal $= \frac{\$1{,}000}{(1.08)^5} \approx \$681$.

  (Note: this NP is not paid in advance or redeemed at terminal period. It is used on the assumption that each of the swap legs could be viewed as a bond.)
- $1,000 – $681 = $319.
- Adding up the discount factors and substituting in the present value equation above, we obtain $\$319 = xR * \$1{,}000\ (4.086)$
- Amount of fixed coupon interest $= xR * \$1{,}000 = \$319/4.086 \approx \$78.07$
- The fixed rate $xR = \$78.07/\$1{,}000$
  $= 0.07807$ with rounding errors.

Note: *xR* = fixed-coupon rate
*zR* = zero-coupon rate
*NP* = Notional Principal (Face value)

## Information Log: Basis Swap (Floating-for-Floating) Contracts

The conventional form of plain vanilla swaps is a fixed-for-floating contract. Numerous other types of interest rate contracts exist. One of these types is a contract that hedges "basis risk"; the risk of loss due to adverse change in two reference rates—e.g., 3-month LIBOR vs. 6-month LIBOR, U.S. Federal Funds Rate vs. LIBOR, or LIBOR vs. EURIBOR (European Interbank Offer Rate). See definitions below.

Basis swaps can be used as an instrument for locking in a particular spread or margin between variable interest-bearing assets and variable interest rate liabilities and could qualify for cash flow hedge accounting, provided that the other hedge accounting qualifying criteria are also satisfied. These criteria are detailed in Chapter 6.

Basis interest rate swap in the *same* currency has (a) a notional amount or principal; (b) the notional amounts are not exchanged; (c) reset dates are pre-specified; (d) settlement periods are pre-specified; and (d) the contract maturity is predetermined. Basis interest rate swap in different currencies is discussed in Chapter Eleven.

## Information Log: Definitions of LIBOR and EURIBOR

LIBOR (**L**ondon **I**nter**B**ank **O**ffer **R**ate) is a daily reference rate based on average interest rates under which banks offer unsecured funds to other banks. It is announced daily at 11:00 a.m., London time by the British Bankers Association as the average rate banks offered other banks during the preceding 24 hours. It is comparable to the *Federal Funds Rate* in the U.S.[26]

EURIBOR (European InterBank Offer Rate) is the rate at which European banks offer each other for unsecured loans within the EMU (European Monetary Union) zone.

In a basis swap, for example, one leg may be indexed to LIBOR and the other leg indexed to EURIBOR.

Definitions of four different benchmarks for the EURIBOR can be found at http://www.euribor-ebf.eu/.

### 5.4.2 Commodity Swaps

While interest rate swaps constitute the majority of over-the-counter derivatives market, dealers and investment banks also write commodity swap contracts. These contracts have the same concept and operate in a similar way to interest rate swaps, but there are several significant differences. There is no parallel to the zero-coupon curve structure in commodity prices; commodities are not as fungible as monetary assets and commodity swap contracts must specify a narrowly defined grade of product quality; the valuation of these swaps poses its own challenges; and the liquidity of commodity swap markets is not as high as that of interest rate swaps.

As an example, the Commonwealth Bank of Australia writes swap contracts on nine different agriculture products. The examples presented in Exhibit 5.14 describe the nature of the commodity swap contracts on wool offered by the bank: one form is for consumers and the other is for producers.

## Exhibit 5.14 Commodity Swaps—Wool Swaps Written by Commonwealth Bank of Australia

### Wool swaps for producers

*'I want the security of a fixed price.'*

**Your need**

You are a producer (seller) of wool. You must have certainty for planning and budgeting. You would therefore like to agree on a fixed price now for when you sell your wool in the future.

**Solution**

A wool swap allows you to receive a fixed commodity reference price for wool.

**How it works**

After credit approval, you enter into a wool swap with the Bank. We will calculate the fixed price based on certain factors, such as the current commodity reference price, the pricing date/s, the transaction amount and transaction period.

**Possible outcomes on the pricing date**

- If the commodity reference price is lower than the fixed price, we must pay you the difference between the fixed price and the commodity reference price.
- If the commodity reference price is higher than the fixed price, you must pay us the difference between the fixed price and the commodity reference price.
- If the commodity reference price is equal to the fixed price, you and the Bank will have no further obligations to each other with respect to the wool swap.

**Benefits**

- You receive price protection by fixing the commodity reference price.
- You can determine the transaction amount and pricing date/s.
- The transactions are cash-settled so there is no need to physically deliver wool to the Bank.
- There are no complex exchange-traded brokerage and margin calls.

**Points to consider**

- You cannot benefit if the commodity reference price moves above the fixed price.
- You are not covered for the basis risk, which is the risk arising from entering into a hedge transaction that is not identical with the risk being covered.
- You may have to pay an amount if the wool swap is terminated prior to its scheduled termination date, depending on its mark to market value.

## Wool swaps for consumers

*'I want the security of a fixed price.'*

**Your need**

You are a consumer (buyer) of wool. It is important for you to have certainty for planning and budgeting. You would therefore like to agree on a fixed price now for when you buy your wool at a future date.

**Solution**

A wool swap allows you to pay a fixed commodity reference price for wool.

**How it works**

After credit approval, you enter into a wool swap with the Bank. We will calculate the fixed price based on certain factors, such as the current commodity reference price, the pricing date/s, the transaction amount and transaction period.

**Possible outcomes on the pricing date**

- If the commodity reference price is higher than the fixed price, we must pay you the difference between the fixed price and the commodity reference price.
- If the commodity reference price is lower than the fixed price, you must pay us the difference between the fixed price and the commodity reference price.
- If the commodity reference price is equal to the fixed price, you and the Bank will have no further obligations to each other with respect to the wool swap.

**Benefits**

- You receive price protection by fixing the commodity reference price.
- You can determine the transaction amount and pricing date/s.
- The transactions are cash-settled so there is no need to physically deliver wool to the Bank.
- There are no complex exchange-traded brokerage and margin calls.

**Points to consider**

You cannot benefit if the commodity reference price moves below the fixed price.

You are not covered for the basis risk, which is the risk arising from entering into a hedge transaction that is not identical with the risk being covered.

You may have to pay an amount if the agricultural swap is terminated prior to its scheduled termination date, depending on its mark to market value.

(Source: http://www.commbank.com.au/business/agribusiness/commodities-risk-management/wool/consumer-swaps.aspx)

## Accounting Log

Why should accountants know how to estimate the values of swap contracts?

The volume of interest rate swaps in the USA is astronomically high. For example, JPMorgan Chase had $80 billion of derivative receivables (after master netting) on December 31, 2010, more than 80% of which was interest rate contracts. Even with that type of volume, interest rate swaps are mostly valued at level 2 (using market information other than price quotes of the same asset) or level 3 (using valuation models) because interest rate swaps are traded over the counter (dealer-to-dealer) and prices are not publicly available. In its annual report of 2010, General Electric, for example, states that the majority of level 2 assets are interest rate contracts.

Even the International Swap Dealers Association does not have direct access to trade data (or does not wish to disclose them) and gathers information about swap trades and values by surveying dealers. The lack of transparency of any information about over-the-counter derivatives is very troublesome. From an economics point of view, how could markets operate efficiently without information? From the accounting and auditing point of view, the absence of transparency requires accountants to know how to value these swap contracts.

## 5.5 Forward Contracts

### 5.5.1 Definition and Concepts

A *forward* contract is an agreement between two counterparties in which a buyer agrees to purchase a stated quantity of a commodity (i.e., natural gas, coffee) or instrument (stocks, options, currency) at a pre-stated future price, at a specific time and place. For commodities, the location of delivery (even when physical delivery is not contemplated) is also an important element of a forward contract and of the accounting for it. In general, the contracting parties know:

1. The quantity of the commodity, instrument or currency, which is called the "notional" amount.
2. The nature of settlement, whether physical delivery or, net settled. Net settlement means the two counterparties exchange only the difference between the contracted forward price and the spot (cash) price at maturity.
3. The location and time of delivery. This is an important element in forward contracts for commodities, even when the parties intend to settle net instead of having physical delivery of the commodity because different delivery locations have different transaction cost.[27]
4. The contracted forward price (also known as delivery price) is to be paid at maturity.
5. No cash (or other assets) is exchanged in advance.
6. In general, forward contracts do not require posting collateral or making a security deposit, but the contracting parties could choose to do so.
7. Both parties are obligated to perform—the seller is obligated to deliver the commodities, the instruments, the currency or the object specified in the contract, and the buyer is obligated to accept delivery. This sale and delivery could mean:

   a. actual physical delivery, or
   b. exchanging price differences to settle net.

As a result of these commitments, forward contracts have a double-sided payoff/risk profile; the contracting parties bear both the upside and downside of price risk, similar to the payoff profile of swaps. Figure 5.11 presents two profiles for different outcomes of forward contracts.

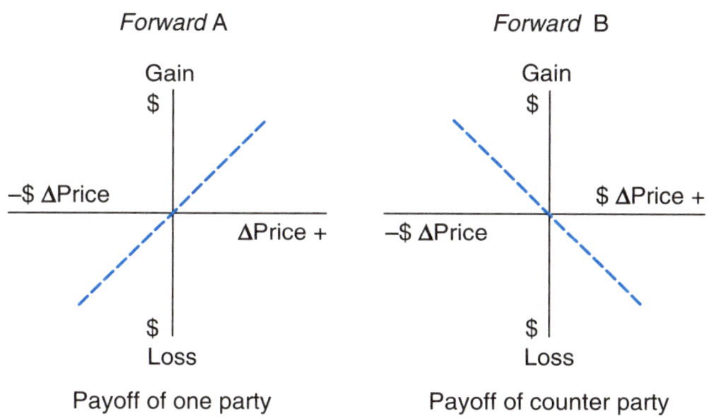


**Figure 5.11** Payoff Profiles of Two Forward Contracts

Forward contracts are not standardized and are customized to meet the needs of both parties to the contract. In general, forward contracts are freestanding instruments, yet they are derivatives because they derive their values from changes in reference prices or indexes.[28]

Typically, the forward price at inception of a forward contract is said to be an arbitrage free contract—i.e., the contractual futures price is equal to the expected or predicted future value of the asset, which is the current spot price at the contract inception plus the cost of financing and the cost of carry (if any, such as in commodity contracts). As a result, a forward contract does not require payment of a premium at inception; it has a value of zero.

## 5.5.2 Valuation of Forward Contracts

*The general concept*: a forward contract premium at any point in time is the present value of future benefits.[29]

For a business enterprise, say Entity A, to enter into a forward contract to sell a (non-perishable) commodity to a counterparty at a future date, both contracting parties determine the forward price based on a set of assumptions:

1. An enterprise or entity that contracts to sell a product at a future date does not necessarily own that product to deliver.
2. The two parties to the contract agree on either physical delivery or settling net.
3. The market is efficient such that there will be no opportunity for arbitrage profits.
4. To set the forward price, traders have to consider the cash price and the cost of carry (financing cost and storage cost) as well as dividends for a dividend-paying instrument.

Given these assumptions, if an entity is to (hypothetically) acquire that product and hold it until delivery time, it will have to finance its acquisition and incur the cost of financing (at an assumed risk-free interest rate).[30]

In addition, if the commodity is non-perishable, the entity will also have to pay the cost of storing it and holding it up to the date of delivery. Therefore, in principle, the price of a commodity forward contract should not (in general) exceed the sum of these three components:

- The spot price of the product.
- The interest cost as a cost of financing that price.
- Cost of carry.

3. More specifically for a financial instrument or a product that is not tangible, that is not generating income, assuming a one-year contract period, the forward price of a commodity forward contract at inception is

$f_{0 \to Td} = S_0\,(1 + r)$, assuming simple interest, or

$f_{0 \to Td} = S_0 e^r$, assuming continuous compounding.

where

$S_0$ = spot price at time $t = 0$.
$r$ = the risk-free interest rate for one year.
$F_{0 \to Td}$ = the forward price at time $t = 0$ (the initiation of the contract), and the time is $T_d$, the delivery time.

The forward price $f_0$ could be thought of as the predicted spot rate at the time of delivery; time $T_d$.[31]

If the forward price is greater than the compounded spot price, i.e., if $f_{0 \to Td} > S_0 e^r$, then profit takers (arbitrageurs) would profit by selling the forward and buying the asset. Similarly, if $f_{0 \to Td} < S_0 e^r$, arbitrageurs will profit by selling the asset and buying the forward. This behavior will continue until the price reaches equilibrium, $f_{0 \to Td} = S_0 e^k$. The contrast between the three conditions is presented in Exhibit 5.15.

## Exhibit 5.15 Impact of Forward Price Deviation from Efficient Pricing

| *Condition if ...* | *Arbitrageurs' behavior* | | *Characteristic* |
|---|---|---|---|
| | *Sell* | *Buy* | |
| $F_{0,T} = S_0 e^{rt}$ | Arbitrageurs are out of the market | Arbitrageurs are out of the market | Equilibrium |
| $F_{0,T} > S_0 e^{rt}$ | Forward contracts on the asset | The asset | Downward pressure on prices of forward<br>Upward pressure on asset prices |
| $F_{0,T} < S_0 e^{rt}$ | The asset | Forward contracts on the asset | Upward pressure on prices of forward<br>Downward pressure on asset prices |

Definitions:
$F_{0,T}$ = The time 0 forward price for delivery at time T.
$S_0$ = The spot (cash) price at time 0.
$e$ = Euler's exponential e.
$r$ = risk-free rate.
$t$ = time period from inception (t = 0) to delivery or terminal time, T.

### 5.5.3 An Illustration of a Commodity Forward Contract

ADM uses agricultural products to produce cattle feed, seed oil, soy, and other products and it fears that an unusually dry season may reduce the harvest yield of soybean leading to higher prices. On October 1, 20x1, ADM decided to enter into a contract with farmers to purchase five million bushels of soybean for delivery on August 1, 20x2. The spot price of soy on October 1, 20x1 is $12.00 a bushel. The risk-free interest rate is 3% per annum and the cost of storing soybeans is 1% a year.

On October 1, 20x1 ($t = 0$), the August 20x2 ($t = T$) forward price of soy is estimated as

$$F_{10/20x1 \to 8/20x2} = \$12.00 * e^{(r+c)*(10/12)}$$

$$f_{10/20x1 \to 8/20x2} = \$12.00 * e^{(0.03+.01)*(10/12)}$$

$$= \$12.4067$$

The $12.4067 is the October 1, 20x1 arbitrage-free (no profit) price of soybean for August 1, 20x2 delivery. At that price, the premium of the forward contract itself on October 1, 20x1 is worth zero.

Prices and cost of carry do not remain stationary as in the example of the contract in Panel A of Exhibit 5.16. Panel B presents the changes in market conditions. Panel C uses the information in Panels A & B to calculate the premium of the forward contract when market conditions change, the gain/loss of ADM and the settlement. It is important to note that "*F*" refers to forward commodity price (value), while "*f*" refers to the forward premium.

## Exhibit 5.16 An Illustration of a Forward Contract

**Panel A: The Forward Contract**

- Contract Date: October 1, 20x1
- Commodity: Yellow Soybean Grade #2
- Notional Amount: 50 million bushels
- Delivery Date: August 1, 20x2
- Delivery Location: Sidney, IL
- Forward Price: $12.4067 per bushel
- Settlement: Physical Delivery or Net
- Spot (cash) Price: $12.00 per bushel.
- Interest Rate: 3% per annum
- Storage Cost: 1% per annum

**Panel B: Events**

- December 1, 20x1: Spot (cash) price increased from $12.00 a bushel to $12.10.
- April 30, 20x2, two changes:
  i. Spot (cash) price increased from $12.10 to $12.50.
  ii. Interest rate increased from 3% to 4% per annum.
- August 1, 20x2. Spot price is $12.71

**Panel C: Valuation and closing the contract**

*Terminology*:

| | |
|---|---|
| $S_t$ | = Spot (cash) price at time *t*. |
| $e$ | = The base of natural logarithm (also known as Euler's $e = 2.718281\ldots$). |
| $r$ | = Risk-free interest rate. |
| $c$ | = Storage cost per year as a percent of notional amount. |
| $(r + c)$ | = The cost of carry. |
| $F_{t \to T}$ | = Forward (delivery) price at time *t* for delivery at *T*, where $t = 0, 1, 2, \ldots T$. |
| | $= F_{t \to T} = S_t * e^{(r + c) * ((T - t)/12)}$ |
| | = arbitrage-free price. |
| $CF_T$ | = The contract forward price for delivery at *T*. |
| $CF_T - S_t$ | = forward points (sometimes referred to as time value of the forward). |
| $f_t$ | = Forward contract premium. |
| $t$ | = current time period. |
| $T$ | = contract terminal period |

**At $t = 0$**

$$CF_T = F_{0 \to T} = S_0 * e^{(r + c) * (T/12)}$$
$$= F_0$$
$$\to f_0 = F_0 - CF_T$$
$$= 0.$$

**At $t = 1$ (December 1, 20x1), the remaining contract period is $T - 1$**

$$F_1 = F_{1 \to T} = S_1 * e^{(r + c) * ((T - 1)/12)b}$$
$$f_1 = F_1 - CF_T$$
$$\to \text{gain or loss} = \Delta f_1 = F_1 - F_0$$

If $\Delta f_1 > 0$ for one party, it is a gain for that party and it would be a loss for the counterparty, i.e., $\Delta f_1 < 0$.

The nominal gain or loss depends on the direction of the newly established forward rate in relationship to the contract price and on whether the party is long (purchasing) or short (selling) the commodity.

The accounting gain or loss is the present value of $f_1$ discounted at the discount rate implicit in the forward contract, which would be the cost of carry. However, if the cost of storage is zero, then the cost of carry is the risk-free interest rate.

**At $t = 2$ (April 30, 20x2), the remaining contract period is $T - 2$**

$$F_2 = F_{2 \to T} = S_2 * e^{(r + c) * ((T - 2)/12)}$$
$$f_2 = C\,F_T - F_2$$
$$\to \Delta f_2 = F_2 - F_1$$

The treatment of $\Delta f_2$ is the same as that of $\Delta f_1$.

For the ADM illustration, applying the above information, we could estimate the premium of the forward contract at different dates as follows.

**On October 1, 20x1**

$F_{Oct\ 1,\ 20x1} = F_{10/20x1 \rightarrow 8/20x2} = \$12.0 * e^{(0.03 + 0.01)*(10/12)} = \$12.4067$

The value of forward sale on this date = \$12.4067 × 50,000,000 = \$620,335,000

$f_{Oct1,\ 20x1}$ = The premium of the forward contract = 0.

**On December 1, 20x1**

$F_{Dec\ 1,\ 20x1} = F_{12/20x1 \rightarrow 8/20x2} = \$12.10 \times e^{(0.03 + 0.01) * (8/12)} = \$12.427007$

The value of forward sale on this date = \$12.427007 × 50,000,000 = \$621,350,369.40

$f_{Dec1,\ 20x1}$ = The premium of the forward contract on this date is
= \$621,350,369.40 – \$620,335,000.00 = \$1,015,369.36
= (12.427007 – 12.4067) × 50,000,000

Nominal Gain for ADM = \$1,015,369.36 (to be realized upon delivery on August 1, 20x2)
However, on December 1, 20x1, ADM will recognise the present value

Present value of the nominal gain = $1{,}015{,}369.36 \times e^{-0.04 * (8/12)}$
= \$988,650.33

This amount is what accounting would recognize as a gain for this period.

**On April 30, 20x2**

$F_{April\ 30,\ 20x2} = F_{4/20x2 \rightarrow 8/20x2}$
$= \$12.50 \times e^{(0.04 + 0.01) * (3/12)}$
= \$12.6572306

The value of forward sale on this date = \$12.6572306 × 50,000,000 = \$632,861,532.20

$f_{April\ 30,\ 20x2}$ = The premium of the forward contract
= \$632,861,532.20 – \$620,335,000.00 = \$12,526,532.20

Present value of nominal gain = $12{,}526{,}532.20 \times e^{-0.04^5 * 3/12} = \$12{,}370{,}925.12$

(Note that the rate implicit in the forward contract is 0.04 + 0.01 = 0.05 and this is the rate used for discounting future values.)

Gain for this period = \$12,370,925.12 – \$988,650.33
= \$11,382,274.79

**On August 1, 20x2—Settlement**

$F_{August\ 1,20x2} = S_{August\ 1,20x2} = \$12.71$

The value of forward sale on this date = \$12.71 × 50,000,000 = \$635,500,000.00

*Settlement amount* = \$635,500,000.00 – \$620,335,000.00
= \$15,165,000.00

Gain for the period = \$15,165,000.00 – \$11,382,274.79 = \$3,782,725.21

## 5.6 Futures

A futures contract is an agreement between two parties to deliver a pre-specified quantity of a specified asset at a pre-determined date in the future.[33] Unlike forward contracts, futures are standardized contracts and are traded on a futures exchange. The futures exchange decides on the contracts to be made available for trade; the futures exchange is the counterparty to every futures contract. As a result, the futures exchange guarantees the contract performance either by asset delivery or by net settlement. To reduce exposure to the credit risk of dealers and traders, the futures exchange has two mechanisms:

1. Requiring a security deposit (margin) that is a function of the size of the contract and the credit risk of the trader.
2. Requiring daily settlement of price differences.

Because of standardization, daily settlement, trading on an exchange, and transparency, futures markets are more liquid than the forwards market.

A futures contract could be closed by taking an offsetting (opposite) position of the same specification as the initial one, and vice versa. Unwinding futures contracts cancels both the economic and legal obligations of the dealer or trader because both the initial and offsetting contracts are written with the futures exchange, which is the same counterparty for both contracts.[34] Under the rules of the exchange, a futures contract is revalued (marked to market) daily and the resulting gains (or losses) change hands every day—i.e., gains are credited and losses are charged to the contracting parties. Exhibit 5.17 compares the futures and forward contracts.

Exhibit 5.18 presents an example of a futures contract that NYMEX offers for U.S. Midwest Domestic Hot-Rolled Coil Steel Index.

### Exhibit 5.17 Differences between Forwards and Futures Contracts

| *Features* | *Forward Contracts* | *Futures Contracts* |
|---|---|---|
| Structure | Self-tailored to match the contracting parties' needs | Standardized |
| Counterparty | A dealer, a bank or another entity | An exchange (clearinghouse) |
| Cash flow | No cash or other assets exchanged until delivery | (i) A security margin is required according to the exchange rules.<br>(ii) Daily settlement of market price difference |
| Trading system | Over the Counter | On an organized exchange |
| Contract size | Customized | Stated in terms of standardized units as designated by the futures exchange |

| | | |
|---|---|---|
| Exposure to counterparty risk | Relatively high credit risk exposure because:<br>(a) The counterparty is a dealer, an individual trader, or a bank.<br>(b) No settlement or exchange of assets until maturity. | Relatively low credit risk exposure because:<br>(i) The counterparty is the exchange or clearinghouse.<br>(ii) The security margin is updated periodically as the risk exchange exposure changes.<br>(iii) Parties exchange price differences every day through the clearinghouse. |
| Contract period | Customized | Standardized |
| Contract type | Negotiated and customized | Standardized, initiated by the exchange and operates on submitting quotes |
| Liquidity | Relatively low due to the unsystematic and unstructured trade over the counter | Relatively high due to the standardized trade, daily settlement, and exchange transparency |
| Valuation | May mark to market if the management intends to use as a derivative. But no valuation is recorded (being an executory contract) if it is considered a "normal way business trade." | Marked to market daily and valuation differences are exchanged (by Clearinghouse rules) |

## Exhibit 5.18 An Example of NYMEX "Net Settled" Futures Contract[35]

**U.S. Midwest Domestic Hot-Rolled Coil Steel Index Futures**

| | | |
|---|---|---|
| Product Symbol | HRC, Clearing: HR | |
| Venue | CME Globex, CME ClearPort | |
| Hours (All Times are New York Time/ET) | CME Globex: | Sunday–Friday 6:00 p.m.–5:15 p.m. (5:00 p.m.–4:15 p.m. Chicago Time/CT) with a 45-minute break each day beginning at 5:15 p.m. (4:15 p.m. CT) |
| | CME ClearPort: | Sunday–Friday 6:00 p.m.–5:15 p.m. (5:00 p.m.–4:15 p.m. Chicago Time/CT) with a 45-minute break each day beginning at 5:15 p.m. (4:15 p.m. CT) |
| Contract Size | 20 short tons | |
| Price Quotation | U.S. dollars and cents per ton | |
| Minimum Fluctuation | $1.00 per short ton | |

| | |
|---|---|
| Floating Price | The floating price for each contract month is equal to the average price calculated for all available price assessments published for that given month by the CRU U.S. Midwest Domestic Hot-Rolled Coil Steel Index. |
| Termination of Trading | Trading terminates on the business day prior to the last Wednesday of the named contract month. |
| Listed Contracts | Trading is conducted in 24 consecutive months. |
| Settlement Type | Financial |
| Position Limits | NYMEX Position Limits |
| Rulebook Chapter | 920 |
| Exchange Rule | These contracts are listed with, and subject to, the rules and regulations of NYMEX. |

Note: The final settlement price will be the Floating Price calculated for each contract month rounded to the nearest $1.00/short ton.

(Source: http://www.cmegroup.com/trading/metals/ferrous/hrc-steel_contract_specifications.html)

## 5.7 Credit Default Swaps

A credit default swap (CDS) is an agreement between two parties to transfer risk from one party to another for a fee. There are three relevant entities in this transaction.

1. *Reference Entity*: This is the subject entity whose credit risk is of concern to the two CDS contracting parties. The reference entity could be a borrower; counterparty to other agreements or derivatives; or a totally unrelated third party.
2. *The Protection Buyer*: This is the one party seeking credit protection (pseudo insurance) against the default of a third party called "the reference entity,"
3. *The Protection Seller*: This is the counterparty to the CDS contract that is providing credit protection (pseudo insurance) by taking over the risk of default.

### 5.7.1 Two Important Qualifications

1. The *Protection Buyer* may be a creditor that supplied credit to the reference entity or may have another contract such as forwards or interest rate swap to which the reference entity is a party. On the other hand, the protection buyer and the reference entity may have no connection whatsoever (in this case, the contract is called naked CDS).

For example, Entity A and Entity Z are far apart and have no connection of trade or contracts, but the management of Entity A has seen some analysis suggesting that Entity Z might be in technical violation of bond covenants. Entity A could benefit by that information and seek credit protection from Entity B. Entity Z does not have to be involved in this contract or even grant permission to either Entity A or Entity B to use Entity Z as the reference entity.

2. For the protection buyer to settle with the protection seller and collect the benefits stipulated in the contract, the reference entity does not have to actually go through default. The contract typically stipulates a set of credit events and any one of them could trigger the obligation of the protection provider to pay the agreed upon amount to the protection buyer. Typical triggering events could be lowering credit ratings by outside agencies, default, restructuring, and violation of bond covenant or having a specified level of total debt to earnings.

### 5.7.2 The Implications

Three important implications follow:

1. CDSs are financial derivatives because they derive their values from the occurrence of credit events.
2. CDSs are not insurance policies in the traditional sense of insurance because the protection buyer may or may not have insurable interest, a fundamental principle of insurance (see Chapter Four). Furthermore, the protection buyer does not have to show suffering any loss in order to collect from the protection seller upon the occurrence of any of the stipulated triggering events.
3. CDSs may not qualify for hedge accounting because of the requirement that a hedge must be for a specific risk; it is practically impossible to define the specific risk being hedged. Therefore, CDSs are considered part of the trading portfolio (as derivatives they could not be classified as held-to-maturity or as available-for-sale).

## Information Log

**The AIG Saga**

AIG (insurance company) had issued an extraordinarily large number of CDSs before the 2007 financial crisis. The company enjoyed the income it generated from collecting quarterly premiums and that was going well until the 2007 crisis hit. The majority of those default swaps had one or more triggering events occur within a few hours. AIG had to deliver a huge sum of money to CDS protection buyers and was about to collapse completely if the Federal government did not intervene to inject an enormous amount of taxpayers' money into AIG. The news media and the web are full of stories about AIG for interested readers.

**The MBIA Pending Crisis with CDS**

MBIA is an insurance company that emerged from a syndicate agreement between several other insurance firms only to specialize in municipal bonds. MBIA had enjoyed AAA credit rating by both Moody's and Standard & Poor and got on the bandwagon of CDSs.

In 2012, the credit rating of MBIA began to deteriorate and was downgraded several times to the level of BBB. Within a few months the downgrading has triggered many of the CDSs to which MBIA is a party. It is reported that MBIA is in need of $7.8 billion in cash to satisfy the calls from CDSs' holders.

## 5.8 Summary of Key Points

- This chapter draws distinction between fundamental securities and financial derivative instruments. Both types represent contracts that create financial rights and obligations. The values of these rights and obligations are the discounted values of their expected future cash flows.
- Financial derivative instruments are contracts that derive their values from the price of the underlying assets or indexes or from credit event. The main derivatives are options (and warrants), swaps, forwards, and futures and credit default swaps.
- Options create rights to the holder (the buyer) and obligations on the writer of the option. These rights could be right to buy (*call* options) or right to sell (*put* options). The basic valuation rule is to estimate the present value of a call or of a put adjusted for risk (volatility). These values are determined by the market price of the underlying asset, the strike price stated in the contract, the volatility of the underlying asset, time to expiration (tenor) of the contract, and risk-free rate of interest. The two most commonly used models in valuation of options are the Black-Scholes model and the Binomial model. As options near expiration, the time value of options vanishes. Market price and strike price differ by the sum of intrinsic value and time value of options. At terminal date, the time value of options vanishes and the difference between market price and strike price would be equal to the intrinsic value. Options can be out-of-the-money (strike price > market price for a call option, or strike price < market price for a put option), or in-the-money when these inequalities reverse. Options are at-the-money when strike price equals market price and in-the-money when the intrinsic value is positive. An information log in the chapter presents a brief discussion of other types of options such as *warrants*, *caps* and *floors*.
- This chapter also presents the basics of Black-Scholes model and Cox-Ross-Rubinstein Binomial model. All these models measure present values of the option contracts more comprehensively than a simple discounting rule by incorporating the main determinants of option values: volatility, the current market price of the underlying asset, the strike price, risk-free rate, and time to expiration. Caps and floors are unique in that they are mainly interest rate options with strike prices set as upper rate for caps (which are European call options in substance) and as lower bound for floors (which are put options in substance). A cap and a floor together form a collar. Sensitivity of option prices (premiums) to changes in the values of state variables or parameters is briefly introduced under the name of Options' Greeks.
- Interest rate swaps are agreements to exchange interest on a stated principal amount called notional. A plain vanilla interest rate swap exchanges fixed rate for a floating rate for a period of time by reference to an interest rate benchmark for a notional amount. For these swaps the floating rate is derived from the zero-coupon curve and is the rate to be determined first. The cash flow stream expected to be generated from the floating-rate leg is then discounted to present value using rates obtained from the zero-coupon curve. The fixed-leg interest rate is solved for by setting the present value of the fixed leg equal to the present value of the floating leg. This process of determining both rates means that the present value of the swap contract at inception is nil. Subsequently, changes in benchmark interest rate alter this and create value for the swap contract. The swap contract price or present value result from the imbalance between the present value of the fixed-rate leg and the present value of the newly developed floating rate.

## Notes

1 Embedded derivatives are discussed in Chapter Nine.

2 LIBOR stands for London InterBank Offer Rate. LIBOR is determined every morning at 11:00 a.m. London time by the averages of the interbank interest rates being offered by members of the British Bankers Association membership. LIBOR is calculated for periods as short as overnight and as long as one year. LIBOR is fixed for the 24-hour period.

There is also EURIBOR, which stands for the European InterBank Offer Rate. It is the rate that 50 large European banks use to offer unsecured loans to one another.

3 There is a form of bonds that give bondholders the right to participate in dividends with common stockholders. These are called "participating bonds" and are known mostly in Europe.

4 This contract is called "weather derivative" and has a special accounting treatment as will be seen later. In particular, it would be accounted for as a derivative and would not qualify for hedge accounting unless it is traded on a recognized exchange.

5 For "call options" note that the holder has the right to make the call—i.e., to choose buying.

6 Options are generally granted at-the-money and the premium is a small amount that is often equal to the time value of the option.

7 There are FLEX Options devised by the Chicago Board of Options Exchange, which are self-tailored contracts.

8 The literature often uses the term "underlying" asset to refer to the asset for which the option could be exercised. However, accounting standards use the term underlying only for the risk driver (price or credit risk) and explicitly states that the subject asset is not an underlying.

9 As discussed below, an out-of-the-money option could still have a non-zero price if the time value of option is non-zero.

10 Time value of option is ignored for the moment.

11 The measure of decay of the time value of options is called Theta. See the Options Greek in section 5.2.7.

12 As the number of periods approaches infinity (i.e., increases to a large number), the option value of the Binomial model equals the option value of the Black-Scholes model.

13 For those who are not familiar with continuous compounding, the analogy with simple compounding are:

Assuming continuous compounding, these values are estimated as follows:

$$u = e^{\sigma\sqrt{t}} \approx 1 * (1 + \sigma)^{\sqrt{t}} \quad \text{for the upward movement,}$$

$$d = e^{-\sigma\sqrt{t}} = 1/u \approx 1/(1 + \sigma)^{\sqrt{t}} \quad \text{for the downward movement.}$$

where all terms are as defined above.

14 "Vega" is not a Greek letter, but it is included in the Options Greek suite.

15 Interest rate swaps based on short LIBOR rates currently trade on the interbank market for maturities up to 50 years. In the swap market a "five-year LIBOR" rate refers to the 3-year swap rate where the floating leg of the swap references 6-month LIBOR ("3-year rate vs. 6-month LIBOR"). The day count convention for LIBOR rates in interest rate swaps is Actual/360, except for the GBP currency for which it is Actual/365.

16 See the International Swaps and Derivatives Association at www.isda.org.

17 General Electric has a large finance entity.

18 Modern development of swap contracts started with an unintentional move by the World Bank and IBM. In 1981 the World Bank and IBM swapped Swiss francs for U.S. dollars to fit the financing needs of each at low cost. The idea of swap contracts has evolved ever since but gained significant momentum by the repeal of the Bucket Shop law on December 21, 2000 which allowed companies to essentially speculate without regulatory constraints or oversight.

19 This feature is different in currency swaps. In currency swaps, the notional amount is exchanged at the inception and at the end of the swap contract.

20 It is reported that initiation of swap contracts took place in 1982 when an investment banker in Salomon Brothers proposed to swap Swiss francs for U.S. dollars to mutually satisfy the currency needs of the World Bank and IBM at a cost lower than direct liquidation of position in open markets (Apte, 2009).
21 This condition is different for some types of interest rate swap contracts in which one party pays in one currency and receives a different currency. See Chapter Ten.
22 It should be noted that in an interest rate swap contract, the notional (principal) amount is not exchanged. However, treating the fixed leg and the floating leg of the swap for each period as two different zero-coupon bonds does not necessarily violate this condition because the present values of the final refund of the (hypothetical) bonds are equal for either type (fixed or floating).
23 These rates are calculated to have equal present values for both legs of the swap.
24 It will be noted in Chapter 7 that, until July 17, 2013, hedge accounting for interest rate swap requires that the swap contract be written with only one of two benchmark interest rates: either LIBOR or Treasury Rates. On July 17, 2013, the FASB added Overnight Index Swap Rate (OIS) as a third acceptable benchmark rage. This change is effective for financial transactions entered into or after July 17, 2013. IFRS do not specify any restrictions.
25 If the fair value of the contract at inception is not zero, then the contract is essentially a loan.
26 This comparability is true only to a point. For example, the Federal Funds Rate is less susceptible to manipulation while litigation and substantial fines have been levied against Barclays Bank, UBS, Royal Bank of Scotland, and JPMorgan Chase for agents who falsely manipulate LIBOR.
27 As we learn more about hedge accounting we will find out the reason for the significance of locational differences in prices of the same commodity. For example, a *forward* contract on natural gas may be priced for delivery at the Henry Hub in Louisiana (the hub used by New York Mercantile Exchange for futures trading), but the delivery location is one of the other 30 major natural gas hubs in the USA. The price differential between these two locations is "a basis" difference and should not be included in the measurement of the risk being hedged or hedge effectiveness. This issue is significant because the volume of derivatives traded on natural gas is estimated to be 12 times the volume of the physical market. See www.naturalgas.org.
28 We shall see that accounting standards give the management of the contracting company the option to consider a forward contract as a "Firm Commitment" that could be hedged or as a derivative that could be used as a hedge. Additionally, a commodity forward contract could fall in the exception from ASC 815 by considering it a "normal purchase or sale contracts."
29 It is essential to distinguish between two prices: (1) The *forward price*, which is the future delivery price of the asset; (2) the *forward premium*, which is the price one pays (or receives) to have the commitment to sell (or buy) the asset at a future date.
30 It is not clear to me why the risk-free rate is the rate of choice.
31 This general concept does not fully apply to perishable goods for which forward prices are primarily a function of the anticipated short-term supply and demand. For example, the June delivery forward price of tomatoes may be lower than the December spot price simply as a result of more supply.
32 The following two chapters will show the accounting for those assets and obligations, which could take one of two possibilities: (1) be valued at fair value with the changes in fair values flow through earnings if the hedge is ineffective, or (2) be valued at fair value with the changes in fair values being posted to Accumulated Other Comprehensive Income if the hedge is highly effective.
33 There is a wide range of assets for which futures contracts are traded. The CME Group (parent of the Chicago Mercantile Exchange) has the widest variety through its Chicago Board of Trade, Chicago Mercantile Exchange, and the New York Mercantile Exchange. These include: Currencies, Interest Rate derivatives; Agricultural Products; Dow Jones Industrial Average; Metals and Energy products.
34 This particular feature has an important implication for hedge accounting as is discussed in the related chapters.
35 NYMEX is New York Mercantile Exchange which is now a member of the CME (Chicago Mercantile Exchange) Group.

# PART III

# ACCOUNTING

CHAPTER 6

# QUALIFICATIONS FOR HEDGE ACCOUNTING

## 6.1 A Brief Recap of Financial Derivatives

As discussed in the preceding chapter, financial derivatives are bilateral contracts having four main features:

1. Their values are derived from, or generated by reference to another factor (an underlying), which is a price change or an event.
2. They create rights for one party and obligations on the counterparty.
3. Holders of rights (assets) and the counterparty having obligations (liabilities) do not necessarily maintain that position; their position can be switched before settlement depending on the behavior of the underlying price.
4. They have definite life spans.
5. Their payoffs are *not* intended to be compensation for damages or losses.

## 6.2 Accounting for Financial Derivatives under Ordinary GAAP

Ordinary (i.e., non-special) GAAP accounting for derivatives falls under two categories: (a) the basis of valuation and (b) choice of the channel that filters the change in values to owners' equity (the geography).

### 6.2.1 Fair Value Is Mandatory

ASC 815 (formerly Statement 133 as amended) and IAS 39 (changing to IFRS 9) require that all financial derivative contracts be valued at fair values using a defensible valuation approach. Fair value is measured according to one of three acceptable measurement levels:[1]

- *Level 1: Fair values as measured by quoted (exit) prices in active markets for identical assets for which the measurement date is clearly established.* Fair values are established with little difficulty for assets traded in liquid markets such as exchange-traded derivatives. (This is *Level 1* in the fair value measurement hierarchy of Statement 157, now ASC 820; IAS 39). This is known as mark-to-market.
- *Level 2: Estimated fair values based on observable inputs other than quoted prices included within Level 1.* These inputs must be either directly or indirectly observable such as quoted prices for

similar assets in active markets, quoted prices for identical or similar assets in inactive markets, and inputs that are derived from observable market data by correlation between prices or by other means. This level primarily includes non-exchange traded derivatives such as over-the-counter commodity forwards and swaps, interest rate swaps, and foreign currency forwards and options (Level 2 in the Fair Value Hierarchy).

- *Level 3: Estimating the present value of expected future cash flow where there is little or no market activity for the asset.* This valuation uses a valuation model and depends heavily on management assumptions and expectations (Level 3).

In some cases, the standards incorporate references to specific models (while not excluding other models) such as Black-Scholes and Cox-Ross-Rubinstein Binomial models for valuation of options. In other cases, the accepted valuation method is suggested by using examples such as the case of valuing interest rate swaps.

The requirement to value financial derivative instruments at fair value is *not a choice* and generally has very few exceptions or exclusions.[2]

### 6.2.2 The Changes in Fair Values Flow through Earnings

Accounting standards require posting changes in the fair values of financial derivatives to earnings (the P&L Statement) periodically. This requirement is *not* conditional either on the realization of the change in value or on contract settlement. As a consequence, under ordinary GAAP, the volatility of the prices of financial derivatives will be reflected in earnings.[3]

Hedge accounting is a modification of this rule; it provides a complex process by which earnings are sheltered from the volatility of financial derivatives. To be eligible to take advantage of this modification, accounting standards set a number of criteria as preconditions that must be met.

Accordingly, volatility of valuation of financial derivative instruments will be reflected in earnings under two sets of circumstances:

1. If business enterprises hedge risk but the hedge does not satisfy the required conditions to permit them to adopt hedge accounting.
2. If business enterprises do not hedge risk and enter into derivative contracts either for investment or for speculation. In this case, the changes in fair values of these contracts will be posted to earnings with the potential of inducing earnings volatility.

## 6.3 Uses of Financial Derivatives

### 6.3.1 Using Derivatives as Investments

Banks and other financial institutions (FI), such as JPMorgan Chase, Goldman Sachs, and Morgan Stanley, make markets in derivatives by writing contracts that meet their customers' needs to mitigate different types of risk: interest rate risk, currency exchange rates risk, commodity price risk, and credit risk. The FI originates these proprietary trading or client derivative portfolios for two purposes: (1) to serve clients to manage their risk exposures, and (2) to generate revenues by subsequently trading on these derivatives.

Enterprises other than FIs may also acquire financial derivatives for trading and profit-making purposes. In this case, these derivatives are typically part of the enterprise's trading portfolio and the accounting for them would be the same as accounting for trading securities: entities would frequently value derivative positions at fair value (mark-to-market or mark-to-model) with intervals of time shorter than 90 days and post changes in values to earnings.[4]

Writing trading derivatives by FIs generates a cycle of events and consequences which can be outlined as follows:

1. The FI writes these derivatives for clients with the goal of generating net profits.
2. After writing these trading derivatives, the market maker (the FI) becomes exposed to additional client credit risk.
3. To manage this additional risk, the FI enters, either concurrently or subsequently, into other derivative contracts to hedge its risk exposure to the derivatives it has written to clients. The risk and cash flow profile of the *hedging* derivatives should be expected to offset the risk and cash flow profiles of the (proprietary) *trading* derivatives.
4. To enhance its profit expectations, the FI sets the terms of these hedge derivatives so that it would be less costly than the derivatives that the FI has written to clients.
5. Entering into these hedging relationships to hedge the trading derivatives means that the FI uses derivative instruments to hedge investments in other derivative instruments.

Using derivatives to hedge the risk exposure of other derivatives creates a unique accounting problem. There are two types of derivatives involved in this process: one is a "trading derivative" and the other is a "hedge derivative" entered into in order to hedge the risk exposure created by trading derivatives. In this situation, the accounting treatment (under current accounting standards) should be as follows:

1. The trading derivatives written by the FI to help clients manage their own risk will have the same accounting treatment as "trading securities." It will be valued at fair value with the changes in fair values being reported in earnings. This is the normal application of ordinary GAAP.
2. The hedge derivative is entered into with a third party (perhaps another FI and other than the client) for the purpose of hedging the risk of the written trading derivatives; a financial derivative intended for use in hedging other derivatives does not qualify for any special hedge accounting treatment.[5] Therefore, the accounting for this third party hedging derivative also follows the common procedure under ordinary GAAP, which is to be valued at fair value with the changes in fair values flowing through earnings. There is no need for hedge accounting, however, because if the hedge is effective, the change in fair value of the *hedge* derivative will offset the change in fair value of the *hedged* derivative without any special accounting.

The story of trading derivatives may be gleaned from disclosures by banks and others; Exhibit 6.1 presents examples from JPMorgan Chase, Barclays PLC and the energy company Dominion Resources, Inc.

## Exhibit 6.1 Examples of Corporate Disclosures of Trading Derivatives

**JPMorgan Chase, Form 10-K 2010, p. 191**

*Trading derivatives*

The Firm makes markets in a variety of derivatives in its trading portfolios to meet the needs of customers (both dealers and clients) and to generate revenue through this trading activity ("client derivatives"). Customers use derivatives to mitigate or modify interest rate, credit, foreign exchange, equity and commodity risks. The Firm actively manages the risks from its exposure to these derivatives by entering into other derivative transactions or by purchasing or selling other financial instruments that partially or fully offset the exposure from client derivatives. The Firm also seeks to earn a spread between the client derivatives and offsetting positions, and from the remaining open risk positions.

(Source: http://www.sec.gov/Archives/edgar/data/19617/000095012311019773/y86143e10vk.htm)

**Barclays PLC Annual Report, 2010, p. 119**

*Traded market risk (audited)*

Traded market risk is predominantly the result of client facilitation in wholesale markets. This involves market making, offering hedge solutions, pre-hedging and assisting clients to execute large trades. Not all client trades are hedged completely, giving rise to market risk. In Barclays Capital, trading risk is measured for the trading book, as defined for regulatory purposes, and certain banking books.

(Source: http://group.barclays.com/about-barclays/investor-relations/financial-results-and-publications/annual-reports)

**Dominion Resources, Inc., Form 10-K, 2010, p. 73**

As part of Dominion's strategy to market energy and manage related risks, it also manages a portfolio of commodity-based financial derivative instruments held for trading purposes. Dominion uses established policies and a procedure to manage the risks associated with price fluctuations in these energy commodities and uses various derivative instruments to reduce risk by creating offsetting market positions.

(Source: https://www.dom.com/investors/pdf/2010_10k.pdf)

### 6.3.2 Using Derivatives to Hedge Risk

In principle, business enterprises can use financial derivatives to hedge any risk the management intends to mitigate. However, not every hedge qualifies for the special treatment of hedge accounting. Accounting standards provide several filters for the type of hedge that would qualify for hedge accounting. These filters are briefly outlined below and will be elaborated in the segments to follow.

1. Hedge accounting is limited to hedging market risk (commodity prices, interest rate, currency exchange rates, and indexed equity prices) and credit risk.
2. Management must designate each hedging relationship as a hedge of a *specific* risk. It must show the fit between the cash flow and risk being hedged and the cash flow and risk profile of the hedge derivative. This leads to classifying hedge derivatives as "designated" or "undesignated."
3. The hedge derivative must satisfy the accounting definition of derivatives, which imposes specific criteria. Whether or not the derivative is designated as a hedge, GAAP requires its valuation at fair value with intervals not longer than 90 days with the changes in fair values flowing through earnings. Business practices refer to these undesignated derivatives, or hedging relationships that do not satisfy the requirement of hedge accounting as an "economic hedge" to disclose them as distinct from the hedge acceptable for hedge accounting.[6]
4. The designated hedge relationships must satisfy additional criteria in order to be accounted for under the special hedge accounting treatment. Those criteria are concerned with documentation and measurement of the success of the hedging relationship (i.e., effectiveness). If it satisfies these criteria, hedge accounting applies to one of three categories discussed below.

### 6.3.2.1 Fair Value Hedge

Hedging the exposure to unexpected value loss that can arise from a specific risk (i.e., unexpected changes in market prices or downgrading of credit worthiness of counterparty) of:

1. A recognized asset (i.e., fixed-interest rate asset).
2. A recognized liability (i.e., fixed-interest rate liability).
3. An unrecognized firm (binding) commitment (i.e., an unrecognized executory contract such as a contract for future sale or purchase of inventories). To qualify for being a hedged item, the standards require that a firm (definite commitment) must have a disincentive (whether implicit or explicit) for nonperformance.

The hedged item is the *asset*, the *liability*, or *firm commitment* whose value changes are being hedged.

In this type of hedge, the risk generator (i.e., change in prices or credit risk) should be caused by forces external to the business entity, not by the business enterprise itself. Additionally, financial contracts with related parties (such as subsidiaries) are not considered derivatives.

### 6.3.2.2 Cash Flow Hedge

A cash flow hedge is the hedging of exposure to unexpected cash flow variability with the following features:

1. It is attributable to a particular risk that is specified in advance of hedging.
2. It is associated with a recognized asset, a recognized liability, or a probable prospective (forecasted) transaction.
3. It has an earnings effect.
4. It is the result of contractual relationship with unrelated parties (with some exception for foreign currency denominated contracts).[7]

Some examples of recognized balance sheet items with variable future cash flows are floating-rate investments that are, for example, classified as available-for-sale, and cash flow of the debt that pays a variable interest.

An example of a forecasted transaction is the anticipated issuance of debt that could be affected by a changing market interest rate. See Exhibit 6.2 for an illustration from Form 10-K of IBM.

## Exhibit 6.2 IBM Cash Flow Hedging of Forecasted Issuance of Debt

**Forecasted Debt Issuance**

The company is exposed to interest rate volatility on future debt issuances. To manage this risk, the company may use forward starting interest rate swaps to lock in the rate on the interest payments related to the forecasted debt issuance. These swaps are accounted for as cash flow hedges. The company did not have any derivative instruments relating to this program outstanding at December 31, 2010 and 2009.

At December 31, 2010 and 2009, net losses of approximately $15 million and $18 million (before taxes), respectively, were recorded in accumulated other comprehensive income (loss) in connection with cash flow hedges of the company's borrowings. Within these amounts $9 million and $10 million of losses, respectively, are expected to be reclassified to net income within the next 12 months, providing an offsetting economic impact against the underlying transactions.

(Source: IBM Annual Report, p. 97. (page 123 within Form 10-K). Available at: ftp://public.dhe.ibm.com/annualreport/2010/2010_ibm_annual.pdf)

If future cash flows are volatile because of changes in credit risk or price changes such as changes in interest rates, we can mitigate unexpected currency prices or commodity prices by using financial derivatives with offsetting cash flow behavior.

In any of these three cases, the unanticipated loss may take the form of potential increase in cash outflow or potential decrease in cash inflow. To take an example, the floating (variable)-coupon-rate bond is indexed to a benchmark interest and when the benchmark rate changes, the cash flow associated with the floating rate of the bond will also change; the present value of the bond will remain unchanged.[8]

### 6.3.2.3 Hedging Net Investment in Foreign Operations

Multinational companies may have subsidiaries and operations in foreign countries whose currencies are not the same as the home currency. For example, a foreign operation for a U.S. company is one whose currency is not the U.S. dollar, and a foreign operation for a Swiss company is one whose currency is not the Swiss franc.[9]

The value of net investments (assets minus liabilities) in foreign operations (assets minus liabilities translated at the current spot rate) is exposed to loss due to currency fluctuation. The enterprise can enter into currency hedging contracts to preserve the value of these net investments. The unique nature of this hedge does not fit the classification of either fair value hedge or cash flow hedge. Rather, it is a category by itself for which the required accounting is distinctly related to the translation of the financial statements of foreign operations.

In the event that either the documentation or the effectiveness test is not satisfied, the special hedge designation will be terminated and these hedging relationships will revert to ordinary GAAP. In this case, the derivatives will be accounted for as if they are trading securities.

The categorization of financial derivatives discussed above is portrayed in Figure 6.1.

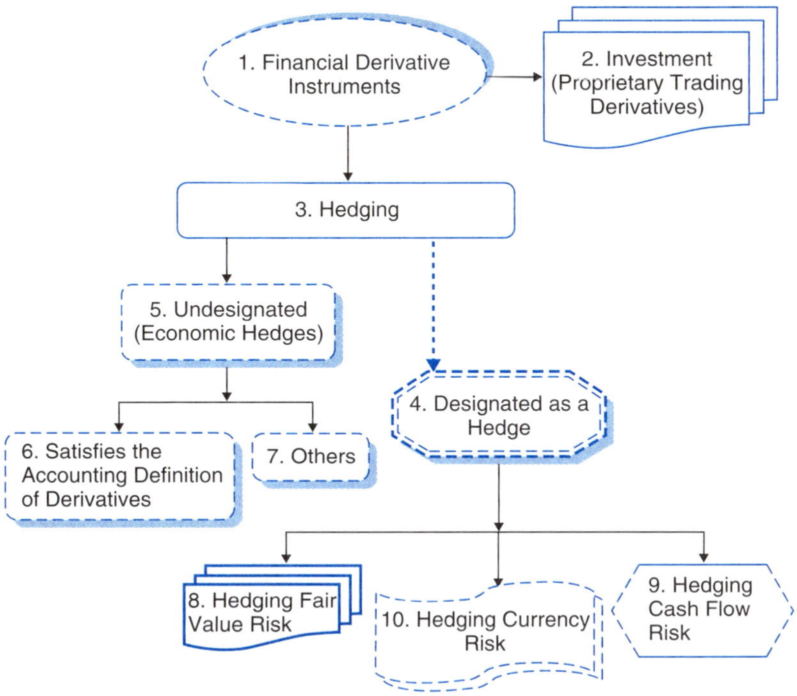


**Figure 6.1** Derivatives Categories in Accounting

Item 1. Financial derivative instruments include all types of derivative instruments irrespective of the accounting scope and exceptions for what constitute a derivative. For example, a forward contract requiring physical delivery is a derivative in an economic sense, but is not accepted as a derivative as accounting defines it. Instead, accounting would treat this type of a contract as an executory contract. An executory contract is a firm agreement awaiting to be performed. In contrast, a forward contract requiring net settlement satisfies the accounting definition of a derivative.

Item 2. Financial derivatives can be written (by banks, for example) or acquired (by any enterprise) for trading and investment purposes. These derivatives constitute a component of the trading portfolio and must be valued at fair value with the changes flowing through earnings.

Item 3. Financial derivatives can be entered into as contracts or can be acquired in the marketplace for the purpose of hedging risk.

Item 4. Hedging derivatives may qualify for hedge accounting and management exercises its discretion to "designate" these derivatives as such. Designating derivatives as hedging instruments is not adequate for applying hedge accounting; other prerequisites must be satisfied. The remainder of this chapter elaborates on these requisite criteria.

Item 5. A segment of derivatives may be "undesignated" and would be accounted for as required by ordinary GAAP. The undesignated derivatives do not qualify for special accounting treatment for hedge relationships. However, at some future date, management may elect to change this treatment by designating a derivative as a hedge for a specific risk. In this case, the type of accounting will depend on whether or not the newly designated hedging relationships satisfy the requisite criteria for applying hedge accounting.

Item 6. A subset of the "undesignated" derivatives that satisfy the definition of derivatives in accounting, but for some reason they are not accounted for as a hedge. This can happen when, for example, the hedge is ineffective, the documentation is incomplete, or the management elects to use the fair value option instead of hedge accounting to avoid cumbersome evaluation and costly administrative processes. It can also happen when measuring effectiveness is costly, such as in the case of credit default swaps. Derivative instruments must be valued at fair value with the change in fair value flowing through earnings.

Item 7. The subset of financial instruments is considered financial derivatives in an economic sense, although not accepted as derivatives in accounting. Under GAAP, these derivatives would be accounted for as other financial instruments.

*The Remainder*: Once a financial instrument satisfies the accounting definition of a "derivative," and the hedge relationship satisfies requirements of documentation and effectiveness, it can be classified in one of three groups:

Item 8. *Fair value hedge*: Hedging the potential loss in the fair value of an asset, an increase in the fair value of a liability, or a change in value of an unrecognized firm (fixed or assured) commitment.

Item 9. *Cash flow hedge*: Hedging the potential increase in cash outflow or the potential decrease in cash inflow associated with a recognized asset, a recognized liability, or a forecasted transaction.

Item 10. *Net foreign investment hedge*: Hedging the potential loss due to currency risk other than transaction risk or operating risk.

## 6.4 What Is Hedge Accounting?

### 6.4.1 Basic Features

As noted in Chapter Four, hedging is a management activity aimed at generating outcomes that are expected to be negatively correlated with specific types of risk. While previous chapters have introduced several definitions and types of risk, all types of risk are of concern to management because each can expose the enterprise to possible losses as well as possible gains. Of particular relevance to accounting is *the risk exposure due to adverse behavior of prices* (commodity prices, interest rate as the price of money, currency exchange rate as the price of currency, equity index as the price of equity), or to *the occurrence of credit risk events that are* precipitated by external factors and unrelated parties.

The special hedge accounting treatment is applicable to a broad scope of contracts and activities and aims to meet the following objectives:

- Disclosure of the risks the enterprise faces, particularly those created by interaction with other systems in the environment.
- Disclosure of the approach and success of management in dealing with these risks.
- Recognition of hedging transactions.
- Measurement of the impact of hedging transactions on assets, liabilities, and owners' equity in accordance with specific accounting standards.

### 6.4.2 Ultimate Goals of Hedge Accounting

Hedging is a purposeful activity that aims at mitigating exposure to unexpected loss due to particular types of risk not caused or created by the enterprise itself. *Hedge accounting* aims at showing the extent to which the management has succeeded in achieving this goal. Two key indicators are relevant in reporting the extent of management success in this area:

1. The process of accounting focuses on measuring and reporting the impact of hedging on earnings in a manner consistent with *management intent*.[10] Accounting must present evidence about how well the risk and cash flow patterns of the hedged item and the hedge derivative offset one another.
2. A successful hedge shelters earnings from the fluctuations of the fair values of derivatives and from any volatility emanating from exposure to the risk being hedged. In fully hedged relationships, income should also be sheltered from both gains and losses of the hedge instrument. While the management could adopt any hedging strategy of its own choice, hedge accounting is permitted only for successful hedging of particular types of risks. The degree of success in hedging is known as hedge effectiveness.

   To achieve these goals, the standards have incorporated certain features:

- Providing a comprehensive look at the use of financial derivatives and instruments for investment and hedging by business enterprises.
- Explicitly recognizing the critical role of risk management by connecting each hedge to the strategy and philosophy of the enterprise risk management.
- Establishing the goal of communicating information to external users about how business enterprises manage their market and credit risk exposures. In this respect, the standards focus on the success of managerial decisions that are explicitly intended to hedge those types of risk.
- Departing from the process of arbitrarily deferring or allocating costs or losses to different periods. Gains and losses attributable to hedging are accounted for periodically and case-by-case.
- Having devoted a standard (that has evolved into a complex set of standards) for a rich and complex activity is in contrast to the previously adopted piecemeal approach.
- Using "management intent" as the anchor for hedge accounting, which is a significant departure from the long-established tradition of seeking independent verification and arms-length exchange as bases for accounting.[11]

## 6.5 Fundamental Premises

Conceptually, hedge accounting embodies two premises with each having a necessary set of conditions:

1. *First Premise*: *Hedge accounting is a privilege, not a right.*

*Necessary Conditions*: This premise has several implications that accounting standards have established as necessary conditions. These conditions are:

- *Intent*: Management must declare its intent to hedge a specific risk before entering into a particular hedging contract.
- *Specificity*: The hedge contract must be specific to an identifiable risk. Management is required to document how the derivative contract is expected to mitigate the specific risk identified.
- *Relevance*: The hedge must be related to the enterprise risk management and philosophy that has been adopted by its Board of Directors—e.g., an *Enterprise Risk Management* system. It is an integral part of this philosophy.
- *Evidence*: All of the above must be documented prior to and following every hedging transaction or contract. Full documentation must be carried out *ex-ante* (prospectively or ahead of the event or time) and *ex-post* (retrospectively, following the event or time).
- *Continuity*: To maintain the privilege of hedge accounting, all of the above must be maintained continually throughout the life of the hedge contract at every reporting period (90-day intervals) or more frequently.
- *Derecognition*: If an entity fails in maintaining any of the above noted five elements for a particular contract, this will lead to termination (derecognition) of the special hedge accounting for the affected contract and hedged item. When a hedge is terminated, the accounting treatment of gains and losses of prior hedge accounting are not reversed and the impact of hedge termination is carried out prospectively.

2. *The Second Premise: Negative Relationship*

To qualify for hedge accounting, every hedging activity must be singularly successful: *the outcome of the hedge instrument must be significantly negatively correlated with the outcome of the risk exposure being hedged.* The operational definition of "highly effective" is achieving at least 80% success.[12]

> *An Example*: Fearing decline in the values of its inventories, the management of the enterprise could enter into financial derivatives contracts (e.g., swaps, forwards, etc.) whose value changes are expected to be highly negatively correlated with future changes in the prices of inventories. If that expectation is realized, the hedge would be considered successful—i.e., highly effective. The issue of interest is to provide an operational definition for what is considered a highly effective or successful hedge.

The premise on effectiveness leads to several implications that have become requisites for adopting hedge accounting. These implications are:

- *Dependency of the hedge and hedged items*: Accounting for hedge instruments cannot be independent of the accounting for the items or events that are causing the entity's initial exposure to risk and that necessitates the move into a hedge relationship.

  *An Example*: An enterprise is hedging the loss of value of inventories due to unexpected price changes. If this hedging relationship is highly effective, and the management elects to use hedge accounting, management must abandon the "lower-of-cost-or-market" as a basis for inventory valuation because hedge accounting requires that inventories be marked to market (only from the initiation of the hedge onward) for hedging relationships that meet all the qualifying criteria.[13]
- *Measurement*: With few exceptions,[14] hedge effectiveness must be measured explicitly and periodically.

- *Methodology*: The measurement of hedge effectiveness must be based on an accepted method that reveals the significance of the negative association between the volatility of prices of the hedge instrument and the volatility of prices of the hedged items.[15]
- *Frequency*: The hedging relationship must be highly effective both *ex-ante* at inception of the hedge and on a continuous *ex-post* basis with frequency and time interval shorter than 90 days.
- *Evidence*: Measurement of hedge effectiveness must be documented at inception and then continuously.
- *Consequences*: Failing the "highly effective" test will lead to termination of hedge accounting prospectively and reverting back to ordinary GAAP.

## 6.6 Hedge Accounting Qualifying Criteria

Hedge accounting aims to measure and report to external users: (1) how the management of the business enterprise manages the risks to which the enterprise is exposed; and (2) the degree of management success in achieving that goal.

Because applying hedge accounting has the effect of smoothing and reducing the volatility of earnings, both the FASB and the IASB consider hedge accounting as an override of normal (or ordinary) GAAP. Therefore, adopting hedge accounting is a privilege not a right or even a requirement. To be able to benefit by that privilege, both U.S. GAAP and IFRS specify strict guidelines[16] that must be satisfied for a hedging relationship to qualify for hedge accounting. These guides consist of four essential requisites, which are outlined and detailed below.

### 6.6.1 An Outline of Qualifying Criteria

1. *Definition*: Contracts of financial derivatives that are accepted for the adoption of hedge accounting must have very specific definitional features. As a result, not all financial derivatives in the financial economics literature or in the practice of finance qualify for hedge accounting.
2. *Scope*: The scope of financial contracts that qualify for hedge accounting is delineated in two ways:
   a. By *exclusion*: stating the set of contracts and transactions that do not fit (ASC 815 refers to these excluded items as "exceptions").
   b. By *inclusion*: This feature relates to identifying, measuring and including embedded derivatives.[17]
3. *Documentation*: It is essential to have detailed documentation of the hedging relationship that has several features:
   a. *Timing*: Both *ex-ante* at inception of the hedge and *ex-post* on an ongoing basis with intervals not exceeding 90 days.
   b. *Fit of Risks*: The fit of three different types of risk must be documented:
      i. The risk being hedged.
      ii. The risk of the hedge instrument.
      iii. The enterprise risk philosophy and management.

4. *Success*: To adopt and continue using hedge accounting, the hedge must be highly effective at inception and on an ongoing basis. Testing hedge effectiveness must be carried out periodically with intervals of time not exceeding 90 days.

## 6.6.2 Necessary Requisites

### *6.6.2.1 The First Requisite: Definition of Derivative Instruments*

Both U.S. GAAP and IFRS (IAS39) define a derivative as a financial contract having *all* of the following features:

- One or more underlying.
- One or more notional (face) amount *or* settlement provision.
- A requirement of net settlement, *or* an arrangement that would have an equivalent effect.
- No initial investment *or* an investment not of a significant nature.[18]

These features encompass complex details, the essence of which is as follows.

1. *One or More Underlying (Risk and Value Generator)*
The FASB defines an underlying (ASC 815 Glossary) as:

> A specified interest rate, security price, commodity price, foreign exchange rate, index of prices or rates, or other variable (including the occurrence or nonoccurrence of a specified event such as a scheduled payment under a contract). An underlying may be a price or rate of an asset or liability but *is not the asset or liability itself* [emphasis added]. An underlying is a variable that, along with either a notional amount or a payment provision, determines the settlement of a derivative instrument.

As noted in Chapter One and in Chapter Three, exposure to risk has two sides: gains and losses. Management is typically concerned with downside risk and the external factors that could adversely impact the enterprise. The factors about which hedge accounting is built are price (market) risk and credit risk, which are known as the underlying. As prices (commodity prices, cost of funds [interest rate or price index], and foreign currency exchange rates) or credit risk change, the risk exposure and cash flow profile of the contract also change. *In this sense, an underlying is both the value and risk generator.*

For example, commodity price changes are the value and risk generator of the enterprise inventory; change in the benchmark (market) interest rate (e.g., LIBOR or U.S. Treasury Rate) is the value and risk generator of a fixed-rate financial instrument; change in the exchange rate between the U.S. dollar and a foreign currency such as the Hong Kong dollar is the value and risk generator of the accounts receivable (or payable) denominated in Hong Kong dollars.

The other important *risk and value generator* in an accounting setting is the credit standing of debtors and counterparties to contracts. Investors in capital markets purchase bonds and redeemable (callable) preferred stock to meet their investment goals, which might include a stable and predictable flow of interest income and simultaneous assurance that issuers of the instruments will redeem the instrument's face value at predetermined future dates. Both bonds and mandatorily redeemable preferred stock are considered obligations of the issuing enterprise (debtor) that is responsible for making those payments to investors. Investors in these instruments are exposed to the risk of loss of their expected cash flow, in part or full, under the terms of the contract if the debtor's ability or willingness to pay is impaired.[19] Therefore, the *debtor's credit risk or creditworthiness is also a value and risk generator.*

2. *One or more notional (face) principal amounts or a payment provision*
A notional or face amount is the "number of units, shares, bushels, pounds, or other units specified in a derivative instrument" (ASC 815 Master Glossary). The notional amount representing the total units being hedged is used jointly with the change in price to determine the amount of funds required for settlement. For example, a forward contract on crude oil has an underlying (the price of oil) but also specifies a quantity (number of barrels) to be delivered. Both the change in oil price (the underlying) and the number of barrels specified in the contract (notional or face amount) determine the amount of money that one party to the contract owes the other.

## Accounting Log: Two substitutes for stating a notional principal amount

A. *Payment Provision*: The standards allow for some conditions under which notional amounts may not be explicitly stated in the contract, but the contract allows for a particular payment provision as an alternative. For example, a forward contract on Midwest Rolled Steel might specify the payment of a sum of money; say $50,000.00, if the spot price of the Midwest Rolled Steel increases by a stated percentage (say, 10%) over the next year. In this case, the underlying remains to be the price of rolled steel, but there is no stated principal or notional amount because specifying a payment provision determines the amount of settlement and is accepted as a substitute for the explicit statement of a notional amount.
B. *Requirement Contract*: A requirement contract is an agreement in which one party (say, Entity D) agrees to provide to the counterparty (Entity E) a quantity of a commodity determined by the production schedule of the counterparty's (Entity E) operations. In those types of contracts, other variables or clauses in the agreement may be used to estimate a quantity that would substitute for stating a notional amount; the history of trading between the parties to the contract could also serve to make this estimate.[20]

3. *No (significant) initial investment*
The third definitional element requires that the derivative contract does not require an initial net investment at inception of the hedge, or it requires an investment *smaller than would be required for contracts having a similar response to changes in market factors.*

This condition could be easily understood by referring to the basic financial instruments presented in Chapter Five. The present value of plain vanilla interest rate swaps at the start of the contract is zero. The terms of the swap agreement are designed such that the present value of the fixed leg equals the present value of the floating leg at inception. Therefore, entering into a new swap contract of this type does not require investment of funds (other than processing costs) from either contracting party. Subsequently, existing swap contracts generate value only because of the unexpected changes in interest rates that occur.[21] The change in values because of changes in the benchmark interest rate or credit risk (assuming everything else is held constant) creates cash flow rights for one party which are at the same time cash flow obligations for the counterparty; the former has gains (and an asset), while the latter has losses (and a liability). The assets and liabilities are to be settled periodically (every day for a *futures* contract) by exchanging funds equal to the difference between changes in values.

## Accounting Log

Some interest rate swaps have contract terms such that the present value of the contract is positive. For example, if the contract stipulates an 8% rate for the fixed leg of the swap when the zero-swap curve shows that the fixed rate (that will generate a present value equal to the present value of the floating leg) should be 5.5%, then the contract will have a value equal to the present value of the discounted difference in cash flows (rates times the notional amount). In this contract, the party that pays a fixed rate receives that present value at inception.[22] The derivatives interpretation guides (now incorporated in ASC 815) provide some ideas about how to account for such an instrument.

- If the present value of the contract at inception is as high as the present value of the notional amount, then this swap contract does not meet the "no investment" criterion required for a derivative to qualify for special accounting treatment of hedge accounting and it is not a derivative for accounting purposes. This swap contract is instead a hybrid debt instrument and the amount paid (received) at inception would be an investment (obligation).
- If the value of the swap and the amount exchanging hands at inception is lower than the present value of the notional amount by a "significant" amount, then the contract meets the requirement of "no initial" investment and would qualify in accounting as a derivative. But there is no clear guidance on the meaning of the term "significant" and the FASB leaves it as a matter of judgment.

Similarly, the intrinsic value of a forward contract at inception is zero[23] because in an efficient market the price of the forward is calculated such that no party would have arbitrage profit at the start of the contract. Therefore, forward contracts also do not require initial investment at the start of the contract.

In this respect, futures and forward contracts are similar, except for three differences:

i. The Futures Exchange is the counterparty to every futures contract.
ii. Upon contracting with the Futures Exchange, business enterprises and dealers must deposit a margin (security deposit) in advance.
iii. *Futures* are settled every day and thereby exposure to credit risk is reduced.

An option contract may be issued at-the-money or even out-of-the-money, but it will have a value equal to the time value of the option; paying the time value of the option is not considered a net investment for the purpose of meeting the criteria defining derivatives in hedge accounting.

4. *Net Settlement (and Equivalent Mechanisms)*
*The General Concept*

The fourth definitional condition of a derivative concerns the nature and mechanism of settling derivative contracts. Typically, the two main approaches for settling a derivative contract are:[24]

i. *Physical delivery*—such as delivering the required number of common shares stipulated in a contract for stock options, the required number of oil barrels for a futures contract on oil, or the required number of cotton bales for a forward contract on cotton.[25]

ii. *Financial or net settlement*—the contract may include an explicit or an implicit agreement to exchange a cash amount equal to the net difference in values at the time of settlement—i.e., the intrinsic values of an option; the difference between the cash flow of the fixed leg and the cash flow of the floating leg of an interest rate swap; the difference between forward and spot prices at the end of the day for a futures contract; or for the settlement of a forward contract on the terminal date.[26]

## Information Log: Mechanisms Equivalent to Net Settlement

ASC 815 provides for some alternative mechanisms that satisfy the criterion of net settlement in substance. Some of those mechanisms are discussed below.

- *Variable Penalties*: A contract may stipulate penalties for nonperformance based on changes in the underlying, the price of the items that are subject of the contract. A *variable* penalty might be in the form of a schedule stating the amount of the penalty for some specific changes in the underlying. For this arrangement to qualify as a substitute for "net settlement," the term "variable" means that any fixed portion of the penalty is not high enough to induce nonperformance.
- *Symmetrical Default Payment*: A derivative contract might stipulate specific actions by the two parties to the contract in the event that either one defaults on delivery—i.e., the seller does not deliver *or* the buyer does not take the asset. Irrespective of which party defaults, there will always be:

  a. a party with a favorable position, and
  b. a counterparty with an unfavorable position.

For example, if *the buyer is the defaulting party*, identifying the party in the favorable position would depend on market conditions:

> *Condition A*: If the spot price is lower than the contract price, the defaulting party would be in a favorable position and the non-defaulting party (the seller in this case) would be in an unfavorable position. Under a *symmetric default provision*, the seller (the non-defaulting party) pays the default penalty.
> *Condition B*: If the spot price is higher than the contract price, the defaulting party (the buyer) would be in an unfavorable position and the non-defaulting party (the seller in this case) would be in a favorable position. Under a *symmetric default provision*, the buyer (the defaulting party) pays the default penalty (see the Information Log below for an example on asymmetric default).

It is necessary to emphasize that in a symmetric default provision, the party that pays the penalty is the losing party, irrespective of who has caused the default condition. Contract provisions that compensate for damages are forms of insurance and are known as asymmetric default provisions. They are distinct from contracts with symmetric provision.

- *Market Mechanism*: The requirement for net settlement would be satisfied if a market mechanism exists to allow the seller and the buyer to transact outside the contract. All of the following five conditions must be fulfilled:

    i. Relieving all parties to the contract of the legal obligation to perform.[27]
    ii. Not entailing a significant transaction cost.
    iii. Not entailing a significant negotiation cost.
    iv. The settlement occurs within the time frame considered normal in the industry for settling this type of contract.
    v. The existence of a market mechanism is assessed at inception of contract and on an ongoing basis.

    The best example of market mechanism is the operation of a Futures Exchange. The Exchange is the counterparty to futures contracts and requires daily settlement by exchanging price differences with the trader. Therefore, unwinding contracts would require dealing with the same counterparty, which relieves the dealer or the trader of both economic and legal responsibility for the first contract. In this case, the Exchange is the market mechanism that facilitates settling net.

- *Transferring Assets Readily Convertible into Cash:* The fourth possible equivalence to settling net is the transfer of an asset that has a ready market such that the buyer could readily convert it to cash and be in a position equivalent to what he/she would have been in if there was a direct net settlement. For the receiver of the asset (the buyer) to be indifferent between settling net and accepting an asset readily convertible to cash, the transfer must not have a significant transaction cost and the market for the asset should be large enough and sufficiently active so that liquidating the asset would not cause shifts in either the supply or the demand functions to a point of influencing market prices.

    For example, assume that a *forward* contract stipulates net settlement in U.S. dollars, but at the time of settlement, the counterparty delivers Japanese yen instead. If the amount of Japanese yen delivered is equivalent to the required amount of U.S. dollars at the spot exchange price, this would be equivalent to net settlement because the yen has a liquid market and is readily convertible into dollars. If, in contrast, the counterparty delivers Egyptian pounds, this would not be equivalent to settling net because the Egyptian pound does not have a market as large or liquid as the Japanese yen.

## Information Log: An Example of Asymmetric Default Provision

Some contracts include a feature to compensate the non-defaulting party for any loss incurred by the defaulting party. This provision is known as "asymmetric default provision" and is not accepted as meeting the criterion of net settlement required in accounting standards. It intends to compensate for loss or damage and is, therefore, a form of insurance.

In 815-30-55-11A (Implementation Guidance and Illustrations), the FASB provides the following example:

A Buyer agreed to purchase 100 units of a commodity from a Seller at $1.00 per unit:

- Case A. Assume the Buyer defaults on the forward contract by not taking delivery and the Seller must sell the 100 units in the market at the prevailing market price of $.75 per unit. To compensate the Seller for the loss incurred as a result of the Buyer's default, the Buyer must pay the Seller a penalty of $25.00 (that is, 100 units × ($1.00 – $.75)).
- Case B. Similarly, assume that the Seller defaults and the Buyer must buy the 100 units it needs in the market at the prevailing market price of $1.30 per unit. To compensate the Buyer for the loss incurred because of the Seller's default, the Seller must pay the Buyer a penalty of $30.00 (that is, 100 units × ($1.30 – $1.00)).

Note that an asymmetrical default provision is designed to compensate the non-defaulting party for a loss incurred. The defaulting party cannot demand payment from the non-defaulting party to realize the changes in market price that would be favorable to the defaulting party if the contract were honored. Under the forward contract in this example, if the Buyer defaults when the market price is $1.10, the Seller will be able to sell the units of the commodity into the market at $1.10 and realize a $10.00 greater gain than it would have under the contract. In that circumstance, the defaulting Buyer is not required to pay a penalty for nonperformance to the Seller, nor is the Seller required to pass the $10.00 extra gain onto the defaulting Buyer. Similarly, if the Seller defaults when the market price is $0.80, the Buyer will be able to buy the units of the commodity in the market and pay $20.00 less than the payment under the contract. In that circumstance, the defaulting Seller is not required to pay a penalty for nonperformance to the Buyer, nor is the Buyer required to pass the $20.00 savings on to the defaulting Seller.

As with many guides, there are some exceptions. For example, 815-3-55-17 notes that writing contracts with asymmetrical provisions could be the pattern of contracting between two parties with the understanding "that there will always be a net settlement." In that situation, those kinds of commodity contracts would meet the characteristic of net settlement in paragraph 815-10-15-100.

### 6.6.2.2 The Second Requisite: Scope Boundaries

The scope of the contracts and the activities to which hedge accounting is applicable is defined in two ways: (1) by explicitly *excluding* specific types of contracts and instruments, and (2) by explicitly *including* an expanded array of embedded derivatives.[28]

#### By Exclusion: Disqualifications and Exceptions

There are two broad categories of exceptions:[29] (a) *umbrella exclusions*, which constitute exclusions of general applicability, and (b) *micro exclusion* of specific types of contracts.

- *Umbrella Exclusion*: Hedge accounting does *not* apply if the hedged item is related to *any* of the following:

1. Assets or liabilities that are measured, or will be re-measured, at fair values with changes in fair values flowing through earnings (e.g., trading securities, or financial assets to which the fair value option is applied).
2. Investments that are accounted for by the equity method.[30]
3. Equity or minority interest in one or more consolidated subsidiaries.
4. Business combination.
5. Equity instrument classified in stockholders' equity.
6. Weather or geological derivatives unless they are exchange traded.
7. *Certain insurance contracts* that only compensate the holder for loss resulting from identifiable insurable events. They *are not based on changes in prices or price indexes*. Examples of this exclusion are traditional property and casualty insurance contracts and traditional life insurance.

- *Micro or Specific Exclusions*: These are contracts or instruments that are explicitly excluded from the scope of hedge accounting (ASC 815). These exclusions generally apply to both parties of the contract.

1. *"Regular-way" security trades*: The securities that are traded and settled in the customary practice of trade are not derivatives, unless

   a. the net settlement is affected by delivery of an asset that has a readily available liquid market, or net settled through market mechanism such as a clearinghouse or a dealer, or
   b. the net settlement is not on trade-date basis or extends beyond the customary trade practice.[31]

2. *Commodity contracts of normal purchase and normal sale* are not considered derivatives *if*

   a. they are purchased or sold within the norms of the customary business transactions for the industry, and
   b. they will likely be settled by physical delivery.

   For example, not all forward contracts are accepted as derivatives covered by the scope of hedge accounting. Forward contracts that provide for the delivery of commodities at future dates for use in normal business activities (as evidenced by delivery time, location and history of use) will probably end up with physical delivery as a means of settlement. Therefore, they are not considered derivatives under current accounting standards and must be treated as "normal purchase or sale contracts."

3. *Derivatives that serve as impediments to sales accounting:* Consider the contract that transfers financial assets but also has a repurchase option (Repo). The repurchase option is a long call option that enables the transfer or repurchase the transferred assets according to prespecified terms and dates. This contract is a loan in substance and is structured in such a way that it appears as if it is a sale but the intent is to circumvent making an actual sale transaction.
4. *Non-exchange-traded contracts* with the underlying being based on any of the following:

   a. *Climatic, geological, or other physical variables* (e.g., temperature, level of snowfall, seismic readings).[32]
   b. The price or value of a *non-financial asset or liability* of one of the parties that is not readily convertible into cash or does not require settlement by delivery of an asset that

is readily convertible into cash (e.g., an option to purchase or sell a specific real estate property that one of the parties owns, or a firm commitment to purchase or sell specialized unique machinery).

c. *Contracts related to volumes of sales or service revenues* of one of the parties (e.g., royalty agreements, which are typically based on the volume sold).
d. *Certain financial guarantee contracts*. In some cases, creditors (such as bank lenders) are offered guarantees against loss due to the failure of the debtor (e.g., borrower of a commercial loan) to meet required payment obligations under the terms of a contract. A financial guarantee contract that provides creditors with protection against losses if the borrower defaults is essentially an insurance contract that compensates for losses and would not qualify for hedge accounting. A financial guarantee contract would not qualify for hedge accounting under the following conditions:

   i. Reimbursing the creditor an amount equal to the defaulting payment.
   ii. The reimbursement is made only for past due payments.
   iii. The creditor was exposed to the risk of default on the asset for which the guarantee is provided.

   Some credit default swaps are guarantee contracts of this type and provide insurance protection and they are subject to accounting under ordinary GAAP, not under hedge accounting.

e. Interest rate risk and prepayment risk of the held-to-maturity securities do not qualify as hedged items (but credit risk does).
f. Investments in affiliates (subsidiaries or associates) that are consolidated in full or proportionately, and investments accounted for by the equity method do not qualify as hedges (unless they are denominated in foreign currencies other than the functional currency).
g. For the enterprise's own-written options, the writer (seller) of the option cannot designate it as a hedge.

### By Inclusion of Qualified Embedded Derivatives

An embedded derivative is a component of a hybrid financial or non-financial contract that alters the cash flow pattern and response of the host instrument.

A hybrid financial instrument is a contract that has debt-like and equity-like features. One of those features is the base feature (the host contract), while the other is the embedded derivative. An embedded derivative grants one of the parties to the contract some specified rights. These rights are similar in nature, but not in the magnitude of cash flow, to the rights of a similar freestanding financial derivative. For example, a callable bond consists of: (1) a straight bond as a host instrument, and (2) a call option giving the issuer the right to redeem the bond earlier than maturity. The redemption feature is a call option purchased by the issuer of the bond. The issuer pays that price by offering a higher yield on the bond (such as issuing the bonds with a discount) than the market yield for a similar risk class.

Two main features distinguish embedded and freestanding derivatives:

1. *Detachability*: The embedded derivative is not detachable from the host contract.
2. *Marketability*: The embedded derivative cannot be traded independent of the host contract.

What is relatively new in accounting standards is the *requirement* (not a choice) to identify all embedded derivatives and account for them in isolation from the non-derivative contracts, provided that specific conditions are satisfied. These are the conditions for bifurcation discussed in Chapter Nine.[33]

### 6.6.2.3 The Third Requisite: Documentation as a Qualifying Criterion

To qualify for hedge accounting, an entity must maintain clear and extensive documentation at inception throughout the life of the hedge. Because of the different nature of fair value and cash flow hedges, some aspects of the required documentations differ.

Common requirements relate to:

a. *Risk*: identification of the risk being hedged, the risk of the hedge instrument, the anticipated degree of offset and the fit in the enterprise risk management philosophy.
b. *Hedged Item and Hedge Instrument(s)*: identification and description of the specification and characteristics of the hedged item, transaction or forecasted transaction. Detailed description of the hedge instrument(s).
c. *Relationships*: Description of the methods to be used in testing hedge effectiveness, both *ex-ante* (prospectively) and *ex-post* (retrospectively) as well as the methods to measure hedge ineffectiveness.
d. *Others*: Some documentation requirement is specific to currency hedges such as consistency between the basis for hedging and measurement of effectiveness (e.g., after tax or before tax) and information about the quantity or amount of currency expected in hedging a forecasted transaction. (See 815-20-25-3.)

In addition, the documentation must evaluate the need for bifurcating (conceptually separating) embedded derivatives, and it must verify that both of the following conditions are satisfied:

1. The hedged item (the asset, liability, firm commitment or sources of prospective cash flow volatility) is *not* a derivative.[34]
2. The hedged item is not an asset or a liability that is valued at fair value under ordinary (otherwise applicable) GAAP with value changes flowing through the income (P&L) statement.

The documentation requirement is simplified when the business firm adopts and maintains an Enterprise Risk Management program such as, for example, the COSO ERM discussed earlier (Chapter Four). Failing to maintain and update the required documentation for any particular hedging relationship would be sufficient grounds to disqualify using hedge accounting for that particular hedge.

### 6.6.2.4 The Fourth Requisite: Evaluating and Testing Hedge Effectiveness

#### The Concept of Effectiveness

As noted earlier, a hedging program aims at managing the risk exposure of a business enterprise by entering into contracts having risk and cash flow payoffs that are expected to have a negative correlation with the risk exposure. The enterprise must report to its investors and stakeholders how successful is its hedging program in offsetting the risk being hedged. The term used to describe this process is "hedge effectiveness."

A perfectly effective hedge is one in which the changes in the value of the hedge instrument completely offset the risk being hedged. The 100% offset is feasible and can be realized, especially in some specific foreign currency hedge contracts. But for all practical purposes, hedge effectiveness is subject to randomness and unpredictable errors. The standards are silent on the extent to which deviations from perfect offset would be acceptable but, with the encouragement of the SEC, best practices suggest an error tolerance of 20%. A hedging relationship is considered highly effective if it achieves at least 80% success. Enterprises are permitted to continue using hedge accounting for a given hedging relationship to the extent that this gauge of success is achieved.[35]

### Assessment of Hedge Effectiveness: Qualitative Approaches

## Information Log

The ultimate benefit of hedge accounting is to allow the management to avoid reporting the volatility of earnings—even for a very large portfolio of derivatives. But hedge accounting cannot be applied unless the hedge is highly effective. For this reason, the management is likely to manage the firm's transactions in derivative instruments to acquire those derivatives with terms that could pass the accounting test of effectiveness. Therefore, the accounting method used in testing hedge effectiveness is more critical for management policies and decisions than the mere judgment of effective/ineffective. By the same token, the management exercises care in selecting the method to be used in testing hedge effectiveness.

1. *The Short-Cut Method*: In an attempt to simplify hedge accounting, the FASB adopted a method to test hedge effectiveness by asserting the negative: there is no ineffectiveness. Once a hedge qualifies for this method, it is assumed to have no ineffectiveness (fully effective) now and until termination without any quantitative evaluation now or at any time during the term of the hedge. Because nothing is required of the management, it is given the name short-cut method.

The standards have tight constraints that must be satisfied to qualify for using the short-cut method. This method is restricted to interest rate swaps in which the following characteristics hold:

a. The contract is a hedge of interest rate risk exposure of a recognized financial asset or financial liability.
b. Neither the hedged item, nor the hedge instrument is pre-payable in cash or by conversion to another instrument.
c. Equal notional amounts of the hedge and the hedged item.
d. The formula for computing net settlements under the interest rate swap is the same for each net settlement. That is, both of the following conditions are met.
    i. The fixed rate is the same throughout the term of the hedge.
    ii. The variable rate is based on the same index and includes the same constant adjustment or no adjustment.

e. The index on which the variable leg of the interest rate swap is based matches the benchmark interest rate designated as the interest rate risk being hedged for that hedging relationship.

f. The use of the *same* yield curve for both the derivative and the hedged item in all three hedge ineffectiveness calculation methodologies.
g. The expiration date of the interest rate swap matches the maturity date of the interest-bearing asset or liability.
h. The counterparty does not default.

In addition to the above noted requirements, a hedging relationship must satisfy a number of detailed requirements. These requirements have led to limiting the application of the short-cut method to certain types of interest rate swaps. Neither the IASB nor the SEC show enthusiasm for the short-cut method. The method is unique to the U.S. GAAP and, if the IASB has its way in converging standards for financial instruments, the short-cut method will very likely disappear.

2. *Critical Terms Match*: By critical terms, the standards mean all the contractual elements that determine value and risk exposure, such as the underlying, the notional amount, the timing and duration of the hedge and the hedged item. If the critical terms of the hedge instrument and the hedged item match, the enterprise does not need to test quantitatively for effectiveness prospectively or *ex-ante*. However, the entity must perform quarterly evaluation of the continuation of whether critical terms match. A change in matching of critical terms means hedge effectiveness should be tested by statistical (quantitative) methods.

## Accounting Log: ASC 815-20-25-84 on Critical Terms Match Criteria

Whether a hedging relationship qualifies as highly effective sometimes will be easy to assess, and there will be no ineffectiveness to recognize in earnings during the term of the hedge. If the critical terms of the hedging instrument and of the entire hedged asset or liability (as opposed to selected cash flows) or hedged forecasted transaction are the same, the entity could conclude that changes in fair value or cash flows attributable to the risk being hedged are expected to completely offset at inception and on an ongoing basis. For example, an entity may assume that a hedge of a forecasted purchase of a commodity with a forward contract will be highly effective and that there will be no ineffectiveness to be recognized in earnings if all of the following criteria are met:

1. The forward contract is for the purchase of the same quantity of the same commodity at the same time and location as the hedged forecasted purchase.
2. The fair value of the forward contract at inception is zero.
3. Either of the following criteria is met:
   a. The change in the discount or premium on the forward contract is excluded from the assessment of effectiveness and included directly in earnings pursuant to paragraphs 815-20-25-81 through 25-83.
   b. The change in expected cash flows on the forecasted transaction is based on the forward price for the commodity.

## Assessment of Hedge Effectiveness: Quantitative Approaches

Quantitative assessment of hedge effectiveness allows the use of a statistical method, but no boundaries are drawn on inclusion or exclusion of some methods.[36] However, there are three basic methods that use quantitative analysis. These are: (1) The dollar offset method (sometimes called the percentage method); (2) The regression analysis method; and (3) The variance reduction method.

1. *The Dollar Offset Method (the Percentage Method):* The dollar offset method is based on the relationship between cumulative changes in values of the derivative instrument, and cumulative changes in the values of the hedged item. Because changes in values of the hedge instrument and the hedged item are expected to be negatively correlated, the dollar offset ratio (DOR) is measured by the absolute value of the ratio Delta calculated as follows:

$$\delta = |c\Delta D / c\Delta H|$$

where $c\Delta D$ = the cumulative change in the fair value of the hedge derivative instrument and $c\Delta H$ = the cumulative change in the fair value of the hedged item.

For a perfect hedge, Delta should be 100%. However, randomness and errors might not yield 100% and, following best practices and at the initiative of the SEC, a 20% tolerance level became an accepted norm.[37] A hedging relationship is considered highly effective if Delta falls within the range of

$$0.80 \leq |c\Delta D/c\,\Delta H| \leq 1.25$$

Because changes in the cash flow of the derivative and hedge item should offset one another, the cash flow of the derivative and the hedged item should move in opposite directions. As the cash flow of one increases, the cash flow of the other declines. Therefore, the sign of $\delta$ should be negative. However, this simple transformation facilitates understanding the range of effectiveness.

For the purpose of measuring effectiveness of a hedging relationship, two observations must be made:

a. In retrospective tests, the relevant measures are generally the cumulative changes in the values of the derivative hedge and cumulative changes in the values of the hedged item.
b. The hedge effectiveness test should only use the components of value changes that are attributable to the specific risk being hedged. Changes in values that arise from other causes are not relevant and should not be used in the measurement of hedge effectiveness.

**Examples:**

1. An enterprise hedges interest rate risk of a fixed-interest rate bond. The bond value could change for one or both of the following reasons: (a) change in the market interest rate, and (b) change in the issuer's credit risk. Similarly, the derivative could change in value due to changes in interest rate or change in the credit risk of the counterparty.[38] In either case, only the risk being hedged—i.e., the change in fair value due to change in interest rates in this example—should be used in calculating the hedge effectiveness test. The same would apply to hedging credit risk; only the change in value due to changes in credit risk should be used to test hedge effectiveness.

2. In testing hedge effectiveness, the management must decide in advance whether to include changes in option prices due to the time value of options. The time value of option depends on both the volatility of the asset whose risk exposure is being hedged and the duration of the remaining time to expiration.
3. In forward contracts, the management could choose between using the spot rate (i.e., exclude the forward points) or the forward rate (i.e., include the forward points) to measure hedge effectiveness for a given hedge.
4. The change in the fair value of a derivative instrument used to hedge net investment in foreign operations is attributable to the difference between currency spot rate and currency forward rate (if certain conditions are met).

There are three practical problems with using the dollar offset method for evaluating hedge effectiveness:

i. The changes in values of the derivative and hedged item might have a very high negative correlation, but if the magnitude of $c\Delta DV$ is small relative to $c\Delta VH$ and the DOR might give false results. In this situation, the implementation guide (that has become ASC 815-20-35-2) recommends the use of regression analysis.
ii. The correlation between $c\Delta DV$ and $c\Delta VH$ might be low, but the correlation (after the change) between $DV$ and $VH$ is high.
iii. Using the intrinsic value of options in the measurement of effectiveness ignores the time value of options and will yield more measures showing highly effective hedges than if the time value of options was included.

2. *The Regression Analysis Method*: Regression analysis is used often in testing hedge effectiveness because it provides descriptive measures of the relationship between $\Delta DV$ and $\Delta VH$, *even when the magnitudes of one of them is consistently smaller than the other.* The regression relationship is of the form:

$$\Delta D = \alpha + \delta \, \Delta H + e$$

where

$\Delta D$ = the change in the fair value of the hedge instrument.
$\Delta H$ = the change in the fair value of the hedged item.
$\alpha$ = the intercept measuring the stable and relationship between $\Delta D$ and $\Delta H$.
$\delta$ = the coefficient showing the slope or the sensitivity of $\Delta D$ to $\Delta H$ (*the sign of this coefficient must be negative*).
$e$ = an error term that has an expected value (average) of zero.

In addition to the estimated intercept ($\alpha$) and slope coefficient ($\delta$), the regression model produces three useful statistics: (i) the correlation coefficient, (ii) the coefficient of determination or *R-squared*, and (iii) the mean squared error.

Under the interpretation of current best accounting practices, a hedge is considered highly effective if the coefficient of determination ($R^2$) is at least 0.80, which has two possible interpretations:

i. *R-squared* of 80% means that the explanatory variable, which is the change in the value of the hedged item ($\Delta H$), explains 80% of the variability of the dependent variable, the change in the value of the hedge derivative ($\Delta D$). This relationship, however, is only statistical and not causal.
ii. An 80% *R-squared* level means an 89% correlation between the changes in the values of the hedge and the hedged item.

An important factor to consider is the time period over which the regression analysis should be conducted. Clearly, one would want a period long enough to reveal the true relationship between the variations in the two prices; the longer the period, the more the possibility of dampening the impact of sharp movements.

Changes in prices can take different patterns. Prices of the hedge derivative and the hedged item may change in opposite directions as anticipated, but the change in prices might not be highly correlated.

## Exhibit 6.3 Using Regression in Testing Effectiveness

**Panel A: Basic Issues in Using Regression to Test Hedge Effectiveness**

In the regression equation, $\Delta D_i = \alpha + \delta \Delta H_i + e_i$

$\Delta D$ = the change in the fair value of the hedge instrument.
$\Delta H$ = the change in the fair value of the hedged item.
$\alpha$ = the intercept measuring the relationship between $\Delta DV$ and $\Delta VH$.
$\delta$ = the coefficient showing the slope or the sensitivity of $\Delta DV$ to $\Delta VH$ (*the sign of this coefficient must be negative*).
e = an error term that has an expected value (average) of zero.
*i* = the time period of collecting the observation

The slope coefficient $\delta$ shows the sensitivity of the change in the fair value of the derivative to the change in the fair value of the hedged item and, on average, is equal to

$$\Delta D/\Delta H = \delta$$

Therefore, the coefficient $\delta$ is essentially the ratio used in the dollar offset method.

If the hedge has any degree of effectiveness, the value of $\delta$ *can fluctuate within the range*

$$-1 \leq \delta \leq 0.$$

However, irrespective of the size of $\delta$, the goodness of fit or the coefficient of determination ($R^2$) measures the proportion of total variation in the dependent variable $\Delta D$ that is explained by the explanatory variable $\Delta H$. The ratio of explained variation is calculated as follows:

$$R^2 = [1 - RSS_D]/TSS_D$$

where

$TSS_D = \sum_{i=1}^{n}(\Delta D_i - \overrightarrow{\Delta D})^2$ is total variation
$\Delta D_i$ = the change in the value of the derivative over period *i*.
$\overrightarrow{\Delta D}_i$ = average change in the value of the derivative over period *i*.
$\sum_i^n e_{i\,D}^2$ = the residual or unexplained variation (= RSS).
$ESS_D = TSS_D - RSS_D$, is explained variation.
The subscript "D" refers to the hedge derivative.
The subscript "*i*" refers to the time period of which the observations are collected.

To provide an example, assume that two financial derivatives (D) may be designated for hedging an asset or a liability (H). Using historical data of price changes over the past 200 days in a regression analysis produced the relationships shown in Figure 6.2.

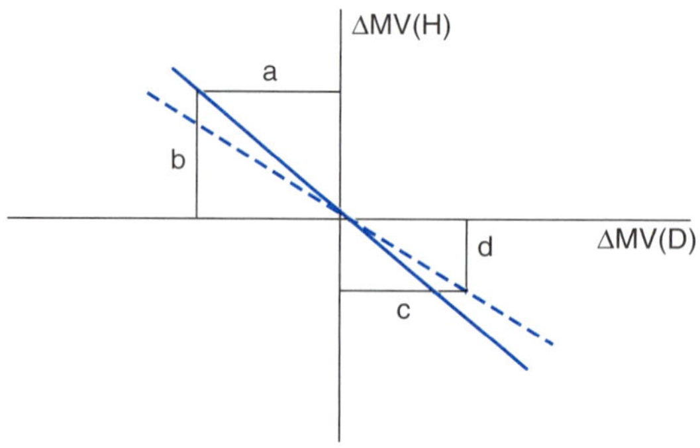


$\Delta$ MV(D) = change in market value of the hedge derivative (a and c).
$\Delta$ MV(H) = change in market value of the hedged item (b and d).
$|\delta| = |a/b| = 1.16 \rightarrow$ means the hedge is effective.
$|\delta| = |c/d| = 1.67 \rightarrow$ means the hedge is ineffective.

**Figure 6.2** Regression Relationships for Price Changes of Two Derivative Instruments and Two Hedged Items

The slopes of the two regression lines are $\delta_{(a,b)}$ and $\delta_{(c,d)}$. These slopes suggest that, on average, one derivative (a,b) moves more in harmony with the hedged item than the other. Furthermore, the relationship is negative and is likely to provide an offset between the absolute values of 0.80 and 1.25.

*Dollar Offset Ratio versus Regression*

Comparing the dollar offset method with the regression method, the ratio of value changes, which is the coefficient $\sigma$, could be small, but the fit and the degree of explained variation is high. This is where the dollar offset method fails: a ratio of change in values lower than the permitted boundary of |0.80| but $R^2$ is high. For this reason, the regression method and the criteria of at least 80% value $R^2$ is preferable to the dollar offset method.

**Panel B: Diagnostics**

For this regression with one explanatory variable, $R^2$ is also the squared value of the correlation coefficient.

The correlation coefficient is given by

$$\rho = \text{cov}\ (\Delta D, \Delta H)/\sigma_{\Delta D} * \sigma_{\Delta H}$$

where

- cov ($\Delta D, \Delta H$) is the covariance of the change in the value of derivatives and the change in the value of the hedged item.
- $\sigma_{\Delta D}$ = the standard deviation of the change in the value of the derivative instrument and is equal to the square root of [$TSS_D/n - 1$].
- $\sigma_{\Delta H}$ = the standard deviation in the value of the hedged item and is equal to the square root of [$TSS_H/n - 1$].
- $n$ = the number of periods over which the accumulation is made – 1, 2 ... n.
- *t-statistic* = a measure of the statistical significance and is measured as slope coefficient divided by the standard error ($= \delta/\sqrt{\sigma_e^2/n}$).

While the regression diagnostics may reduce the problems of using the dollar offset method, using regression to test hedge effectiveness creates different issues:

- There is a need for symmetry in the dates used for accumulating $\Delta D$ and $\Delta H$—using a three-month LIBOR means that both $\Delta D$ and $\Delta H$ are measured on the basis of three-month LIBOR.
- Obtaining a sufficient number of observations might require collecting data from the distant past when the economic conditions and regimes were materially different.
- Estimating regression based on time-series observations will be serially correlated and corrections for serial correlation might be needed before using the results of the regression as valid diagnostics.

3. *The Volatility Reduction Ratio (VRR)*: This method compares the volatility of the hedged item against the volatility of a portfolio consisting of the hedged item and the hedge derivative. Consider the following definitions:

$\sigma_H^2$ = The variance of changes in the value of the hedged item.
$\sigma_D^2$ = The variance of changes in the value of the hedge derivative.

Therefore, the sum of the variance of the Hedged item (H) and the hedge Derivative (D) is

$$\sigma_P^2 = \sigma_H^2 + \sigma_D^2 + \text{cov}(D, H)$$

and the standard deviation is

$$\sigma_p = \sqrt{\sigma_p^2}$$

The subscript "$D$" is for derivative, "$H$" is for hedged item, and "$P$" is for portfolio.
Then the volatility reduction ratio is measured by

$$VRR = [\sigma^2_H - \sigma^2_p]/\sigma^2_H$$
$$= 1 - \sigma^2_p/\sigma^2_H$$

### 6.6.2.5 Measurement Issues with Cash Flow Hedging

Hedge effectiveness is an evaluation of the degree to which a hedge succeeds in mitigating a specific risk. In the cash flow hedge treatment, the hedged item is the volatility of anticipated future cash flows; it is a feature without a value attached to it. Accordingly, the changes in the values of the hedge instruments do not always have counter measures of changes in the hedged "feature." In an effort to fill in this void, both the FASB and IASB adopted the concept of "hypothetical derivative" to stand for the hedged item. As the name connotes, a hypothetical derivative is an imaginary contract structured to generate imaginary cash flows moving in the opposite direction of the changes in the cash flows of the hedge instrument. By construction, cash flow hedge are in this case highly effective as a result of this mechanical process rather than real economic events. Additionally, when the cash flow of the hedged feature could be estimated, there could be a case of overhedge when the change in the fair value of the derivative is greater than the change in the fair value of the changes in the cash flow of the hedged feature. There could also be underhedge. The accounting treatment for overhedge and underhedge is discussed in Chapter Seven.

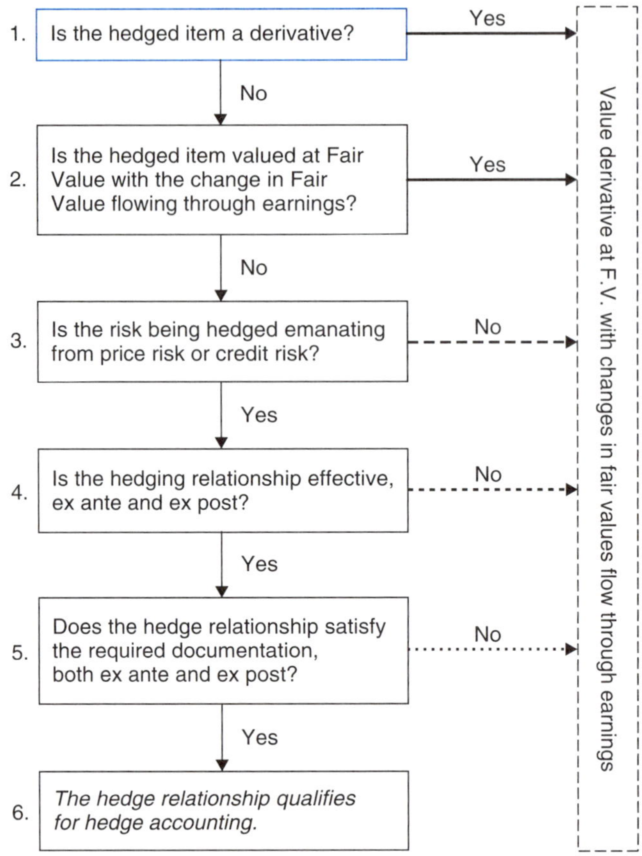


**Figure 6.3** A Flowchart Summary for Eligibility for Hedge Accounting

## Exhibit 6.4 Description of Hedge Accounting at IBM

### Derivative Financial Instruments

All derivatives are recognized in the Consolidated Statement of Financial Position at fair value and are reported in prepaid expenses and other current assets, investments and sundry assets, other accrued expenses and liabilities, or other liabilities. Classification of each derivative as current or noncurrent is based upon whether the maturity of the instrument is less than or greater than 12 months. To qualify for hedge accounting, the instruments must be effective in reducing the risk exposure that they are designated to hedge. For instruments that hedge cash flows, hedge effectiveness criteria also require that it be probable that the underlying transaction will occur. Instruments that meet established accounting criteria are formally designated as hedges. These criteria demonstrate that the derivative is expected to be highly effective at offsetting changes in fair value or cash flows of the underlying exposure both at inception of the hedging relationship and on an ongoing basis. The method of assessing hedge effectiveness and measuring hedge ineffectiveness is formally documented at hedge inception. The company assesses hedge effectiveness and measures hedge ineffectiveness at least quarterly throughout the designated hedge period.

Where the company applies hedge accounting, the company designates each derivative as a hedge of: (1) the fair value of a recognized financial asset or liability or of an unrecognized firm commitment (fair value hedge); (2) the variability of anticipated cash flows of a forecasted transaction or the cash flows to be received or paid related to a recognized financial asset or liability (cash flow hedge); or (3) a hedge of a long-term investment (net investment hedge) in a foreign operation. In addition, the company may enter into derivative contracts that economically hedge certain of its risks, even though hedge accounting does not apply or the company elects not to apply hedge accounting. In these cases, there exists a natural hedging relationship in which changes in the fair value of the derivative, which are recognized currently in net income, act as an economic offset to changes in the fair value of the underlying hedged item(s).

(Source: IBM Form 10-K, 2010 Annual Report, p. 75. Available at: ftp://public.dhe.ibm.com/annualreport/2010/2010_ibm_annual.pdf)

## 6.7 How Important Are Derivative Instruments?

The volume of financial derivatives has increased by more than 3,500% over the past 20 years. In the first quarter of 2012, the Office of U.S. Comptroller of the Currency Administrator of National Banks (OCC's Report) reports a notional amount of $243 trillion for the volume of derivatives in the top 25 U.S. commercial banks. Figure 6.4, reproduced from the OCC's Report, presents the growth in derivatives during the 10 years ending the first quarter of 2012, which is very likely greater than any other man-made phenomenon. This growth is in spite of the reported decline in 2012: "The notional amount of derivatives contracts held by insured U.S. commercial banks in the

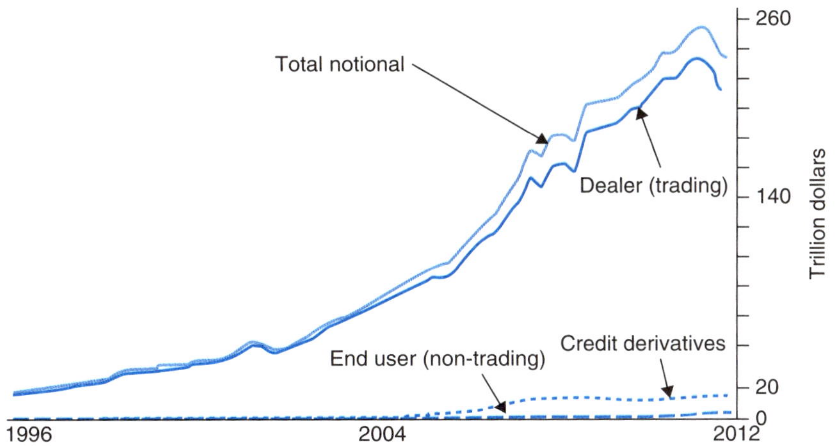


**Figure 6.4** OTC erivative Notional Accounts by Type of User (Insured U.S. Commercial Banks and Savings Associations)

(Source: http://www.occ.gov/topics/capital-markets/financial-markets/trading/derivatives/dq112.pdf, Graph 1, p. 11. First Quarter 2012)

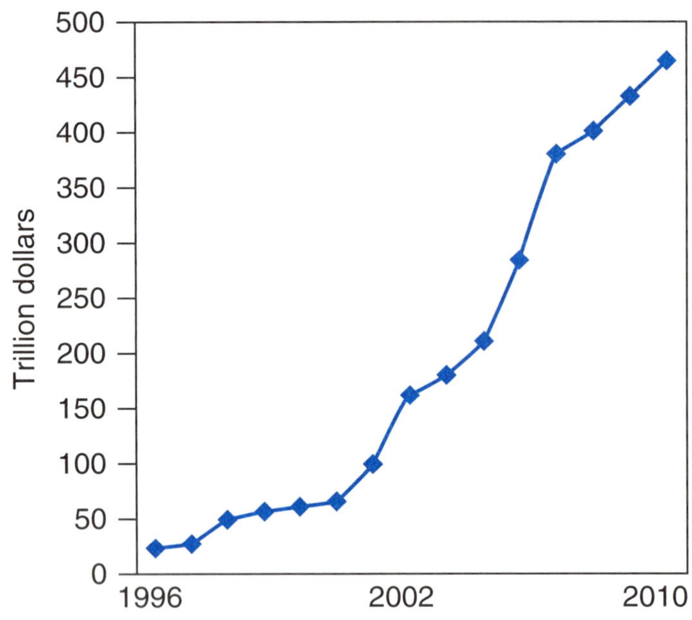


**Figure 6.5** Volume of Notional Amounts of OTC Derivatives as Reported by ISDA

(Source: Compiled from ISDA = International Swap Dealers Association, http://www.isda.org/statistics/recent.html)

fourth quarter fell by $17.2 trillion (6.9%) to $230.8 trillion from the third quarter. Notionals had also fallen 0.6% during the third quarter."[40]

Figure 6.5 shows the volume of the derivatives notional (face) amounts as reported by the International Swap Dealers Association (ISDA). The size of the market has increased from $20 trillion in 1996 to about $500 trillion in the first half of 2010. The true volume is probably even greater than that being reported simply because the volume is an estimate based on surveying dealers and not all dealers had responded. Of this total, the size of trade for the largest 14 global derivatives dealers was $355 trillion and the volume for the five largest U.S.-based dealers was $172 trillion.[41]

The notional amount is a measure upon which the payoff of a derivative is based. It does not represent the amount at risk. While the estimated fair values amount to about 4% of notional amount, if one assumes that only 2% represent the amount at risk, this amounts to $10 trillion, about 80% of the U.S. Gross Domestic Product (GDP).

## Exhibit 6.5 Cases Describing the Volume of Derivatives in Financial and Non-Financial Institutions

### 1. Derivatives at JPMorgan Chase

*Balances of Notional Amounts:*

As of 2010, the total notional amount of derivatives is $78.9 trillion, of which $63.6 trillion are for interest rate contracts, and $7.7 trillion are for foreign currency contracts.

**Carrying Assets and Liabilities as of December 31, 2010**

| Total recognized freestanding trading derivatives | Receivable | Payable |
|---|---|---|
| Not designated as hedges (in billion dollars) | 1,520 | 1,481 |
| Designated as hedges (in billion dollars) | 9.5 | 4 |
| Netting adjustment (in billion dollars)[(a)] | (1,529) | (1,485) |
| Carrying fair value on the balance sheet (in billion dollars) | 80.5 | 69 |

**Income Statement Effects of Hedge Derivative**

| | | |
|---|---|---|
| Fair Value Hedges | Gain on derivatives (in millions of dollars) | 1,069 |
| | Loss on hedged items (in millions of dollars) | (384) |
| | Net impact on earnings (in millions of dollars) | 686 |
| Cash Flow Hedges | Recorded in OCI (in millions of dollars) | 247 |
| | Reclassified from OCI to earnings (in millions of dollars) | 384 |

(a) Netting assets and liabilities of contracts with the same counterparty under the terms of the ISDA for all over-the-counter derivatives. Netting is permitted under U.S. GAAP where there is a counterparty Master Agreement that would be enforceable in the event of bankruptcy.

(Source: JPMorgan Chase, 2010 Form 10-K, pp. 192–195. Available at http://www.sec.gov/Archives/edgar/data/19617/000095012311019773/y86143e10vk.htm)

**2. Derivatives Assets and Liabilities at Barclays PLC (2010)**

| | *Gross assets (£ million)* | *Counterparty netting[(a)] (£ million)* | *Net exposure (£ million)* |
|---|---|---|---|
| Interest rate | 272,386 | 224,124 | 48,262 |
| Foreign exchange | 60,494 | 49,405 | 11,089 |
| Credit derivatives | 47,017 | 39,786 | 7,231 |
| Equity and stock index | 14,586 | 10,523 | 4,063 |
| Commodity derivatives | 25,836 | 16,629 | 9,207 |
| Total derivative assets | 420,319 | 340,467 | 79,852 |
| Total collateral held | | | 37,289 |
| Net exposure less collateral | | | 42,563 |
| Derivative liabilities | 405,516 | — | — |

(a) Under IFRS, netting is also permitted only if (i) the enterprise has a legally enforceable right to offset the recognized amounts; and (ii) the enterprise intends to either settle on a net basis, or realize the asset and settle the liability simultaneously.

(Source: Barclays PLC, Annual Report 2010, p. 111. Available at http://group.barclays.com/about-barclays/investor-relations/financial-results-and-publications/annual-reports)

### 3. Derivative Instruments at IBM (2010)

| | *Fair value of derivative assets (US$ million)* | *Fair value of derivative liabilities (US$ million)* |
|---|---|---|
| Interest rate contracts | 548 | — |
| Foreign exchange contracts | 530 | 1,003 |
| Equity contracts | 12 | 3 |
| Total | 1,100 | 1,006 |
| The reported numbers for these contracts are the fair values. (Source: IBM, 2010 Annual Report, Form 10-K, p. 99. Available at ftp://public.dhe.ibm.com/annualreport/2010/2010_ibm_annual.pdf) | | |

### Gain (Loss) Recognized in Earnings ($ millions)

| | *Recognized* | | *Attributable to Risk* | |
|---|---|---|---|---|
| *For the year ended December 31:* | *2010* | *2009* | *2010* | *2009* |
| Derivative instruments in *fair value hedges*: | | | | |
| Interest rate contracts cost of financing interest expense | 241 | (172) | (70) | 344 |
| Derivative instruments not designated as hedging instruments | 160 | (97) | (46) | 193 |
| Foreign exchange contracts | | | | |
| Other (income) and expense | 299 | (128) | N/A | N/A |
| Equity contracts SG&A expense | 105 | 177 | N/A | N/A |
| Total | 805 | (219) | (116) | 537 |
| Gain (loss) Recognized in Accumulated Other Comprehensive Income | | | | |
| Effective Portion Recognized in AOCI | $549 | | | |
| Reclassified from AOCI | $(203) | | | |
| Ineffective and amounts excluded from effectiveness | $(7) | | | |
| (Source: IBM, Form 10-K, 2010, p. 101. Available at ftp://public.dhe.ibm.com/annualreport/2010/2010_ibm_annual.pdf) | | | | |

## 6.8 Sources of Complexity in Hedge Accounting

Financial derivatives differ from most other assets in several respects:

1. They are rights and obligations conveyed by contracts.
2. They do not generate their values from fundamentals as common stocks (earnings and dividends).

3. These contracts can be structured in many combinations and terms.
4. New structured contracts can be (and are) developed every day.
5. The rights and obligations conveyed by these contracts depend critically on the terms of the contracts and relationship to the value and risk generators.
6. As a result, the first difficult aspect of accounting for derivatives and hedging is the ability to sort out and identify the basic elements of each contract so that rights and obligations can be identified.
7. The second most difficult aspect of accounting for these contracts is the valuation of assets and liabilities. These valuations are essential since the historical cost of most derivatives is zero or negligible. These measurements will depend on the interpretations of the contracts and the uncertainties involved.

Once these elements are determined, it becomes a simple exercise to book the assets, liabilities, earnings, and equity. Yet this exercise is significant because of the differential impact on assets, liabilities, earnings, and owners' equity.

To illustrate this complexity, Exhibit 6.6 presents two of the numerous examples addressed by the FASB Derivatives Implementation Group (DIG).

## Exhibit 6.6 Two Examples of Seemingly Simple Contracts from the FASB Derivatives Implementation Group

### 1. Derivatives Implementation Group (2006). "Statement 133 Implementation Issue No. A1"

QUESTION

If an entity enters into a forward contract that requires the purchase of 1 share of an unrelated company's common stock in 1 year for $110 (the market forward price) and at inception the entity elects to prepay the contract pursuant to its terms for $105 (the current price of the share of common stock), does the contract meet the criterion in paragraph 6(b) related to initial net investment and therefore meet the definition of a derivative for that entity? If not, is there an embedded derivative that warrants separate accounting?

RESPONSE

Paragraph 6(b) of Statement 133 specifies that a derivative requires either no initial net investment or a smaller initial net investment than would be required for other types of contracts that would be expected to have a similar response to changes in market factors. If no prepayment is made at inception, the contract would meet the criterion in paragraph 6(b) because it does not require an initial net investment but, rather, contains an unexercised election to prepay the contract at inception. Paragraph 8 further clarifies paragraph 6(b) and states that a derivative instrument does not require an initial net investment in the contract that is equal to the notional amount or that is determined by applying the notional amount to the underlying. If the contract gives the entity the option to "prepay" the contract at a later date during its 1-year term (at $105 or some other specified amount), exercise of that option would be accounted for as a loan that is repayable at $110 at the end of the forward contract's one-year term.

If, instead, the entity elects to prepay the contract at inception for $105, the contract does not meet the definition of a freestanding derivative. Paragraph 8, as amended, indicates that if the initial net investment of the contract (after adjustment for the time value of money) is less, by more than a nominal amount, than the initial net investment that would be commensurate with the amount that would be exchanged to acquire the asset related to the underlying, the characteristic in paragraph 6(b) is met. The initial net investment of $105 is equal to the initial price of the 1 share of stock being purchased under the contract and therefore is equal to the investment that would be required for other types of contracts that would be expected to have a similar response to changes in market factors. That is, the initial net investment is equal to the amount that would be exchanged to acquire the asset related to the underlying.

However, the entity must assess whether that nonderivative instrument contains an embedded derivative that, pursuant to paragraph 12, requires separate accounting as a derivative unless a fair value election is made pursuant to Statement 155. (Note that Statement 155 was issued in February 2006 and allows for a fair value election for hybrid financial instruments that otherwise would require bifurcation. Hybrid financial instruments that are elected to be accounted for in their entirety at fair value cannot be used as a hedging instrument in a Statement 133 hedging relationship.) *In this example, the prepaid contract is a hybrid instrument that is composed of a debt instrument as the host contract (that is, a loan that is repayable at $110 at the end of the forward contract's 1-year term) and an embedded derivative based on equity prices. The host contract is a debt instrument because the holder has none of the rights of a shareholder, such as the ability to vote the shares and receive distributions to shareholders.* (Refer to paragraph 60 of Statement 133.) Unless the hybrid instrument is remeasured at fair value with changes in value recorded in earnings as they occur, the embedded derivative must be separated from the host contract because the economic characteristics and risks of a derivative based on equity prices are not clearly and closely related to a debt host contract, and a separate instrument with the same terms as the embedded derivative would be a derivative subject to the requirements of Statement 133.

Available at http://www.fasb.org/derivatives/issuea1.shtml; emphasis added)

**2. Derivatives Implementation Group (2003). "Statement 133 Implementation Issue No. C10"**

QUESTION

In what instances can the normal purchases and normal sales exception in paragraph 10(b) (as amended) be applied to (1) purchased option contracts (including net purchased options) and written option contracts (including net written options) that would require delivery of the related asset at an established price under the contract only if exercised, and, (2) forward contracts with optionality features?

BACKGROUND

Paragraph 10(b) of Statement 133 (as amended by Statement 149) states, in part:

> Normal purchases and normal sales are contracts that provide for the purchase or sale of something other than a financial instrument or derivative instrument that will be delivered in quantities expected to be used or sold by the reporting entity over a reasonable period in the normal course of business. The following guidance should be considered in determining whether a specific type of contract qualifies for the normal purchases and normal sales exception:

(1) *Forward contracts (non-option-based contracts).* Forward contracts are eligible to qualify for the normal purchases and normal sales exception. However, forward contracts that contain net settlement provisions as described in either paragraph 9(a) or paragraph 9(b) are not eligible for the normal purchases and normal sales exception unless it is probable at inception and throughout the term of the individual contract that the contract will not settle net and will result in physical delivery.* Net settlement (as described in paragraphs 9(a) and 9(b)) of contracts in a group of contracts similarly designated as normal purchases and normal sales would call into question the classification of all such contracts as normal purchases or normal sales. Contracts that require cash settlements of gains or losses or are otherwise settled net on a periodic basis, including individual contracts that are part of a series of sequential contracts intended to accomplish ultimate acquisition or sale of a commodity, do not qualify for this exception.
(2) *Freestanding option contracts.* Option contracts that would require delivery of the related asset at an established price under the contract only if exercised are not eligible to qualify for the normal purchases and normal sales exception, except as indicated in paragraph 10(b)(4) below.
(3) *Forward contracts that contain optionality features.* Forward contracts that contain optionality features that do not modify the quantity of the asset to be delivered under the contract are eligible to qualify for the normal purchases and normal sales exception. Except for power purchase or sales agreements addressed in paragraph 10(b)(4), if an option component permits modification of the quantity of the assets to be delivered, the contract is not eligible for the normal purchases and normal sales exception, unless the option component permits the holder only to purchase or sell additional quantities at the market price at the date of delivery. In order for forward contracts that contain optionality features to qualify for the normal purchases and normal sales exception, the criteria discussed in paragraph 10(b)(1) must be met.
(4) *Power purchase or sales agreements.* Notwithstanding the criteria in paragraph 10(b)(1) and 10(b)(3), a power purchase or sales agreement (whether a forward contract, option contract, or a combination of both) that is a capacity contract also qualifies for the normal purchases and normal sales exception if it meets the criteria in paragraph 58(b).

Contracts that are subject to unplanned netting (referred to as a "book out" in the electric utility industry) do not qualify for this exception except as specified in paragraph 58(b).

The contracts addressed in this Issue do not have a price based on an underlying that is not clearly and closely related to the asset being purchased, nor do they require cash settlement of gains or losses as stipulated in paragraph 10(b).

In some circumstances, an option contract may be combined with a forward contract. In some cases, the optionality feature in the forward contract can modify the quantity of the asset to be delivered under the contract. In other cases, the optionality feature in the forward contract can modify only the price to be paid or the timing of the delivery.

RESPONSE

Paragraph 10(b) of Statement 133, as amended by Statement 149, indicates that purchased option contracts (including net purchased options) and written option contracts (including net written options) that would require delivery of the related asset at an established price under the contract only if exercised are generally not eligible to qualify for the normal purchases and normal sales exception, except as indicated in paragraph 10(b)(4) and the related guidance in paragraph 58(b), as amended, and Statement 133 Implementation Issue No. C15, "Normal Purchases and Normal Sales Exception for Option-Type Contracts and Forward Contracts in Electricity." The normal purchases and normal sales exception applies only to contracts that provide for the purchase or sale of something other than a financial instrument or derivative instrument that will be delivered in quantities expected to be used or sold by the reporting entity over a reasonable period in the normal course of business. Option contracts only contingently provide for such purchase or sale since exercise of an option contract is not assured. Thus, in accordance with paragraph 10(b)(2) of Statement 133, as amended, freestanding option contracts (including in-the-money option contracts) are not eligible to qualify for the normal purchases and normal sales exception. Furthermore, because of the contingent nature of an option contract (whose potential exercise is typically dependent upon future changes in the underlying); an entity cannot determine at the inception of the option contract that it will be probable throughout the term of the contract that physical delivery will result. Thus, option contracts cannot meet the requirement in paragraph 10(b) that it be "probable at inception and throughout the term of the individual contract that the contract ... will result in physical delivery." The normal purchases and normal sales exception applies only to forward contracts. However, as indicated in paragraph 10(b)(3), forward contracts that contain optionality features would be eligible to qualify for the normal purchases and normal sales exception only if the optionality feature could not modify the quantity of the asset to be delivered under the contract. (Refer to the following discussion.)

The following are examples of forward contract with optionality features:

1. Company A enters into a forward contract to purchase on a specified date a specified quantity of a raw material that is readily convertible to cash. The purchase price is the current market price on the date of purchase, neither to exceed a specified maximum price (a cap) nor to be less than a specified minimum price (a floor).
2. Company B enters into a forward contract to purchase on a specified date a specified quantity of a raw material that is readily convertible to cash. The contract's purchase price is a fixed amount per unit that is below the current forward price; however, if the market price on the date of purchase has fallen below a specified level, Company B's purchase price would be adjusted to a higher fixed amount significantly in excess of the current forward price at the inception of the contract. (The contract entered into by Company B is a compound derivative consisting of a forward contract to purchase raw material at the original fixed price and a written option that obligates Company B to purchase the raw material for the higher adjusted price if the market price of the raw material falls below the specified level. In exchange for the written option, Company B received a premium representing the difference between the purchase price in the contract and the forward market price of the raw material at the inception of the contract.)
3. Company C enters into a forward contract to purchase on a specified date a specified quantity of a raw material that is readily convertible to cash. The contract's purchase price is a fixed amount per unit that is below the current forward price. However, if the market price on the date of purchase has fallen below a specified level that is below the contract's fixed

purchase price, Company C would be required to purchase a specified additional quantity of the raw material at the contract's fixed purchase price (which is above the current market price on the date of purchase). (The contract entered into by Company C is a compound derivative consisting of a forward contract to purchase raw material at the original fixed price and a written option that obligates Company C to purchase additional quantities of the raw material at an above-market price if the market price of the raw material falls below the specified level.)

In the above cases, the optionality feature must be analyzed to determine whether it could modify the quantity of the asset to be delivered under the contract. In doing so, the conclusion as to whether the contract is eligible for the normal purchases and sales exception applies in the same way to both counterparties—the purchaser and the writer of the option (within the forward contract).

In cases in which the optionality feature in the forward contract can modify the quantity of the asset to be delivered under the contract, if that option feature has expired or has been completely exercised (even if delivery has not yet occurred), there is no longer any uncertainty as to the quantity to be delivered under the forward contract. Accordingly, following such expiration or exercise, the forward contract would be eligible for designation as a normal purchase or normal sale, provided that that the other conditions in paragraph 10(b) are met.

In Example 1, the optionality feature cannot modify the quantity to be delivered; thus, the contract is eligible to qualify for the normal purchases and normal sales exception.

Similarly, the contract in Example 2 is also eligible to qualify for the normal purchases and normal sales exception because the optionality feature in the contract cannot modify the quantity to be delivered.

The contract in Example 3 is not eligible to qualify for the normal purchases and normal sales exception since the optionality feature in the contract can modify the quantity of the asset to be delivered under the contract.

(http://www.fasb.org/derivatives/issuec10.shtml)

## 6.9 Summary of Key Points

### 6.9.1 Previous Chapter

The preceding chapter presented the main financial derivative instruments, how they create rights and obligations. The next natural step in thought would be to ask the question: now we know there are many types of risk, is volatility the only treatment measure of risk? Alternatively do we know of alternative approaches to measure each type? Financial instruments can be used as investments or as risk-hedging tools. The accounting treatment is very different for these two types of uses. Although accounting for financial instruments is not new, hedge accounting is relatively new, starting in 2000, with the issuance of FAS 133 (now ASC 815), and has spilled over to all other accounting standards.

Hedge accounting allows the management to smooth earnings volatility and, as such, it is a privilege and the enterprise must earn the right to use it by adhering to a set of qualifying criteria.

### 6.9.2 Key Issues

This chapter addresses two different topics.

#### *6.9.2.1 Qualification for Hedge Accounting*

- Financial instruments may be used for investment, hedging risk exposure, or speculation.
- The derivative instruments used as investment in the trading portfolio do not qualify for hedge accounting.
- The derivative instruments used for speculation do not qualify for hedge accounting and can be a component of the "undesignated" derivatives—often referred to as "economic hedges."
- Not all financial derivatives could qualify for hedge accounting; only those derivatives that meet specific qualifications:
    - Meeting the accounting definition of a derivative (one or more underlying, notional amount or payment provision, no initial investment made, and settle net).
    - The instrument is not subject to explicit exclusion from the scope of applying the standard.
    - It is not limited to freestanding instruments; it could be embedded.
    - The hedge is fully documented as a hedge.
    - The hedging relationship is highly successful (effective) in mitigating the risk being hedged.
- All financial derivatives are to be valued at fair value.
- The risk exposure permitted for hedge accounting is limited to the risk arising from unexpected price changes or credit risk that may lead to loss in value or volatility of cash flow and that have effects on earnings.
- Hedging success is measured by the extent to which the risk being hedged is offset by the price behavior of the derivative instrument. Accounting distinguishes between successful (highly effective) hedges and unsuccessful (ineffective) hedges; the application of hedge accounting is permitted only for the highly effective hedge.
    - Effectiveness may be "declared" qualitatively: the short-cut method and critical terms match.
    - Effectiveness may be measured qualitatively by one of the following methods:
        1. Dollar offset ratio.
        2. Regression analysis.
        3. Volatility reduction method.
- Hedging exposure to currency risk could be treated as hedging fair value loss (of a specific asset, liability or firm commitment), cash flow volatility (of an asset, liability or forecasted transaction), or the loss of the value of net assets of foreign operations. Hedging "net" assets of foreign operations is the only exception permitting hedge accounting to net assets and liabilities as a hedgeable position.
- The accounting treatment for financial derivative contracts that result in highly effective hedge should reflect management's intent in using these derivatives to actually hedge risk exposure.

- Provided that the hedge is highly effective and the other criteria are satisfied, accounting must distinguish between hedging the risk exposure to (current or contemporaneous) loss in value versus the risk exposure to cash flow volatility. The former is classified as *fair value hedge*, while the latter is classified as *cash flow hedge*. The different classification will result in different accounting treatments, as the next chapter will discuss.

### 6.9.2.2 Significance of Financial Derivatives

The statistics about the volume of financial derivatives is unfathomable. The reported statistics show that the notional amounts of the OTC derivatives have grown from $20 trillion in about the year 2000 to nearly $650 trillion in 2012, of which the U.S. insured commercial banks hold about $243 trillion. This segment ends by showing the volume of derivatives at several larger corporations.

## Notes

1 Transfers between levels of fair values are acceptable to the extent to which quoted prices, active markets, or input data availability changes.
2 Deciding that a derivative contract represents "normal purchase or normal sale" is an exception recognized by ASC 815 that could be elected if the contract satisfies certain criteria, including a requirement that physical delivery of the underlying commodity is probable. For example, having a forward contract to purchase a specified quantity of a specific commodity at a future date would qualify for this exception if physical delivery is probable. Adopting this exception simply means this forward contract will not be accounted for as a derivative. Instead it would be accounted for as an executory contract which would be recognized upon performance.
3 This end result has been a source of contention between management and standard setters and has affected the way in which standards have evolved.
4 Because management has a wide latitude in the determination of fair value under Level 3, some analysts refer to Level 3 as "mark-to-management."
5 This is done by explicit exclusion from the scope of hedge accounting.
6 In principle, derivatives are acquired for trading (speculation) or hedging. It follows that all hedging relationships are undertaken for economic reasons whether or not the hedge relationship satisfies the accounting conditions for the adoption of special hedge accounting.
7 Foreign currency denominated intercompany contracts expose the entity to cash flow risk due to fluctuations in currency exchange rates. This risk is acceptable to be hedged as a cash flow hedge.
8 Except for accrued interest amounts.
9 It is assumed that the U.S. dollar is the functional currency for the U.S. company and the Swiss franc is the functional currency for the Swiss company.
10 Throughout this book, it will be noted that using management intent as a guide for establishing accounting standards could lead to suboptimal behavior.
11 This is perhaps the weakest link in the entire system and accounting standards.
12 Further detail on measures of hedge effectiveness follows.
13 The full set of conditions necessary to affect this treatment will follow in later sections.
14 The short-cut method of interest rate hedge does not require continuous measurement of effectiveness.
15 Three of these methods are provided in the guides to standards and are detailed later in this chapter.
16 To a large extent, U.S. GAAP and IFRS are very similar in this respect.
17 Embedded derivatives are discussed in more detail in Chapter Nine.

18 "Significant nature" in this context means a price lower than what could be paid for a freestanding derivative with the same cash flow and risk characteristics.
19 Willingness to pay is a legal matter that we do not consider.
20 However, before making a decision on the appropriate accounting method, the transaction has to be evaluated to see if it fits the exception to ASC 815 for purchase and sale in the normal way.
21 Value changes could also occur because of inaccuracy of the published yield curve used, forward rates, or the evaluation of the credit risk of the counterparty.
22 This present value is an "effective notional" for the special arrangement of contracting at a fixed rate higher than the zero-swap rate. This amount is essentially a loan and should be accounted for as debt that should be amortized over the term of the swap contract. It will adjust the nominal interest rate of 8% to become an effective rate of 5.5%. Enron had a swap contract of this type with Citi for which Enron was paid about $2 billion. Given the inclination of Enron's management, the $2 billion were accounted for as "gain" for the period in which the swap contract originated. This was improper because it should have been accounted for as a liability, not as an equity account.
23 The forward upfront points are not considered a price or an investment that would violate this requirement and discussion of these forward points is ignored for the moment.
24 The metals' futures traded on NYMEX are designated as either cash settled or physical delivery settlement: *Cash Settled Contracts*: Asian Gold; Asian Platinum; Asian Palladium; miNY Gold; Asian Platinum; Asian Palladium; miNU Gold; miNY Copper; and miNY Silver. *Physically Settled Contracts*: Gold; Copper; Silver; Aluminum; Platinum; Palladium. www.nymex.com
25 NYMEX, the major cotton futures market is located in New York. The unit of trade is 50,000 pounds or 100 statistical bales.
26 In some cases, holders of call options may prefer to pay the strike price of the options and receive the number of shares specified in the contract if the holder of the option wants to actually hold the stock and wants to avoid incurring additional transaction cost. For example, this could be an investor who wants to increase the influence of his/her voting power. In most cases, however, it is more cost effective for the writer of the option to pay the holder a cash amount equal to the intrinsic value of the option (spot market price at the time of exercise minus the strike price) at expiration. After settling net, the option holder will have a sufficient amount of money (what could have been paid as an exercise price plus the intrinsic value received at settlement) to purchase the stock in the open market if he or she chooses to do so.
27 Unwinding a sale (purchase) contract by entering into a purchase (sale) contract with similar terms does not relieve the contracting party from legal obligations unless both contracts are written with the same counterparty. For example, unwinding a futures contract always satisfies this condition because the Futures Exchange would be the counterparty for both contracts, but this may not be the case for unwinding forward contracts.
28 Embedded derivatives are the subject of Chapter Nine.
29 By the term "exceptions" ASC 815 means disqualification from hedge accounting.
30 Except investments that are denominated in foreign currency and are exposed to currency risk which could be hedged, such as hedging net investment in foreign operations (Chapter Eleven).
31 Securities of the type "when issued" such as in the case of mortgage-backed securities are considered regular-way trade and hedge accounting would not apply to them.
32 It should be noted that the exclusion of weather derivatives from hedge accounting is not an absolute ban; exchange-traded weather derivatives are accepted.
33 Because embedded derivatives are not detachable, the FASB does not use the term "separation" and instead uses the term "bifurcation." More details in Chapter Nine.
34 Strictly speaking, this statement could be confusing because in some cases the hedged items are what might be called "derivatives." The embedded call option in callable debt could be designated as the hedged item if is not bifurcated (isolated) from the host instrument. Similarly, a swaption is a contract that gives the holder the option to enter into a swap contract. In this case, it was ruled that the option could be a

hedge derivative with the hedged item being the written swap contract; the underlying is the value of the swap, and the settlement of the option is net.

35 The FASB circulated an exposure draft of a revision that would change "highly effective" to "moderately effective." Also, there has been some difference in historical development at IASB and FASB. The IASB approach was to require a 100% prospectively, but would accept the 80–100% range for retrospective tests. The differentiation between prospective and retrospective hedges has changed to allow the same range for both tests.

36 As of the time of writing this book, both the IASB and the FASB were considering the possibilities of softening the quantitative measures of hedge effectiveness.

37 It is not clear how the upper limit became 1.25. There are stories that this range is what was given in a speech by an SEC official. Alternatively, one could think of the ratio of full effectiveness to the lower bound as 1.00/0.80 = 1.25. This range, however, might become history since lobbyists are increasing the pressure on the FASB and IASB to accept a management judgment call of "reasonably effective" as the benchmark. Irrespective of whether there is or is not a quantitative measure, the basic accounting for effective and ineffective hedge will remain the same.

38 Impact of credit risk changes on the value of the derivative is minimal for futures because of the security margin and daily settlement.

39 A firm commitment is an executory contract (a contract awaiting performance) which accounting standards have not fully addressed. As a result, the values of these contracts are not reported. But the changes in values of these contracts are recognized in a fair value hedge if they are hedged and the hedge is effective.

40 Source: Office of Comptroller of the Currency (2012). "OCC's Quarterly Report on Bank Trading and Derivatives Activities First Quarter 2012" Washington, D. C., p. 10. Available at: http://www.occ.treas.gov/news-issuances/news-releases/2012/2012-96a.pdf

41 www.isda.org/statistics/

# CHAPTER 7

# HEDGE ACCOUNTING I (SINGLE CURRENCY)

## 7.1 The Two Types of Accounting Standards

### A Caveat

There is only one U.S. GAAP (Generally Accepted Accounting Principles) and one international GAAP called IFRS (International Financial Reporting Standards). In reality, however, corporate adoption of hedge accounting is an override of GAAP; for a company to apply the special guides provided by hedge accounting and be able to smooth earnings is a privilege; it is neither a right nor an obligation. An entity becomes eligible to adopt hedge accounting if it meets a very specific set of rules; that is, the management could opt to take or leave this special accounting treatment. These choices are not available in any other accounting standard.

Therefore, to facilitate the discussion and the presentation, let us informally partition the set of accounting standards into two categories: (a) hedge accounting, and (b) everything else that could be referred to as "ordinary GAAP."

## 7.2 Ordinary GAAP versus Hedge Accounting

As discussed in Chapter Six, a financial instrument is considered a "derivative" if it meets four criteria:[1]

1. It drives its value (and risk) from the behavior of one or more "underlyings": changes in prices, indexes or credit risk.
2. It has one or more notional amounts or a payment provision.
3. It requires minimal or no initial investment.
4. It allows for settling net.

Furthermore, valuation and recognition of changes in value will depend on whether the financial instrument is: (i) an asset, (ii) a liability, or (iii) equity.

## 7.2.1 Financial Assets

### *7.2.1.1 A General Concept*

A financial asset is cash or the right to receive cash. For example, accounts and notes receivable are financial assets because they constitute the right to receive cash. Investments in marketable securities are financial assets because all investment in securities (whether held-to-maturity (amortized cost), held-for-trading (fair value through earnings), or available-for-sale (fair value through Other Comprehensive Income (OCI)) have the right to receive cash upon sale or maturity. Even investing in mandatorily convertible bonds that grant the issuers the right to convert the bonds into common equity shares are financial assets because common stock is a financial asset; the stockholder has the right to receive cash in the form of dividends. In contrast, physical assets, such as property, plant, and equipment, are held for use, not for conversion into cash, and are therefore not financial assets.

### *7.2.1.2 Types of Financial Assets*

- Other than cash, receivables and investment in loans are the first and simplest types of financial instruments. Both types carry the right to receive cash. If these rights are exercisable in the near term (within a year), these instruments would be valued at collectible (exit) amounts. Longer-term receivables and loans are valued at the present value of future cash flow using discount rates appropriately adjusted for the credit risk of counterparties.
- The second type of financial asset falls in the category of securities held-for-trading. This category includes two types of instruments: (i) financial assets that are held-for-trading and (ii) *all* financial derivative instruments that are not designated as hedging instruments.
- The third category consists of the securities for which the management elects applying the fair value option at the time of acquisition or at the time of remeasurement to fair value.
- The measurement of fair values must be consistent with the three levels of measurement set forth in accounting standards, ASC 820, IAS 39, and IFRS 7, that require the use of known market prices if available (Level 1) or other market information to estimate the sale price of an asset (Level 2). Only when such externally generated information is not available can management use an acceptable valuation model (Level 3). Level 1 is available for exchange-traded derivatives such as options and futures. Most over-the-counter derivatives, such as interest rate swaps use Level 2, and Level 3 is used for other derivatives such as forward contracts. The choice of applying the fair value option for any financial instrument is irrevocable.
- Financial instruments that are acquired with the intent (and ability) of holding them to maturity are valued at amortized cost. These securities must have maturity dates. (*Financial derivative instruments are excluded from this classification.)*
- Financial instruments that do not fit the classification of either held-for-trading or held-to-maturity are considered "available-for-sale." Financial instruments classified in this category should be valued at fair value with the changes in fair values parked in OCI. When transactions in these securities affect earnings, the related revaluation accounts will be reclassified from OCI to earnings. *(Financial derivative instruments are excluded from this classification.)*

### 7.2.2 Financial Liabilities

As liabilities, derivative financial instruments are valued at fair value with the changes in fair values flowing through earnings. Other financial instruments are valued at amortized cost unless the fair value option is elected (or the inventory is hedged). Changes in values of liability financial instruments also flow through earnings.

#### *7.2.2.1 Constraints and Guides*

- If financial assets or financial liabilities are valued at fair values, this valuation must be updated frequently with valuation intervals not exceeding 90 days.
- Financial derivatives may not be used as hedged items (although swaption contracts are permitted to be hedged items).
- Deviation from ordinary GAAP is allowed in accounting for financial derivatives (as defined above) only if the following two conditions hold:

  i. The derivative qualifies as instrument for hedging the exposure to one of the accepted hedgeable risks (price risk, interest rate risk, currency risk, and credit risk).
  ii. The hedge is highly effective and is properly documented.

- Because hedge accounting reduces earnings volatility by sheltering earnings from the fluctuations of derivative prices, adoption of hedge accounting is a privilege permitted for use by enterprises that adhere to a set of prescribed, and often restrictive, criteria.
- The most convenient way of thinking about hedge accounting in relationship to ordinary GAAP is to view hedge accounting as an override of GAAP.[2]

## 7.3 Risk and Hedge Accounting

### 7.3.1 Two Main Types of Risk Exposure

As discussed throughout this book, hedging is not for predictable risk exposures because these types of risk could be strategically managed or insured. Rather, it is the unexpected exposure to risk that leads management to invest in financial instruments as a means for reducing this exposure. Accounting standards identify the hedgeable risks that may qualify for special hedge accounting and categorizes them on the basis of their economic impact along two dimensions: value and cash flow.

To illustrate the difference between hedging value and cash flow risks, we could compare the response of fixed-rate and floating-rate instruments to changes in market interest rates, the underlying, or the value and risk generator.

When the market benchmark interest rate changes (Chapter Two):

- Fixed-rate financial instruments, such as a bond with a fixed-rate coupon, will change values in opposite directions but preserve cash flow.
- Floating-rate financial instruments, such as a bond with a coupon rate indexed to the prime rate of interest, to LIBOR, to Treasury rate or any other index, will change cash flows (in the direction of changes in interest rates) but preserve levels of fair values.

Panel A of Exhibit 7.1 shows these responses to interest rate changes for the fixed-rate instrument from the viewpoints of both the investor (the debtholder) and the debt issuer. As the benchmark interest rate increases, the values of fixed-rate instruments decline. In this event, the change in value is a gain to the issuer and a loss to the investor. Conversely, a decline in the benchmark interest rate leads to an increase in the value of the fixed-rate instrument, which would be a gain to investors and a loss to issuers.

Panel B of Exhibit 7.1 shows the response of floating-rate instruments to changes in benchmark interest rate. A rise in the benchmark rate increases the coupon of the floating-rate financial instrument and the interest paid by the issuer to investors. This increase in interest rate is, therefore, a gain to investors and a loss to the issuer. In contrast, a drop in the benchmark interest rate reduces the cash flow the issuer pays to investors, which is a gain to the issuer and a loss to the investor.

### 7.3.2 Hedging Objectives

The financial and economic literature presents different arguments for the motivation to hedge. Factors such as risk reduction, tax avoidance, managing cash flow, and lowering financing cost among other factors are cited as motivation. However, accounting standards filter these reasons down to two major factors:

1. Mitigating anticipated value loss.
2. Smoothing cash flow volatility.

## Exhibit 7.1 Relationship of Risk, Values, and Cash Flow in Response to Changes in Interest Rate

**Panel A: Response of a Fixed-Rate Instrument to Changes in Market Interest Rate (Assuming No Change in Credit Risk)**

| | Investment (for debtholders) | Liability (for debt issuers) |
|---|---|---|
| Rise in market interest rate | Decrease in value = loss<br>*(No change in cash flow)* | Decrease in value = gain<br>*(No change in cash flow)* |
| Decline in market interest rate | Increase in value = gain<br>*(No change in Cash Flow)* | Increase in value = loss<br>*(No change in Cash Flow)* |

**Panel B: Response of a Floating-Rate Instrument to Changes in Market Interest Rate (Assuming No Change in Credit Risk)**

| | Investment (for debtholders) | Liability (for debt issuers) |
|---|---|---|
| Rise in market interest rate | Increase in cash inflow = gain<br>*(No change in fair value)* | Increase in cash outflow = loss<br>*(No change in fair value)* |
| Decline in market interest rate | Decrease in cash inflow = loss<br>*(No change in fair value)* | Decrease in cash outflow = gain<br>*(No change in fair value)* |

### 7.3.2.1 *Hedging Potential Loss in Value*

The comparison between fixed-rate and floating-rate instruments noted above provides a good start not only for comparing the two main types of hedging, but also for emphasizing the prevalence of one common goal: to offset the adverse effects of changes in market prices (interest rates). For example, since the adverse movement in interest rate is reflected in the changing value of the fixed-rate instrument, hedging exposure to this loss requires entering into a contract whose value responds to change in market interest rates in an offsetting (opposite) direction.

## A General Principle

Success of hedging depends on the expectation of high negative correlation (covariance) between price changes of the hedge and price changes of the hedged item.

For example, if an enterprise is hedging a fixed-rate debt on its balance sheet, a decrease in the benchmark interest rate will increase the fair value of the debt. To hedge this risk exposure, the enterprise may enter into a contract whose fair value changes in response to the decrease in interest rate in an offsetting manner (e.g., hold fixed-rate investment or purchase interest rate cap). Accounting classifies hedging activities that fit in this category as fair value hedge, which can be defined as follows:

A fair value hedge is a hedge of exposure to adverse changes in the fair value of:

1. a recognized asset;
2. a recognized liability; or
3. an unrecognized fixed-price firm commitment (executory contract) to exchange assets.

These changes must:

- be attributable to a particular risk; and
- have an expected negative correlation between changes in the values of the hedge and changes in the values of the hedged item (i.e., highly effective).

### 7.3.2.2 *Smoothing Cash Flow Volatility*

The second type is the floating-rate instrument that exposes the enterprise to the risk or volatility of cash flow. Hence, hedging the risk arising from adverse movements in interest rates requires entering into a contractual agreement where cash flow patterns respond to changes in the market in the opposite direction. For example, when investing in a floating-rate instrument, an unexpected decrease in interest rates will decrease cash inflow and earnings. To hedge that exposure, an entity might acquire a put option (a floor) that it could exercise if the market rate falls below a specified level. For interest rates, this type of put option is called a "floor."

This would be a cash flow hedge that we can define as follows:

A cash flow hedge is a hedge of the exposure to volatility of cash flows:

- that is attributable to a particular risk for a recognized asset or a recognized liability;
- that arises from a probable forecasted (anticipated) transaction;
- that can also have an earnings effect.

### 7.3.3 Hedgeable Risks

#### Information Log

Some students are not clear on the role of accounting in hedging. The decisions to buy or sell financial instruments and the decisions to designate or not designate an instrument as a hedge are the prerogatives of management, not the accountants. Every enterprise faces a large number of risks with varying degrees of significance. For example, country risk might be relevant to the McDonald's Corporation or to General Electric Company, but it might not be relevant to others that do not have large presence in any foreign country. Similarly, compliance risk is important for banks, other financial institutions and companies whose businesses have implications for public safety such as The Boeing Company, but is of less significance to a retail company such as Macy's, for example.

Some of the risks facing the enterprise could be hedged and others could not. Commodity price risk could be hedged, while reputation risk could be managed but not hedged. Of the set of risks being hedged, some would qualify for the application of hedge accounting, while others would not. The accountants' role begins after the management makes decisions on hedging. This role typically begins by identifying that segment of hedged risk that qualifies for the special treatment of hedge accounting, which is a subset of all the risks facing the enterprise.

It is useful to note that: (a) the boundaries of the risks facing an enterprise are not well defined and are shrouded in uncertainty; (b) some types of risk could be managed, insured, hedged, or ignored; (c) the types of risk that could be hedged are identifiable; and (d) the hedgeable risks that could qualify for hedge accounting constitute a subset of the last type, but identification of that subset is subject to management choices and the plasticity of accounting guides.

The above described process is theoretical, however, because in reality the relevance of accounting comes sooner in the decision-making process; managers structure their hedging contracts to achieve particular accounting outcomes.

The above discussion distinguishes between hedging (i) value loss exposure and (ii) the exposure to cash flow volatility. The discussion is developed around fixed-rate and floating-rate financial instruments, but an enterprise's risk exposure extends to all assets, liabilities, and events. In principle, the enterprise could "economically" hedge the risk exposure associated with many of the risks it faces. However, not all the risks that affect values or cash flow qualify for hedge accounting. To elaborate, let us consider hedgeable risk for various categories of assets, liabilities, and contracts in the context of the following issues:

1. Financial assets
    a. Trading securities and instruments (FVNI)
    b. Available-for-sale securities (FVOCI)
    c. Held-to-maturity securities (Amortized Cost)
2. Financial liabilities
3. Executory contracts
4. Inventory and commodity price risk
5. Currency risk
6. Partial hedging
7. Hedging aggregates

### *7.3.3.1 Financial Assets*

#### **Accounting Log: Changing the Classification of Financial Securities**

Currently, the FASB has an Exposure Draft a summary of which is provided by the accounting firm of Deloitte & Touche, LLP is reproduced (with permission) in the Appendix to Chapter Seven.

The classification presented below represents GAAP as of November 2012.

#### Trading Securities and Instruments

These are financial instruments that are held for the purpose of making profits and benefitting by a fast turnover; they consist of loans, receivables, and securities held for trade.

- *Accounting*: "Held-for-trading" instruments are valued at fair value with value changes flow through earnings.
- *Hedging:* Enterprises are not permitted (for accounting purposes) to hedge securities held for trade under the general guidance that excludes hedge accounting financial assets or liabilities that are normally valued at fair value with the changes in values flow through the income statement (under ordinary GAAP).

#### Available-for-Sale

- *Risks*: The securities and instruments designated as available-for-sale (are as fair value through OCI) are exposed to the following risks:
    - *Interest rate risk*: adverse movement in interest rates.
    - *Prepayment risk:* if an enterprise invests in "available-for-sale" instruments or securities, the counterparty classifies them as investment in debt instruments. The counterparty may redeem the debt before maturity when market interest rate declines to the point that it

would be more profitable to refinance the liabilities at lower interest rates. The early prepayment of debt would leave investors (who were debtholders) with funds that they would have to reinvest at lower interest rates. Because the decline in market interest rate is the main motivation for the prepayment of debt, the prepayment risk facing investors is closely tied to interest rate risk.

  - *Credit risk*: The risk of deterioration of creditworthiness of the counterparty and increasing the probability of default.

- *Accounting*: Available-for-sale investment in securities and financial instruments are valued at fair value and the changes in fair values are deferred in OCI. These changes are reclassified from OCI to earnings by the extent to which transactions in the available-for-sale portfolio (e.g., sale) affect earnings.
- *Hedging*: Hedge accounting is permitted if these securities and instruments satisfy the required criteria, but the management of the enterprise must exercise care in designating which specific risk it is being hedged.
  - *Hedge designation*: Accounting standards under GAAP and IFRS require that a hedging relationship must designate the *particular* risk being hedged.
  - *Hedging interest rate risk:* When interest rate risk is hedged, only the change in values or cash flow of the available-for-sale instruments attributable to changes in interest rate would qualify for the hedge accounting treatment. The changes in value attributable to other risks remain subject to ordinary GAAP for this type of asset.
  - *Hedging credit risk*: When credit risk is hedged and the hedge is successful (i.e., highly effective) changes in values attributable to credit risk are subject to hedge accounting. The changes in value attributable to other risks remain subject to the application of ordinary GAAP.

#### Held-to-Maturity (HTM)

HTM are financial instruments with definite lives and which the enterprise and the management have the *ability* and the *intent* to hold to maturity.

- *Accounting*: HTM instruments are valued at amortized cost. Except for asset impairment, recognition of changes in value is not permitted.
- *Hedging*: Instruments held under this designation also face interest rate risk, prepayment risk, and credit risk. Having the intent and ability to hold them to maturity means that exposure to interest rate risk (including related prepayment risk) does not affect the income statement. Therefore, hedge accounting is not permitted for hedging the interest rate risk of HTM.

  However, HTM is subject to impairment because of exposure to credit risk. Since impairment impacts earnings, hedging and hedge accounting are permitted for mitigating credit risk exposure of HTM securities.

### *7.3.3.2 Financial Liabilities*

Financial liabilities are securities and instruments that are issued by the enterprise and that create obligations to settle by transferring cash to external parties. As financial obligations, these instruments are also exposed to interest rate risk and the issuer's own liquidity and credit risks. Whether or not hedge accounting is permitted depends on the nature of the liability and the method of valuation being used for each type of security or instrument.

- *Accounting at amortized cost*: Hedge accounting is permitted for non-trading and non-derivative liabilities that are accounted for, under ordinary GAAP, at amortized cost.
- *Accounting at fair value*: Hedge accounting is not permitted for liabilities that are valued at fair value with the changes in fair values posted to earnings. These are financial derivatives, trading liabilities, and the liabilities for which management elects applying the fair value option.

### *7.3.3.3 Executory Contracts*

An executory contract is an agreement between the enterprise and counterparty to perform specific services, or to receive or deliver a specific commodity under the conditions specified in the agreement. This contract is fulfilled by performance. As such, executory contracts create rights and obligations for performance yet to be fulfilled and for which (economic) assets or liabilities actually exist but are not recognized in accounting. For example, a contract committing an oil producer to deliver natural gas to an end user is an executory contract that is not recognized on the books of either entity (under ordinary GAAP), although it gives rise to rights (the right of the end user to receive the gas and the right of the oil producer to receive the cash price) and obligations (the obligation of the producer to deliver and the obligation of the buyer to pay).

- *Accounting*: With few exceptions, ordinary GAAP does not recognize the rights or obligations associated with executory contracts until performance occurs.[3]
- *Hedging*: There are risks associated with executory contracts—e.g., price risk, delivery risk, and credit risk. Business enterprises are able to hedge some of these risks. Hedge accounting is permitted for hedging the changes in value (though unrecognized initially) that arise from exposure to price or credit risk of some executory contracts; these are contracts for which there is a fixed price, firm and non-cancelable commitment to perform. In this case, the recognition is limited to changes in fair values that are associated with effective hedges.

### *7.3.3.4 Inventory and Commodity Price Risk*

Inventories of raw materials and finished goods are subject to various risks. Some of these risks can be managed, including the risk of fire, obsolescence, shrinkage, or theft. However, the risk of change in value due to change in commodity prices is not insurable, is not under the management's control and is unpredictable. This includes the risk of loss due to selling the inventory at lower prices because of unexpected commodity price decline, or the risk of loss by restocking the inventory at higher cost due to unexpected commodity price increase. This exposure is a commodity price risk that is not under the control of management and for which there is no insurance. The management could manage the price risk of the inventory in stock by engaging in a fair value hedge, or by managing the risk of prospective inventory purchase or sale by engaging in a cash flow hedge; the choice is essentially a management decision.

- *Accounting*: Under ordinary GAAP, inventory is valued at lower-of-cost-or-market with "cost" being based on any of the following cost flow assumptions: FIFO, (LIFO in the USA only), average, specific identification, or allocated manufacturing cost. Market is defined as the net realizable value.

- *Hedging*: The general rule is that the risks of assets reported at fair value are not hedgeable if the changes in fair value flow through earnings. It is therefore important to note that the valuation of inventory at the lower-of-cost-or-market is not equivalent to valuation at fair value. [4]

### *7.3.3.5 Currency Risk*

As discussed earlier in this book there are 178 currencies in the world. As a result of this diversity, complex processes and outcomes arise from the transfer of funds across borders by entities involved in global commerce, tourism and other international activities. These funds transfers require pricing one currency in terms of another currency. As discussed in more detail in Chapter Ten, currency prices are quoted by reference to a base currency using a three-letter designation for each currency. For example, the price of one U.S. dollar in Canadian dollars is expressed by the ratio USD/CAD, where USD and CAD are the internationally agreed upon trade symbols of these currencies. Each of the 178 currencies in the world has a unique three-letter identification. The first currency in the ratio of foreign currency exchange (FX) is called the base currency and the second currency is called the "quote" currency. The ratio indicates how many units of the quote currency are required in exchange for one unit of the base currency. The U.S. dollar is the base currency for most currency price quotes followed by the euro and the sterling.

From 1944 to 1973, currency exchange rates (prices) were pegged to the U.S. dollar and the U.S. dollar was pegged to the price of gold. That period is known as the period of the "gold standard" which was the result of the 1944 Bretton Woods Treaty. In 1973, the United States unilaterally abrogated the treaty that created the gold standard and most countries followed, which changed the pricing of currency exchange rates from fixed to floating. Although some currencies are still pegged to the U.S. dollar (e.g. Hong Kong dollar), most currencies are allowed to change rates with changing market conditions that determine the supply and demand for each currency.

Operating in a regime of floating currency prices reduces the predictability of currency exchange realizations for any type of currency transfer. For example, an exporter from one country may sell its products with the sale price expressed or denominated in a foreign currency. At the time of sale, the sales contract could also be expressed in domestic currency units by converting (translating) the foreign currency sales to domestic currency at the exchange rate that existed at the time of the transaction. The exporter will collect only the number of foreign currency units at which the sale was made, irrespective of changes in the currency exchange rates. Between the time of sale and the time of collection of the sale price, the exchange rate from foreign to domestic currency will be different from the exchange rate at the time of sale. Although the exporter would collect the same foreign currency units specified in the sale contract, the collected amount may be converted to a larger or a smaller amount of domestic currency, depending on the movement of currency exchange rates between the time of sale and the time of collection. A decrease in the amount of domestic currency collected means a loss to the exporter while an increase is a gain. The reverse is true for an importer. The exposure to loss due to this sort of trade is called "transaction risk." In this book, I will refer to it as "transaction settlement risk" because the risk of loss arises from the adverse movement of currency exchange rates between sale and settlement.

Adverse movements in currency exchange rates may also extend to future periods and thereby affect the revenues and costs that are expressed in domestic currency units. Exposure to future loss of revenues or future increase in cost due to adverse currency movements is referred to as "currency operating risk."

The third type of exposure to currency risk arises from the effect of adverse movement of currency prices between domestic currency and foreign currencies of countries or regions in which the domestic enterprise has operations. For example, establishing a subsidiary in a foreign region means that the enterprise will have assets and liabilities represented in a foreign currency for each of its foreign operations. A multinational enterprise with foreign operations is exposed to currency risk by the extent to which adverse currency exchange rate movements would negatively impact the value of net assets of foreign operations when converted (translated) to domestic currency units. This conversion to domestic currency is necessary for reporting consolidated financial statements and for managing foreign operations. Exposure to this type of loss is called "currency translation loss" or "accounting loss" because it arises from the interaction of adverse movement in currency rates and the accounting method used for the conversion or translation of the foreign currency. Different accounting treatments of currency risk of foreign operations are presented in Chapters Ten and Eleven.

### *7.3.3.6 Partial Hedging*

Accounting standards distinguish between financial and non-financial items in hedging parts of an asset or a liability.

- Hedge accounting is permitted for hedging the risk exposures of financial assets and liabilities in full or in part. For example, investments in fixed-rate instruments that are designated as available-for-sale are subject to interest rate risk, prepayment risk, and credit risk. An enterprise might hedge only interest rate risk of the securities in the portfolio that have the same exposure to interest rate risk, or it might hedge only a proportion of these securities. Similar guidelines apply to hedging risks other than interest rate risk.
- Different guidelines apply for non-financial items with some basic restrictions. Hedging price risk of a non-financial asset is permitted only for hedging the "full price" risk exposure either for the full asset or for a *proportion* of it. *The proportion being hedged must have the same risk exposure as the full asset.* While accounting permits hedging a proportion or a percentage of the full asset risk exposure, it *prohibits* hedging the risk exposure of an ingredient in non-financial assets. The example often cited is the commodity price risk of the tires inventory of an auto company, where hedging the price risk of the rubber component only is not permitted.[5]

### *7.3.3.7 Hedging Aggregates (Macro Hedge)*

A collection of assets or liabilities (a portfolio) may be aggregated for hedging *only* if those assets or liabilities in a given collection have the same risk exposure. Accounting criteria do not permit hedge accounting for portfolios that consist of aggregated items having different risk exposures.[6]

#### Summary

Exhibit 7.2 presents a summary and classification of the hedgeable risks accepted for the application of hedge accounting, provided that the other hedge criteria are also met.

## Exhibit 7.2 Hedgeable Fair Value Risks Acceptable for Accounting (ASC 815-20-25-12(f))

| *Hedgeable items* | *Type of risk* | *Characterization of the hedged risk* |
|---|---|---|
| *Financial items:*<br>1. Asset<br>2. Liability<br>3. Firm (enforceable) commitment | Price Risk | The risk of changes in the overall fair value of the entire hedged item. |
| | Interest Rate Risk | The risk of changes in the fair value of the hedged item attributable to changes in the designated benchmark interest rate (either LIBOR or U.S. Treasury Rate). |
| | Foreign Currency Exchange Rate Risk | The risk of changes in the fair value of the hedged item attributable to changes in the related foreign currency exchange rates. |
| | Credit Risk | The risk of changes in its fair value attributable to *both* of the following<br>(a) Changes in the obligor's creditworthiness.<br>(b) Changes in the spread over the benchmark interest rate with respect to the hedged item's credit sector at inception of the hedge. |
| | Mixed Risks | • Two or more of interest rate risk, foreign currency exchange risk, and credit risk may simultaneously be designated as the risk being hedged.<br>• Hedging a portion of the risk or cash flow is permitted |
| *Non-financial assets and liabilities* (not including recognized loan servicing right or a non-financial firm commitment having financial components) | Full price risk | Entire price of the hedged item |
| | An ingredient of the hedged item | *Not permitted unless* it is a tandem hedge having:<br>• The entire change in the fair value of the derivative is expected *ex-ante* to be highly effective in offsetting the entire change in the fair value the hedged item.<br>• All of the remaining hedge criteria are met. |
| | A percentage of the entire full price risk | Permitted |
| | A combination of an asset and a liability | Not permitted |
| | A combination of assets or of liabilities | Permitted if they all have similar risk and similar cash flow response to market conditions. |

## 7.4 Why Hedge Accounting?

To explain why we use hedge accounting, we must examine the conventional matching principle in accounting that refers to the periodic matching of revenues (benefits) with the cost (expended effort) of generating them. The need for the principle arises when the indefinite life of the firm is partitioned into finite accounting periods in which the inflow and outflow of activities are not properly aligned. Expenses are incurred in one period but revenues and benefits may be realized in other periods. Hence, the concepts of accrual and matching became necessary conventions.

In recent years, the accounting focus on risk has led to an expanded view of the matching concept. The motivation for this expansion has come about from questioning the rationale for according different accounting treatments to transactions or balance sheet items with essentially the same risk exposure. This problem is discussed next as one of the main motivation for deviating from ordinary GAAP and for inventing hedge accounting methods. Three important concepts explain the motivation that gave rise to the development of hedge accounting:

1. Similar risk exposure but different accounting treatment
2. Mismatching flows and value changes
3. Mismatching timing of flows

### 7.4.1 Similar Risk Exposure but Different Accounting Treatment

#### The Setting

Changes in commodity prices, currency rates, or interest rates are market-wide phenomena that we expect to have similar effects on financial assets and financial liabilities. That is, the economic effects of changing prices on assets and liabilities are synchronous, but GAAP ignores this synchronicity and accounts for the financial assets and liabilities differently. Exhibit 7.3 illustrates this problem under two different scenarios:

1. If, for example, financial assets are included in the available-for-sale portfolio, they would be valued at fair value with the change in fair value being posted to OCI (an equity account). However, similar "economic" changes in financial liabilities are ignored unless the fair value option is elected. Even in the latter case, the changes in fair values flow through earnings, not OCI, which is another source of mismatching.
2. If financial assets or financial liabilities consist of derivatives, they will be valued at fair value. The changes in fair values are posted to earnings even for long-term derivatives (i.e., 15-year interest rate swap) and filter to owners' equity through retained earnings.

In both cases the reported change in the fair value of financial assets is not matched by reporting the corresponding change in financial liabilities. Instead, changes in fair values of financial liabilities are ignored when liabilities are booked at amortized cost. The result is an accounting mismatch with greater income volatility and unfaithful representation of the financial position of the enterprise.

## Exhibit 7.3 Effects of Mismatching the Valuation of Financial Assets and Financial Liabilities

| | *Financial Assets* | | *Financial Liabilities* |
|---|---|---|---|
| Valuation | Fair Value | | Amortized Cost |
| | *If Available for Sale Investments* | *If Financial Derivatives* | |
| Impact of Δ Values | • Δ Other Comprehensive Income<br>Δ Owners' equity (OCI) | • Δ Net Income,<br>• Δ Retained Earnings<br>Δ Owners' equity | Ignored* |
| | Mismatch of outcomes<br>For Assets and Liabilities having similar Risk Exposure | | |

* Except for deterioration in own credit risk

### The Accounting Solution

This type of mismatch, shown in Exhibit 7.3, is created by accounting and may be resolved by adapting accounting standards to value financial liabilities at fair value: (i) through OCI for those liabilities with the same risk exposure as available-for-sale investments, or (ii) through earnings for other financial liabilities.

The FASB and IASB indicated that they aim to move in that direction, but they have currently adopted the following two remedial approaches:[7]

- *The Fair Value Option:* The management of an enterprise has the option to elect valuation of financial liabilities (or assets) at fair value with the changes flow through earnings.
- *Hedge Designation:* This treatment requires management to designate the financial derivative (that are acquired as hedge instruments) as a hedge of a specific risk exposure of financial liabilities and requires the management to reflect the impact of this risk exposure on the value of the hedged liabilities through earnings.

In both cases, the decision to mitigate the impact of an accounting mismatch is left up to management discretion.[8] However, the two approaches are not the same. Electing to adopt the fair value option is *irrevocable*. Once management decides to adopt the fair value option for a given liability (or asset), it cannot change it. But the second approach is revocable; management can voluntarily elect to de-designate a hedge.[9] Additionally, the second approach is costly to implement because it requires documentation and periodic testing of hedge effectiveness.

## 7.4.2 Mismatching Flows and Value Changes

This type of mismatch is structural rather than a creation of accounting. To illustrate, consider four possible situations:

1. $A_x \neq L_x$: Unequal fixed-interest-rate assets and fixed-interest-rate liabilities.
2. $A_f \neq L_f$: Unequal floating-interest-rate assets and floating-interest-rate liabilities.
3. $A_x$ & $L_f$: Earning fixed interest rate on financial assets, but paying floating rates on financial liabilities.
4. $A_f$ & $L_x$: Earning floating interest rate on financial assets but paying fixed interest rate on financial liabilities.

Each of these cases poses a different type of (mismatch) risk exposure in any given accounting period.

### *7.4.2.1 $A_x \neq L_x$: Unequal Fixed-Rate Financial Assets and Fixed-Rate Financial Liabilities*

The fair value of the fixed-interest-rate assets and the fair value of fixed-interest-rate liabilities respond to changes in interest rate in similar ways, but have opposite impact on the firm value. There would be immunization of value changes if the fair values of these assets and liabilities were equal (assuming same durations); otherwise the enterprise would be exposed to fair value loss. With unequal fixed-rate assets and fixed-rate liabilities, the impact on the enterprise can be one of four outcomes as presented in Exhibit 7.4.

**Exhibit 7.4 Different Effects of Changing Interest Rate for Fixed-Rate Financial Assets and Fixed-Rate Financial Liabilities**

| Interest Rate | $A_x$ | $L_x$ | $A_x = L_x$ | $A_x > L_x$ | $A_x < L_x$ |
|---|---|---|---|---|---|
| ↑ | *Fair Value Loss* | *Fair Value gain* | ***Impact = 0*** | *Net Loss* | *Net Gain* |
| ↓ | *Fair Value Gain* | *Fair Value Loss* | ***Impact = 0*** | *Net Gain* | *Net Loss* |

$A_x$ = Fixed-rate financial assets
$L_x$ = Fixed rate financial liabilities

Therefore, unless the total amount of fixed-rate financial assets equals the fixed-rate financial liabilities, the enterprise is exposed to the potential of fair value loss whether interest rates increase or decrease, depending on the size of assets in relationship to liabilities. To hedge this risk exposure, management can enter into derivative contracts that it expects to offset the impact of changes in interest rate on fair values. The enterprise management enters into this derivative contract to achieve an effective fair value hedge. The types of derivative contracts will depend on management's expectations about the direction of interest rate changes given the enterprise's net financial asset position.

*This is a case of fair value hedge: hedging exposure to adverse changes in interest rates on the fair value of a recognized financial asset or a recognized liability.*

### 7.4.2.2 $A_f \neq L_f$: Unequal Floating-Rate Financial Assets and Liabilities

In this situation, the interest rates on assets and liabilities are indexed to one or more reference market interest rates; the enterprise earns variable interest on its financial assets and pays variable interest on its financial liabilities. Changes in the reference rate will impact both cash inflow for the interest earned on assets and cash outflow for interest paid on debt; fair values would not change. With inequality, the impact on the enterprise's cash flow could be one of four outcomes as presented in Exhibit 7.5.

**Exhibit 7.5 Different Effects of Changing Interest Rate for Floating-Rate Financial Assets and Floating-Rate Financial Liabilities**

| **Interest Rate** | $A_f$ | $L_f$ | $A_f = L_f$ | $A_f > L_f$ | $A_f < L_f$ |
|---|---|---|---|---|---|
| ↑ | *Cash inflow* ↑ | *Cash outflow* ↑ | ***Impact*** = 0 | ***Net Gain*** | ***Net Loss*** |
| ↓ | *Cash inflow* ↓ | *Cash outflow* ↓ | ***Impact*** = 0 | ***Net Loss*** | ***Net Gain*** |

$A_f$ = Floating rate financial assets
$L_f$ = Floating rate financial liabilities

#### Consequences

Unless floating-rate financial assets equal floating-rate financial liabilities, the enterprise is exposed to potential loss due to the difference between the change in cash inflow (income) and the change in cash outflow (expense). To hedge this risk exposure, the enterprise can enter into derivative contracts with the expectation that they will generate offsetting cash flows. An enterprise enters into this derivative contract to achieve effective hedge of cash flow volatility and the types of derivative contracts will depend on management's expectations about the direction of interest rate changes given the enterprise's net financial asset position.

*This is a case of cash flow hedge: hedging exposure to adverse changes in interest rates on the net cash flow position of the enterprise.*

### 7.4.2.3 $A_x$ & $L_f$: Fixed-Rate Assets and Floating-Rate Liabilities

In this situation, the enterprise earns a fixed (pre-determined) interest rate on financial assets, but pays out floating interest (indexed to a reference market interest rate) on liabilities. This combination leads to mixed effects of changes in interest rate; as interest rates change, the fair value of the financial assets change (cash inflow remains the same) and the cash outflow for the financial liabilities changes (fair value remains the same). The resulting combination is as presented in Exhibit 7.6.

## Exhibit 7.6 Different Effects of Changing Interest Rate for Fixed-Rate Financial Assets and Floating-Rate Financial Liabilities

| **Interest Rate** | $A_x$ | $L_f$ | *All Combinations* $A_x = L_f; A_x > L_f; A_x < L_f$ |
|---|---|---|---|
| ↑ | ↓ *Fair Value* | *Cash outflow* ↑ | *Fair Value Loss & Net Cash Flow Loss* |
| ↓ | ↑ *Fair Value* | *Cash outflow* ↓ | *Fair Value Gain & Net Cash Flow Gain* |

$A_x$ = Fixed-rate financial assets
$L_f$ = Floating rate financial liabilities

### Consequences

To hedge exposure to loss, the enterprise needs to enter into contracts that provide fair value hedge (for assets) and other contracts that provide cash flow hedge (for liabilities).

### *7.4.2.4 $A_f$ & $L_x$: Floating-Rate Assets and Fixed-Rate Liabilities*

In this situation, the enterprise earns floating interest (indexed to a reference market interest rate) on financial assets, but pays out fixed (pre-determined) interest rate on liabilities. As in the preceding case, this combination leads to mixed effects; as interest rates change, the cash inflow from interest earned on financial assets changes (fair value remains unchanged), but the fair value of financial liabilities changes (cash outflow remains the same). The resulting combination is presented in Exhibit 7.7.

## Exhibit 7.7 Different Effects of Changing Interest Rate for Floating-Rate Financial Assets and Fixed-Rate Financial Liabilities

| **Interest Rate** | $A_f$ | $L_x$ | *All combinations* *Af = Lx; Af > Lx; Af < Lx* |
|---|---|---|---|
| ↑ | ↑ *Cash inflow* | ↓ *Fair Value* | *Fair Value Gain & Net Cash Flow Gain* |
| ↓ | ↓ *Cash inflow* | ↑ *Fair Value* | *Fair Value Loss & Net Cash Flow Loss* |

$L_x$ = Fixed rate financial liabilities
$A_f$ = Floating rate financial assets

## Consequences

As in the preceding case, to hedge exposure to loss, the enterprise needs to enter into two types of contracts that: (a) provide fair value hedge (for liabilities), and (b) provide cash flow hedge (for assets).

## The Accounting Problem

In the four cases noted above changes in interest rate could affect either fair value or cash flow or both. To mitigate exposure to loss, each case requires different hedging instruments and strategies. Under ordinary GAAP (in absence of special hedge accounting), reporting the success or failure of hedging fair value or cash flow risk could run into two problems:

1. Under ordinary GAAP, the enterprise books the financial asset or financial liability whose exposure to the fair value risk is being hedged at amortized cost so that the change in fair value is not recognized in earnings.[10] If this accounting treatment is retained, accounting reports will fail to show management's efforts in hedging exposure to value loss because only the changes in the fair values of the hedge instrument (the derivative) will be reported through earnings.

Therefore, the special hedge accounting for *fair value hedges* requires adapting ordinary GAAP by changing the reported values of the hedged item (asset or liability) from amortized cost to fair value and reporting the changes in fair values through earnings. This adaptation is what is called "accounting for fair value hedge" in ASC 815 for U.S. GAAP and IAS 39 and IFRS 9 for IFRS.

However, because of the special nature of this change in GAAP, applying a fair value hedge requires meeting all the following five conditions:

i. The hedged item is not normally valued at fair value where the changes in fair values ordinarily flow, or are expected to flow, through earnings. Trading securities is a prime example of this type; these securities do not qualify for hedge accounting.
ii. Changes in fair values in earnings of the hedged item are recognized upon adopting fair value hedge accounting.
iii. Changes in fair value of the hedged item are recognized from inception of the effective hedge onward.
iv. Implementation of this accounting treatment requires that the hedging relationship be highly effective (i.e., successful).
v. In each reporting period, the enterprise must re-evaluate changes in the values of both the hedge derivative and the hedged item and post these changes to earnings, which should be documented periodically.

*Conclusion*: Fair value hedge accounting

- accounts for hedging potential loss of value;
- is an adaptation of ordinary GAAP;
- departs from ordinary GAAP for the hedged item; but
- retains ordinary GAAP accounting treatment for derivative instruments.

The flowchart in Figure 7.1 illustrates the above discussion of departure from ordinary GAAP to provide a special accounting treatment for fair value hedge.

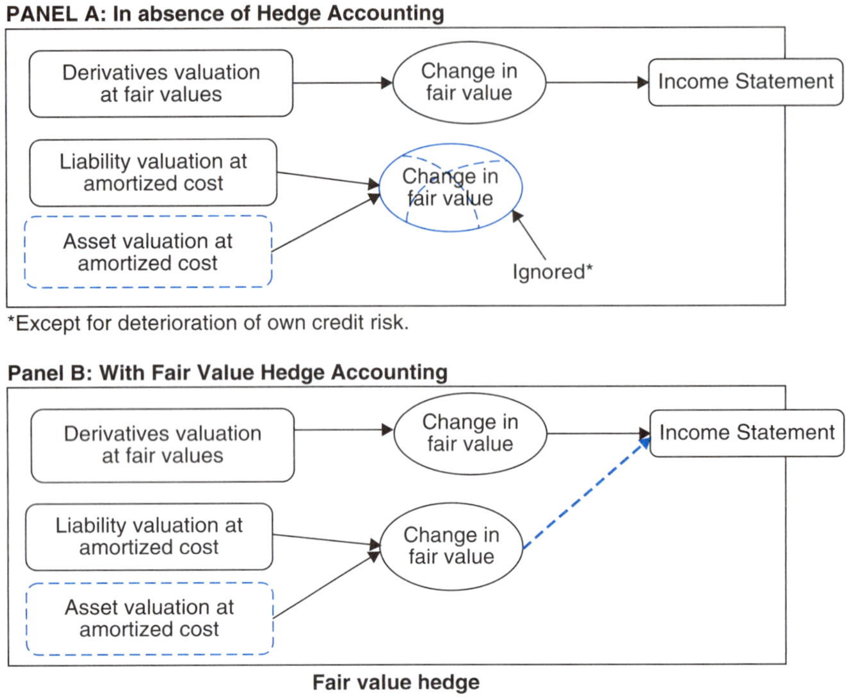


**Figure 7.1** Fair Value Change Mismatching Due to the Mixed-Attribute Accounting Model

2. Change in interest rate impacts cash flow. Hedging the change in cash flow will require entering into derivative contracts with the expectation of generating cash flow that is negatively correlated with the cash flow of the hedged item (asset or liability). An accounting system that couples the earnings recognition of the cash flow of the hedge contract with the earnings recognition of the cash flow of the hedged item (asset or liability) will be offset in accounting reports. If cash flow outcomes of the hedged item and of the hedge derivative are *non-synchronous* (i.e., mismatched), aligning the earnings recognition requires a special adaptation of ordinary GAAP. This adaptation is elaborated in the following case of mismatch of timing earnings recognition and cash flow.

### 7.4.3 Mismatching Timing of Flows and Earnings Recognition

Enterprises can mitigate the impact of mismatching on earnings through natural hedging, as in the case when the interest-rate-gap is zero—that is, assuming same durations—floating-rate financial assets (i.e., interest-rate-sensitive assets) equal floating-rate liabilities (i.e., interest-rate-sensitive liabilities). A zero interest-rate-gap is a desired objective from the standpoint of both liquidity management and accrued interest income and charges. It offers a natural hedge against the volatility of earnings arising from the effects of interest rate on cash flow and earnings. For a non-zero interest-rate-gap, volatility of cash flow and earnings will increase with a changing interest rate in proportion to the magnitude and sign of the interest-rate-gap as noted earlier.

If interest-rate-gap is non-zero and natural hedging is costly, the enterprise could enter into derivative contacts to hedge the potential cash flow volatility induced by interest rate changes. However, accounting reports under ordinary GAAP (i.e., when there is no special treatment for hedge accounting) may not reflect the achieved reduction in volatility if the realization of cash flow and the recognition of earnings are non-synchronous (i.e., if they do not occur during the same accounting period). The illustration below will be useful in understanding this concern.

### Illustration

Assume that *Enya, Inc.* has interest-rate-gap = $0 (interest-rate-sensitive assets equal interest-rate-sensitive liabilities) in the current period (Period 1), but the management anticipates that the interest-rate-gap will be –$100,000 in Period 2; i.e., interest-rate-sensitive assets will be lower than interest-rate-sensitive liabilities by $100,000. Assume that *Enya, Inc.* has interest-rate-gap = $0. The management fears an increase in LIBOR or having a negative interest-rate gap; either one will increase cash outflow. In Period 1, the management anticipated changes resulting in the interest-rate-gap = –$400,000 in Period 2; i.e., interest-rate-sensitive assets will be lower than interest-rate-sensitive liabilities by –$400,000. However, the management of *Enya, Inc.* does not anticipate any changes in LIBOR. The floating-rate debt of *Enya, Inc.* averages 0.5% above LIBOR. When LIBOR = 2%, the interest rate for *Enya, Inc.* would be 2.5% in Period 1. Assume that the management obtained a reliable forecast predicting LIBOR At this rate, the negative interest-rate-gap (i.e., increase in interest-sensitive liabilities) will cost *Enya, Inc.* an additional interest expense of $10,000 in Period 2, reflecting an increase in cash outflow and an increase in accrued interest expense. If Entity *Enya* does not take action to hedge this possible increase, each of earnings (before tax) and cash flow will decline by $10,000.

To reduce exposure to this risk, *Enya, Inc.* buys (long) in Period 1 call options that would provide positive cash inflow which the management hopes to offset the cash flow effect of having negative interest rate gap. The timing of this cash flow may take one of three scenarios that are contrasted with the Status Quo scenario as shown in Table 7.1.

**Table 7.1** Cataloging Different Timing of Cash Flow and Accruals (*Enya, Inc.* when there is no special accounting for hedging)

| | *Accounting Period 1* | | | *Accounting Period 2* | | |
|---|---|---|---|---|---|---|
| *Scenarios* | *Cash inflow from the Option Derivative* | *Cash outflow for decrease in Interest-Rate-Gap* | *Impact on Earnings* | *Cash inflow from the Option Derivative* | *Cash outflow for decrease in Interest-Rate-Gap* | *Impact on Earnings* |
| A: Status Quo | N/A | 0 | 0 | N/A | ($10,000) | ($10,000) |
| B: Hedging | $9,500 | 0 | $9,500 | 0 | ($10,000) | ($10,000) |
| C: Hedging | $6,000 | 0 | $6,000 | $3,500 | ($10,000) | ($6,500)* |
| D: Hedging | 0 | 0 | 0 | $9,500 | ($10,000) | ($500) |

* This is the net of $10,000 increase in interest expense less $3,500 gain on the derivative in period 2.

In the Status Quo scenario, *Enya, Inc.* does not enter into hedging contracts and will account for the increase in cash outflow related to the increase in interest cost (a negative interest-rate-gap and a 1% increase in the reference interest rate). This will produce a net cash outflow of $10,000 in Period 2 and an increase in accrued expense of $10,000. Therefore, net income before tax will decline by that amount.

In Scenarios B, C, and D, *Enya, Inc.* buys call options whose payoff is expected to generate a positive cash flow of $9,500 if LIBOR increases by 1%. This positive cash flow will offset most of the anticipated increase in cash outflow if the interest rate rises.[11] Under ordinary GAAP, without special hedge accounting, the impact on earnings will follow the cash flow pattern. This pattern is different under different scenarios (if there is no special accounting treatment for hedging).

- In Scenario B, all the cash inflow from options is realized in Period 1. The result is an increase in earnings by $9,500 in Period 1, and a decrease in earnings by $10,000 in Period 2. Here the cash flow is non-synchronous, resulting in an accounting mismatch that will increase earnings volatility.
- In Scenario C, the cash inflow from option contracts is generated over two periods: $6,000.00 in Period 1 and $3,500 in Period 2. The impact of this cash flow pattern is to report an increase in earnings by $6,000 in Period 1 and report a decrease in earnings of $3,500 in Period 2. Once again, this timing mismatch will result in earnings volatility, although to a lesser degree than in Scenario B.
- In Scenario D, the entire cash inflow from the option contracts is realized in Period 2. Thus, there is no incremental impact on cash flow or on earnings in Period 1, but there is a 95% offset of each, cash flow and earnings, in Period 2. The net earnings effect is zero for Period 1, but declines by $500 in Period 2 only.

### The Accounting Problem

Under ordinary GAAP and without any special treatment for hedging, this non-synchronicity (mismatching of timing) of the cash flow of the hedge instrument and earnings impact (accruals) related to the hedged item will have two results:

1. Higher earnings volatility.
2. Failure to convey to users of financial statements the degree to which the management of the enterprise is successful in hedging risk.

### The Accounting Solution

The solution offered by standard setters is to deviate from ordinary GAAP and adopt the special accounting treatment for cash flow hedges. While hedge accounting could not alter the cash flow pattern, it alters the pattern of earnings recognition. Under scenarios B and C above, the cash inflow from the hedge came in the first period either in full or in part, while the cash outflow being hedged took place in the second period. The accounting solution is to take the cash inflow as it comes in, but defer the recognition of that gain in earnings until the second period when the hedged item affects the income statement. It must be emphasized that real events remain the same, but the accounting recognition changes.

This solution is described in Table 7.2 and Figure 7.2 for scenario B in the above illustration. The table compares the cash flow and earnings consequences with and without hedge accounting.

**Table 7.2** The Impact of Applying Cash Flow Hedge Accounting on Cash Flow and Earnings (Scenario B of the Example of *Enya, Inc.*)

| Panel A: *Effect on earnings without special hedge accounting* | | |
|---|---|---|
| | *Period 1* | *Period 2* |
| Cash inflow from the option (increase in earnings) | $9,500 | $0 |
| Expected cash outflow for debt (decrease in earnings) | 0 | ($10,000) |
| Impact of change in GAP on cash flow | $9,500 | ($10,000) |
| Impact of change in GAP on earnings | $9,500 | ($10,000) |

| Panel B: *when there is special hedge accounting* | | |
|---|---|---|
| ***Impact on Cash Flow*** | | |
| Increase in cash inflow from options | $9,500 | 0 |
| *Deferral of earnings recognition (Posting to OCI, not earnings)* | 9,500 | 0 |
| Impact of increase in benchmark interest rate on cash flow | 0 | (10,000) |
| *Net Change in Cash flow* | 9,500 | (10,000) |
| ***Impact on Earnings*** | | |
| *Reclassification of Period 1 gain from OCI to earnings* | 0 | 9,500 |
| *Decrease in Earnings from the hedged item* (negative interest-rate-gap) | 0 | (10,000) |
| *Income impact of increase in benchmark interest rate* | 0 | ($500) |

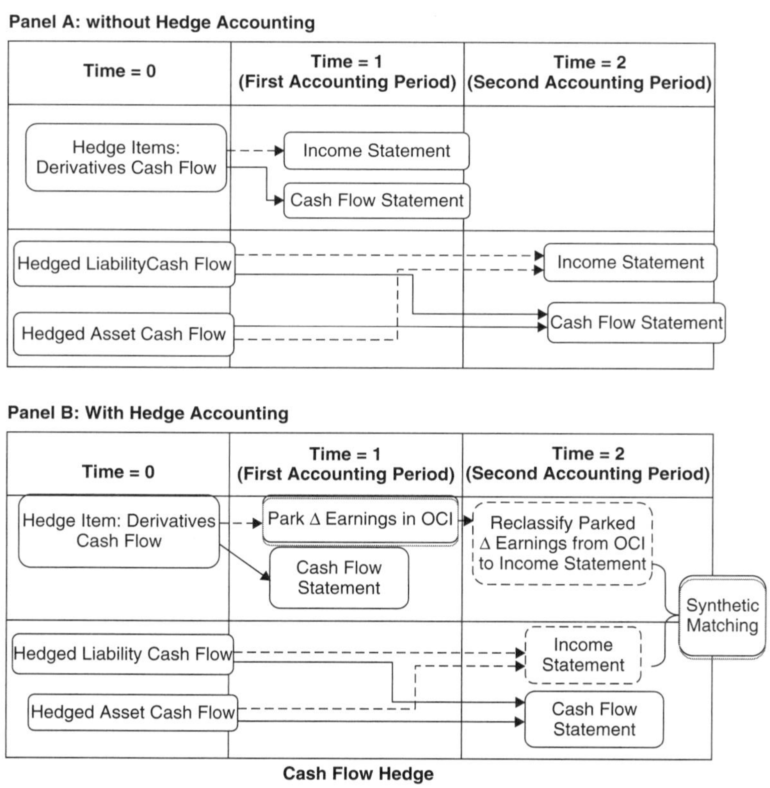


**Figure 7.2** Mismatching Due to the Accounting Mixed-Attribute Model in the Presence of Hedging but in Absence of Hedge Accounting

## Exhibit 7.8 Effects of Hedge Accounting on Applying Ordinary GAAP

| | *Fair Value Hedge* | *Cash Flow Hedge* |
|---|---|---|
| Derivative Instruments → | No Change in GAAP(b)<br>✓ Assets/Liabilities<br>▪ Post to Earnings | Change in GAAP(a)<br>✓ Assets/Liabilities<br>❖ *Post to AOCI* |
| Hedged Item → | Change in GAAP<br>❖ *Fair Value Assets & Liabilities*<br>▪ Post to Earnings | No Change in GAAP<br>↔ Follow ordinary GAAP |

❖ Changed condition.
(a) The derivative instrument is still accounted for at fair value, but the Δ in fair Value is posted to OCI instead of earnings.
(b) Hedge item is revalued to Fair Value and Δ Fair Value are posted to earnings.
(a) & (b) Requiring that the hedge meet the effectiveness test.

### 7.4.4 Centrality of Management Intent

Classification of hedging relationships into *cash flow hedge* or *fair value hedge* has significant implications for the measurement and reporting of assets, liabilities, earnings, and owners' equity. It is therefore of relevance to know the process by which the management adopts one classification or the other. For some contracts, classifying a hedging relationship as either *cash flow hedge* or *fair value hedge* can depend on one of two factors:

1. The nature of the transaction.
2. Management's declaration of intent.

For example, the hedge of a forecasted issuance of interest-bearing debt (as the IBM disclosure presented in Chapter Six, section 6.2.2) can only be accounted for as a cash flow hedge because of the uncertainty associated with carrying out a forecasted transaction. In other cases, the nature of the transaction is not the determining classification factor. For example, in hedging the inventory of finished goods, *the classification is essentially a management choice because the standards call for the accounting treatment to be aligned with management intent.* Management might declare its intention to hedge the value of finished goods inventory in order to preserve the value reported on the balance sheet; it then hedges the value of an asset to qualify for *fair value hedge* accounting treatment. Alternatively, the management might intend to lock in a sale price and hedge the anticipated sale of the inventory at that price to ensure having a certain level of revenues. In this case, the hedging relationship would qualify as *cash flow hedge* because, without having a firm commitment, the sale of inventory (for which there are no written contracts) is only a forecasted transaction.

### Conclusion

*The natures of some contractual arrangements lend themselves to be classified either as cash flow hedge or fair value hedge accounting treatment. In other cases, the choice is based on (the rather unverifiable) management intent.*

The above example of hedging inventory is for finished goods inventory where the choice would be between preserving the value of the asset and locking in a forecasted sales price. The situation would not be much different if the inventory consists of raw materials. In this case, the choice of the hedge classification will also depend on *management intent*. Management could intend to hedge the value of the inventory as an asset and account for it as fair value hedge. Alternatively, management could intend to hedge the forecasted cost of restocking the inventory and treat the transaction as a cash flow hedge.

Management's ability to make this choice is subject to a limited number of conditions. In particular, the occurrence of the forecasted transaction must be judged to be probable. In this setting, the "term *probable* requires a significantly greater likelihood of occurrence than the phrase *more likely than not*" (ASC 815-20-25-16). While the standards do not require providing evidence in support of the forecoast, the management of an enterprise could justify its probability judgment by reference to some supporting factors such as the following:

- Frequency of occurrence of similar transactions in the past.
- The enterprise's financial capability of completing the transaction.
- The length of time expected before the forecasted transaction is carried out.

It should not be difficult to show that these evidential matters would be supportive of management's intent to sell finished goods or to purchase raw materials for use in an ongoing production. But for other types of forecasted transactions such as the forecasted issuance of a fixed-rate bond or the forecasted importation of commodities from another country, these supporting factors would not score high in judging the probability of occurrence. In these cases, management's declared intent would be a dominant factor in determining the appropriate accounting method. To give one example, this would be the case if management plans to fund capital budgeting projects for which its intent is the only known factor and for which there are also alternative sources of funding.

## 7.4.5 Special Issues about Cash Flow Hedge (Overhedge and Underhedge)

- A cash flow hedge is hedging the risk (volatility) of cash flow associated with a recognized asset, a recognized liability, or a forecasted transaction whose realization is probable.
- Therefore, the hedged item is a "feature" rather than an asset or a liability.
- In an effective cash flow hedge, one should defer in an equity account the gain or loss on a hedge derivative that is attributable to the specific risk being hedged (OCI) until such time when the hedged transaction has an effect on earnings.
- Gains or losses on the hedge item might be equal to, or different from the gains or losses of the hedged position.
- A case of overhedge is said to exist if the gain or loss on the hedge instrument exceeds the fair value of the expected change in cash flow of the hedged item.
- A case of underhedge is said to exist when the gain or loss on the hedge instrument is below the change in the fair value of the expected cash flow of the hedged position.
- Hedge accounting rules have five simple propositions:

1. Overhedge is an indication of the extent of hedge ineffectiveness.
2. Overhedge amounts should not be deferred in an equity account.
3. The amounts of overhedge should be recognized in earnings in the period it occurs.
4. Underhedge should be ignored.
5. In a cash flow hedge, the amount to be deferred in OCI should be the lower amount of the following two measures as presented in Figure 7.3:[12]
   i. The absolute value of cumulative gain or loss on the hedging instrument from inception of the hedge.
   ii. The absolute value of cumulative change in the fair value or present value of the expected cash flow of the hedged position from inception of the hedge.

- The standards (both ASC in the U.S. and IFRS) present this over/underhedge rule by reference to the cumulative change.

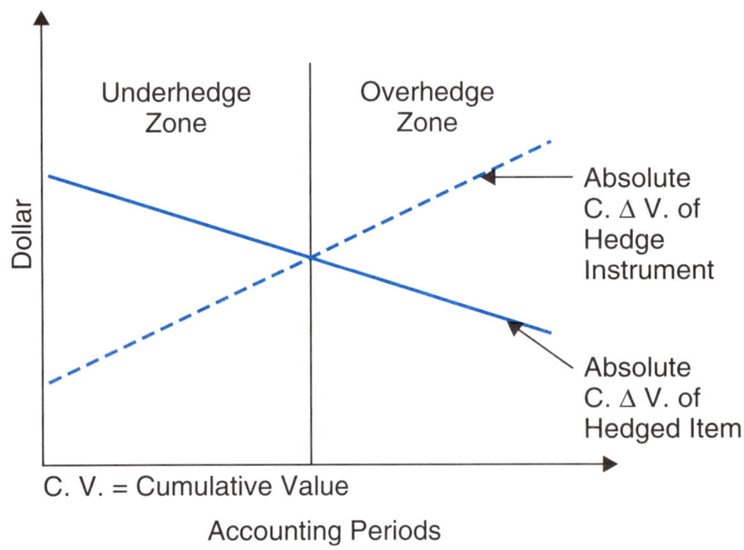


**Figure 7.3** Overhedge and Underhedge in Cash Flow Hedging

## 7.5 Hedging Inventory

### Information Log: Roadmap to the Illustrations in Chapter Seven

The illustrations in this chapter address the following issues:

- Illustrating hedge accounting when the hedge is *effective* for market conditions of either *contango* or *normal backwardation*.[13]
- Comparing the accounting impact of *designating* versus *not designating* a derivative as a hedge for accounting purposes.

- Comparing the impact on cash flow and earnings of *cash flow hedge* versus *fair value hedge* for a given hedging relationship.
- The set up and general facts are used in most cases in order to facilitate comparisons between different accounting treatments.
- Illustrating the *termination* of hedge accounting due to *ineffectiveness* of the hedging relationship.
- Analyzing the impact of hedge accounting on *financial ratios and liquidity*.
- Showing that the accounting treatment does not *change the reality* of cash and product flows; it only changes the timing and locations on the financial statements (i.e., *accounting geography*) resulting in differing financial reports.
- Providing examples of *underhedge* and *overhedge* in cash flow hedging relationships. The case of overhedge is designed to show reclassifying earnings charges of prior periods overhedge.
- All illustrations provide simple representations of the required management documentation and testing effectiveness.

## 7.5.1 Fair Value Hedge of Inventory (1)

### 7.5.1.1 Scenario C (FVH): *Decreasing Forward Prices & Effective Hedge*

This illustration shows hedge accounting when the far futures' price declines as the contract approaches maturity (i.e., forward prices decreasing, as when the market is experiencing *contango*).

- On October 1, 20x1, *Milsom Farms, Inc.* has 100,000 bushels of soybean in inventory, which it acquired at a cost of $12.00 a bushel.
- The company plans to sell this inventory in six months' time.
- Current market prices as of October 20x1 are:
    - Spot (cash): $13.03 a bushel.
    - Futures (March delivery): $13.10 a bushel.
- *Milsom Farms, Inc.* management is concerned that the spot price in March might be lower than $13.10 because of the good soybean harvest in Argentina and the increased likelihood of dumping Argentinean soybean in US markets.
- To lock in the sale price at $13.10, the company entered into a futures agreement with CBOT, contract *FSB12G*, to sell 20 March futures contracts of Grade 2 American soybean at $13.10 a bushel.[14]
- The company settled the futures on March 31, 20x2 as the contract stipulates.
- On April 20, 20x2, *Milsom Farms* sold the inventory to a soybean crushing company for $12.55 a bushel.

### *7.5.1.2 The Accounting*

The management of *Milsom Farms, Inc.* designated the futures contracts as a fair value hedge of soybean inventory. The company documented this specific hedge to be consistent with its policy and accounting standards requirements (under FASB and IFRS). The documentation is shown in Exhibit 7.9.

## Exhibit 7.9 Hedging Documentation for *Milsom Farms, Inc.*

| | |
|---|---|
| Risk Management Objectives: | The risk management of *Milsom Farms, Inc.* has the goal of reducing exposure to inventory value loss due to adverse commodity price movement. This goal is consistent with the management risk philosophy of *Milsom Farms, Inc.* and the risk management system that was adopted by the Board of Directors in its meeting in April 20x0. |
| Hedged Item | The inventory of 100,000 bushels of American Yellow Grade 2 soybean. |
| Hedge Instrument | CBOT futures agreement, contract *FSB12G*. The company purchased 20 contracts (the standard soybean futures contract is 5,000 bushels). |
| Starting Date | October 1, 20x1. |
| Duration | Six months to March 31, 20x2. |
| Hedge Designation | The management of *Milsom Farms, Inc.* decided to designate contract *FSB12G* as a fair value hedge of the 100,000 bushels of soybean inventory. |
| Testing Hedge Effectiveness | Dollar offset ratio (DOR) method will be used for testing hedge effectiveness.<br>DOR = \|Δ value of the futures/Δ value of the inventory\|<br>The values used for testing hedge effectiveness exclude the time value of futures contracts. |

During the six-month period of the contract, spot and futures prices changed as shown in Table 7.3.

**Table 7.3** Soybean Spot and Future Price Movements (Fair Value Hedge No Ineffectiveness)

| | *Price per Bushel* | | |
|---|---|---|---|
| | *October 20x1* | *December 20X1* | *March 20X2* |
| Spot price | $13.03 | $12.796 | $12.55 |
| March 2x02 Futures Price | $13.10 | $12.821 | $12.55 |
| Δ Spot price | — | $(0.234) | $(0.246) |
| Δ March Futures price | — | $0.279 | $0.271 |

Based on these changes we have the following values:

| | *December 20X1* | *March 20X2* |
|---|---|---|
| Fair value of the futures contract. | $ 27,900 | $55,000 |
| Δ Fair value of the futures | $ 27,900 | $27,100 |
| Δ Fair value of inventory | ($23,400) | ($25,600) |
| Time value of futures[(a)] | $4,500 | $2,500 |
| Margin Deposit[(b)] | $14,000 | $14,000 |

*Notes:*

(a) The Time Value of Futures is calculated as the difference between futures and spot prices. This calculation is based on the assumption of efficient markets with traders clearing arbitrage profits in which case the futures price is determined as

$$F_{t \to t+6\text{ month}} = S_t * e^{c \times (6/12)}$$

Where $F_{t \to t+6\text{ month}}$ = Futures price six months hence.
$S_t$ = spot price at time t (October 20x1 in this example)
$c$ = the cost of carry (as the sum of (%) interest rate and storage cost.)
(6/12) = the time period (six months from October 20x1 in this example).

Therefore, the difference between spot and futures prices is due to the cost of carry which is positive for time > 0.

(b) The Margin is determined by the Futures Exchange. It is usually a function of the size of the contract, expectation of price movement and the credit risk of the trader. In this example, we assume that the Exchange requires a $14,000 margin for this transaction (The Exchange has a formula for determination of the Margin, which the counterparty has to accept).

## Accounting for the First Period from October 1, 20x1 to December 31, 20x1

- The change in fair value of inventory is calculated as the change in spot prices times the notional principal amount of 100,000 bushels:

  $(13.03 - 12.796) \times 100,000 = \$23,400$

  for the period from October 20x1 to December 20x1.
- Fair value of the futures contract is calculated as the difference in futures prices times the notional amount:

  $(13.10 - 12.821) \times 100,000 = \$27,900$

  for the period from October 20x1 to December 20x1.

  Recording these changes on the books of *Milsom Farms, Inc.* is as follows.

| *Date* | *Transaction* | *Dr* | *Cr* |
|---|---|---|---|
| 10/1/20x1 | Memorandum<br>*Milsom Farms, Inc. entered into 20 futures contracts (5,000 bushels each) with CBOT to sell 100,000 bushels of American Yellow Grade 2 soybean at $13.10 a bushel. The contract number is FSB12G.* | — | —<br>— |
| 10/1/20x1 | Receivable—Futures Exchange margin *FSB12G*<br>Cash<br>*Depositing the required margin with the Futures Exchange for contract FSB12G* | 14,000 | <br>14,000 |

| | | | |
|---|---|---|---|
| 12/31/20x1 | Other gains/losses on soybean inventory<br>  Inventory—soybean<br>*To recording the loss on inventory as spot prices dropped from $13.03 to $12.796 per bushel for the inventory of 100,000 bushels* | 23,400 | <br>23,400 |
| 12/31/20x1 | Receivables—CBOT for futures contract *FSB12G*<br>  Other gains/losses on futures<br>*To record the gain on the short futures contracts FSB12G as the futures prices dropped from 13.10 to $12.821 per bushel* | 27,900 | <br>27,900 |
| 12/31/20x1 | Cash<br>  Receivables—CBOT for futures contract *FSB12G*<br>*To record collecting the receivable from CBOT*[a] | 27,900 | <br>27,900 |
| 12/31/20x1 | Other gain or loss on futures<br>  Other gain/loss on soybean inventory<br>  Other gains/losses (time value of futures)<br>*Recording the ineffective component of the hedge which is the effect on earnings* | 27,900 | <br>23,400<br>4,500 |
| 12/31/20x1 | Other gains/losses (time value of futures)<br>  Earnings<br>*To record the net effect of hedging on earnings.* | 4,500 | <br>4,500 |

[a] In reality this amount is added electronically as adjustments to the margin deposited by the client.

### Accounting for the Second Period between December 31, 20x1 and March 31, 20x1

- Fair value of the futures contract is calculated as the difference in futures prices times the notional amount.
- The total change since signing the contract is equal to 100,000 bushels times the contract price of $13.10 minus the current futures price for same delivery time which is $12.55,

  $$(13.10 - 12.55) \times 100{,}000 = \$55{,}000$$

  for the period from October 20x1 to March 20x2. From that amount, $27,900 was already recognized in the previous period, leaving $27,100 for this period.
- Although the futures price has dropped, these changes in fair value are gains for *Milsom Farms, Inc.* because the futures contract obligates the Futures Exchange to purchase the soybean at $13.10. Under the agreement, the Futures Exchange would have to pay *Milsom Farms, Inc.* any drop in price below. Conversely, *Milsom Farms, Inc.* would pay the Futures Exchange any increase in the price above $13.10. (Also refer to the Appendix to Chapter One.)
- The change in fair value of inventory is calculated as the change in spot prices between December 31, 20x1 and March 20x2 times the notional principal amount of 100,000 bushels:

  $$(12.796 - 12.55) \times 100{,}000 = 24{,}600$$

  for the period from October 20x1 to March 20x2.

  The journal entries recording these changes on the books of *Milsom Farms, Inc.* are as follows.

| *Date* | *Transaction* | *Dr* | *Cr* |
|---|---|---|---|
| 3/31/20x2 | Other gains/losses on soybean inventory<br>  Inventory—soybean<br>*To record the loss on inventory as spot price declined from $12.796 to $12.55 per bushel* | 24,600 | <br>24,600 |
| 3/31/20x2 | Receivables—CBOT for futures contract *FSB12G*<br>  Other gains/losses on futures<br>*To record the gain on the short futures contract as futures prices have dropped from $12.821 to $12.55* | 27,100 | <br>27,100 |
| 3/31/20x2 | Other gain or loss on futures<br>  Other gain/loss on soybean inventory<br>  Other gains/losses (time value of futures)<br>*To record the effective and ineffective components of the gain on futures contract* | 27,100 | <br>24,600<br>2,500 |
| 3/31/20x2 | Cash<br>  Receivables—CBOT for futures contract *FSB12G*<br>  Receivables—Futures Exchange margin *FSB12G*<br>*Collecting the receivables owed by the Futures Exchange for the margin deposit and for gains on the futures contract.** | 41,100 | <br>27,100<br>14,000 |
| 4/20/20x2 | Cost of goods sold<br>  Inventory—soybean<br>*Costing the sales of 100,000 bushels of soybean ($1,200,000 less the losses of $48,000)* | 1,152,000 | <br>1,152,000 |
| 4/20/20x2 | Receivables—Trade<br>  Sales revenue<br>*Recording the sale of soybean inventory* | 1,255,000 | <br>1,255,000 |

* In reality, the Futures Exchange settles every day with the counterparty (*Milsom Farms, Inc.*). In this illustration we assumed that settlement is made at once for simplification.

## Analysis

### 1. Hedge Effectiveness

Hedge documentation states that the DOR (i.e., Δ value of the futures/Δ value of the inventory) is the method to be used for testing effectiveness. Excluding the time value of futures as noted in documentation of the hedge, retrospective effectiveness would be measured using dollar offset as follows:

a. For the period October 1, 20x1 to December 31, 20x2:

$$|\$23{,}400/\$23{,}400| = 1.00$$

b. For the period December 31, 20x1 to March 31, 20x2:

$$|\$25{,}600/\$25{,}600| = 1.00$$

On the other hand, if forward points were included in the effectiveness test, we would have

c. For the period October 1, 20x1 to December 31, 20x2:

$$|\$27{,}900/\$23{,}400| \approx 1.19$$

d. For the period December 31, 20x1 to March 31, 20x2:

$$|\$27{,}100/\$25{,}600| \approx 1.06$$

As discussed in Chapter Six, a hedge does not have to be 100% offsetting to be classified as highly successful; the SEC and best practice allow for a 20% error resulting in an acceptable zone of Dollar Offset Ratio (DOR),

$$0.80 \le |DOR| \le 1.25$$

Therefore, the hedge is considered highly effective and hedge accounting is applicable.

**2. Sales**

The company sold the inventory at the spot market price of the day on sale, April 20, 20x1.[15] In all futures contracts, the Futures Exchange is the counterparty. For this transaction, *Milsom Farms, Inc.* collected $69,000 cash from the Futures Exchange (CBOT) representing the gain of $55,000 plus the $14,000 margin (deposit). Therefore, the $55,000 is the profit it earned on the soybean futures contract. It also sold its inventory of soybean at spot market prices on the date of sale, March 31, 20x2, which is $12.55 per bushel, resulting in having trade receivables in the amount of $1,255,000. Therefore, the increase in liquid assets in the amount of $1,310,000 consists of two components:

| | |
|---|---|
| + Cash (gain on futures) | $55,000 (27,900 in 20x1 + 27,100 in 20x2) |
| + Receivable-Trade | $1,255,000 |
| Total | $1,310,000 |

The combination of sale at the spot market price shortly after the end of the contract term and the gain on the hedge allowed *Milsom Farms, Inc.* to effectively sell its inventory of soybean at the desired price of $13.10 a bushel.

**3. Cost of Sales**

The inventory was carried on the books at cost in the amount of $1,200,000. Upon designating the inventory as a fair value hedge item, the company did not automatically reset the carrying amount to fair value. Instead, *only the changes in fair values that are attributable to the hedged risk (which is the change in price from its level at hedge inception)* will be reflected in the carrying value of the inventory (provided that the hedge is highly effective and other hedging requirements are satisfied).

When the inventory was carried on the books at $1,200,000, its (unrecognized) fair market value was $1,303,000. Designating the inventory as a hedge item in a fair value hedge means *taking into account the changes in fair value from inception of the hedge onward*—the change above or below the $1,303,000. These changes in fair values will be applied as adjustments to the $1,200,000 carrying amount of inventory. Figure 7.4 shows the two different approaches of arriving at this cost.

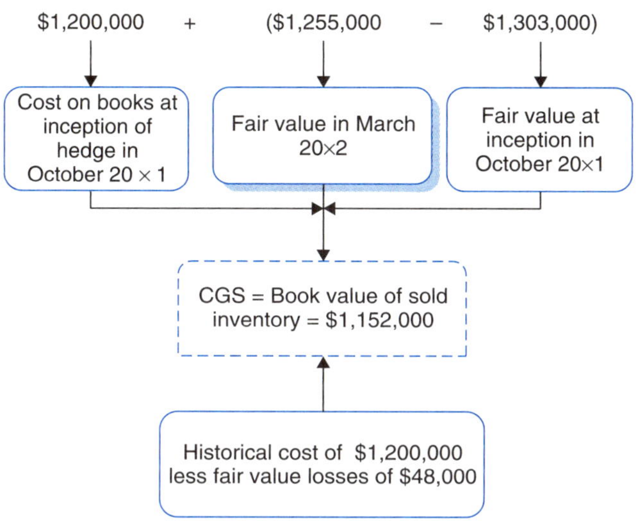


**Figure 7.4** Two Approaches to Measuring CGS

### 4. Earnings

The effects of hedging on income amounted to the following:

- Ineffectiveness due to time value of futures (the difference between futures price and spot price at inception) increased earnings by $4,500 and $2,500 in 20x1 and 20x2, respectively.
- The combined net income from the sale of soybean inventory equals the desired income goal of $110,000, which is effectively equal to $1,310,000 (contractually) desired sales less the $1,200,000 cost of inventory. However, actual sales revenues amounted to only $1,255,000 which is the fair market value at the time of sale; the desired income level is achieved as a result of having an effective hedge. This is shown as follows:

| | |
|---|---|
| Sales | $1,255,000 |
| Cost of goods sold | ($1,152,000) |
| Gross profit | $103,000 |
| + gain (time value) | $7,000 |
| | $110,000 |

### 5. Financial Analysis

Table 7.4 presents comparisons of three situations:

C1 When there is no derivative instrument.
C2 There is a derivative but it is not designated as a hedge.
C3 The derivative (futures) contract is designated as a fair value hedge.

**Table 7.4** A Comparison of Different Conditions of Using Financial Derivatives (*Milsom Farms, Inc.*)

| | *No Derivative* | *Futures (forward) Derivative* | |
|---|---|---|---|
| | | *Undesignated Hedge* | *Effective Hedge* |
| | C1 | C2 | C3 |
| Sales | $1,255,000.00 | $1,255,000.00 | $1,255,000.00 |
| Gross Profit | $55,000.00 | $55,000.00 | $103,000.00 |
| Gross Profit Margin (Gross Profit / Sales) | **4.28%** | **4.28%** | **8.2%** |
| Net Profit | $55,000.00 | $110,000.00 | $110,000.00 |
| Net Profit/Sales | **4.28%** | **8.76%** | **8.76%** |
| Futures Time Value | N/A | $7,000.00 | $7,000.00 |
| Impact of the Futures Derivative on Profits | N/A | $48,000.00 | 0.00 |
| Effective Sale Price per bushel | $12.55 | $13.10 | $13.10 |

- C1—*The Case of No Derivative:* If there were no derivative involved, *Milsom Farms, Inc.* could sell the inventory at the spot market price (cash price) at the time of sale, and the impact on gross profit and net income would be—the difference between sales revenues of $1,255,000 and the carrying cost of $1,200,000. The resulting gross profit margin equals the net profit margin (before tax), which is 4.28%. This is also the profit margin (holding everything else constant).
- C2—*Undesignated Derivative:* When *Milsom Farms, Inc.* enters into a futures contract to sell the soybean inventory, the management can designate this contract as a hedge or keep it undesignated.

  The management of *Milsom Farms, Inc.* entered into derivative contracts ostensibly to hedge the commodity price risk of the inventory but it may elect to use these contracts as an "economic hedge." These contracts are hedge instruments, but in that case they would not be recognized as such in accounting. The derivative will be accounted for as "trading securities" that should be valued at fair value with the changes in fair values posted to earnings. In this case, the sale of soybean inventory would not be impacted by any activity related to the derivatives. Therefore, gross profit would be $55,000 as in C1 (the case of no derivative), but net income is different. Given the facts in the case, the income in C1 will increase by another $55,000 that is collected from the Futures Exchange as the difference ($13.10 – $12.55) × 100,000. The gains from dealing with the Futures Exchanges consists of $7,000 due to time value of the futures ($13.10 – $13.03) × 100,000 plus $48,000 due to the commodity price impact on the futures contract ($13.03 – $12.55) × 100,000. Therefore, while the gross profit margin would be 4.28% as is the case in C1, the net profit margin (before tax) would increase to 8.76%.
- C3— *Designating the Derivative as a Hedge:*In the last column of Table 7.4, *Milsom Farms, Inc.* designated the futures contracts as fair value hedge, prepared the necessary documentation and anticipated, based on historical data, that the hedge would be highly effective. In this case, the

gross profit increased to $103,000 ($55,000 for the difference between the forward price and the spot price at final settlement date ($13.10 – $12.55) × 100,000 plus $48,000 as the excess of fair value and cost at inception of the hedge ($13.03 – $12.00) × 100,000)). The $103,000 gives the company a gross profit margin of 8.2% ($103,000/1,255,000), but adding the $7,000 time value of futures resulted in $110,000 net profits.

Three observations relate to these situations should be made:

a. In both cases C2 and C3, when *Milsom Farms, Inc.* has acquired derivatives, these contracts increased income by $55,000 whether the derivative was or was not designated as an accounting hedge.
b. In both cases, the $55,000 gain on the derivative consists of $7,000 futures time value and $48,000 response to commodity price changes.
c. The difference between C2 and C3 is reporting the impact on different performance indicators—i.e., disclosure geography.

### Impact on Financial Ratios

The three conditions presented in Table 7.4 affect financial ratios in different ways.

1. *Current Ratio (CA/CL):* In a highly effective hedge and when the DOR is not 100%, entering into futures derivative contracts will have an impact on current ratio by the extent of the hedge ineffectiveness. In the first period of this example, accounts receivable (and eventually cash) increased by $27,900 in 20x1, but inventory book value decreased by $23,400 with the difference being the ineffective component of the hedge.

If the hedging relationship was, in total, ineffective, accounts receivables would have increased by $27,900 in 20x1, but the inventory book value will remain unaffected.

2. *Liquidity Ratio:* In this example, the futures contract is treated as a current asset. Therefore, whether or not the derivative is designated as a hedge, futures contracts (assets) are valued at fair value. Entering into the futures contract (in this case) improves the liquidity ratio whether or not hedge accounting is adopted. However, market prices of soybean could have increased, and *Milsom Farms, Inc.* would owe money to the Futures Exchange and the enterprise liquidity condition worsens.

3. *Profit Margin:* When futures derivative contracts are undesignated as a hedge, the change in the value of the derivative will not affect the gross profit margin. This situation changes when the derivative is designated as a hedge and the hedge is effective (and properly documented). In this case, the change in value is specifically designated as hedging commodity price risk and it will have an effect on inventory values and cost of goods sold as is the case in C3 in Table 7.4. The result was an increase in gross profit margin from 4.28% to 8.2%. However, the *net profit margin* 8.76% is realized when the enterprise has derivatives having cash flow expectations opposite of the risk exposure whether or not the derivative is designated as a fair value hedge.[16]

## 7.5.2 Cash Flow Hedge of Forecasted Sale of Inventory (2)

### 7.5.2.1 Scenario D (CFH): *Decreasing Forward Prices & Effective Hedge*

This is the same transaction and basic information of *Milsom Farms, Inc.* in Scenario C (VFH) above except for assuming that the management of *Milsom Farms, Inc.* decided to designate the futures as hedging *the volatility of future prices* that could be realized by selling the inventory; this is a cash flow hedge. An outline of basic information is as follows:

- On October 1, 20x1, *Milsom Farms, Inc.* has 100,000 bushels of soybean in inventory.
- The inventory is booked at $1,200,000, a cost of $12.00 a bushel.
- On October 1, 20x1, *Milsom Farms, Inc.* contracted with CBOT (the Futures Exchange) to sell 20 futures contracts of soybean for March 31 delivery at $13.10 a bushel (each futures contract has a standard size of 5,000 bushels). This contract is given the code "contract *FSB12G*" for ease of identification.
- On October 20x1 the spot (cash) price is $13.03 a bushel.
- *Milsom Farms, Inc.*designated the futures contract as a cash flow hedge of the forcasted sale of inventory.

The documentation is shown in Exhibit 7.10.

### Exhibit 7.10 Cash Flow Hedging Documentation for *Milsom Farms, Inc.*

| | |
|---|---|
| Risk Management Objectives | The risk management of *Milsom Farms, Inc.* has the goal of reducing exposure to future cash flow volatility due to adverse commodity price movements. This goal is consistent with management risk philosophy and the Enterprise Risk Management System that was adopted by the Board of Directors of *Milsom Farms, Inc.* in its meeting in April 20x0. |
| Hedged Item | The future sale price of 100,000 bushels of American Yellow Grade 2 soybean currently held in the inventory. |
| Hedge Instrument | CBOT futures agreement, contract *FSB12G*. The company purchased 20 contracts (the standard soybean futures contract is 5,000 bushels). |
| Starting Date | October 1, 20x1 |
| Duration | Six months to March 31, 20x2 |
| Hedge Designation | The management of *Milsom Farms, Inc.* decided to designate contract *FSB12G* as a cash flow hedge of the 100,000 bushels of soybean inventory. |
| Testing Hedge Effectiveness | Delta or DOR method will be used for testing hedge effectiveness. Dollar Offset Ratio (DOR) = \|Δ value of the futures/Δ FV of expected cash flow from sales\| The values used for testing hedge effectiveness exclude the time value of futures contracts. |

During the six-month period of the contract, spot and futures prices change as shown in Table 7.5.[17]

**Table 7.5** Soybean Spot and Future Price Movements (Fair Value Hedge No Ineffectiveness)

| | | *Price per Bushel* | |
|---|---|---|---|
| | *October 20x1* | *December 20X1* | *March 20X2* |
| Spot price | \$13.03 | \$12.796 | \$12.550 |
| March 2x02 Futures Price | \$13.10 | \$12.821 | \$12.550 |
| Δ Spot price | — | \$(0.234) | \$(0.246) |
| Δ March Futures price | — | \$0.279 | \$0.271 |

Based on these changes we have the following values:

| | *December 20X1* | *March 20X2* |
|---|---|---|
| Fair value of the futures contract. | \$27,900 | \$55,000 |
| Δ Fair value of the futures | \$27,900 | \$27,100 |
| Δ Fair value of inventory | (\$23,400) | (\$25,600) |
| Time value of futures[(1)] | \$4,500 | \$2,500 |
| Margin Deposit[(2)] | \$14,000 | \$14,000 |

*Notes:*

(1) The Time Value of Futures is calculated as the difference between futures and spot prices. This calculation is based on the assumption of efficient markets with traders clearing arbitrage profits in which case the futures price is determined as

$$F_{t \to t+6\text{ month}} = S_t * e^{c \times (6/12)}$$

Where $F_{t \to t+6\text{ month}}$ = Futures price six months hence.
$S_t$ = spot price at time t (October 20x1 in this example)
$c$ = the cost of carry (as the sum of (%) interest rate and storage cost.)
(6/12) = the time period (six months from October 20x1 in this example).

Therefore, the difference between spot and futures prices is due to the cost of carry which is positive for time > 0.

(2) The Margin is determined by the Futures Exchange. It is usually a function of the size of the contract, expectation of price movement and the credit risk of the trader. In this example, we assume that the Exchange requires a \$14,000 margin for this transaction (The Exchange has a formula for determination of the Margin, which the counterparty has to accept).

### Accounting for the First Period from October 1, 20x1 to December 31, 20x1

- In a cash flow hedge, the change in fair value of inventory is ignored.
- Fair value of the futures contract during this period is calculated as the difference in futures prices times the notional amount:

$$(13.10 - 12.821) \times 100{,}000 = \$27{,}900$$

for the period from October 20x1 to December 20x1.

The journal entries recording the cash flow hedge on the books of *Milsom Farms, Inc.* are as follows.

| *Date* | *Transaction* | *Dr* | *Cr* |
|---|---|---|---|
| 10/1/20x1 | Memorandum<br>*Milsom Farms, Inc. entered into 20 futures contracts (5,000 bushels each) with CBOT to sell 100,000 bushels of American Yellow Grade 2 soybean at $13.10 a bushel. The contract number is FSB12G.* | — | — |
| 10/1/20x1 | Futures—CBOT Contract *FSB12G M* argin<br>Cash<br>*Depositing the required margin with the Futures Exchange for contract FSB12G* | 14,000 | <br>14,000 |
| 12/31/20x1 | Futures—CBOT Contract *FSB12G*<br>Other gains/losses on futures<br>*To record the gain on the short futures contracts FSB12G as the futures prices dropped from 13.10 to $12.821 per bushel* | 27,900 | <br>27,900 |
| 12/31/20x1 | Cash<br>Futures—CBOT Contract *FSB12G*<br>*To record collecting the receivable from CBOT*<br>*Collection of the amounts owed by the Futures Exchange (this amount could be different if the CBOT requested adjustment to the margin).* | 27,900 | <br>27,900 |
| 12/31/20x1 | Other gains/losses on futures<br>OCI—hedging future sales, Futures Contract *FSB12G*<br>Other gains/losses (time value of futures)<br>*Recording the ineffective component of the hedge which is the effect on earnings* | 27,900 | <br>23,400<br>4,500 |
| 12/31/20x1 | Other gains/losses (time value of futures)<br>Earnings<br>*To record the net effect of hedging on earnings.* | 4,500 | <br>4,500 |

## Accounting for the Second Period between December 31/20x1 and March 31/20x1

The total change since signing the contract is equal to

- ($13.10 – $12.55) × 100,000 bushels= $55,000 for the two periods from October 20x1 to March 20x2. From that amount, $27,900 was recognized in the previous period, leaving $27,100 for this period.
- Although the futures prices have dropped, these changes in fair value are gains for *Milsom Farms, Inc.* Under the agreement, the CBOT would have to pay *Milsom Farms* any drop in price below the contract price in order to provide the company with sufficient funds to compensate for the opportunity cost.

The journal entries recording these changes on the books of *Milsom Farms, Inc.* are as follows.

| Date | Transaction | Dr | Cr |
|---|---|---|---|
| 3/31/20x2 | Futures—CBOT Contract *FSB12G*<br>Other gains/losses on futures<br>*To record the gain on the short futures contract as futures prices have dropped from $12.821 to $12.55* | 27,100 | <br>27,100 |
| 3/31/20x2 | Other gains/losses on futures<br>OCI—hedging inventories, Futures *FSB12G*<br>Other gains/losses (time value of futures)<br>*To record the effective and ineffective components of the gain on futures contract* | 27,100 | <br>24,600<br>2,500 |
| 3/31/20x2 | Cash<br>Futures—CBOT Contract *FSB12G*<br>Futures—CBOT Contract *FSB12G* margin<br>*Collecting the receivables owed by the Futures Exchange for the Margin deposit and for gains on the futures contract.* | 41,100 | <br>27,100<br>14,000 |
| 4/20/20x2 | Cost of goods sold<br>OCI—hedging inventories, Futures *FSB12G*<br>Inventory—soybean<br>*Costing the sales of 100,000 bushels of soybean* | 1,152,000 | <br><br>1,200,000 |
| 4/20/20x2 | Receivables—Trade<br>Sales Revenue<br>*Recording the sale of soybean inventory* | 1,255,000 | <br>1,255,000 |

## Analysis

**1. Hedge Effectiveness**

Hedge effectiveness could be measured by the Dollar Offset Ratio comparing the changes in prices of the acquired futures and the changes in prices of: (a) a hypothetical derivative, or (b) cash requirements of the hedged position (see Chapter Six).[18] The latter approach is used with the "cash requirements" being represented by the changing prospective sale prices. In practical terms (for this illustration), the DOR used here is equivalent to that used in the fair value hedge. (i.e., $\Delta$ value of the futures/$\Delta$ hedged cash flow position).

Excluding the time value of futures as noted in documentation of the hedge, retrospective effectiveness would be measured using dollar offset as follows:

a. For the period October 1, 20x1 to December 31, 20x2:

$$|\$23,400/\$23,400| = 1.00$$

b. For the period December 31, 20x1 to March 31, 20x2:

$$|\$25,600/\$25,600| = 1.00.$$

On the other hand, if the forward points were included in the effectiveness test, we would have

c. For the period October 1, 20x1 to December 31, 20x2:

$$|\$27{,}900/\$23{,}400| \approx 1.19$$

d. For the period December 31, 20x1 to March 31, 20x2:

$$|\$27{,}100/\$25{,}600| \approx 1.06.$$

As discussed earlier, a hedge does not have to be 100% offsetting to be classified as highly successful; the SEC and best practice allow for a 20% error resulting in an acceptable zone of

$$0.80 \leq |DOR| \leq 1.25$$

**2. Sales**

In all futures contracts, the Futures Exchange is the counterparty. For this transaction, *Milsom Farms, Inc.* collected $69,000 cash from the Futures Exchange representing what the Exchange owes *Milsom Farms, Inc.*, which includes the $14,000 margin (deposit). Therefore, the $55,000 is the gain it earned on the soybean futures contract. However, unlike the preceding case of fair value hedge, in a cash flow hedge, this gain did not affect earnings until the inventory was sold. The company also sold its inventory of soybeans at spot market prices on the date of sale, July 20, 20x2, which is $12.55 per bushel, resulting in having trade receivables of $1,255,000.[19] Therefore, the increase in liquid assets of $1,310,000 consists of two components:

| | |
|---|---|
| + Cash (gain on futures) | $55,000 {27,900 in 20x1 + 27,100 in 20x2) |
| + Receivable-Trade | $1,255,000 |
| Total | $1,310,000 |

The combination of sale at the spot market price at the end of the contract term and the gain on the hedge allowed *Milsom Farms, Inc.* to effectively sell its inventory of soybean at the desired price of $13.10 a bushel.

**3. Cost of Sales**

The inventory was carried on the books at cost in the amount of $1,200,000, which was the lower-of-cost-or-market. The cost of goods sold is $1,152,000, which is the inventory value adjusted by the gain accumulated in OCI.

**4. Earnings**

The effects of hedging on income amounted to the following:

- Ineffectiveness due to time value of futures (the difference between futures price and spot price) increased earnings by $4,500 and $2,500 in 20x1 and 20x2, respectively.
- The net income from the sale of soybean inventory equals the desired income goal of $110,000, which is equal to $1,310,000 desired sales less the $1,200,000 cost of inventory. However, actual sales revenues amounted to only $1,255,000; the desired income level is achieved as a result of having an effective hedge. This is shown as follows:

| | |
|---|---|
| Sales | $1,255,000 |
| Cost of goods sold | ($1,152,000) |
| Gross profit | $103,000 |
| + gain (time value) | $7,000 |
| | $110,000 |

The cost of goods sold is equal to the initial carrying value of the inventory of $1,200,000 less the $48,000 loss on the fair value hedge of commodity price risk.

**5. Financial Analysis—What Is the Difference?**

A reasonable question to be asked relates to the difference between the fair value hedge and the cash flow hedge accounting treatments if the cost of goods sold and net profits under cash flow hedge accounting are the same.

Several observations could be made in response to this query.

- For the same facts, the ultimate results should be the same whether the accounting treatment is the fair value hedge or cash flow hedge.
- Differences between the two accounting treatments are in the "geography" or location of gains or losses or recognized assets and liabilities on the balance sheet *before* the final settlement of the hedge.
- To show this difference consider the impact of each accounting treatment in the financial statements for the period ended December 31, 20x1:

| | *Under fair value hedge* | *Under cash flow hedge* | *Difference* |
|---|---|---|---|
| Book value of inventory | $1,176,600 | $1,200,000 | ($23,400) |
| Fair value of futures (Receivable) | 0 | 0 | 0 |
| Impact on cash | $13,900 | $13,900 | 0 |
| Impact on earnings (time value) | $4,500 | $4,500 | 0 |
| Impact on OCI | | ($23,400) | $23,400 |

- Similarly, the impact on the financial statements for the period ended March 31, 20x2 (before selling the inventory):

| | *Under fair value hedge* | *Under cash flow hedge* | *Difference* |
|---|---|---|---|
| Book value of inventory | $1,152,000 | $1,200,000 | ($48,000) |
| Fair value of futures (receivable) | 0 | 0 | 0 |
| Impact on cash | $41,100 | $41,100 | 0 |
| Impact on earnings (time value) | $2,500 | $2,500 | 0 |
| Balance of OCI | | ($48,000) | $48,000 |

## 7.5.3 Fair Value Hedge of Inventory (3)

### 7.5.3.1 Scenario E: *Forward Prices Decreasing, Presence of Hedge Ineffectiveness*

Assume that *Malthus Farms* is in a similar situation to that of *Milsom Farms, Inc.* discussed in *Scenario C* above. On October 1, 20x1, *Malthus Farms* has 100,000 bushels of soybean in the inventory that it had acquired at a cost of $12.00 a bushel. The company plans to sell this inventory after six months. The current market prices as of October 1, 20x1 are:

- Spot (cash) $13.03 a bushel.
- Futures (March delivery) $13.10 a bushel.

The management of *Malthus Farms* is concerned that the spot price of soybean is declining and might fall below the futures price of $13.10. To lock in the sale price at $13.10, the company entered into a futures contract with CBOT to sell 20 March contracts of Grade 2 American Soybean at $13.10 a bushel. The company documented this specific and detailed information as required by accounting standards.[20]

Assume that the contract spot and futures prices changed as reflected in the price movements shown in Table 7.6.[21]

**Table 7.6** Soybean Spot and Future Price Movements (Fair Value Hedge Presence of Ineffectiveness)

| | | *Price per Bushel* | |
|---|---|---|---|
| | *October 20x1* | *December 20X1* | *March 20X2* |
| Spot price | $13.03 | $12.796 | $12.550 |
| Futures Price | $13.10 | $12.880 | $12.550 |
| Δ Spot price | — | $0.234 | $0.246 |
| Δ Futures price | — | $0.220 | $0.330 |

Based on these changes we have the following values:

| | *December 20X1* | *March 20X2* |
|---|---|---|
| Fair value of futures contract[(a)] | $22,000 | $55,000 |
| Δ Fair value of futures | $22,000 | $33,000 |
| Δ Fair value of inventory[(b)] | ($23,400) | ($24,600) |
| Δ Time value of futures[(c)] | ($1,400) | $0 |
| Margin Deposit[(d)] | 46,000 | $46,000 |

*Notes:*

(a) Fair value of the futures contract is calculated as the difference in futures prices times the notional amount:
(13.10 – 12.88) x 100,000 = $22,000 for the period from October 20x1 to December 20x1.
(13.10 – 12.55) x 100,000 = $55,000 for the period from October 20x1 to March 20x2.
Although the futures price has dropped, these changes in fair value are gains for Malthus Farms, Inc. because it has signed with the Futures Exchange to sell Soybeans at $13.10. Under the agreement, the Futures Exchange would have to pay Malthus Farms, Inc. any drop in price below that in order to provide Malthus Farms, Inc. with sufficient funds to compensate for actual loss.

(b) The change in fair value of inventory is calculated as the change in spot prices times the notional principal amount of 100,000 bushels:
(13.03 – 12.796) x 100,000 = 23,400 for the period from October 20x1 to December 20x1.
(12.796) – 12.55) x 100,000 = 24,600 for the period from October 20x1 to March 20x2.

(c) Time Value of Futures is calculated the same way as in Table 7.3. as follows: On October 1, 20x1: \$13.10 – \$13.03) × 1,000; and on December 31: \$12.88 – \$12.796) × 1,000
(d) The Futures Exchange determines the Margin, which is usually a function of the size of the contract, the expectation of price movement, and the credit risk of the trader. In this scenario, we assume that the Exchange require a \$46,000 Margin for this transaction.

## Accounting for the First Period from October1, 20x1 to December 31, 20x1

- The change in fair value of inventory is calculated as the change in spot prices times the notional principal amount of 100,000 bushels:

  (13.03 – 12.796) × 100,000 = \$23,400

  for the period from October 20x1 to December 20x1.
- Fair value of the futures contract is calculated as the difference in futures prices times the notional amount:

  (13.10 – 12.88) × 100,000 = \$22,000

  for the period from October 20x1 to December 20x1.

The journal entries for the above transactions and events are as follows:

| *Date* | *Transaction* | *Dr* | *Cr* |
|---|---|---|---|
| | Memorandum<br>*Malthus Farms, Inc. entered into 20 futures contracts (5,000 bushels each) with CBOT to sell 100,000 bushels of American Yellow Grade 2 soybean at \$13.10 a bushel. The contract number is FSB12G.* | — | — |
| 10/1/ 20X1 | Futures—CBOT Contract *FSB12G*— Margin<br>Cash<br>*Depositing the required margin with the Futures Exchange for contract FSB12G* | 46,000 | 46,000 |
| 12/31/20x1 | Other gains/losses on soybean inventory<br>Inventory—soybean<br>*To record the loss on inventory as spot prices dropped from \$13.03 to \$12.796 per bushel for the inventory of 100,000 bushels* | 23,400 | 23,400 |
| 12/31/20x1 | Futures—CBOT Contract *FSB12G*<br>Other gains/losses on futures (earnings)<br>*To record the gain on the short futures contracts FSB12G as the futures prices dropped from \$13.10 to \$12.88 per bushel* | 22,000 | 22,000 |
| 12/31/20x1 | Cash<br>Futures—CBOT Contract *FSB12G*<br>*To record collecting the receivable from CBOT*[a] | 22,000 | 22,000 |

| | | | |
|---|---|---|---|
| 12/31/20x1 | Other expenses—financing<br>Other gains/losses on soybean inventory<br>*Recording the ineffective component of the hedge which is the effect on earnings due to increase in cost of carry.* | 1,400 | <br>1,400 |
| 12/31/20x1 | Earnings—income statement<br>    Other expenses—financing<br>*To record the net effect of hedging on earnings.* | 1,400 | <br>1,400 |

(a) In reality this amount is added to the margin account of the client and adjustments are made electronically.

### Accounting for the Second Period between December 31, 20x1 and March 31, 20x2

- Fair value of the futures contract is calculated as the difference in futures prices times the notional amount:
- The total change since signing the contract is equal to 100,000 bushes times the contract price of \$12.10 minus the current futures price for same delivery time which is \$12.55.

  $$(13.10 - 12.55) \times 100{,}000 = \$55{,}000$$

  for the period from October 20x1 to March 20x2. From that amount, \$22,000 was recognized in the previous period, leaving \$33,000 for this period.
- Although futures prices have dropped, these changes in fair value are gains for *Malthus Farms, Inc.* because they have signed with the Futures Exchange to sell soybean at \$13.10. Under the agreement, the Futures Exchange would have to pay *Malthus Farms, Inc.* any drop in price below that in order to provide *Malthus Farms* with sufficient funds to compensate for actual loss.
- The change in fair value of inventory is calculated as the change in spot prices between December 31, 20x1 and March 20x2 times the notional principal amount of 100,000 bushels:

  $$(12.796 - 12.55) \times 100{,}000 = 24{,}600$$

  for the period from October 20x1 to March 20x2.

  The journal entries recording these changes on the books of *Malthus Farms, Inc.* are as follows.

*Testing hedge effectiveness for the period ended March 31, 20x2 revealed that the hedge was ineffective during the period between December 31, 20x1 and March 31, 20x2. See the test results in the notes below.*

| | | | |
|---|---|---|---|
| 3/31/20x2 | Futures—CBOT Contract *FSB12G*<br>    Other gains/losses on futures<br>*To record the gain on the short futures contract as futures prices have dropped from \$12.88 to \$12.55. This gain consists of two components: the change in the intrinsic value by \$24,600 and the change in time value of futures by \$8,400* | 33,000 | <br>33,000 |
| 3/31/20x2 | Other gain or loss on futures<br>    Earnings—Income Statement<br>*To record ineffective components of the gain on futures contract* | 33,000 | <br>33,000 |

| | | | |
|---|---|---|---|
| 3/31/20x2 | Cash<br>Futures—CBOT Contract *FSB12G*<br>Futures—CBOT Contract *FSB12G*—margin<br>*Collecting the receivables owed by the Futures Exchange for the margin deposit and for gains on the futures contract** | 79,000 | <br>33,000<br>46,000 |
| 4/20/20x2 | Cost of goods sold<br>Inventory—soybean<br>*Costing the sales of 100,000 bushels of soybean* | 1,176,600 | <br>1,176,600 |
| 4/20/20x2 | Receivables—Trade<br>Sales revenue<br>*Recording the sale of soybean inventory* | 1,255,000 | <br>1,255,000 |

## Analysis

**1. Hedge Effectiveness**

Historical patterns of price changes showed that the hedge would be highly effective prospectively (*ex-ante*). On December 31, 20x1, at the end of the first period, a retrospective effectiveness test showed that the hedge relationship was effective using the Dollar Offset Ratio. This was highly effective because it falls within the accepted range of 0.80–1.25. Effectiveness would be measured using dollar offset.

The absolute value of the dollar offset ratio as follows:

a. In the period from October 20x1 through December 20x1:

$$|\Delta \text{ Futures Price}/\Delta \text{ Inventory Price}|$$
$$= |0.22/-0.234| = 0.94 \text{ per bushel.}$$

b. In the period from December 31, 20x1 through March 31, 20x2:

$$|\Delta \text{ Futures Price}/\Delta \text{ Inventory Price}|$$
$$= |0.33/-0.246| = 1.34.$$

This is *outside the accepted range* of 0.80–1.25 and the hedge relationship failed the effectiveness test.

**Result**

- Hedge accounting was applied for the first period (October 20x1 through December 20x1). But was terminated for the second period (December 31, 20x1 through March 31, 20x2).
- During the first period, *Malthus Farms, Inc.* recognized market value changes in both the futures contract and the inventory.
- During the second period, *Malthus Farms, Inc.* did not recognize changes in the fair value of the inventory, but recognized the change in the fair value of the futures and reported this change in earnings because ordinary GAAP requires that derivatives be valued at fair values and the change in fair value must be reported in earnings. This is the default accounting when the hedge is ineffective.

**2. Sales**

The same analysis from *Scenario C* of *Milsom Farms, Inc.* applies to *Malthus Farms*. The Futures Exchange is the counterparty. By the end, *Malthus Farms* collected $55,000 from the Futures Exchange, which represents the profits it earned on the soybean futures. It also sold its inventory of soybeans at spot market prices on the date of sale, March 20x2, which is $12.55 per bushel. This results in having trade receivables equal to $1,255,000. Therefore, the increase in liquid assets in the amount of $1,310,000 consists of two components:

| | |
|---|---|
| + Cash (gain on futures) | $55,000 |
| + Receivable-Trade | $1,255,000 |
| Total | $1,310,000 |

The combination of sale at the spot market price and the gain on the hedge allowed *Malthus Farms* to effectively sell its inventory of soybean at the desired price of $13.10 a bushel.

**3. Cost of Sales**

At inception of the hedge, the inventory was carried on the books at cost in the amount of $1,200,000, which was the lower-of-cost-or-market. After the company designates the inventory as a fair value hedge item, the changes in fair values (attributable to the hedged risk, which is the change in prices in this case) will be reflected in the carrying amount of the inventory (provided that the hedge is effective and other hedging requirements are satisfied).

The hedge was effective in the first period (from October to December 20x1) at which time the fair value of the inventory declined from $1,303,00 to $1,279,600, which is a loss of $23,400. Because the hedge was effective during that period, the inventory value was written down to reflect this change in fair value. *However, during the second period (from December 20x1 to March 20x2), the hedge was not effective and it was therefore terminated and the change in the fair value of inventory during that period was ignored.* When the inventory was sold in March 20x2, the cost of goods sold was $1,176,600 as shown in Figure 7.5.

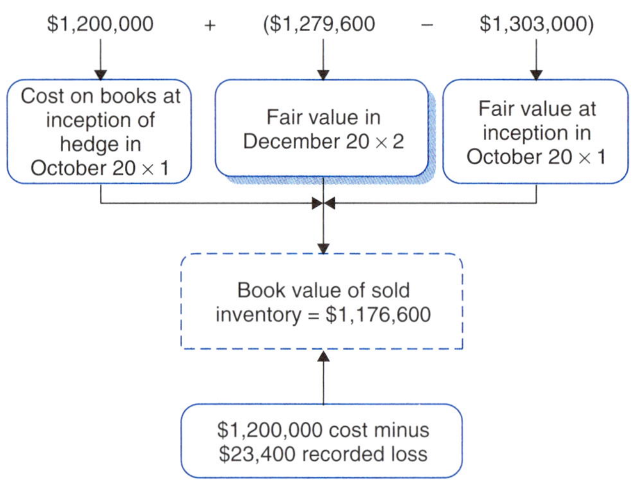


**Figure 7.5** Calculation of the Cost of Goods Sold for *Malthus Farms, Inc.*

**4. Earnings**

The effects of hedging on income amounted to the following:

- In 20x1, ineffectiveness due to the time value of futures (the difference between futures price and spot price) reduced earnings by $1,400 in 20x1. In 20x2, earnings increased by $33,000, which is total change in the fair value of the futures.
- The net income from sale of soybean inventory equals the desired goal:

| | |
|---|---|
| Sales | $1,255,000 |
| Cost of goods sold | $(1,176,600) |
| Gross profit | $78,400 |
| + change in time value | $(1,400) |
| | $77,000 |
| + Gain on financial derivatives | $33,000 |
| Net profit | $110,000 |

This is equal to the notional amount (i.e., the number of bushels of 100,000) times $1.10, the net difference between the desired sale price of $13.10 and the unadjusted book value of $12.00 per bushel.

**5. Financial Analysis**

Comparison of *Malthus Farms* in *Scenario E* where the hedge became ineffective with *Milsom Farms, Inc.* in *Scenario C* where the hedge was highly effective reveals two observations:

i. Net profits (before tax) are the same amount of $110,000, because the facts are the same; the difference is in the accounting treatment.
ii. The "geography" of reporting this net profit differs between the two scenarios. In *Scenario C*, Gross Profit was $103,000, but in *Scenario E*, Gross Profit was only $78,000.

This comparison between effective (*Scenario C*) and ineffective (*Scenario E*) hedges is highlighted further in Table 7.7.

**Table 7.7** Comparisons of Conditions and Scenarios Related to Presence or Absence of Hedge Effectiveness

| | | *Futures (forward) Derivative* | | |
|---|---|---|---|---|
| | *No Derivative* | *Undesignated Hedge* | *Effective Hedge* | *Ineffective Hedge* |
| Sales | $1,255,000.00 | $1,255,000.00 | $1,255,000.00 | $1,255,000.00 |
| Gross Profit | $55,000.00 | $55,000.00 | $103,000.00 | $78,400.00 |
| Gross Profit Margin | 4.38% | 4.28% | 8.2% | 6.2% |
| Net Profit | $55,000.00 | $110,000.00 | $110,000.00 | $110,000.00 |
| Net Profit Margin | 4.38% | 8.76% | 8.76% | 8.76% |
| Futures Time Value | N/A | $7,000.00 | $7,000.00 | $7,000.00 |
| Impact of Futures Derivative on Profits | N/A | $48,000.00 | 0 | $24,600.00 |
| Effective Sale Price per Bushel | $12.55 | $13.10 | $13.10 | $13.10 |

This comparison shows the impact of hedge accounting under the conditions of effective and ineffective hedges.

- The reality is that both *Milsom Farms, Inc.* and *Malthus Farms, Inc.* paid $1,200,000 for the inventory that it later sold for $1,255,000. Hedging does not change these facts.
- Anticipating "decreasing forward prices," where future prices will be lower than current spot prices, the management wanted to lock in sales at the high prices lest they decline.
- The futures contract assured the company it would achieve this goal and the net profit that *Malthus Farms* is expecting should be $13.10 less $12.00 per bushel, totaling $110,000.
- Of this $110,000, there is $7,000 total time value of the futures contract.
- By hedging, *Malthus Farms, Inc.* has locked in the sale price at $13.10 per bushel, but 0.07 of this price is time value of futures, leaving out $13.03, which is the spot price at inception (October 20x1). The difference between the value of the inventory at spot price at time *t* (October 20x1) and the cost is $1,303,000 – 1,200,000 = $103,000.
- Hedge accounting will then help the management of *Malthus Farms, Inc.* to choose how to recognize this $103,000 difference in values. Without using any special accounting for hedging with the futures contracts as undesignated hedge, this value difference would be allocated as follows:

  $55,000 for gross profit ($1,255,000 – $1,200,000)
  $48,000 for other income to be recognized in earnings

- With hedge accounting, the allocation of the $103,000 to different components on the income statement depends on hedge effectiveness. The above allocation of $55,000 and $48,000 would be the same if the hedge were totally ineffective from inception as it would be if special hedge accounting was not allowed. If the hedge were effective as in *Scenario C*, the entire $103,000 would be the gross profit. The situation is different for *Scenario E* under which the hedge was effective for the first period but became subsequently ineffective. Of the $103,000, $78,400 is allocated to gross profit and $24,600 is recognized in earnings as other income from trading derivatives. This accounting difference led to showing different gross margins of 8.2% for highly effective hedges, to 6.2% due to the hedge having one effective and one ineffective period. If the hedge was totally ineffective or if the management did not designate the derivative as a hedge, the gross margin would have been 4.38% ($55,000/$1,255,000).
- In all cases, the $7,000 futures time value is recognized in earnings as other income.

## 7.5.4 Fair Value Hedge of Inventory (4)

### *7.5.4.1 Scenario F: (FVH): A Case of Increasing Forward Prices*

In the scenarios presented above, futures and spot prices were declining over time, which placed *Milsom Farms, Inc.* in a position of loss of inventory value. In the case of increasing prices, i.e., *increasing forward prices*, the enterprise would be in a position of having increased fair value of inventory and having holding gains. In this case, the futures contract designed for hedging the inventory would be in a loss position, if in fact the hedge is effective. To illustrate this situation, consider the case of *Cecil Pigou Enterprises, Inc.*, which faces a different market in which futures prices are increasing as shown in Table 7.8. Other than having different movements of futures prices (decreasing for *Milsom Farms, Inc.* and increasing for *Cecil Pigou Enterprises*), the remaining facts of Table 7.8 are the same as those of *Milsom Farms, Inc.* presented in Table 7.6. These two different behaviors are called *contango* and *normal backwardation*, which were explained earlier (see note 13).

**Table 7.8** Soybean Spot and Future Price Movements for *Cecil Pigou Enterprises* (Fair Value Hedge when Prices Are Increasing)

| | *October* | *December* | *March* |
|---|---|---|---|
| Spot price | $13.03 | $13.191 | $13.47 |
| March Futures Price | $13.10 | $13.235 | $13.47 |
| Δ Spot price | — | $0.161 | $0.279 |
| Δ March Futures price | — | $(0.135) | $(0.235) |

Based on these changes we have the following values:

| | *December 20X1* | *March 20X2* |
|---|---|---|
| Fair value of the futures contract[(a)] | $13,500 | $37,000 |
| Δ Fair value of futures | $13,500 | $23,500 |
| Δ Fair value of inventory[(b)] | ($16,100) | ($27,900) |
| Amortized time value of futures[(c)] | $2,600 | $4,400 |
| Margin Deposit[(d)] | $45,000 | $45,000 |

*Notes:*

(a) Fair value of the futures contract is calculated as the difference in futures prices times the notional amount:
(13.10 –13.235) x 100,000 = –$13,500 for the period from October 20x1 to December 20x1.
(13.10–13.47) x 100,000 = –$37,000 for the period from October 20x1 to March 20x2.
Futures prices have increased. Since *Cecil Pigou Enterprises*, Inc. has agreed to sell soybean at $13.10, an increase in futures prices means that *Cecil Pigou Enterprises*, Inc. owes the Futures Exchange the difference in prices.

(b) The change in fair value of inventory is calculated as the change in spot prices times the notional principal amount of 100,000 bushels:
(13.191 – 13.03) x 100,000 = 16,100, for the period from October 20x1 to December 20x1.
(13.47 – 13.03) x 100,000 = 44,000, for the entire six month period from October 20x1 to March 20x2.
The difference ($44,000–$16,100 =) $27,900 is the change in fair value during the December 20x1 to March 20x2 period.

(c) Time Value of Futures is calculated as the difference between futures and spot prices. As in the preceding cases, this calculation is based on the assumption of efficient markets with traders clearing arbitrage profits in which case the futures price is determined as the spot price plus the cost of carry.

(d) The Margin (security deposit) is determined by the Futures Exchange. It is usually a function of the size of the contract, expectation of price movement and the credit risk of the trader. In this example, we assume that the Exchange requires $45,000 Margin for this transaction.

The journal entries of the above transactions and events for *Cecil Pigou Enterprises* are as follows.

| *Date* | *Transaction* | *Debit* | *Credit* |
|---|---|---|---|
| 10/1/20x1 | Futures—Futures Exchange margin<br>Cash<br>*Depositing the required margin with the Futures Exchange* | 45,000 | <br>45,000 |
| 12/31/20x1 | Inventory—soybean<br>Other gain/loss on soybean inventory<br>*Recording gain on the inventory as spot price increased from $13.03 to $13.191* | 16,100 | <br>16,100 |
| 12/31/20x1 | Other expense—gain/loss on futures<br>Futures—payable<br>*Recording gain on futures as futures prices change from $13.10 to $12.88 per bushel* | 13,500 | <br>13,500 |
| 12/31/20x1 | Other gain/loss on soybean inventory<br>Other income—income statement<br>*Recording the ineffective component of the hedge which is the effect on earnings* | 2,600 | <br>2,600 |
| 12/31/20x1 | Other gain/loss on soybean inventory<br>Other expense—gain/loss on futures<br>*Closing income statement accounts related to the effective hedge* | 13,500 | <br>13,500 |
| 3/31/20x2 | Inventory—soybean<br>Other gain/loss on soybean inventory<br>*Recording the change in the fair value of inventory between October 20x1 and December 20x1.* | 27,900 | <br>27,900 |
| 3/31/20x2 | Other expense—gain/loss on futures<br>Futures—payable<br>*Recording the gain on the short futures contract as futures prices have dropped from $12.88 to $12.55 per bushel* | 23,500 | <br>23,500 |
| 3/31/20x2 | Other gain/loss on soybean inventory<br>Other Income—income statement<br>*Recording the effective and ineffective components of the gain on futures contract* | 4,400 | <br>4,400 |
| 12/31/20x1 | Other gain/loss on soybean inventory<br>Other expense—gain/loss on futures<br>*Closing income statement accounts related to the effective hedge* | 23,500 | <br>23,500 |

| | | | |
|---|---|---|---|
| 3/31/20x2 | Futures—payable<br>Cash<br>Receivables—Futures Exchange margin<br>*Collecting the receivables owed by the Futures Exchange for the margin deposit less the amount owed the Futures Exchange for loss on the futures contract* | 37,000<br>8,000 | <br><br>45,000 |
| 4/20/20x2 | Receivables—trade<br>Cost of goods sold<br>Inventory—soybean<br>Sales revenue<br>*Recording the sale of soybean inventory* | 1,347,000<br>1,244,000 | <br><br>1,244,000<br>1,347,000 |

## Analysis

In this setting, the spot price of soybeans has increased from $13.03 to $13.47 a bushel. Unlike the cases of decreasing forward prices, if *Cecil Pigou Enterprises, Inc.* did not hedge, net profits would have been higher than they are with hedging.

### 1. Hedge Effectiveness

Historical patterns of price changes showed that the hedge would be highly effective prospectively (*ex-ante*). On December 31, 20x1, at the end of the first period, a retrospective effectiveness test showed that the hedge relationship was effective using the Dollar Offset Ratio (DOR), which is |Δ Futures Price/Δ Inventory Price| = |0.135/–0.161| = 0.838. In the second period, the hedge was also effective retrospectively; DOR = |0.235/–0.0279| = 0.84. In each case, DOR falls within the accepted range of 0.80–1.25 for highly effective hedges.

### 2. Sales

To close this transaction, *Cecil Pigou Enterprises, Inc.* collected $8,000 cash from the Futures Exchange, which represented the net receivables that the Exchange owed the company (for the margin deposit of $45,000 less the loss on the futures contract of $37,000 that *Cecil Pigou Enterprises, Inc.* owed the Exchange. Note that we assured that the company was not required to replenish its margin deposit.). The company sold its inventory of soybeans at spot market prices on the date of sale, March 31, 20x2, which is $13.47 per bushel. This sale resulted in trade receivables equaling $1,347,000. Therefore, the increase of $1,310,000 in current assets consists of two components:

| | |
|---|---|
| + Receivable-Trade | $1,347,000 |
| – Payables to the Futures Exchange (loss) | ($37,000) |
| Total | $1,310,000 |

The combination of the sale at the spot market price and the loss on the hedge allowed *Cecil Pigou Enterprises, Inc.* to effectively sell its inventory of soybean at the initially desired price of $13.10 a bushel, which was the sale price the management wanted to achieve when the hedge began in October 20x1. To clarify, this is a loss for *Cecil Pigou Enterprises, Inc.* in relationship to the spot price at the time of sale, but the management initially intended to hedge the downside risk using futures, which is a two-sided payoff contract. When the price of soybean went against management expectation, management actually lost by hedging.

### 3. Cost of Sales

At the inception of the hedge, the inventory was carried on the books at cost in the amount of $1,200,000, which was the lower-of-cost-or-market. Upon designating the inventory as a fair value hedge item, the company saw the changes in fair values (attributable to the hedged risk, which is the change in prices in this case) reflected in the carrying value of the inventory (provided that the hedge is effective and other hedging requirements are satisfied).

The hedge was *effective in the first period* (from October to December 20x1) at which time the fair value of inventory was $1,244,000. Because the hedge was effective during that period (based on DOR), the inventory value was written up to market. The difference calculations of cost of goods sold are presented in Figure 7.6.

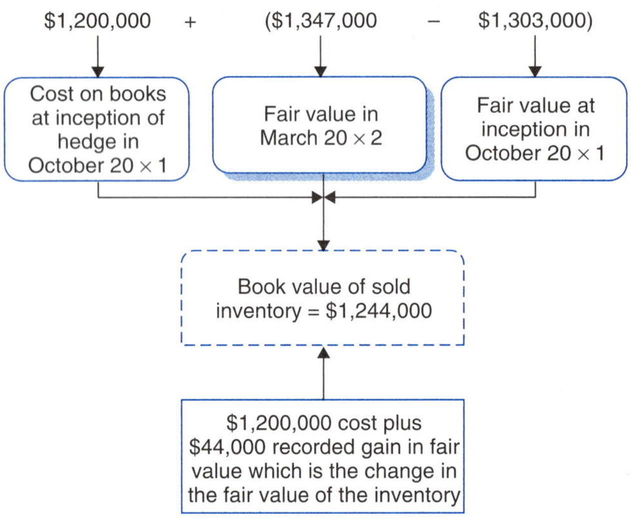


**Figure 7.6** Calculation of the Cost of Goods Sold for *Cecil Pigou Enterprises, Inc.* (A Different Scenario)

### 4. Earnings

The effects of hedging on income amounted to the following:

- In 20x1, ineffectiveness due to time value of futures (the difference between futures price and spot price) reduced earnings by $2,600 in 20x1 and $4,400 in 20x2. With hedging, earnings are lower by $37,000 than they would have been without hedging. Again, this is due to market movement opposite of management expectations.
- The net income from sale of soybean inventory equals the desired goal:

| | |
|---|---|
| Sales | $1,347,000 |
| Cost of goods sold | $(1,244,000) |
| Gross profit | $103,000 |
| + Gain (time value) | $7,000 |
| | $110,000 |

This is equal to the notional amount (i.e., the number of bushels of 100,000) times $1.10, the net difference between the forward sale price of $13.10 and the unadjusted book value of $12.00 per bushel.

**5. Financial Analysis**

Table 7.9 presents a comparison of *Cecil Pigou Enterprises, Inc.*'s situation without hedge and with effective hedges in this scenario.

**Table 7.9** A Comparison of Conditions With and Without Hedging *Cecil Pigou Enterprises*, Inc. (Inventory Prices Follow Increasing Forward Prices Condition)

| | *Without hedging* | *With effective hedging* |
|---|---|---|
| Sales | 1,347,000.0 | 1,347,000.0 |
| Cost of goods sold | 1,200,000.0 | 1,244,000.0 |
| Goss profit | 147,000.0 | 103,000.0 |
| Gross profit margin | 10.9% | 7.6% |
| Time value of futures | — | 7,000.0 |
| Net profit | 147,000.0 | 110,000.0 |
| Net profit margin | 10.9% | 8.17% |
| Effective Sale Price | $13.47 | $13.10 |

- The reality is that *Cecil Pigou Enterprises, Inc.* paid $1,200,000 for the inventory that it sold for $1,347,000. Hedging does not change these facts.
- The management anticipated "decreasing forward prices," where future prices will be lower than anticipated futures prices, but market forces did not support this expectation and the setting was increasing forward prices.
- The futures contract assured the company it would achieve its desired goal at inception of the hedge irrespective of price movement, which is expecting profits totaling $110,000.
- Of this $110,000, there is $7,000 total time value of the futures contract. This is determined by the difference between the futures price and the spot price at the inception of the contract ($13.10 – $13.03) – 100,000 bushels.
- By hedging, *Cecil Pigou Enterprises, Inc.* has locked in the sale price at $13.10 per bushel, but 0.07 of this price is time value of futures, leaving out $13.03, which is the spot price at inception of the hedge. The difference between the value of the inventory at spot price at inception of the hedge (October 20x1) and the book value equals $1,303,000 – 1,200,000 = $103,000.
- Hedge accounting will then help the management of *Cecil Pigou Enterprises, Inc.* to choose how to recognize this $103,000 difference in values.

  - Without hedging, gross profit is (1,347,000 – 1,200,000) = $147,000
  - Less the loss on futures used to hedge <u>$44,000</u>
  - Gross profit with effective hedging fair value and cost at inception of hedge $103,000
  - Plus time value of futures <u>$7,000</u>

## 7.6 Cash Flow Hedge

### 7.6.1 Hedging a Prospective Transaction (*A Case of Underhedge Followed by Overhedge*)

*Cherokee, Inc.* is a soybean crusher and purchases its input from a distributor of farm products in Moline, Illinois. *Cherokee, Inc.* and the distributor have a long-term customer/supplier relationship, but "brown stink" beetles[22] invaded the Midwest crop and the management of *Cherokee, Inc.* fears a supply shortage and a price rise. The management decides to lock in a purchase price for soybean a year ahead of production needs.

On April 19, 20x4, *Cherokee, Inc.* entered into a futures contract with the Chicago-based CME Globex to have 100 futures contracts (a contract of soybean futures is 5,000 bushels) of American Yellow Grade 2 soybean for delivery in September 20x4 at a price of $11.94 a bushel, which is the April 20x4 forward price for September delivery. At inception of the hedge, the spot price of soybean was $11.50 a bushel. *Cherokee, Inc.* did not incur any cost for the contract (other than simple processing fees), but deposited the required margin of $140,000 with the Futures Exchange.

At the end of September 20x4, *Cherokee, Inc.* purchased 500,000 bushels of American Yellow Grade 2 soybean at the market price of $11.45 plus $0.03 for transaction cost (a total cost of $11.48) per bushel.

By November, China signed contracts with three large U.S. grain companies (*Cargill, Archer Daniels Midland*, and *Bunge*) to buy 2.2 million metric tons of American Yellow Grade 2 soybean, which led to a sharp rise in prices. *Cherokee*'s management decided to sell 200,000 bushels at the high market price of $14.76 a bushel and replace its soybean crushing production needs by imported Brazilian soybean Grade 1 which has about the same level of oil and protein content as the American Yellow Grade 2.

### *7.6.1.1 Analysis of the Hedging Relationship*

## Exhibit 7.11 Hedge Documentation: *Cherokee, Inc.*

| | |
|---|---|
| Transaction | A forecasted purchase of 500,000 bushels of American Yellow Grade 2 soybean on September 30, 20x4. |
| Risk | *Cherokee, Inc.* is exposed to price risk of forecasted purchase of soybean for production because the management is predicting a shortage of supply due to brown stink beetle infestation (BMSB) of the soybean crop. This hedge is consistent with the management philosophy and approach to managing risk as documented in *Cherokee's Enterprise*'s risk management program. |
| Hedging contracts | 100 long CME contracts for delivery on September 30, 20x4 (contract number *LS7Y*) of American Soybean Grade 2 (each contract is 5,000 bushels) at a price of $11.94 a bushel. |
| Date of designating the hedge | April 19, 20x4. |
| Hedge Effectiveness | The dollar offset method is the method to be used for testing hedge effectiveness. This involves comparing the cumulative changes in the price of futures contracts with cumulative changes in the expected cash outflow for the forecasted purchase of 500,000 bushels of soybean. Based on historical patterns of the behavior of soybean prices, *ex-ante* changes in the cash flow of soybean futures are expected to provide a highly effective hedge of price risk exposure of forecasted purchase. |

The quantitative information related to this cash flow hedge is presented in Table 7.10. Panel A of this table shows the behavior of soybean prices (at inception of the hedge this behavior is assumed and we will use that information as if it is also realized). Panel B presents the changes and cumulative changes of the futures contracts prices. Panel C presents the changes in cumulative changes of anticipated cash outflow for the forecasted transaction. Finally, Panel D shows the measurement of overhedge.

**Table 7.10** Measurement of the Amount of Overhedge

***Panel A:*** *Soybean price behavior*

| | *Date* | *Spot price* | *Expected Cash Outflow for Purchasing in September* | *September Futures price* |
|---|---|---|---|---|
| | | *C1* | *C2* | *C3* |
| Row A | April 19, 20x4 | $11.50 | $11.96 | $11.94 |
| Row B | June 15 | $11.30 | $11.76 | $11.76 |
| Row C | September 12 | $11.45 | $11.48 | $11.45 |

***Panel B:*** *Soybean Futures Prices*

| | | *C4* | *C5* | *C6* |
|---|---|---|---|---|
| | | *April 20x4* | *June 20x4* | *September 20x4* |
| Row D | Futures Price per Bushel | $11.94 | $11.76 | $11.45 |
| Row E | Change in Futures Prices per Bushel | — | $0.18 | $0.31 |
| Row F | Change in Value of Futures[(a)] (Equal to Row E times the notional amount of 500,000 bushels) | — | ($90,000) | ($155,000) |
| Row G | Cumulative Change in Fair Value of Futures Contracts (The lesser amount is in bold)[(b)] | — | (**$90,000**) | ($245,000) |

***Panel C:*** *Assumptions about Cash Outflow for the Anticipated Purchase of Soybean (this equal to spot price plus necessary transaction cost).*

| | | *C7* | *C8* | *C9* |
|---|---|---|---|---|
| Row H | Expected Cash Outflow for Purchasing Soybean per Bushel (including transaction costs) | $11.96 | $11.76 | $11.48 |
| Row I | Change in Expected Cash Outflow for Purchasing Soybean per Bushel | — | $0.20 | $0.28 |
| Row J | Total Change in Expected Cash Outflow for | — | $100,000.00 | $140,000.00 |

| | | | | |
|---|---|---|---|---|
| | Purchasing Soybean[c] (Equal to Row I times the notional amount of 500,000 bushels) | | | |
| Row K | Cumulative Change in Expected Cash Outflow for Purchasing Soybean per Bushel (Row G, C 6 versus Row K, C9; the lesser amount is in bold) | — | $100,000.00 | **$240,000.00** |

***Panel D:*** *The Lesser of the Cumulative Amount of the Change to Determine the Amounts to Be Deferred in Other Comprehensive Income and the Amounts to Be Recognized in Earnings (ASC 815-30)*

| | | | *C10* | *C11* |
|---|---|---|---|---|
| Row L | The Lesser Cumulative Absolute Amount of Futures or Expected Cash Outflow[d] (Row G C5 & C6 versus Row K C8 and C9) | — | **$90,000** | **$240,000** |
| Row M | Amount to be posted to Other Comprehensive Income[e] (The differences (i) Row L, C10 – Row L, C9 and (ii) Row L, C11 – Row L, C10) | — | $90,000 | $150,000 |
| Row N | Amount to be posted to earnings as Overhedge[f] | — | 0 | $5,000 |

*Notes:*

a) The changes in fair values of futures prices between April and June 20x4, and between June 20x4 and September 20x4 are calculated as the change in futures price per bushel times the size of the contracts: 500,000 bushels.

b) The cumulative change is added over the two periods noted above.

c) As a cash flow hedge, the hedged transaction is only a forecast. Instead of using the hypothetical derivative approach to represent the hedged transaction, Cherokee elected to use the expected cash outflow for the forecasted purchase which is based on, but is not equal to, predicted spot prices. The change in expected cash outflow for this purpose is calculated for the two periods (between April and June 20x4, and between June 20x4 and September 20x4) as the change in expected cash outflow per bushel times the size of the contracts which add up to 500,000 bushels. These numbers are accumulated over the hedge period in order to identify overhedge.

d) The lesser of the two cumulative numbers of the change in futures prices or the change in anticipated cash outflow is identified for each period. For the period between April and June 20x4, the lesser amount is the change in futures prices ($90,000), while for the period between June and September, the lesser number is the cumulative change in anticipated cash outflow for the purchase of 500,000 bushels of soybean, which is $240,000.

e) The amounts to be deferred in OCI (provided that other hedge criteria are met) are $90,000 for the first period and $150,000 for the second period.

f) The cumulative change in the futures prices is $245,000, which is $5,000 more than the total amount posted to OCI. This $5,000 is an overhedge and should flow through earnings.

At the end of September 20x4, the purchased soybean costs $11.48 a bushel, as projected. In November 20x4, *Cherokee* sold 200,000 bushes for total revenues of $2,952,000. The cost of goods sold for this transaction is $2,392,000 which consists of $2,296,000 actual price of the inventory plus the $96,000 reclassified from OCI for the deferred related hedge cost (= $240,000 total hedge loss deferred in OCI times 2/5, the sold proportion of the inventory).

The journal entries for this hedge transaction are as follows.

| *Date* | *Transaction* | *Dr* | *Cr* |
|---|---|---|---|
| April 19, 20x4 | Receivable—Futures Exchange margin<br>Cash<br>*Depositing the required margin with the Futures Exchange* | 140,000 | <br>140,000 |
| June 30, 20x4 | Other gains/losses – loss on soybean futures<br>Payable—Futures Exchange<br>*Recording loss on soybean futures (0.18 price change – 500,000 bushels)* | 90,000 | <br>90,000 |
| June 30, 20x4 | Other Comprehensive Income—futures<br>Other gains/losses—loss on soybean futures<br>*Posting the loss on short futures as the futures prices to OCI* | 90,000 | <br>90,000 |
| 9/30/20x4 | Other gains/losses – loss on soybean futures<br>Payable—Futures Exchange<br>*Recording the loss on futures contract (0.31 price change × 500,000 bushels)* | 155,000 | <br>155,000 |
| 9/30/20x4 | Other Comprehensive Income—loss on futures<br>Other expenses—income statement<br>Other expenses—loss on soybean futures<br>*Posting the effective portion of the loss on soybean futures to OCI* (150,000) *and recognizing the overhedge portion of loss in earnings* | 150,000<br>5,000 | <br><br>155,000 |
| 9/30/20x4 | Payables—Futures Exchange<br>Receivables—Futures Exchange Margin<br>Cash<br>*Settling with the Futures Exchange by crediting the margin and paying off the difference of $105,000.* | 245,000 | <br>140,000<br>105,000 |
| 9/30/20x4 | Inventory—soybean<br>Cash<br>*To record purchase of soybean inventory at $11.48 a bushel ($11.48 × 500,000)* | 5,740,000 | <br>5,740,000 |
| 11/30/20x4 | Cost of goods sold<br>Inventory—Soybean<br>Other Comprehensive Income—soybean futures<br>*Recording the use of the purchased soybean in the cost of sale* | 2,392,000 | <br>2,296,000<br>96,000 |
| 11/30/20x4 | Receivables—Trade<br>Sales<br>*Sale of 200,000 bushels at $14.76 a bushel* | 2,952,000 | <br>2,952,000 |

## Analysis

- *Hedge Effectiveness*: Two approaches are possible for selecting the comparison basis applying the Delta or the regression method to test effectiveness:

  1. Using a hypothetical derivative to represent the hedged position.
  2. Using a projection of the cash flow needed to complete the forecasted transaction being hedged.

  *Cherokee, Inc.* elected to use the projected cash outflow.
  The DOR is selected for testing hedge effectiveness. Using historical data, the prospective (*ex-ante*) measure of DOR was within the accepted range of 0.80–1.25.
  Retrospective (*ex-post*) hedge effectiveness is measured as follows:

  |–90,000/100,000| = 0.90 for the period of April to June 20x4; and

  |–155,000/140,000| = 1.11 for the period from June to September 20x4.

  The absolute value of both measures fall within the accepted scope of 0.80–1.25.
- *Over Hedge and Under Hedge*: There is underhedge in the first period because the change in the fair value of the hedge instrument fell $10,000 short of the change of the fair value in anticipated cash flow (hedged item). The amount of change in fair value that is deferred in OCI is $90,000; *the $10,000 underhedge is not recorded.* The second period has overhedge because the change in the fair value of the hedge instrument is $15,000 greater than the change in the fair value of the anticipated cash flow of the hedged transaction. *However, the amount that should be reported as overhedge is a different amount because it has to be measured cumulatively. It is determined by the lesser of the cumulative changes.*

  - The cumulative changes over Period 1 and Period 2 are $245,000 for the change in the futures fair value (the hedge instrument) and $240,000 for the cumulative change in the fair value of the anticipated cash outflow for the hedged item. The $240,000 is selected for classification in OCI based on the criterion of selecting the lesser cumulative amount. From that amount, $90,000 has already been recorded in the first period, leaving $150,000 to be recorded in OCI in the second period. The total of $240,000 is $5,000 below the change in fair value of the futures contract (the hedge instrument) and it is the amount of overhedge representing the ineffectiveness of the hedging relationship and should be recognized in earnings.

- The $240,000 loss will remain classified in OCI until one of two events occur:

  1. The inventory is sold, assuming that the forecasted (hedged) transaction is executed and the inventory is purchased. The related balance in OCI will be reclassified as an adjustment to cost of goods sold.
  2. The forecasted inventory purchase did not occur, and the balance in OCI will be reclassified to earnings as other expense.

In this illustration, *Cherokee, Inc.* sold only 200,000 bushels, which is 2/5 of the inventory. A proportionate amount ($96,000) of the loss that was deferred in OCI will be reclassified to earnings (as adjustment to the cost of sold goods).

## 7.6.2 Cash Flow Hedge of Prospective Transaction (*Recapturing Over Hedge Charges*)

The case described in this illustration is one in which the amount of overhedge occurring in the first period is posted to earnings, but is "recaptured" from earnings and is reclassified in OCI when events revert in future periods. The amount "recaptured" is limited by the amount of overhedge that was charged to earnings in prior periods. To illustrate this situation, assume the same set up of *Cherokee, Inc.* as before except for the behavior of soybean prices (the facts here are different from 7.6.1).

- On April 19, 20x4, *Cherokee, Inc.* entered into 100 futures for delivery on September 30, 20x4 contracts with CME Globex (a contract of soybean futures is 5,000 bushels) to purchase American Yellow Grade 2 soybean for delivery at a price of $11.94 a bushel.
- The spot price of soybean on April 19, 20x4 was $11.96 a bushel, which is equal to the quoted price of $11.927 plus 0.033 for transportation.
- *Cherokee, Inc.* did not incur any cost for the contract (other than simple processing fees).
- The company deposited the required margin of $140,000 with the Futures Exchange.
- At the end of September 20x4, *Cherokee, Inc.* purchased 500,000 bushels of American Yellow Grade 2 soybean at the market price.
- Because of the unexpected demand from China, market prices increased sharply and the management of *Cherokee* decided on October 15, 20x4 to sell 200,000 bushels at the market price of $14.76 a bushel and replace its crushing production needs by imported Brazilian soybean Grade 1 which has about same level of oil and protein.
- The relevant quantitative information is in Table 7.11.

**Table 7.11** Assumption and Information Related to Hedging Forecasted Purchased of Soybean for Crushing

***Panel A:*** *Assumptions about Futures Prices*

| | | *April 20x4* | *June 20x4* | *September 20x4* |
|---|---|---|---|---|
| | | *C1* | *C2* | *C3* |
| Row a | Futures Price per Bushel | $11.94 | $12.11 | $12.376 |
| Row b | Change in Futures Prices per Bushel | — | $0.17 | $0.266 |
| Row c | Change in Value of Futures (Row b x 500,000 notional amount) | | $85,000.00 | $133,000.00 |
| Row d | Cumulative Change in Fair Value of Futures Contracts (= *C2* + *C3*) | | $85,000.00 | **$218,000.00** |

***Panel B:*** *Assumptions about Cash Outflow for the Anticipated Purchase of Soybean (this equal to spot price plus necessary transaction cost).*

| | | *C4* | *C5* | *C6* |
|---|---|---|---|---|
| Row e | Expected Cash Outflow for Purchasing Soybean per Bushel (observed price in the market plus transportation cost for delivery) | $11.96 | $12.116 | $12.409 |
| Row f | Change in Expected Cash Outflow for Purchasing Soybean per Bushel (*C5* minus *C4* and *C6* minus *C5*) | | ($0.156) | ($0.293) |

| | | | |
|---|---|---|---|
| Row g | Change in Expected Cash Outflow for Purchasing Soybean (Row f x 500,000 the notional amount) | ($78,000) | ($146,500) |
| Row h | Cumulative Change in Expected Cash Outflow for Purchasing Soybean (= *C5* + *C6* of Row i) | ($78,000) | ($224,500) |

***Panel C:*** *Analysis of the Lesser (absolute value of the) Cumulative Amount of the Change to Determine the Amounts to be Deferred in Other Comprehensive Income and the Amounts to be Recognized in Earnings (ASC 815-30)*

| | | *C7* | *C8* |
|---|---|---|---|
| Row i | The Lesser Cumulative Absolute Value of Futures or Expected Cash Outflow (Comparing Row d versus Row h) | **$78,000** | **$218,000** |
| Row j | Amount to be posted to Other Comprehensive Income | $78,000 | $140,000 |
| Row k | Amount to be posted to earnings (Comparing Row d and Row h C5 and) comparing Row c, C3 with Row j, C8 | $7,000 | ($7,000) |

## Explanatory Notes

1. The changes in fair values of futures contracts between April and June 20x4 and between June and September 20x4 is calculated as the product of the change in futures price per bushel times the size of the contracts, 500,000 bushels (the notional amount).
2. In the first period, the change in the fair value of futures is $85,000 (Row d, Column C2), but the change in the fair value of anticipated cash flow needs is only $78,000 (Row g, Column C5). In the second period the cumulative change in fair value of the futures contracts of $218,000 (Row i, Column C8) is less than the cumulative change in the fair value of anticipated cash flow of $224,500 (Row i, Column C6).
3. As a cash flow hedge, the hedged transaction is only a forecast. Instead of using the hypothetical derivative approach to represent the hedged transaction, Cherokee's management elected to use the expected cash outflow needs. Expected cash outflow for forecasted purchase is based on, but not equal to, predicted spot prices. The change in expected cash outflow for this purpose is calculated for the two periods (first, between April 19 and June 30, and second between June 30 and September 30) as the product of the change in expected cash outflow per bushel times the size of the contracts, 500,000 bushels. These numbers are accumulated over the hedge period in order to apply the test of identifying overhedge.
4. The lesser of the two (absolute) cumulative numbers of the change in futures prices or the change in anticipated cash outflow is identified for each period. For the period between April and June 30, 20x4, the lesser amount is the change in futures prices ($78,000). For the second period between June and September, the lesser number is the cumulative change in anticipated cash outflow for the purchase of 500,000 bushels of soybean, which is $218,000.
5. Given the above information and the standards (both ASC in the USA and IFRS internationally), the amounts to be deferred in OCI (provided that other hedge criteria are met) are $78,000 for the first period, which is less than the change in the fair value of the futures contracts by $7,000.

Therefore, this is a case of overhedge; the $7,000 increase in the value of the futures should be recognized in earnings and only $78,000 should be classified (deferred) in OCI in this period.

6. In the second period, the (absolute) cumulative change in fair values is $218,000 for the fair value of the futures, and $224,500 for the fair value of the projected cash flow needs. Under the test of "the lesser cumulative amount" the amount to be classified in OCI should not exceed $218,000 in total. Therefore, the amount to be deferred in OCI in the second period is $140,000, which is the difference between the full amount of $218,000 and the previously recognized amount.
7. The change in the fair value of the futures contracts in the second period is $133,000, which is less than the $140,000 amount to be deferred in OCI. The difference between the two numbers is $7,000 (=140,000 – 133,000). This is a case of an underhedge. It turned out in this illustration that the amount of overhedge in the first period is $7,000—is exactly the same amount of underhedge as in the second period. Therefore, the entire $140,000 should be classified (deferred) as gains in OCI with the debit side of the journal entry consisting of the $133,000 for the change in the fair value of the futures contracts and $7,000 to recapture (reclassify) the amount of overhedge previously recognized in earnings.
8. At the end of September 20x4, the purchased soybean costs $12.409 per bushel, which is the spot rate in the market. But this is not the cost of the inventory to *Cherokee* because it is not adjusted for the impact of the hedge. The total cost is effectively the following amount: $6,204,500 (500,000 bushels × $12.409) minus $218,000 gains on the hedge = $5,986,500 in total or $11.973 per bushel. This is the cost that *Cherokee* aimed to achieve when it began the hedging relationship: it is equal to the contracted futures price of $11.94 + 0.03 for transportation cost.
9. In October 20x4, *Cherokee* sold 200,000 bushes for total revenues of $2,952,000. The cost of goods sold for this transaction is $2,307,400 which consists of $2,394,600 actual price of the inventory minus $87,200 reclassified gains from OCI (218,000 × 0.40 for the deferred related hedge cost (= $218,000 total hedge loss deferred in OCI times 2/5, the sold proportion of the inventory).

The journal entries for this hedge transaction are as follows.

| | | *Dr* | *Cr* |
|---|---|---|---|
| April 19, 20x4 | Receivable—Futures Exchange margin<br>  Cash<br>*Depositing the required margin with the Futures Exchange* | 130,000 | <br>130,000 |
| June 30, 20x4 | Receivables—Futures Exchange<br>  Other income—gain on soybean futures<br>*Recording gain on soybean futures* | 85,000 | <br>85,000 |
| June 30, 20x4 | Other income—gain on soybean futures<br>  OCI—gain on futures<br>  Earnings statement—overhedge gain<br>*Recording gain on futures net of overhedge amount* | 85,000 | <br>78,000<br>7,000 |
| September 30, 20x4 | Receivables—Futures Exchange<br>  Other income—gain on soybean futures<br>*Recording the gain on futures* | 133,000 | <br>133,000 |

| | | | |
|---|---|---|---|
| September 30, 20x4 | Other income—gain on soybean futures<br>Other expenses/gains<br>OCI—futures on soybean<br>Posting the gain on soybean hedge and reclassifying the previously charged amount of overhedge. | 133,000<br>7,000 | <br><br>140,000 |
| September 30, 20x4 | Cash<br>Receivables—Futures Exchange—margin<br>Receivables—Futures Exchange—soybean futures contracts | 348,000 | <br>130,000<br>218,000 |
| September 30, 20x4 | Soybean—inventory<br>Cash | 6,204,500 | <br>6,204,500 |
| October 13, 30x4 | Cost of goods sold<br>OCI—soybean<br>Inventory—soybean | 2,307,400<br>87,200 | <br><br>2,394,600 |
| October 13, 30x4 | Cash<br>Sales revenues<br>*To record the sale of 200,000 bushels for $14.76 a bushel* | 2,952,000 | <br>2,952,000 |

## Analysis

- *Hedge Effectiveness*: To measure cash flow hedge effectiveness, the standards allow two approaches:

  1. The use of a hypothetical derivative to represent the hedged position.
  2. The use of a projection of the cash flow that would be required to complete the forecasted transaction being hedged.

  *Cherokee, Inc.* elected to use the projected cash outflow. The Delta (dollar offset) method is selected. Using historical data, the prospective (*ex-ante*) measure of Delta for the period of April to June 20x4 is

  $$|85{,}000/78{,}000| = |1.09|$$

which falls within the accepted scope of |0.80–1.20|. Therefore, the hedge is expected to be highly effective.

  - At the end of the first period, all data suggest that the hedge will continue to be effective prospectively.
  - For the period from June to September 20x4, the dollar offset ratio is equal to |133,000 / 146,000| = 0.91, which indicates high effectiveness. Cumulatively, the dollar offset ratio over the entire period is |218,000 / 224,500| = 0.97, which indicates high effectiveness.

- *Over hedge and Under hedge*: There is an overhedge in the first period because the change in the fair value of the hedge instrument is greater than the fair value of the hedged (forecasted) transaction by $7,000. This overhedge is posted directly to earnings as "other gains."

- In Period 2, the cumulative changes are $218,000 for the change in the futures fair value (the hedge instrument) and $224,500 for the cumulative change in the fair value of the anticipated cash outflow for the hedged item. The "cumulative value test" requires using the lesser (absolute value) of the two amounts, which is $218,000. From that amount $78,000 was recorded in the first period, which leaves $140,000 to be added to OCI in the second period. However, this amount is greater than the $133,000 change in the fair value of the futures contracts during that period by $7,000.
- The $7,000 deficit in the change in the value of the hedge instrument compared to the expected cash outflow needs is an underhedge, but it is equal to the amount of the overhedge in the first period. To account for the effective hedge properly, the $7,000 is reclassified (recaptured) from earnings to OCI in the second period.
- The $218,000 loss classified in OCI will remain there until one of two events occur:

    1. The inventory is sold out and the related balance in OCI is reclassified as an adjustment to cost of goods sold.
    2. If the forecasted inventory purchase did not occur, the balance in OCI will be reclassified to earnings as other gains/losses.

- The company sold 200,000 bushels of soybean (that is 40% of the purchase) in October when prices increased and reclassified $87,200 from OCI to earnings (through adjustment to the cost of goods sold). This amount is equal to 40% of the total accumulated in OCI.

## 7.7 Summary of Key Points

- Financial derivative instruments are not permitted to be classified as HTM or as available-for-sale. They are to be booked at fair value with the valuation updated periodically with a frequency not less than quarterly and the change in fair values are recognized in earnings (Profit & Loss Statement).
- The differential impact on earnings of the hedge item and the hedging derivative arises from non-synchronicity or mismatching of changes in values and cash flows.
- The task of hedge accounting is to provide synthetic synchronicity (synthetic matching) when the actual events do not match.
- The very nature of derivative instruments is that they derive their values from changes in other prices or indexes. Changes in commodity prices, interest rate, currency exchange rates and credit risk are both value and risk drivers of financial derivative instruments.
- Accounting for hedging transactions aims at achieving two goals: (a) sheltering earnings from the volatility induced by valuation of financial derivatives, and (b) informing external users of the success of management in mitigating risk.
- The risk exposures that are outside the control of the management are related to price movement and credit risk. The management could not successfully manage the unexpected risks related to these externally determined events.
- Accounting classifies all these risks into three buckets: (i) the risk of losing value; (ii) the risk of exposure to cash flow volatility; and (iii) the risk of losing on investment in foreign operations.

- The last bucket is deferred to Chapter Eleven. This chapter and the next chapter are devoted to risk exposures—exposure to value loss and cash flow volatility only in single currency.
- If a recognized asset or a recognized liability is valued normally, or is expected to be valued, at fair value, then the changes in fair values induced by unexpected price movements will be normally reflected in earnings. Thus, there is no need to provide a special hedge accounting for these items.
- Special hedge accounting treatment could only apply to value changes or the cash flow volatility associated with recognized assets and recognized liabilities that are not valued at fair value if the changes in fair values are recognized in earning.
- Two additional items could be hedged (in accounting): changes in the values of executory contracts that create rights for, or obligations on, the entity, and forecasted transactions. The former is like exposure to probable loss in value, while the latter is probable exposure to cash flow volatility.
- In a fair value hedge:
    - Changes in the values of the hedging derivative instrument are accounted for as normal under GAAP—it is recognized in earnings.
    - The changes in the fair values of the hedged item (a recognized asset, a recognized liability, or an executory contract) that are attributable to the risk being hedged and to the extent of hedge effectiveness are recognized in earnings.
    - If the hedging relationship is successful, the above noted items should offset one another and the volatility of derivative values would have little or no impact on earnings.
    - Successful hedging is measured by "effectiveness"; the extent to which price movement of the hedge instrument offsets the price movement of the hedged item.
    - The ineffective component of the hedge would flow through earnings without offset.
- In a cash flow hedge:
    - The hedged item is a future event or condition that would have earnings effect in future periods.
    - The derivative instrument used to hedge this condition or prospective transaction need not impact earnings until the hedged item does or the forecasted transaction is no longer probable.
    - Therefore, if the management designates the derivative as a hedge and the hedge is successful, the changes in the fair values of the financial derivative would be parked in Accumulated Other Comprehensive Income and deferred until the hedged item impacts earnings.
    - This deferral creates synthetic matching in the sense that it only defers the earnings effect of derivatives until the hedged item impacts earnings.
- Over the entire hedge horizon, accounting methods do not matter in a real sense because accounting does not change the facts over the life of an instrument or a contract. What changes is the distribution of the timing of gains and losses over different periods within the horizon of the hedging relationship.

## Notes

1 Bonds also derive their values from changes in interest rate (the price of funds) but they are not derivatives because they do not satisfy the remaining criteria.
2 The accounting for embedded derivatives could be viewed as part of ordinary GAAP. With or without hedging, embedded derivatives are to be separated (bifurcated) from host instruments and accounted for separately. This requirement is not contingent on hedge accounting and is now part of GAAP. See Chapter Nine.
3 With few exceptions, ordinary GAAP does not recognize the assets or liabilities associated with executory contracts. The exceptions include leases and (employees') pensions and share-based compensation.
4 Other risks, such as fire hazard, shrinkage, obsolescence, or spoilage, are either managed or insured.
5 To repeat, the management could hedge the rubber component in this case, but it would not be accepted for the application of hedge accounting in hedging the price of the inventory of tires.
6 There is, however, pressure on the IASB by various industry groups to change this restriction which is, in turn, bringing pressure on the FASB to do the same.
7 In addition, there is a problem about recognition of gains as a result of deterioration in own credit risk. As of this time, both the FASB and IASB are debating the appropriate accounting for this particular problem.
8 The hedge applied in this case would be the fair value hedge.
9 This particular feature is the subject of a proposed repeal.
10 Unless the management elects the fair value option.
11 Over-the-counter interest rate options could settle periodically. This is illustrated in Chapter Eight.
12 Taking the absolute value is only for the decision rule, not for record-keeping purposes.
13 The behavior of futures' price movement may be in contango or normal backwardation.
Contango is the case when forward prices are higher than expected spot prices. No one really knows the level of expected spot prices but if futures prices decline over time, it signifies the market's adaptation to the divergence between futures prices and expected spot prices. Because on the day of delivery, the futures' price of delivery must equal the spot price, downward adjustment of futures prices to the spot price at delivery is an indication that the market is in contango.
Normal backwardation is the reverse. Futures prices are lower than expected spot prices. Since the latter is unknown, the state of the market could be inferred from the adaptation behavior of futures prices as the contract approaches maturity. In a case of normal backwardation, futures prices will rise to the level of spot prices at delivery date.
14 A futures contract consists of 5,000 bushels or about 136 metric tons.
15 It is assumed that the price did not change between March 31, 20x1 and April 20, 20x2 for simplicity. Additionally, the sale in the illustration is recorded at the end of the quarter in the interim financial statements of June 30 could show the comparison between the case of using fair value hedge and the case of using cash flow hedge.
16 As will be discussed later, this will be true in the cash flow hedge by the extent to which the hedge is ineffective because in a highly effective cash flow hedge, the gain on the derivative is deferred in OCI until the sale of the hedged commodity impacts earnings.
17 This is the same table as 7.3 and is reproduced here to facilitate reading and to avoid flipping pages back and forth.
18 The hypothetical derivative is in the adopted standards both in ASC and IFRS. However, it is unsupported by any theoretical basis and, in the view of this author, is essentially "make believe" accounting.
19 Under the simplifying assumption that prices had not changed between March and July.
20 Assume that the documentation is similar to what has been presented above for Milsom Farms and it would not add information to include it here.

21 Note: the table is not the same as the previous one. The objective is to introduce a different accounting treatment for mostly similar facts but change enough to move from effective hedge to ineffective hedge.

22 The scientific name is *Halyomorpha halys* Stål, but the common name is the "brown marmorated stink bug" (BMSB), and is different from the southern green stink bug (*Nezara viridula*). BMSB is a native of China, Japan and Korea (http://entnemdept.ufl.edu/creatures/veg/bean/brown_marmorated_stink_bug.htm).

# CHAPTER 8

# HEDGE ACCOUNTING II (SINGLE CURRENCY)

## 8.1 Hedging Interest Rate Risk

### Information Log: Roadmap to Chapter Eight

Chapter Eight contains hedge accounting illustrations of the following issues:

- Discussing interest rate swaps as mere substitutions of risk: taking on fair value risk by hedging cash flow risk, or taking on cash flow risk by hedging fair value risk.
- Presenting a working example of valuation of an interest rate swap contract in a fair value hedge and the related accounting after:
  - upward shifts in the yield curve
  - downward shift in the yield curve.
- Showing the effect of terminating accounting for a fair value hedge and the management decision to accrete the fair value of debt by reversing accounting for the balance of the gains already recognized.
- Presenting a numerical example of the valuation and accounting of an interest rate swap contract as a cash flow hedge for a forecasted transaction.
- Cases of accounting for hedging interest rate risk of available-for-sale securities under conditions of:
  - effective hedge;
  - ineffective hedge; and
  - change in default risk.
- Providing a numerical example of the valuation and accounting for hedging interest rate risk using interest rate floors (OTC options) with periodic settlement and changes in benchmark interest rate.

Business enterprises issue and invest in financial instruments whose values and cash flow are directly or indirectly impacted by market changes in interest rate. As a result of financial engineering and the activism of Wall Street, numerous instruments have been, and continue to be, developed to help managers and investors mitigate their exposure to interest rate risk. The issuance of FAS 133 (now ASC 815) in 1989 and the corresponding changes in IAS 32 and IAS 39 have set in motion a complex system for recognizing and classifying the impact of hedging the risk of changes in interest rates on assets, obligations, and equity. The role of these standards in the 21st-century information environment is unclear; the volume of derivatives has increased more than 40 times since 2000 and the standards have been more responsive to management needs.[1]

### 8.1.1 Types of Interest Rate Risk Exposure

As discussed in the preceding chapters, exposure to interest rate risk arises from the impact of changes in interest rate on one or both of the following:

1. *Exposure to potential loss in value*: For fixed-rate instruments, changes in the value of the financial instrument are negatively correlated with changes in interest rate (see Chapter Two). As interest rate increases, the value of fixed-rate instruments drop to the point of equating the yield on the instrument with market yield; the equilibrating process also takes place with decreasing interest rates.
2. *Exposure to cash flow volatility*: Unexpected volatility of interest rates could adversely affect the cash flow and negatively affects the present value of the enterprise. The different impact of changes in interest rate on fixed-rate and floating-rate instruments is outlined in the following tabulation.

| *Interest rate* | *Fixed-rate instruments* | | *Floating-rate instruments* | |
|---|---|---|---|---|
| | *Value* | *Cash flow* | *Value* | *Cash flow* |
| Increases | Declines | *No Change* | *No Change* | Increases |
| Decreases | Increases | *No Change* | *No Change* | Decreases |

As the price of using funds, interest rate is determined by forces of supply and demand as is the case with setting the price of any other commodity. The demand for money is determined by investment opportunities and trade policies. The supply of money depends on the national monetary policy that is managed mostly by central banks (the Federal Reserve Bank in the USA), and fiscal policy that is the responsibility of the executive branch of the government. Other external factors that are not directly related to government actions include intervention by international organizations such as the International Monetary Fund. While this description is an over simplification, it highlights the main point that interest rates are determined by factors outside the control and influence of any particular business enterprise. As a result, business enterprises in general are interest rate-takers rather than interest rate-makers.

Interest rate risk exposure could then be defined as the possible loss in firm value or future cash flow arising from changes in interest rate that are caused by external forces.

The changes in market interest rates are either predictable, at least in direction, or are unexpected surprises. Prudent corporate governance is expected to have policies in place to allow the management to take actions and make borrowing and lending decisions that would mitigate the probable negative impacts of these predictable changes. For example, as noted in earlier chapters, financial institutions manage their short-term exposure to interest-rate volatility by a targeted management of interest-rate-gap—the difference between interest-rate-sensitive assets and interest-rate-sensitive liabilities (Chapter Three). Expected increases in interest rate would have a positive impact on cash flow and on the value of the enterprise if interest-rate-gap is positive, but would have a negative effect if interest-rate-gap is negative—i.e., interest-rate-sensitive liabilities are greater than interest-rate-sensitive assets. The reverse is, of course, true: a drop in interest rates would have a positive effect on the present value of the enterprise and on cash flow for firms with negative interest-rate-gap, and vice versa.

Managing interest-rate-gap is one form of natural hedging for near-term exposure to interest rate risk, but there is also a longer-term exposure that could be managed by setting credit limits, managing liquidity, and making borrowing and lending decisions with matching duration (Macaulay's Duration as presented in Chapter Three) to reduce the negative consequences of unexpected interest rate movement on the enterprise's net worth. However, planning and implementing these policies could be more complex when the assets or liabilities are denominated in multiple currencies (which is the subject of Chapter Ten and Chapter Eleven).

As noted earlier, natural hedging could be costly because actual borrowing, lending or investing in different projects or regions require actual deployment of resources and taking on other risks such as credit and liquidity risk. Conversely, hedging using financial instruments does not require mobilization of capital and is viewed as a low-cost approach to manage interest rate risk,[2] a factor that could explain the phenomenal growth in interest rate swaps. According to the Bank for International Settlements, the estimated volume of notional amounts and fair values of over-the-counter derivatives as of the last quarter of 2011 is as follows.[3]

*Notional Amounts*

- Over-the-counter derivatives (total) $647 trillion
- Over-the-counter interest rate derivatives $504 trillion

*Gross (Fair) Market Value*

- Over-the-counter derivatives (total) $27 trillion
- Over-the-counter interest rate derivatives $18 trillion

Additionally, interest rate swaps represent about 80% of the notional amounts ($403 trillion) and 70% of the gross estimated fair value ($12 trillion).

## 8.1.2 Interest Rate Swaps

### *8.1.2.1 A Brief Review of Related Concepts*

Chapter Five included some essential concepts about interest rate swaps. The following is a summary of these key elements:

a. Interest rate swaps in the real world vary in duration from a relatively short period to a period possibly as long as 25 years, but settlements of interest rate differences take place periodically and frequently such as monthly, quarterly, or semi-annually.

b. Unlike financial options, plain vanilla interest rate swaps have a two-sided payoff function. Since both counterparties are obligated to perform in accordance with the terms of the contract, one party must lose and the other wins. The difference between the gains of one party and the losses of the counterparty is the transaction cost consisting mainly of the swap dealer's spread.
c. Like forward contracts, swap contracts are not standardized and can be customized to fit the counterpartys' needs. But unlike forward contracts, swap contracts settle interest rate differences frequently enough to reduce credit risk exposure of either counterparty. However, counterparty credit risk of swap contracts is relatively lower than the counterparty credit risk of forward contracts because interest rate swap contracts settle more frequently than forward contracts. Extending this comparison to futures, it is clear that both swap and forward contracts bear higher counterparty risk than futures. Futures require making a deposit (margin) and settling differences daily.
d. Valuation of interest rate swaps follows the same basic valuation rule: the fair value of a swap contract is the present value of the rights to receive cash or obligations to deliver cash. The difference between valuation of a swap contract and a simple discounting rule emanates from the complexity of the terms of the contract and the impact of macroeconomic factors (e.g., change in the yield curve). To review the valuation process presented in Chapter Five, several issues need to be outlined.

   In designing and accounting for a swap contract, it is useful to view it as a series of staggered payments that take the following pattern:

```
(1)  -------------|
(2)  --------------------------|
(3)  ----------------------------------------|
(4)  -----------------------------------------------------|
     and so on ...
```

   In this structure, item (1) is the period from inception to the time of the first settlement; item (2) is the period from inception to the time of the second settlement; item (3) is the period from inception to the time of the third settlement, and the rest follows this cascading order. This disaggregation of one swap contract appears like a series of zero-coupon instruments—one instrument is due at each settlement date. It is possible, therefore, to view a swap contract as a series of forward contracts. The disaggregated time of the swap corresponds to the zero-coupon curve for the same risk class.
e. Because the swap value at inception must be nil, the present value of the cash flow from the floating leg must equal the present value of the cash flow from the fixed leg, both discounted at the zero-coupon rate (using the yield curve for the same risk class). This information is then employed in deriving the fixed rate that would generate this equality (see the example provided later in this section). For the fixed leg, the settlement amount is known, the present value of the cash flow is known (it is the market price of the instrument), and the discount rates factors are known (based on the zero-coupon rates). The only variable that is not known is the constant amount of cash flow that would be generated as the product of the face [notional] amount times the fixed interest rate that should be determined. For one unknown in one equation, imputing the interest rate for the fixed leg follows a simple rearrangement of terms to allow solving for the one unknown.

Equality of the present values of the cash flow from the floating leg and fixed leg guarantees that the fair value of the swap contract at inception is nil. The fair value of a swap contract becomes non-zero (a gain for one party and a loss for the counterparty) only after initiation of the agreement when the yield curve changes in ways to alter the cash flow generated by the variable leg.

### 8.1.2.2 Interest Rate Swaps as Substituting One Risk for Another

Abstracting away from the intermediary role of swap dealers, in a plain vanilla interest rate swap, one of the parties to the contract receives fixed rate and pays variable rate, and at the other end, the counterparty receives variable rate and pays fixed. Therefore, the same swap contract has two different functions for the two counterparties. We examine these functions from the perspective of a debt issuer and the investor.

#### If the Hedged Item is a Liability

These are similar to the cases presented in Figure 8.1.

1. Company *Beatriz Ltda* pays fixed rate at 8% p.a. on debt to capital markets. To convert this fixed rate into a variable rate, the company entered into a swap agreement with a dealer to receive 8.1% fixed rate and pay LIBOR + 0.2% variable rate. According to the terms of this agreement, the company has effectively changed the 8% annual interest rate commitment to paying LIBOR + 0.1% (the sum of LIBOR + 0.2% for the floating rate and 0.1% for the difference between two fixed-rate flows for the interest paid on the debt and for the interest received from the swap dealer).

*Analysis*: The management of this company was fearful that a decrease in market yield would increase the fair value of its debt, which would be a loss. By entering into this swap, the value of its debt will not be affected by market movement because as LIBOR decreases, the cash outflow the company incurs for payment of interest declines to match market movements. But the company is also taking the risk that the management's prediction will not materialize and LIBOR may instead increase. In this case, the cash outflow for the payment of interest increases.

*Conclusion*: The management of *Beatriz Ltda.* hedged the change in fair value of debt but took on exposure to cash flow volatility.

2. Company *Clea, NV* pays a variable interest rate of LIBOR + 0.7% on the debt it has borrowed from capital markets. The management of *Clea, NV* believes that an increase in LIBOR is likely and the interest payment will demand more cash that would have to be diverted from other uses. The company enters into a swap contract to convert this floating rate into a fixed rate. The contract calls for the company to receive LIBOR + 0.5% and pay fixed at 7.9%. The result is to change the interest cost to the company from LIBOR + 0.7 to fixed rate equal to 8.1% (which is the sum of 7.9% paid to the dealer plus 0.2% difference between the floating rate received from the swap dealer and the floating rate the company pays on the debt).

*Analysis*: The management of this company was fearful that an increase in LIBOR would expose it to cash flow risk. By entering into this swap, the company receives floating rate from the swap dealer, takes this inflow and pays it to bondholders. Thus, the company has a predictable outflow, and the prospect of facing volatile cash flow and shortage of cash is now removed.

With the swap, the company is facing a fixed cash outflow schedule. If the management forecast materializes and LIBOR actually increases, there will be no change in cash flow, but the fair value of the debt will decrease. On the other hand, if the management's forecast is wrong and LIBOR actually decreases, there will still be no cash flow consequences to *Clea, NV*, but the fair value of the debt increases because the debt has, in effect, been converted to a fixed-rate debt.

*Conclusion*: The management of *Clea, NV* hedged the exposure to interest rate cash flow volatility, but took on fair value risk.

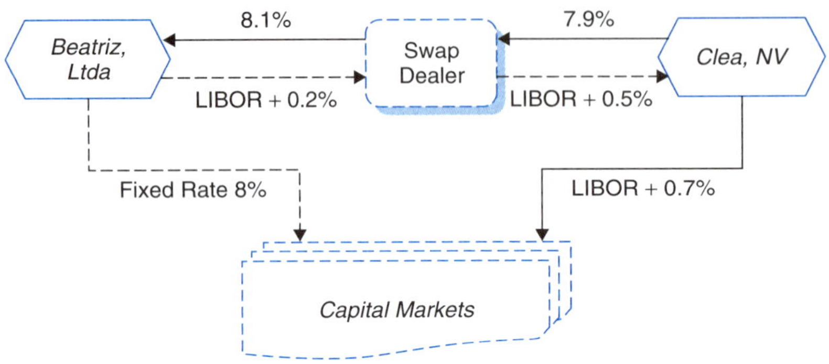


Notes

Company *Beatriz, Ltda*:

- This company has two contracts: a fixed-rate bond, and a swap contract to receive fixed, pay floating.
- The combination of the bond and swap contracts (if effective) results in converting the company's fixed-rate interest into a floating rate.
- Assuming an effective hedge, the company has as a result hedged the fair value risk, but assumed the cash flow risk.

Company *Clea, NV*:

- This company has two contracts: a variable-rate bond and a swap contract to receive variable, pay fixed.
- The combination of the bond and swap contracts (if effective) results in converting the company's floating-rate interest into a fixed rate.
- Assuming an effective hedge, the company has as a result hedged the cash flow risk, but assumed fair value risk.

**Figure 8.1** Hedging A Liability: Fixed for Floating Interest-Rate Swaps

## If the Hedged Item Is an Asset

This scenario is represented by the cases in Figure 8.2.

1. Company *Montague SA* earns fixed income of 6% on its investment in available-for-sale (AFS) securities. If the company remains locked into a fixed-rate investment, it will not be able to benefit from possible increases in market yield. The management acted on this expectation and entered into an interest rate swap agreement with a swap dealer to pay 5.8% fixed and receive floating rate of LIBOR + 0.4%. By entering into this swap, the company succeeds in converting the fixed rate income into LIBOR + 0.6% per annum (which is the swap contract rate of LIBOR + 0.4% plus the difference between the 6% the company earns and the 5.8% it pays for the swap).

*Analysis*: The management of *Montague SA* is holding a fixed-income asset and will be penalized if market interest rate increases because the change in the value of AFS is inversely related to the change in interest rates. This possible decrease in value is the result of sacrificing the higher return by holding a fixed-income AFS. By entering into this swap, the value of its AFS will not be affected by market movement, but the cash flow will. The management was hopeful that the market yield would increase and its earnings on the combination of AFS and the swap would also increase. However, the company is also taking on the risk that the management's prediction will not materialize and LIBOR will decrease instead. In this case, the cash inflow from the combination of AFS and the swap will decline.

*Conclusion*: Although this is an asset, the company is facing the same situation as *Beatriz, Ltda* with its debt. The management of *Montague SA* hedged the change in fair value of AFS but took on exposure to cash flow volatility.

Company *La Sierra* earns variable interest rate of LIBOR on its investment in AFS. The management of this company has access to some prediction showing that LIBOR may decrease, thereby reducing cash inflow and disrupting the company's ability to meet its obligations. The management entered into an interest rate swap agreement with a swap dealer to pay LIBOR and receive fixed 2.50%. By having this contract, the company succeeds in converting the floating-rate income into a 2.50% fixed return.

*Analysis*: The management of this company hedged a probable decrease in LIBOR that may expose it to cash flow shortages. By entering into this swap, the company receives fixed rate from the swap dealer and pays floating rate. If LIBOR goes up, the company will collect the increase in interest above LIBOR from the swap dealer. Thus, the prospect of facing a shortage of cash is now stabilized. With the swap, the company is facing a schedule of fixed cash inflow. Thus, this company is facing a situation similar to *Clea, NV* in connection with its debt issue.

*Conclusion*: *La Sierra* hedged the exposure to cash flow volatility, but took on fair value risk.

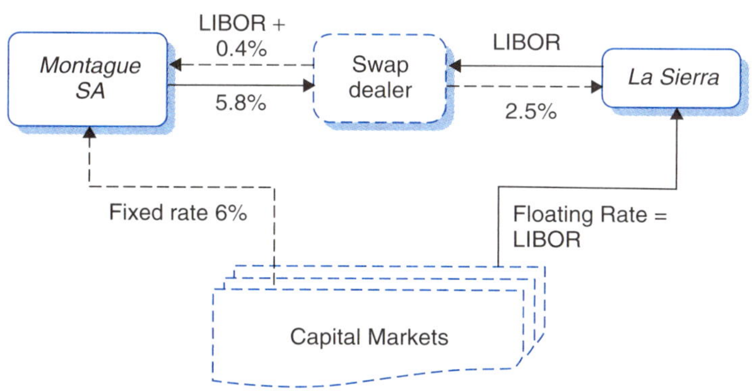


Notes

*Company Montague SA*:

- This company has two contracts: a fixed-rate AFS investment and a swap contract to receive floating and pay fixed.
- The combination of the investment and swap contracts (if effective) results in converting the company's fixed-rate income into a floating rate.
- Assuming an effective hedge, the company has as a result hedged the fair value risk, but assumed the cash flow risk.

*Company La Sierra*:

- This company has two contracts: a variable-rate investment security (AFS) and a swap contract to receive fixed and pay floating
- The combination of the bond and swap contracts (if effective) results in converting the company's floating-rate interest into a fixed rate.
- The company has as a result hedged the cash flow risk, but assumed fair value risk.

**Figure 8.2** Hedging Value and Cash Flow Risk of an Asset: Fixed for Floating Interest-Rate Swaps

In these examples, each of the four enterprises has succeeded in converting the contractual streams of cash flow (a contractual rate of interest payment on the debt or income from fixed-rate investments) into other streams of cash flow that are consistent with management's risk appetite and the firm's strategic risk. However, none of these four swap contracts provides a complete hedge of exposure to interest rate risk. When an enterprise switches from one cash flow stream to another, it is giving up the risk exposure of the surrendered cash flows and is assuming the risk exposure of the acquired cash flows. If an enterprise converts a fixed flow to a variable flow (such as *Beatriz, Ltda* in Figure 8.1 in the case of debt and *Montague SA* in Figure 8.2 in the case of assets), the enterprise is hedging the risk of adverse changes in value but accepting the risk of cash flow volatility.

Similarly, when an enterprise converts a variable cash flow stream to a fixed stream (such as the cases of *Clea, NV* in Figure 8.1 and *La Sierra* in Figure 8.2), the enterprise is, in effect, hedging or mitigating the exposure to cash flow volatility but, in the meantime, accepting exposure to the risk of changes in fair values.

Exhibit 8.1 presents a summary of these cases.[4]

## Exhibit 8.1 Interest Rate Swaps as Affecting Risk Substitution

| | *Hedged item* | |
|---|---|---|
| | *A liability* | *An asset* |
| Receive fixed, pay variable | • Convert a fixed rate to variable rate<br>• Hedge fair value risk<br>• Take on cash flow risk<br>**Example**: *Beatriz, Ltda* | • Convert a variable rate to a fixed rate<br>• Hedge cash flow risk<br>• Take on fair value risk<br>**Example**: *La Sierra, SAS* |
| Receive variable, pay fixed | • Convert a variable rate to fixed rate<br>• Hedge cash flow risk<br>• Take on fair value risk<br>**Example**: *Clea, NV* | • Convert a fixed rate to variable rate<br>• Hedge fair value risk<br>• Take on cash flow risk<br>**Example**: *Montague, SA* |

## 8.2 Illustrations of Accounting for Hedging Using Interest Rate Swaps

### 8.2.1 Hedging a Fixed-Rate Debt

On January 1, 20x1, *BetaCo*, a U.S.-based company, sold 1,000 bonds (*Debt Contract No KA50T*) at face value of $1,000 each, coupon rate of 3.9525% per annum and five-year maturity. Interest is payable annually at year end.[5]

Having observed some unexpected movements in macroeconomic indicators, the management of *BetaCo* feared loss of value due to probable decline in market interest rate and the concurrent increase in the fair value of its debt. In the event that this decline takes place and the company continues to pay bondholders the fixed rate of 3.9525%, it will be incurring an opportunity cost equal to the present value of the difference between the value underlying the 3.9525% fixed rate and the value determined by any market rate below 3.9525%. To avoid exposure to this potential value loss, concurrent with selling the bonds to investors in the marketplace, the management of *BetaCo* negotiated and entered into a swap agreement (*Swap Contract No. W215*) with a swap dealer, *SwapWhale Ltd* , to receive fixed rate and pay floating rate. The company's credit rating is "AA," and for this level of credit rating, *SwapWhale* does not charge points for credit risk. *Swap Contract No. W215* has the following terms:

- Notional principal is $1,000,000.
- *BetaCo* pays *SwapWhale* at LIBOR.[6]
- *BetaCo* receives from *SwapWhale* 3.9525% per annum.
- The swap contract is settled periodically on the last day of each year.
- The swap floating interest rate is reset on the same day of settlement.
- The swap contract terminates in five years (unless *BetaCo* unwinds it earlier or enters into a contract having opposite terms).

On January 1, 20x1, *BetaCo* has two financial instruments: a fixed-rate debt contract and a swap contract to receive fixed and pay floating. Figure 8.3 shows the flow of funds between *BetaCo* and both the capital market and *SwapWhale, Ltd.*

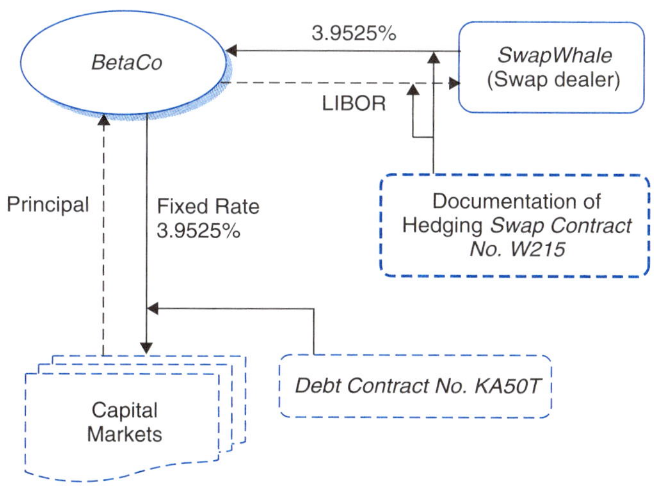


**Figure 8.3** Hedging Fixed-Rate Debt using Interest Rate Swap

## 8.2.2 Determination of Swap Rates

Exhibits 8.2 and 8.3 present the process of determining the floating and fixed rates of the interest rate swap contract of *BetaCo*. This calculation is preceded by a short review of the process, and the reader is reminded of the presentation in Chapter Five.

## Deriving Forward Rates

The first step is to estimate the periodic cash flow of the floating leg of the swap. This is determined by estimating the implied change in the benchmark interest rate using the zero-coupon curve for the same risk class as that of the payee. To show this process, let

$t$ = the time period, $t = 1, 2, \ldots, T$.
$NP$ = the face value, the principal or notional amount of the instrument.
$T$ = *maturity* which is five years.
$xR$ = the fixed-rate coupon.
$zR_t$ = the zero-coupon rate for the same risk class at time $t$.
$fR_t$ = the implied forward-rate at time $t$.
$fR_{t+1}$ = the implied forward-rate at time $t + 1$.

Then, for any period $t$, the forward rate for $t + 1$ is calculated as follows:

$$fR_{t\to t+1} = [(1+zR_{t+1})^{t+1}/(1+zR_t)^t] - 1 \qquad \text{(Eq. 5.1)}$$

*and* $fR_{t\to t+1}$ is estimated for each period as shown in Exhibit 5.12.

For example, calculation of these rates for *BetaCo* is shown in Exhibit 8.2.

## Exhibit 8.2 Deriving the Floating Rates for the Term of the Swap

Using Information of *BetaCo*

| | | | | *Zero-Coupon Rate(*) per Period* | | | | |
|---|---|---|---|---|---|---|---|---|
| | | | | $t=1$ | $t=2$ | $t=3$ | $t=4$ | $t=5$ |
| | | | | 0.025 | 0.03 | 0.035 | 0.0375 | 0.04 |
| Forward Rates | $t$ | $fR_{t\to t+1}$ | Calculation of forward rates | | | | | |
| | 1 | 2.5% | $fR_{(0,1)} = 0.025$ | | | | | |
| | 2 | 3.502% | $fR_{(1,2)} = [(1+0.03)^2/(1+0.025)] - 1$ | | | | | |
| | 3 | 4.507% | $fR_{(2,3)} = [(1+0.035)^3/(1+0.03^2] - 1$ | | | | | |
| | 4 | 4.504% | $fR_{(3,4)} = [(1+0.0375)^4/(1+0.035)^3] - 1$ | | | | | |
| | 5 | 5.01% | $fR_{(4,5)} = [(1+0.04)^5/(1+0.0375)^4] - 1$ | | | | | |

* The zero-coupon rate is obtained from the zero-spot curve available in the market place for interest rates of zero-coupon bond of different duration and same risk sector.

### 8.2.3 Determination of the Fixed-Leg Rate

Having determined the floating-leg rates, the periodic floating-leg cash flow is then calculated as the product of the implied interest rates times the notional principal amount. The calculation below will determine the fixed rate of interest that will result in a present value equal to the present value of the floating-rate-leg. Equality of present values is necessary because at inception of the swap, the value of the swap contract is zero—i.e., no accrued asset (rights) or liabilities (obligations).[7]

To facilitate the presentation, as is the case in Chapter Five, we will carry out the calculation *as if* each leg (the floating and the fixed) is a bond that will settle the principal amount of \$1,000.00 upon termination of the contract such that the following equity holds:

*PV* of the fixed leg = *PV* of the floating leg

We now have the following information:

- present value of the fixed leg,
- time to maturity,
- frequency of interest payment,
- discount factor as determined by the relevant zero-coupon curve,

but we are still missing the amount of periodic cash flow that the fixed leg will generate. This amount is equal to the known notional amount (principal) times the fixed rate. Therefore, the only variable that needs to be determined is the fixed (coupon-equivalent) rate. The determination of this rate for *BetaCo* is shown in Exhibit 8.3.

This means that the present value of each (hypothetical) bond is \$1,000. In Exhibit 8.3, we use this information to derive the fixed rate of interest that satisfies the conditions of present value equality.

## Exhibit 8.3 Deriving the Coupon Rate for the Fixed Leg of the Swap

*xR* = fixed coupon rate; *zR* = zero-coupon rate; *NP* = Notional Principal (face value)

Each bond in the portfolio has a face value of \$1,000. The fixed interest rate that satisfies equality of present value to face value of the bond is *xR* and the objective of the derivation below is to find out the numerical value of *the* fixed rate *xR*.

The equality:

$$\$1{,}000 = \frac{xR*1{,}000}{(1+zR_1)} + \frac{xR*1{,}000}{(1+zR_2)^2} + \frac{xR*1{,}000}{(1+zR_3)^3} + \frac{xR*1{,}000}{(1+zR_4)^4} + \frac{xR*1{,}000}{(1+zR_5)^5} + \frac{1{,}000}{(1+zR_5)^5}$$

$$\$1{,}000 = xR*\$1{,}000)\left[\frac{1}{1.025} + \frac{1}{(1.03)^2} + \frac{1}{(1.035)^3} + \frac{1}{(1.0375)^4} + \frac{1}{(\$1.04)^5}\right] + \frac{\$1{,}000}{(1.04)^5}$$

$$\$1{,}000 = xR*\$1{,}000)\ [0.9756 + 0.9426 + 0.902 + 0.86307 + 0.822] + \$821.927$$
$$\$1{,}000 = [xR*\$1{,}000) \times 4.50527] + \$821.927$$

(Note: The number 4.50527 is the sum of the dicount factors and the zero-coupon rates are obtained from the information in Exhibit 8.2.)

The present value of the terminal settlement (the notional principal) is

$$\frac{\$1,000}{(1.04)^5} \approx \$821.927.$$

Therefore, the present value of cash flow of the interest component in the above equation is equal to

$$\begin{aligned}&\$1,000 - \$821.927\\&= \$178.073\end{aligned}$$

&

$$\$178.073 = 4.50527 * (xR * \$1,000)$$

It follows that

$$\begin{aligned}xR * \$1,000 &= \$78.073/4.50527\\&= \$39.525\end{aligned}$$

For the fixed rate bond, the periodic cash flow would be $39.525 annually. This means that the coupon rate is 3.9525%.

### 8.2.4 Some Financial Considerations

1. The fixed-rate bond issue means that the cash outflow that *BetaCo* incurs in servicing the debt obligation does not change with changes in market rates.
2. Because the bond issue is a plain vanilla bond without optionality, the fair value of the bond will change for one of two reasons: interest rate risk, and credit risk.[8]
3. The payoff function of the swap contract is two sided: *BetaCo* will be penalized if LIBOR increases and will benefit if LIBOR decreases.
4. The swap contract allowed *BetaCo* to convert a stream of fixed interest rate payments to a variable cash outflow.
5. The net result is that *BetaCo* will end up paying interest cost referenced to LIBOR as the benchmark rate and, therefore, any drop in LIBOR will benefit *BetaCo* and vice versa.
6. The swap contract between *BetaCo* and *SwapWhale* is a fair value hedge of a recognized liability.
7. Together the bond indenture and the swap contract have allowed *BetaCo* to hedge fair value risk and take on cash flow risk.

## 8.3 The Accounting Processes and Analysis

Accounting for the swap agreement and performance takes several steps in each cycle:

1. Designation of the hedge and the hedging relationship.
2. Prospective testing of hedge effectiveness at inception of the hedge for the forthcoming period.
3. Recording transactions.

4. Retrospective testing of hedge effectiveness at each quarterly reporting date (or more frequently).
5. Prospective testing of hedge effectiveness for forthcoming period.
6. Exchanging cash amounts equal to interest rate differences over the settlement period.
7. Recognizing the gain or loss on the swap and posting it to earnings to the extent it is effective hedge within the range 0.80–1.25 or 0.80 *R2*.
8. Recognizing the *change* in value of the fixed asset and post it to earnings if the hedge is highly effective.
9. Resetting the floating rate of interest.
10. Starting a new payment cycle.

### 8.3.1 Hedge Designation

As discussed in Chapter Six, accounting standards require that each hedging relationship be specifically designated and have full documentation at inception of the hedge and on an ongoing basis. Important elements of the documentation are to designate the item, the risk being hedged, the nature of the hedge relationship, and the fit of the hedge to the enterprise approach to risk management and mitigation. It must also detail the characteristics of the hedge instrument, the methods and measurements to be applied in testing hedge effectiveness.[9]

In compliance with these requirements, *BetaCo* has designated and documented the hedge using *Swap Contract W215* as shown in Exhibit 8.4.

#### Exhibit 8.4 *BetaCo* Initial Hedge Documentation (*Interest Rate Risk Swap Contract W215*)

| | |
|---|---|
| *Date* | *January 1, 20x1* |
| *The hedged risk* | *Interest rate risk.* Exposure to possible loss due to increased fair value of debt contract *Bonds KA50T* due to volatility of interest rates in the market place. *Bonds KA50T* pay a fixed-rate coupon at 3.9525% p.a. |
| *Hedge objective* | • Eliminating the fair value risk associated with unexpected decline of the benchmark interest rate (i.e., LIBOR).<br>• *Swap Contract W215* converts periodic payments of interest from fixed to variable to be consistent with management strategy to maintain balance between fixed charge commitments and forecasted earnings. |
| *Risk management* | The management of *BetaCo* believes that exposure to the hedged risk is probable and the hedging relationship is consistent with the enterprise's risk management program that has recently been approved by the Board of Directors to hedge probable risk exposure if the risk identification and hedging are cost effective. |
| *Hedge instrument* | The hedge instrument is interest rate *Swap Contract W215* agreed upon with *SwapWhale*, the swap dealer for a period of five years, January 1, 20x1 through December 31, 20x5. The terms of the swap are: notional amount of $1,000,000; *BetaCo* pays LIBOR as of the time of periodic |

| | |
|---|---|
| | settlement; *BetaCo* receives 3.9525% fixed rate; periodic settlement takes place once a year at year end; and the floating rate is reset for the following year also at year end. |
| *The hedged item* | Debt contract *Bonds KA50T*. The debt is booked at amortized cost and the book value of this debt is $1,000,000. |
| *Assessment of hedge effectiveness prospectively* | Prospective hedge effectiveness is assessed by the Dollar Offset Ratio (DOR) method using the *as if* the zero-coupon rate parallel shifts upward (and downward) scenarios to estimate the changes in the value of the swap contract ( *Swap Contract W215*) and the changes in the fair value of the hedged item ( *Bonds KA50T*). |
| *Retrospective test of hedge effectiveness* | Retrospective hedge effectiveness is assessed by DOR using the ratio of cumulative past change in the fair value of the swap contract ( *Swap Contract W215*) to the cumulative change in the fair value of the debt being hedged ( *Bonds KA50T*). |
| Other hedge criteria | All other criteria required for fair value hedge are satisfied. |

## 8.3.2 Conclusion of Prospective (*Ex-Ante*) Assessment of Hedge Effectiveness

As noted in the documentation, hedge effectiveness will be measured prospectively by DOR or the ratio of changes in values under different scenarios. Because, in a hedge, the two fair values of the hedged debt and the hedge instruments are expected to move in opposite directions, DOR should have a negative sign. To facilitate presentation and discussion, it is useful to take the absolute value of the ratio so that it could be evaluated against the range of what is considered "highly effective" hedge (of 0.80–1.25).[10] Row B22 in Panel C of Exhibit 8.5 shows that the ratio of the change in the value of the swap to the change in the value of debt = 1.00, which is a perfect hedge.[11]

## Exhibit 8.5 For *Swap Contract W215* to hedge *Debt Contract KA50T*[12]

**Panel A**: Verifying that the Present Value of the Swap Contract at Inception is Nil

| | | *20x1* | *20x2* | *20x3* | *20x4* | *20x5* |
|---|---|---|---|---|---|---|
| B1 | $zR_0$: zero-coupon rate as of 1/1/20x1 | 0.025 | 0.03 | 0.035 | 0.0375 | 0.04 |
| B2 | $fR_{1,S+}$: Floating rate imputed from the zero-coupon curve | 0.025 | 0.035024 | 0.045067 | 0.045036 | 0.05006 |
| B3 | $CF_{VR,\, t=0}$: Cash outflow to be paid for the floating leg of the swap | 25,000 | 35,024 | 45,067 | 45,036 | 50,060 |

| | | | | | | |
|---|---|---|---|---|---|---|
| B4 | PV of the cash flow of the floating leg of the swap (total = $178,066) | 24,390 | 33,013 | 40,648 | 38,869 | 41,146 |
| B5 | $CF_{Fx,\, t=0}$: Cash flow to be received for the fixed leg of the swap (excluding principal amount) | 39,525 | 39,525 | 39,525 | 39,525 | 39,525 |
| B6 | PV of cash flow from the fixed leg of the swap (total = $178,066) excluding settlement of principal amount | 38,561 | 37,256 | 35,649 | 34,113 | 32,487 |
| B7 | Difference in cash flow between floating and fixed legs (= Row B3 – Row B5) | (14,525) | (4,501) | 5,542 | 5,511 | 10,535 |
| B8 | PV of difference in cash flow between the floating and fixed legs (PV of Row B7. These numbers are the same as Row B4 – Row B6) | (14,170) | (4,243) | 4,999 | 4,756 | 8,659 |
| | $\sum PV\ (Row\ B8) = 0$ | | | | | |
| | *Conclusion*: Present value of the fixed leg equals present value of the floating leg. | | | | | |

Note: The numbers are subject to rounding errors

**Panel B**: Prospective (*Ex-Ante*) Test of Hedge Effectiveness

*The Scenario*: Change in present value of interest rate swap *as if* the zero-coupon curve has an upward parallel shift by 100 Basis Points[13]

| *Entry No.* | *Transaction* | *20x1* | *20x2* | *20x3* | *20x4* | *20x5* |
|---|---|---|---|---|---|---|
| B9 | What the zero-coupon curve would look like under the *as if* scenario of an increase by 100 Basis Points | 0.035 | 0.04 | 0.045 | 0.0475 | 0.05 |
| B10 | Future value factor | 1.035 | 1.0816 | 1.141166 | 1.20397 | 1.27628 |
| B11 | The forward (swap) rates *as if the zero-coupon curve shifted* 100 Basis Points upward. | | | | | |

| | | | | | | |
|---|---|---|---|---|---|---|
| | These numbers are derived in the same way as Exhibit 8.3 | 0.035 | 0.04502 | 0.05507 | 0.055036 | 0.06006 |
| B12 | The cash flow that would be paid for the floating leg *after* upward shift by 100 Basis Points | 35,000 | 45,025 | 55,070 | 55,036 | 60,060 |
| B13 | The cash flow to be received for the fixed leg (excluding Principal Amount) | 39,525 | 39,525 | 39,525 | 39,525 | 39,525 |
| B14 | Cash flow difference (Row B11 – Row B12) | (4,525) | 5,500 | 15,542 | 15,511 | 20,535 |
| B15 | Present value of the floating leg cash flow difference (calculated as Row B14*)[14] (1/Row B10) | (4,372) | 5,085 | 13,620 | 12,885 | 16,090 |
| | $\sum$ *of* Row B15 = $43,308 | | | | | |

Note: The numbers are subject to rounding errors

**Panel C**: The Debt Instrument—*Bonds KA50T*

*The Scenario*: Change in present value of debt *as if* the zero-coupon curve has a parallel shift by 100 Basis Points

| | | *20x1* | *20x2* | *20x3* | *20x4* | *20x5* |
|---|---|---|---|---|---|---|
| B16 | Fixed-leg cash flow for interest payment on debt | 39,525 | 39,525 | 39,525 | 39,525 | 39,525 |
| B17 | Zero-coupon rate after upward shift by 100 Basis Points | 0.035 | 0.04 | 0.045 | 0.0475 | 0.05 |
| B18 | Future value factor | 1.035 | 1.0816 | 1.141166 | 1.20397 | 1.27628 |
| B19 | $PV_{B,0}$: Present value of the cash flow in Row B16 | 38,188 | 36,543 | 34,636 | 32,829 | 30,969 |
| B20 | Present value of principal amount (needs to be recalculated at the new zero-coupon rate) | | | | | 783,527 |

<table>
<tr><td>B21</td><td>Present value of interest plus principal amount (Total = $956,692)</td><td>38,188</td><td>36,543</td><td>34,636</td><td>32,829</td><td>814,496</td></tr>
<tr><td rowspan="3">B22</td><td rowspan="3">Difference between present value in Row B20 and present value at inception (i.e., change in the fair value of the bond)</td><td colspan="3">Present value on 1/1/20x1</td><td colspan="2">$1,000,000</td></tr>
<tr><td colspan="3">Present value after 100 Basis Points upward parallel shift</td><td colspan="2">$956,692</td></tr>
<tr><td colspan="3">Change in fair value of the bond</td><td colspan="2">($43,308)</td></tr>
<tr><td colspan="2">Testing hedge effectiveness DOR as if the zero-coupon curve shifted upward by 100 Basis Points.</td><td colspan="5">|Δ fair value of the swap/Δ fair value of the debt|<br><br>|Row 15/Row B22 = |$43,308/$43,308| = 1.00</td></tr>
</table>

Note: The numbers are subject to rounding errors

## 8.3.3 Performance of the Hedge

### *8.3.3.1 Year One of the Hedge—Fiscal Year 20x1*

Under this scenario, the only (related) transactions that took place are the following:

1. Accrual and payment of interest on the debt.
2. First period settlement by exchanging funds equal to interest rate differences for the year.

Although this is the first year and the swap contract value was zero, there is interest differential because the two legs of the swap have different patterns of cash flow: it increases over the five years for the floating leg, but remains the same for the fixed leg.

On December 31, 20x1, *BetaCo* received (in theory) $39,525 and paid *SwapWhale* (in theory) $35,000. However, this is only theoretical and executing the settlement here does not involve actual delivery of all interest amounts both ways. To settle, the two counterparties exchange only the difference in amounts of interest. For the first year, settlement means *BetaCo* receives $4,525 from *SwapWhale*, which is the net difference between $39,525 for interest on the fixed leg that *BetaCo* pay *SwapWhale* less the $35,000 the company receives as interest on floating leg.

The following journal entries provide a recording of these events.

**Fiscal Year 1/1/20x1–31/12/20x1**

| *Entry No.* | *Date* | *Explanation* | *Debit* | *Credit* |
|---|---|---|---|---|
| C1 | 1/1/20x1 | Cash<br>Bonds Payable<br>*BetaCo issued 1,000 bonds under Bond Contract KA50T at face value of $1,000 each and an annual interest rate of 3.9525%. The bonds are sold at par and are payable in full in five years.* | 1,000,000 | <br>1,000,000 |
| C2 | 1/1/20x1 | *Memorandum*<br>*The management of BetaCo entered into a contract (Swap Contract W215) with SwapWhale, Ltd to exchange interest cash flows on a notional amount of $1,000,000. For a period of five years, BetaCo will receive fixed to SwapWhale and pay floating. The fixed rate is 3.9525% p. a. and the floating rate is LIBOR. Settlement of cash for interest differences and resetting the rates is at year end.* | — | — |
| C3 | 12/31/20x1 | Interest Expense[15]<br>Interest Payable<br>*To record accrued interest on Bond Contract KA50T calculated as $1,000,000 @ 3.9525%* | 39,525 | <br>39,525 |
| C4 | 12/31/20x1 | Accounts Receivable—*SwapWhale*<br>Interest Rate Settlement—*Swap Contract W215*<br>*To record the difference in cash flow arising from difference in terms of Swap Contract W215. The difference between the $39,525 that SwapWhale is required to pay BetaCo and the $35,000 that BetaCo is required to pay SwapWhale on 12/31/20x1.* | 4,525 | <br>4,525 |
| C5 | 12/31/20x1 | Interest Payable<br>Cash<br>*To record the disbursement of interest payable to bondholders.* | 39,525 | <br>39,525 |
| C6 | 12/31/20x1 | Cash<br>Accounts Receivable—*SwapWhale*<br>*To record the collection of the debt owed by* SwapWhale. *This is the result of cash differential between the fixed and floating rates.* | 4,525 | <br>4,525 |
| C7 | 12/31/20x1 | Interest Rate Settlement—*Swap Contract W215*<br>Interest Expense<br>*Recording the interest rate differential as an adjustment to interest expense* | 4,525 | <br>4,525 |

The net result of the transactions above:

- Interest cost is $35,000, which is the cost at LIBOR as the management of *BetaCo* intended to accomplish.
- The cash flow decreased by $35,000
- No additional assets or liabilities are recorded.

### 8.3.3.2 Year Two of the Hedge—20x2

At the start of the second period of the swap contract, macroeconomic conditions changed such that the yield curve shifted upward.[16] The shift was not parallel and was more like a "bend" shift: the shift increases with maturity. The change in the zero-coupon curve will change the cash flow of the floating leg by the same process described in Exhibit 8.3. The new rates and cash flow are as follows:

| *Year* | *20x2* | *20x3* | *20x4* | *20x5* |
|---|---|---|---|---|
| Initial ${}_{p}zR_{0}$: zero-coupon rate as of 1/1/20x1 | 0.030 | 0.035 | 0.0375 | 0.040 |
| Current $zR_{1}$: zero-coupon rate after the shift as of 1/1/20x2 | 0.035 | 0.042 | 0.050 | 0.060 |
| Implied forward rate after the shift in yield curve (calculated in the same way as in Exhibit 8.3. For example, the rate in 20x4 is equal to $[(1.05)^3 / (1.042)^2] - 1 = [1.1576/1.08576] - 1$ | 0.035 | 0.049047 | 0.06618 | 0.0906 |

Note: The numbers are subject to rounding errors

Evaluating hedge effectiveness *ex-ante* (prospectively) requires comparison of the change in present value of the swap contract against the change in the present value of the bond.

Exhibit 8.6 has three panels to calculate the required measures:

- Panel A shows the change in value of the swap contract.
- Panel B shows the change in fair value of the bond.
- Panel C shows the measurement of *ex-ante* hedge effectiveness.

## Exhibit 8.6 Prospective Assessment of Hedge Effectiveness

**Panel A:** Estimating the change in value of the swap contract (the hedge instrument)

| | | *20x2* | *20x3* | *20x4* | *20x5* |
|---|---|---|---|---|---|
| D0 | Past ${}_{p}zR_{0}$: Zero-coupon rate as of 1/1/20x1 | 0.03 | 0.035 | 0.0375 | 0.04 |
| D1 | Current $zR_{0}$: Zero-coupon rate after the shift as of 1/1/20x2 | 0.035 | 0.042 | 0.05 | 0.06 |
| | *Discount Factors* | 0.9662 | 0.921 | 0.8638 | 0.7921 |
| D2 | Implied forward rate after the shift in yield curve (calculated in the same way as in Exhibit 8.3) | 0.035 | 0.049047 | 0.06618 | 0.0906 |

| | | | | | |
|---|---|---|---|---|---|
| D3 | Expected cash flow for the floating leg (the rate in Row D2 times the notional amount of $1,000,000) | 35,000 | 49,047 | 66,181 | 90,600 |
| D4 | Cash flow of floating leg expected before the shift in the yield curve (from Row B3 in Exhibit 8.5) | 35,000 | 45,067 | 45,036 | 50,060 |
| D5 | Difference in cash flow between cash flow of the floating leg before the shift in the yield curve and after the shift (excluding principal amount) (Row D3 – Row D4) | 0 | 3,980 | 21,145 | 40,540 |
| D6 | Present value of cash flow differences discounted using the zero-coupon rates after the shift in the yield curve (Row D5 discounted at the discount factors generated from the zero-coupon rates in Row D2. For example, the present value for year 20x5 = $40,540/(1.06)^4$) | 0 | 3,666 | 18,265 | 32,111 |
| D7 | The sum of changes in the present value of *Swap Contract W215* = (3,666 + 18,265+ 32,111) – 0 = 54,042 | | | | |

Note: The numbers are subject to rounding errors

**Panel B**: Calculation of change in present value of debt (hedged item)

| | *Year* | *20x2* | *20x3* | *20x4* | *20x5* |
|---|---|---|---|---|---|
| D8 | Cash flow of the fixed leg (interest)<br>(Principal) | 39,525<br>— | 39,525<br>— | 39,525<br>— | 39,525<br>1,000,000 |
| D9 | *Discount Factors* | 0.9662 | 0.921 | 0.8638 | 0.7921 |
| D10 | Present value of fixed leg discounted based on the zero-coupon rates after shift in the yield curve (Interest) →<br>(Principal) → | 38,188<br>— | 36,403<br>— | 34,143<br>— | 31,308<br>792,100 |
| D11 | Present value of the debt (hedged item) using the new yield curve.<br>= PV of interest + PV of principal<br>= 140,042+ 792,100<br>= 932,142 | | | | |
| D12 | Change in present value of debt = 932,142 – 1,000,000<br>= (67,858)<br>The fair value of the bond decreased as the yield curve shifted upward.<br>Note: A decrease in the fair value of the debt is a gainto *BetaCo*. | | | | |

Note: The numbers are subject to rounding errors

**Panel C**: Prospective Assessment of Hedge Effectiveness
Per the documentation of designating *Swap Contract W215*, *ex-ante* (prospective) hedge effectiveness is assessed by the present value of DOR against the accepted range of 0.80–1.25. In this case,

$$
\begin{aligned}
\text{DOR} &= |\Delta \text{ fair value of the swap}/\Delta \text{ fair value of the debt}| \\
&= |54{,}042\ /{-67{,}858}| \\
&\approx 0.80
\end{aligned}
$$

Under the shift in the yield curve, designating *Swap Contract W215* as a hedge for *Bonds Contract KA50T* is expected to be highly effective in offsetting the hedged interest rate risk.

## Accounting for the Second Year, 20x2

Assuming that all went as predicted, on the first day of the year:

- *BetaCo* accrued and paid $39,525 interest due on the bond issue.
- *BetaCo* receives the difference in interest from *SwapWhale* equal to $4,525 (= 39,525 – 35,000).
- Recognition of the change in the fair value of the debt.
- Recognition of the change in the fair value of the swap.

### Recording Transactions

| *Date* | *Transaction* | *Debit* | *Credit* |
|---|---|---|---|
| 12/31/20x2 | Interest expense | 39,525 | |
| | Interest payable | | 39,525 |
| | *Accruing the interest expense on Bonds Contract KA50T.* | | |
| 12/31/20x2 | Accounts Receivable—*SwapWhale* | 4,525 | |
| | Interest Rate Settlement—*Swap Contract W215* | | 4,525 |
| | *Exchanging interest differential according to the contract agreement.* | | |
| | *The swap is net settled; the only physical flow is the net difference. This amount is what the swap dealer owed BetaCo; it is equal to what could have been interest inflow from the swap contract in the amount of $39,525 less what could have been outflow to the swap dealer in the amount of $35,000.* | | |
| 12/31/20x2 | Interest Rate Settlement—*Swap Contract W215* | 4,525 | |
| | Interest Expense | | 4,525 |
| | *Adjusting accrued interest to the interest rate differential in the first period. Interest expense for the period is then 39,525 minus 4,525 = 35,000, which is LIBOR.* | | |

| | | | |
|---|---|---|---|
| 12/31/20x2 | Bonds payable<br>  Other income/expense<br>*To record the decline in the value of debt as a gain. The change in the fair value of the bond due to rise in the zero-coupon rate.*<br>*This information is from Row D12 in Exhibit 8.6, Panel B.*<br>*It is calculated as the fair value at year end minus fair value at the beginning of the year:*<br>  *$932,142 – $1,000,000 = –67,858.*<br>*A decline in the fair value of debt is gain to the debtor.* | 67,858 | <br>67,858 |
| 12/31/20x2 | Other income/expense<br>  Fair value of derivatives—*Contract W215*<br>*To record the loss on Swap Contract W215. The present value of the excess of cash outflow for the swap based on the increased zero-coupon rate over the present value of the fixed cash inflow.*<br>*This amount is calculated in Panel A of Exhibit 8.6, Row D7.* | 54,042 | <br>54,042 |
| 12/31/20x2 | Interest payable<br>  Cash<br>*Paying off interest obligation* | 39,525 | <br>39,525 |
| 12/31/20x2 | Cash<br>  Accounts Receivable—*SwapWhale*<br>*Collecting receivable owed to us by SwapWhale* | 4,525 | <br>4,525 |

### A Summary of Transactions in Year 20x2

- Net Interest Expense charged to earnings = $39,525 – $4,525 = $35,000
- Net cash payment related to the bond and hedge = ($39,525 – $4,525) = $35,000
- The bond issue *KA50T* is reported at a book value of $932,142 because of gain by $67,858.
- The balance sheet would have a liability for the fair value of the swap (loss), which is $54,042.
- Earnings (before taxes) increased by $13,816, the balance remaining in the gains on debt net of the loss of the swap contract. This balance is the ineffective component of the hedging relationship.
- Retrospective test of hedge effectiveness should be carried out explicitly. However, we have seen how this test is done and, for simplicity and desire to move to a newer issue, we assume that the zero-coupon rates changed only once at the beginning of the second year. This means that the retrospective (*ex-post*) test of hedge effectiveness will be identical to the prospective (*ex-ante*) effectiveness check.

## *8.3.3.3 Year Three of the Hedge—20x3*

At the beginning of this year, there was a downward parallel shift in the zero-coupon yield curve by 50 Basis Points. The first task is to assess *ex-ante* (prospective) hedge effectiveness under this change. The information for this test is presented in Exhibit 8.7.

## Exhibit 8.7 Assessment of *Ex-Ante* (Prospective) Hedge Effectiveness with a Downward Shift of Zero-Coupon Rate by 50 Basis Points

| | | *20x3* | *20x4* | *20x5* |
|---|---|---|---|---|
| F1 | (Old) Previous zero-coupon rate before the downward shift | 0.042 | 0.05 | 0.06 |
| F2 | (New) The zero-coupon rate after the downward shift | 0.037 | 0.045 | 0.054 |
| F3 | The new implied forward rate | 0.037 | 0.05306 | 0.07223 |
| F4 | Expected cash flow for the floating leg of the swap under the new interest rate regime<br>(new floating interest rate times notional amount of $1,000,000) | 37,000 | 53,060 | 72,230 |
| F5 | Earlier expected cash flow for the floating leg of the swap under the previous interest rate regime<br>(From Panel A of Exhibit 8.6, Row A3) | 49,047 | 66,181 | 90,060 |
| F6 | Difference in expected cash flow for the floating leg (Row F4 – Row F5) | (12,047) | (13,121) | (17,830) |
| F7 | Present (fair) value of cash flow difference for the floating leg (sum of these PVs is 38,860) | (11,617) | (12,015) | (15,228) |
| F8 | Cash flow for the fixed leg of the swap | 39,525 | 39,525 | 39,525 |
| F9 | PV of cash flow for the fixed leg of the swap<br>Interest<br>Principal (face = $1,000,000)<br>*PV of fixed leg = PV of interest + PV of principal*<br>*= $108,062 + $854,040*<br>*= $962,102* | <br>38,115<br>— | <br>36,194<br>— | <br>33,756<br>854,040 |
| F10 | Before the change in the yield curve, the present value of debt was $935,250 (Row D10 in Exhibit 8.7, Panel B). Therefore, the change in the value of debt would be<br>$962,102 – $935,142 = $29,960<br>Increase in the fair value of debt is a loss | | | |
| F11 | *Effectiveness*<br>Effectiveness is measured by DOR:<br>DOR = absolute value of (Δ fair value of hedge/Δ fair value of debt)<br>= 38,860/29,960<br>= 1.297<br>This ratio is outside the accepted range of 0.8–1.25. Therefore, with the 50 Basis Points downward shift in the zero-coupon yield curve, the hedge is ineffective and should be terminated. | | | |

### 8.3.4 Hedge Ineffectiveness and Termination

The prospective test of effectiveness shows that the hedge will be ineffective, given the new change in LIBOR. The hedging relationship should be terminated.

**Accounting Log**

Ineffectiveness is not the only reason to de-designate a hedge; a hedging relationship could be terminated for any of the following reasons:

a. The hedge relationship fails to meet the test of high effectiveness. ASC 815-25-40-1 through 40-4.
b. The management decides, at will and for whatever reason of its own, to de-designate the hedge.[17]
c. The hedged item (asset, liability) no longer exists.
d. The firm commitment or the hedged forecasted transaction is no longer probable (this is for the cash flow hedge, which has its own termination rules).
e. The counterparty becomes insolvent or declares bankruptcy.

In the illustration at hand for *BetaCo*, the *Swap Contract W215* to hedge the fair value of debt (*Bond Contract KA50T*) failed the prospective effectiveness test in the third year, year 20x3. Upon termination or de-designation of the hedging relationship, the management must decide on actions related to the hedge instrument (*Swap Contract W215*) and the hedged item (*Bond Contract KA50T*).

#### *8.3.4.1 Possible Actions Related to the Hedge Instrument (Swap Contract W215)*

- Retaining the swap instrument as an investment in the "trading securities" portfolio.
- Re-designating the swap instrument as a hedge of the risk exposure of another hedgeable item for which this instrument would be effective.
- Unwinding the swap contract by discounting the remaining payments for the tenor of the swap and settling up with the counterparty. Alternatively, *BetaCo* could enter into another swap agreement with opposite flows. In the first case, unwinding the swap alleviates *BetaCo* from both economic and legal obligations for any future activities related to the swap (i.e., default of the counterparty) because both counterparties have settled their position. In the second case, entering into another swap contract with another counterparty relieves *BetaCo* from the economic obligation but does not relieve it from the legal obligation to the counterparty of the swap agreement in the event that the counterparty of the second contract defaults.
- Terminating the swap contract by exchanging its present value.

#### *8.3.4.2 Possible Actions Related to the Hedged Item (Debt issue KA50T)*

- Accounting for the debt will be independent of this swap contract.
- The book value of the debt would include the amount of write-down that was recorded when the hedge was effective.

- If the debt is to be retained to maturity, the difference between the settlement amount of the debt at retirement, which is $1,000,000, and the carrying book value, which is $932,142, is $67,858. This amount should be amortized in order to accrete the book value of the bond to reach the settlement amount.
- Enter into another derivative contract that could be highly effective in hedging the value change of this debt.

## 8.3.5 The Management Decision

Watching drop in LIBOR led the management to terminate the hedge by recontracting with *SwapWhale, Ltd*. In this case, the management would pay *SwapWhale, Ltd* a cash amount equal to the fair value of the swap, which is $54,042.

The book value of debt should be accreted by $67,858 over three years in order to bring it up to a level equal to the settlement amount.

- There is an implicit discount rate (i.e., internal rate of return) that would discount the expected cash outflow (three payments of $39,525 each and one payment three years ahead of $1,000,000) to a present value of $932,142.
- The internal rate of return used to cover the interest coupon payments and also accrete the $932,142 to the level of $1,000,000 is 6.51758%.
- Of the interest calculated at that rate, $39,525 will be paid in cash (credit the cash account), the excess of interest calculated at the implicit internal rate of return over the $39,525 will be charged as a liability (credit *Bond Contract KA50T*) and added to the accrued interest expense. Examples of these entries are shown below.

Table 8.1 shows the pattern of amortization and expensing the cost of debt. From there on, journal entries are straightforward conventional financial accounting.

**Table 8.1** Interest Expense and Accreting Book Value of Debt for the Remaining Term of *Bond Contract TA50T* (Effective interest rate is 6.518%)

| *Year* | *20x3* | *20x4* | *20x5* |
|---|---|---|---|
| *Bond Contract TA50T* Settlement Amount | $1,000,000 | | |
| Book Value as of January 1, 20x3 | $932,142 | $953,370 | $975,982 |
| Amount that should Be Amortized | $67,858 | $46,630 | $24,018 |
| Implicit Internal Rate of Return to Pay the Coupon and Amortize the Balance | 6.51758% | | |
| Accrued Interest Expense | $60,753 | $62,137 | $63.543[(a)] |
| Interest Payment | $39,525 | $39,525 | $39,525 |
| Amount accreted to the Bond Contract *KA50T* | $21,228 | $22 ,612 | $24,018[(a)] |
| Bonds Payable Ending Balance – Contract *KA50T* | $953,370 | $975,982 | $1,000,000 |

(a) Numbers are subject to rounding errors.

**Recording Year Three, 20x3:**

| *Date* | *Transaction* | *Debit* | *Credit* |
|---|---|---|---|
| 12/31/20x3 | Fair value of derivatives—*Contract W215*<br>Cash<br>*To record the termination of Swap Contract W215. The contract was terminated due to ineffectiveness and possible reversal in interest rate movements.* | 54,042 | <br>54,042 |
| 12/31/20x3 | Interest expense<br>Interest payable<br>Bonds payable—*Bond Contract KA50T*<br>*Accruing the interest expense on Bonds Contract KA50T and accreting the balance of bonds payable to amortize the previously recognized gains on the related swap* | 60,753 | <br>39,525<br>21,228 |
| 12/31/20x3 | Interest payable<br>Cash<br>*Paying off interest obligation* | 39,525 | <br>39,525 |
| 12/31/20x4 | Interest expense<br>Interest payable<br>Bonds payable—*Bond Contract KA50T*<br>*Accruing the interest expense on Bonds Contract KA50T and accreting the balance of bonds payable to amortize the previously recognized gains on the related swap* | 62,137 | <br>39,525<br>22,612 |
| 12/31/20x3 | Interest payable<br>Cash<br>*Paying off interest obligation* | 39,525 | <br>39,525 |
| 12/31/20x5 | Interest expense<br>Interest payable<br>Bonds payable—*Bond Contract KA50T*<br>*Accruing the interest expense on Bonds Contract KA50T and accreting the balance of bonds payable to amortize the previously recognized gains on the related swap (numbers are subject to rounding errors)* | 63,543 | <br>39,525<br>24,018 |
| 12/31/20x5 | Interest payable<br>Cash<br>*Paying off interest obligation* | 39,525 | <br>39,525 |
| 12/31/20x5 | Bonds payable—*Bond Contract KA50T*<br>Cash<br>*Paying off the obligations on Bond Contract KA50T.* | 1,000,000 | <br>1,000,000 |

## 8.4 Hedging Interest Rate Risk in a Cash Flow Hedge

Interest rate swaps and interest rate options are the dominant instruments in hedging interest rate risk. Contracts using both types of instruments could be structured to allow the hedging party to apply either fair value hedge or the cash flow hedge accounting treatment.

To illustrate the accounting for cash flow hedge, a new swap contract between *La Sierra* and *The SwapBank*, a swap dealer, is presented below.

Assume that, on 1/1/20x1, the one-year LIBOR was 2.5%.[18] On that day, *La Sierra, Inc.* made the following transactions:

**Debt Issue:**

- Issued 1,000 bonds, *DBond23*, at face value of $1,000 each.
- These bonds mature in three years.
- The coupon is LIBOR plus 0.5% (starting at 3%).
- The coupon rate is reset at LIBOR on December 31.
- The interest payment to be made on December 31.

**Swap:**

- The company entered into an interest rate *Swap Contract No. OTCZebra8* with *The SwapBank Co.*, a local swap dealer.
- The notional amount is $1,000,000.
- The agreement is for *La Sierra* to receive LIBOR and pays fixed rate at 2.5%.
- The amount of settlement is determined by LIBOR on the settlement date.
- LIBOR rates are used for rate reset at December 31.
- At the time of this agreement, LIBOR was 2.5%.

The effect of these contracts combined is to maintain the cost of debt to the company at 3% under different scenarios. For example, if LIBOR increases by 50 or 100 Basis Points, the relationship between receiving LIBOR and paying fixed combined with the cost of debt will result in costing the company interest at 3% annually. This could be illustrated as follows:

| *Market conditions* | *No change* | *Increases 50 Basis Points* | *Increases 100 Basis Points* |
|---|---|---|---|
| Receive LIBOR | 2.5% | 3% | 3.5% |
| Pay fixed | (2.5%) | (2.5%) | (2.5%) |
| Pay LIBOR + 50 BP | (3%) | (3.5%) | (4%) |
| Net interest rate | 3% | 3% | 3% |

### 8.4.1 Management Decision on the Accounting

These decisions would concern two questions:

1. Does this hedge qualify for hedge accounting?
2. If it does, should this hedge be accounted for as a cash flow hedge or a fair value hedge?

To answer these questions, the management would have to evaluate the risk being hedged, the fit of the hedge in the enterprise system of risk management and the method of testing hedge effectiveness. The management indicated that the terms of this hedge qualify for the short-cut method (see Chapter Six) because all the terms match, there is no prepayment clause, no optionality, and no ineffectiveness at inception. As a result, the hedge is considered perfectly effective and no quantitative measures of effectiveness are required.

## Exhibit 8.8 *La Sierra* Initial Hedge Documentation (*Interest Rate Swap Contract H3A7*)

| | |
|---|---|
| *Date* | *January 1, 20x1* |
| *The hedged risk* | *Interest rate risk*. Exposure to cash flow volatility. If LIBOR (the benchmark index) increases above the 2.5% the cost servicing the debt contract *DBonds15* will increase. |
| *Hedge objective* | Eliminating the risk associated with increased cash outflow and unexpected volatility of benchmark interest rate. |
| *The hedged item* | Debt contract *DBonds15* that has face amount of $1,000,000.00 and pays variable coupon rate at LIBOR + 0.50. The bonds are due in three years. |
| *Hedge instrument & strategy* | *Swap Contract No. OTCZebra8*with *The SwapBank*, a local swap dealer, on a notional amount of $1,000,000.00. The company receives LIBOR at settlement date and pays 2.5% fixed rate. The swap contract is for a three-year period. |
| *Risk management* | The management of *La Sierra* believes that the hedged risk is probable and the hedging relationship is consistent with the enterprise risk management system that has been recently approved by the Board of Directors to hedge probable risk exposure if the risk identification and hedging are cost effective. |
| *Assessment of hedge effectiveness* | The hedge relationship qualifies for the short-cut method. There is no ineffectiveness and the contract satisfies all qualifications for the short-cut method. No quantitative measure of effectiveness is required under US GAAP. |
| *Other cash flow hedge criteria* | All other criteria required for the cash flow hedge accounting treatment are satisfied. |

### Events and Transactions in 20x1

- On 1/1/20x1, LIBOR rate was 2.5%, which is the benchmark.
- On 12/31/20x1, there was a parallel upward shift in the zero-coupon curve by 0.50%.
- LIBOR increased to 3%. This increase in LIBOR has two consequences:

  i. *La Sierra* and *The SwapBank* must settle the difference: *The SwapBank* pays *La Sierra* $5,000 which is 0.5% rate difference times the notional amount of $1,000,000.

  ii *La Sierra, Inc.* has expectation of a stream of cash inflow reflecting the difference in LIBOR and the fixed rate that *La Sierra* is obligated to pay.

- Based on these changes, on December 31, 20x1, *La Sierra* estimated the fair value of the swap contract at $9,567, calculated as follows:

  Assuming no additional change in market rates, every year, *La Sierra* will receive $5,000 from *The SwapBank*, which is estimated to have following present value:
  $PV = (5000/1.03) + (5000/1.03^2)$
  $= \$9{,}567$ (The numbers are rounded to the nearest dollar)

  At the end of 20x1, *La Sierra* records these events as follows:

| *Date* | *Transaction* | *Debit* | *Credit* |
|---|---|---|---|
| 1/1/20x1 | Cash<br>Bonds Payable<br>*Issuing 1,000 bonds of contract DBonds15 at face value of $1,000. The bond pays a coupon equal LIBOR plus 0.5%* | 1,000,000 | <br>1,000,000 |
| 1/1/20x1 | Memorandum<br>*Today, we have signed a three-year swap contract with The SwapBank to receive LIBOR and pay 2.5% fixed. Swap Contract No. OTCZebra8 has a notional amount of $1,000,000; periodic settlement, and resetting interest rate takes place at year end.* | — | — |
| 12/31/20x1 | Interest expense<br>Interest payable<br>*To record the accrual of interest on the bond issue at the new LIBOR rate of 3% plus 0.5%.* | 35,000 | <br>35,000 |
| 12/31/20x1 | Accounts receivable—*The SwapBank*<br>Gain/loss on the swap[19]<br>*To record the right of La Sierra, Inc. in the collection of the LIBOR-fixed rates.* | 5,000 | <br>5,000 |
| 12/31/20x1 | Gain/loss on the swap<br>Interest Expense<br>*Paying off accrued interest liability for the period.* | 5,000 | <br>5,000 |

| | | | |
|---|---|---|---|
| 12/31/20x1 | Swap fair value—Contract *No. OTCZebra8*<br>OCI—Swap Account for Contract No. *OTCZebra8*<br>*To recognize the fair value change of the swap contract with The SwapBank calculated as*<br>PV = (5000/1.03) + (5000/1.03²)<br>*under the assumption that the yield curve will not shift.* | 9,567 | <br>9,567 |
| 12/31/20x1 | Interest payable<br>Cash<br>*Paying off accrued interest liability for the period.* | 35,000 | <br>35,000 |
| 12/31/20x1 | Cash<br>Accounts receivable—*The SwapBank*<br>*Collection of the right to interest rate difference resulting from LIBOR change.* | 5,000 | <br>5,000 |

## Year Two: 20x2

In the second year, there was no change in LIBOR after it had increased last year; it remained at 3%. This means the expected right to collect the $5,000 difference from *The SwapBank* has not changed. But there is a difference in timing between the end of year 1 and the end of year 2 so that the fair value of the swap contract has changed. On December 31, 20x2, right before settlement, the fair value of the swap contract is

$5000 + $5000/1.03 = $9,845

The change in fair value is equal to $9,845 – $9,567 = $287, which should be accrued. La Sierra records the following entries

| | | | |
|---|---|---|---|
| 12/31/20x2 | Interest expense<br>Interest payable<br>*To record the accrual of interest on the bond issue at the new LIBOR rate plus 0.5%.* | 35,000 | <br>35,000 |
| 12/31/20x2 | Accounts receivable—*The SwapBank*<br>Gain/loss on the swap<br>*To record the right of La Sierra, Inc. in the collection of the LIBOR-fixed rates.* | 5,000 | <br>5,000 |
| 12/31/20x2 | Gain/loss on the swap<br>Swap fair value—Contract No. *OTCZebra8*<br>*Closing the account of swap* Contract No. *OTCZebra8* | 5,000 | <br>5,000 |
| 12/31/20x2 | Swap fair value—Contract No. *OTCZebra8*<br>OCI—*Swap Account* Contract No. *OTCZebra8*<br>*Recording the change in the fair value of the swap due to timing difference only. At year end, the present value of the swap contract is*<br>*5000 + 5000/1.03 = 9,854, which is an increase by $287.* | 287 | <br>287 |

| | | | |
|---|---|---|---|
| 12/31/20x2 | OCI—Swap account<br>  Interest expense<br>*To record adjusting the variable cost of interest on contract DBonds15* | 5,000 | <br>5,000 |
| 12/31/20x2 | Interest payable<br>  Cash<br>*To record paying off interest obligations to The SwapBank.* | 35,000 | <br>35,000 |
| 12/31/20x2 | Cash<br>  Accounts receivable—*The SwapBank*<br>*To record collection of the right to interest rate difference from the counterparty.* | 5,000 | <br>5,000 |

## Year Three: 20x3

- No change in LIBOR or contract.
- The only change is the time value of the deferred gain on the swap. The fair value of the swap will increase by the difference in the time value of money. The year-end fair value is $5,000, but the balance of the account is $4,854.

| *Date* | *Transaction* | *Debit* | *Credit* |
|---|---|---|---|
| 12/31/20x3 | Interest expense<br>  Interest payable<br>*To record the accrual of interest on the bond issue at the new LIBOR rate plus 0.5%.* | 35,000 | <br>35,000 |
| 12/31/20x3 | Accounts receivable—*The SwapBank*<br>Gain/loss on the swap<br>*To record the right of La Sierra, Inc. in the collection of the LIBOR-fixed rates.* | 5,000 | <br>5,000 |
| 12/31/20x3 | Swap fair value—Contract No. *OTCZebra8*<br>  OCI<br>*Recording the change in the fair value of the swap due to timing difference only. At year end, the present value of the swap contract is*<br>*4854 × 1.03 = $5,000 which is an increase by $146.* | 146 | <br>146 |
| 12/31/20x3 | OCI—*Swap Account* Contract No. *OTCZebra8*<br>  Interest expense<br>*To record adjusting the variable cost of interest on contract DBonds15* | 5,000 | <br>5,000 |
| 12/31/20x3 | Gain/loss on the swap<br>  Swap fair value—Contract No. *OTCZebra8*<br>*Closing the account of swap* Contract No. *OTCZebra8* | 5,000 | <br>5,000 |
| 12/31/20x3 | Interest payable—*The SwapBank*<br>  Cash<br>*Paying off the liability to bondholder* | 35,000 | <br>35,000 |

| | | | |
|---|---|---|---|
| 12/31/20x3 | Cash<br>Accounts receivable—*The SwapBank*<br>*Collecting the rights to interest rate difference for Swap Contract No. OTCZebra8* | 5,000 | <br>5,000 |
| 12/31/20x3 | Bonds payable<br>Cash<br>*Paying off bond obligation* | 1,000,000 | <br>1,000,000 |

## 8.5 Hedging Securities Valued at Fair Value through Other Comprehensive Income (Available for Sale)

The available for sale (AFS) portfolio consists of securities valued at fair value through OCI. Because the changes in fair values do not flow through earnings, these securities are eligible (in accounting) to be designated as hedged items. These securities may be equity or debt instruments; financial derivatives are not permitted to be included in this group of securities.

As is the case with financial securities, the investing enterprise is exposed to several types of risk:

- *Price risk*: unexpected changes in prices due to market conditions—all types of securities whether equity or debt.
- *Interest rate risk*: unexpected adverse changes in interest rate—debt instruments.
- *Prepayment risk*: debtors repay the debt instruments before maturity—which is mostly related to interest rate risk.
- *Default risk*: the risk that debtors will default on interest or interest and principal—debt instruments.

An enterprise may enter into derivative contracts to hedge any or all of these risks. Other than credit default swaps, most other financial derivatives could be designated as hedge instruments that could qualify for hedge accounting, provided that all the hedge accounting requisites are met.

### 8.5.1 Fair Value Hedge of Interest Rate Risk (For Marketable Securities (AFS) in Absence or Presence of Credit Default Risk)

Hedging these securities could qualify for fair value hedge accounting treatment or cash flow hedge accounting treatment (for floating rate securities). However, hedging fair value risk of these securities has a unique feature in that not all changes in prices could be accounted for as an element of the hedging relationship. To illustrate, consider four scenarios:

#### *8.5.1.1 Scenario A: No Hedging*

An enterprise has a portfolio of AFS securities that include fixed rate bonds. Assume in accounting period 1, market interest rate increased such that the fair value of the portfolio declined by $6,000.

If this portfolio is not hedged, the enterprise records the following journal entries:

| | Debit | Credit |
|---|---|---|
| Loss on AFS<br>AFS Portfolio<br>*To record the decline in fair value of available-for-sale securities* | 6,000 | <br>6,000 |
| OCI—AFS value changes<br>Loss on AFS<br>*To record classification of loss in fair value of AFS in Other Comprehensive Income* | 6,000 | <br>6,000 |

*Notes:*
The effect of these entries:

- Income statement: no effect
- On the Balance Sheet:
  - The assets decrease by 6,000
  - OCI (an equity account) decreases by $6,000

## 8.5.1.2 Scenario B: Highly Effective Hedging

If the portfolio is hedged against interest rate risk and the hedge is considered *ex-ante* highly effective—100% DOR. In the first accounting period, the price of the hedged securities decreased by $6,000 and the fair value of the swap increased by $6,000. These changes are offsetting and the journal entries would be as follows:

| | Debit | Credit |
|---|---|---|
| Receivable—swap dealer<br>Gains/losses on swap<br>*To recognize the gain on the financial derivative* | 6,000 | <br>6,000 |
| Cash<br>Receivable—swap dealer<br>*To report collection of the amount of derivative settlement* | 6,000 | <br>6,000 |
| Loss on AFS<br>AFS portfolio<br>*To record the decline in fair value of available-for-sale securities* | 6,000 | <br>6,000 |
| Gain /loss on the swap<br>Loss on AFS<br>*Closing the gain on the hedge and the loss on the hedged item* | 6,000 | <br>6,000 |

Both accounts of gains/losses on Swap & Loss on AFS will be closed in the income statement.

*Notes:*
The effect of these entries:

- On Income Statement: no impact
- On the Balance Sheet:
- The marketable securities assets portfolio decreases by 6,000.
- The cash account increases by $6,000.

### 8.5.1.3 Scenario C: Highly Effective Hedging and a Loss Due to Default Risk

If the portfolio is hedged against interest rate risk and the hedge is considered *ex-ante* highly effective—100% DOR. In the first accounting period, the price of the hedged securities decreased by $10,000 and the fair value of the swap increased by $6,000. The $4,000 difference between the decline in the fair value of the portfolio and the increase in the fair value of the swap is due to a change in the credit risk of the bond issuer. These changes are not offsetting and the journal entries would be as follows.

| | *Debit* | *Credit* |
|---|---|---|
| Receivable—swap dealer | 6,000 | |
| Gains/losses on swap | | 6,000 |
| *To recognize the gain on the financial derivative* | | |
| Cash | 6,000 | |
| Receivable—swap dealer | | 6,000 |
| *To report collection of the amount of derivative settlement* | | |
| Loss on AFS | 10,000 | |
| AFS portfolio | | 10,000 |
| *To record the decline in fair value of AFS securities* | | |
| OCI—AFS value changes | 4,000 | |
| Loss on AFS | | 4,000 |
| Gains/losses on swap | 6,000 | |
| Loss on AFS | | 6,000 |
| *To close the loss on AFS and the related gain on the swap* | | |

*Notes:*

The effect of these entries:

- On the income statement: No impact.
- On the Balance Sheet:
  - The marketable securities asset decreases by 10,000
  - Cash increases by $6,000
  - OCI—AFS value changes decrease by $4,000

### 8.5.1.4 Scenario D: Hedging in Presence of Ineffectiveness and Loss Due to Default Risk

If the portfolio is hedged against interest rate risk and the hedge is considered *ex-ante* highly effective—80% Dollar Offset Ratio (DOR). In the first accounting period, the price of the hedged securities decreased by a total of $10,000, composed of $4,800 decline in value due to interest rate changes, and $5,200 because of default risk. In the meantime, the change in fair value of the swap increased by $6,000. The DOR is 4,800/6,000 = 0.80, therefore the hedge is effective and hedge accounting may continue.

This is a case of overhedge because the fair value of the derivative is greater than the change in the fair value of the hedged position. The $5,200 difference between the decline in the fair value of the portfolio and the increase in the fair value of the swap is due to a change in the credit risk of the bond issuer. These changes are not offsetting and the journal entries would be as follows:

| | Debit | Credit |
|---|---|---|
| Receivable—swap dealer<br>  Gains/losses on swap<br>*To recognize the gain on the financial derivative* | 6,000 | <br>6,000 |
| Cash<br>  Receivable—swap dealer<br>*To report collection of the amount of derivative settlement* | 6,000 | <br>6,000 |
| Loss on AFS<br>  AFS portfolio<br>*To record the decline in fair value of available-for-sale securities* | 10,000 | <br>10,000 |
| OCI—AFS value changes<br>  Loss on AFS<br>*To record the loss in AFS fair value due to default risk (unhedged) as an adjustment to OCI* | 5,200 | <br>5,200 |
| Gains/losses on swap<br>  Income statement<br>  Loss on AFS<br>*To record the ineffective portion of the hedge (overhedge)*<br>*Close the gain on the swap* | 6,000 | <br>1,200<br>4,800 |

*Discussion of hedge effectiveness*:

The decline in AFS portfolio consists of two components:

- $5,200 due to credit risk.
- $4,800 due to interest rate risk.

Credit risk was not hedged.

- The $4,800 is the loss due interest rate risk.
- Gains from hedging interest rate risk amounted to $6,000.
- Therefore, the $4,800 change in the fair value of AFS is 0.80 of the change in the fair value of AFS and the hedge is highly effective.
- As a result, the gain on hedging interest rate risk will be allocated as follows:
  - $4,800 to offset the loss in the fair value of AFS.
  - $1,200 credit to earnings as the ineffective component of the hedge.

### 8.5.2 Hedging Cash Flow Risk Using Interest Rate Floors

As noted in Chapter Five, interest rate options consist of floors, caps and collars. An enterprise investing in floating rate assets could protect the levels of its cash inflow from a decline in the benchmark interest rate by buying floors. If the reference interest rate falls below the floor, the dealer will pay the difference between the specified floor and the market rate. Similarly, an enterprise that has floating rate debt could limit the amount of cash outflow for servicing the debt by buying interest rate caps. If the reference rate increases above the specified cap, the dealer would pay the enterprise the excess of the market rate over the specified cap. Purchasing a cap and a floor guarantees the buyer any interest rate within a corridor for interest rate between a cap and a floor. Because caps, floors and collars are customized instruments and have longer durations than exchange traded options, counterparties to these contracts agree on periodic settlement in the same sense as interest rate swaps. As a result, a floor could be considered a series of European put options (each is called floret) that expire at different durations. Similarly, a cap is a series of European call options that expire at different durations.

Given this characterization, it would not be difficult to see how these floors and caps are valued. Each floret is valued as a put option and the value of the floor would be the sum of the values of all of its florets. Each caplet is also valued as a call option and the value of the cap would be the sum of the values of all of its caplets. Option valuation models such as Black-Scholes or Cox-Ross-Rubinstein Binomial model can be used to estimate these values in the same way as the illustrations in Chapter Five use these models. However, this is not how the illustration below values interest rate floors. To focus on the accounting features of treating interest rate floors, I will follow accounting standards' setters and adopt a simple present valuation (discounting) model.

An illustration: The *Unlimited Chips Company* is a microchips manufacturer located in San Mateo, California. The company has been successful and accumulated large sums of cash but the management is wary of the economic conditions in the nation and decided, on January 1, 20x1, to invest $100 million in financial securities that could be liquidated when the economy improves and the company may need the cash to finance specific projects. The company classified these investments as AFS to be valued at fair value with the changes in fair value to be reported in OCI. Anticipating higher inflation and the related increase in interest rate, the management of *Unlimited Chips* decided to invest $40 million in equity and $60 million in floating-rate bonds that are due in December 20x2 (2 years down the road from the time of purchase). The bonds are indexed to six-month LIBOR and bear a coupon rate of six-month LIBOR plus 100 Basis Points. The interest is collectable, and is reset, on June 30 and December 31. On January 1, 20x1, six-month LIBOR was 2.5%.

The interest rate risk facing the company is the possibility of a decline in LIBOR and the attendant decrease in the cash inflow from AFS investments. To hedge this downside risk, the company purchased interest rate floors, which are essentially like put options where the seller (writer of the floor) compensates the buyer of the floor (holder of the option) if LIBOR falls below the stated benchmark.

As to the transactions of the *Unlimited Chips Company*, the information about the investment in debt securities and the interest rate floors (options) are as follows:

| | |
|---|---|
| 1. *AFS investment in bonds* | $60 million |
| • Interest rate earned | Six-month LIBOR plus 100 basis points. |
| • Interest collection/reset | June 30 and December 31. |
| 2. *Interest rate floors notional amount* | $60 million |
| • The strike interest rate | 2.50%. |
| • Settlement and reset dates | June 30 and December 31. |
| • Maturity | Two years ending December 31, 20x2. |
| • Floors premium | $95,000 |

Assume that the zero-coupon curve has the following behavior:

**Table 8.2** Assumptions about Movements of the Zero-Coupon Curve and Time Value of Options

| *Observation Date* ↓ / *Settlement Date* → | *1/1/20x1* | *6/30/20x1* | *12/31/20x1* | *6/30/20x2* | *12/31/20x2* |
|---|---|---|---|---|---|
| 1/1/20x1 | 0.025 | 0.026 | 0.0264 | 0.0266 | 0.027 |
| 6/30/20x1 | — | 0.023 | 0.024 | 0.023 | 0.023 |
| 12/31/20x1 | — | — | 0.022 | 0.023 | 0.024 |
| 6/31/20x2 | | | | 0.0205 | 0.020 |
| 12/31/20x2 | | | | | 0.020 |
| Floors Time Value | $95,000 | $40,000 | $15,000 | $5,000 | 0 |
| Use of Time Value | 0 | $50,000 | $30,000 | $10,000 | $5,000 |

See Table 8.3 for Calculation of Intrinsic Values of Interest Rate Floors

**Table 8.3** Calculation of Intrinsic Values of Interest Rate Floors

A. Present Value of Interest Rate Floors
On the first day of settlement, June 30, 20x1, Six-Month LIBOR dropped from the benchmark level of 2.5% to 2.3%. For one half year, the dealer owes Unlimited Chips $60,000. Assuming the change will remain flat, the company anticipates $60,000 for every settlement period.

| | | | | | |
|---|---|---|---|---|---|
| | | $60,000 | 60,000 | 60,000 | 60,000 |
| P. V. Factor 6/30/x1 Based on Zero Coupon Rates | | 0.98863 | 0.97643 | 0.96628 | 0.9553 |
| $ PV 6/30/x1 | | 59,318 | 58,586 | 57,977 | 57,318 |
| Sum PV on 6/30/x1 | | 233,198 | | | |

B. Present Value of the Floors on December 31/20x1
By December, the hedged rate dropped to 2.2% . The Interest Rate Floor Dealer must compensate Unlimited Chips for the difference between 2.5% and 2.2%. For one-half year, this amount is $90,000.

| | | | | | |
|---|---|---|---|---|---|
| | | | 90,000 | 90,000 | 90,000 |
| P.V. Factor 12/31/x1 | | | 0.989 | 0.97739 | 0.9648 |
| $ PV 12/31/x1 | | | 89010 | 87,965 | 86,836 |
| Sum PV on 12/31/x1 | | | 263,811 | | |

C. Present Value of the Floors on June 30/20x2
Same situation as above because the relevant LIBOR rate dropped to 2.0%.

| | | | | | |
|---|---|---|---|---|---|
| | | | | 135,000 | 135,000 |
| P.V. Factor 6/30/x2 | | | | 0.978 | 0.9565 |
| $ PV 6/30/x2 | | | | 132,030 | 129,127 |
| Sum PV on 6/30/x2 | | | | 261,157 | |

D. Present Value of the Floors on December 31/20x2
Same situation as above because the relevant LIBOR rate dropped to 2.0%.

| | | | | | |
|---|---|---|---|---|---|
| | | | | | 150,000 |
| P.V. Factor 12/31/x2 | | | | | 0.97561 |
| $ PV 12/31/x2 | | | | | 146,342 |

The journal entries for these four periods are as follows.

| *Date* | *Transaction* | *Debit* | *Credit* |
|---|---|---|---|
| 1/1/20x1 | AFS Securities<br>  Cash<br>*Purchasing $40 million equity investment and $60,000 floating-rate bonds.* | 100,000,000 | <br>100,000,000 |
| 6/30/20x1 | Fair value of interest rate floors<br>  Cash<br>*Purchasing interest rate floors (put options) to guarantee the income on the bond portfolio in AFS.*<br>*This premium is the time value of options because at this time, the floors are at-the-money.* | 95,000 | <br>95,000 |
| 6/30/20x1 | Fair value of interest rate floors<br>Financing expense—AFS interest income<br>  OCI—Account of interest rate floors<br>*To record the intrinsic value change of interest rate floor derivatives including write-down of $50,000 of the options premium (time value of options)* | 183,198<br>50,000 | <br><br>233,198 |
| 6/30/20x1 | Cash<br>OCI—Account of interest rate floors<br>  AFS interest income<br>*Recognition of interest earnings on AFS Bonds*<br>  = ($60 M × 0.033 × (6/12)<br>*Plus the settlement on Interest Rate Floors*<br>  = $60 M × (0.023 – 0.025) × (6/12)<br>*This is because six-month LIBOR dropped below the 2.5% benchmark of the floors* | 990,000<br>60,000 | <br><br>1,050,000 |
| 6/30/20x1 | Cash<br>  Fair value of interest rate floors<br>*Collection of interest rate difference for the period* | 60,000 | <br>60,000 |
| 12/31/20x1 | Fair value of interest rate floors<br>Financing expense—AFS interest income<br>  OCI—account of interest rate floors<br>*To record the intrinsic value change of interest rate floor derivatives including write-down of $30,000 of the options premium (time value of options)* | 60,613<br>30,000 | <br><br>90,613 |
| 12/31/20x1 | Cash<br>OCI—Account of interest rate floors<br>  AFS interest income<br>*Recognition of interest earnings on AFS Bonds*<br>  = ($60 M × 0.032 × (6/12)<br>*Plus the settlement on interest rate floors*<br>  = $60 M × (0.022 – 0.025) × (6/12)<br>*This is because six-month LIBOR dropped below the 2.5% benchmark of the floors.* | 960,000<br>90,000 | <br><br>1,050,000 |
| 12/31/20x1 | Cash<br>  Fair value of interest rate floors<br>*Collection of interest rate difference for the period* | 90,000 | <br>90,000 |

| | | | |
|---|---|---|---|
| 6/30/20x2 | Fair value of interest rate floors<br>Financing expense—AFS interest income<br>  OCI—Account of interest rate floors<br>*To record the intrinsic value change of interest rate floor derivatives including write-down of $30,000 of the options premium (time value of options).* | 77,346<br>10,000 | <br><br>87,346 |
| 6/30/20x2 | Cash<br>OCI—Account of interest rate floors<br>  AFS interest income<br>*Recognition of interest earnings on AFS Bonds*<br>=($60 M × 0.0305 × (6/12)<br>*Plus the settlement on Interest Rate Floors*<br>= $60 M × (0.0205 – 0.025) × (6/12)<br>*This is because six-month LIBOR dropped below the 2.5% benchmark of the Floors* | 915,000<br>135,000 | <br><br>1,050,000 |
| 12/31/20x2 | Cash<br>  Fair value of interest rate floors<br>*Collection of interest rate difference for the period* | 135,000 | <br>135,000 |
| 12/31/20x2 | Fair value of interest rate floors<br>Financing expense—AFS interest income<br>  OCI—Account of interest rate floors | 15,185<br>5,000 | <br><br>20,185 |
| 12/31/20x2 | Cash<br>OCI—Account of interest rate floors<br>  AFS interest income<br>*Recognition of interest earnings on AFS Bonds*<br>= ($60 M × 0.03 × (6/12)<br>*Plus the settlement on interest rate floors*<br>= $60 M × (0.020 – 0.025) × (6/12)<br>*This is because six-month LIBOR dropped below the 2.5% benchmark of the floors* | 900,000<br>150,000 | <br><br>1,050,000 |
| 12/31/20x2 | Fair value of interest rate floors<br>  OCI—Account of interest rate floors<br>*To record the change in fair value of interest floors* | 3,658 | <br>3,658 |
| 12/31/20x2 | Cash<br>  Fair value of interest rate floors<br>*Collection of interest rate difference for the period* | 150,000 | <br>150,000 |

- The objective of this illustration is to show how the accounting treatment of Cash Flow Hedge is implemented when interest rate floors are used as the hedge instrument.
  - As shown, changes in the fair value of the hedge instrument are parked in OCI and are reclassified to earnings each period when the related interest income is collected.
  - Hedge effectiveness is not explicitly calculated. However, if the "hypothetical derivative" approach is used for evaluating effectiveness, it is virtually guaranteed that the hedge will be highly effective.23
  - Success of the hedging relationship reveals that *Microchips Unlimited* has always earned $1,050,000 interest every six months. This income shows that, in spite of a continuous

decline in LIBOR, the company has maintained earning 3.5% annual interest rate—the level of LIBOR at the time of making investment plus 100 basis points.

- The Company could earn more than 0.035 annual interest income if LIBOR were to increase above 2.5% in which case the interest rate floors are not relevant and no measurement of hedge effectiveness is necessary.
- If the company had issued debt instead of investing in debt instruments, interest rate caps would have been the appropriate hedge instrument.
- Because these instruments have floating rates, only their cash flow changes with the change in LIBOR but the fair value remains unchanged. Therefore, the Cash Flow Hedge accounting treatment is the only permissible method (provided that all the qualifying criteria noted in Chapter Six are satisfied).
- Option valuation models are the appropriate models to use for valuation. However, to simplify the illustration for accounting purposes, discounting of expected future flows is employed to estimate the present value of interest rate floors (refer to Chapter Five for option valuation models and illustrations).

## 8.6 Summary of Key Points

This chapter consists of two main components: (i) accounting for interest rate swaps and (ii) hedging marketable securities held as investment.

### 8.6.1 Accounting for Interest Rate Swaps

Interest rate risk is the enterprise's exposure to cost or opportunity cost because of movements in interest rates. The impact of changes in interest rates on the financial conditions of an enterprise depends on several factors, most notably interest-rate-gap and management business plans. Mitigating this risk exposure might take the form of natural hedging, but since the late 1990s, financial derivatives have been the most common method used in managing interest rate risk.

According to the statistics provided by the Bank for International Settlements, interest rate derivatives constitute over 80% of all over-the-counter derivatives and are estimated to have a notional amount of over $504 trillion and an estimated fair value of about $20 trillion. This chapter addresses the accounting for two main interest rate derivative instruments: interest rate swaps and interest rate options.[20]

#### 1. Interest Rate Swaps

Interest rate swaps vary in complexity from the simple vanilla swaps to more complex structured contracts. The focus of this chapter is on vanilla swaps since they have sufficient richness for the purpose of understanding the accounting treatment.

A plain vanilla interest rate swap is an agreement to exchange floating interest rate for a fixed rate. If one party pays the floating rate, this party would be receiving the fixed and the counterparty would be paying fixed rate and receiving floating rate.

A significant effort is made in this chapter to show that interest rate swaps effectively substitute one risk exposure for another. By exchanging floating rate for fixed, the entity is effectively hedging interest rate volatility but is taking on fair value risk. Similarly, by paying fixed rate and receiving variable rate, the entity is hedging fair value risk but is taking on interest rate volatility.

Determining the fair value of interest rate swaps is an important application of either Level 2 or Level 3 of fair value measurement hierarchy for several reasons. First, interest rate swap agreements are customized contracts and the terms of each contract are uniquely determined by the two contracting parties. Second, these instruments are traded over-the-counter and there is no disclosure (almost of any kind) about the transactions that take place. Relying on dealers' quotes to estimate fair value is not adequate because each swap contract is uniquely customized. These limitations place greater emphasis on the accountant's knowledge and ability to estimate the present values of swap contracts.

The basic method of estimating these present values makes use of zero-coupon curves and implied forward rates as presented in Chapter Five. This method is repeated in this chapter in connection with specific illustrations of accounting for these swaps.

Unless the management makes decisions to achieve specific accounting results, accounting per se does not change transactions and facts. Therefore, over the total life of a swap contract, the financial position or results of performance do not change whether or not the enterprise uses hedge accounting; applying hedge accounting changes the distribution of these financial results over the different accounting periods covered by the interest rate contract. The longer the tenor of the contract, the more important is the periodic measurement and reporting of performance. The special hedge accounting for interest rate swaps permits smoothing this distribution over time. However, the implementation and the mechanics of this "smoothing" process are far too complex to comprehend without specific illustrations.

The illustrations used in this chapter make use of plain vanilla swap contracts and interest rate options. In general, the accounting treatment of these contracts is guided by the risk exposure being hedged as the probability of value loss (fixed rate) or the probability of exposure to high cash flow volatility. Regardless to which risk is being hedged, the accounting requirements include:

- Preparing hedge documentation.
- Measurement of prospective and retrospective effectiveness.[21]
- Measurement and reporting the impact of hedging on earnings and financial position for the accounting periods intervening between inception and final settlement of the contract.
- Accounting treatment of terminating a hedge before contract maturity.

### 2. Hedging Marketable Securities Held as Investment

Securities held as investments are also subject to loss in value and cash flow volatility arising from unexpected price and interest rate changes. The available for sale (AFS) securities are valued at fair value with the changes in fair values reported in Other Comprehensive Income (OCI) until the securities are sold or affect earnings. Hedging these securities poses some unique issues because the change in the fair value of these securities may result from the hedged risk as well as from other factors.

This section addresses hedging the fair value of fixed debt securities held in AFS. The presentation considers different conditions to illustrate the accounting treatment when interest rate risk is hedged, but the fair value of the securities in the investment portfolio changes because of interest rate movement and deterioration of default risk.

Finally, there are also different types of interest rate derivatives. In this segment, interest rate floors are used to illustrate the accounting for hedging cash flow risk of floating rate debt that is held in the AFS marketable securities. An interest rate floor has periodic (sequential) settlements and is, therefore, treated as a sequence of European put options. To highlight the accounting treatment options pricing models were not used and present values were calculated using a simplified method.

## Notes

1 www.isda.org

2 I use the word "viewed" on purpose because there is no risk-free hedge; hedging one type of risk exposes the enterprise to another.

3 Available at: http://www.bis.org/statistics/otcder/dt1920a.pdf. Although not all countries were included in the report; only in 2011, Australia and Spain began reporting to BIS estimates of the derivative activities within their sovereign regions.

4 This point is belabored because it is often missed and numerous students continue to have issues with this substitution notion.

5 Normally, coupon payments are made more frequently. The principle applied is the same whether it is annual or quarterly. Using annual payments simplifies the calculation and reduces the number of periods used for analysis.

6 LIBOR is the benchmark interest rate, which is one of two rates that were permitted under ASC 815 for an interest rate swap to qualify for hedge accounting. However, on July 17, 2013, the FASB issued an Accounting Standards Update 2013-10 adding Overnight Index Swap Rates (OIS). The other rate is the U.S. Treasury Rate.

7 There are swap contracts with positive present value at inception, but it is not the norm. *On July 17, 2013, the FASB added OIS for all transactions entered into on or after July 17. This addition is made by the following amendment*:

**815-20-25-6A** In the United States, currently only the interest rates on direct Treasury obligations of the U.S. government and, for practical reasons, the London Interbank Offered Rate (LIBOR) swap rate and the **Fed Funds Effective Swap Rate** (also referred to as the Overnight Index Swap Rate) are considered to be benchmark interest rates. In each financial market, generally only the one or two most widely used and quoted rates that meet these criteria may be considered benchmark interest rates. The Fed Funds rate, the Prime rate, the Federal National Mortgage Association (FNMA or Fannie Mae) Par Mortgage rate, and the Securities Industry and Financial Markets Association Municipal 5 Swap Index (formerly called the Bond Market Association index) shall not be used as the benchmark interest rate in the United States. See, FASB ASU 2013-10. The accounting treatment of these types of contracts is discussed later on in this chapter.

8 Prepayment risk is a function of both of these risks.

9 In real life, the documentation is very detailed and could be costly in terms of labor and processing.

10 More discussion on hedge effectiveness is in Chapter Six.

11 To be totally in compliance with the standards, we need to have the process applied for other *as if* scenarios such as a downward shift in the yield curve or shifts of different magnitudes. I will not bring in this additional analysis because the process is the same as the one presented above, it will only vary in numbers.

12 These names are arbitrary but they are used to highlight the accounting standards requirement to specifically identify the hedge designation in documentation and in performing various related processes.

13 There are three possible forms the yield curve could take: (i) parallel, (ii) tilt (increasing in near term and decreasing in far term), and (iii) bend (increasing in near term and decreasing in far term). Typically, more than one scenario is required to properly carry out sensitivity analysis and examine hedge effectiveness under different scenarios. However, if one understands this scenario, constructing others would not be that difficult.

14 This $43,308 would be the fair value of the swap.

15 Interest expense should be accrued every reporting period. We used one year instead of quarterly in order to concentrate on the main issue, which is hedge accounting.

16 We assume that the change took place on day one to simplify the calculations, especially for prospective hedge effectiveness.

17 This provision is perhaps one of the most troublesome aspects of hedge accounting.

18 Normally, the rates are used for shorter periods because of quarterly reporting depending on the contract and the reset dates. For simplicity of calculation, we will use one year time.

19 The names of accounts used in this book are not intended to convey the exact names used in practice. Instead, the intent is to offer names that describe the related events.

20 http://www.bis.org/statistics/derstats.htm.

21 While the method of "hypothetical derivative" is accepted in both IFRS and US GAAP, it cannot be justified by theories or factors other than the desire to show derivatives as if they are highly effective hedges.

# CHAPTER 9

# HYBRID INSTRUMENTS AND EMBEDDED DERIVATIVES

## 9.1 Basic Features of Hybrids

A hybrid security is a financial instrument that has two or more components of the following features:

- Equity-like features that offer the holder residual interest or claim in the enterprise.
- Debt-like feature that establishes an obligation on the enterprise to transfer assets to the holder of the instrument.
- Derivatives that create rights (assets, equity) for the enterprise or obligations (debt) on the enterprise.

Examples of hybrids are convertible bonds or convertible preferred stocks that give the holder the right to convert the security into common stock. Several hybrid instruments with different features are discussed in this chapter before we begin the presentation of accounting for embedded derivatives.

An embedded derivative is a component feature in a hybrid instrument having four characteristics:

1. The hybrid instrument in its entirety is not a financial derivative.
2. The hybrid has a base (host) instrument, which is either a debt or an equity instrument.
3. The embedded feature component alters the risk and cash flow characteristics of the base instrument.
4. The embedded feature has the characteristics of a financial derivative (as defined in accounting and presented in Chapter 6).

Accounting standards refer to the base contract as the "host" contract that could be, for example, a debt or equity financial instrument, a purchase or sale contract, an insurance contract, or a lease contract. Exhibit 9.1 shows two examples: (a) a convertible bond consisting of a debt host instrument and a conversion option, and (b) a callable bond (or mandatorily redeemable preferred stocks) consisting of debt host instrument and a call option. Embedded derivatives are not limited to securities, however. For example, a purchase (or sale) contract giving one party to the agreement the right to terminate or change the terms of the contract under specified conditions is a hybrid security with an embedded option.

## Exhibit 9.1 The Composition of Hybrid Instruments

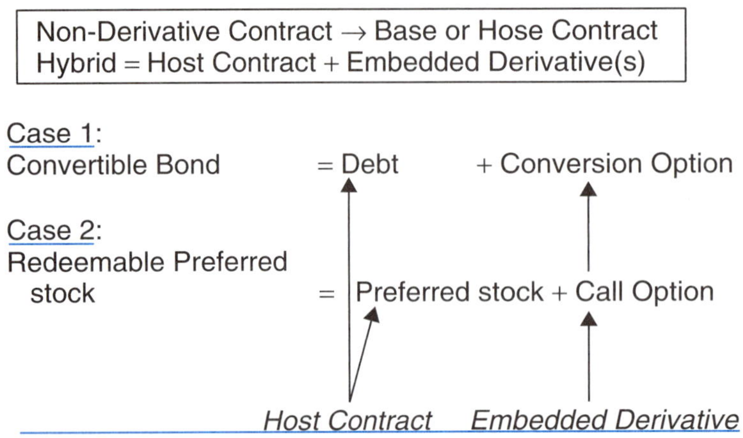


Financial contracts that include embedded derivatives can be used as a way of masking the derivatives' features and limiting the transparency about the enterprise's exposure to risk. For this reason, accounting standards (ASC 815 in U.S. GAAP and IAS 39 in IFRS) have developed a detailed process to account for embedded derivatives. The second segment of this chapter provides more discussion of this subject along the following outline:

- Embedded derivatives that are *not clearly and closely related* to the host contract (and that satisfy some other conditions to be discussed) should be bifurcated (separated) from the host contract and accounted for separately.
- For the embedded feature to be considered a financial derivative and be separated from the host contract, it must meet the (accounting) definitional characteristics of a derivative and would be classifiable as a derivative if it were freestanding.
- Bifurcated embedded derivatives should have the same accounting treatment as that of free-standing derivative instruments—i.e., to be valued at fair value with the changes in fair values flow through earnings periodically (at least every 90 days).
- The fair value of the embedded derivative is established at inception and the balance of the consideration given to the hybrid would be a measure of the fair value of the host contract.
- The host contract could be equity-like and classified as equity if the holder of the contract has residual claim or residual interest in the enterprise that has issued the contract.
- Other host contracts having potential claims on assets are classified as liabilities.[1]

## 9.2 Examples of Hybrid Securities

*Equity-Linked Securities* (*ELKS*) are a class of hybrid instruments that derive the changes in their values and risk either in full or in part from changes in the price of the enterprise's common equity shares.[2] Some examples of *ELKS* are described below.

### 9.2.1 Bonds with Detachable Warrants

This type of security is a single contract that could be physically separated into two components or instruments: (a) a host contract, which is the debt instrument for which there is a similar straight (plain vanilla) bond without optionality, and (b) detachable warrants that are option-like contracts to purchase common (or preferred) stock shares of the issuing enterprise at a specific (subscription or strike) price during a specific period.[3] Detachable warrants are often separated and traded independent of the host contract, although there is nothing that prevents the two parties to the contract from agreeing on different arrangements.

Although warrants are option-like instruments, they have longer maturities than options, are considered securities, could have a more frequent reset subscription (strike) price (such as step-up adjustment to provide warrant holders with incentives to purchase the stocks), and are traded over-the-counter as well as on stock exchanges.

Warrants to be exercised on the issuer's own equity are separate (not embedded) instruments that could be traded independent of the main or host contract (the debt) unless the terms of the contract state otherwise. These two instruments, the bond and the warrant, have different generators of risk and value: interest rate is the underlying for the debt, while stock price is the underlying for the warrant. Having different drivers of value and risk means that the debt host instrument is accounted for as a liability, but the warrants may or may not be accounted for as equity depending on other terms of the contract. As discussed in Chapter Five, these detachable warrants are valued as freestanding options.

The intrinsic value of the warrant is

$$W_d = \text{Max}\{0, \text{N} * (P_s - X)\}$$

where

$W_d$ = the intrinsic value of a detachable warrant.
$N$ = the number of shares to which a warrant entitles the owner.
$P_s$ = the price of the stock.
$X$ = the subscription or exercise price of the warrant.

The value of the warrant could be estimated by one of the option pricing models (such as Cox-Ross-Rubinstein Binomial or Black-Scholes Model). The market price of a warrant could be higher than the intrinsic value because of the time value of the warrant, which is a function of the remaining time to expiration.

## Summary Note

- Detachable warrants are freestanding derivative securities.
- Being option-like, warrants derive their values from changes in stock prices.
- Bonds derive changes in their values from changes in interest rate, the issuer's credit risk, settlement value, and prepayment risk (as well as currency risk if they are denominated in different currencies).
- There is no embedded derivative in a bond contract issued with detachable warrants.

### 9.2.2 Bonds with Non-Detachable Warrants

A warrant attached to a bond is a non-detachable option to purchase common or preferred stock and is embedded so that it could not be separated or traded independent of the host contract. Investors in bonds with non-detachable warrants have the right to purchase common (or preferred) equity shares at a strike price stated in the contract and at a particular time or during a specified period. Exercising these warrants differs from the conversion of convertible bonds because investors in bonds with non-detachable warrants may continue to hold their bond instruments as investments after exercising the warrants. If bondholders must surrender the bonds to exercise the warrants, then the contract is essentially similar to a convertible bond.

Before exercising the warrants, the value of the hybrid should be greater than the value of an option-free bond with similar terms issued by an entity having the same risk class. That is,

*Value of a Bond with a Warrant = Value of Bond + the Option Value of Warrant*

If the hybrid is traded in an active market, the market price provides a reliable measure of the fair value of the combined instrument. The proceeds collected from issuing the hybrid could be partitioned into its components according to one of three processes:

1. Estimating the fair value of the warrant using an option pricing model (such as the Binomial or Black-Scholes Model).
2. Estimating the fair value of the option as the difference between the proceeds received from issuing the hybrid and the fair value of the host instrument.
3. A process that follows two steps:[4]

   - Estimate the fair value of the host (debt) contract and the fair value of the embedded derivative.
   - Partition or allocate the proceeds collected from issuing the hybrid to the host (bond) and to the embedded derivative in proportion to the relative fair value of each.

#### Information Log: Bonds with Non-Detachable Warrants

*The Host Contract*: Debt instrument.
*The Host Contract Value Driver*: Interest rate, credit risk of the issuer, and settlement value.
*Embedded Derivative*: Call option sold by the issuer and held by the investor.
*The Value Driver of the Derivative*: Stock price.

### 9.2.3 Convertible Bonds

A convertible bond is a hybrid security that combines a standard corporate bond (a host contract) with an embedded option allowing the holder of the hybrid to convert the bond into common (or preferred) stock shares. The number of common equity shares to which a single bond could be converted is called the *conversion ratio*, which may or may not be a fixed number stated in the contract.[5] The bond component of the hybrid is the host instrument and the conversion option is the embedded derivative. Investors in convertible bonds are protected from downside risk by a boundary or a floor equal to the value of the straight bond component.

If conversion is at the election of the investor (holder), the right to convert the debt into stock is an embedded call option written (sold) by the issuer of the debt (the borrower) and could be held by the bondholder (the investor).[6] In the general case where investors (debtholders) also hold the call option to convert the bond into common stock, investors are also acquiring a privilege for which there is a price or a premium. This price is paid in the form of an adjustment to coupon rate. In particular, convertible bonds have lower yield than the yield on an equivalent non-convertible bond (of the same risk class) because the bondholder is compensated for the difference in yield by owning an option to convert the debt into common equity shares.[7]

Convertible bonds offer benefits to both sides of the contract. Investors benefit by having diversified-risk in one instrument because changes in equity markets do not affect convertible bonds as much as they impact stocks, and changes in debt markets do not affect convertible bonds as much as they affect straight debt instruments. In addition, convertible bonds facilitate reducing information asymmetry between the issuer and investors. Finally these instruments offer investors assured steady investment income while retaining the option to become shareholders.

Issuers of convertible bonds have other types of benefits. They could obtain lower financing cost than issuing stock when stock prices are highly volatile and lower financing cost than the cost of straight debt because the conversion feature reduces the sensitivity of convertible bonds to issuers' risk. Additionally, issuing convertible bonds allows the management to access capital markets to finance risky projects. Once projects show promise of success, the issuers could force the conversion into equity. Finally, convertible bonds provide investors with the flexibility of managing their debt capacity and their debt-to-equity ratio in terms of: (a) managing compliance with debt covenants, (b) reducing fixed-charge ratio (income to recurrent fixed charges), and (c) managing the issuers' own liquidity and credit risk.

Bonds with a conversion option have two underlyings (i.e., two value and risk generators): interest rate for the host contract, and stock price for the conversion feature. Accordingly, the intrinsic value of the conversion option increases with the increase in stock price and the option would be in-the-money if the value of the hybrid is higher than the value of a straight bond. Similarly, the value of the conversion feature declines with the decline in the value of the stock but, as is the case with call options, this decline is bounded from below at zero (intrinsic value of the conversion call option could not be negative).

Measuring *conversion value* as the spot price of common stock times the conversion ratio, the option would be: (i) *in-the-money* if the conversion value is greater than the value of an option-free bond; (ii) *out-of-the-money* if the conversion value is below the price of an option-free bond; or (iii) *at-the-money* if the conversion value equals the value of an option-free bond.

When the conversion option is out-of-the-money, the hybrid bond would be more debt-like (a substitute for straight debt) and the holders of convertible bonds would be subject to both interest rate risk and the issuer's credit risk. When the conversion option is in-the-money, the hybrid would be more equity-like because the value and risk generators in this region are driven by the change in stock prices. Therefore, convertible bonds in this region would be subject to equity market risk (i.e., volatility of the issuer's common share prices).

The option value is a function of stock price and the premium of the conversion option is always non-negative because a convertible bond must be worth at least as much as the straight bond alone. Because the *convertible bond price* could not fall below *bond investment value*, the latter is also known as the *convertible bond price floor*.

## Summary Note

In a convertible bond, the following definitions hold:

- *Host contract* is the debt instrument
- *Embedded derivative* is a call option.
- *Convertible price*: Fair value of the convertible bond as a hybrid.
- *Bond value* (or *bond floor*): The price of a plain vanilla bond (an option-free bond with otherwise similar features).
- *Conversion ratio*: the number of common shares exchangeable for one bond.
- *Conversion* (*strike*) *price*: face value of the bond/conversion ratio.
- *Conversion value*: current common share price * conversion ratio.
- *Conversion premium* ($): convertible price – conversion value.
- *Conversion premium* (%): [convertible price/conversion value] – 1.

### 9.2.4 Callable and Puttable Debt

Bonds may be redeemed or retired prior to their stated maturity if they are callable or puttable. A bond is callable if early redemption is at the option of the issuer (the debtor), and is puttable if early redemption is at the option of the investor (the bondholder).

A callable bond is a compound security consisting of a host contract (debt) and an embedded feature granting the issuer the right to redeem or retire the bond before maturity under some conditions. The yield on a callable bond is higher than the yield on a similar straight bond; the price at which an issuer would sell a callable bond in the marketplace is lower than the price of a similar straight bond (bond without optionality) because the issuer pays investors (bondholders) a price for holding the right to redeem the bond before maturity.

The debt issuer may call the bond for redemption when the conditions are favorable to them, which could be caused by one or more of the following states:

- A fall in the market rate of interest that would permit the issuer to refinance the debt at a lower interest rate—i.e., to refund the bond.
- The issuer's need to navigate out of a binding debt covenant.
- The need to rearrange the capital structure of the enterprise.

The terms of this type of contract typically specify a protection or lockout period during which the issuer may not call the bond for redemption. Outside that period, the debt may be called according to any one of many schemes such as calling the debt on any date before maturity (e.g., an *American-style option*), on the date of interest payment (*Bermudian or Bermudan option*), or at a pre-specified date only (a *European-style option*).

The terms of a callable bond contract also offer different types of early bond retirement choices:

- *Optional redemption* in which the call is made at the election of the issuer given the conditions stipulated in the contract. These terms include the call period, the protection period, the call price, and a provision that accruing or paying interest will cease upon making the call (this latter provision is necessary in order to force the investor to accept retiring the debt early).
- *Event-driven redemption* that allows the issuer to call the bond if a particular and pre-specified event takes place.

- *Sinking fund redemption*, which requires the issuer to set aside installments for gradual retirement of the bond. The requirement to set up a sinking fund for redeeming the bond before maturity may be stated explicitly in the contract or may be the result of another loan covenant stipulated in the loan contract.

Exhibit 9.2 provides an illustration using the 2011 *Prospectus* filing by *Time Warner Cable, Inc.* in conjunction with a $2.25 billion debt offering. This disclosure presents the terms of the contract:

a. A statement of the call period.
b. A statement describing the method of estimating the present value of the called bonds.
c. The nature of the interest rate to be used in calculating accrued interest upon calling the debt.
d. The provision that interest payment will cease upon making the call.

## Exhibit 9.2 Embedded Options—Callable Bonds Case of Time Warner Cable, Inc. Public Offering Prospectus on 9/8/2011

**Optional Redemption**

Unless we specify otherwise in the applicable prospectus supplement, we may redeem any of the debt securities as a whole at any time or in part from time to time, at our option, on at least 30 days, but not more than 60 days, prior notice mailed to the registered address of each Holder of the debt securities to be redeemed, at respective redemption prices equal to the greater of:

- 100% of the principal amount of the debt securities to be redeemed, and
- the sum of the present values of the Remaining Scheduled Payments, as defined below, discounted to the redemption date, on a semi-annual basis, assuming a 360 day year consisting of twelve 30 day months, at the Treasury Rate, as defined below, plus the number, if any, of basis points specified in the applicable prospectus supplement; plus, in each case, accrued interest to the date of redemption that has not been paid (such redemption price, the "Redemption Price").

*"Comparable Treasury Issue"* means, with respect to the debt securities, the United States Treasury security selected by an Independent Investment Banker as having a maturity comparable to the remaining term ("Remaining Life") of the debt securities being redeemed that would be utilized, at the time of selection and in accordance with customary financial practice, in pricing new issues of corporate debt securities of comparable maturity to the Remaining Life of such debt securities.

*"Comparable Treasury Price"* means, with respect to any redemption date for the debt securities: (1) the average of two Reference Treasury Dealer Quotations for that redemption date, after excluding the highest and lowest of such Reference Treasury Dealer Quotations; or (2) if the Trustee obtains fewer than four Reference Treasury Dealer Quotations, the average of all quotations obtained by the Trustee.

*"Independent Investment Banker"* means one of the Reference Treasury Dealers, to be appointed by us.

*"Reference Treasury Dealer"* means four primary U.S. Government securities dealers to be selected by us.

*"Reference Treasury Dealer Quotations"* means … [Details omitted].

*"Remaining Scheduled Payments"* means … [Details omitted].

> "*Treasury Rate*" means, with respect to any redemption date for the debt securities: (1) the yield, under the heading which represents the average for the immediately preceding week, appearing in the most recently published statistical release designated "H.15(519)" or any successor publication which is published weekly by the Board of Governors of the Federal Reserve System and which establishes yields on actively traded United States Treasury debt securities adjusted to constant maturity under the caption "Treasury Constant Maturities," for the maturity corresponding to the Comparable Treasury Issue; provided that if no maturity is within three months before or after the maturity date for the debt securities, yields for the two published maturities most closely corresponding to the Comparable Treasury Issue will be determined and the Treasury Rate will be interpolated or extrapolated from those yields on a straight line basis, rounding to the nearest month; or (2) if that release, or any successor release, is not published during the week preceding the calculation date or does not contain such yields, the rate per annum equal to the semiannual equivalent yield to maturity of the Comparable Treasury Issue, calculated using a price for the Comparable Treasury Issue (expressed as a percentage of its principal amount) equal to the Comparable Treasury Price for that redemption date. The Treasury Rate will be calculated on the third business day preceding the redemption date.
>
> On and after the redemption date, interest will cease to accrue on the debt securities or any portion thereof called for redemption, unless we default in the payment of the Redemption Price, and accrued interest. On or before the redemption date, we shall deposit with a paying agent, or the applicable Trustee, money sufficient to pay the Redemption Price of and accrued interest on the debt securities to be redeemed on such date. If we elect to redeem less than all of the debt securities of a series, then the Trustee will select the particular debt securities of such series to be redeemed in a manner it deems appropriate and fair.
>
> *Source*: Time Warner SEC filing. Time Warner Cable. Filing 424B5 on September 8, 2011. http://www.sec.gov/Archives/edgar/data/893657/000095012311083334/g27997b5e424b5.htm

### 9.2.5 Convertible Callable and Puttable Bonds

A *callable convertible* bond is a contract with a conversion feature that also gives the issuer the right to redeem the bond prior to maturity at a pre-specified price. By including the call provision, the issuer does not give investors full discretion over the timing of conversion. Bondholders would voluntarily convert a bond into common stock only if it is to their benefit—e.g., if the stock is expected to earn a higher rate of return than the bond. However, including a provision permitting the issuer to call the bond for redemption enables the issuer to force investors to convert bonds into common shares when it is to the benefit of the issuer.

Upon calling the bonds for redemption before maturity, investors in callable convertible bonds have to make a choice between two actions:

1. Redeeming the bonds and receiving the call price.
2. Converting the bonds and receiving common equity shares.

A conflict of interest between the entity issuing the callable convertibles and investors could develop when interest rates fall below the coupon rate on the bond. In this case, it would not be advantageous for investors to take on the investment risk by accepting to retire the bonds before maturity and investing the proceeds at interest rates below what they currently earn. In the meantime, it is to the benefit of the issuer to call the bonds for redemption because the issuer could retire the bonds and refund them from the marketplace at lower coupon rates. Because neither party would want to assume the investment risk, investors would prefer converting the bonds into common stock in the event of falling interest rates and when the issuer calls the bonds for redemption.

The reverse occurs when interest rates increase, if investors did not act, they would bear all investment risk. It is therefore anticipated that they would put the bonds back to the issuer and reinvest the proceeds at the higher interest rate, which incentivizes the issuer to convert the bonds (if the bonds are both puttable and convertible, the conversion is more likely to be at the election of the issuer).

In effect, the puttable convertible bond essentially places the conversion decision in the hands of the issuer, while the callable convertible bond places the conversion decision in the hands of investors. But there are other defense mechanisms that investors in callable convertible bonds (or callable convertible preferred stock) may use to reduce the possible adverse impact of redeeming convertible bonds when it is not to their advantage. One of those defenses is stating in the bond indenture the type of "call" the issuer could make, which could be one of three types:

1. *A soft call*: A requirement that the change in the stock price be above a pre-specified trigger level, say 20% for example.
2. *A hard call*: A prohibition on initiating the call during the early life of the contract (the lockout period would be specified in the contract).
3. *A Parisian-type call*: Requiring the call for redemption to be initiated when the stock price falls within a stated range and remains in that range for a certain period of time.[8]

## Valuation

The early redemption call feature is a *call option* held by the issuer of a callable convertible bond for which the issuer pays a price by offering a higher yield than the yield offered by a similar (risk sector) option-free bond. The interest rate is the underlying (i.e., the value and risk generator) for this call option.

These features result in the following relationship of values:

*Value of Callable Convertible Bond = Value of Convertible – Call Option*

$$VB_{call,\,conv} = VB_{conv} - OP_{call}$$
$$= VB + O_{conv} - OP_{call}$$

where

| | |
|---|---|
| $VB$ | = value of plain vanilla bond or the bond floor. |
| $VB_{call,\,conv}$ | = value of the callable convertible bond. |
| $VB_{conv}$ | = value of the convertible bond. |
| $OP_{call}$ | = value of the redemption call option. |
| $OP_{conv}$ | = value of the conversion option. |

$VB_{conv}$ is higher than the value of a similar plain vanilla bond if, as in the general case, the conversion is at the option of investors (holders).

$VB_{conv}$ is lower than the value of a similar plain vanilla bond if the conversion is at the option of the issuer (borrower).

Investors in puttable convertible bonds (creditors/bondholders) have the right to sell the bonds back to the issuer before maturity according to terms pre-specified in the bond indenture. The put option provides an advantage to the holder (the investor) when market interest rates rise because investors could put the bonds back to the issuer for redemption and reinvest the proceeds at interest rates higher than the coupon rate on the bond. However, bondholders could also use the put option to force the issuer to convert the bonds into common shares. The investor pays a price for the put option by paying a premium to the issuer or by accepting a lower yield.

*Value of Puttable Convertible Bond = Value of Convertible + Put Option*

$$VB_{put,\ conv} = VB_{conv} + OP_{put}$$

where

$VB_{put,\ conv}$ = the value of the putttable convertible bond.
$VB_{conv}$ = the value of the convertible bond.
$OP_{put}$ = the value of the put option.

$VB_{conv}$ is higher than the value of a similar plain vanilla bond if, as in the general case, the conversion is at the option of investors (holders).

$VB_{conv}$ is lower than the value of a similar plain vanilla bond if the conversion is at the option of the issuer (borrower).

The characteristics of adding the put or call feature to a convertible bond are summarized in Exhibit 9.3.

## Exhibit 9.3 Characteristics of Adding a Put or a Call Option to Convertible Securities

| *Other option added to conversion →* | *+ Call* | *+ Put* |
|---|---|---|
| Who is the writer of the added option? | The investor (bondholder) | The issuer (debtor) |
| Who has the right to exercise the added option? | The issuer (debtor) | The investor (bondholder) |
| What is the objective of the added option? | To force conversion when it is more profitable to the issuer | To force conversion when it is more profitable to the investor |
| What is the impact of the added option feature on the value of the convertible bond? | Decreases the fair value of the hybrid (higher yield) | Increases the fair value of the hybrid (lower yield) |

## Summary Note

**Callable Bonds:**

| | |
|---|---|
| *Host instrument*: | Debt |
| *Embedded derivative*: | Call option, written by the investor, held by the issuer. |
| *Valuation*: | Value of Debt – Value of Call Option |

**Convertible Callable Bonds**

| | |
|---|---|
| *Host instrument*: | Debt |
| *Embedded derivatives*: | Call option, written by the investor, held by the issuer.<br>Conversion option, written by issuer, held by the investor |
| *Valuation*: | Value of Debt – Value of Call Option + Value of Conversion Option |

**Puttable Bonds:**

| | |
|---|---|
| *Host instrument*: | Debt |
| *Embedded Derivative*: | Put Option, written by the issuer, held by the investor. |
| *Valuation*: | Value of Debt + Value of Put Option |

**Convertible-Puttable Bonds:**

| | |
|---|---|
| *Host instrument*: | Debt |
| *Embedded Derivatives*: | Put option, written by the issuer, held by the investor.<br>Conversion option, written by issuer, held by the investor. |
| *Valuation*: | Value of Debt + Value of Put Option + Value of Conversion Option |

### 9.2.6 Debt Exchangeable for Common Stock (DECS)[9]

*DECS* is a form of mandatorily convertible debt contracts that are indexed either to the issuer's own share prices or to the share prices of a third party that are held in the issuer's portfolio of available-for-sale securities. One form of those types of instruments is a bond that is convertible into common equity shares at the option of the issuer and according to different rules for sharing in equity price changes, depending on the nature of changes in price. These types of instruments are also called mandatorily convertible bonds (see the example of *Deutsche Telekom* below) and have several unique features:

- The issuer collects the principal (generally the face value).
- The issuer pays interest based at a stated coupon rate.
- At maturity, the principal is not repaid to the investor.
- Instead, at maturity, the bond is converted into common equity shares.
- Conversion has two boundary strike prices, depending on the behavior of stock prices to which the conversion feature is indexed in relationship to the investment in the instrument: a lower strike price and an upper strike price.
- The magnitude of the conversion ratio depends on changes in stock prices. There are three types of conversion ratios at three different states of price changes: stable (below the lower strike price), declining (between upper and lower strike prices), and increasing or stable (above the upper strike price, this level may or may not be the same as the stable level below the lower strike prices).

- As a result, this type of mandatorily convertible bonds has three levels of payoff representing three different conversion ratios:

  1. *Declining payoff zone*: Full 100% participation below the lower strike price—i.e., the downside risk (this zone has a stable conversion ratio).
  2. *Stable payoff zone*: This is the region between lower and upper strike prices. In this zone, the conversion value is equal to the issue price, even though the underlying price of the stock is increasing (this zone reflects a declining conversion ratio).
  3. *Increasing payoff zone*: This is the upside of the stock—the region in which the stock price increases above the upper strike price. Conversion will be at fractional participation in share prices, say for example 75%, reflecting less than full participation in the stock price upside (this zone has a stable conversion ratio, but at a lower level than the average conversion ratio in the declining conversion zone).

---

The three levels of participation have three payoff values that Arzac (1979) has described as follows:[10]

$$V_m = S_m * CR_L \quad \text{if } S_m \leq X_L$$
$$V_m = S_m * CR_B \quad \text{if } X_L < S_m < X_U$$
$$V_m = S_m * CR_U \quad \text{if } S_m \geq X_U$$

Where

$V_m$ = value at maturity.
$S_m$ = stock price at maturity.
$CR_B$ = conversion ratio between the lower and upper strike prices.
$CR_L$ = conversion ratio at the lower strike price.
$CR_U$ = conversion ratio at the upper strike price.
$X_L$ = the lower strike price.
$X_U$ = the upper strike price.

---

Typically, these bonds are issued at-the-money representing the lower strike price. Between that level and the upper strike price, the conversion ratio will be changing such that the value of the common shares to be acquired remains stable and equal to the issuance price of the bond. When prices deviate from the stable conversion value (i.e., declining conversion ratio), bonds will have 100% participation in falling prices and below 100% participation in rising prices.

Figure 9.1 presents the general shape of the payoff function of this particular type of mandatorily convertible instrument which is known as *DECS* (Debt Exchangeable for Common Stock, or Dividend Enhanced Convertible Securities). This figure shows that the slope of the payoff function in the zone of declining prices is equal to one (full participation), while the slope of the payoff functions for the upside risk is less than one. Enterprises may issue debt that is exchangeable for their own common stock or for the common stock of a third party that is being held as investment in the marketable securities portfolio.

An illustration of *DECS* that are issued by companies on their own common stock is the case of *Deutsche Telekom*, which issued *DECS* under the description of "Guaranteed Mandatory

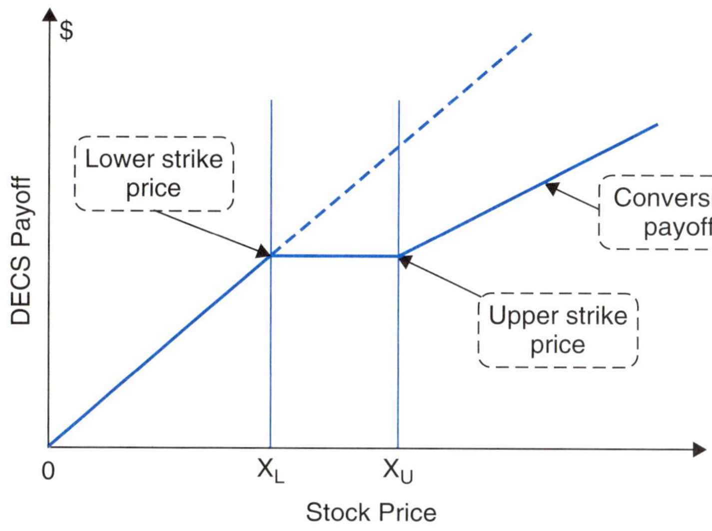


**Figure 9.1** A Typical Payoff Profile of Debt Exchangeable for Common Stock

Convertible Bonds." The difference between the bonds sold by *Deutsche Telekom* (Exhibit 9.4) and other forms of mandatorily convertible bonds is the risk exposure and payoff structure which is exactly the structure of *DECS* described in Figure 9.1.

## Information Note

| | |
|---|---|
| *Instrument*: | *DECS* (Debt Exchangeable for Common Stock) |
| *Host Contract*: | Long stock (at lower strike price). |
| *Embedded derivatives*: | Long and out-of-the-money call option.<br>Short and at-the-money put option |
| *Nature*: | A compound instrument having at least two embedded derivatives. |
| *Valuation of DECS*: | By replicating portfolio |
| *Fair value* = | The value of a call with upper strike price times the upper conversion ratio<br>– value of a put with lower strike price times the lower rate<br>+ present value of the risk-free par value<br>+ present value of the risk coupon payments. |

(Source: Arzac, 1997; Ammann and Seiz, 2006)

To provide a real-life illustration, Exhibit 9.4 presents excerpts from the 2003 prospectus filed by *Deutsche Telekom AG* concerning a June 2006 scheduled conversion of €2,288,500,000 debt (6.5% Guaranteed Mandatory Convertible Bonds) into common stock.[11] It is crucial to note that the Prospectus specifies the three different levels of conversion ratios corresponding to three exercise states: maximum (for upper strike), minimum (for the lower strike) and medium (for the region between the upper and lower strike prices). In its financial statements, *Deutsche Telekom AG* reports this transaction on the balance sheet as *contingent capital*, which is a mezzanine category similar to the *temporary capital* classification in the U.S. GAAP.[12]

## Exhibit 9.4 *Deutsche Telekom AG* Issuance of Debt Exchangeable for Common Stock (*DECS*)

**€2,288,500,000 6½% Guaranteed Mandatory Convertible Bonds Due 2006**

The Guaranteed Mandatory Convertible Bonds due 2006 (the "Bonds") shall be mandatorily converted into ordinary registered shares of Deutsche Telekom AG on June 1, 2006.
*Principal Amount* is €50,000
*Initial Share Price* means €11.80
*Conversion Price* means €14.632
*Closing Price* means, on any date of determination, the closing auction price of the Shares in Deutsche Börse AG.
*Maturity Share Price* means the arithmetic average of the daily Closing Prices of the Shares on the twenty consecutive Trading Days ending on the third Trading Day immediately preceding the Final Conversion Date rounded to the nearest full cent, with 0.005 being rounded upwards.

Unless previously (voluntarily) converted, each Bond outstanding on the *Final Conversion Date*, June 1, 2006 shall be mandatorily converted into ordinary registered shares in Deutsche Telekom AG with a notional par value of € 2.56 each (the*"Shares"*) at the *Mandatory Conversion Ratio* of (a), (b), or (c).

*Maximum Conversion Ratio*: If the Maturity Share Price (as defined below) is less than or equal to the Initial Share Price the conversion ratio shall be equal to 4,237.2881

*Minimum Conversion Ratio*: If the Maturity Share Price (as defined below) is equal to or greater than the Conversion Price, the conversion ratio shall be equal to 3,417.1679 (Principal Amount divided by the Conversion Price).

*Medium Conversion Ratio*: If the Maturity Share Price (as defined below) is neither less than or equal to the Initial Share Price nor equal to or greater than the Conversion Price the conversion ratio shall be equal to the Principal Amount divided by the Maturity Share Price.

(Source: Adapted from *Deutsche Telekom AG* Bonn, Federal Republic of Germany as Guarantor for the Bonds issued by *Deutsche Telekom International Finance B.V.* Amsterdam, The Netherlands, pp. 119–121. Available at www.telekom.com/static/-/54298/3/mandatory-convertible-bond -2006-si

### 9.2.6.1 *Conversion Ratios Implied by* DECS

As noted above, the conversion ratios implicit in *DECS* are not stationary and take on, at least, three levels:

1. A constant conversion ratio when stock prices are below the lower strike price at some level. Call this "the high conversion level."

2. A declining conversion ratio when stock prices are in the region between the lower and upper strike prices.
3. A constant conversion ratio when stock prices are above the upper strike price, but at a lower level than the "high level" or the "mid-range level" of the preceding two segments. Call this "the lower level."

## Accounting Log

The accounting section of this chapter below presents a criterion called "fixed-for-fixed" exchange or conversion. The fixed-for-fixed rule requires that a conversion to common equity would qualify for equity classification if: (a) it requires exchanging a fixed amount for a fixed number of common shares, and (b) it would be classified in common stockholders' equity if it were freestanding.

The varying conversion ratios of *DECS* instruments do not satisfy the first condition. More is discussed later in this chapter.

### *9.2.6.2 Conversion Ratios for Deutsche Telekom AG*

From the information disclosed in the Prospectus, we could outline the important features and relate them to the graph of *DECS* in Figure 9.2.

- The lower strike price is €11.80.
- The upper strike price is €14.632.
- The face value of the Notes is €50,000.00.
- The three conversion ratios are:

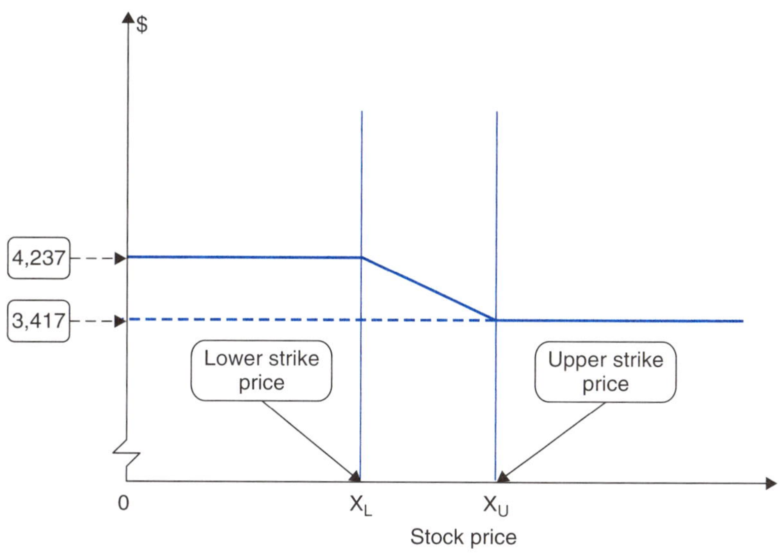


**Figure 9.2** The Varying Conversion Ratios of the *Deutsche Telekom AG* Issue Debt Exchangeable for Common Stock ( *DECS*)

1. High-level conversion ratio is 4,237.2881 common shares per note.
2. Low-level conversion ratio is 3,417.1679 common shares per note.
3. Medium-level conversion ratio is declining between 4,237.2881 and 3,417.1679 with an average of 3,827.228.

Figure 9.2 shows the behavior of the conversion ratio over the three regions. Because the conversion ratio is unlike the payoff profile shown in Figure 9.1, it is sometimes referred to as the "mysterious conversion ratio."

### 9.2.7 Equity-Linked Notes

An equity-linked note (*ELN*) combines the risk and return characteristics of (a) a debt instrument and (b) an equity-like option linked to the performance of common stock prices or to another reference asset. Regardless of the structure that *ELN* takes, these types of instruments are generally unsecured debt securities that provide investors with the potential of earning significantly high yields. *ELN* are also called "structured notes" because the terms of these notes are customized and could take many forms and combinations.

The first two structured notes presented in Table 9.1, for example, show the following features:

- The investor is guaranteed redemption of 100% of the principal at a future date as specified in the contract.
- No interest payment is made until maturity.
- For the first note, the payoff is structured on the basis of increases in the issuer's common equity stock price.
- For the second note, the payoff is based on increases in the S&P 500 index.

Each of the two cases presented in Table 9.1 combines a zero-coupon bond (debt) and a call option whose value depends on the movement of the issuer's own equity price in the first note,

**Table 9.1** Two Examples of Structured Equity-Linked Notes

*Panel A: Notes linked to own equity performance* (Face Value = $1,000)

| *Change in Sock price* | *ELN Participation* | *ELN Payoff at Maturity* |
|---|---|---|
| Above 60% | 40% | $1,000 + $1,000*0.40 = $1,400 |
| 40% | 25% | $1,000 + $1,000*0.25 = $1,250 |
| 25% | 12% | $1,000 + $1,000*0.12 = $1,112 |
| < 25% | 0 | $1,000 |
| Below zero | 0 | $1,000 |

*Panel B: Notes linked to an External Reference Index* (Face Value = $1,000)

| *Change in S & P 500* | *ELN Participation* | *ELN Payoff at Maturity* |
|---|---|---|
| Above 25% | 40% | $1,000 + $1,000*0.40 = $1,400 |
| Above 10% | 5% | $1,000 + $1,000*0.5 = $1,050 |
| < 10% | 0 | $1,000 |

and on an external market reference in the second note. For the issuer, the embedded option in the first note is equity-like (assuming no other contingencies) but it is not accounted for as equity because it involves cash payment to settle and is therefore an obligation.[13] The embedded option in the second note is debt-like and will be accounted for as debt. (There is more about accounting treatments in the second half of this chapter.)

In both cases, the investor participates in the upside risk but is protected on the downside by having a "floor" value equal to the principal. The payoff of this type of ELN is similar to the payoff of a plain vanilla option, except that the payoff function is increasing in piece-wise linear form.

### 9.2.8 Adjustable, Step-up, Callable Financial Instruments[14]

Step-up instruments may start at a fixed or floating rate and adjust the rate according to either pre-specified steps of rate increase or steps determined on the basis of some other reference index or criteria. In many cases, this type of debt is issued for investment income as in the case of adjustable rate debt issued by One Financial of Canada and guaranteed by BNP Paribas Bank.[15] Other issuers of these types of bonds or notes may have low credit ratings and offer the step-up feature to compensate investors for accepting higher credit risk and to encourage them to continue refinancing.[16]

Two examples could be presented to illustrate the step-up and adjustable features. The first is the case of *Aegon, N.V.* (presented in Exhibit 9.5), which issued preferred stock with an adjustable dividends rate staring at 4.00% or three-month LIBOR plus 0.875%, whichever is higher.[17]

The second illustration is the Variable Step-up Bonds ™ offered by *BNP Paribas S.A.* (Canada) through One Financial.[18] These bonds are structured as follows:

- The offer price is $100.00 and is fully redeemable at maturity.
- Maturity is seven years.
- Interest rates:
    - 3% guaranteed at inception, but increasing up to 8%.
    - In 4th year before maturity, rate could go up to 8%.
    - In 3rd year before maturity, rate could go up to 11%.
    - In 2nd year before maturity, rate could go up to 12%.
    - Last year before maturity, rate could go up to 13%.

Another type of step-up note, the level to which the rates are stepped up is linked to the return on a basket (portfolio) of stocks of 40 selected global corporations. Step-up bonds provide investors with the potential for a high rate of return while guaranteeing the principal if the bond is not called for early redemption.[19]

Valuation of step-up bonds is complex when the steps are tied to the performance of other instruments. However, the valuation of simple structured notes may not be that complicated. Consider, for example, a bond that has a face value of $10,000.00, a starting coupon rate of 4% per annum and a three-year maturity. The bond is sold at face value. The step-up agreement calls for increasing the coupon rate at every year end by 1.00%. Valuation of this bond could be measured as the sum of its elements of: (a) a three-year bond at a fixed rate of 4% per annum, (b) the present value of a two-year zero-coupon bond for a face value of $100.00, and (c) the present value of a three-year zero-coupon bond, which is $100.00 in this illustration.

Since the debt in this example is redeemable at face value, unless the Fair Value Option was adopted, the $10,000.00 bond is classified as debt and is valued at amortized cost according to ordinary GAAP.[20] The problem is whether or not to bifurcate the two embedded zero-coupon bonds. As we shall learn in the second part of this chapter, these instruments are clearly and closely related to the host contract and should not therefore be bifurcated. This question is addressed after presenting the criterion for bifurcation.

## 9.2.9 Preferred Stock

### *9.2.9.1 Types of Preferred Stocks*

Enterprises issue preferred stock securities to raise capital from investors who have a particular risk preference. Issuing conventional (plain vanilla) preferred stock aims at attracting funds from those investors who seek stable income but accept only a moderate risk. The income is in the form of preferred dividends, but preferred stockholders have liquidation preference over common shareholders and are, therefore, not residual claimants. The mix of features offered to investors in preferred stock has evolved to convey various rights:

- *Cumulative*: Unpaid dividends accumulate and become due when the level of earnings permits making a distribution.
- *Participative*: In addition to their own specified preferred stock dividends, preferred stockholders participate in the dividend distribution to common shareholders.

### *9.2.9.2 Derivatives Embedded in Preferred Stocks*

- *Convertible*: This provision grants preferred stockholders the right or option to convert their preference shares into common stock. Investors are presumed to hold the conversion option, but the terms of the contract might make this right contingent on the occurrence of events or on achieving specific benchmarks. In addition, it is possible to have contractual terms that give the issuer the right to make the call for conversion.
- *Redeemable (callable)*: If the preferred stock contract includes the possibility of redeeming and retiring preferred stock, the issuer is presumed to hold that option. In this case, the redeemable preferred stock is like callable preferred stock. However, the contract could stipulate that investors hold the option rights to call for redeeming preferred stock. Given this duality, a redeemable preferred stock is not necessarily equivalent to a callable preferred stock.
- *Mandatorily Redeemable*: In this contract, the issuer is under obligation to redeem preferred stock, and the investor is under obligation to accept. Typically, the issuer makes the call and, being mandatory, the issuer has an obligation, not a choice, to redeem preferred stock according to the terms of the contract.
- *Retractable (Puttable)*: This is a relatively less common type of preferred stock for which redemption is at the option of stockholder (not the issuer) according to the terms stated in the contract.
- *Perpetual Preferred Stock*: These are preference shares without maturity date or options to redeem them. Terms of preference in this case include dividends rights and renewing the stock under the same terms or under different agreed upon terms. Absent other options or conditions, the presumption is that perpetual preferred stock is similar to common stock in equity financing.

The various combinations of rights and obligations are common examples of what might lead to structuring contracts in relatively individualistic ways. For example, in April 2011, U.S. Bank Corporation floated $44 million of non-cumulative perpetual preferred stock that combines fixed and floating rates to determine preferred stock dividends.[21] The offer states "commencing on April 15, 2012, at a rate *per annum* equal to 6.500% from the date of issuance to, but excluding, January 15, 2022, and thereafter at a floating rate *per annum* equal to three-month LIBOR plus a spread of 4.468%."

Similarly, perpetual preferred stock contracts might include other features that negate the presumption of permanence. These features are about redemption, either voluntary or mandatory, and conversion. Two examples are the preferred stocks issued by *Aegon, N.V.* and *Xerox Corporation*. Exhibit 9.5 presents segments of disclosures by these two companies showing issuance of redeemable perpetual preferred stock by *Aegon, N.V.* and convertible perpetual preferred stock by *Xerox Corporation*.

## Exhibit 9.5 Examples of Perpetual Preferred Stock Issues

**Panel A**: *Aegon, N.V.*

Floating Rate *Perpetual Capital Securities*, liquidation preference $25 per share, *redeemable at the issuer's option* on or after 12/15/2010 at $25 per share plus accrued and unpaid dividends, with no stated maturity, and with floating rate distributions paid quarterly on 3/15, 6/15, 9/15 & 12/15 to holders of record on 3/1, 6/1, 9/1 & 12/1 respectively (*Note*: the ex-dividend date is at least 2 business days prior to the record date). The annual floating rate distributions will be reset quarterly and will be the greater of 4.00% or the three-month LIBOR plus 0.875%. In regards to payment of dividends and upon liquidation, the preferred shares rank equally with other preferreds and senior to the common shares of the company. See the IPO prospectus for further information on the preferred stock. [Emphasis added]

(Source: http://www.quantumonline.com/search.cfm?tickersymbol=AEB&sopt=symbol)

**Panel B**: *Xerox Disclosure*

**Note 18 – Preferred Stock**

**Series A Convertible Preferred Stock**

In connection with the acquisition of ACS in February 2010 (see Note 3—Acquisitions for additional information), we issued 300,000 shares of Series A convertible perpetual preferred stock with an aggregate liquidation preference of $300 and a fair value of $349 as of the acquisition date to the holder of ACS Class B common stock. The convertible preferred stock pays quarterly cash dividends at a rate of 8 percent per year and has a liquidation preference of $1,000 per share. Each share of convertible preferred stock is convertible at any time, at the option of the holder, into 89.8876 shares of common stock for a total of 26,966 thousand shares (reflecting an initial conversion price of approximately $11.125 per share of common stock and is a 25% premium over $8.90, the average closing price of Xerox common stock over the 7-trading day period ended on September 14, 2009 and the number used for calculating the conversion price in the ACS merger agreement), subject to customary antidilution adjustments. On or after the fifth anniversary of the issue date, we have the right to cause, under certain circumstances, any or all of the convertible preferred stock to be converted into shares of common stock at the then applicable conversion rate. The convertible preferred stock is also convertible, at the option of the holder, upon a change in control, at the applicable conversion rate plus an additional number of shares determined by reference to the price paid for our common stock upon such change in control. In addition, upon the occurrence of certain fundamental change events, including a change in control or the delisting of Xerox's common stock, the holder of convertible preferred stock has the right to require us to redeem any or all of the convertible preferred stock in cash at a redemption price per share equal to the liquidation preference and any accrued and unpaid dividends to, but not including the redemption date. The convertible preferred stock is classified as temporary equity (i.e., apart from permanent equity) as a result of the contingent redemption feature.

(Source: http://services.corporate-ir.net/SEC.Enhanced/SecCapsule.aspx?c=104414&fid=7398918 (Xerox Corporation page 97 of the Annual Report for 2010, note 8))

## 9.3 Accounting for Hybrid Instruments

### 9.3.1 The Challenge for Accounting

The preceding overview of hybrids aims at introducing basic forms of contractual features of hybrids and embedded derivatives that significantly impact accounting measurement and reporting. The nature of contractual terms and the economics of the contract determine the approach to accounting. This consideration has led to a world in which a contract having the form of legal ownership could be reported as a liability, while a contract having the legal form of obligations could be reported as equity. Accounting standards have evolved to account for contracts differently based on their risk exposure and economic substance. Furthermore, accounting for the rights and obligations created by these contracts from the points of view of the two parties to a contract is not always symmetrical. A contract could generate an obligation on one party but may not be considered an asset for the counterparty.

As far as compound contracts and hybrids are concerned, the challenge that accountants face in this respect involves several issues:

- Identification of each embedded derivative in a given contract or hybrid.
- Making assessment as to whether each component of the hybrid, the base (host) contract and the embedded derivatives, is debt or equity.
- Deciding on a valuation and measurement basis for each component.
- Evaluating the hedge relationship if any component of the hybrid is designated either as a hedge instrument or a hedged item.
- Evaluating and accounting for the impact of each of the above elements on earnings (the income statement) and the balance sheet.
- Understanding the types and forms of disclosure that would be most useful to external users in understanding:

  a. the risks facing the enterprise;
  b. the methods used and efforts expended by the management to manage and mitigate those risks; and
  c. the degree to which these methods and efforts are successful.

## 9.3.2 Definitions from Master Glossary of Accounting Standards Codification

A *financial instrument* is

Cash, evidence of an ownership interest in an entity, or a contract that both:

a. Imposes on one entity a contractual obligation either:
   1. To deliver cash or another financial instrument to a second entity.
   2. To exchange other financial instruments on potentially unfavorable terms with the second entity.
b. Conveys to that second entity a contractual right either:
   1. To receive cash or another financial instrument from the first entity.
   2. To exchange other financial instruments on potentially favorable terms with the first entity.

*Assets/Liabilities*

Contractual rights and contractual obligations encompass both those that are conditioned on the occurrence of a specified event and those that are not. All contractual rights (contractual obligations) that are financial instruments meet the definition of asset (liability) set forth in FASB Concepts Statement No. 6, Elements of Financial Statements, although some may not be recognized as assets (liabilities) in financial statements—that is, they may be off-balance-sheet—because they fail to meet some other criterion for recognition.

*Freestanding Financial Instrument*

A financial instrument that meets either of the following conditions:

It is entered into separately and apart from any of the entity's other financial instruments or equity transactions.
It is entered into in conjunction with some other transaction and is legally detachable and separately exercisable.

*Hybrid Instrument*

A contract that embodies both an embedded derivative and a host contract.

*Embedded Derivative*

Implicit or explicit terms that affect some or all of the cash flows or the value of other exchanges required by a contract in a manner similar to a derivative instrument.

815-10-15-83

A derivative instrument is a financial instrument or other contract with all of the following characteristics:

- Underlying, notional amount, payment provision. The contract has both of the following terms, which determine the amount of the settlement or settlements, and, in some cases, whether or not a settlement is required:

- One or more underlyings.
- One or more notional amounts or payment provisions or both.
- No initial net investment. The contract requires no initial net investment or an initial net investment that is smaller than would be required for other types of contracts that would be expected to have a similar response to changes in market factors.
- Settling net or equivalent. The contract can be settled net by any of the following means:

    - Its terms implicitly or explicitly require or permit net settlement.
    - It can readily be settled net by a means outside the contract.
    - It provides for delivery of an asset that puts the recipient in a position not substantially different from net settlement.

## 9.4 Three Building Blocks

The building blocks for accounting for freestanding instruments and embedded derivatives are:

1. *Distinction between Liability and Equity*: The decision on whether either the hybrid instrument in its entirety or the embedded derivative is debt or equity is based on contract terms and characteristics, not the form of the hybrid and its components (ASC 480).
2. *Bifurcating (Splitting) Hybrid Instruments*: If the hybrid and the embedded derivative are not considered either debt or equity under the criteria of ASC 480, a decision has to be made as to whether they fall within the scope of hedge accounting and whether the embedded derivative should be bifurcated and accounted for its components separately.
3. *Specific Exemption from Hedge Accounting*: The scope exceptions discussed here are:

    a. Contracts classified in their entirety as liabilities.
    b. Contracts that are equity derivatives.
    c. Extreme risk interest rate-linked derivatives.

### 9.4.1 Distinction between Liabilities and Equity

Accounting for hybrid instruments and embedded derivatives has two main building blocks with each block having multiple aspects.

The general concept underlying the distinction between debt and equity consists of two guides based on differences in sharing cash flow rights and bearing risk as well as whether the issuer or the investor has the discretion over decisions concerning these instruments.[22]

1. A liability exists if there is an obligation to transfer cash or other assets to a party external to the enterprise.
2. Equity exists if the counterparty has residual interest in the enterprise.

The conditions under which the financial instruments should be classified as liabilities are built around having *the obligation to transfer cash or other assets to external parties*. For example:

- The issuer has an unconditional obligation to redeem the instruments by transferring cash or other assets at a specified or determinable date, or upon the occurrence of an event not controlled by the issuer. This is the case for bonds, debt, payables and mandatorily redeemable preferred stock.
- The entity has an unconditional obligation to repurchase its equity shares and is required or may be required to settle such obligation by transferring assets. This is the case of *put options or forward contracts written by the issuer to repurchase its own shares and also the case of puttable stock, puttable warrants, or warrants that give the holder the right to purchase issuer's shares which are themselves puttable.*
- The entity is obligated to issue a variable number of equity shares having fair value equal to a fixed monetary amount specified in the contract. An example of this situation is when the contract obligates the enterprise to deliver shares for a stated amount or to deliver a number of shares that have a particular fair value when issued.
- The issuer is obligated to issue a variable number of equity shares based on an index other than the fair value of their own equity or the fair value of inverse floater such as, for example, debt instruments that pay a stated interest rate minus 50% of LIBOR.

The accounting standard on distinguishing between liabilities and equity (ASC 480-10-15-3) applies to any freestanding financial instrument or embedded derivative, including one that: (a) comprises more than one option or forward contract, or (b) having the characteristics of both liability and equity (and assets in some circumstances).[23] This particular standard applies to any contract such as warrants, convertible preferred stock, convertible debt, puttable stock, and mandatorily redeemable preferred stock.

## Accounting Log

- The fact that a financing contract takes the form of a debt instrument does not necessarily mean it will be accounted for as a liability. Similarly, instruments issued in the form of equity may not be accounted for as equity.
- The nature, not the form, of the instrument is the relevant criterion.
- The terms of the contract determine the nature of the instrument, the structure of the payoff, holders of the rights, and assignment of the obligations.

### *9.4.1.1 Specific Cases*

#### Case 1: Perpetual Preferred Stock

The shareholders of plain vanilla preferred stock have cash flow rights in the form of dividends. In the cases of non-cumulative preferred stock, the issuer is not under obligation to transfer cash to shareholders unless the income level permits the board of directors to declare dividends. The conditional nature of the cash flow rights of shareholders (a contingency under the control of the issuer) does not create unconditional obligations on the issuer and, as a result, this type of preferred stock is classified as equity.

This conclusion may not be applicable to perpetual preference shares. These are financial instruments that have no specified maturity and without options for redemption or conversion. It is therefore presumed that this type of preference shares will continue in perpetuity and that shareholders will have residual interest in the enterprise. However, dividends on perpetual preferred stock may be accounted for differently, depending on the terms of the contract. If the issuer is not obligated to pay dividends, preferred stock dividends would not then create an obligation on the entity and would not therefore be a liability. Instead, these dividends are distribution of profits in the same way as common stock dividends.

In contrast, cumulative preferred stock dividends create unconditional obligation on the issuer to transfer funds, which results in two accounting effects:

1. Preferred stock dividends are treated as interest expense.
2. The present value of expected dividend payments would be recognized as liability.

If the contract requires paying dividends in perpetuity, the present value of dividends might be equal to the entire fair value of preferred stock and the entire amount would therefore be recorded as a liability. Although this result might appear to be counterintuitive, it is a direct application of the standards (ASC 480 in the USA and IAS 32 in IFRS).

### Case 2: Redeemable Preferred Stock

Shareholders of plain vanilla preferred stock have cash flow rights in the form of dividends that obligate the issuer to pay. But the rights of shareholders and the obligations of the issuer are altered significantly if preferred stocks are redeemable, whether this feature is at the option of the issuer (callable) or at the option of the holder (puttable).

Accounting standards distinguish between two states:

1. The redemption is at the option of the holder (the investor).
2. The redemption is at the option of the issuer.

The Accounting Series Release, ASR 268 (now ASC 480-10-S99), provides that redeemable securities should be classified outside the *permanent equity section if* they are redeemable: (a) in cash or other assets; (b) in fixed or determinable price or at a fixed date; (c) at the option of the holder; or (d) upon the occurrence of an event that is not solely under the control of the issuer. These instruments are classified outside permanent equity, but they could be classified as temporary equity if the redemption is at the option of the issuer, or as a liability if the redemption is at the option of the holder.

### Case 3: Mandatorily Redeemable Financial Instruments

Adding the feature that obligates the issuer to redeem preferred stock alters the cash flow and risk characteristics of the instrument: the issuer is under obligation to unconditionally transfer cash or other assets at some specified time to entities external to the enterprise according to certain conditions. Similarly, the stockholder is under obligation to surrender the stock certificate and accept the redemption of preferred stock at the value specified in the contract. While the *form* of mandatorily redeemable preferred stock differs from the *form* of a bond, they are equivalent in an economic sense and should be accounted for as a liability (ASC 840-10-25-4). The liabilities should be reported at fair value measured at inception and the preferred dividends on mandatorily redeemable preferred stock should be accrued as interest expense through the income statement in a similar manner as interest on bonds.

#### Case 4: Debt Instruments with Non-Detachable Warrants

The host instrument could be a bond or a mandatorily redeemable preferred stock with non-detachable warrants as embedded options granting the holders additional rights. Of the various types of warrants that could be granted, the following types are warrants giving investors in mandatorily redeemable preferred stock or investors in bonds the right to purchase one of the following instruments:

1. Type A: Mandatorily redeemable preferred stock at a given (strike) price on or before a certain date or period.
2. Type B: The issuer's common shares at a given (strike) price on or before a certain date or period.
3. Type C: The issuer's common shares having a specified fair market value at exercise date.
4. Type D: The issuer's common shares valued by reference to an index external to the issuer's stock or operations, i.e., $10.00 × 1 + % change in S&P 500 index over past year.

In each of these cases, accounting for warrants will be different. From the standpoint of the issuer, these warrants will (under current accounting standards) be accounted for differently.

- Type A warrants that grant the holder the right to purchase mandatorily redeemable preferred stock should be classified as liability because they are options to acquire liability instruments. These warrants will be recognized at fair value when issued and revalued to fair value every reporting period with the changes in values flow through earnings.
- For Type B warrants, the contract specifies a strike price for exercising these warrants to purchase common shares of the issuer. Therefore, there is an implicit fixed conversion ratio and the warrants are considered indexed to the issuer's common shares and are therefore treated as equity.
- As to Type C warrants, the contract specifies a fair market value at the time of exercising the warrant. The number of common shares to be exchanged for a warrant will be different at different dates because of changes in market prices. This contract, therefore, does not qualify for classification as equity.[24]
- Finally, for Type D warrants, the warrants are a liability because the contract is not indexed to the issuer's common shares or operations and does not therefore qualify for equity treatment.

### 9.4.2 Bifurcation of Hybrid Instruments

Once a determination is made that the contract under consideration is not subject to the accounting standard outlining the criteria for distinguishing between equity and liability (ASC 4800), then a question arises as to whether the hybrid should be accounted for as a unit or should be split into its components and each accounted for separately. There are three choices:

1. Bifurcate (split) the host and derivative features of the contract.
2. Do not bifurcate due to exceptions to the standards and special provisions.
3. Account for hybrid in its entirety.

### 9.4.2.1 Splitting or Bifurcating Hybrids

Bifurcation is a general concept denoting "separation."[25] In the context of hybrid financial instruments, the term "bifurcation" refers to the abstract separation of the instrument into its components. In general, a hybrid instrument has a host (main or base) instrument and one or more embedded derivatives. Under some specific conditions, the enterprise is required to bifurcate the hybrid instrument and account for the host and the derivative components differently. The adopted accounting should be consistent with the risk and economic characteristics of each component. The bifurcated derivative will be accounted for as a liability (or as an asset), valued at fair value, and the changes in fair values flow through earnings. To make the decision on bifurcation, the contract features must be examined in connection with three criteria, two of which relate to the nature of the contract and the third relates to the valuation basis used before the hedge commenced. *All three criteria must be satisfied for the host and the derivative to be bifurcated.*

#### First Bifurcation Criterion

> The economic characteristics and risks of the embedded derivative instrument and of the host contract are not clearly and closely related.

The judgment on the strength of the connection between the host contract and the embedded derivative is based on the risk and cash flow characteristics of the two components and the similarity or differences in their responses to changes in market conditions. Both the FASB and the IASB expanded on this concept by providing a set of illustrations. The examples provided below should facilitate understanding this concept.

**1. Examples of Clearly and Closely Related Host and Embedded Derivative**

A *callable bond* consists of a debt host contract and an embedded call option that grants the issuer the right to redeem the bond before maturity. The interest rate is the underlying of both the host contract and the call option. After the protection (blackout) period ends, the issuer considers alternative financing options. If market interest rates for the same risk class and credit risk are higher than the coupon on the bond, the issuer would not have the economic incentive to call the bond for redemption. On the other hand, if market interest rates drop and the issuer could refinance at rates below the coupon rate, the issuer could make the call, redeem the bond and issue a new bond at the lower coupon rate.[26]

In this scenario, the host contract and the call option generate their values and risk from changes in market interest rate—they have the same underlying. Therefore, the embedded call option and host contract are closely and clearly related; they should not be bifurcated even if the other two criteria are met.

A second example is about some types of *step-up bonds* in which the step-up condition is determined on the basis of interest rates. This is the first of the two illustrations presented earlier on step-up notes. This is the case of the bond that is sold at face value of $1,000.00, has a starting coupon rate of 4% per annum and a three-year maturity. The step-up agreement in this contract calls for increasing the coupon rate at every year end by 1.00%. The value of this bond should be the sum of its elements of: (a) a three-year bond having a face value of $1,000.00 and earning $40.00 a year (a fixed rate of 4% per annum), (b) the present value of a two-year zero-coupon bond for a face value of $10.00, and (c) the present value of a three-year zero-coupon bond for $10.00. While the hybrid consists of several instruments, all are indexed to market interest rate and therefore respond to interest rate changes in a way similar to the host instrument. Therefore, the embedded features in this instrument are clearly and closely related to the host contract.

**2. Examples of Not Clearly and Closely Related**

*Equity returns contingent step-up bonds*. The contingency basis for deciding on the increasing steps could be any variable. In the above case, it was the interest rate. In the case of the note issued by *PNB Paribas Bank S.A.* (Canada), for example, the steps are indexed to the rate of return earned on a selected (and disclosed) portfolio of 40 global stocks. Thus, while the host instrument is indexed to interest rate, the embedded features of this contract are indexed to equity prices (return). Therefore, the embedded features and the host contract do not respond to changes in market conditions of either the interest rate or equity prices—they are not clearly and closely related and could be bifurcated (if the two remaining criteria are satisfied).

*Convertible bonds*: A convertible bond has a host (debt) instrument and a call option that gives the investor the right to convert the bond into common shares (assuming that the conversion is made at the option of the holder). The conversion feature typically states the strike price, the fair value, or the number shares to which a bond could be converted. The decision to convert to common stock is typically made at the discretion of the investor (the bondholder) and investors make the call when the option is in-the-money; the intrinsic value of the option increases with increases in common share prices. Therefore, the underlying of the option is the price of the stock, while the underlying of the debt (the host instrument) is interest rate. Accordingly, the host instrument and the embedded option respond to changes in interest rate and in stock price differently; their economic and risk characteristics are not closely related.

It must be noted that convertible bonds are used here only for illustration of what is meant by clearly and closely related, but convertible bonds of the type described above could be exempted from hedge accounting and bifurcation if: (a) the conversion is for a fixed number of shares, and (b) if the option would qualify for equity classification if it were a freestanding derivative.

### Second Bifurcation Criterion

> A separate freestanding instrument with the same terms as the embedded derivative is accounted for as a derivative as defined in accounting.

This second criterion requires that the embedded feature has the characteristics that qualify an instrument or a contract as a derivative (under accounting standards). These characteristics are presented in more detail in Chapter Six but may be summarized as follows:

- One or more underlyings and one or more notional amounts, or payment provision.
- No net investment or a net investment less than would be required for other contracts having similar response to changes in underlying(s).
- Permits net settlement, i.e., can be readily settled net by means outside the contract, or, provides for delivery of an asset that makes the recipient indifferent between settling net and receiving the asset.

### Third Bifurcation Criterion

The hybrid (combined) instrument is not valued or remeasured at fair value with the changes in fair values reported in earnings.

Ordinary GAAP requires that derivatives be measured at fair value through earnings. The hybrid instrument may or may not be measured at fair value under ordinary GAAP or because of the management's election of the fair value option. If the hybrid is already measured at fair value through earnings, then separating the embedded derivative does not accomplish anything different in terms of impact on earnings volatility. For example, marketable securities classified as trading securities and any security to which the fair value option has been elected do not qualify for bifurcation of embedded derivatives because their values are remeasured at fair values with the changes in fair values flow through earnings.

## An Important Caveat

- Bifurcation of embedded derivatives is *not* a choice.
- If an embedded derivative meets the three criteria specified in the standard, they must be bifurcated and accounted for separately.

If all three criteria are met, the hybrid security must be bifurcated into a host and embedded derivatives with separate accounting.

A summary of the process of bifurcation is described in the flow chart in Figure 9.3

### The Necessity of Bifurcation

Bifurcation of structured instruments in real life is not as simple as the examples discussed above; it actually could be very complex. It is therefore reasonable to ponder the benefits of bifurcating hybrids and accounting for the embedded features separately. At least four accounting-related reasons could be noted.

1. *Impact on Valuation of Assets and Liabilities*: If an embedded derivative is bifurcated, it must be valued at fair value periodically (at least every quarter) with the changes in fair values reported in earnings.
2. *Impact on Measure of Earnings*: Whether it is an asset or a liability, changes in fair values of derivatives are reported in earnings (income statement). Even when an embedded derivative is used as a hedge instrument, the changes in fair values are to be reported in earnings concurrently with the changes in values of the hedged items. The adverb "concurrently" in this context has two different meanings:

   - In a fair value hedge: concurrently means contemporaneously and immediately.
   - In a cash flow hedge: concurrently means when the hedged forecasted transaction or cash flow change affects earnings.

3. *Impact on Hedging*: Embedded derivatives cannot be used as hedge instruments unless they are bifurcated from the host contract and accounted for separately.

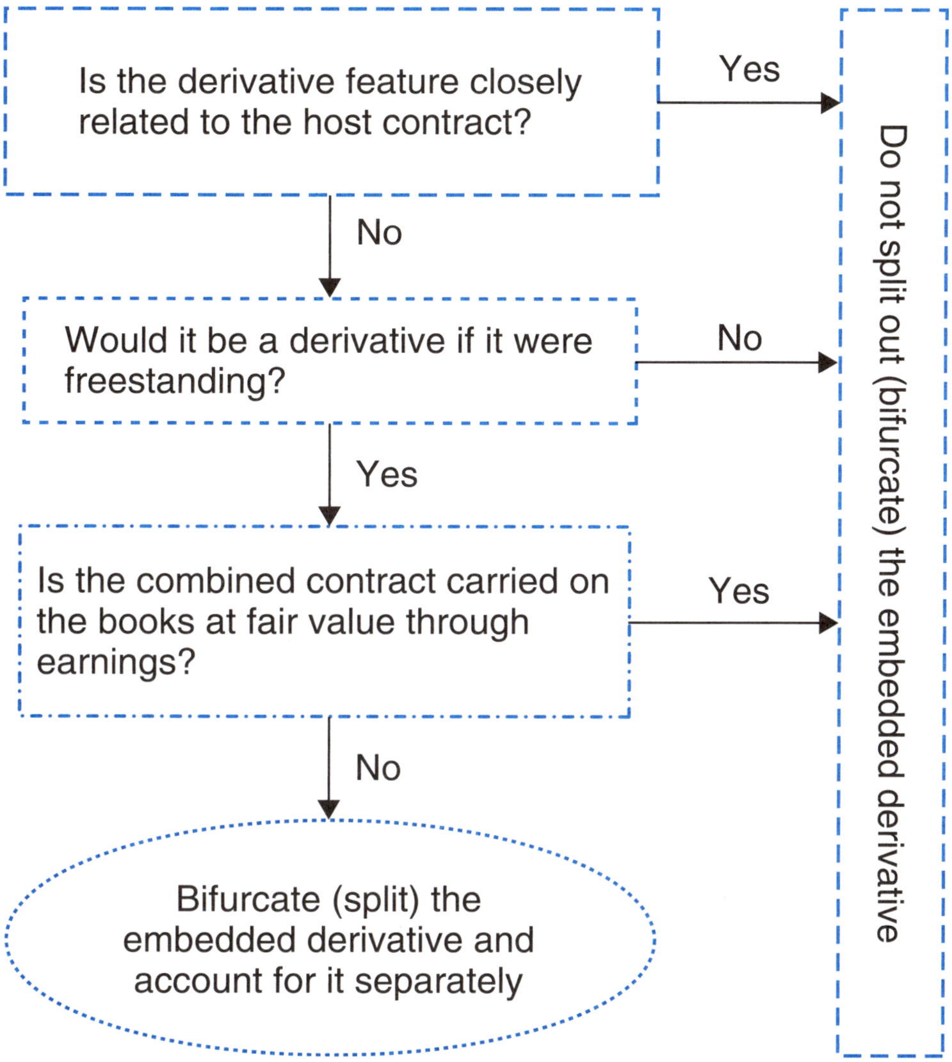


**Figure 9.3** The Decision on Bifurcating Embedded Derivatives

4. *Informing External Users*: Reporting and accounting for derivatives will provide users a better picture of the risks that the enterprise is facing and how they are managed.

### 9.4.3 Multiple Embedded Derivatives

Hybrid securities could have more than one derivative in such cases, for example, as having puttable or callable features in a convertible bond (e.g., DECS). Multiplicity of embedded derivatives in a single contract complicates the accounting and might compel the accountant to take one of two actions:

1. Combine all embedded derivatives in one bundle.
2. Account for the entire hybrid at fair value through earnings.

Exhibit 9.6 presents the case of *ConMed* which issued a hybrid with two embedded derivatives.

## Exhibit 9.6 ConnMed Disclosure of Convertible and Puttable Notes with Embedded Derivatives

We have outstanding $112.1 million in 2.50% convertible senior subordinated notes due 2024 ("the Notes"). During 2010, we repurchased and retired $3.0 million of the Notes for $2.9 million and recorded a loss on the early extinguishment of debt of $0.1 million. During 2009, we repurchased and retired $9.9 million of the Notes for $7.8 million and recorded a gain on the early extinguishment of debt of $1.1 million net of the write-offs of $0.1 million in unamortized deferred financing costs and $1.0 million in unamortized Notes discount. The Notes represent subordinated unsecured obligations and are convertible under certain circumstances, as defined in the bond indenture, into a combination of cash and CONMED common stock. Upon conversion, the holder of each Note will receive the conversion value of the Note payable in cash up to the principal amount of the Note and CONMED common stock for the Note's conversion value in excess of such principal amount. Amounts in excess of the principal amount are at an initial conversion rate, subject to adjustment, of 26.1849 shares per $1,000 principal amount of the Note (which represents an initial conversion price of $38.19 per share). As of December 31, 2010, there was no value assigned to the conversion feature because the Company's share price was below the conversion price. The Notes mature on November 15, 2024 and are not redeemable by us prior to November 15, 2011. Holders of the Notes have the right to put to us some or all of the Notes for repurchase on November 15, 2011, 2014 and 2019 and, provided the terms of the indenture are satisfied, we will be required to repurchase the Notes. If the Notes are put to us on November 15, 2011, we expect to utilize our $250.0 million revolving credit facility for payment of the Notes. The Notes contain two embedded derivatives. The embedded derivatives are recorded at fair value in other long-term liabilities and changes in their value are recorded through the consolidated statements of operations. The embedded derivatives have a nominal value, and it is our belief that any change in their fair value would not have a material adverse effect on our business, financial condition, results of operations, or cash flows.

(Source: ConnMed Form 10-K , 2010, p. 52. Available at: http://www.faqs.org/sec-filings/100225/CONMED-CORP_10-K/)

## Exhibit 9.7 Examples of Hybrids with Embedded Derivatives

| *Instrument* | *Host contract* | *Embedded Derivative* |
|---|---|---|
| A two-year fixed-quantity sales contract including maximum and minimum pricing limits | Purchase contract | Pricing collar in relation to the item being sold or purchased |
| Debt paying interest quarterly based on an equity index | Debt instrument | Four forward contracts per year based on an equity index |

| | | |
|---|---|---|
| A loan which pays interest based on changes in the S&P 500 index | Loan | Interest calculation based on changes in the S&P 500 Index |
| A loan with the provision for early payment with penalty | Debt instrument | A call option held by the borrower |
| A loan contract for a period of time with granting the borrower the right to extend the loan period | Debt instrument | A call option |
| Convertible debt | Debt instrument | A call option to be accounted for as equity under specific criteria |
| A contract to purchase natural gas with the price linked to the price of electricity | Purchase/sale contract | The pricing formula |

## 9.5 Embedded Derivatives Not Subject to Hedge Accounting

### 9.5.1 Contracts Classified in their Entirety as Liabilities

#### *9.5.1.1 Contract A: Share Repurchase Commitment*

Share repurchase is a method enterprises use to achieve different objectives related to cash rights or control rights. Repurchase could be an open market operation or executing a contractual agreement. Of particular interest in distinguishing between equity and liability is the forward contract that commits the enterprise to repurchase its own shares. For this type of contract, the standards[27] state that

> An entity shall classify as a liability (or an asset in some circumstances) any financial instrument, other than an outstanding share, that, at inception, has both of the following characteristics:
>
> a. It embodies an obligation to repurchase the issuer's equity shares, or is indexed to such obligation.
> b. It requires or may require the issuer to settle the obligation by transferring assets.

This standard requires the accounting for contracts obligating the enterprise to repurchase its own shares as an obligation with a concurrent reduction in equity.

> [T]he reporting entity shall not consider the following contracts to be derivative instruments for the purpose of this Subtopic
> [...]
> *Forward contracts that require settlement by the reporting entity's delivery of cash in exchange for the acquisition of a fixed number of its equity shares (forward purchase contracts for the reporting entity's shares that require physical settlement).*[28]
>
> (ASC 815-10-15-74)

This forward contract is different from puttable shares: a forward contract obligating the enterprise to repurchase its own shares is a freestanding instrument, while the put features in puttable shares is an option that permits the investor to put the shares back to the issuer under some conditions.

Because the forward contract agreement to repurchase the entity's own shares obligates the issuer to transfer assets to shareholders, it gives rise to a liability. Also, because the transfer of funds to shareholders will result in reacquiring the issuer's own common shares, owners' equity should be reduced by the stated amount. The accounting for this type of contract is illustrated below by an example.

### An Illustration

The management of *XAR, Inc.*, a publicly held company, wanted to reduce the concentration of shareholders voting rights by reallocating ownership of common equity stock. On 1/1/20x1, the company signed an agreement with *UKAN*, a major investor who owns 22% of outstanding shares, to repurchase 10,000 shares. Relevant information includes the following:

- On 1/1/20x1 the stock price was $25.00.
- The forward contract is to repurchase 10,000 shares from *UKAN*.
- The settlement (purchase) price is $30 per share.
- The transaction will be executed and settled on December 31, 20x2.

### Assumptions and Analysis

Assume that *XAR, Inc.* does not pay dividends and the contract was executed as intended.

*Analysis*:

- This agreement is a forward contract requiring the management to pay $300,000 to *UKAN, Inc.* on December 31, 20x2.
- The required transfer of assets is unconditional on the occurrence of any contingency other than passage of time.
- The *unconditional* nature of the contract creates an *obligation* on *XAR* to transfer cash to *UKAN, Inc. XAR, Inc.* must recognize this obligation on 1/1/20x1 and account for it as a liability.
- The liability is measured at fair value at inception and the recognized amount is accreted (i.e., increased or made larger) by the interest implicit in the contract. The total amount of interest to be accreted over the entire period is the excess of the obligation over the fair value. To apply this clause, the rate of interest implicit in the contract must be imputed from the terms of the agreement.

*Specific Information*:

- The 1/1/20x1 market price of $25.00 per share is assumed to be the present value of the forward contract price of $30.
- The implicit discount rate of interest (the rate at which $25.00 would accrete or grow in value to become $30 in two years) is calculated to be 9.5479%.
- Common shares have par value of $1.00.

### Accounting on the books of *XAR, Inc.*

(This is the issuer that is under obligation to transfer cash and reacquire its own shares).

| | | | |
|---|---|---|---|
| 1/1/20x1 | Capital<br>Additional paid-in capital<br>Obligation to *UKAN, Inc.*<br>*To record the transfer of $250,000 from equity to liability to recognize the creation of the unconditional obligation to repurchase 10,000 shares of XAR, Inc. at $30.00 on December 31, 20x2.* | 10,000<br>240,000 | <br><br>$250,000 |
| 12/31/20x1 | Interest expense<br>Obligation to *UKAN, Inc.*<br>*To accrue the interest expense* ($250,000 × 0.09545) | 23,860 | <br>23,860 |
| 12/31/20x2 | Interest expense<br>Obligation to *UKAN, Inc.*<br>*To accrue interest expense implicit in the contract for the obligation of $273,860* [(250,000 + 23,860) × 0.09545] | 26,140 | <br>26,140 |
| | Obligation to *UKAN, Inc.*<br>Cash<br>*To record the settlement of the forward contract* | 300,000 | <br>300,000 |

## 9.5.1.2 Contract B: A Put Option to Issue a Variable Number of Shares[29]

Some financial instruments obligate the issuer of equity shares to settle the contract by issuing a number of shares (unknown in advance) having a stated fair value. This type of contract has two related value measures: (1) the fixed amount received as a price, and (2) the fair value of the shares to be delivered. The latter is unknown at the start of the contract and the known obligation is the fixed monetary amount of cash the issuer has received. No equity is recorded before settlement because the only exchange that took place up to that point in time is the transfer of cash from the investor to the issuer of common shares. The amount received would be an obligation on the issuer and will be recorded as a liability until contract settlement.

The fair value at settlement is likely to be different from the fixed amount of cash already received by the issuer. But that fair value amount at the time of settlement is not relevant in this case. At settlement (issuance of shares as required in the contract), equity will increase only by the amount initially received from the investor and recognized as a liability.

### An Illustration[30]

The management of *Magna, Inc.* signs a contract (contract No. *CT2M4*) *with* an investor, *Star, Inc.*, having the following terms.

- On 1/1/20x5, *Star Inc.* pays *Magna, Inc.* $100,000 for a forward contract.
- The contract obligates *Magna, Inc.* to deliver to *Star, Inc.* at the end of January a sufficient number of common shares of *Magna, Inc.* worth $110,000 at the market price on 1/31/20x5.

### Accounting

- Assume that common shares of *Magna, Inc.* have par value of $1.00.
- At inception of the contract, on 1/1/20x5, *Magna, Inc.* collects the $100,000 and records it as an obligation.
- At the end of the month, on 1/31/20x5, assume that the price of *Magna, Inc.*'s shares was $20.00.
- On 1/31/20x5, *Magna, Inc.* issues 5,500 new common shares (from the shares that have been authorized and registered) to *Star, Inc.*

The following journal entries describe this transaction.

| | | | |
|---|---|---|---|
| | Cash | 100,000 | |
| | Liability— *Star, Inc.* | | 100,000 |
| | *To record receiving $100,000 from Star, Inc. for the commitment to deliver equity shares worth $110,000 at month end in accord with the agreement No. CT2M4.* | | |
| 1/31/20x5 | Obligation— *Star, Inc.* | 100,000 | |
| | Capital stock | | 5,500 |
| | Additional paid-in capital | | 94,500 |
| | *Issuing 5,500 common shares to Star, Inc. to settle forward contract No. CT2M4.* | | |

## 9.5.2 Contracts that Are Equity Derivatives

### *9.5.2.1 Hybrids with Conversion Option*

#### Detachable (and Attached) Warrants

Debt securities (including mandatorily redeemable preferred stock) may be issued with detachable warrants granting the holder the right to purchase the company's own common shares at a specified price (perhaps below the market) according to a timetable set in the contract. Because of the benefits given by the warrants, the funds collected by the issuer from the bond issue are, in an economic sense, payments for both the debt (the host instrument) and the warrants, which are freestanding derivatives. Therefore, the issuer must allocate these funds between these two financial instruments. The accepted method of allocation is in proportion to their relative fair values.

These warrants are detachable and are therefore like freestanding options. They could be separated from the host instrument and, depending on the terms of the contract, debtholders may be able to trade them separately from the bond. Typically, warrants have the following features:

- They have an exercise or a strike price.
- They are exchangeable for common stock whose price and historical volatility measures are known or could be established.
- They can be exercised during a certain period or at a given time.

This information, along with the risk-free rate, provides the variables required for estimating the fair value of the warrant using one of the option pricing models (e.g., the Binomial Model or Black-Scholes Model). The fair value of the debt could be estimated by the fair value of a plain vanilla bond (a bond without additional features) having the same terms as the host instrument and the same credit risk class or sector.

Assuming that *fvw* is the fair value of the warrant and *fvd* is the fair value of the debt, then the proceeds collected from issuing the bond with detachable warrants are to be allocated in the following proportions:[31]

- For the warrants: *fvw*/ (*fvd* + *fvw*).
- For the debt: *fvd*/(*fvd* + *fvw*).

The total of the values assigned to all the warrants represents a discount on the bond and an increase in equity through additional paid-in capital. The following illustration is based on the examples provided by ASC 470-55.

*Case 1 Illustration*: Debt with Detachable Warrants

On 1/1/20x1 the common stock of *Company ABC* is traded on the exchange for $10.00. On that date, *Company ABC* issues 10,000 convertible bonds having par value of $100 each. The bonds are sold at par value and each bond has 10 detachable warrants for a total of 100,000 warrants. Each warrant grants the debtholder the option to purchase one common stock of *Company ABC* at $10.00.

Using the Binomial option pricing model (see Chapter Five), the warrants are valued at fair value of $300,000. Additionally, based on market information, a bond having the same features as the debt host instrument without warrants is valued at an estimated amount of $900,000. Therefore, relative proportions of fair values are 0.25 for the warrants and 0.75 for the debt. The proceeds of $1.00 million will therefore be allocated according to these proportions: $250,000 for the warrants and $750,000 for the debt.

*Company ABC* will record this transaction as follows:

| | *Case 1 Illustration* | *Debit* | *Credit* |
|---|---|---|---|
| 1/1/20x1 | Cash | 1,000,000 | |
| | Discount (warrants) | 250,000 | |
| | Bonds | | 1,000,000 |
| | Additional paid-in capital | | 250,000 |
| | *Recording the issuance of 10,000 bonds at $100.00 each. The bonds have 100,000 detachable warrants, bear a coupon rate of 3% per annum payable semiannually, and have 20-year maturity. The warrants are exercisable at or after the fifth anniversary at an exercise price of $10.00 each.* | | |

The discount of $250,000 will be amortized over the 20-year term of the bond as an adjustment to interest cost. This adjustment is required in order to bring the accrued interest expense in line with the cost of debt; it is a recognition that bond investors had accepted a coupon rate lower than the coupon on the debt of an issuer having similar credit risk because of the benefits granted by the detachable warrants. (The reader may refer back to the illustration of amortization using implicit internal rate of return shown in Table 8.1 and the entries that follow in Chapter Eight).

*Case 2 Illustration*: Debt with warrants and conversion option

Assume the same information as in Case 1 but, in addition to the warrants, the bonds that *Company ABC* issued are also convertible to common stock of *Company ABC*. The warrants remain detachable, but the conversion feature is an embedded call option that could be exercised at the election of investors according to the terms of the contract. The debt is convertible into common stock on or after 1/1/20x5 at a conversion price of $10.00 so that the conversion ratio is 9 common shares for each bond.

The allocation of the $1 million proceeds is the same as in Case 1: $250,000 for warrants and $750,000 for the debt. In addition, the intrinsic value of the embedded conversion option must be determined and accounted for because the conversion option is a *beneficial feature*. The standards provide a short-cut for this valuation that could be described in the following steps:[32]

- At the time of issuance, $750,000 of the proceeds is allocated to the debt component.
- This allocation means that each bond is valued at $75.00.
- Because each bond could be converted into 9 common shares, the *effective conversion price* is $8.33 a share.
- Since the conversion exercise price is $10, and then compared with the effective conversion price, the implicit intrinsic value of the option is $1.27, which is calculated as $10.00 – $8.33. Therefore, the total intrinsic value of the conversion feature for the entire bond issue is $114,300 (calculated as 10,000 bonds × 9 shares conversion ratio × $1.27 implicit intrinsic value).

The conversion feature assumes no other constraints on the holder in exercising the option to convert. Therefore, there is a possibility that bondholders will have residual interest in *Company ABC* if they decide to exercise the option to convert. Because having *residual interest* is the key criterion for equity classification, the entire amount of $114,300 should be accounted for as equity. As in Case 1, the discounts for the warrants and the conversion feature will be amortized as an adjustment (increase) to interest expense.

The journal entries below capture this process.

| | *Case 2 Illustration* | *Debit* | *Credit* |
|---|---|---|---|
| 1/1/20x1 | Cash | 1,000,000 | |
| | Discount (warrants) | 250,000 | |
| | Discount (conversion feature) | 114,300 | |
| | Bonds | | 1,000,000 |
| | Additional paid-in capital | | 364,300 |
| | *Recording the issuance of 10,000 convertible bonds with 100,000 detachable warrants at $100.00. The bonds have a coupon rate of 3% per annum payable semiannually and have 20-year maturity.* | | |
| | • *The warrants are exercisable at or after the fifth anniversary of issuance at an exercise price of $10.00 each.* | | |
| | • *The conversion option grants bondholders 9 common shares per bond that may be exercised at or after 1/1/20x5 at an exercise price of $10.00 each.* | | |

*Case 3 Illustration*: Conventional Convertibles

Conventional convertibles (both convertible debt and convertible mandatorily redeemable preferred stock) are exempted from the scope of hedge accounting (ASC 815-40-25). In conventional convertibles, the conversion feature is more akin to equity than debt because of the presumption that debtholders will seek physical delivery and are therefore potential residual claimants. Furthermore, there is a difference in risk bearing between conventional and nonconventional convertibles. This difference is highlighted in an SEC statement about convertibles:

- In conventional convertibles, the risk of loss due to market fluctuations is borne by debtholders (investors) because the conversion is set for a fixed number of shares (not value) that is known at the time the convertible security was issued.
- In nonconventional convertibles, the issuer and shareholders bear the risk of market fluctuations, while debtholders are protected because they will receive a number of shares that guarantees them a predetermined fixed market value.

## Accounting Log: Excerpts from the SEC Information Statement

In a conventional convertible security financing, the conversion formula is generally fixed—meaning that the convertible security converts into common stock based on a fixed price.

By contrast, in less conventional convertible security financings, the conversion ratio may be based on fluctuating market prices to determine the number of shares of common stock to be issued on conversion. A market price based conversion formula protects the holders of the convertibles against price declines, while subjecting both the company and the holders of its common stock to certain risks. Because a market price based conversion formula can lead to dramatic stock price reductions and corresponding negative effects on both the company and its shareholders, convertible security financings with market price based conversion ratios have colloquially been called "floorless," "toxic," "death spiral," and "ratchet" convertibles.

(Source: http://www.sec.gov/answers/convertibles.htm)

The criteria adopted for identifying conventional convertible hybrids are as follows:[33]

- The entire proceeds of the conversion are to be exchanged for *a fixed number of shares* (not a variable number and not a conversion formula). This means a stable *conversion ratio*, except for the effects of standard antidilution provisions.
- Based on the choice of the issuer only, settlement of conversion by an equivalent cash value of a fixed number of shares would be an acceptable substitute for the requirement of a fixed number of shares. In this case, there is no obligation on the issuer to settle in cash because bondholders could not force the issuer to settle in cash and therefore these convertible hybrids do not create a liability.
- The conversion is in exchange for *the entity's own shares* (not for the shares of a third party).
- The issuer's degree of control over the events that trigger the reset of prices or over the likelihood of occurrence of the reset is not relevant.
- Ability to exercise the option for a fixed number of shares is conditional on passage of time or the occurrence of a future contingency or event.

The two flowcharts in Figures 9.4 and 9.5 present the steps required for making a decision on whether a convertible hybrid is or is not conventional convertible and the fit of that decision in the process of bifurcating embedded derivatives. It should be noted that the codified accounting standards discuss the decision on whether or not the convertible is conventional as a scope exception at the end of the bifurcation process. In Figure 9.5, the decision on whether convertibles are or are not conventional precedes the start of the bifurcation process. This is a more reasonable and less costly approach because it makes little sense to go through the entire process of bifurcation if, indeed, the hybrid fits the scope exception.

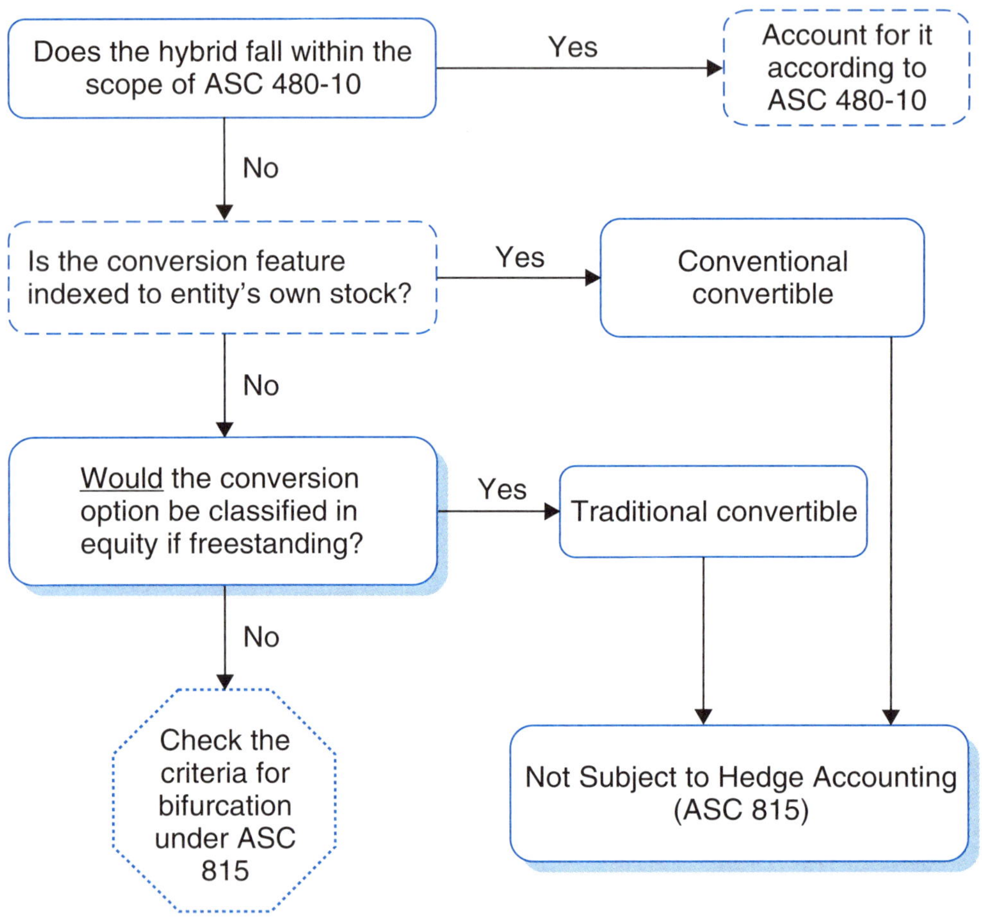


**Figure 9.4** A Flowchart for Accounting Decisions Related to Convertible Debt

## Other Illustrations

Example A: Convertible Debt
On 1/1/20x1, enterprise *WXW* issues 10,000 bonds with the following terms:

- Face value is $1,000, each.
- Bond is issued at face value (no discount or a premium).
- Coupon rate is 4% payable semiannually.
- Maturity is 5 years.

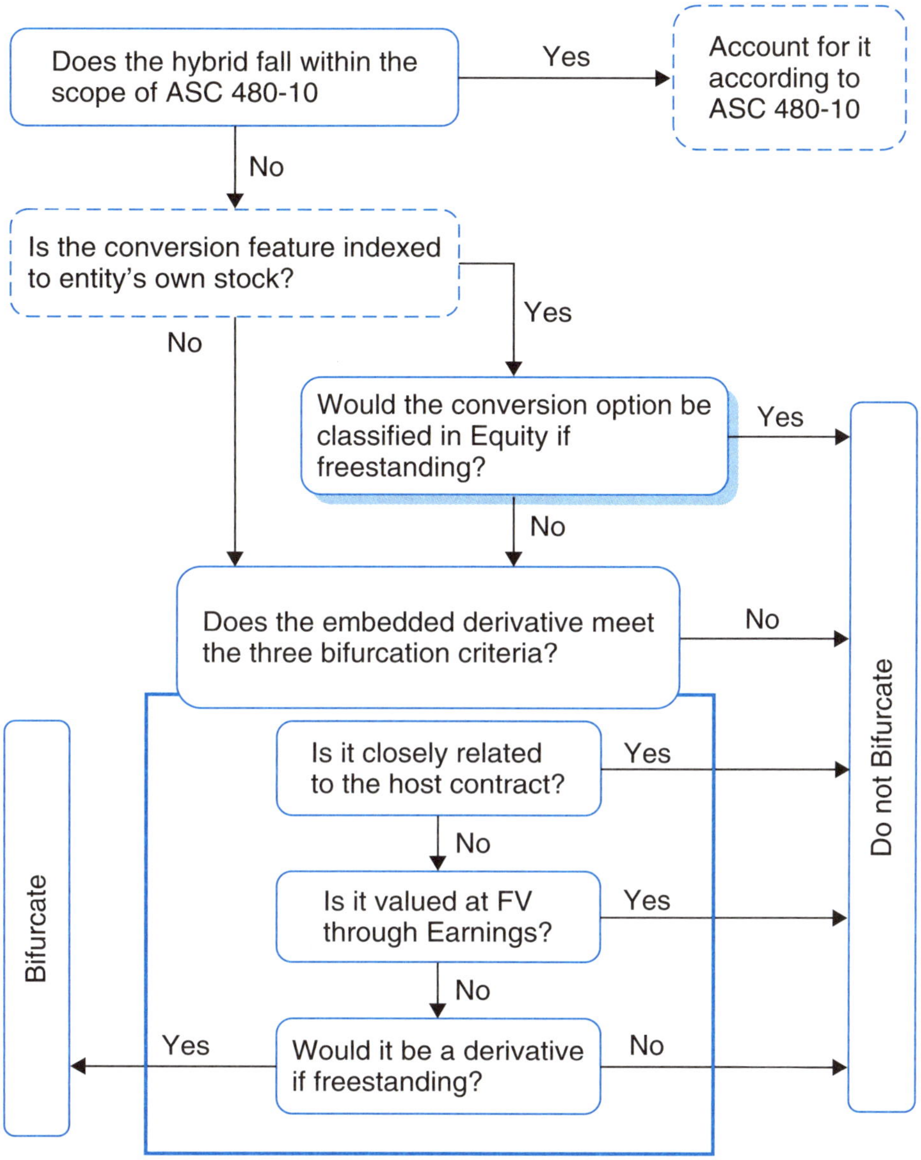


**Figure 9.5** A Flowchart for Bifurcation of Embedded Derivatives in the Presence of Conventional Convertible Debt

- On the third anniversary of the issue, bonds could be converted into common shares of *WXW*.
- The conversion ratio is 50.
- Common shares of *WXW* are traded on the NYSE.

*Supporting Material*
The interest rate for a borrower having the same credit risk as *WXW* is 6% annually with semi-annual payment. At that rate, discounting the present value of payments of *WXW* will yield a PV of $917 ($170 for interest and $747 for principal).

*Relevant Questions*

- For the issuer:

  Q1. Is the conversion option indexed solely to the issuer's stock?
    A. Yes, the conversion option is solely indexed to *WXW* stock.

  Q2. Would the conversion option be classified in equity if it were a freestanding derivative?
    A. Yes, it would be classified in equity.

  Q3. Is the bond issue carried on books at fair value with the changes in fair value flow through earnings?
    A. No, it is not carried out at fair value.

*Decision*

- For the issuer:
  - Separate the conversion option feature from the debt host instrument and account for it as equity.
  - Allocate values as follows: If the bond issue was not convertible (and has no other option features), the coupon rate that the issuer would have had to pay is 6%. We now need to use this interest rate to calculate the present value of an annuity of 10 payments of $20.00 each (5 years times payment twice a year) plus the present value of principal. This present value is $917.00. The allocation of the convertible bond issue between debt (the host contract) and equity (the conversion feature) per bond is to assign $917 to the debt and $83.00 to equity.

  The journal entry on the issuer's books would be

| | | |
|---|---|---|
| Cash | $1,000,000 | |
| Bonds | | 917,000 |
| Paid-in capital | | 83,000 |

- For the holder:
  - Because of the conversion feature, the holder is not permitted to classify convertible debt in the held-to-maturity category; the option to convert might be exercised before maturity.
  - If the holder is accounting for this investment as trading securities, the investment is valued at fair value with the change in fair value flowing through earnings. Therefore, the holder must account for this investment in its entirety and no special consideration is given to the conversion option.
  - If the holder is accounting for this investment as AFS, the analysis will center on whether the embedded derivative of conversion option should be bifurcated under the requirement of ASC 815. Analysis of the steps of bifurcation will show that:

    a. The embedded derivative is not clearly and closely related to the host instrument. In particular, the value and risk drivers of the host instrument are interest rate and credit risk of the issuer, but the value driver of the conversion option is the price of the common stock of the issuer.

b. The hybrid security has a liquid market and a conversion feature and could be treated as a derivative if it were freestanding—i.e., similar to warrants.
c. The price paid for the conversion option is much lower than the price of the consideration given.

*Decision*:

- Bifurcate the embedded derivative and account for it separately.

*Question*:
Both the host instrument and the embedded derivative are investments for the holder, what difference does this bifurcation make? The host instrument is valued at fair value with the changes in fair value being reported in OCI (because it is in the AFS portfolio), and the embedded derivative is also valued at fair value but the changes in fair values flow through earnings.

**Example B:**
In the previous example, the strike price is \$20.00 calculated as \$1,000 principal (face) value divided by the conversion ratio of 50. Assume the same facts as Example 1 except that the conversion ratio is determined to be 105% of the fair value of the bond. Given that the strike price is set at \$20.00, the number of shares to be issued is unknown and would vary with the market.

For the issuer, the variable number of shares violates the standard that requires a fixed number of shares to be predetermined to permit treating the convertible bond as conventional convertible. The entire amount should be treated as debt with one of two treatments: (a) value the entire hybrid at fair value with the changes in value flowing through earnings, or (b) evaluate the applicability of ASC 815 for bifurcating the embedded derivative and account for it separately. This evaluation examines the bifurcation criteria:

- The embedded derivative derives its value from the stock price and its volatility, but the host instrument derives its value from the interest rate changes. Therefore, they are not clearly and closely related.
- The embedded derivative is exchangeable for an asset that is readily convertible to cash.
- The value of the embedded derivative is not significant because it consists of the time value of the option only.

*Decision*:
The embedded derivative should be bifurcated and accounted for as a liability under ASC 815. The bifurcated derivative is to be valued at fair value with the changes in fair value flowing through earnings.

*Case 4 Illustration*: Fixed-for-Fixed Exchange
Some equity-linked instruments that could be considered derivatives otherwise are explicitly exempted from the application of hedge accounting because the terms of the contract render them more as equity-like type of financial instruments. In particular, these are contracts that satisfy the following two conditions:[34]

1. Being indexed to the company's own stock.
2. Would be classified in stockholders' (permanent or temporary) equity in the company's own balance sheet.

### 9.5.2.2 *The Meaning of Indexed to Own Stock*

#### Evaluation of Conversion Contingencies

Except for the standard antidilution provision, indexing to own stock would be supported if:

a. There are no exercise contingencies.
b. These contingencies refer to any benchmark related to *one* of the following:
   i The issuer's observable market value of own stock.
   ii The issuer's observable own operations such as sales, earnings or cash flow.[35]

Reference to any observable index, benchmark or variable not related to the above-stated factors would not support a conclusion that the contract is indexed to own stock.

Consider the following examples:

| *Contract terms* | *Is it indexed to own stock?* |
|---|---|
| A. A warrant or an option is exercisable if the stock price of the issuer increases by 10% over four months. | Yes: it is an observable index and the index is the company's own stock. |
| B. A warrant or an option is exercisable if the S&P 500 Index increases by 10% over four months. | No. It is an observable index other than the company's own stock. |
| C. A warrant or an option is exercisable if the stock price of the U.S. Treasury Rate increases by 10% over four months. | No. It is an observable index other than the company's own stock. |
| D. A warrant or an option is exercisable if the sales volume of the issuer increases by 10% over four months. | Yes. It is an observable index, and it is related to the company's own operations. |
| E. Entity A purchases net settled call option to buy 100 of its own common shares at $10 per share when the share price exceeds $15.00 per share.** | Yes. No contingency and the determinant of settlement value is the stock price which is a factor or a variable in an option pricing model. |
| F. Entity A issues warrants to permit the holder to buy 100 shares of its common stock any time during the next 10 years at $10 per share and if Entity A obtains FDA approval for specific drug during the following five years. If drug approval does not occur, Entity A purchases the warrants back at $2 each.** | No. There is no exercise contingency but there is a settlement contingency—the regulatory approval. That contingency is not based on Entity A stock price. |
| G. Entity A issues American-style options to permit the holder to buy 100 shares of its own common stock at $10 per share at any time during the next 10 years. | Yes. The option value changes with the change in stock price and stating an exercise period is not a contingency. |

** Illustrations in ASC 815-40-55

### 9.5.3 Extreme Risk Interest Rate-Linked Derivatives (The Double-Double Test)

For interest rate-linked hybrids such as callable bonds and similar notes, the embedded derivative and the debt host contract share interest rate as the common underlying that generates risk and value. Therefore, when determining whether or not to bifurcate the embedded derivative in these types of hybrids, the criterion of "clearly and closely related" is deemed to be met. However, this general inference does not apply in situations when the embedded derivative exposes the holder (the investor) to a significantly higher risk than the risk normally generated by the underlying. Both U.S. GAAP and IFRS acknowledge this problem and prepared the conditions for exempting high-risk embedded derivatives in interest rate-linked notes from bifurcation.[36]

An embedded derivative in interest rate-linked notes is deemed to bear significantly higher risk than the risk of exposure to interest rate if the investor "could" either lose a substantial amount of the investment in the host contract, or gain an unusually high return.

- *The Extreme Loss Condition*: Any "possibility whatsoever that the investor's (the holder's or the creditor's) undiscounted net cash inflows over the life of the instrument would not recover substantially all of its initial recorded investment in the hybrid instrument under its contractual terms."

  This boundary applies only to those situations in which the investor (creditor) could be forced by the terms of a hybrid instrument to accept settlement at an amount that causes the investor not to recover substantially all of its initial recorded investment.
- *The Extreme Gain Condition*: This condition contains two measures, both of which must be satisfied.

  1. The embedded derivative contains a provision that could at least double the investor's initial rate of return on the host contract under any, even a remote, possibility.
  2. The embedded derivative could result, under any interest rate scenario, in a rate of return that is at least double the initial rate of return for a similar contract (same terms as the host contract and same credit risk as the issuer's).

The hybrid instruments that could fall under the umbrella of this exception are similar to some forms of structured notes, such as step-up bonds or step-up notes discussed in the first segment of this chapter if the principal is at risk and the interest rate step-up is large enough to make the investment attractive to investors with high risk appetite. For example, the disclosure of *Aegon*,N.*V.* notes that "The annual floating rate distributions will be reset quarterly and will be the higher of 4.00% or the three-month LIBOR plus 0.875%." If, in addition, the principal was not guaranteed, there could be situations in which the investor could lose a substantial amount of the investment, or gain double the initial rate of return if the three-month LIBOR increases to above 4.572%.

The flowchart in Figure 9.6 shows this process of deciding on whether or not a hybrid bears extreme risk and, therefore, should not be subject to bifurcation.

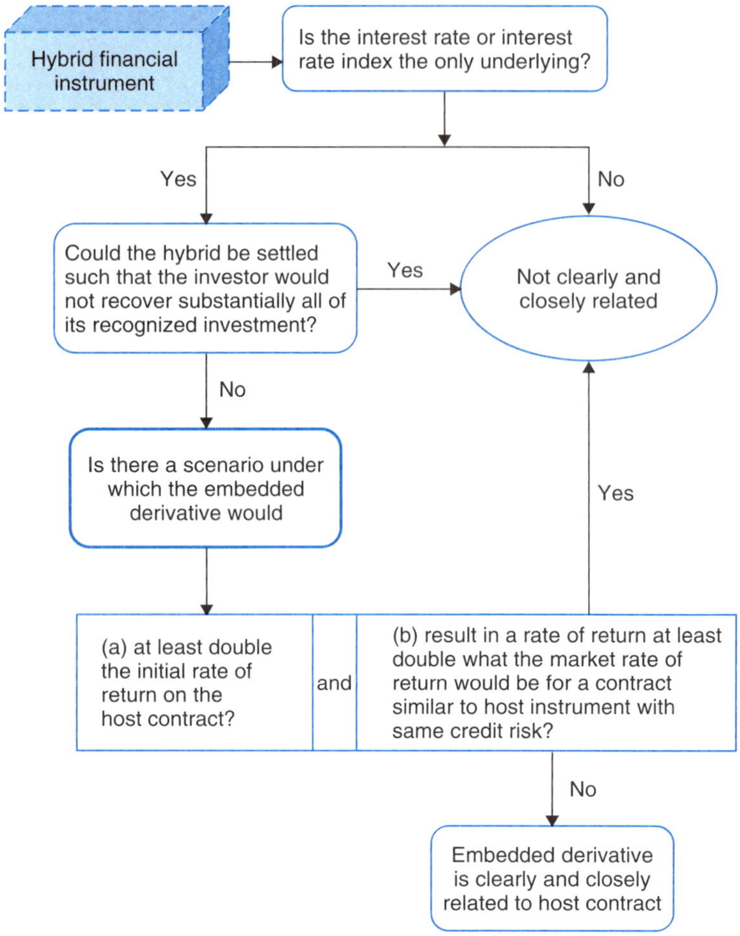


**Figure 9.6** Flowchart of the Decision on the Clearly and Closely Related Criterion for Extreme Risk Interest-Rate-Linked Instruments (The Double-Double Test)

## 9.6 Summary of Key Points

### 9.6.1 Types of Derivatives

- Financial derivative instruments are either freestanding or embedded other host contracts. Chapter Five presented the plain vanilla types of freestanding derivatives—options, swaps, forwards, futures, and credit default swaps. Embedded derivatives are the subject matter of this chapter. Distinction between freestanding and embedded derivatives is highlighted by looking at warrants which could be either freestanding or non-detachable from the host contract.
- Typically, the literature defines hybrid securities as an instrument with debt-like and equity-like features. In this chapter, the definition of hybrid securities is extended to include contracts having a combination of the two of the following: either equity-like or debt-like features and embedded derivatives. The non-derivative component of this type of hybrid instrument is called the "host" contract.
- Of relevance is the fact that embedded derivatives could be a component of any contract and could extend beyond financial securities—e.g., embedded derivatives could be components of purchase or sale contracts such as the cancelation option or take-or-pay contracts.

- Simple forms of embedded derivatives include the option to convert bonds (or preferred stock) to equity (or preferred) stock; this type of option could be a *call* option (issuers make the call) or a *put* option bondholders. More complex instruments include bonds having multiple embedded derivatives: callable and convertible features; debt-exchangeable-for-equity instruments and other equity-linked embedded derivatives.
- Preferred stocks have their own unique features in that embedded options determine whether they should be classified as debt or equity.

## 9.6.2 Accounting for Embedded Derivatives

- Both the U.S. GAAP and IFRS require accounting for embedded derivatives, although both boards are in the process of simplifying it.
- Accounting for embedded derivatives consists of several elements

  - Evaluation of whether the embedded derivative should be separated from the host contract. The separation is abstract only in a financial accounting sense and is referred to as "bifurcation."
  - There are specific criteria for bifurcation. The most critical ones are whether or not the embedded derivative (a) is "clearly and closely related" to the host contract; (b) is valued (as part of the combined contract) at fair value with changes reported in earnings; (c) could be derivative if freestanding; (d) is normally classified or expected to be classified in owners' equity; or (e) the contractual terms bear extreme risk that could generate double-return or substantially lose the investment. Every public entity is required (it is not a choice) to identify and assess the separability of all embedded derivatives in new or old contracts and account for them accordingly.
  - If bifurcated, the derivative is to be valued at fair value and the changes are to be reported in earnings in a similar manner to accounting for freestanding derivatives. An embedded derivative can be used to hedge other contracts that are not themselves derivatives.

## Notes

1 Potential claims on assets might also be classified as *temporary equity* (or *contingent capital* under IFRS) which is reported in the "mezzanine" section between debt and equity and is not included in the ownership equity section.

2 There are literally hundreds of different variations of these hybrids. The instruments presented here capture different features that should give the reader an idea of the elements of different contracts and how accountants could analyze them.

3 There are warrants that grant the holder the right to purchase a third-party common equity shares. This type of warrant is excluded from this discussion at this time.

4 For debt with detachable warrants, accounting standards require adopting the two-step process of allocating the proceeds in proportion to relative fair value of each component.

5 This is a very critical feature in accounting for convertible bonds as we will see below in the segment on conventional convertibles and the fixed-for-fixed criterion.

6 In most convertible bonds, investors hold the option to convert, but in other cases, the issuer has the right to convert the bonds into stock under certain conditions or the right to call the convertible bond for redemption and force the conversion.

7 Whether the issuer actually offers a yield lower than the yield on a straight bond with similar features or sells the bond at a premium above the face value, the investor pays for the conversion feature and the yield on a convertible bond would be lower than the yield on a plain vanilla bond without the option to convert. The difference in approach could have accounting implications.

8 This is a cross between *Asian* and *Barrier* options and is called the Parisian down-and-in option or Parisian up-and-in option.

9 *DECS* is one form of mandatorily convertible securities that was introduced by Salomon Brothers. Some variations of *DECS* were introduced by other firms. *ACES* (Automatically Convertible Equity Securities), *PRIDES* (Preferred Redemption Increased Dividend Equity Securities), *FELINE* PRIDES (Flexible Equity-Linked Exchangeable *PRIDES*), *DECS*, *SAILS* (Stock Appreciation Income-Linked Securities), *MARCS* (Mandatory Adjustable Redeemable Convertible Securities), and *TAPS* (Threshold Appreciation Price Securities) are examples of mandatory convertibles with a payoff structure similar to *PEPS*. *CHIPS* (Common-linked Higher Income Participating debt Securities), *EYES* (Enhanced Yield Equity Securities), *TARGETS* (Targeted Growth Enhanced Term Securities), and *YES* (Yield Enhanced Stock). More are developed every day because the development of such instruments is not costly. Therefore, accounting for these instruments critically depends on detailed analysis of each contract to determine the embedded rights, obligations, and their measurements (see Note, 2 in Arzac, 1997).

10 See also Ammann and Seiz, 2006.

11 I used the 2003 disclosure in order to follow through to know about the conversion. As it turns out, this practice continues.

12 On p. 63 of the 2005 Annual Report it states: "Contingent capital I was used in 2003 to issue convertible bonds amounting to approximately EUR 2.3 billion that will be converted into shares of Deutsche Telekom common stock at maturity (June 1, 2006). The convertible bonds were issued by Deutsche Telekom's financing company in the Netherlands—Deutsche Telekom International." A similar situation is reported in 2009 financial statements.

13 More on the accounting details will be discussed in the next segment of this chapter.

14 This type of instrument is one of those that could satisfy the "double-double" test criteria of accounting for embedded derivatives as is discussed below.

15 See an example of variable step-up bonds at http://www.one-financial.com/en_investment_solutions_variable_step_up_bonds_series_1.asp.

16 http://riskinstitute.ch/00010641.htm

17 See "AEGON N.V., Floating Rate Perpetual Capital Securities" at http://www.quantumonline.com/search.cfm?tickersymbol=AEB&sopt=symbol.

18 Source: One Financial at http://www.one-financial.com/en_investment_solutions_variable_step_up_bonds_series_1.asp.

19 *BNP Paribas S.A.* is the seventh largest bank in the world and is promoting this form of Notes as an investment. This type of instrument is relevant for accounting when it comes to implementation of the double-double test.

20 The Fair Value Option is an accounting standard that permits the management to elect to value any financial asset or liability (other than Held to Maturity) at fair value. However, the choice is irrevocable.

21 U.S. Bancorp 6.5% Fixed to Floating Perpetual Preferred Stock (Non-Cumulative) http://www.dividendyieldhunter.com/USBM.html

22 With the issuance of FAS 150 (ASC 480) in the USA and the development of IAS 32 (now IFRS 7) internationally, accounting standards continue to evolve in this domain and have reached a reasonable, but still incomplete, stage of differentiating between debt and equity. However, the continuing flow of new instruments in the marketplace has given rise to unanticipated complexity.

23 In some circumstances, the derivative may also have characteristics of an asset (for example, a forward contract to purchase the issuer's equity shares that is to be net cash settled). Accordingly, ASC 480 does not address the case of an instrument that has only the characteristics of an asset.
24 The contract violates the fixed-for-fixed criterion discussed below.
25 The term "bifurcation" is used in many contexts to mean branching, splitting or separating. The context determines the specific meaning. For example, Karl Marx and Joseph Schumpeter wrote about bifurcation of society into the upper elites and the masses. In biometrics, bifurcation refers to the point in a fingerprint where a ridge branches out to form two other ridges; in geography, it refers to the forking of a river into its tributaries; and in mathematics it is used to describe separation of hyperplanes.
26 "Refunding" is the term used for issuing new bonds when existing bonds are redeemed.
27 The topic of distinguishing liability and equity, ASC 480-10-25.
28 This criterion does not apply to the counterparty to this contract. In other words, the issuer would account for this contract as a liability while the investor would account for this contract as an asset and equity.
29 480-10-25-14
30 The illustration of *Magna, Inc.* below is based on ASC 840-10-55-22.
31 ASC 470-20-25-2
32 The terms *beneficial feature* and *effective conversion price* are relevant in accounting standards. The illustration used here is based on ASC 470-20-55-11.
33 Codified Accounting Standards (ASC 815-40-25-39).
34 This is known as exception ASC 815-10-15-74.
35 Neither passage of time nor the occurrence of an event related to the enterprise's own stock or operations violate the indexation requirement.
36 This is my own interpretation of ASC 815-15-25-26 through -25-29.

CHAPTER 10

# CURRENCY TYPES AND RISK

## Hedging Transaction-Settlement Risk

## 10.1 An Overview of Currency Matters

According to the CIA World Fact Book, there are 178 different currencies in use around the world. Each country or region (e.g., Eurozone) has its own currency. Entities that are domiciled in a given country or region employ the local currency as a medium of exchange and as a store of value and they may or may not use the same currency as a unit of measure. Most known currencies are convertible into one another at exchange rates that currency (FX) traders in world markets constantly renegotiate; while others are pegged to the US dollar.

A currency exchange rate is the *ratio* of two currencies: the amount of one currency (the quote currency) that can be exchanged for one unit of another currency (the base currency). Decision-making requires information about the price of one currency in units of another or knowledge of the currency conversion. For example, in making decisions on pricing different cars in local currency, an auto dealer in Hong Kong would want to know the exchange prices of the Hong Kong dollar into the currencies used by car manufacturers: e.g., the Japanese yen, the euro and U.S. dollar.

Currency exchange prices are quoted in pairs taking the form of C1/C2, where C1 is the *base currency* and C2 is the *quote* or *counter* currency. There is a *direct quote* and an *indirect quote* format by reference to home or domestic currency. In a *direct currency quote* the domestic currency is the base currency and the foreign currency is the quote currency. For example, the quote C1/C2 is direct for residents of the country whose currency is C1 but is indirect for residents of the country whose currency is C2. To state that USD/JPY = 80 is a *direct quote* for a U.S. trader, but is an *indirect quote* for a Japanese trader. We could avoid the possible confusion that may result from using the terms direct and indirect by setting the base currency equal to one unit and using the following rule of thumb:

> The expression C1/C2 states the number of C2 units needed to be exchanged for one unit of C1.

In foreign currency exchange markets, currency prices are designated by three-letter identifiers, not by the currency symbol. The convention is to use the first two letters for the country name or code and the third letter for the type of currency of that country. For example, the United

Kingdom currency is quoted by GBP (for Great British pound) not by the symbol £. Based on this convention, USD stands for U.S. dollar; AUD stands for Australian dollar; and SAR stands for Saudi Arabian real. For most currency quotations, the USD is the base currency when the U.S. Dollar is one of the currency pair. A convention in financial markets is to use the U.S. dollar as the base currency, except for the euro, GBP, AUD, NZD (the New Zealand dollar) and currencies of a few other Commonwealth countries. Exhibit 10.1 shows some forms of currency quotations used in FOREX markets.[1]

## Exhibit 10.1 Comparison of *Direct* and *Indirect* Quotes

**Base Currency: U.S. Dollar, USD** on April 9, 2012

| Currency | Code | Direct Quote | Indirect Quote |
|---|---|---|---|
| | | 1USD/ Units C2 | C2 Unit/ Units of USD |
| Canadian Dollar | CAD | 0.9976 | 1.0034 |
| Swiss Franc | CHF | 0.9174 | 1.0912 |
| British Pound | GBP | 0.6302 | 1.5878 |
| Japanese Yen | JPY | 81.6777 | 0.012258 |

In this example, USD is C1 and C2 is one of these four foreign currencies.

A currency quote takes on two values; a value for the *bid price* and a value for the *ask price*. For example, the exchange rate USD/SEK means the number of Swedish Krona that can be exchanged for one U.S. dollar. On April 9, 2012 the values were *Kr* 6.75590 for bid price and *Kr* 6.76040 for ask. A *bid quote* is the price (i.e., exchange rate) in one currency at which a dealer will buy another currency. An *ask quote* is the price (i.e., exchange rate) at which a dealer will sell the other currency. For a given dealer, the *bid* (buy) price is slightly lower than the *ask* (sell) price by a spread representing the dealer's profit. Changes in currency rates are quoted to four decimal places; the smallest change is one Pip, which is 0.01%.

A *cross currency* quote is one that does not use USD as either a *base* or a *quote* currency, e.g., ARS/BRL (Argentinean pesos/Brazilian real). One could convert a cross currency quote to a direct quote by double conversion as in the following example that converts ARS/BRL to a direct quote of USD/BRL as follows USD/BRL = ARS/BRL * USD/ARS.

## 10.2 Changing Currency Exchange Rates

### 10.2.1 The Gold Standard

Up until 1973, economic policy makers of industrial nations believed that fixing currency exchange rates to a known standard would facilitate both international trade and the flow of capital across borders. They assumed that stationary exchange rates would offer the high degree of predictability that often comes with stability. This belief was formalized in an international treaty in July 1944 when delegates from 41 allied nations gathered in Bretton Woods, New Hampshire and agreed to stabilize currency markets by fixing currency exchange rates. They accomplished this by pegging (i.e., indexing or attaching) the currencies of the countries represented at the Summit. These countries became signatories to the Bretton Woods Treaty that pegged other currencies to the U.S. dollar, while the U.S. dollar was pegged to the price of gold. The resulting arrangement became known as the Gold Standard.

At that time, the price of gold was about U.S. $35.00 an ounce and the U.S. owned more than 90% of the world's then-known gold supply. Over the years, the U.S. control over gold supply diminished as other nations gathered sufficient economic power to acquire large quantities of it. As the flow of gold out of the USA accelerated, the artificially imposed stationary exchange rates were no longer reflecting international economic conditions and it became clear that the Gold Standard was constraining international trade. In 1971 the United States decided to unilaterally abrogate both the Gold Standard and the Bretton Woods treaty in favor of free-floating exchange rates. Shortly thereafter, other countries followed suit and, by March 1973, most of the world major currencies had free-floating exchange rates that are, by and large, determined by market forces.[2]

## 10.2.2 The Currency-Floating Regime: Causes of Changing Rates

The annulment of the Gold Standard intensified economists' and financial specialists' interest in the reasons for changes in currency exchange rates. They developed several theories in an effort to explain the causes of these currency movements, although all these theories appear to seek different explanations for the forces that alter the supply of, and demand for, currencies. Some of these theories are briefly outlined below.

### *10.2.2.1 Market Forces*

The currency of a country is like any other commodity in the world market—its price is determined by supply and demand forces. Absent regulatory or targeted intervention in markets, the currency exchange rate would be the equilibrium price at which markets for that currency clear. For example, if country ABC trades with other countries around the world, there will be inflows and outflows of its currency with the balance of payment (the net effect) reflecting excess demand, excess supply, or equality of supply and demand.

The elements of the balance of payment (*BoP*) are exports (*X*), capital inflows (*CI*), financial inflows (*FI*), imports (*I*), capital outflow (*CO*), and financial outflows (*FO*). That is,

$$BoP = (X + CI + FI) - (I + CO + FO).$$

From the viewpoint of any particular country, the trading partners could be any other country in the world. A positive (surplus) *BoP* of a particular currency is an indication of more inflow than outflow of that currency for the country with positive *BoP* and other countries in the world will have shortage of the currency causing an increase in exchange rates. Conversely, if *BoP* is negative (deficit), the rest of the world will have more of the currency of that country and its value will decrease relative to other currencies. For example, the USA has more imports (cash outflow) from China than exports (cash inflow) and thereby reducing the value of the US dollar in relationship to the Chinese renminbi. Absent intervention in the market by governments or other financial agencies (such as the World Bank or International Monetary Fund), the increase and decrease in the price of the domestic currency of a country will alter the terms of trade and the related flow of funds until *BoP* is brought back to equilibrium. This adjustment would occur faster in a floating-exchange-rate regime than in a rigid-exchange-rate environment because in a floating-exchange-rate regime, currency exchange rates adjust to changes in economic forces faster than commodity prices.

To illustrate, compare the movements in USD/JPY exchange rates over time. These movements illustrate the impact of changes in currency supply and demand. In January 2002, one U.S. dollar was exchanged for 134 Japanese yen. Since then, the U.S. has imported more commodities from Japan (sending out more U.S. dollars) than it has exported (receiving Japanese yen). As a result, the Japanese yen appreciated against the U.S. dollar and the exchange rate dropped to about 80 Japanese yen for one U.S. dollar as of May 22, 2012.

#### 10.2.2.2 Purchasing Power Parity (PPP)

With the free mobility of commodities, services, and funds across national boundaries, changes in the prices of a basket of commodities in one country is compared with changes in the prices of the same basket of commodities in another country. If commodity prices in domestic markets are lower than the prices of similar goods in other countries, merchants in domestic markets will have the incentive to export their products to these foreign countries. This will continue until prices in one country, when converted to the currency of the other country, will be equal. For this to happen, the exchange rate between two currencies will have to be equal to the ratio of their price levels so that, in equilibrium, the two countries would have the same purchasing power.

There are two versions of PPP theories: the first deals with the change in price levels and is called *absolute PPP*; the second deals with the percentage of change in prices and is called *relative PPP*. Both of these versions assume: (a) risk neutrality; (b) ability to compare prices of the same basket of goods and services in both countries; (c) no transportation cost; (d) no transaction cost; and (e) no tariffs or regulatory restrictions on the flow of funds and goods across borders. Since these restrictive assumptions do not match reality, economists argue that the law of one price does not hold in real life. However, currency exchange rates appear to be more volatile than the prices of real commodities because currency exchange rates adjust more rapidly to changes in economic conditions than do commodity prices.

The other version of Purchasing Power Parity is relative PPP theory. This theory posits that the percentage change in exchange rate from a given base period must equal the difference between the percentage change in the domestic price level and the percentage change in the foreign price level. Measures of relative PPP depend on the determination of the base period used for calculating the change and on the reference basket of goods and services for which prices are measured and compared. The limitations and assumptions related to relative PPP are generally similar to those of absolute PPP. In particular, trade restrictions, regulatory interventions and the disparity between financial markets and commodity markets limit the diagnostic validity of relative PPP in describing the forces that change the determination of exchange rates.[3]

#### 10.2.2.3 Interest Rate Parity

The third prominent theory of exchange-rate determination is *interest rate parity* (*IRP*). Under this theory, the forward currency exchange rate reflects only the interest rate differential between the two

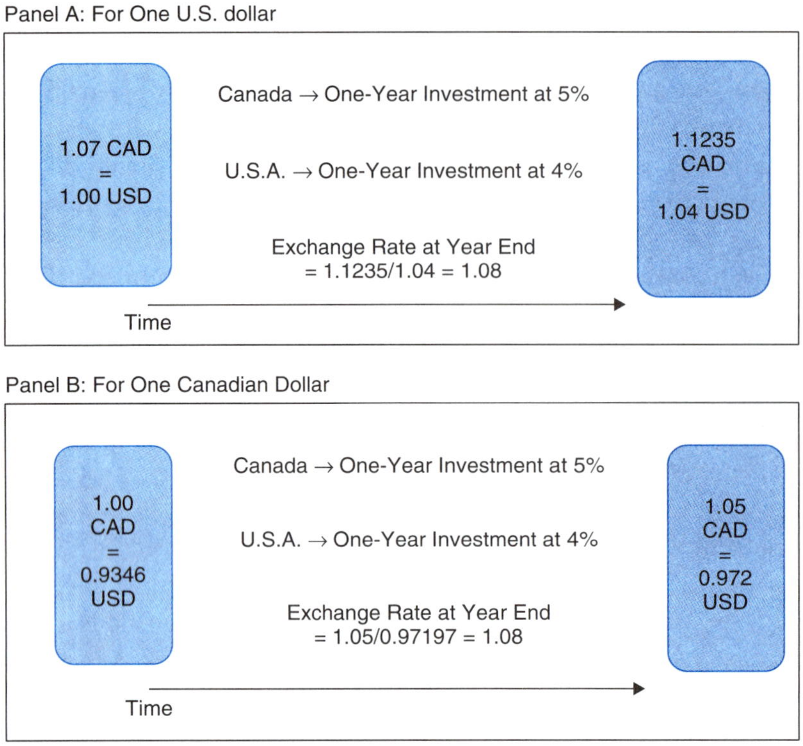


**Figure 10.1** An Illustration of Interest Rate Parity and Exchange Rate (Exchange rate numbers are rounded)

countries. To illustrate, in Figure 10.1 the spot exchange rate between the Canadian dollar and the U.S. dollar (USD/CAD) is assumed to be 1.07. That is, 1.07 Canadian dollars are required to buy one U.S. dollar. It also assumes that the interest rate one could earn by investing in Canada is 5% per annum, and the interest rate one could earn by investing in the U.S. is 4.00% per annum. At the beginning of the year, an investor has CAD100. If she invests this fund in Canada, she should expect to accumulate CAD105 by the end of one year. Alternatively, she could convert the CAD100 to U.S. dollars and invest the proceeds in a risk-free financial instrument. At the exchange rate of 1.07, converting CAD100 into USD will provide USD93.458 (= 100/1.07). The investment in the U.S. will earn 4.00% per annum and, at the end of one year, she should expect to accumulate USD97.196 (USD93.458 * 1.04). The difference in investment outcome would be expected to yield 1.0802 (= 105/97.196) currency exchange rate at year end. The CAD1.0802 exchange rate for USD1.00 is the expected spot rate by year end. At the beginning of the year, this expected year-end spot rate is the forward exchange rate.

### 10.2.2.4 The International Fisher Effect

In any country, the Fisher Effect states that the nominal interest rate changes in response to inflation. But inflation rates differ between countries which should result in corresponding differences in nominal interest rates. The result in Figure 10.1 can also be explained by the *International Fisher Effect*, which states that the expected change in currency exchange rates between two countries is a function of the difference in expected inflation rate because inflation rate differentials are the sources of differences in nominal interest rates. The International Fisher Effect remains a theoretical construct not supported by empirical evidence.[4] However, the International Fisher Effect yields essentially the same result as the *Relative Purchasing Power Parity* theory.

- Interest rate in country A = true cost of capital + expected inflation in A.
- Interest rate in country B = true cost of capital + expected inflation in B.
- Currency exchange rate CA/CB will change to reflect the relative change in expected inflation.

## 10.3 Consequences of Changing Currency Exchange Rates

The domestic or local currency may depreciate or appreciate in relationship to other currencies. A depreciation of domestic currency exchange rate against foreign currency has the following implications:

- Increasing prices of imports and increasing costs (decreasing profits) to importers.
- Improving competitiveness for exporters by having foreign-currency-denominated prices of exports expressed in lower amounts of local currency.
- Increasing the cost of servicing foreign-currency-denominated debt.
- Increasing values (measured in domestic currency) of investments in foreign-currency-denominated assets.

An appreciation of domestic currency would have the opposite effects. If the U.S. dollar appreciates against the Indian rupee, imports that are priced at a given number of rupees will require fewer U.S. dollars to satisfy. Therefore, an appreciation of the domestic currency would lower the cost of imports as measured in units of domestic currency. The other side of this effect is the impact on exports. The U.S. products that cost $X will, after appreciation of the dollar, require more foreign currency units to satisfy. Therefore, exports become more expensive to foreign buyers.

At the micro level, the changes in currency lead managements of business enterprises to reassess their business strategies and how they manage currency risk in an effort to reduce the negative impact of changes in currency rates on the income statement (profitability) and the balance sheet of their enterprises. The consequences of currency rate changes on balance sheets and income statements may result from current transactions (creating currency transaction risk exposure) or from impact on future operations (giving rise to operating risk exposure).

## 10.4 Types of Exchange Rate Changes

### 10.4.1 Currency Changes

Currency exchange rates reflect the change of one currency in relationship to another currency in one of two directions: it either becomes more valuable (appreciates) or less valuable (depreciates). As noted above, these directions are referred to as *appreciation* and *depreciation* of currency, respectively.

- *Appreciation*: The currency of country X becomes stronger than the currency of country Y if more units of Y would be required for one unit of X. For example, in 2011 US$1.00 was exchangeable for €0.71 ($1.40845 for €1.0) but since then the dollar has appreciated against the euro and, on July 26, 2012, the EUR/USD stands at €0.814 ($1.2285 for €1.0).[5]
- *Depreciation*: The currency of country W becomes weaker than currency of country Z if a larger number of W is required for one unit of Z.

The depreciation and appreciation of currency depends on the country's point of view. An American businessman would consider the depreciation of the U.S. dollar in relationship to the Canadian dollar if more units of the U.S. dollar were needed to acquire one Canadian dollar. On the other hand, the "depreciation" of the U.S. dollar in relationship to the Canadian dollar is at the same time an "appreciation" of the Canadian dollar with respect to the U.S. dollar.

Furthermore, appreciation of currency may or may not be beneficial, depending on the nature of international trade and cash flow patterns. For an exporter of real goods, currency appreciation makes these goods more expensive to consumers in other countries and will therefore reduce the demand and the volume of exports. In contrast, appreciation of currency would benefit importers because goods imported from abroad will cost less in units of domestic currency. By the same token, depreciation of currency is a beneficial feature for exporters, but not for importers.

The effects of depreciation or appreciation of domestic currency on imports and exports also apply to the flow of other funds so long as this flow requires conversion to or from other currencies. The *BoP* of a country will reflect the net impact of changes in imports and exports as well as changes in the flow of other funds.

Exhibit 10.2 summarizes the impact of currency appreciation or depreciation on importers and exporters.

## Exhibit 10.2 Impact of Type of Change in Currency Exchange Rates

| Currency Change status (from the point of view the holder of U.S. dollars) | From the Standpoint of | |
|---|---|---|
| | An Importer | An Exporter |
| *Appreciation*<br>*Old: $10 = 12 Euros After Appreciation of U.S. Dollar: $10 = 14 Euros* | Pay fewer USD for each unit imported (foreign products become cheaper for domestic buyers). | Collect fewer U.S. dollars for each exported unit (domestic products become more expensive to foreign buyers; more foreign currency per unit). |
| | Volume of imports will increase. | Volume of exports will decrease. |
| *Depreciation*<br>*Old: $10 = 12 Euros After Depreciation of U.S. Dollar: $10 = 10 Euros* | Pay more USD for each unit imported (foreign products become more expensive for domestic buyers). | Collect more U.S. dollars for each exported unit. For a U.S. product sold in Europe at 120 Euros, the U.S. Exporter will collect $120 after currency depreciation instead of the $100 before the depreciation.<br>Or, an American product that sells for $100 will now sell for 100 Euros instead of 120 Euros. |
| | Volume of imports will decrease. | Volume of exports will increase. |

## 10.5 Types of Currency Prices

Prices of a given currency differ by reference to time, place, and function.

### 10.5.1 Currency Prices by Reference to Time

#### *10.5.1.1 Spot, Current and Future*

The term "spot exchange rate" refers to the rate at which one currency can be exchanged for another currency at the present time—it is the cash price for immediate delivery. However, in reporting financial statements, the term "current exchange rate" refers to the spot rate that existed at the time of preparing financial statements.[6] The "forward" or "futures currency exchange rate" is the predicted spot rate at a specific future date—future delivery price. If we stand at time $t = 0$ and the period in question ends at time $t = T$, then $S_0$ denotes the spot rate at time $t = 0$ and $F_{0\rightarrow T}$ denotes the arbitrage-free forecast of what the spot rate is expected to be at time $T$. This is the forward rate at time t = 0 for delivery at time $T$; that is, $F_{0\rightarrow T} = E(S_T)$.

#### *10.5.1.2 Past and Current*

Exchange rates of transactions that have been carried out in the past are historical or past prices, while exchange rates of transactions that are carried out contemporaneously are spot or current rates. It is important to note that the term "current rate" may have a different meaning in accounting for translating financial statements that are denominated in foreign currencies. Accounting standards refer to exchange rates that prevail on the date of preparing financial statements as the "current rates."

Consolidating financial statements that include foreign operations requires converting the financial statements of foreign operations into the functional (reporting) currency of the consolidated entity. As Chapter Eleven on currency translation details, accounting standards distinguish between currencies on the basis of the time dimension:

1. *Current Rate Method*: This approach uses the currency spot exchange rate known at the end of the period for which the financial statements are prepared. Under the Current Rate Method, three different types of currency rates are applied to financial statements: (i) all assets and liabilities are translated from foreign currency to the parent's functional currency at currency spot exchange rate on the closing date of financial statements; (ii) owners' equity elements are translated at historical rates; (iii) income statement items are translated at a weighted average of the currency exchange rates for the period of operations covered by the income statement. In the context of consolidating financial statements, applying the Current Rate Method is referred to as " *translation* of financial statements."
2. *Temporal Method*: This method uses the currency exchange rates that existed when the assets and liabilities of the foreign operation were acquired. All financial assets and financial liabilities could be liquidated at the current exchange rate and are therefore assumed to be acquired "currently"; they are translated at the current rate. All other items on the balance sheet are translated at historical rates—the rates that were in effect when the transactions that resulted in generating these assets or liabilities took place. The income statement items are translated at

a weighted average rate. In the context of consolidating financial statements, restating the foreign-currency-denominated financial statements in the currency of the reporting entity using the Temporal Method is called *remeasurement.*

## Translation vs. Remeasurement

*Translation* is the term used when the Current Rate Method is applied; it is the process of converting the financial statements of foreign operations into the currency used in reported consolidated financial statements.

*Remeasurement* is the term used when the Temporal Rate Method is applied for the purpose of consolidation with the parent's financial statements, which would be under one of the following situations: converting the currency of foreign operations that (i) are not autonomous; (ii) are located in a highly inflationary economy; (iii) have the U.S. dollar as its functional currency, or (iv) is accounted for by the equity method.

## 10.5.2 Currency Type by Reference to Function

### *10.5.2.1 Functional Currency*

#### Definition of Functional Currency

> An entity's functional currency is the currency of the primary economic environment in which the entity operates; normally, that is the currency of the environment in which an entity primarily generates and expends cash.
>
> (ASC 830-10-45-2)

The functional currency may or may not be the local currency of the foreign operation or the currency in which the subsidiary keeps its books. The term *functional currency* is a concept and does not refer to any specific type of currency that has legal or physical substance in exchange. The FASB invented the functional currency concept in 1981 in order to facilitate changing the accounting for currency translation (changing from FAS No. 8 to FAS No. 52) that existed before that time.[7] Because a functional currency is the currency in which an entity generates its own revenues and cash flow, an enterprise is permitted to change the identified functional currency only if there is a change in the dominant currency for its economic activities.

It is mandatory: Identifying and adopting the appropriate functional currency *is not a choice; it is a requirement.*

#### Determinants of Functional Currency

Both the FASB (FAS 52, now ASC 830) and the IASB (AIS 21) fundamentally agree on the notion that the functional currency is the dominant or primary currency of the economic activities of an entity and have provided general guides for enterprises in determining their functional currencies. However, the FASB adds, "It is neither possible nor desirable to provide unequivocal criteria to identify the functional currency of foreign entities under all possible facts and circumstances and still fulfill the objectives of foreign currency translation" (ASC 830-10-45-3). Specific indicators summarize the broad criteria offered (ASC 830-10-55-5).

IFRS outlines the determinants of the functional currency in a slightly different way. Under IFRS, there is a hierarchy of primary and secondary determinants. The secondary determinants are applied only if the primary factors fail to identify a functional currency.

Panel A of Exhibit 10.3 presents the general criteria of U.S. GAAP, and Panel B presents the hierarchy of the two sets of criteria that IFRS requires. Exhibit 10.4 shows examples of determining functional currency.

## Exhibit 10.3 Determinants of Functional Currency

**Panel A:** Functional Currency Determinants in U.S. GAAP

| | |
|---|---|
| Cash Flow | Cash flows related to the foreign entity's individual assets and liabilities are primarily in the foreign (local) currency and do not directly affect the parent entity's cash flows |
| Sales | Sales prices for the foreign entity's products are not primarily responsive on a short-term basis to changes in exchange rates but are determined more by local conditions—competition or local government regulation. |
| Market | There is an active local sales market for the foreign entity's products, although there also might be significant volume of exports. |
| Expenses | Labor, materials, and other costs for the foreign entity's products or services are primarily local costs, even though there might be imports from other countries also. |
| Financing | Financing is primarily denominated in foreign currency, and funds generated by the foreign entity's operations are sufficient to service existing and normally expected debt obligations. |
| Intercompany transactions | Intercompany transactions are not frequent or extensive. |

**Panel B:** The IFRS Hierarchy of Factors for Identifying the Functional Currency

| | |
|---|---|
| *Primary Factors* | |
| Output | The currency that influences determination of sales prices and in which sales prices for its goods and services are denominated and settled. |
| Environment | The currency of the country whose regulations and market forces mainly determines sales prices. |
| Input | The currency that mainly influences the cost of input (labor, material and other costs). |
| *Secondary Factors* [(a)] | |
| Financing | The currency of financing activities (i.e., issuing debt and equity instruments). |
| Operations | The currency in which receipts from operating activities are usually retained. |

[(a)] The secondary factors are to be considered only when the primary factors fail in the determination of the functional currency or when their application produces mixed results.

## Exhibit 10.4 Examples of Determining Functional Currency

**Example 1**

Styles-International is a U.S. multinational company. Its reporting currency is the U.S. dollar. Styles-International owns 100% of a subsidiary in Italy, named Styles-Italy. Retail shops throughout Europe are the main buyers of Styles-Italy's products.

In this case, the euro is the functional currency because most of the cash flow is generated in euros, which is the primary currency of the economic environment in which Styles-Italy operates.

**Example 2**

Styles-International owns 100% of a subsidiary in Thailand called Styles-Asia. The clientele of Styles-Asia are mostly residents of mainland China and use the Chinese yuan to pay for their purchases.

Although the subsidiary operates in Thailand and hires domestic workers who are paid in baht, 90% of the sales revenues are transacted in the Chinese renminbi. In this case, the Chinese renminbi (yuan) is the functional currency.

**Example 3**

Styles-International owns 100% of a third subsidiary in Lebanon called Styles-MidE. The clientele of Styles-MidE are mostly from the Middle East. About 35% of revenue is generated in Lebanese liras, 40% in Egyptian pounds, and the remaining 25% in Indian rupees.

To decide on the functional currency, the management of Styles-MidE has to consider other supporting factors. It turns out that 83% of the payroll of that subsidiary is carried out in Lebanese liras, which is the appropriate currency to be designated as the functional currency of Styles-MidE.

### *10.5.2.2 Reporting or Presentation Currency*

#### Currency of Reporting Entity

In general, the term "reporting entity" refers to the entity for which the consolidated (or group) financial statements are presented and the term "reporting currency" refers to currency in which the reporting entity presents its financial statements. For multinational enterprises, the reporting entity typically incorporates financial statements of other affiliated entities and may reflect the following:

- The financial statements of one or more foreign operations by combination, consolidation, or equity accounting.
- Foreign currency transactions.

Although entities must measure financial statements in the identified functional currency, the reporting currency does not need to be the same as the functional currency. The entity has two possibilities:

1. *Most Common*: Using the functional currency for reporting or presentation.
2. *Less Common*: Having two different currencies for functional and reporting.

A specific example of the latter possibility is the case of the Icelandic company *Landsvirkjun*. The company uses the U.S. dollar as its functional currency and the Icelandic *Krona* as the reporting currency.

### Accounting Log: *Landsvirkjun*: Changing the functional, but not the reporting, currency

The Icelandic enterprise *Landsvirkjun* generates electric power from natural geothermal and waterfalls for distribution and sale to end users. Until 2007, the Icelandic krona (ISK) was the currency used in the financial statements of the company. With the switch from Icelandic GAAP to IFRS in 2007, the management was faced with the requirement to confirm whether or not its reporting currency is also its functional currency as IAS 21 requires. The first step in this process was to define the economic environment in which the company operates and the currency in which the company generates its cash inflow. This assessment revealed the following relevant facts:

a. *Landsvirkjun*'s clients are mostly aluminum producers.
b. Many of these clients are U.S.-registered companies such as Alcoa and Alcan.
c. The majority of the contracts of *Landsvirkjun* are denominated in the U.S. dollar.

As a result, the management concluded that the U.S. dollar is the functional currency of *Landsvirkjun*. Since determination and use of the identified functional currency is an accounting requirement and not a choice, *Landsvirkjun* changed its functional currency from Icelandic krona to the U.S. dollar in 2008 and from that point onward, reported its financial statements in both krona and U.S. dollars.

#### Currency of the Foreign Entity

A foreign entity consists of any foreign operations that are the activities of a subsidiary, associate, joint venture, or a branch whose activities are based on a currency other than the functional currency of the reporting entity. The financial statements of a foreign entity are (a) prepared in a currency other than the reporting currency of the reporting entity, and (b) combined or consolidated with, or accounted for on the equity basis in the financial statements of the reporting entity.

As with the reporting entity, the foreign entity has both a functional currency and a reporting currency that may or may not be the same currency. The functional currency of a foreign entity may or may not be the same as the functional currency of the reporting entity. Translation, remeasurement, and hedging of foreign currency are the subject matters of Chapter Eleven.

## 10.6 Currency Risk Exposure

### 10.6.1 Definition and Types of Currency Risk

Currency risk is the *exposure* to loss due to adverse movements of currency exchange rates. The increased internationalization of business and the volatility of the free-floating exchange rates regimes have contributed to a significant increase in business firms' exposure to currency risk. Currency exposure is usually classified into three types: transaction, operating, and translation. Economic exposure is the combination of transaction (settlement) and operating exposures.

Exhibit 10.5 and Figure 10.2 present an outline of the types of currency risk exposure.

## Exhibit 10.5 An Outline of the Risks Created by Changing Currency Rates

Changing currency exchange rates create several types of risk (as depicted in Figure 10.2), outlined as follows:

*Currency Transaction-Settlement Risk*

International commerce and exchange of services lead enterprises to carry on transactions and exchanges denominated in foreign currencies. Transaction exposure arises whenever an enterprise expects cash inflow or outflow in a foreign currency at an amount determined at an unknown future exchange rate.

Transaction risk is the probable exposure to loss (measured in units of the functional currency of the reporting entity) arising from unexpected adverse movements in exchange rates between the time a transaction (buying, selling, borrowing, lending, providing or receiving services) took place and the time of settling the account.

Currency transaction risk may consist of one or both of the following:

- Loss in value of a foreign-currency denominated contract or a transaction as measured by domestic currency.
- Potential loss that arises from cash flow volatility as measured in units of domestic currency emanating from unexpected movement in currency exchange rates.

Accounting standards (ASC 830 and IAS 21) require organizations to recognize the currency gain or loss on foreign-currency-denominated transactions in earnings (the income statement) at the current (spot) rate.

*Currency Operating Risk*

Currency operating risk is the exposure to unexpected loss or unexpected reduction in the present value of future cash flow related to future operations (e.g., buying or selling) that could result from adverse movement in currency exchange rates. This risk may occur because of unexpected changes in revenues, costs or cash flow from operations.

*Currency Translation Risk*

Currency translation risk is often referred to as the "currency accounting exposure" because measurement of the exposure is a result of the accounting methods used for converting the financial statements of foreign operations into the currency of the reporting entity. The risk exposure in this context refers to the fact that net investments in foreign operations are denominated in currencies that might suffer a loss in value. However, the measure of this exposure is a result of some specific accounting guides.

Multinational firms operate in different countries through subsidiaries, which tend to use or report in foreign currencies—i.e., currencies other than the functional currency of the reporting entity. A foreign subsidiary or activity may operate using the local currency or the currency of a third country. In either case, the units of measure in which the financial statements of foreign operations are presented differ from the reporting currencies of the reporting entity. To consolidate foreign operations with the parent's operations, all these foreign-currency-denominated financial statements of a defined foreign operation must be converted (translated or remeasured) into the functional currency of the reporting entity.

Two types of translation exposure:

- *Current Operations Exposure*: Revenues, expenses, gains or losses of the foreign operation are translated as part of the income statement. Therefore, the net gain or loss on translating the income statement is included in the consolidated income statement.
- *Financial Position Exposure*: This exposure is called *currency translation adjustment* and is posted (parked) in an equity account in the accumulated other comprehensive income.

The accounting guides for translation of foreign currency statements are discussed in Chapter Eleven.

*Economic Exposure*: is the sum of transactions' and operating exposures.

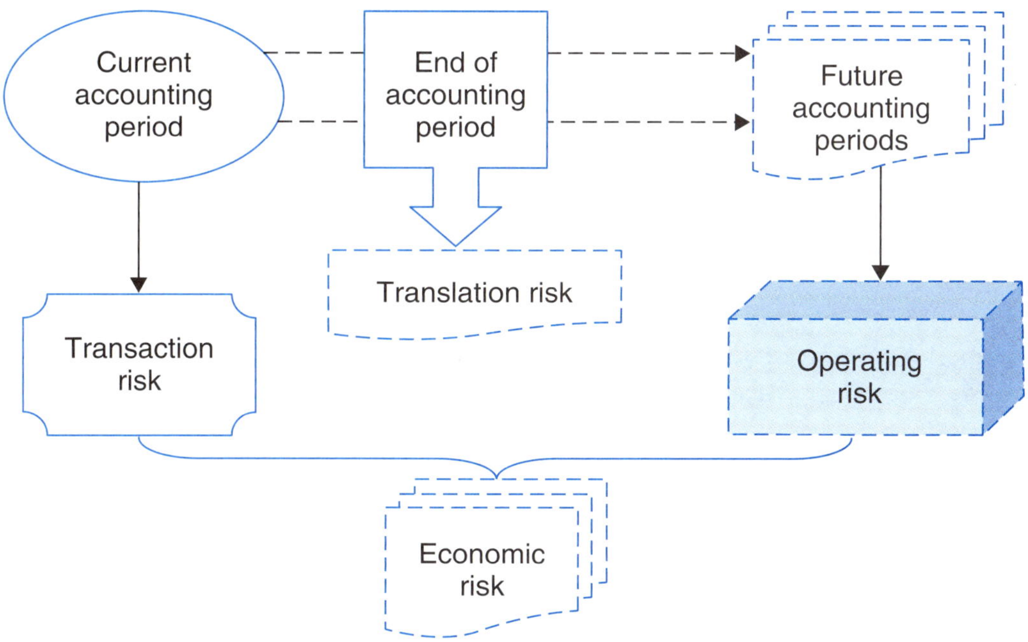


**Figure 10.2** Relationships between Different Currency Risk Exposures

## 10.7 Currency Transaction-Settlement Risk

As noted above, currency transaction risk exposure refers to the possibility of incurring gains or losses from contracts denominated in a foreign currency when settled at future dates. These transactions can be any foreign-currency-denominated transaction for which there is a deferred payment, such as credit purchasing (as in importing), selling (as in exporting), exchanging services, borrowing or lending funds, or being party to an executory contract or instrument. The risk exposure arises during the interval of time from initiating and settling these foreign-currency-denominated contracts. For example, a U.S. importer with a contract denominated in Japanese yen could end up paying more U.S. dollars to settle if, before settling the contract, the Japanese yen appreciates against the U.S. dollar. In contrast, a U.S. exporter selling products to Japan would be exposed to a similar currency risk if the Japanese yen depreciates in value before settling yen-denominated contracts. Similarly, issuing or purchasing debt instruments denominated in a foreign currency exposes the domestic party in the contract to currency loss; for any movement in currency exchange rate, one party to the contract will incur loss and the other will realize gains. Currency gain or loss on these contracts is treated as a financing item.[8]

### 10.7.1 Sources of Currency Transaction-Settlement Risk

An enterprise need not have foreign subsidiaries to be a party to contracts denominated in a foreign currency. An enterprise located in the U.S. (whose functional currency is the U.S. dollar) may sell products to be shipped from Miami, San Francisco, or some other port to buyers in other countries or regions having currencies different from the U.S. dollar. Similarly, enterprises within the U.S. purchase raw materials and finished goods and acquire services from foreign enterprises located in other countries. This exchange is not limited to physical commodities, but extends to financial transactions; foreign banks might provide loan facilities to business firms within the U.S. and vice versa. These types of activities are major components of both international trade and of the flow of funds across borders.

The foreign-currency-denominated contracts between an enterprise whose functional currency is the U.S. dollar, for example, and foreign counterparties may be written in one of three types of currencies:

1. The functional currency of the reporting entity (the U.S. dollar). In this case, the U.S. enterprise does not bear currency risk. Instead, it is the counterparty that bears currency settlement risk.
2. The currency of the country in which the counterparty is domiciled. In this case, the exposure to currency risk is borne by the U.S. enterprise.
3. The currency of a third country. In this case, both parties to the contract are exposed to currency risk.

The simple contract presented below illustrates these three scenarios.

### 10.7.2 Examples of Currency Transaction-Settlement Risk

#### *10.7.2.1 A Common Setting for Three Types of Contracts*

*P&K, Inc.*, a U.S. company based in Ohio, has the U.S. dollar as its functional currency. On March 1, 20x1, *P&K, Inc.* entered into an agreement with *Ozi Mining, Ltd.*, an Australian company whose functional currency is the Australian dollar, to purchase 5,950 metric tons of rock phosphate at AUD184.69 a ton. All contracts were written for 30-day net. On March 1, 20x1, the time of executing the contract, the exchange rate of AUD/USD was 0.91 (91 U.S. cents for one Australian dollar). At the end of 30 days, the exchange rate increased to 0.95 (the U.S. dollar depreciated and the AUD appreciated).

At the AUD/USD currency exchange rate on March 1, 20x1, this contract could be written and settled on that date for USD1,000,000 or AUD1,098,901. But by having credit terms, *P&K, Inc.* may or may not realize currency gains or losses, depending on the currency in which the contract is denominated. There are three possible currencies that *P&K, Inc.* and *Ozi Mining, Ltd.* could choose from:

1. The U.S. dollar (Contract One)
2. The Australian dollar (Contract Two).
3. A third currency of another country or region (Contract Three).

(Note: in all three contracts, credit risk is ignored in this illustration.)

### 10.7.2.2 Contract One—A Contract Denominated in U.S. Dollars

For this type of contract, the fact that the Australian counterparty has a different currency is not relevant to *P&K, Inc.*, the U.S. buyer. Because the contract is denominated in the functional currency of *P&K, Inc.*, the company does not bear currency risk; instead *Ozi Mining, Ltd.* bears all currency exchange risk. *P&K* will record the initiation and termination of this contract in exactly the same way as it records the contracts written with counterparties in the U.S.

#### Records of *P&K, Inc.* Contract One

Assume that the rock phosphate purchase contract between P&K, Inc. and *Ozi Mining, Ltd.* is payable in U.S. dollars (USD) in 30 days. If the contract were settled on the date of purchase, *P&K, Inc.* would transfer USD1,000,000 to pay for the transaction and the Australian company would record the sale and collection transactions at the spot rate of USD0.91 for AUD1.00 for a total amount of AUD1,098,901 (= USD1,000,000/0.91).

However, the contract was written for settlement in 30 days. At the time of purchase, *P&K, Inc.* will record inventory purchases and payables in the amount of USD1,000,000 while the Australian counterparty will record receivables and sales revenues equal to the value of the contract converted at the spot rate as AUD1,098,901. At the end of 30 days, currency exchange rates have changed such that the U.S. dollar has depreciated and the exchange rate AUD/USD increased to 0.95. This change, however, would have no impact on *P&K, Inc.* because the company will still pay off the note payable to *Ozi Mining* by transferring USD1,000,000. From the viewpoint of *Ozi Mining, Ltd.*, the USD1,000,000 could now be converted to AUD1,052,631 (= 1,000,000/0.95). *Ozi Mining* would record receiving AUD1,052,631, which is below the recorded receivable by AUD46,270. This difference is a currency loss for *Ozi Mining, Ltd.*, which is a result of a change in currency exchange rates during the period of credit. (Note that all numbers are rounded to the nearest one unit of currency.)

Accounting for Contract One on the Books of Both *P&K* and *Ozi Mining*

| *P&K, Inc.* (U.S.) | | | *Ozi Mining, Ltd.* (Australia) | | |
|---|---|---|---|---|---|
| In 1,000 U.S. dollars | | | In 1,000 Australian dollars | | |
| | Debit | Credit | | Debit | Credit |
| 3/1/20x1 | | | 3/1/20x1 | | |
| Purchases—Inventory | 1,000 | | Receivable—*P&K* | 1,098.90 | |
| Payable—*Ozi Mining* | | 1,000 | Sales Revenues | | 1,098.90 |
| *Purchase of 5,950 metric tonnes of rock phosphate from Ozi Mining, Ltd.* | | | *Sale of 5,950 metric tonnes of rock phosphate to P&K, Inc. in the U.S.* | | |
| 3/31/20x1 | | | 3/31/20x1 | | |
| Payable—*Ozi* | 1,000 | | Cash | 1,052.63 | |
| Cash | | 1,000 | Currency Loss— *P&K,* | 46.27 | |
| *Paying off Ozi Mining payable* | | | Accounts Receivable—*P&K* | | 1,098.90 |
| | | | *Collecting A/R and recording currency loss due to changing rates* | | |
| | | | Currency Loss—*P&K, Inc.* | 46.27 | |
| | | | Other Gains/Losses—Earnings | | 46.27 |
| | | | *To record currency settlement loss* | | |

### 10.7.2.3 Contract Two: A Contract Denominated in Australian Dollars

Assume the following information:

- *P&K, Inc.* has the U.S. dollar as its functional currency.
- *Ozi Mining, Ltd.* has the Australian dollar as its functional currency.
- On March 1, 20x1, *P&K, Inc.* entered into an agreement with *Ozi Mining, Ltd.* to purchase 5,950 metric tons of rock phosphate at AUD184.69 a ton.
- The contract is written for 30-day net.
- On March 1, 20x1, the time of executing the contract, the exchange rate of AUD/USD was 0.91 (91 U.S. cents for one Australian dollar).
- On March 31, 20x1, the exchange rate was 0.95 (the USD depreciated and AUD appreciated).

### Implication

This contract was payable in Australian dollars. Therefore, *Ozi Mining, Ltd.* will always receive AUD1,098,901. If the contract was written for cash instead of credit, *P&K, Inc.* would have paid a total of USD1,000,000 on March 1, 20x1. But settling the contract at the end of 30 days when the exchange rate increased from 0.91 to 0.95 meant that *P&K, Inc.* would have to pay USD1,043,956. In this case, the change in currency exchange rate has no impact on *Ozi Mining, Ltd.* but *P&K, Inc.* loses USD43,956.

### Accounting for Contract Two on the Books of Both *P&K* and *Ozi Mining*

| *P&K, Inc.* (U.S.) | | | *Ozi Mining, Ltd.* (Australia) | | |
|---|---|---|---|---|---|
| In 1,000 U.S. dollars | | | In 1,000 Australian dollars | | |
| | Debit | Credit | | Debit | Credit |
| 3/1/20x1<br><br>Purchases—Inventory<br>Accounts Payable<br><br>*Purchase of 5,950 metric tonnes of rock phosphate from Ozi Mining, Ltd. on 30-day credit.* | <br><br>1,000 | <br><br><br>1,000 | 3/1/20x1<br><br>Accounts Receivable<br>Sales Revenues<br><br>*Sale of 5,950 metric tonnes of rock phosphate to P&K, Inc. in the U.S.* | <br><br>1,098.90 | <br><br><br>1,098.90 |
| 3/31/20x1<br><br>Accounts Payable<br>Currency Loss<br>Cash<br><br>*Paying off the Payable and recording currency loss due to changing rates* | <br><br>1,000<br>43.956 | <br><br><br><br>1,043.956 | 3/31/20x1<br><br>Cash<br>Accounts Receivable<br>*Collecting A/R* | <br><br>1,098.90 | <br><br><br>1,098.90 |
| 3/31/20x1<br><br>Other Gains/Losses—Earnings<br>Currency Loss<br>*To record currency loss in earnings as a financing cost* | <br><br>43.956 | <br><br><br><br>43.956 | | | |

## *10.7.2.4 Contract Three: A Contract Denominated in a Third Currency*

Assume the following facts for this contract.

- *P&K, Inc.* has the U.S. dollar as its functional currency.

- *Ozi Mining, Ltd.* has the Australian dollar as its functional currency.
- On March 1, 20x1, *P&K, Inc.* enters into an agreement with *Ozi Mining, Ltd.* to purchase 5,950 metric tons of rock phosphate at NZ$235.295 a ton.
- The contract is written for 30-day net.
- The contract is denominated in New Zealand dollars for NZD1,400,000 (*P&K, Inc.* would pay *Ozi Mining, Ltd.* in New Zealand dollars).
- On March1, 20x1,
    - AUD/NZD = 1.20 (NZD1.20 for each Australian dollar) and
    - USD/NZD = 1.40 (NZD1.40 for each U.S. dollar).
- On March 31, 20x1,
    - AUD/NZD = 1.24 (NZD1.24 for each Australian dollar) and
    - USD/NZD = 1.47 (NZD1.47 for each U.S. dollar).

### Implications

- From the standpoint of *P&K, Inc.*:
    - At the time of purchase, March 1, 20x1, the contract was worth USD1,000,000 (equivalent to NZD1,400,000).
    - But at the time of settlement on March 31, 20x1, *P&K, Inc.* had to pay NZD1,400,000 which would be equal to USD952,381, a gain of USD47,619 (NZD70,000/1.47).
- From the standpoint of *Ozi Mining, Ltd.*:
    - At the time of purchase, March 1, 20x1, the NZD1,400,000 would be equal to AUD1,166,667.
    - But at the time of settlement on March 31, 20x1, the NZD1,400,000 would be equal to AUD1,129,032 (1,400,000/1.24); *Ozi Mining Ltd.* will collect less in units of its local currency than what it sold. This is a loss of AUD37,635.
- When the contract is denominated in a third currency (not the functional currency of either party to the contract), both parties to the contract are exposed to currency transaction-settlement risk.
    - In this contract, because the debt of *P&K, Inc.* was denominated in NZ dollars, the depreciation of NZ currency against the U.S. dollar has resulted in a gain for *P&K, Inc.*
    - On the other hand, because the receivable of *Ozi Mining, Ltd.* was denominated in NZ dollars, the depreciation of NZ dollar against the Australian dollar has resulted in loss for *Ozi Mining, Ltd.* because the sales contract was denominated in NZ dollars.

Accounting for Contract Three in the Books of Both *P&K, Inc.* and *Ozi Mining, Ltd.*

| *P&K, Inc.* (U.S.) | | | *Ozi Mining, Ltd.* (Australia) | | |
|---|---|---|---|---|---|
| *In U.S. dollars* | | | *In Australian dollars* | | |
| | Debit | Credit | | Debit | Credit |
| 3/1/20x1 | | | 3/1/20x1 | | |
| Purchases—Inventory | 1,000,000 | | Accounts Receivable | 1,166,667 | |
| Accounts Payable | | 1,000,000 | Sales Revenues | | 1,166,667 |
| *Purchase of xx quantity of phosphate* | | | *Sale of xx quantity of phosphate* | | |
| 3/31/20x1 | | | 3/31/20x1 | | |
| Accounts Payable | 1,000,000 | | Cash | 1,129,032 | |
| Currency Gain | | 47,619 | Currency Loss | 37,635 | |
| | | | Accounts Receivable | | 1,166,667 |
| Cash | | 952,381 | | | |
| *Paying off the Payable* | | | *Collecting A/R and recording currency loss due to changing rates* | | |
| 3/31/20x1 | | | 3/31/20x1 | | |
| Currency Gain | 47,619 | | Other Gains/Losses— Earnings | 37,635 | |
| Other Gains/Losses— Earnings | | 47,619 | | | |
| | | | Currency Loss | | 37,635 |
| *To record the currency gain in earnings as a financing cost* | | | *To record the currency loss in earnings as a financing cost* | | |

### *10.7.2.5 Comparing the Three Contracts*

1. In a contract denominated in the domestic currency, the foreign counterparty bears all currency exchange risk.
2. In a contract denominated in the currency of the foreign counterparty, the domestic counterparty bears all currency exchange risk.
3. In a contract denominated in a third currency (not the currency of either party), both parties to the contract bear currency exchange risk.

## 10.8 Mitigating Currency Transaction-Settlement Risk

Enterprises can manage their exposure to currency transaction-settlement risk in several ways, including, but not limited to, the following four approaches:

1. Parallel or back-to-back loans.
2. Matching inflows and outflows.
3. Money market hedge.
4. Hedging using financial derivatives (or non-derivatives as permitted).

### 10.8.1 Parallel (or Back-to-Back) Loans

#### *10.8.1.1 Description of Parallel Loans*

There was a period in the twentieth century when British government officials believed that restricting the flow of British currency outside the United Kingdom would enhance domestic investment. As a result of acting on this belief, it was illegal under the law for a British enterprise to use British pounds to invest in other countries. The law was intended to promote deploying British capital at home to finance domestic growth and to help create the type of employment that accompanies a healthy economy.

A side effect of this law was that U.K. multinational enterprises had difficulty carrying out certain business transactions abroad, even with their own subsidiaries. While these early regulations had prevented a British company from extending finance to its own subsidiary operating in a foreign country, they did not prevent a company from extending loans in British pounds to subsidiaries of foreign companies operating in the U.K. A form of finance bartering was developed and evolved. It became known as parallel or back-to-back loans.[9]

#### *10.8.1.2 An Illustration of Parallel Loans*

To illustrate parallel loans as a way of managing exposure to currency risk, consider the situation of a British company that has a subsidiary in Canada, and a Canadian company that has a subsidiary in the United Kingdom. To provide financing to these subsidiaries without transferring funds from one country to the other, a bank in the U.K. could provide a loan to the Canadian subsidiary in London and a bank in Canada could provide a loan with equivalent terms to a British subsidiary in Canada. Assume that the exchange rate of GBP/CAD is CAD1.50 for each British pound. The U.K. company would provide a 5% loan in the amount of £5,000.00 (in British pounds) to the Canadian subsidiary located in the U.K. and, simultaneously, the Canadian company would provide a loan at 5% interest in the amount of CAD7,500 to the British subsidiary located in Canada. The British subsidiary in Canada would make debt payments to the Canadian lender in Canadian dollars, while the Canadian subsidiary in the U.K. would make the debt payment of interest and principal to the U.K. company in British Sterling (pounds). Therefore, changes in currency exchange rates would not have significant effects on either party. In an economic sense, these two loans are related, but they are not connected when it comes to accounting.[10]

Figure 10.3 illustrates the cash flow of these two parallel loans and this is followed by an illustration of the booking of the transaction.

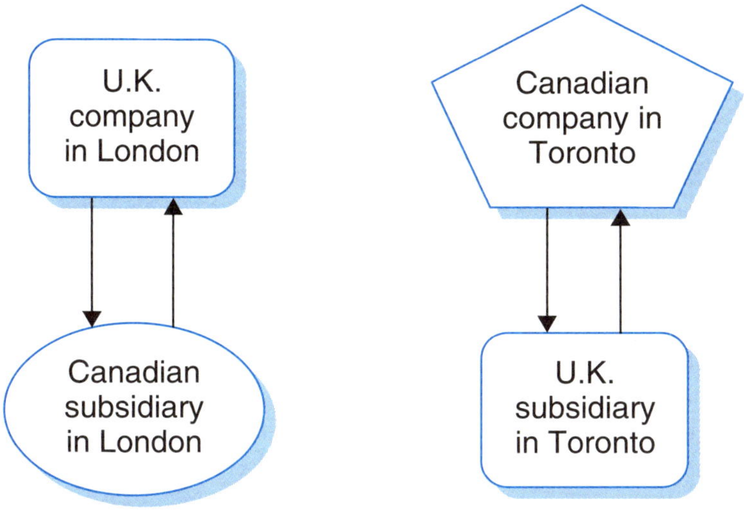


**Figure 10.3** An Illustration of Parallel Loans

### *10.8.1.3 Accounting for the Parallel Loans between the U.K. and Canadian Companies*

| *Records of the U.K. company in London* | | | *Records of the Canadian company in Toronto* | | |
|---|---|---|---|---|---|
| Loan Receivable<br>Cash<br>*Extending a loan to the Canadian subsidiary in London* | £5,000 | <br>£5,000 | Loan Receivable<br>Cash<br>*Extending a loan to the U.K. subsidiary in Toronto* | $7,500 | <br>$7,500 |
| Cash<br>Loan Payable<br>*Borrowing by the U.K. subsidiary in Canada* | £5,000 | <br>£5,000 | Cash<br>Loan Payable<br>*Borrowing by the Canadian subsidiary in London* | $7,500 | <br>$7,500 |
| Cash<br>Interest Income<br>*Interest earnings on the receivable extended to the Canadian subsidiary in London* | £250 | <br>£250 | Cash<br>Interest Income<br>*Interest earnings on the loan to the U.K. subsidiary in Toronto* | $375 | <br>$375 |
| Interest Expense<br>Cash<br>*Cost of borrowing by our subsidiary in Canada* | £250 | <br>£250 | Interest Expense<br>Cash<br>*Cost of borrowing by our subsidiary in London* | $375 | <br>$375 |

Financial Statements: Effects of Parallel Loans

| *In United Kingdom* | *In Canada* |
|---|---|
| • The U.K. company would show an increase of £5,000.00 asset (loan extended to Canadian company) and a decrease of £5,000.00 in cash.<br>• The Canadian subsidiary would show an increase in loans (liability) of £5,000.00 and an increase in cash of £5,000.00.<br>• The consolidated balance sheet of the U.K. company will have an increase in assets by £5,000.00 and an increase in liabilities by £5,000.00.<br>• Similarly, the income statement will show an interest expense of £250.00 and an interest income of £250.00. | • The Canadian company would show an increase of CAD7,500.00 in asset (loan extended to the U.K. company) and a decrease of CAD7,500.00 in cash.<br>• The U.K. subsidiary in Canada would show an increase in loans (liability) of CAD7,500.00 and an increase in cash of CAD 7,500.00.<br>• The consolidated balance sheet of the Canadian company will have an increase in assets by CAD7,500.00 and an increase in liabilities by CAD7,500.00.<br>• Similarly, the income statement will show an interest expense of CAD375.00 and an interest income of CAD375.00. |
| No net effect | No net effect |

In addition to complying with the British law (which is no longer in effect), these two parallel loans shelter both the U.K. company and the Canadian company from movements in currency exchange rate from its level of CAD1.50 for £1.00, the currency exchange rate at the time of the loan. Assume that the exchange rate changes to CAD1.40 for £1.00 at the time the loans are settled. The Canadian company would have a gain of CAD500 on paying off the payable, which would be offset by a loss of CAD500 from collecting the receivable. The U.K. company would have a gain of £357.14 on collecting the receivables, which would be offset by the loss of £357.14 for paying off the loan. Therefore, neither company would be affected by changes in currency exchange rates. But each item must be reported separately. The only real incremental cost for both companies is for negotiating the loans and processing the periodic payments of principal and interest on both sides of the Atlantic. However, from the perspective of financial analysis, parallel loans change the financial ratios and relationships within and between the balance sheet and the income statement.

### 10.8.2 Matching Inflows and Outflows in the Same Currency

Another approach to managing exposure to currency risk is to manage financing and business transactions so as to have correspondence of the amounts and patterns of cash inflows and outflows of a particular foreign currency. An enterprise can balance its receivables and payables in the same currency or manage taking long and short positions in the same currency. Enterprises can also implement more complex matching of flows by multilateral agreements and by strategically managing leads and lags of inflows and outflows.

For example, exporting commodities to the Eurozone can neutralize currency risk of euro-denominated purchases of commodities of equal amounts of euros. Similarly, issuing a foreign-currency-denominated debt can be matched by investing an equal amount in the country or region of that currency. In this case, currency appreciation (increased value) would mean both enhancing the income from the investment as well as increasing the cost of maintaining the debt. Conversely, currency depreciation (drop in value) leads to both decreasing returns on investment but also decreasing debt service obligations. In both cases, the changes of inflows would offset the changes in outflows.

This approach is a form of "natural hedging" and can be implemented in different ways. For example, in its Form 10-K of 2011, the management of McDonalds Corporation notes, "where practical, the Company's restaurants purchase goods and services in local currencies resulting in natural hedges." It continues: "Certain foreign currency denominated debt is used, in part, to protect the value of the Company's investments in certain foreign subsidiaries and affiliates from changes in foreign currency exchange rates."[11]

Although this currency hedging approach has survived the test of time, entering into additional investment or borrowing transactions in foreign currencies to match the inflows and outflows entails higher transaction cost than the transaction cost of using financial derivatives. This proposition seems to reflect the sentiment of General Electric Company's management, for example, as the statement in Form 10-K implies:

> As a matter of policy, we use derivatives for risk management purposes, and we do not use derivatives for speculative purposes. A key risk management objective for our financial services businesses is to mitigate interest rate and currency risk by seeking to ensure that the characteristics of the debt match the assets they are funding. If the form (fixed versus floating) and currency denomination of the debt we issue do not match the related assets, we typically execute derivatives to adjust the nature and tenor of funding to meet this objective. The determination of whether we enter into a derivative transaction or issue debt directly to achieve this objective depends on a number of factors, including market related factors that affect the type of debt we can issue.
>
> (General Electric, Form 10-K, 2011 p. 166; http://www.ge.com/investors/financial_reporting/index.html)

In the early 1980s, the use of derivatives began to take over matching cash flows just as it did for parallel loans, but these tools exist and continue to be utilized by enterprises whose managements would not want to deal with financial derivatives and possible exposure to other types of risk.

The results of mismatching currency flows can be serious. A classic example is the case of Lakers Airlines (Smithson, 1998, pp. 7–8). In the 1970s, the U.S. dollar was weak in relationship to the British Sterling. It was relatively inexpensive for British citizens to travel and tour the USA. Lakers Airlines wanted to capitalize on this pattern and purchased several airplanes to service this market by borrowing money in U.S. markets. Lakers Airlines' hopes were dashed when the dollar gained strength against British currency. Tourism from the U.K. to the USA dropped and Lakers needed much more money in British pounds to service its U.S. dollar-denominated debt. This was double jeopardy and led to Lakers Airlines' bankruptcy.

## 10.8.3 Money Market Hedge

### *10.8.3.1 A Description of Money Market Hedge*

A money market hedge (MMH) consists of borrowing and lending transactions in different currencies in order to lock in (fix to a known level) the home currency value of a foreign currency asset, liability or transaction. While the intent of using MMH is to hedge currency risk exposure, making a direct link between borrowing and lending in different currencies is not part of the structure of accounting systems. Illustrations in this section are developed for one case, *UImporte* Company, in order to facilitate comparison between the effects of different methods. We use this case to illustrate applying MMHs for the purpose of comparison with the use of financial derivatives, discussed in the next segment in this chapter.

#### 10.8.3.2 The Case

On June 1, 20x8, *UImporte Company*, a motorcycle dealer located in the USA purchased 250 motorbikes, model BR2G, from the Brazilian producer *BraziBikes, Ltda.* for R$1,000,000 when the spot exchange rate was US$1.00/R$1.53846. To pay for the transaction in cash at the time of purchase, *UImporte* would have had to transfer US$650,000.00 (the numbers are subject to rounding errors). But *UImporte* was short of cash and purchased the goods on credit by giving the exporter in São Paulo an interest-free note payable due on or before August 31, 20x8. During that period, *UImporte* was exposed to the possibility of loss if the Brazilian real[12] appreciated against the U.S. dollar, which would require transferring an amount of funds greater than the initial debt of $650,000 to pay off the note payable.

#### 10.8.3.3 The Money Market Hedge Contract

The management of *UImporte* had considered the possibility that currency exchange movements between the U.S. dollar and the Brazilian real would have adverse effects on earnings and cash flow. The management decided to plan for this contingency by investing in Brazil an amount of funds such that the principal and interest would accumulate to R$1,000,000 in three months. *UImporte* would then use this R$1,000,000 to pay off the note payable to *BraziBikes, Ltda* without being impacted by changes in currency exchange rates.

The management of *UImporte* identified a bank in Brazil that pays interest at 6% per annum (which is 0.015 for 90 days) on commercial deposits. Assuming simple compounding of interest, the 90-day present value of R$1,000,000 equals R$985,221.67 (=1,000,000/1.015). At the prevailing spot exchange rate on the date of purchase (which is equal to 0.65 U.S. dollar for R$1.00 or R$1.53846 for US$1.00), *UImporte, Inc.* must deposit an amount equal to US$640,394.09 (= R$985,221.67 × 0.65) as an investment in the Brazilian Bank. To avoid diverting funds away from normal business activities, *UImporte, Inc.* borrowed US$640,394.09 from The Trade Bank in Chicago at 8% per annum and transferred the entire amount to the bank in Brazil on June 1, 20x8. At the currency spot exchange rate on June 1, 20x8, the amount of Brazilian reals actually deposited in the bank in Brazil was R$985,221.67 (US$640,394.09 × 1.53846) as planned.

At the end of the reporting period (June 30, 20x8) and at the end of 90 days, *UImporte* had additional transactions in both Brazil and the USA.

##### Transactions in Brazil

- During the period from June 1, 20x8 through August 31, 20x8, the investment in Brazil earned *UImporte* R$14,788.33 interest income.
- The sum of the initial investment of R$985,221.67 and the earned interest income of R$14,778.33 equals R$1,000,000.

- *UImporte* withdraws the R$1,000,000 from the bank in Brazil and uses these funds to pay off the Note Payable to *BraziBikes, Ltda.*

Transactions in the USA

- At an annual interest rate of 8%, *UImporte* accrues three months' interest at a cost of US$12,807.88 (= 640,394.09 × 0.08/4) on the loan it had borrowed from The Trade Bank in Chicago.
- *UImporte* pays The Trade Bank a total of US$653,201.97 to pay off the loan principal plus the interest it owed.

### *10.8.3.4 A Summary of the Money Market Hedge Contract*

Figure 10.4 shows the flow of funds of this illustration of a money market hedge. There are several different types of transactions in this system: (a) purchasing inventory; (b) borrowing funds in U.S. capital markets; (c) investing funds in Brazil; (d) accruing interest expense on the loan to The Trade Bank; (e) accruing interest income on the deposit in Brazil Bank; and (f) paying off both obligations to *BraziBikes, Ltda* and to The Trade Bank in Chicago. At the end, the total cost related to the purchase of *BraziBikes* inventory amounted to $653,201.97, of which $3,201.97 is treated as a financing cost. Therefore, the cost of this MMH to *UImporte* is $3,201.97; the MMH has locked in the cost at that level irrespective of the behavior of the currency exchange rate. *UImporte* has thus succeeded in paying off the note payable in Brazilian reals at a predetermined cost of financing the credit purchase.

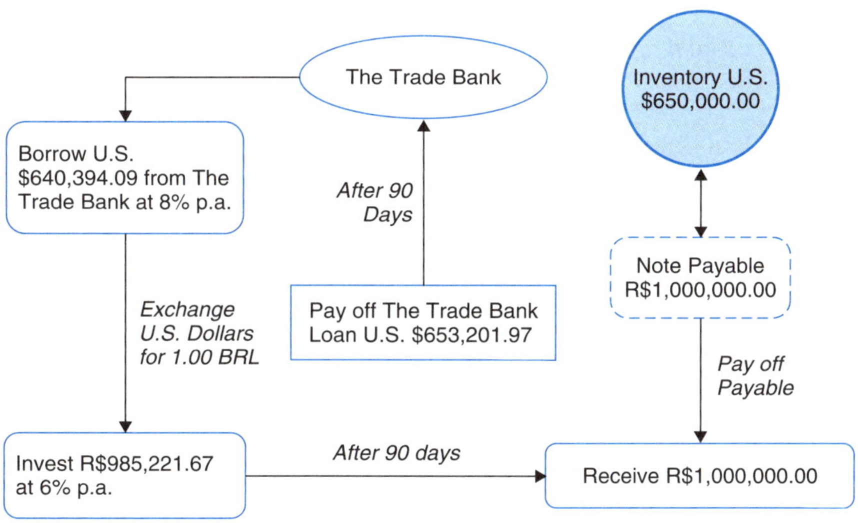


**Figure 10.4** The Flow of Funds for a Money Market Hedge

### *10.8.3.5 Accounting for Money Market Hedge*

As in the case of parallel loans, the accounting treatment of an MMH does not link the borrowing and investing transactions. In the above illustration, the *three transactions of inventory purchase, borrowing from The Trade Bank in Chicago, and investing in the Brazilian Bank are treated as if they are unrelated*. Inventory purchase is a commodity transaction, while the transactions with the U.S. and Brazilian banks are financing transactions that do not affect the cost of inventory or the cost of goods sold. The gain or loss on these financing transactions should be posted directly to earnings.

### Recording Money Market Hedge Transactions

In the illustration presented above, *UImporte, Inc.* would record the following journal entries:

| *Date* | *Transactions* | *Debit* | *Credit* |
|---|---|---|---|
| June 1, 20x8 | Inventory<br>Notes Payable—*BraziBikes, Ltda*<br>*Purchase of inventory from Brazil denominated at R$1,000,000. The exchange rate was U.S.$1.00/R$1.53846.* | 650,000.00 | 650,000.00 |
| June 1, 20x8 | Cash<br>Bank Loans—The Trade Bank in Chicago<br>*Borrowing from The Trade Bank in Chicago for 90 days at 8% interest rate per annum. This loan is obtained for the purpose of depositing the funds in the Brazilian Bank in order to build up funds to pay off the note payable.* | 640,394.09 | 640,394.09 |
| June 1, 20x8 | Investment in Bank Brazil<br>Cash<br>*Investing in Bank Brazil to accumulate funds to payoff BraziBikes, Ltda.* | 640,394.09 | 640,394.09 |
| June 30, 20x8 | Investment in Bank Brazil<br>Interest income—deposit in Brazil<br>*Accruing interest earnings during the quarter ended June 30* | 3,202.00 | 3,202.00 |
| June 30, 20x8 | Interest Expense<br>Interest Payable—The Trade Bank in Chicago<br>*Accruing the interest payable to The Trade Bank in Chicago for the quarter ended in June 30, 20x8* | 4,269.36 | 4,269.36 |
| June 30, 20x8 | Other Expense/Income—deposit in Brazil<br>Financing cost—Earnings Statement | 3,202.00 | 3,202.00 |
| June 30, 20x8 | Financing Cost—Earnings Statement<br>Other Expense/Income—The Trade Bank in Chicago | 4,269.36 | 4,269.36 |
| August 30, 20x8 | Interest expense<br>Interest Payable<br>*Accruing the interest payable to The Trade Bank in Chicago* | 8,538.52 | 8,538.52 |

| | | | |
|---|---|---|---|
| August 30, 20x8 | Investment—income on deposits in the Brazilian Bank<br>Gain on investment in the Brazilian Bank<br>*Accruing the interest earned on the deposits in the Brazilian Bank* | 6,402.91 | 6,402.91 |
| August 30, 20x8 | Cash<br>Investment in Brazil<br>*Liquidating the deposit in the Brazilian Bank* | 650,000.00 | 650,000.00 |
| August 30, 20x8 | Notes Payable<br>Cash<br>*Paying off the note payable to the vendor in Brazil* | 650,000.00 | 650,000.00 |
| August 30, 20x8 | Bank Loan<br>Cash<br>*Pay off the loan from The Trade Bank in Chicago* | 653,201.97 | 653,201.97 |
| September 30, 20x8 | Gain on investment in the Brazilian Bank<br>Other Income/Expense—Income Statement<br>*Recognizing the gain on the deposits with the Brazilian Bank as a financing gain* | 6,402.91 | 6,402.91 |
| September 30, 20x8 | Other Income/Expense—Income Statement<br>Interest Expense<br>*Recognizing the interest paid to The Trade Bank in Chicago as a financing cost* | 8,538.52 | 8,538.52 |

#### *10.8.3.6 MMH and Qualification for Hedge Accounting*

The objective of an MMH is to shelter the enterprise from unexpected fluctuations in currency exchange rates, as is the case with parallel loans. In that sense, an MMH is also an economic hedge, although not accounted for as such. The system of MMH as described above does not have a financial derivative instrument. However, under current accounting standards in US and IFRS, it is permitted to use a non-derivative financial item to hedge foreign-currency-denominated debt and it is permitted to apply hedge accounting if the hedge is designated and the hedging relationship satisfies other hedge requirements with respect to documentation and effectiveness.

## **10.9** Hedging Using Financial Derivatives

### 10.9.1 Accounting Qualifying Criteria for Hedging Currency Risk

The purpose of a foreign currency hedge is to mitigate risk exposure due to uncertain (unexpected) future changes in exchange rates of currencies other than the entity's own functional currency. The financial instruments used to affect hedging strategies include financial derivatives similar to those discussed earlier in this book—futures contracts, forwards, swaps, and options, as well as various combinations and variations thereof. However, applying hedge accounting for multiple currencies is more complex than the accounting for hedging in a single currency. This complexity arises because of the interdependence among currencies and because of the intersection between currency accounting standards pre-FAS 133, which are mainly ASC 830 (FAS 52) for U.S. GAAP and IAS 21 for IFRS.

#### 10.9.1.1 A Necessary Condition

Provided that other hedging criteria (detailed in Chapter Six) are met, exposure to currency risk exists only to the extent to which recognized assets, liabilities, contracts, forecasted transactions, and net investment in foreign operations are denominated in currencies *other than* the hedging entity's functional currency. A U.S. enterprise, for example, whose functional currency is the U.S. dollar may hedge currency risk of any item or transaction denominated in euros, but a U.S. enterprise whose functional currency is the euro may hedge the currency risk of any item or transaction denominated in U.S. dollars, but not the ones denominated in euros. In the former case, the enterprise is exposed to the currency risk of the euro, while in the latter case the enterprise is exposed to the currency risk of the U.S. dollar. *In either case, a necessary condition for adopting hedge accounting is that the entity is exposed to currency risk that could impact earnings or asset/liability values.*

A change in the functional currency of an entity alters its exposure to currency risk. For example, the experience of the Icelandic company *Landsvirkjun* is a case in point. Up until 2008, the company used the Icelandic krona as its functional currency. In anticipating the switch from Icelandic GAAP to IFRS, the management recognized the need to change its functional currency from krona to the U.S. dollar. Most of the company's revenues come from selling electric power to U.S. aluminum companies and these sale contracts are typically denominated in U.S. dollars. In 2006, the company changed its functional currency to the U.S. dollar.[13]

When the Icelandic krona was the reporting (and functional) currency of *Landsvirkjun*, the company could hedge exposure to the risk of variability in the value of the U.S. dollar, but could not hedge variability in the exchange rate of the krona. After changing the functional currency, *Landsvirkjun* could hedge the risk exposure to variability of the krona, but not to the variability of the U.S. dollar.

#### 10.9.1.2 Implications

These necessary condition noted above adds complexity to the hedge qualifying criteria discussed in Chapter Six. It is necessary for the hedging entity (the parent company, a subsidiary or a defined foreign operation) to be part to the hedging contract and the risk exposure must be in a currency other than the functional currency of the hedging unit that could impact earnings. The standard (ASC 815-20-25-30) states:

a. For consolidated financial statements, either of the following conditions is met:
   1. The operating unit that has the foreign currency exposure is a party to the hedging instrument
   2. Another member of the consolidated group that has the same functional currency as that operating unit is a party to the hedging instrument and there is no intervening subsidiary with a different functional currency.
b. The hedged transaction is denominated in a currency other than *the hedging unit's* functional currency.

### 10.9.2 Other Unique Features

Currency hedging is also influenced by earlier standards on currency matters related to currency translation. To be consistent with earlier standards, the guides on hedge accounting provide several unique features for hedging currency risk. These features are summarized as follows:

1. *Permitting Hedging Net Position*: An essential feature of hedge accounting in general is to *account for hedging a specific risk*, which rules out hedging net positions (an asset less a liability) because each component faces a different type of risk. This feature was modified in currency hedging to permit designating Net Investment in Foreign Operations (and foreign investments that are accounted for using the Equity Method) as a hedge item.
2. *Non-derivative Financial Instruments as a Hedge*: In all other areas, hedge accounting treatment is permitted only if the hedge instrument is a financial derivative and the hedge item is not a derivative. But an exception is made for hedging currency risk. Foreign-currency-denominated non-derivative financial instruments that can generate currency gain or loss (i.e., have earnings impact) are permitted to be used as hedge instruments for hedging currency risk exposure in the following situations:

   a. Hedging a foreign-currency-denominated non-financial item.
   b. Hedging a firm commitment denominated in a foreign currency only when applying the fair value hedge treatment.
   c. Hedging net investment in foreign operations and foreign-currency-denominated investments that are accounted for by the Equity Method.

3. *Restrictions on Hedging the AFS Securities*: Unlike the case with hedging currency risk exposure of foreign-currency-denominated financial assets and liabilities, fair value hedge model only is permitted to account for hedging foreign-currency-denominated AFS, provided that two other conditions are met. These conditions are as follows:

   a. The AFS security is not traded on an exchange (or other established marketplace) on which trades are denominated in the enterprise's own functional currency.
   b. Dividends or other cash flows to holders of the security are denominated in the same foreign currency as the currency the enterprise expects to receive upon sale of the security.[14]

4. *Dual Treatment*: In principle, adopting the cash flow hedge or the fair value hedge accounting treatment is permitted under three conditions:

   a. The risk being hedged is, in effect, the risk exposure of the entity; a cash flow hedge is permitted if the entity faces the risk of volatility of cash flow, and a fair value hedge is permitted if the entity faces the possibility of loss of value.
   b. The risk being hedged is identifiable and quantifiable.
   c. The chosen hedge accounting treatment is consistent with management intent.

   In some cases, a recognized asset or liability might be exposed to both cash flow risk and the risk of value loss. In those cases, the standards permit using both the cash flow hedge to hedge the probable volatility of cash flow and fair value hedge to hedge the probable loss in value.

The unique adaptation of these rules to hedging currency risk permits management to choose either the cash flow hedge treatment or the fair value hedge treatment for each of the following:

a. Foreign-currency-denominated firm commitment.
b. Foreign-currency-denominated recognized asset or liability

5. *Currency Translation Adjustment*: Neither cash flow hedge, nor fair value hedge applies accounting treatment to hedging: (a) net investment in foreign operations nor (b) investments accounted for by the equity method. Gain or loss on effective hedging of net investments is treated as an adjustment to Accumulated Translation Adjustment in OCI.
6. *Intercompany Transaction*: The general rule for allowing the application of hedge accounting is that the hedge instrument as well as contracts designated as hedged items must be contracts with external counterparties; and intercompany transactions are reconciled in the consolidated financial statements. However, an exception is made for hedging currency risk, which came about by considering the implications of adopting the concept of functional currency. *The enterprise would be exposed to currency risk if forecasted intercompany transactions were denominated in a currency other than the enterprise's functional currency.*
7. *Special Provision for Highly Liquid Currency*: A foreign-currency (not a functional currency)-denominated forward contract for a highly liquid currency (e.g., Japanese yen) is considered a derivative even if it must be settled by delivery of units of that currency because a highly liquid currency can be easily converted into cash units of functional currency. It follows that a forward contract for an illiquid currency is not considered a derivative eligible for hedge accounting.
8. *Remeasurement is not a Revaluation to Fair Value*: The general rule in hedge accounting is to prohibit fair valued (marked-to-market) items whose changes in value flow through earnings from being designated as hedge items. However, a special case exists with respect to foreign-currency-denominated items. Under ASC 830, foreign-currency-denominated assets or liabilities for which currency transaction gains or losses are recognized in the income statement are to be remeasured using the spot currency exchange rate; this is what we have presented earlier as transaction–settlement risk. For the purpose of applying hedge accounting, this remeasurement does not constitute a revaluation to fair value. For example, in the above illustration (in 10.7.2) of the transaction between *P&K Co.* and *OZi Mining, Ltd.*, either one or both companies had to remeasure the value of receivables or payables to reflect the changes in currency exchange rates between the time of the transaction and settlement. The gain or loss on this currency transaction-settlement was posted to earnings. The remeasurement that took place for this purpose is not considered a revaluation to fair value that would prohibit the application of hedge accounting. Therefore, these foreign-currency-denominated assets and liabilities can be designated as hedge items in either cash flow hedges or fair value hedges, provided that all other hedge accounting criteria are satisfied.
9. *Forecasted Transactions*: Foreign exchange transaction risk associated with forecasted purchase or sale of a non-financial item is a hedgeable risk.

Exhibit 10.6 outlines these accepted hedgeable currency risks, the hedge instruments allowed for each case, and the hedge accounting method.

## Exhibit 10.6 Hedgeable Currency Risk and Hedging Approaches

| Hedgeable item or position | Hedging model | Hedge instrument |
|---|---|---|
| Hedging a financial item—recognized financial asset or a recognized financial liability denominated in foreign currency (except AFS securities) | *Both,*<br>Fair value hedge<br>Cash flow hedge | Only financial derivative instruments |
| AFS securities denominated in a foreign currency | Only fair value hedge | |
| Hedging a foreign-currency-denominated non-financial item | *Both,*<br>Cash flow hedge<br>Fair value hedge | Financial derivative<br>OR |
| Hedging currency risk in a firm commitment | Fair value hedge | Foreign-currency-denominated non-derivative financial instrument |
| Intercompany forecasted transaction if denominated in a foreign currency other than the functional currency | Cash flow hedge | Financial derivatives only |
| Hedging a forecasted transaction denominated in a foreign currency | | |
| Hedging net assets in foreign investment<br>Foreign investments accounted for by the equity method | Neither cash flow hedge, nor fair value hedge<br>Gain or loss on effective hedging is treated as an adjustment to accumulated translation adjustment in OCI | Financial derivatives<br>OR<br>Foreign-currency-denominated non-derivative financial instrument |

### 10.9.3 Examples of Hedging Currency in some Enterprises

Multinational enterprises differ from one another in the extent to which each one uses currency derivatives. For example, total fair value of all financial derivatives at McDonalds Corporation amounted to $355 million in 2011. By comparison to other multinationals of the same size, this volume is modest and may be due to a stated management policy: "The Company does not use derivatives with a level of complexity or with a risk higher than the exposures to be hedged and does not hold or issue derivatives for trading purposes."[15]

Examples from Merck & Co., Inc. and General Electric provide information for comparison. In its 2011 Annual Report, Merck & Co., Inc. reported the amounts of currency risk for which hedge accounting is applied: at €5.6 billion and fair value is (€246) million. The corresponding numbers for which hedge accounting *is not* applied are €1.2 billion and (€7.8) million.

Currency hedging activities at General Electric Company are presented in Exhibit 10.7. In 2011, the fair value (not the national amount) value of financial derivatives assets exceeded $15 billion and the fair value of financial derivatives liabilities was $5 billion. The corresponding numbers for 2010 are $5.5 billion and $1.30 billion, respectively. It must be emphasized that these numbers are after master account netting, which was more than $3.0 billion of assets and liabilities in each of these two years.[16] Before netting, the total fair value of currency hedges in 2011 was about $5.5 billion, of which only $4.2 billion was designated as hedges and was accounted for using hedge accounting. The balance was considered an "economic hedge." Overall, currency derivatives account for about 50% of the fair value of all derivatives recognized on the balance sheet of General Electric Company.

## Exhibit 10.7 Excerpts from General Electric 2011 Form 10-K

The notional amounts of derivative contracts represent the basis upon which interest and other payments are calculated and are reported gross, except for offsetting foreign currency forward contracts that are executed in order to manage our currency risk of net investment in foreign subsidiaries. Of the outstanding notional amount of $328,000 million, approximately 89% or $292,000 million is associated with reducing or eliminating the interest rate, currency or market risk between financial assets and liabilities in our financial services businesses. The remaining derivative activities primarily relate to hedging against adverse changes in currency exchange rates and commodity prices related to anticipated sales and purchases and contracts containing certain clauses that meet the accounting definition of a derivative. The instruments used in these activities are designated as hedges when practical. When we are not able to apply hedge accounting, or when the derivative and the hedged item are both recorded in earnings currently, we deem the derivatives economic hedges and hedge accounting is not applied. This most frequently occurs when we hedge a recognized foreign currency transaction (e.g., a receivable or payable) with a derivative. Since the effects of changes in exchange rates are reflected currently in earnings for both the derivative and the transaction, the economic hedge does not require hedge accounting.

The following table provides information about the fair value of our derivatives by contract type, separating those accounted for as hedges and those that are not.

| | At December 31, 2011 | | At December 31, 2010 | |
|---|---|---|---|---|
| | Fair value | | Fair value | |
| *(In millions)* | Assets | Liabilities | Assets | Liabilities |
| **Derivatives accounted for as hedges** | | | | |
| Interest rate contracts | $9,446 | $1,049 | $5,959 | $2,675 |
| Currency exchange contracts | 4,189 | 3,174 | 2,965 | 2,533 |
| Other contracts | 1 | 11 | 5 | – |
| | 13,636 | 4,234 | 8,929 | 5,208 |
| **Derivatives not accounted for as hedges** | | | | |
| Interest rate contracts | 319 | 241 | 294 | 552 |
| Currency exchange contracts | 1,309 | 425 | 1,602 | 846 |
| Other contracts | 381 | 137 | 531 | 50 |
| | 2,009 | 803 | 2,427 | 1,448 |

| | | | | |
|---|---|---|---|---|
| **Netting adjustments**[(a)] | (3,294) | (3,281) | (3,867) | (3,857) |
| **Cash collateral**[(b)(c)] | (2,310) | (1,027) | (2,043) | (1,385) |
| Total | $10,041 | $729 | $5,446 | $1,414 |

Derivatives are classified in the captions "All other assets" and "All other liabilities" in our financial statements.

(a) The netting of derivative receivables and payables is permitted when a legally enforceable master netting agreement exists. Amounts included fair value adjustments related to our own and counterparty non-performance risk. At December 31, 2011 and 2010, the cumulative adjustment for non-performance risk was a loss of $13 million and $10 million, respectively.

(b) Excludes excess collateralization of $579 million at December 31, 2011 and an insignificant amount at December 31, 2010.

(c) Excludes securities pledged to us as collateral of $10,574 million and $5,577 million at December 31, 2011 and 2010, respectively.

Source: http://ir.10kwizard.com/files.php?source=329&welc_next=1&page=1&ext=, p. 166.

## 10.10 Currency Hedge Accounting Illustrations

### 10.10.1 Using Forward Contracts to Hedge Foreign-Currency-Denominated Debt

#### *10.10.1.1 The Setting*

- *UImporte Company* is an American company that uses the U.S. dollar as its functional currency.
- On June 1, 20x8, *UImporte* purchased 250 motorbikes from the Brazilian *BraziBikes, Ltda* company for R$1,000,000.
- Also on June 1, 20x8, the spot exchange rate was USD1.00/BRL1.5384, or US$0.65 for each R$1.00.
- The purchase of motorbikes was on credit by giving a note payable in three months.
- By delaying the settlement after the contract date, *UImporte* is exposed to currency risk because the purchase agreement with *BraziBikes, Ltda* is denominated in Brazilian currency.

#### *10.10.1.2 The Hedge*

On the day of the purchase of motorcycles, the management of *UImporte* was concerned about a possible appreciation of the Brazilian currency against the U.S. dollar and decided to hedge the currency settlement risk associated with the note payable *UImporte* made to *BraziBikes, Ltda*. On 6/1/20x8, *UImporte* entered into a currency forward contract (contract *C81FZ*) with the currency dealer DFX to purchase R$1,000,000 at the forward price of R$1.541 for US$1.00 (or US$0.64829 for each R$1.00) for delivery on August 31, 20x8.

Table 10.1 presents the movements of spot and forward exchange rates of the Brazilian real for the U.S. dollar and the changes in values of the note payable and the currency forward during the contract period.

## Information Note: Reading this Table

The data in Table 10.1 are discussed and used for analysis following the table. To be able to follow this table, the reader may look first at Row A and Row E, and then begin to read the analysis and return to different cells in the table as you go.

**Table 10.1** Price Behavior of Currency Exchange Rate between the Brazilian Real and the U.S. Dollar

Panel A for the Spot Rate Movement

| | | *Brazilian Real Rate (R$ for US$1.00)* | | *Brazilian Real Rate (US$ for R$1.00)* | | | |
|---|---|---|---|---|---|---|---|
| | Column 1 | Column 2 | Column 3 | Spot Rate | | | |
| | | Spot (Amount of R$ for one USD) | Forward (Amount of R$ for one USD) | Column 4 FX Rate No. of USD for R$1.00 | Column 5 Δ Value: (Period to period) In US$ | Column 6 ΔValue due to unexpected Currency change in US$ | Column 7 Balance of change period -to-period From in US$ |
| Row A | 6/1/ 20x8 | 1.5384 | 1.541 | 0.650 | — | — | — |
| Row B | 6/30/20x8 | 1.512 | 1.515 | 0.661376 | (11,376) | (11,019) | (11,376) (Row B of Column 5) |
| Row C | 7/15/20x8 | 1.5268 | 1.527 | 0.654965 | 6,411 | 6,906 | (4,966) (Rows B + C of Column 5) |
| Row D | 8/31/20x8 | 1.5236 | 1.5236 | 0.65634 | (1,375) | (1,290) | (6,340) (Rows B+ C+ D of Column 5) |

Panel B for the Forward Contract (*C81FZ*)

| | | Brazilian Real Rate in US$ | | |
|---|---|---|---|---|
| | Column 8 | Column 9 | Column 10 | Column 11 |
| | *Date* | *Forward FX Rate* | *ΔValue (period to period)* | *Fair Value of Forward* |
| Row E | 6/1/ 20x8 | 0.648929(a) | | |
| Row F | 6/30/20x8 | 0.660066 | 11,137 | 11,063 |
| Row G | 7/15/20x8 | 0.654879 | (5,187) | 5,923 |
| Row H | 8/31/20x8 | 0.65634 | 1,488 | 7,411 |

Notes:

a. First Period: June 1 – Jun 30:
   - Actual change in the value of debt = (0.65 – 0.0661376) x R$1,000,000 = (US$11,376) a loss (Row B, Column 5).

- o The change in the value of currency forward = (0.648929 - 0.660066) x R$1,000,000 = US$11,137 a gain (Row F, Column 10).

  The carrying cost is 4% p.a. (the risk free rate). Discounting the US$11,137 at 4% for one month gives us a present value of US$11,063 (Row F, Column 11).

b. Second Period: (June 30 – July 15):
   - o Change in the value of the debt = (0.661376 – 0.654965) * R$1,000,000 = US$6,411 a gain (Row C, Column 5)
   - o The net change in the value of the debt = US$11,376 – US$6,411 = US$4,965 (Row c, column 7)
   - o Change in the forward = (0.654879 – 0.660066) * R$1,000,000 = (US$5,187) a loss (Row G, Column 10).
   - o Over the entire period, the change is 0.654879 – 0.648929 *R$1,000,000 =US$5,950.
   - o At 0.04, the present value for the remaining six weeks is US$5,923 (Row G, Column 11)
   - o Therefore, the change in the present value is US$11,063 – US$5,923 = US$5,140.

c. Third period 7/15/20x8 – 8/31/20x8

   Because the hedge was ineffective in the second period, the management kept the currency forward as a trading security. More details below.

## 10.10.2 Processing and Accounting Documentation

### *10.10.2.1 First Period of Exchange Rate Change: June 1–June 30*

#### Change in the Fair Value of Debt

- For the purpose of this analysis, using the exchange rate of the Brazilian real to the U.S. dollar or using the exchange rate of the U.S. dollar to the Brazilian real will achieve the same results; in either case, transaction costs are ignored.
- Comparing the spot and forward rates, *the forward points represent the difference between the spot and forward rates of currency exchange*. On June 1, 20x8, the spot rate is USD1.00/BRL1.538 and the forward rate is USD1.00/BRL1.541. The forward contract has higher exchange rate than the spot contract by the forward points of R$0.003 for each US$1.00 for the three months from June 1 to August 31. This is the anticipated rate of change.

### Information Log: The Nature of the Forward Points

Forward points represent the difference between the spot exchange rate and the forward exchange rate. They are determined by the interest rates prevailing in the two currencies (see IRP earlier in this Chapter and Chapter Five for discussion of forward contracts). Given IRP, the currency of the higher yield country will have negative forward points and the currency of the lower yield country will have positive forward points. In this example, the USA is the country with higher yield relative to Brazil. Given the parity, arbitrageurs could not earn abnormal (arbitrage) profits. Forward points are quoted in Pips (0.00001 or 1/10,000) of the spot rate. For example, if the forward rate is higher than the spot rate by 0.001648, it would be quoted as "plus 16.48." Similarly, if the forward rate is lower than the spot rate by 0.001648, it would be quoted as "minus 16.48."

- Looking at it from the viewpoint of *UImporte*, the buyer in the USA, the spot rate on June 1, 20x8 is US$0.65 for each R$1.00 and the forward rate is US$0.648929. Therefore, the positive forward points from the Brazilian vantage point are negative from the vantage point of the *UImporte*.

- In either case, the forward price is the predicted (equilibrium) spot price. If the forward rate is the prediction that will be actually realized, currency markets predict that *UImporte* will have to transfer $648,929 to *BraziBikes* to settle the R$1,000,000 payable on August 31 (if everything else remains unchanged). The difference between US$650,000 and US$648,929 is US$1,071.
- Using this information, the expected rates of decline in currency exchange rate (from the U.S. *UImporte* standpoint) are as follows:
    - (0.65 – 0.648929)/0.65 = 0.001648 for the three-month period;
    - 0.001648/3 ≈ 0.0005493 per month.

    To verify this information, consider the following:

    Total forward points are $1,071 and can be calculated in either of the two approaches below:

    i. 0.00054935 × US$650,000 = 357 per month and 357 × 3 ≈ $1,071 for the entire period.
    ii. (0.65 – 0.648929) × R$1,000,000 = $1,071

- It would be to the benefit of *UImporte* that the exchange rate declines, but what concerns the management of *UImporte* is the unexpected rise in exchange rate (the downside risk) which may require more than US$650,000 to settle the payable.
- It is important to note that neither *UImporte* nor the currency dealer DFX pays or receives the forward points at the time of signing the contract.
- As it turned out, both the spot rate and the forward rate increased (from the standpoint of *UImporte*) by the end of the month. The spot rate increased from US$0.65 for R$1.00 to US$0.661376, which means that, if *UImporte* did not have a forward contract, it would have had to transfer US$661,376 to settle the payment— which would be a loss of US$11,376.
- As noted above, the US$11,376 would be the total loss of which only US$357 gain was anticipated by the forward rate. Therefore, the unexpected currency loss would be US$11,376 – US$357 = US$11,019.
- A summary of change in fair value of debt (Row B in the Table):

    Total $11,376 → $357 expected (gain)
    Total $11,376 → $11,019 unexpected (loss)

### Change in the Fair Value of the Forward Contract—contract *C81FZ*

- The fair value of the forward is the change in exchange rate from the contract price discounted to the present value at the "cost of carry," which is assumed to be the risk-free rate. The annual risk-free rate (based on LIBOR) is 4%.
- The total change in the forward contract fair value would be

    (0.660066 – 0.648929) × R$1,000,000 = US$11,137. (Row F)

- If everything remains the same, the US$11,137 would be the gain on the forward contract that *UImporte* will realize on August 31, 20x8.
- But on June 30, 20x8, the forward contract is not worth US$11,137. It is worth the present value of this amount; discounted for a two-month period at the risk-free rate of 4% p.a. and the discounted value is

    $11,137/(1 + (0.04 \times 2/12)) = \$11,063$

### Retrospective Test of Hedge Effectiveness as of June 30, 20x8

In the hedge documentation, the management decided to exclude the forward points from the measurement of hedge effectiveness. Using the dollar offset ratio (DOR), effectiveness of the hedge is

$$|-11,063/11,019| = 1.004.$$

*Conclusion*: the hedge is highly effective because the DOR falls within the accepted range of 0.80–1.25.

If the management included the forward points in measuring the effectiveness, the DOR would have been |–11,376/11,137| = 1.02, which is still highly effective.

### Journal Entries for the Period June 1, 20x8 through June 30, 20x8

| | *Journal Entries* | *Debit (in U.S. dollars)* | *Credit (in U.S. dollars)* |
|---|---|---|---|
| 6/1/20x8 | Inventory—Motorbikes model BR2G<br>Note Payable—*BraziBikes, Ltda*<br>*To record the purchase of 250 motorbikes from Brazil at R$1,000,000 translated to US$ at the spot currency exchange rate.* | $650,000 | <br>$650,000 |
| 6/1/20x8 | Memorandum: *UImporte entered into a currency forward contract (contract C81FZ) with DFX Dealer to purchase R$1,000,000 at R$1.541 for US$1.00 for delivery on August 31, 20x8.* | — | — |
| 6/30/20x8 | Currency Gain/Loss<br>Note Payable—*BraziBikes, Ltda*<br>*To record the loss resulting from the increase in the fair value of the note payable to BraziBikes, Ltda due to change of currency rates from R$1.5384 per US$1.00 to R$1.515 currency loss.* | 11,376 | <br>11,376 |
| 6/30/20x8 | Forward Contract—Currency Dealer Accounts-DFX<br>Currency Gains/Losses—*Forward c ontract C81FZ*<br>*To record the gain on the currency forward contract entered into with DFX for the purpose of hedging the value of debt to BraziBikes, Ltda as the forward exchange rate for August 30 delivery of Brazilian real has changed from R$1.541 for US$1.00 to R$1.515 for US$1.00.* | 11,063 | <br>11,063 |

On 6/30/20x8:

The loss on inventory of $11,376 and the gain on the forward contract of $11,063 will be closed in the statement of income for the period ended June 30, 20x8. The $313 difference could be considered financing expense, or a cost of the inventory.

## *10.10.2.2 Second Period of Exchange Rate Change: June 30–July 15*

### Change in the Fair Value of Debt

- Using the information in Table 10.1, the expected rates of decline in currency exchange rate (from the U.S. *UImporte* standpoint) are as follows:
- On June 30, the expected decline in the exchange rate for the remainder of the contract is (from Row B, Column & Row F, Column 9 in Table 10.1):

(0.661376 – 0.660066)/0.661376
= 0.0019807, which is 0.0002476 per week (0.0019807/8).

- For the two weeks until July 15 when the exchange rate changed again, the expected decline is 0.00197 × 2weeks/8weeks = 0.000495; and the dollar amount is R$1,000,000 × 0.000495 = US$495.
- The actual change in currency is equal to 0.654965 – 0.661376 = –6,411

  This is a decline in the fair value of the debt; i.e., a gain for *UImporte*.

- The anticipation was to lose $495, but the net result is a gain of US$6,411, which means the total gain is actually 6,411 + 495 = $6,906. In other words, the US$6,411 gain is effectively the net after covering the US$495 expected loss.

### Change in the Fair Value of the Forward Contract

- The fair value of the forward is change in exchange rate from the contract price discounted to the present value at the "cost of carry," which is assumed to be the risk-free rate. The annual risk-free rate (based on LIBOR) is 0.04.
- The total change in the forward contract fair value for the two-week period is (Row G, Column 9 & Row F, Column 9 in Table 10.1) equal to

  (0.654879 – 0.660066) × R$1,000,000 = (US$5,187).

- At the beginning of June, *UImporte* agreed to buy R$1,000,000 for US$648,929. When the currency rate increased to 0.660066, the currency dealer would have had to pay *UImporte* for the increase in cost, which is US$11,137 and that was treated as a currency gain. But in the first two weeks of July, the rate declined from 0.660066 to 0.65634, which means the currency dealer DFX would have to claim back the difference from *UImporte*. Over the entire period from June 1, 20x8 to July 15, 20x8, the change in the currency rate is equal to

  (0.654879 – 0.648929) × R$1,000,000 = US$5,950

- The US$5,950 is the dollar amount that *UImporte* would pay on August 31, 20x8 *if everything remains the same*. But, on July 15, 20x8, the forward contract is only worth the present value of $5,950. Discounting this amount for the six-week period at the 4% annual rate results in

  5,950/1+ (0.04 × 6 weeks/52 weeks) ≈ US$5,923

- In order for the present value of the balance of the fair value of the contract to drop from US$11,063 to $5,923, the change in the fair value of the forward should be equal to US$5,140 (the difference between the balance forwarded from preceding period of US$11,063 and the present value of US$5,923).

### Retrospective Test of Hedge Effectiveness as of July 15, 20x8.

In the hedge documentation, the management decided to exclude the forward points from the measurement of hedge effectiveness.

Using DOR, effectiveness of the hedge is

|–5,140/6,906| = 0.744

*Conclusion*: The hedge is ineffective and hedge accounting must be terminated.

### Management Decision

Given that the management of *UImporte* must terminate the hedge, decisions must be made on the following:

1. Whether or not to keep the forward contract.
2. Whether or not to pay off the debt early.
3. If the debt is not paid off before August 31, 20x8, how much of the change in the fair value of the debt should be accounted for?

### Assumptions

Assume that the management decided to keep the currency forward contract (*contract C81FZ*) as part of the trading securities portfolio. Also assume further analysis showed that the hedge became ineffective on July 15.

*Result*: Account for the hedge as usual until July 15, 20x8 only and adjust the book value of the debt to fair value until July 15, 20x8.

### Journal Entries for the Period June 30 through July 15, 20x8

| *Date* | *Transactions* | *Debit (in U.S. dollars)* | *Credit (in U.S. dollars)* |
|---|---|---|---|
| 7/15/20x8 | Note Payable— *BraziBikes, Ltda*<br>Currency Gain/Loss<br>*To record the gain resulting from the increase in the fair value of the note payable to BraziBikes, Ltda due to change of currency rates from R$1.512 per US$1.00 to R$1.5268 currency loss.* | 6,411 | 6,411 |
| 7/15/20x8 | Currency Gains/Losses— *Forward contract C81FZ*<br>Forward Contract—Currency Dealer Accounts-DFX<br>*To record the loss on the currency forward contract entered into with DFX for the purpose of hedging the value of debt to BraziBikes, Ltda as the forward exchange rate for August 30 delivery of Brazilian real has changed from R$1.541for US$1.00 to R$1.515 for US$1.00.* | 5,140 | 5,140 |

July 15, 20x8 is not the end of a reporting period.

The gain on the fair value of inventory of $6,411 and the loss on the forward contract in the amount of $5,140 will be closed in the income statement on September 30, 20x8. The $1,271 difference could be considered financing expense (IFRS), or a cost of the inventory (U.S. GAAP).

## *10.10.2.3 Period 3 from July 15, 20x8 through September 30, 20x8*

### Valuation of Debt

No additional change in values of the hedged item since the hedge is terminated. By August 31, 20x8, the book value of debt is $654,966 (= 650,000 +11,376 – 6411). However, *UImporte* will settle the note payable at the currency exchange rate of 0.65634 prevailing on August 31, 20x8 and recognize a currency loss of the difference, $1,375.

### The Derivative Contract

Although the hedge is terminated, the currency forward contract *C81FZ* is a financial derivative and will continue to be accounted for at fair value and the change in fair value will be recognized directly in earnings. The change in fair value is the difference in currency rates between July 15 and August 31 times R$1,000,000 and is calculated in three steps:

1. Total change in value since inception = (0.65634 – 0.648929) × 1,000,000 = US$7,411.
2. Balance of currency forward as of July 15, 20x8 is US$5,923.
3. The excess of total change over the beginning balance is 7,411 – 5923 = $1,488

Currency dealer DFX has a debit balance of $7,411 (11,063 – 5,140 + 1,488). The forward contract is settled net on August 31, 20x8. On December 30, 20x8, the end of the reporting period, the Currency Gains/Losses—Forward Contract *C81FZ* will be closed in the earnings statement.

### Journal Entries

| *Date* | *Transaction* | *Debit (in US dollars)* | *Credit (in US dollars)* |
|---|---|---|---|
| 7/15/20x8 | Currency Gain/Loss—<br>Note Payable—*BraziBikes, Ltda*<br>*To record the gain resulting from the increase in the fair value of the note payable to BraziBikes, Ltda due to change of currency rates from R$1.512 per US$1.00 to R$1.5268 currency loss.* | 1,375 | <br>1,375 |
| 8/31/20x8 | Forward Contract—Currency Dealer Accounts-DFX<br>Currency Gains/Losses—Forward Contract *C81FZ*<br>*To record the gain the Currency Forward Contract C81FZ entered into with BraziBikes, Ltda. During this period, the hedge was ineffective and the Currency Gain in the amount of 1,488 will be recognized in earnings as Other Income.* | 1,488 | <br>1,488 |

The hedge was ineffective as of July 15, 20x8. Therefore, the gain of $1,488 on the forward contract will be recognized in earnings on September 30, 20x8 as gain on trading securities.

| | | | |
|---|---|---|---|
| 8/31/20x8 | Notes Payable—BraziBikes, Ltda<br>Cash<br>*Paying off the note payable to BraziBikes, Ltda at the prevailing currency rate of US$0.65634 for R$1.00*<br>*Because the hedge during this period is ineffective, the Currency Settlement Loss will be recognized in earnings as other expense. It should not be charged to inventory cost.* | 656,341[a] | <br>656,341 |
| 8/31/20x8 | Cash<br>Currency Dealer Accounts–DFX<br>*To record collection of the foreign currency dealer's debt.* | 7,411 | <br>7,411 |

a. Rounding errors of $1.00.

#### 10.10.2.4 Analysis

##### Cash Flow

- The company paid US$656,341 to settle the note payable, which is US$6,341 higher than the company would have paid at the time of purchase.
- However, the company collected US$7,411 from the currency dealer for the currency forward.
- The net cash outflow for the company is 656,341 – 7,411 = $648,930, which is the cost the company intended to pay by entering into the forward contract (there is $1.00 rounding error). Termination of the hedge did not change there facts.
- The cash paid for the note payable is less than what could have been paid at the time of purchase by 650,000 – 648,930 = $1,070, which is the amount of the forward points at the inception of the hedge.

##### Earnings

- The net amount recognized in the earnings statement is $1,071, which is calculated as follows:
  - Credit: $1,271 adjustment to financing cost on 9/30/20x8
    $1,488 gain on the forward contract at settlement (a trading security at that time)
  - Debit: 313 financing expense on June 30, 20x8
    $1,375 currency loss on settling the note payable on August 30, 20x8
- The net effect on earnings is an increase by $1,071.

##### Conclusion

The impact on earnings and cash is equal to the contract's forward points.

#### 10.10.2.5 The Alternative Measure of Hedge Effectiveness

When documenting the hedge, the management could have decided *ex-ante* to use cumulative changes (rather than period-by-period change) to evaluate hedge effectiveness. If that choice was made, the evaluation will show:

DOR = |cΔ Forward Contract Value/cΔ Value of the Debt|

Using the data in Table 10.1, we have:

On June 30 = Row B, Column 7/Row F, Column 11
= |11,063/11,376| = 0.97
On July 15 = Row C, Column 7/Row G, Column 11
= |4,966/5923| = 0.838

In this case, the hedge is highly effective in both periods and *UImporte* could continue to use hedge accounting.

The analysis for both periods ending June 30 and July 15 will be the same as above, except concluding that the hedge meets the effectiveness test. The difference in analysis and reporting will be in the third period, between July 15 and August 31.

## 10.11 Summary of Key Points

- A currency exchange rate is the number of units of one currency to be exchanged for one unit of another currency. Currency exchange rates are always stated in pairs.
- The Gold Standard prevailed between 1944 and 1973; the U.S. dollar was pegged to the price of gold and other currencies were pegged to the U.S. dollar. Since 1973 most countries have allowed their currencies to fluctuate with market conditions. Allowing currency exchange rates to fluctuate has given rise to different types of currency prices:

    1. *Spot Rate*: The exchange rate at a given point in time. Sometimes referred to as the cash rate.
    2. *Forward Rate*: The rate at which one currency can be exchanged for another on a future date.
    3. *Current Rate*: In accounting contexts, the term "current rate" refers to the spot rate on the date of the financial statements.

- There are also two types of currency:

    1. *Exchange Currency*: This is the actual currency of a country or a region and is the currency used for trade and for settling obligations.
    2. *Functional Currency*: This is the (exchange) currency in which the enterprise carries out its major revenue-generating activities, costing or financing transactions. This currency is used for accounting purposes—consolidation and hedge designation.

- Numerous factors affect changes in currency exchange rates, including *BoP* (net cash flows of a country in relationship to others), differences in inflation rates, and differences in interest rates, government policies and tariffs.
- In frictionless efficient markets, currency exchange rates reflect both expected inflation and differential change in interest rates between the two countries of the currency pair. Therefore, it is the unexpected changes in currency rates that expose an enterprise to risk of loss.
- Enterprises face three types of currency risk that arise from changes in currency exchange rates:

    1. *Transaction-settlement risk*: The probability of loss in the settlement of foreign-currency denominated transaction if the settlement and transaction dates are different (other than the three-day allowed for regular-way-settlement).
    2. *Operating risk*: The risk of incurring future losses by losing revenues or by increasing cost of operations.
    3. *Translation risk*: Incurring losses in the net assets invested in foreign operations.

- Enterprises can manage currency risk either by a form of natural hedging or by financial hedging.

    A. Natural hedging may require one of the following (among others):

        i. Balancing the inflows and outflows in a given currency.
        ii. Entering into a money market hedge.
        iii. Undertaking parallel loans.

    B. Financial hedging involved using financial derivatives to hedge currency risk exposure.

- This chapter focuses on transaction settlement risk and provides illustrations of the accounting and mechanics of recording hedging transactions using currency futures and forward contracts. Chapter Eleven covers hedging operating risk and translation risk.

## Notes

1 In many circles, a *direct* currency quote is one in which the "home country" currency is the *base* currency; the currency quotation is *indirect* when the "home country" currency is the counter or quoted currency. Other than market convention, any currency could be a base currency or a quote currency. See http/// www.oanda.com/currency/table

2 There is, however, a concern that Chinese renminbi is not allowed to change with supply and demand because it appears to be pegged to the U.S. dollar and is subject to the Chinese government controls.

3 Purchasing Power Parity theory does not fully explain the determinants of the supply and demand for a given commodity in an economy. An explanation that interested financial economists is the productivity-consumption theory (see Balassa, 1964; Samuelson, 1964). Under this theory, productivity in an economy biases PPP because a country will have a higher overall price level if it is highly productive in traded goods, relative to its own non-traded goods, and relative to the traded goods of other countries.

4 But the empirical evidence is generated from historical observations obtained from environments that do not satisfy the *ceteris paribus* assumption.

5 In Forex markets, the euro is always quoted as the *base currency*.

6 This distinction between *spot* and *current* is perhaps unique in the jargon of accounting for foreign currency translation.

7 The new standard was SFAS No. 52, which is now ASC 830. SFAS No. 8 is the standard that was in effect before 1981. Applying that standard required taking all currency gains and losses to earnings, which caused more earnings volatility as well as extensive lobbying by preparers of financial statements to change the standard.

8 This would be under the accounting guidance that contracting and settling are two different transactions.

9 Parallel loans and back-to-back loans are a bit different but are very similar.

10 This was the normal practice in accounting for parallel loans until the amending of FAS 133 and the corresponding adaptation of IAS 39 to permit designating non-derivative financial assets and liabilities as a hedge item. If either the U.K. or the Canadian company in this example designate the loan or the asset denominated in the foreign currency as a hedge of another hedged item, and if the hedge is effective, accounting for the loan or the asset designated as a hedge would be linked to the hedged item.

11 McDonalds Corporation, Form 10-K, 2011, pp. 24 and 34. http://markets.financialcontent.com/stocks/quote/filings/quarterly?Symbol=MCD

12 Since 1994, the Brazilian currency is the *Brazilian real* (plural is *reais or reals*), each real consists of 100 *centavos*. It has the three-letter FX code BRL and currency symbol R$.

13 http://www.landsvirkjun.com/about-us/reports/

14 This dual accounting treatment of hedging firm commitment is allowed only in foreign-currency-denominated contracts. See, ASC 815-20-55-136 and ASC 815-20-55-137.

15 2011 Form 10-K, page 20, http://markets.financialcontent.com/stocks/quote/filings/quarterly?Symbol=MCD

16 It is allowable to net assets and liabilities for derivative transactions with same counterparty through the ISDA to Master Agreement. See, www.isda.org

# CHAPTER 11

# OPERATING AND ACCOUNTING CURRENCY RISK

## 11.1 A Brief Review

A number of economists maintain that currency exchange rates embody expectations about different determinants—i.e., inflation rates, interest rate, balance of payment, etc., while others claim that the known models have failed to outperform the simple *random walk* models.[1] Under either scenario, any nonzero difference from expectations would be unexpected surprises that could expose the enterprise to currency risk. Hedging currency risk is one of the main approaches that multinational companies use to mitigate this risk.

As noted in Chapter Ten, currency exchange rates are dynamic because the determinants of these rates are not stationary. These determinants include:

- Changes in the country's balance of payment.
- Inflation differences in different regions.
- Changes in interest rates and cost of capital across national boundaries.
- Government actions and regulatory interventions.
- Political risk and regional instability.

Having foreign operations exposes multinational enterprises to the possibility of loss caused by the effects of adverse movements of exchange rates on transactions, investments, or expected future operations. Neither the exposure to currency risk nor the need to manage it is new; however, the methods and approaches employed in mitigating and accounting for it are of relatively of recent origin, especially for derivative instruments that have been growing at exponential rates since late 1990s.

## 11.2 Volume of Currency Derivatives

Over-the-counter derivative trading is so far a "dark market" in the sense that only the players know what is going on. Unfortunately, dealers are not required to disclose any information to the public; there is no regulation of any kind and there is no transparency of any sort. However, derivatives' dealers do not mind self-reporting on their own activities.[2] The International Swap Dealers Association has been collecting survey data from large derivative dealers since the late 1990s.[3] Other groups collect survey data as well. In 2004, the Foreign Exchange Committee (FEC), a trade organization, began collecting information about foreign-currency markets in North America.[4] At the time this chapter was written, the most recent survey was dated October 2011. An abridged summary of the results is reported in Table 11.1. This survey reports an average *daily* (notional amounts) volume of trade of about $976.7 billion of which about 40% consists of currency derivative instruments and 60% consists of spot transactions.

**Table 11.1** Volume of Currency Trade in North America (Foreign Currency Committee, October 2011)

| *(all numbers are in million US dollars)* | *Average Daily Amount in Million US Dollars* | *Average Monthly Amount in Million US Dollars* |
|---|---|---|
| Spot Transactions | 564,466 | 11,853,760 |
| Forward Transactions | 135,291 | 2,841,079 |
| Foreign Exchange Swaps Transactions | 245,173 | 5,148,667 |
| Over the Counter Options | 31,816 | 668,158 |
| **GRAND TOTAL** | 976,746 | 20,511,664 |

Source: http://www.newyorkfed.org/FXC/volumesurvey/

## 11.3 Currency Operating Risk

### Information Log: Plan of Presentation

Chapter Three and Chapter Ten identify three types of currency risk:

1. *Transaction-settlement risk* related to the settlement of past and current transactions denominated in foreign currency.
2. *Operating risk* related to the impact of currency movements on future revenues and costs.
3. *Translation (accounting) risk* related to reporting investments in other currencies.

Economic risk is the combination of transaction-settlement risk and operating risk. Transaction-settlement risk is the focus of Chapter Ten, while operating risk and translation risk are the focus of this chapter.

Currency operating exposure refers to the negative impact of exchange rate movements on future revenues and expenses that will have adverse effects on the firm's present value. Unlike transaction-settlement risk, operating risk exposure is prospective and of longer term. In general, managements of multinational enterprises must make assumptions about currency exchange rates to use as a benchmark for forecasting foreign-currency-denominated sales, purchases, and services. Currency operating risk arises due to unexpected deviations from that benchmark. It is difficult to quantify this risk because it relates to future expectations rather than to current or past specific events or transactions. Therefore, one way of mitigating currency operating risk is to hedge forecasted transactions of sales, purchases, and services.

### 11.3.1 Hedging Forecasted Sales and Purchases

A feature of a well-managed enterprise is preparing a master budget for the next period(s) activities, which typically begins with forecasting sales and estimating the types of resources required to support the budgeted sales in different regions and different currencies. During this process, management forms predictions of the sales volume it expects to sell, the exchange price in foreign-currency units, and the expected currency exchange rates. These elements are required for the purpose of expressing forecasted foreign sales in units of local currency. Deviations from forecasts would occur due to unexpected changes in volume, sale price, or currency exchange rates. These factors are interconnected, however. Changing commodity prices could change the quantity demanded by consumers (the extent of which depends on the elasticity of demand). Commodity prices respond to changing demand and multinational enterprises need to be strategic in trying to sell (or buy) a budgeted quantity. As a result, foreign-currency-denominated sales (or purchases) expose the enterprise to two types of hedgeable price risk: commodity price risk and currency exchange rate risk. These risks differ for the exporter and the importer.

To show how the importer and the exporter experience opposite effects of changes in currency exchange rates, assume, for example, that commodity X2Y is produced in Germany and it is normally marketed at the price of €100.00 per unit. At the time a U.S. company is setting its budget for next quarter, the currency exchange rate EUR/USD is $1.50 for €1.00, which means that the price of commodity X2Y in U.S. dollars is $150.00 per unit. Depending on the currency denomination of the contracts, either the exporter in Germany or the importer in the USA are exposed to currency operating risk if actual currency exchange rates in future periods differ from the budgeted rate of $1.50 for €1.00.

The currency operating risk exposures will have opposite effects on the importer and the exporter:

- If the U.S. dollar appreciates and currency exchange rate changes to become $1.45 for €1.00 the price of commodity X2Y will be $145.00. The $5.00 difference would be a loss to the exporter in Germany and a gain for the importer in the USA.
- If the U.S. dollar depreciates and currency exchange rate changes to become $1.56 for €1.00, the price of commodity X2Y will be $156.00. The $6.00 difference would be a gain for the exporter in Germany and a loss to the importer in the USA.

Both the exporter in Germany and the importer in the USA (in this example) have the incentive to hedge this currency operating risk and both sides of the hedge would qualify for hedge accounting if, under both U.S. GAAP and IFRS, the following hedge accounting qualification criteria are met:

1. The hedgeable risk is well identified and quantifiable.
2. The realization of the hedged forecast is probable.
3. There would be an earnings effect due to the volatility of exchange rates or prices.
4. The hedge instrument is a financial derivative that:

    a. has an underlying—the exchange rate;
    b. has a notional amount or payment provision;
    c. has an insignificant initial investment;
    d. can be settled net or has a market mechanism for settlement.

5. The hedge is expected (*ex-ante*) to be highly effective.
6. For hedging forecasted transaction, changes in the fair value of the hedge instrument are deferred in an equity account (OCI) and are transferred to earnings when the hedged transaction (the forecasted sale) affects earnings.
7. The hedge instrument may also be a non-derivative financial contract denominated in a currency other than the entity's functional currency.

The different risk exposures of the importer and the exporter translate into different hedging strategies. Panel A of Figure 11.1 shows the currency risk profile of the exporter: loss with lower prices and gain with higher prices. To hedge the downside risk, the exporter would buy *put* options. In contrast, Panel B of Figure 11.1 shows the risk profile of the importer: gain with lower prices and loss with higher prices. To hedge the downside risk exposure, the importer would buy *call* options. These are simple strategies and are provided to illustrate the motivation for taking different hedging positions.

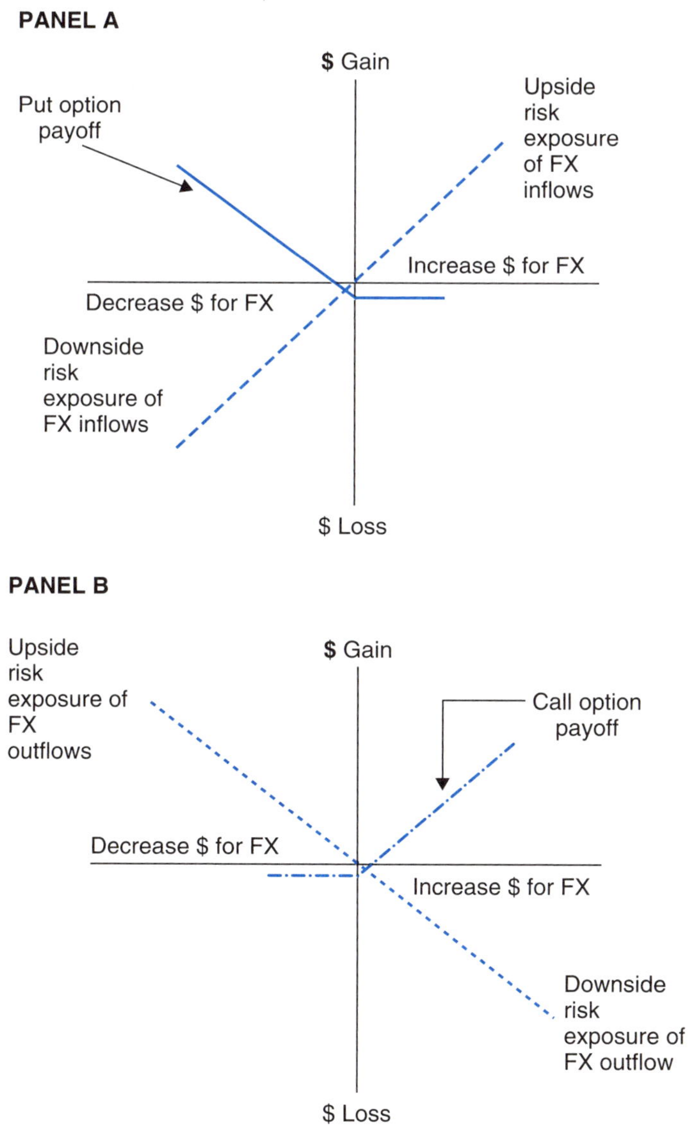


**Figure 11.1** Using Options to Hedge FX Downside Risk

## 11.4 An Illustration of Hedging a Forecasted Foreign Purchase (Using Currency Options)

American Flooring Distributors, Inc., (AFDI) a U.S. company based in Chicago, uses the U.S. dollar as its functional and reporting currency. The company imports hardwood flooring from Brazil for distribution to retailers in North America. On November 1, 20x1, the management of AFDI completed the master budget for the first quarter of 20x2, which calls for importing 20,000 bundles of Santos Mahogany hardwood flooring. The company anticipates purchasing the flooring materials from a Brazilian manufacturer at a cost of R$400 a bundle.[5] The Brazilian manufacturer does not usually bear currency transaction risk and has all of its contracts denominated in Brazilian reals.[6] On November 1, 20x1, the prevailing currency exchange rate was US$0.50 for R$1.00. At that rate, the dollar cost of this transaction would be R$8,000,000 × US$0.50 = US$4,000,000.

The management of AFDI is concerned, however, that the Brazilian real has been appreciating in value against the U.S. dollar. Local financial advisors suggested that the exchange rate could revert back to its average of R$1.96 for US$1.00 (or US$0.5102041 for R$1.00). If that expectation materializes, the cost of the forecasted purchase in U.S. dollars would increase by more than $81,600.00. The management of AFDI observed in 2009, for example, Brazil's government imposed a 2% tax on foreign-currency inflows into Brazil in an effort to slow down the appreciation of the real.

As a result of this concern, the management decided to lock in the exchange rate at US$0.50 for R$1.00 to avoid being exposed to this downside risk. Here is the sequence of events:

- On November 1, 20x1, the currency exchange rate was US$0.50 for R$1.00.
- On November 1, 20x1, AFDI purchased 4,000 currency *call* options (*Contract No. OP17BR*) from JPMorgan Securities. Each contract is US$1,000.
- AFDI would receive R$8,000,000 on March 31, 2012.
- The strike price is US$4,000,000.00.
- AFDI paid a premium of $10,000.00 for these option contracts. (This is the time value of the options.)
- Physical delivery of currency is possible, but settling net is anticipated.

### Information Check

1. Does this contract meet hedge accounting definition of derivatives?
   Yes, the Characteristics of the Contract:

   a. It has a notional amount of R$8,000,000.
   b. It has an underlying—the currency exchange rate.
   c. At the time of entering the contract, it has an intrinsic value of zero. The contract does not require making an initial investment (paying the time value of option is not a violation of the accounting requirement of "no" initial investment).
   d. The contract could be settled net.

2. Is the risk of the option contracts consistent with the risk being hedged?
   Yes, the contract calls for purchasing Brazilian reals at the spot rate on the date of entering into the agreement. If it costs more, AFDI would lose on the forecasted purchase but would gain an equivalent amount on settling the options, and vice versa. Therefore, the risk exposure and the hedged risk match and the cash flows are expected to be fully offsetting.
3. For what type of hedge accounting treatment does this transaction qualify?
   Cash Flow Hedge; there is no purchase or a commitment to purchase. The purchase of flooring materials is only an expectation (a forecasted transaction) and the risk facing AFDI is the volatility of cash flow due to changing currency exchange rates. Cash flow hedge is the appropriate accounting treatment.

AFDI's management designated this transaction as a cash flow hedge of a forecasted foreign-currency-denominated purchase (ASC 815-20-25-29 and 30). The critical terms of the options and forecasted purchase match; therefore, AFDI's management anticipated a highly effective hedging relationship and no quantitative test of prospective effectiveness was required. The cash flow from the change in the intrinsic value of the options was expected to completely offset the change in the cost of forecasted transaction arising from currency fluctuations. AFDI's management also noted that exchange rates could change for other reasons, but any changes unrelated to the hedged risk would not be relevant in the accounting for the hedging relationship. The management also decided to exclude the time value of option from assessment of hedge effectiveness because that would increase the possibilities of achieving effective hedge.

As planned, on March 31, 20x2, the company purchased the 20,000 bundles of hardwood flooring (for R$400 a bundle (33 bd. ft)) at a total cost of R$8,000,000 (FOB-Destination). On that day, the currency exchange rate was US$0.5045 for each R$1.00, and management recorded the transaction on the books at US$4,036,000 (= R$8,000,000 × 0.5045).

On June 15, 2011, AFDI sold the entire 20,000 bundles to a Seattle construction company for US$325.00 a bundle.

## Information Note

When AFDI exercised the options on March 31, the exchange rate was US$0.5045 for R$1.00, the option contracts were in-the-money because AFDI has fixed strike-price contracts with JPMorgan Securities at a strike rate of US$0.50 for R$1.00. If AFDI did not have the hedge agreement, or if (for some reason) JPMorgan Securities did not honor its obligation (credit risk concerns), AFDI would have had to go to cash currency markets and pay US$4,036,000.00 to purchase R$8,000,000.00. But JPMorgan Securities is obligated and is able to honor the contracts and could settle net by paying the company US$36,000.00 to make up for the price difference between spot exchange rate at the time of exercise and the strike price.

### 11.4.1 Accounting for the Hedging Relationship

The first step in the accounting cycle is to provide detailed documentation of the hedge and the hedging relationship. This is to be followed by an *ex-ante* evaluation of hedge effectiveness. In this case, prospective test of hedge effectiveness is not required because the critical terms of the hedge and the hedged position match.

### *11.4.1.1 Documentation*

## Exhibit 11.1 American Flooring Distributor, Inc., Initial Hedge Documentation (Call Options *Contract No. OP17BR*)

| | |
|---|---|
| *Date* | *November 1, 20x1* |
| *The hedged risk* | Exposure to possible loss due to appreciation of the Brazilian real in relationship to a forecasted purchase of 20,000 bundles of Santos Mahogany from Brazil. |
| *Hedge objective* | Eliminating the currency risk associated with unexpected volatility of currency exchange rates between the U.S. dollar and the Brazilian real. |
| *Risk management* | The management of AFDI believes that the hedged risk is probable and the hedging relationship is consistent with the enterprise's risk-management policy to hedge probable risk exposure if the risk is identifiable and the hedge is likely to be cost effective. |
| *Hedge instrument* | The hedge instrument consists of 4,000 currency call options purchased from J.P.Morgan Securities, *Contract No. OP17BR*, for the period of five months, November 20x1 through March 20x2, to purchase R$8,000,000 on March 31, 20x2 at the currency exchange rate of US$0.50 for each R$1.00 (or R$2.00 for each US$1.00). The options are purchased at-the-money (zero intrinsic value) for a premium of $10,000.00. |
| *The hedged item* | The foreign exchange option is designated as currency cash flow hedge of the R$8,000,000 forecasted purchase of 20,000 bundles of Santos Mahogany flooring from Brazil, which is planned for March 31, 20x2. The management of AFDI examined the circumstances related to the forecast and concluded that realization of the forecasted transaction is probable. |
| *Assessment of hedge effectiveness* | The critical terms of the hedged forecasted transaction and the hedge instrument match such that the changes in the options' intrinsic value is expected to completely offset the change in the expected cash flows of the hedged position based on changes in the currency exchange spot rate. |
| *Retrospective test of hedge effectiveness* | The management of AFDI decided to exclude the time value of options from the measurement of hedge effectiveness and will perform retrospective (*ex-post*) measurement of hedge effectiveness based on the cumulative changes in the intrinsic values of the options in relationship to the cumulative changes in expected cash flows of the forecasted transaction. |
| *Other cash flow hedge criteria* | All other criteria required for cash flow hedge are satisfied. |

## Information Note

At any point in time, the management does not know what currency spot exchange rates will be at future periods. However, to simplify the illustration, we will provide all that information at once, recognizing that, in real time, the management obtains that information as it occurs.

Assume that the currency exchange rates, time value of options, and intrinsic values have changed in accordance with the pattern shown in Table 11.2.

**Table 11.2** The Effect of Currency Exchange Rates of BRL to USD on Time Value and Intrinsic Value of Options (*Contract OP17BR*)

| *1* | *2* | *3* | *4* | *5* | *6* | *7* | *8* | *9* |
|---|---|---|---|---|---|---|---|---|
| | *Spot Rate in US$* | *Contract Price at Current Spot Rate*[(a)] | *Intrinsic Value in US$*[(b)] | *Δ in Intrinsic Value in US$*[(c)] | *Time Value of Option in US$*[(d)] | *Δ in Time Value of Options* | *Balance of Time value in US$*[(d)] | *Fair Market Value in US$*[(e)] |
| 11/5/20x1 | $0.50 | $1,000.00 | 0 | 0 | $10,000 | 0 | $10,000 | $10,000 |
| 11/30/20x1 | $0.5012 | $1,002.40 | $9,600 | $9,600 | $8,600 | $1,400 | $8,600 | $18,200 |
| 12/31/20x1 | $0.5022 | $1,004.40 | $17,600 | $8,000 | $3,000 | $5,600 | $3,000 | $20,600 |
| 3/1/20x2 | $0.503 | $1,006.00 | $24,000 | $6,400 | $500 | $2,500 | $500 | $24,500 |
| 3/31/20x2 | $0.5045 | $1,009.00 | $36,000 | $12,000 | 0 | $500 | 0 | $36,000 |

*Currency*:
$ = the U.S. dollar and is also written as US$ or USD
R$ = the Brazilian real and is also written as BRL

Notes:
(a) Strike price is US$1,000.00 for each of the 4,000 option contracts purchased.
(b) Intrinsic value of options is measured in accordance with the definition as the excess of spot price over the strike price.
(c) Change in fair market value of options is the first difference between two fair values between two adjacent periods.
(d) The time value of an option is a function of the time to maturity, volatility, and risk-free rate of interest as described in Chapter Five. It represents investors' expectations that options could be deeper in-the-money by the time they mature.
(e) The fair market value of options is measured by applying Black-Scholes option pricing model using currency spot rate, strike price, volatility of the exchange rates of US$/R$ during the past 200 days, five months' maturity, and the 3-month LIBOR.

### On November 1, 20x2:

- AFDI purchased 4,000 currency call option contracts from JPMorgan Securities. Each contract has a strike price of R$1,000.
- The premium for all contracts is $10,000.00. This is the time value of options which is the excess of market price over the intrinsic value.
- Expiration Date is 3/31/20x2.

### First Price Change Period: 11/1/20x1–11/30/20x1

During this period:

- Time value of options declined by $1,400.[7]
- Currency exchange rate changed from $0.50 to $0.5012 for each R$1.00.
- The intrinsic value of option contracts at the current spot price is

  (0.5012 – 0.50) × R$8,000,000 = $9,600.

- For AFDI to acquire R$8,000,000 in the cash market it would have to pay $18,200 ($9,600 intrinsic value plus $8,600 balance of time value of options).
- The $9,600 increase in intrinsic value is a gain for AFDI that would have to be collected from JPMorgan Securities if AFDI were to exercise the options on 11/30/20x1. However, the options are not exercised and AFDI cannot collect any funds from JPMorgan Securities. In fact it would more profitable for AFDI to sell the options than exercise them if the company decides to terminate the hedge for one reason or another.
- The gain of $9,600 will be recognized because derivatives are to be valued at fair value.

### Journal Entries in AFDI's Books for the First Period

| *Date* | *Journal Entries in AFDI's Books* | *Debit (in US$)* | *Credit (in US$)* |
|---|---|---|---|
| 11/5/20x1 | Currency Options—*Contract No. OP17BR*<br>Cash<br><br>*To record the options premium on 4,000 currency option contracts purchased from JPMorgan Securities. Each contract has a strike price of $1,000.00 to acquire 2,000.00 Brazilian reals* | $10,000 | <br>$10,000 |
| 11/30/20x1 | Financing Expenses<br><br>Currency Options—*Contract No. OP17BR*<br><br>*To record erosion in time value of options.* | $1,400 | <br><br>$1,400 |
| 11/30/20x1 | Currency Options—*Contract No. OP17BR*<br>Gain on Currency Hedging<br><br>*Recording the gain on the currency options acquired from JPMorgan Securities.*<br><br>Calculation: *Measured as the excess of currency spot exchange rates over the strike price times the number of options (=$2.40 × 4,000 contracts or (0.5012 – 0.50) × R$8,000,000.00.* | $9,600 | <br>$9,600 |

### Second Price Change Period: 11/30/20x1–12/31/20x1

During this period:

- Currency exchange rates of US$/R$ increased from $0.5012 for R$1.00 to $0.5022.
- This change increases the intrinsic value of the options by $8,000 (=$0.001 × 8,000,000).
- The $8,000 gain for this period of price change increases the total intrinsic value of the options to $17,600.00.
- The time value of options decreased by $5,600.00.
- This second period ended on December 31, which is the end of a reporting period and the balance of the account of gains on options should be posted to the special equity account in OCI.

### Journal Entries in AFDI's Books for the Second Period

| *Date* | *Journal Entries in AFDI's Books* | *Debit (in US$)* | *Credit (in US$)* |
|---|---|---|---|
| 12/31/20x1 | Financing Expenses<br>Currency Options—*Contract No. OP17BR*<br>*To record erosion in time value of options.* | $5,600 | <br>$5,600 |
| 12/31/20x1 | Currency Options—*Contract No. OP17BR*<br>Gain on Currency Hedging<br>*Recording the gain on currency options.*<br>Calculation: *Measured as the excess of currency spot exchange rates over the strike price times the number of options less the amount recognized earlier [($4.4 × 4,000) – $9,600.00] or as [(0.0522 – 0.50) × R$8,000,000.00] – $9,600.00* | $8,000 | <br>$8,000 |
| 12/31/20x1 | Gain on Currency Hedging<br>Other Comprehensive Income—cash flow hedge<br>*Posting gain on cash flow hedge options—*<br>Contract No. *OP17BR to OCI at end of this reporting period.*<br>*This is the balance of the accumulated gain. It is deferred (parked) in OCI until the forecasted transaction affects earnings.* | $17,600 | <br>$17,600 |

### Third Price Change Period: 12/31/20x1–3/31/20x2

During this period there were two price changes on the first and the last day of March. These price changes are reported as they occur.

1. First price change in the third period:

   - On 1/31/20x2, time value of options declined by $2,500.
   - Currency exchange rates of USD/BRL increased from $0.5022 for R$1.00 to $0.503.
   - On that day, the intrinsic value of options increased by $6,400.00,

[(0.503 – 0.5022) × R$8,000,000.00]

2. Second price change in the third period:

- Time value of options declined by $500.00.
- Currency exchange rates of USD/BRL increased from $0.503 for R$1.00 to $0.5045.
- The intrinsic value of options increased by $12,000.00,

[(0.5045 – 0.503) × R$8,000,000.00]

### Journal Entries in AFDI's Books for the Third Period

| *Date* | *Journal Entries in AFDI's Books* | *Debit (in US$)* | *Credit (in US$)* |
|---|---|---|---|
| 3/1/20x2 | Financing Expenses<br>Currency Options—*Contract No. OP17BR*<br>*To record further erosion in the time value of options* | $2,500 | <br>$2,500 |
| 3/1/20x2 | Currency Options—*Contract No. OP17BR*<br>Gain on Currency Hedging<br>*To record the gain on currency options*<br>Calculation: *Measured as the excess of currency spot exchange rates over the strike price times the number of options less the amount recognized earlier [($6.00 × 4,000) – 17,600].* | $6,400 | <br>$6,400 |
| 3/31/20x2 | Financing Expenses<br>Currency Options—*Contract No. OP17BR*<br>*To record further erosion in the time value of options* | $500 | <br>$500 |
| 3/31/20x2 | Currency Options—*Contract No. OP17BR*<br>Gain on Currency Hedging<br>*To record the gain on currency options*<br>Calculation: *Measured as the excess of currency spot exchange rates over the strike price times the number of options less the amount recognized earlier.* | $12,000 | <br>$12,000 |
| 3/31/20x2 | Gain on Currency Hedging—*Contract No. OP17BR*<br>Other Comprehensive Income<br>*Posting gain on cash flow hedge options—Contract No. OP17BR to OCI at end of this reporting period.* | $18,400 | <br>$18,400 |
| 3/31/20x2 | Cash<br>Currency Options—*Contract No. OP17BR*<br>*Exercising the options and collecting the intrinsic value from JPMorgan Securities* | $36,000 | <br>$36,000 |
| 3/31/20x2 | Inventory—purchases<br>Cash<br>*Purchasing 20,000 bundles of Santos Mahogany hardwood flooring (for R$400 a bundle (33 bd. ft) from Brazil at R$8,000,000 translated at spot price on March 31, 20x1.* | $4,036,000 | <br>$4,036,000 |

### Sale of the Inventory: 6/15/20x2

Costing Goods Sold:

- The cost of goods sold will be the cost of the inventory plus/minus the accumulated balance in the equity account OCI—currency options *Contract No. OP17BR.*
- The amount paid for inventories is $4,036,000.00.
- The $36,000.00 increase in the inventory cost over the planned price is equal to the amount of cash AFDI collected from JPMorgan Securities for the intrinsic value of the options.
- The accumulated balance in OCI related to this contract is a credit of $36,000.
- Therefore, the cost of goods sold equals $4,000,000.00, which is exactly the cost of the inventory as if AFDI purchased the inventory at the spot price on 11/5/20x1. By hedging, the company achieved its objective of locking in the price.

### Journal Entries in AFDI's Books for the Time of Sale

| *Date* | *Journal Entries in AFDI's Books* | *Debit (in US$)* | *Credit (in US$)* |
|---|---|---|---|
| 6/15/20x2 | Cost of goods sold | $4,000,000 | |
| | Other Comprehensive Income—Currency Options | $36,000 | |
| | Inventory | | $4,036,000 |
| | *Costing the goods sold after adjusting for the gain on currency hedging which was deferred in OCI.* | | |
| 6/15/20x2 | Cash | $6,500,000 | |
| | Sales Revenues | | $6,500,000 |
| | *To record the sale of 20,000 bundles of Santos Mahogany hardwood flooring (for US$325 a bundle (33 bd. ft).* | | |

## 11.4.2 Consequences of Hedge Effectiveness

In the fourth quarter of 20x1, the management of AFDI forecasted the purchase of 20,000 bundles of the Brazilian Santos Mahogany, which is priced at R$400.00 a bundle (the price is quoted FOB—Destination) and the manufacturer guarantees this price to any buyer for 18 months. Since there is no commodity price risk at least for 18 months, the risk of paying higher cost for the product can arise mainly from currency exchange rate movements. Therefore, the objective of hedging the exposure to the volatility of the Brazilian real against the U.S. dollar was to lock in the rate $0.50 for each R$1.00 to ensure purchasing the flooring materials at U.S. $200.00 per bundle.

As the management of AFDI expected, the Brazilian real appreciated in value and the currency exchange rate increased reflecting the appreciation of the real between the forecasted purchase and the time of actual purchase from $0.50 to $0.5045 for R$1.00. Without hedging, AFDI would have paid an additional $36,000.00 to buy the 20,000 bundles. But with an effective hedge, this increase in the price of the product was offset by the gain on the hedge instrument (currency options purchased from JPMorgan Securities). The gain on the hedge was credited to the cost of goods sold when AFDI sold the flooring materials so the cost of goods sold was exactly $4,000,000.00, which was the price the management intended to lock in.

In this illustration, the hedging relationship succeeded in achieving the management's objective, but it was not costless. AFDI paid $10,000.00 options premium that has been charged to earnings as financing expense. However, the effect cost of the inventory is $410,000.00

### 11.4.3 What if the Options Were Out-of-the-Money?

In the above illustration, purchased call options were at-the-money when purchased and were in-the-money in every period thereafter. On that basis, it was possible to assess hedge effectiveness by comparing the cumulative change in intrinsic value of the options and the cumulative change in the cash flow that would be required for the forecasted purchase. The hedging relationship was perfectly effective because the critical terms of the options and the forecasted purchase (in terms of amounts, timing, and final settlement) match. The cumulative change in options completely offset the variability of the cash flow of the forecasted purchase.[8]

Because the options' payoff function is one-sided, hedge effectiveness can be evaluated only when the options are in-the-money. This unique feature of options raises the question about evaluating hedge effectiveness when options are out-of-the-money. This scenario can occur if currency exchange rates fall below the USD0.50/BRL1.00 in the above illustration, which would result in a decline in the price of the anticipated purchase (which would be a gain to AFDI on the planned transaction) and the currency options would be out-of-the-money—i.e., the intrinsic value is zero. In this case, it would be assumed that options are not hedge instruments, the balance of the premium would be charged to earnings, and there would be no hedging relationship (the hedge is suspended) until options become in-the-money and the enterprise redesignates them as a hedging instrument for this forecasted purchase or another transaction. During the period in which options are out-of-the-money, no gains or losses are recognized (on hedge or hedged item); other than charging the premium to earnings, neither earnings nor OCI are affected. The amounts accumulated in OCI while the option was in-the-money will remain in OCI until one of four events takes place:

1. The forecasted transaction is no longer probable.
2. The hedge is terminated due to changing forecasts.
3. Changes in the hedged transaction could have an effect on earnings.
4. Management voluntarily decides to terminate the hedge.[9]

If any of these events occurs, the related amounts in OCI would be reclassified to earnings.

## 11.5 Hedging a Firm (Binding) Commitment

An executory contract (to purchase or sell a product) between an enterprise and a foreign entity constitutes a firm (enforceable, non-cancelable) commitment that could qualify for hedge accounting. Chapter Ten notes that accounting for hedging currency risk of a firm commitment is not exactly the same as hedge accounting for a firm commitment in a single currency, as shown in the segment below which is borrowed from Exhibit 10.6.

| | | |
|---|---|---|
| Hedging currency risk of a firm commitment | Fair value hedge | Financial derivatives<br>OR<br>Foreign-currency-denominated non-derivative financial instrument |
| | Cash flow hedge | Financial derivatives only |

While the firm (binding) commitments an enterprise makes in a single currency may qualify for the fair value hedge treatment only, the foreign-currency-denominated firm commitment may qualify for either cash flow hedge or fair value hedge because the volatility of currency exchange rates exposes the enterprise to cash flow volatility as well as to value loss. In addition, either a financial derivative or a currency non-derivative financial item may be designated as a hedge in a fair value hedge accounting treatment of a foreign-currency-denominated binding commitment.

## 11.5.1 Using Forward Contracts to Hedge Firm Commitment[10]

A foreign-currency-denominated commitment is hedgeable only if the contract satisfies the following necessary conditions.

1. The counterparty is an external entity—not a subsidiary or an affiliated entity.
2. The contract has a fixed price.
3. The price is denominated in a currency other than the domestic entity's functional currency.
4. The contract is non-cancelable and is legally enforceable.
5. The contract specifies the quantity to be exchanged, timing of the transaction, and other significant terms of the agreement.
6. An element of the contract provides for large enough disincentives for nonperformance so as to render performance probable.
7. The currency fluctuations of the contract will impact earnings (for the cash flow volatility condition).

In this type of foreign-currency-denominated contract, the domestic entity is exposed to currency risk because the contract is not in the domestic party's functional currency and the fluctuation of the contract currency will impact earnings. One condition is specific to hedging foreign-currency-denominated firm commitments: the enterprise may choose to account for the contract as a fair value hedge or as a cash flow hedge.

- If the fair value hedge accounting treatment is elected, the management of the enterprise is permitted to use either one of the following as a hedge instrument:

i. A derivative contract such as futures, forwards, options, or swaps.
ii. A foreign-currency-denominated non-derivative financial instrument such as debt or AFS securities that give rise to a foreign-currency transaction gain or loss.

- If the cash flow hedge is adopted, only financial derivative instruments may be used as hedge instruments.

## 11.5.2 An Illustration of Hedging Currency Risk of a Firm Commitment

The use of forward currency contracts is illustrated by a contract between a Chinese company called *KChina*, a producer of kitchen products and equipment in China, and a U.S. enterprise called *USKitchen Company* which is an intermediary between *KChina* and retailers in the U.S. On 1/1/20x1, *USKitchen* signed a contract with *KChina* (*Contract P2JCNY*) to purchase 1,000 sets of kitchen wares (style *LM Glorious*) before July 1, 20x1 for ¥720,000.[11] At the time of the contract, the currency exchange rate was ¥7.0922 for $1.00 or $0.141 for ¥1.00.

Because the purchase agreement with *KChina* is denominated in renminbi yuan, the *USKitchen Company* (whose functional currency is the U.S. dollar) is exposed to currency risk. Hedging this exposure allows the company to use either fair value hedge or cash flow hedge.[12] On the day of the agreement, the management of *USKitchen* was concerned about adverse movement of the renminbi exchange rate against the U.S. dollar and, on 1/1/20x1, the company entered into a currency forward contract (*Contract No. FX30FW*) to purchase ¥720,000 at the forward rate of $0.143 for each ¥1.00 (or ¥6.993 for each $1.00) for delivery on June 30, 20x1.

Assume that the movements of spot and forward exchange rates of the renminbi (CNY) for $1.00 (USD) during the contract period were as follows:

| | *USD/CNY spot rate** | | *USD/CNY forward rate** | |
|---|---|---|---|---|
| | *¥ for $1.00* | *$ for ¥1.00* | *¥ for $1.00* | *$ for ¥1.00* |
| 1/1/20x1 | 7.0922 | 0.141 | 6.993 | 0.143 |
| 2/28/20x1 | 7.353 | 0.136 | 7.3099 | 0.1368 |
| 3/31/20x1 | 7.46269 | 0.134 | 7.4349 | 0.1345 |
| 6/30/20x1 | 7.6336 | 0.131 | 7.6336 | 0.131 |

* For delivery on July 1, 20x1. The numbers are subject to rounding errors.

On June 30, 20x1, *USKitchen* purchased the agreed upon 1,000 units from *KChina*, and on November 7, 20x1, the company sold all of the 1,000 units to *Restaurants-R-US* for $221,000.

### *11.5.2.1 Accounting for the Hedging Relationship*

The accounting begins by documenting the hedge designation.

## Hedge Documentation

### Exhibit 11.2 *USKitchen Company*: Initial Hedge Documentation (Forward *Contract No. FX30FW*)

| | |
|---|---|
| *Date* | *January 1, 20x1* |
| *The hedged risk* | Volatility, and the likely appreciation, of the renminbi yuan against the U.S. dollar. |
| *Objective of the hedge* | To lock in the currency exchange rate at U.S.$0.143 for each ¥1.00. |
| *Risk management* | *USKitchen* has established an enterprise risk-management system that calls for identifying, measuring, and controlling the different types of risk facing the enterprise to the extent that any given risk could potentially impact earnings and the present value of the company adversely. Hedging currency risk of a purchase commitment is consistent with this philosophy. |
| *Hedge instrument* | Forward *Contract No. FX30FW* to purchase ¥720,000 at $0.143 for ¥1.00 on June 30, 20x1. |
| *The hedged item* | A firm (binding) commitment with *KChina* of Shanghai (*Contract P2JCNY*) to purchase 1,000 units of kitchenware product *LM Glorious* for delivery on June 30, 20x1 at ¥720 each unit. The contract is denominated in renminbi yuan. |
| *Hedge accounting* | The fair value hedge accounting treatment is adopted. |
| *Assessment of hedge effectiveness* | The spot and forward currency rates are different at inception of the hedge by an amount equal to forward points. Changes in the forward rate of exchange are used to assess hedge effectiveness. |
| *Retrospective test of hedge effectiveness* | The management of *USKitchen* decided to test hedge effectiveness based on the cumulative change in the present values of the forward in relationship to the cumulative changes in expected cash flows to meet the firm commitment. |
| *Other fair value hedge criteria* | All the criteria specified in the ASC 815 to qualify for fair value hedge are documented in detail and are deemed satisfied. |

## Estimating the Discount Rate Implicit in the Forward

### Information Note

Whaley (2006) shows that the cost of carry of a currency forward contract is the difference between the domestic and foreign risk free rates. However, for our purposes we could assume that this difference is the cost of carry "c" in the valuation formula below. The valuation relationship for the period of interest (which is six months in this illustration) is described simply as:

$$F_{Jan\text{-}Jun,\ 20x1} = S_{jan} \times e^{c}$$

where:

$F_{Jan\text{-}Jun,\ 20x1}$ is the January 1 start of the contract for delivery on June 30/20x1.
$S_{jan}$ = the spot rate on January 1.
e = the exponential function
$c$ = the cost of carry or interest rate (difference) in this case (simple discounting).
$c^{*}$ = the cost of carry (continuous compounding)

Rearranging the terms we have:

$$e^{c} = F_{Jan\text{-}June,\ 20x1}/S_{jan}$$
$$ln\ (e^{c}) = 1 + c^{*}$$

Applying this simple transformation to our case of *USKitchen*, we have
$1.43 = 1.41e^{c}$
$e^{c} = 1.43/1.41 = 1.01418$. The interest rate implicit in the forward contract i0.01418 for a six-month period.

## Measurement of Changes in Values

**Table 11.3** Measurement of the Fair Value of the Forward Contract and Change in Firm Commitment

Panel A: Calculation of the change in the fair value of the firm commitment

| | | *1/1/20x1* | *2/28/20x1* | *3/31/20x1* | *6/30/20x1* |
|---|---|---|---|---|---|
| A | Currency Spot Rate in ¥ (Yuan) for US$1.00 | 7.0922 | 7.353 | 7.46269 | 7.6336 |
| B | Currency Spot Rate in US$ for ¥1.00 | 0.141 | 0.136 | 0.134 | 0.131 |
| C | Δ spot rate in units of US dollars | — | (0.005) | (0.002) | (0.003) |
| D | Δ in value of firm commitment | 0 | 3,600 | 1,440 | 2,160 |
| E | Cumulative change in Firm Commitment | 0 | 3,600 | 5,040 | 7,200 |
| F | The fair value of cumulative change in firm commitment at the 0.04% risk free rate | | 3,553 | 4,990 | 7.200 |
| G | Change in fair value of firm commitment | | 3,553 | 1,437 | 2,210 |

Panel B: Calculating the fair value of the forward contract

| | | | | | | |
|---|---|---|---|---|---|---|
| H | Forward Rate for June. 30 Delivery (in ¥ for US$1.00) | ¥ → | 6.993 | 7.3099 | 7.43494 | 7.6336 |
| I | Forward Rate for June. 30 Delivery (in US$ for ¥1.00) | $ → | 0.143 | 0.1368 | 0.1345 | 0.131 |
| J | Δ | $ → | — | 0.006 | 0.0023 | .00035 |
| K | Forward Contract Nominal Value in US$ | $ → | 0 | 4,320 | 6,120 | 8,640 |
| L | Fair Value of Forward Contract in US$ (the present value of F) | $ → | 0 | 4,280[(a)] | 6,077[(b)] | 8,640 |
| M | Δ Fair Value of Forward | $ → | 0 | 4,280 | 1,797 | 2,563 |

Panel C: Notes to Table T11.3

(the actual calculation assumed continuous compounding)
Calculations of present values using the implicit rate (Row K and Row L)
(a) $4,320/1 + (0.01418 × 4/6) = $4,280
(b) $6,120/1 + (.01418 × 3/6)) = $6,077

## Measurement of Hedge Effectiveness

- *Period 1 (1/1/20x1–2/28/20x1)*: change in the fair value of the hedge derivative is $4,280 and the change in the fair value of the hedged item is $3,553.

  The DOR is $4,280/$3,553 = 1.20
  *Conclusion*: The hedge is effective because the DOR falls within the accepted range of 0.80–1.25.

- *Period 2 (2/28/20x1–3/31/20x1)*: The change in the fair value of the hedge derivative is $1,797 and the change in the fair value of the hedged item is $1,437.

  The DOR is = $1,797/$1,437 = 1.25
  *Conclusion*: The hedge is effective because the DOR falls within the accepted range of [0.80, 1.25].

- *Period 3 (3/31/20x1–6/30/20x1)*: The change in the fair value of the hedge derivative is $2,563 and the change in the fair value of the hedged item is $2,210.

  The DOR is $2,563/$2,210 = 1.16
  *Conclusion*: The hedge is effective because the DOR falls within the accepted range of [0.80–1.25].

## Recording

**First Case: Assuming the company adopted the fair value hedge treatment.**

| | *Journal Entries* | *Debit (in US dollars)* | *Credit (in US dollars)* |
|---|---|---|---|
| 1/1/20x1 | *Memorandum*: *USKitchen* signed an agreement with *KChina* to purchase 10,000 units of *LM Glorious* product for ¥720,000 before July1, 20x1. | — | — |
| | *Memorandum*: *USKitchen* entered into a forward contract the dealer Dunedin, Ltd. to purchase ¥720,000 at $0.145 per ¥1.00 for delivery on June 30, 20x1. | — | — |

| | | | |
|---|---|---|---|
| 2/28/20x1 | Loss on currency forward | 4,280 | |
| | Accounts payable—dealer Dunedin, Ltd. | | 4,280 |
| | *To record the loss on currency forward as the forward rate dropped from $0.143 to $0.1368*<br>*Calculation*: (¥720,000 × ($0.143 – $1.368) = $4,320 discounted at annual interest rate of 0.028369% (the rate implicit in the forward/spot relationship) for five months<br>$4,320/1 + (0.01418 × 4/6) = $4,280 | | |
| 2/28/20x1 | Firm commitment to *KChina* | 3,553 | |
| | Gain on firm commitment | | 3,553 |
| | *To record the gain on firm commitment using the change in the forward rate*: a *drop from $0.141 to $0.136.*<br>*The ineffective portion of the hedge is considered a financing expense*<br>*Calculation*: (¥720,000 × ($0.141 – $0.136) = $3,600 discounted at annual risk-free interest rate of 4% for five months<br>$3,600/1 + (0.04 × 4/12) = $3,553 | | |
| 3/31/20x1 | Loss on currency forward | 1,797 | |
| | Accounts payable—dealer Dunedin, Ltd. | | 1,797 |
| | *To record the loss on currency forward as the forward rate dropped from $0.1368 to $0.1345.*<br>*Calculation*: This process involves three steps:<br>i. Calculate the cumulative change in value.<br>= ¥720,000 × ($0.143 – $1.345) = $6,120<br>ii. Discount this amount at 1.418% (the six-month rate) for a period of three months:<br>$6,120/(1 + (0.01418 × 3/6)) = $6,077<br>iii. Subtract the amount recognized earlier<br>$6,077 – $4,280 = $1,797<br>This is the amount that belongs to this period. | | |
| 3/31/20x1 | Firm commitment to *KChina* | 1,437 | |
| | Gain on firm commitment | | 1,437 |
| | *To record the gain on firm commitment using the change in the forward rate which dropped from $0.136 to $0.134.*<br>*Calculation*: This calculation is (0.136 – 0.134)* ¥720,000 = $5,040 for the cumulative change in normal value.<br>• Discount this amount at the annual risk-free rate of 4% for the period of three months.<br>• $5,040/(1 + (0.04 × 3/12)) = $4,990<br>• Subtract the amount recognized earlier.<br>• $4,990 – $3,553 = $1,437<br>This is the amount that belongs to this period. | | |

| | | | |
|---|---|---|---|
| 3/31/20x1 | Gain on Firm Commitment to *KChina*<br>Earnings—Financing Expense<br>Loss on Currency Forward<br>Recording the offset for the effective hedge and posting the ineffective component to earnings.<br>Alternatively, the gains and losses could be recorded directly in the income statement. Notice this ineffective component is part of the forward points | 4,990<br>1,087 | <br><br>6,077 |
| 6/30/20x1 | Loss on currency forward<br>Accounts payable—dealer Dunedin, Ltd.<br>*To record the loss on currency forward as the forward rate dropped from $0.140 to $0.131.*<br>*Calculation*:<br>(¥720,000 × ($0.143 – $1.31) = $8,640<br>Subtract the amounts recognized earlier<br>$8,640 – $6,077 = $2,563 | 2,563 | <br>2,563 |
| 3/31/20x1 | Firm commitment to *KChina*<br>Gain on firm commitment<br>*To record the gain on firm commitment using the change in the spot rate which has dropped from $0.134 to $0.131*<br>*Calculation*: The total change over the period is (0.131 – 0.141) × ¥720,000 = $7,200.<br>From that amount, $4,990 has been accounted for in the previous periods and the remainder of $2,210 belongs to this period. This is the settlement period and the discount factor is one. | 2,210 | <br>2,210 |
| 6/30/20x1 | Inventory purchase from *KChina*<br>Cash<br>*To record the purchase of 10,000 kitchenware units from KChina in accordance with the agreement for ¥720,000 at the spot exchange rate of $0.131 for ¥1.00.* | 94,320 | <br>94,320 |
| 6/30/20x1 | Accounts payable—dealer Dunedin, Ltd.<br>Cash<br>*To record payment of the balance owed to the dealer Dunedin, Ltd. on the forward contract.*<br>Note this is the balance that the dealer Dunedin, Ltd. owes the firm and this amount is equal to ($0.143 – $.131) × ¥720,000. | 8,640 | <br>8,640 |
| 6/30/20x1 | Gain on Firm Commitment to *KChina*<br>Earnings—Financing Expense<br>Loss on Currency Forward<br>Recording the offset for the effective hedge and posting the ineffective component to earnings.<br>Alternatively, the gains and losses could be recorded directly in the income statement. Notice the ineffective component is the balance of the forward contract points. | 2,210<br>353 | <br><br>2,563 |

| | | | |
|---|---|---|---|
| 11/7/20x1 | Cost of goods sold<br>Inventory purchase from *KChina*<br>Firm commitment to *KChina*<br><br>*To record costing the goods sold on November 20, 20x2.* | 101,520 | <br>94,320<br>7,200 |
| 11/7/20x1 | Cash<br>Sales revenues<br><br>*To record the sale of 10,000 units of LM Glorious at $22.10 a unit.* | 221,000 | <br>221,000 |

### 11.5.3 Analysis of the of the Fair Value Hedge Illustration

The objective of the hedge is to lock in a price for the Chinese renminbi in terms of units of U.S. dollars; the management of *USKitchen* does not want to pay for surprises. The firm (binding) commitment the enterprise made on January 1, 20x1 to the supplier, *KChina*, is to purchase 1,000 units of *LM Glorious* model and pay for them on June 30, 20x1. To have an assured rate of currency exchange on that date, the management entered into a forward contract to lock in the price of the yuan at $0.143. If the rate goes above that (the dollar depreciates), *USKitchen* will end up paying only $0.143. Conversely, if the dollar depreciates in value it will require less than $0.143 to buy one renminbi. For example, if the U.S. dollar depreciates in value and it takes only $0.147 for one yuan, the cost of the purchase in U.S. dollars will increase to $105,840 instead of $102,960 and the company could have lost $2,880. By locking in the price at $0.143, the currency dealer would compensate the company for the $2,880 so that the company's cost of the currency would be only $1.43; the management has covered the downside risk.

The management is therefore safe on the downside risk and implicitly agreed to bear a financing cost equal to the forward points, which is forward rate minus the spot rate at the time of the contract (0.143 – 0.141) × ¥720,000 = $1,440. These forward contract points have been charged to earnings as $1,087 at the end of the first quarter and $353 at the end of the second quarter.

At the end of the hedge, the cost of the purchased inventory equals the purchase amount at the spot rate on June 30, 20x1. However, this is not the cost of goods sold. The cost of goods sold will be the actual price paid, which is $94,320, plus the balance of firm commitment, which is $7,200. The total cost of goods sold, therefore, will be $94,320 + $7,200 = $101,520. The $101,520 is equal to the spot price at the time of signing the contract, which is $0.141 times the notional amount of ¥720,000. That is, the cost of goods sold is identical to the cost the company would have incurred if it had paid the price at the time of signing the contract.

## 11.6 Accounting for Currency Swaps

A currency swap is a contract between two parties dealing with different currencies, one domestic and the other foreign, in which the two parties agree on exchanging either coupon or basis in two different currencies.[13] The domestic party makes a domestic-currency-denominated loan to the foreign party and borrows a foreign-currency-denominated loan from the same counterparty. Using the spot exchange rate at inception, the terms of the two swaps are set such that the present values of these two loans are equal. At the end of the swap period, the two loans are paid off and the respective currencies take reverse flows. During the period of the swap, the two parties periodically net settle the differences between interest payments in accordance with the terms of the contract.

The currency exchange rate used at inception is the spot rate, but the rate of currency exchange used at termination of the swap could be the spot rate at that time or the forward currency rate that existed at the start of the swap, depending on the agreement between the counterparties. Therefore, this type of cross-currency swap could be viewed as consisting of two loans: one at the spot exchange rate at inception, and the other is either at the inception forward rate or the termination spot rate.[14]

For simplicity, different types of swaps are identified by different definitions:

a. A *currency swap* refers to cases where both legs of the swap are fixed: fixed-for-fixed.
b. A *cross-currency swap* refers to cases where one of the swap legs is fixed while the other leg is floating. This is the case whether it is a case of fixed-for-floating or floating-for-fixed.
c. A *currency basis swap* refers to the currency swap contracts that exchange floating-for-floating.
d. *Differential swaps* are contracts that exchange interest payments only.
e. *Circus swaps* are contracts consisting of a combination of a cross-currency coupon swap and a single-currency coupon swap.[15]

### 11.6.1 Design and Valuation of Currency Swaps

The terms of most swap contracts are set for the swap contract to have a value of zero at inception.[16] In the case of interest rate swap in a single currency (as in Chapter Five and Chapter Eight), the process of designing a plain vanilla swap contract follows specific steps:

1. The zero-coupon yield curve is used to estimate the forward rates for the risk class or sector of the parties to the contract. The forward rate is the floating rate of the swap agreement.[17]
2. The forward rates and the notional amount are used to estimate the floating cash flow for the variable leg.
3. The present value of the fixed-rate cash flow is set to be equal to the present value of the floating-rate cash flow.
4. Since the fixed interest rate is the only unknown in this equality, it can be determined by rearranging the terms of the model.
5. The derived fixed rate is the rate of the fixed leg of the swap that would yield a present value equal to the present value of the floating leg.
6. In both cases, the discount factor used to arrive at a present value is based on the zero-coupon rate for this class or sector.

There are multiple combinations of contracts and three possible accounting treatments. One of these treatments is not to use hedge accounting. The other two treatments show the combinations in Exhibit 11.3.

## Exhibit 11.3 The Intersection of Cross-Currency Type and Accounting Treatment

| | *Currency* | | *Type of Hedge* | |
|---|---|---|---|---|
| *Type of swap* | *Currency 1 (receive)* | *Currency 2 (pay)* | *Cash flow hedge* | *Fair value hedge* |
| A. | Fixed | Fixed | ✓ | |
| B. | Fixed | Floating | | ✓ |
| C. | Floating | Fixed | ✓ | |
| D. | Floating | Floating | | ✓ |

### 11.6.2 An Illustration: Fixed-for-Fixed Currency Swap (Foreign-Currency-Denominated Liability)

*FlowinWaters Enterprises* is a US-based company that operates a ferry service between Boston and Halifax, Canada. On January 1, 20x1, the company concluded negotiations with the Greek shipbuilder of *RoRo Ropax* ferry boats and purchased a boat model HSS949 for immediate delivery at a price of €1,460,000. To finance the purchase, *FlowinWaters Enterprises* paid €460,000 in cash and borrowed €1,000,000.00 from *BankAthena* in Athens. The loan carries 6% p.a. interest coupon and is due in full at the end of three years. The currency exchange rate was $1.35 for €1.00.

The management of *FlowinWaters Enterprises* was concerned about further depreciation of the U.S. dollar value against the euro. If the exchange rates were, for example, to increase to $1.40 for €1.00, *FlowinWaters Enterprises* would have to transfer to *BankAthena* additional annual interest payments of $3,000 a year and an amount of $50,000 for repayment of the principal. This concern led the management of *FlowinWaters Enterprises* to enter into a currency swap agreement (*Contract No. FX7Euro*) with the French bank: *BankFrance*. The swap contract is a fixed-for-fixed type requiring the following:

a. *FlowinWaters Enterprises* and *BankFrance* exchange the principal at the start of the contract using the currency spot exchange rate on that date: *FlowinWaters Enterprises* pays €1,000,000 and receives $1,350,000 at inception.
b. *FlowinWaters Enterprises* pays *BankFrance* 5.5% on $1,350,000 and receives 6% on €1,000,000 interest payments to be settled once a year at year end.[18]
c. At the end of three years, *FlowinWaters Enterprises* and *BankFrance* will once again exchange the principal amounts in opposite flows: *FlowinWaters Enterprises* receives €1,000,000 and pays $1,350,000.[19] At that time, *FlowinWaters Enterprises* would also repay the loan to *BankAthena*.

In this process, *FlowinWaters Enterprises* would have locked in the exchange rate of $1.35 for €1.00, which was the currency exchange spot rate at the time of making the initial loan.
This dual flow of funds of principal and interest across borders is depicted in Figure 11.2.

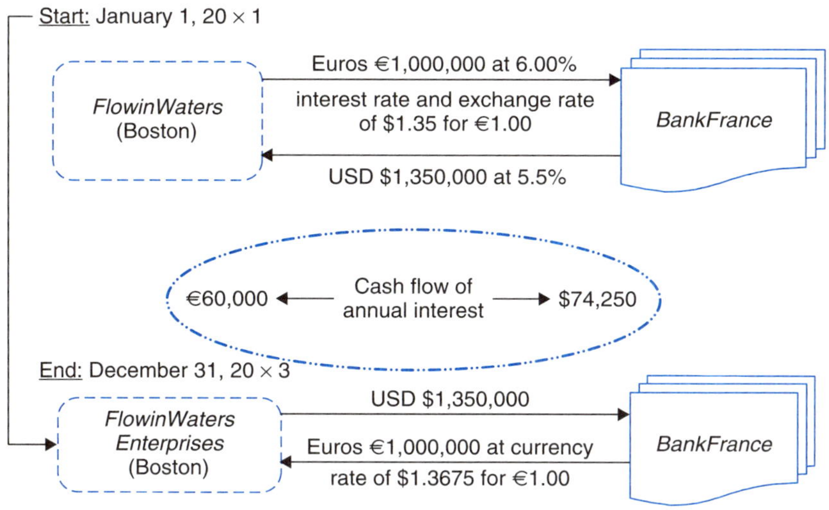


**Figure 11.2** Flow of Funds for Swap *Contract No. FX7Euro*

Note: The exchange is not a "physical" transfer. The counterparties settle net.

### *11.6.2.1 Accounting Processes*

To account for the hedge instrument, the hedged item, and the hedging relationship, the first question asked is whether this hedge qualifies for hedge accounting.

Information Check:

1. Is there a notional amount?
   Yes.
2. Was an initial investment made to acquire the derivative?
   No.
3. Is there a provision for net settlement?
   Yes
4. Is the hedge documented?
   Yes, and the documentation is summarized in Exhibit 11.4.
5. Does the risk of hedge item match the risk of the hedged item?
   Yes.
6. Is the hedge effective prospectively?
   Yes, based on the short-cut method.

*Conclusion*: Yes, the hedging relationship qualifies for the application of hedge accounting.

Table 11.4 provides summary information about the hedging relationship and calculation of the fair value of the swap contract for each of the three years.

### 11.6.2.3 A Summary of the Hedge Components and Estimating the Fair Value of the Swap Contract

**Table 11.4** The Present Value of Swap Contract No. *FX7Euro*

| | | *1/1/20x1* | *12/31/20x1* | *12/31/20x2* | *12/31/20x3* |
|---|---|---|---|---|---|
| Currency Exchange **Spot Rate**: U.S. Dollars for €1.00 | | $1.35 | $1.359 | $1.364 | $1.3675 |
| Currency Exchange **Forward Rate**: U.S. Dollars for €1.00 For delivery on December 31.20x3 | | $1.375 | $1.378 | $1.371 | $1.3675 |
| *Spot Interest Rate* | U.S. Dollar | 5.5% | 5.7% | 5.9% | — |
| | Euro | 6.2% | 6.1% | 6.3% | — |
| *FlowinWaters' Cash flow Related to Swap* | Principal | $1,350,000 €(1,000,000) | — | — | €1,000,000 ($1,350,000) |
| | Interest in Euros | — | €60,000 | €60,000 | €60,000 |
| *BankFrance Cash flow Related to the Swap* | Principal | €1,000,000 ($ 1,350,000) | — | — | $1,350,000 (€1,000,000) |
| | Interest | — | $(74,250) | $(74,250) | $(74,250) |
| Fair (present) value of the swap | | — | $11,482[a] | $15,250[b] | $17,500[c] |
| Change in the fair value of the swap | | | $11,482[a] | $3,768 | $2,250 |

**Calculation of the Value of Currency Swap contract FX7A3Euro:**

(These calculations followed the approached recommended by the FASB to simplify the calculations by assuming a flat zero-coupon yield curve).

(a) On 12/31/20x1 = Present value of cash received minus the present value of Cash paid out.
[€60,000 / 1.061 + €60,000/(1.061)$^2$ + €1,000,000/(1.061)$^2$] × 1.359
minus [$74,250/1.057 + $74,250/ (1.057)$^2$ + $1,350,000/(1.057)$^2$]
= $1,356,511 – $1,345,029 = 11,482

(b) On 12/31/x2 = [€60,000/ 1.063 + € 1,000,000/1.063] × 1.364
minus [$74,250 /1.059 + $1,350,000/1.059]
= $1,360,150 – $1,344,900= $15,250
The change that belongs to this period is $15,250 – 11,482 = $3,768

(c) On 12/31/20x3 = [€1,000,000 × $1.3675] – $1,350,000 = $17,500
From that amount, $15,250 has been recognized, leaving $2,250 for the current period.

*(These numbers are rounded to the nearest dollar)*

**Some Relevant Notes:**

1. There is one U. S. buyer, *FlowinWaters Enterprises*.
2. *FlowinWaters Enterprises* deals with two banks:

- *BankAthena* from which *FlowinWaters Enterprises* borrowed a loan to finance the purchase of a RoRo Ropax ferry boat from the Greek shipbuilder.
- *BankFrance* with which *FlowinWaters Enterprises* has a currency swap contract. (Greece and France are members of the Euro Zone and they use the Euro as the official currency.)

3. This cross currency swap contract provides two hedges:
    - A hedge of interest rate risk.
    - A hedge of currency exchange rate risk.
4. The currency swap contract is designated as a hedge of the loan from *BankAthena* against adverse movement in the exchange rate between the U. S. Dollar and the Euro.
5. Other than *FlowinWaters Enterprises* making the hedging connection, the two banks and the two contracts are unrelated.
6. The currency swap contract calls for the swap of (a) the notional amounts at inception converted to the counterparty's currency at the then prevailing spot currency exchange rate, (b) swapping the difference between the interest cost of each leg, and (c) swapping the notional amounts at the end of the contract using the spot currency exchange rate at the time of final settlement.
7. The purpose of the currency swap is to neutralize the effects of currency exchange rates between the Euro and the U. S. Dollar so that the final cost of the purchase of the ferry boat from Greece would be the contracted price at the exchange rate that prevailed at the time of purchase contract.
8. Currency swap contracts could take many forms. For instance, the contract might specify that the final settlement is to be at the forward currency exchange rate at inception. In this case, *FlowinWaters Enterprises* would be looking at obtaining a swap contract that locks in the forward rate.

### *11.6.2.2 Documentation*

## Exhibit 11.4 *FlowinWaters Enterprises* Hedge Documentation (For Cross-Currency Swap *Contract FX7Euro*)

| *Date* | *January 1, 20x1* |
|---|---|
| Risk being hedged | Exposure to loss due to unexpected variability of the exchange rate between the U.S. dollar and the euro. |
| Hedge objective | Eliminating exposure to variability in future cash flows arising from changes in the exchange rate between the euro and the U.S. dollar. |
| Risk management | The management estimates that the currency risk exposure is probable and that the hedge *Contract FX7Euro is* effective in offsetting the risk of the hedged note payable to the Greek shipbuilder of *RoRo* |

| | |
|---|---|
| | *Ropax* boats. Both types of risk and hedge relationship fit within the enterprise's risk-management philosophy described by the adopted *FlowinWaters Enterprises* system-wide risk-management system. |
| Hedged item | The hedged item in this case is *Contract No. E5x2Y*, which is for a loan from *BankAthena* in Athens, Greece. The terms of the loan are:<br>a. Face value is for €1,000,000.00<br>b. Interest rate is fixed at 6%.<br>c. Three-year term and is due for full payment on December 31, 20 x 3. |
| Hedge instrument | • Fixed-for-fixed currency swap *Contract No. FX7Euro.*<br>• Between *FlowinWaters Enterprises* and *BankFrance* in Paris.<br>• The swap is tantamount to lending *BankFrance* €1,000,000 and borrowing from *Bank France* $1,350,000.<br>• *BankFrance* pays *FlowinWaters Enterprises* 6% interest on the euro-denominated loan, and *FlowinWaters Enterprises* pays *BankFrance* 5.5% interest on the dollar-denominated borrowing.<br>• Interest payments are exchanged and differences are settled on December 31 of every year.<br>• On December 31, 20x3, the termination of the contract, *FlowinWaters Enterprises* receives €1,000,000 from *BankFrance* and pays *BankFrance* $1,350,000. |
| Hedge effectiveness | The terms of the hedge and hedged items match perfectly: same notional amount, same interest rate, same duration.<br>The management of *FlowinWaters Enterprises* concluded that this hedge qualified for the short-cut method and, thereby, no quantitative testing is required.<br>(Note: the short-cut method is not permitted in IFRS.) |

### *11.6.2.4 Accounting for the Loan* (BankAthena) *and the Currency Swap* (BankFrance)

#### Accounting at Inception

Information:

- Borrowing the loan from *BankAthena*
- Entering into an interest rate swap contract with *BankFrance*. Terms of the agreement:
    - Initial exchange: *FlowinWaters Enterprises* receives $1,350,000 and pays *BankFrance* €1,000,000.

- Interest rate: *FlowinWaters Enterprises* pays 5.5% on $1,350,000 and receives 6% on €1,000,000 from *BankFrance*.
- Interest rate: *FlowinWaters Enterprises* pays *BankAthena* 6% on €1,000,000 loan used to finance the purchase of the ferry boat.
- Termination: *FlowinWaters Enterprises* receives €1,000,000 and pays $1,350,000.

### Recording Journal Entries

| *Entry No.* | | *Journal Entries* | *Debit (in US dollars)* | *Credit (in US dollars)* |
|---|---|---|---|---|
| 1. | 1/1/20x1 | Cash<br>Bank loan—*BankAthena*<br>*Recording loan Contract No. E5x2Y borrowed from BankAthena to purchase RoRo Ropax ferry boat from Greek shipbuilders.* | 1,350,000 | <br>1,350,000 |
| 2 | 1/1/20x1 | *Memorandum*<br>Today we entered into a currency swap agreement with *BankFrance*. Terms of the agreement:<br>• Initial exchange: *FlowinWaters Enterprises* receives $1,350,000 and pays €1,000,000.<br>• Interest rate: *FlowinWaters Enterprises* pays 5.5% and receives 6% payable annually. | — | — |

### First Period: 1/1/20x1–12/31/20x1

- Payment of interest on the debt to *BankAthena* (loan *Contract No. E5x2Y*), which is $81,540 and is calculated as €60,000 × $1.359 (spot currency exchange rate at the end of the year).
- Present value of the swap equal to the present value of the cash to be received minus the present value of cash to be paid out.

  - The cash to be received discounted at the Euribor (the European) spot rate of interest times the currency exchange rate:

    = [€60,000/$1.061 + €60,000/($1.061)$^2$ + €1,000,000/($1.061)$^2$] × $1.359
    = $1,356,511.

  - The cash to be paid is discounted at the spot interest rate of the USA
    = [$74,250/1.057 +$74,250/(1.057)$^2$ + $1,350,000/(1.057)$^2$]
    = $1,345,029.
  - Present value of the swap = $1,356,511 – $1,345,029 = 11,482.

- Accruing and paying the interest on the debt to *BankAthena*, which is €1,000,000 × 6% translated at the spot rate on December 31, 20x1 which is $1.359 for each €1.00. Interest expense would be $81,540.
- During this period, the amount of net interest exchanged between *FlowinWaters Enterprises* and *BankFrance* is equal to:
  - The interest on the European debt (*BankFrance*) times the currency spot rate on December 31, 20x1. This is equal to €60,000 × $1.359 (spot currency exchange rate), which amounts to $81,540.00
    Minus
  - The fixed interest rate of the counterparty, which is $1,350,000 × 0.055, which amounts to $74,250.00.
    This difference between what would be received and what would be paid is $81,540 – $74,250 = $7,290, which is the amount to be exchanged or swapped as a result of hedging the interest rate risk component of the swap contract and is, therefore, treated as an adjustment to interest expense on the hedged loan.
  - Finally, the book value of the debt of *FlowinWaters Enterprises* to *BankAthena* is subject to remeasurement (currency translation) because of currency exchange rate changed. The spot currency exchange rate has increased from $1.35 to $1.359 for one euro. At the new rate, settling the debt owed *BankAthena* will cost *FlowinWaters* $9,000 more. This translation loss impacts earnings as an adjustment to accrued interest rate expense.

### Journal Entries for 1/1/20x1–12/31/20x1

| *Entry No. Number* | *Date* | *Journal Entries* | *Debit (in US dollars)* | *Credit (in US dollars)* |
|---|---|---|---|---|
| 3. | 12/31/20x1 | Interest expense<br>Accrued interest payable—*BankAthena*<br>*To record the accrual of interest owed BankAthena on the loan (Contract No. E5x2Y), which is calculated as €60,000 × 1.359 (spot currency exchange rate on 31/12/20x1).*<br>*Information Note*: Noting that the critical terms of the hedge and the hedged item match means that the amount of the debt being hedged is equal to the principal of the swap and that they both have the same interest rate and duration. | 81,540 | 81,540 |
| 4. | 12/31/20x1 | Swap interest receivable—*BankFrance*<br>Interest expense<br>*To record the* net settlement *amount of swapping (exchanging) interest payments. This amount is calculated as the interest the counterparty owed us less the interest that we owed the counterparty at currency spot rate. This is equal to €60,000 × 1.359 (spot currency exchange rate) = $74,250.* | 7,290 | 7,290 |

| | | | | |
|---|---|---|---|---|
| 5. | 12/31/20x1 | Currency swap fair value—*Contract No. FX7Euro*<br>Currency gain/loss—swap<br>*To record the fair value of the swap contract, which is calculated as the present value of the cash flow that BankFrance owes us using Euribor less the present value of the cash flow we owe BankFrance using US Libor as shown in Table 11.4.* | 11,482 | 11,482 |
| 6. | 12/31/20x1 | Accrued interest payable—*BankAthena*<br>Cash<br>*To record the payment of accrued interest* | 81,540 | 81,540 |
| 7. | 12/31/20x1 | Cash<br>Swap interest receivable—*BankFrance*<br>*Collecting accrued interest differential as recorded in Journal Entry No. 5.* | 7,290 | 7,290 |
| 8. | 12/31/20x1 | Translation account (gain/loss)<br>Bank loan—*BankAthena*<br>*To record adjusting the fair value of debt by recognizing the currency translation loss on the debt, which is the amount of loan balance times the difference in currency exchange spot rate between end and beginning of the period.*<br>*This loss is calculated as. €1,000,000 × (1.359 – 1.35)*<br>*Information Note*: ASC 830 for currency matters as well as IAS 21 requires translating financial assets and financial liabilities at the current (spot) rate on the date of consolidated financial statements. An increase in the translated value of debt is a loss. | 9,000 | 9,000 |
| 9. | 12/31/20x1 | Currency (gain/loss)—swap<br>Other comprehensive income—currency swap<br>Translation account (gain/loss)<br>*To defer recognition of currency gain in excess of translation loss until the hedged transaction impacts earnings.* | 11,482 | 2,482<br>9,000 |

### Second Period:[20] 1/1/20x2–31/12/20x2

- Accruing and paying the interest on the debt to *BankAthena* (loan *Contract No. E5x2Y*), which is \$81,840, calculated as €60,000 × \$1.364 (spot currency exchange rate at the end of the year).
- Calculate the present value of the swap as equal to the present value of the cash to be received minus the present value of cash to be paid out.

    - The cash to be received is discounted at the European spot rate of interest and multiplied by the spot currency exchange rate on 12/31/20x2

      = [€60,000/\$1.063 + €1,000,000/(\$1.063)] × \$1.364 = \$1,360,151.

    - The cash to be paid is discounted at the spot interest rate of the USA on December 31, 20x2.

      = [\$74,250/1.059 + \$1,350,000/(1.059)] = \$1,344,901.

    - Present value of the swap = \$1,360,151 – \$1,344,901 = \$15,250. But the change in the fair value of the swap that belongs to this accounting period is the incremental amount which is equal to \$15,250 – \$11,482 = \$3,768.
    - During this period, the amount of net interest (the difference) exchanged between the counterparties is equal to the interest on the European debt times the currency spot rate on December 31, 20x1 minus the fixed interest rate of the counterparty. This is equal to

        - €60,000 × 1.364 (spot currency exchange rate).
          Minus
        - The fixed interest on the U. S. currency-denominated leg \$1,350,000 × 0.055.
        - The difference is \$7,590. This is the amount of interest difference to be exchanged between the two parties as a result of hedging interest rate risk component of the swap contract and is, therefore, treated as an adjustment to interest expense on the hedged loan.

- Finally, the debt to *BankAthena* is subject to remeasurement (currency translation). The spot currency exchange rate changed from \$1.359 to \$1.364 for one euro. At the new rate, settling the debt owed to *BankAthena* for \$1,367,500 implies a currency translation loss of \$3,500.

### Journal Entries for the Period: 1/1/20x2–12/31/20x2

| *Entry No. Number* | *Date* | *Journal Entries* | *Debit (in US dollars)* | *Credit (in US dollars)* |
|---|---|---|---|---|
| 10. | 12/31/20x2 | Interest Expense | 81,840 | |
| | | Interest Expense Payable—*BankAthena* | | 81,840 |
| | | *The record the accrual of the fixed interest owed BankAthena on the loan (Contract No. E5x2Y), which is calculated as €60,000 × 1.364 (spot currency exchange rate on 12/31/20x2).* | | |

| | | | | |
|---|---|---|---|---|
| 11. | 12/31/20x2 | Interest expense payable—*BankAthena*<br>Cash<br>*To record the payment of interest accrued in Journal Entry No. 10* | 81,840 | 81,840 |
| 12. | 12/31/20x2 | Swap interest receivable<br>Interest Expense<br>*To record the net settlement amount of swapping (exchanging) interest payments. This amount is calculated as the interest the counterparty owed us less the interest that we owed the counterparty at currency spot rate. This is equal to €60,000 × 1.364 (spot currency exchange rate) – the fixed dollar amount of the interest $74,250.* | 7,590 | 7,590 |
| 13. | 12/31/20x2 | Cash<br>Swap interest receivable<br>*To record the collection of interest differential recorded.* | 7,590 | 7,590 |
| 14. | 12/31/20x2 | Currency swap fair value—*Contract No. FX7Euro*<br>Currency gain/loss—swap<br>*To record the change in fair value of the swap contract, which is calculated as the present value of the cash flow that Bank-France owes us using Euribor less the present value of the cash flow Flowin-Waters Enterprises owe BankFrance using U.S. LIBOR as shown in Table 11.4 after subtracting the amount of $11,482 which has already been recognized.* | 3,768 | 3,768 |
| 15. | 12/31/20x2 | Translation account (gain/loss—*BankAthena*)<br>Bank loan—*BankAthena*<br>*To record the currency translation loss on the debt, which is the amount of loan balance times the difference in currency exchange spot rate between end and beginning of the period. This loss is calculated as. €1,000,000 × (1.364 – 1.359).* | 5,000 | 5,000 |
| 16. | 12/31/20x2 | Currency gain/loss swap<br>Other comprehensive income—currency swap<br>Translation account (gain/loss—*BankAthena*)<br>*To close the translation loss of the debt to BankAthena.* | 3,768<br>1,232 | 5,000 |

### Third Period: 1/1/20x3–12/31/20x3

- Accruing and paying the interest on the debt to *BankAthena* (loan *Contract No. E5x2Y*), which is \$82,050 (calculated as €60,000 × \$1.3675 spot currency exchange rate at the end of the year).
- Calculating the present value of the swap as equal to the present value of the cash to be received minus the present value of cash to be paid out.

    - At the terminal point of the contract, the cash to be received on 12/31/20x3 is

      €1,000,000 × \$1.3675 = \$1,367,500

    - The cash to be paid on December 31, 20x2 is \$1,350,000.
    - Present value of the swap = \$1,367,500 – \$1,350,000 = \$17,500.
    - The change in the fair value of the swap that belongs to this accounting period is equal to \$17,500 – \$15,250 = \$2,251.
    - During this period, the amount of net interest (the difference) exchanged is equal to:

        - The interest on the European debt times the currency spot rate on December 31, 20x1 minus the fixed interest rate of the counterparty, which is \$82,050.
          Minus
        - The fixed interest on the U. S. currency-denominated leg (\$1,350,000 × 0.055) = \$74,250.
        - The difference is \$7,800. This is the settlement for hedging interest rate risk.

- Finally, the debt owed to *BankAthena* is subject to remeasurement (currency translation). The spot currency exchange rate changes from \$1.364 to \$1.3675 for one euro. At the new rate, settling the debt to *BankAthena* for \$1,367,500.

### Journal Entries for the Period: 1/1/20x3–12/31/20x3

| *Entry No. Number* | *Date* | *Journal Entries* | *Debit (in US dollars)* | *Credit (in US dollars)* |
|---|---|---|---|---|
| 17. | 12/31/20x3 | Interest expense | 82,050 | |
| | | Interest expense payable—*BankAthena* | | 82,050 |
| | | *To record the accrual of interest owed BankAthena on the loan (Contract No. E5x2Y), which is calculated as €60,000 × 1.3675 (spot currency exchange rate on 12/31/20x2).* | | |
| 18. | 12/31/20x3 | Interest expense payable—*BankAthena* | 82,050 | |
| | | Cash | | 82,050 |
| | | *Payment of interest accrued in Journal Entry 17.* | | |

| | | | | |
|---|---|---|---|---|
| 19. | 12/31/20x3 | Swap interest receivable<br>  Interest expense<br>*To record the net settlement amount of swapping (exchanging) interest payments. This amount is calculated as the interest the counterparty owed us less the interest that we owed the counterparty at currency spot rate. This is equal to €60,000 × 1.3675 (spot currency exchange rate) – $74,250.* | 7,800 | <br>7,800 |
| 20. | 12/31/20x3 | Cash<br>  Swap interest receivable<br>*To record collecting the interest differential recorded in Journal Entry No. 19.* | 7,800 | <br>7,800 |
| 21. | 12/31/20x3 | Currency swap fair value—<br>*Contract No. FX7Euro*<br>  Currency gain/loss—swap<br>*To record the* change *in fair value of the swap contract, which is calculated as the present value of the cash flow that Bank-France owes us using Euribor less the present value of the cash flow we owe BankFrance using U.S. LIBOR as shown in Table 11.4 after subtracting the amount of $15,249 which has already been recognized.* | <br>2,251 | <br><br>2,251 |
| 22. | 12/31/20x3 | Translation account (gain or loss)<br>  Bank loan—*BankAthena*<br>*To record the currency translation loss on the debt, which is the amount of loan balance times the difference in currency exchange spot rate between end and beginning of the period. This loss is calculated as €1,000,000 × (1.3675 – 1.364).*<br>*See Journal Entry No. 8 for reference to ASC 830.* | 3,500 | <br>3,500 |
| 23. | 12/31/20x3 | Currency gain/loss—swap<br>Other comprehensive income—swap<br>  Translation account (gain/loss)<br>*To reclassify the balance of OCI—swap and close the account for this contract.* | 2,251<br>1,249* | <br><br>3,500 |

* Subject to rounding errors.

| | | | | |
|---|---|---|---|---|
| 24. | 12/31/20x3 | Cash<br>Currency swap fair value—*Contract No. FX7Euro*<br>*Final swap settlement of currency swap Contract No. FX7Euro by collecting the fair value of the contract from BankFrance and closing the swap asset account on our books.* | 17,500 | 17,500 |
| 25. | 12/31/20x3 | Bank Loan—*BankAthena*<br>Cash<br>Paying off the debt obligation to *BankAthena* for loan *Contract No. E5x2Y* | 1,367,500 | 1,367,500 |

### *11.6.2.5 Analysis of the Hedging Relationship*

1. Under this currency swap contract, the U.S. company *FlowinWaters Enterprises* did not make any investment (present value of the swap is nil) and did not use any funds of its own to enter into the swap contract (except perhaps for a minor transaction processing cost). The U.S. dollar amounts received from *BankFrance* are the amounts of money used to obtain the €1,000,000 at the prevailing spot rate to pay off the debt to *BankAthena*.
2. The terms of the swap correspond to the terms of the loan contract with *BankAthena*. The euro-denominated interest of €60,000 which *FlowinWaters Enterprises* receives from the swap contract is used to pay off the interest on the loan. Since interest rate, notional amount, duration, collections, and payments of the debt to *BankAthena* and setting the swap with *BankFrance* occur at about the same time and they are exchanged at the prevailing spot currency exchange rate, *FlowinWaters Enterprises* has decided to use the short-cut method for hedge effectiveness.[21]
3. By entering into this swap agreement, *FlowinWaters Enterprises* has essentially locked in (a) the interest cost on the debt and (b) the notional amount at the exchange rate of $1.35 for €1.00, which was the spot rate at the inception of the transaction. Thus, both the interest that *FlowinWaters Enterprises* pays on the debt and the final debt settlement amount are protected from the downside risk of currency exchange rate fluctuations. At the end of the term of the swap, *FlowinWaters Enterprises* will receive €1,000,000 from *BankFrance* and pays $1,350,000. There is no physical delivery of currency and the parties will settle the differences between (what could have been cash flow of notional amounts) at the prevailing currency spot rate, which was $1.3675 for each $1.00.
4. At settlement, the dollar equivalent of €1,000,000 would be $1,367,500. Therefore, *BankFrance* must compensate *FlowinWaters Enterprises* by an amount equal to $17,500. This is actually equal to the settlement of the swap at termination.

## **11.7** Translation (Accounting) Risk

Consolidated financial statements and financial reports of multinational corporations are presented in a single currency for the entire enterprise (parent entity, branches, subsidiaries, and all domestic and foreign operations), which is usually but not always the functional currency of the parent entity. This means that the financial statements consolidation process must convert the financial statements of the enterprise's foreign subsidiaries and operations from the currencies of other countries into the reporting currency of the parent entity. This process is generically referred to as "currency translation" and requires using the currency exchange rates between the foreign currency and currency of the parent entity.

> *Accounting currency translation risk* is the risk of loss in the net asset exposure of foreign currency operations as reported by the accounting currency translation.[22]

### 11.7.1 Relevant Types of Currency Exchange Rates

The financial position of any given enterprise is the result of past transactions; the assets, liabilities, and equities shown on the balance sheet are the net result of thousands of past decisions that took place at different times. Currency exchange rates change constantly depending on forces of supply and demand for the currency as well as on tariffs and government intervention. Therefore, various components of assets, liabilities, and owners' equity are the result of decisions made at different periods when currency exchange rates were different. In contrast, consolidation of financial statements including foreign operations takes place at one point in time, at the end of accounting period. Therefore, converting the financial statements of foreign operations with varying currency histories into the reporting currency of the consolidated entity poses a dilemma about which currency exchange rates should be used for the components of assets, liabilities, and equity or income statement items.

For all practical purposes, there are two relevant regimes of currency exchange rates for the purpose of consolidating financial reports of foreign operations of the parent entity. Both regimes are time dependent.

1. *Time-of-Transaction Exchange Rate*: The currency exchange rates in effect at the time of the transactions, i.e., the rate in existence when the foreign operation acquired the asset, when it incurred the liability, when it sold the inventory, or when it paid wages. This approach is the historical perspective and is thus often referred to as "*temporal.*"
2. *End of Consolidation Period Exchange Rates*: The rates of exchange at the date of consolidation—end-of-accounting-period date. This is the current rate perspective.

Two other approaches also exist. These are based on the nature of the item whose book value is being converted to the reporting currency of the parent.

3. *Monetary and Non-Monetary*: Under this system, monetary assets and liabilities are considered contemporaneous in the sense that they could be liquidated currently and exchanged at the ongoing spot rate. Non-current items do not have the same feature and are anchored in the past. For these items, the rates of currency exchange at transaction times are considered the appropriate rates to capture the book value of these items in the converted currency.
4. *Current and Non-current*: Under this view, current assets and liabilities have the feature that allows the management to liquidate them currently. Therefore the current spot exchange rate is considered the appropriate index of currency conversion. But non-current assets are

captured by past transactions because management does not intend to liquidate or transfer them outside the enterprise. Therefore, according to this reasoning, the current exchange rate is not relevant for converting the currency expression of non-current assets.

The role of accounting standards in this consolidation process is to specify the conditions under which any of these approaches to currency translation would be adopted. As discussed below, the accounting standards currently in effect adopt something from each of the above four classifications.

## 11.7.2 Relevance of Organizational Influence

Identifications of the functional currency of the reporting entity and the functional currencies of foreign operations are essential to the currency translation standards (See Chapter Ten for the definition and identification of functional currency). When an entity chooses a method of converting the currency of the foreign operations for consolidation with the parent's financial statements, it must take into account the extent to which the cash flow of foreign operations influences or is influenced by the reporting entity's functional currency.[23] As a starting point, accounting standards distinguish between types of foreign operations on the basis of the influence the management of the parent entity can exert over various foreign operations. In the case that the parent entity has a significant influence, the foreign operation in question would be more like an extension of the parent entity's operations than an autonomous, self-contained entity. In the cases when a parent entity has little or no influence over its foreign operations, the management of the foreign operations in question will be engaged in business activities *as if* it is managing an autonomous entity that is able to generate and disburse cash without regard to movement in the functional currency of the parent entity. The reality, however, is that the foreign operations of a multinational enterprise are legal and integral parts of the enterprise; the extent to which a parent entity could exert influence over its foreign operations does not alter the reality of the enterprise's legal structure. However, this reality may not correspond to the methods by which these foreign operations conduct their business transactions.

The degree of influence the parent entity exercises is not necessarily uniform for all of the foreign operations of any given multinational enterprise; it may be strong in one region of the world, but weak in another. As a result, accounting standards aim at expressing the economic reality of the operations and neither the legal form nor the organizational structure of the enterprise matters for this purpose. Instead, the approach applied in consolidating foreign operations with the parent's financial reports depends on whether or not the decision-making sphere of the foreign operation is self-sustained and autonomous from the influence of the parent entity.

### *11.7.2.1 Applying Type I*

If the *foreign operation of a multinational enterprise has less autonomy and functions more like an extension* of the parent's activities, two outcomes are considered:

1. The activities of the foreign operation will have an impact on the parent entity's functional currency cash flow; foreign operations could readily remit to the parent the cash available to it at any time.

2. The results of the activities of this type of foreign operation should flow through the income statement of the parent and the balance sheet items recorded contemporaneously—i.e., they should be treated *as if* they were conducted by the parent entity.

The functional currency of this type of foreign operations is the functional currency of the parent entity. Generally, this would be the U.S. dollar for foreign operations for a U.S. multinational, for example, and the British Sterling (GBP) for foreign operations of a U.K. multinational.[24] In these circumstances, if the financial statements of foreign operations are reported in a currency other than that of the parent entity, consolidation will require conversion of the financial statements from the foreign (reporting) currency to the reporting currency of the parent. Because of the dependency of the foreign operations on the parent, this conversion should be *only a change in the unit of measure and should not change the attributes of the items being converted.* For this reason, this process is referred to as *remeasurement*.

The assets acquired by the foreign operations will be remeasured *as if* the parent itself had acquired them, and the liabilities of the foreign operations will be remeasured *as if* the parent had incurred the related obligations. If the parent entity acquired these assets from foreign sources, it would have recorded them at the currency exchange rates in effect when it acquired the assets. This is Type I currency conversion: applying the *transaction time exchange rates* which are also the rates employed in consolidating the parent-dependent, non-autonomous foreign operation. Because applying these rates is aligned with the times of the transactions, the currency conversion method used is called the *temporal method.*[25]

### 11.7.2.2 Applying Type II

*If a foreign operation is autonomous* and the management of the parent entity has little influence on the day-to-day decisions, this foreign operation is viewed *as if* it is an independent entity. In this case, the process of consolidating the financial statements of the parent and foreign operations is treated *as if* two separate companies are being merged at year end and their financial statements are pooled together (consolidated) on that date. For that type of consolidation, only the *consolidation period exchange rates* are relevant (these are the currency exchange rates at the end of the accounting period for the balance sheet and the average rate during the period for the income statement). In this case, the relevant exchange rates are not the past currency exchange rates when the foreign entity acquired an asset or incurred a liability.

This is the approach used in converting the financial statements of an autonomous foreign operation from a foreign currency to the reporting currency of the parent entity. The financial statements of these foreign operations will be treated *as if* the parent entity acquires an independent foreign entity. For this assumption to be valid, however, three requirements should be met:

1. If the financial statements of the foreign operations are presented in a local currency other than the functional currency of either the parent or the foreign operations, these statements must first be recast; remeasured from the reporting currency to the foreign functional currency.

2. The translation of autonomous foreign operation's financial statements for the purpose of consolidation requires translation from a *foreign functional currency* to *the parent's functional (reporting) currency*.
3. The translation from foreign functional currency to the parent's functional currency is implemented by using Type II currency conversion *consolidation period exchange rates*. For this reason, this method is referred to as the *current rate method*.

## An Example

Assume a U.S. multinational has foreign operations in Canada that use the Canadian dollar as well as other currencies for transactions. Also assume that the management of the Canadian operations prepares financial statements in Canadian dollars. Assume further that the Canadian operation acquired an asset for CAD1,000 when the exchange rate was CAD1.15 for every USD1.00 and at the time of consolidation, the year-end currency rate was CAD1.08 for USD1.00. On the financial statements of the Canadian operation, this asset will be reported at CAD1,000. In consolidating these financial statements with the parent's financial statements, headquarters must determine the Canadian operations' degree of autonomy when it reports this asset on the consolidated balance sheet:

- If the Canadian operations are not considered autonomous and semi-independent, the asset would be reported on the balance sheet of the consolidated financial statements at USD896.57 [calculated as CAD1000/1.15] as if the parent entity acquired it on the same date it was actually purchased. This is Type I currency conversion—*remeasurement*.
- If the Canadian operations are (a) considered autonomous and semi-independent but (b) the functional currency of these operations is the U.S. dollar (because most of the revenues are generated from sales to U.S. companies and the contracts are denominated in U.S. dollars), the asset would be reported on the balance sheet of the consolidated financial statements at USD896.57 [calculated as CAD1000/1.15] as if the parent entity acquired it on the same date it was actually purchased. This is Type I currency conversion—*remeasurement*.
- If the Canadian operations are considered autonomous and semi-independent and the functional currency is not the U.S. dollar, the asset would be reported on the balance sheet of the consolidated financial statements at USD925.26 [calculated as CAD1000/1.08] as if the parent entity acquired it on the date the financial statements are consolidated. This is Type II currency conversion—*translation*.

The next two figures may help summarize this process. Figure 11.3 portrays three processes required for currency *remeasurement*. Figure 11.4 presents a flow chart showing the decision-making sequence of the process of currency conversion as *remeasurement* and as *translation*.

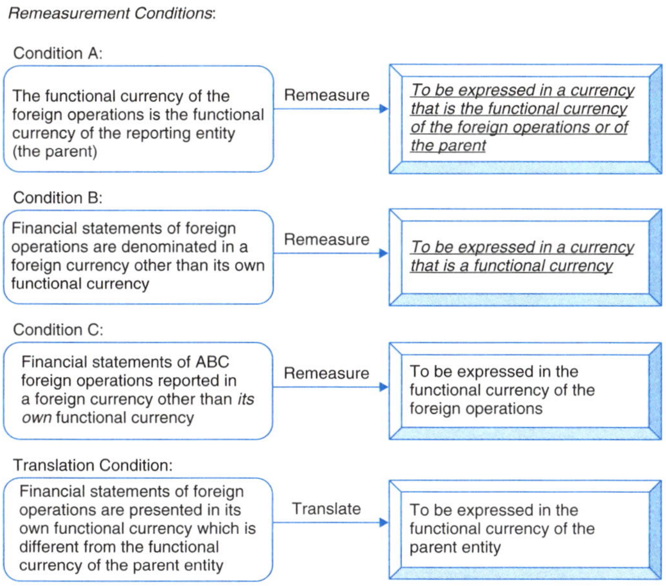


**Figure 11.3** General Remeasurement/Translation Rules

Remeasurement:
Apply the **temporal method**—current exchange rate for monetary items, historical exchange rates for the remainder of balance sheet items, and average exchange rates for the income statement items.

Translation:
Apply the **current rate method**—current exchange rate for all assets and liabilities, historical exchange rates for equity components, and average exchange rates for the income statement items.

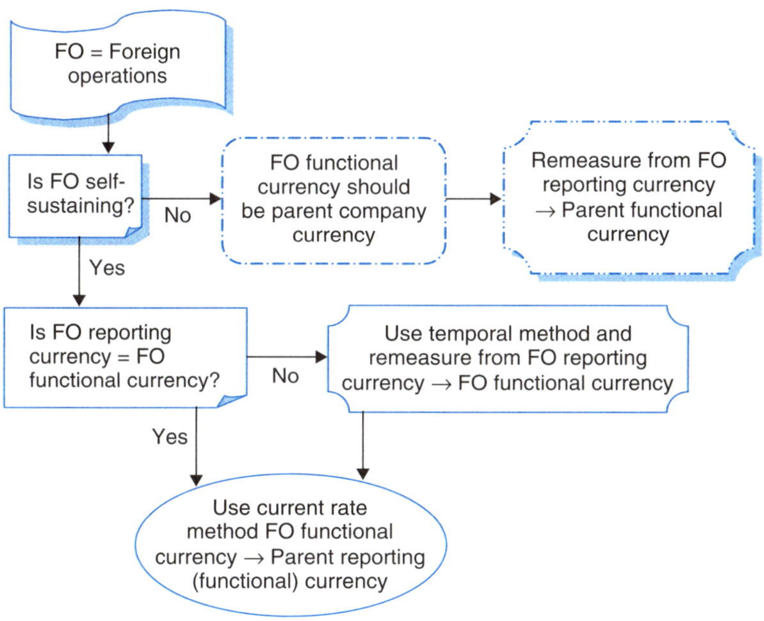


**Figure 11.4** The Process of Currency Translation to Consolidate Financial Statements of Parent and Subsidiaries*

*In the accounting and financial economics literature, the term "currency translation" is used in a broad context; it is a reference to both the **translation** using the current rate method and the **remeasurement** using the temporal method.

Assumption: Parent company functional currency is also its reporting currency.

## Exhibit 11.5 An Outline of Currency Conversion Guides

| *General procedures* | *Temporal method (remeasurement)* | *Current rate method (translation)* |
|---|---|---|
| (a) Monetary assets & liabilities | Current rate | End of period (current) rate |
| (b) Non-monetary assets & liabilities | Historical rate | End of period (current) rate |
| (c) Equity stock (common, preferred, additional paid-in capital, etc.) | Historical rate | |
| (d) Retained earnings | • Beginning balance is translated at historic rates (the rate applied to the ending balance of the previous period).<br>• Income additions to retained earnings since the date of investment are translated using the weighted-average rate of the related accounting period.<br>• Dividend reductions to retained earnings are translated using the historical rates at the date of declaration of the dividend. | |
| (e) Sales | Weighted-average rate for the accounting period | |
| (f) Expenses | | |
| (g) Cost of goods sold | Weighted average for purchases, historical for beginning and ending inventory | Weighted-average rate for year |
| (h) Depreciation, amortization | Historical | Weighted-average rate for year |
| (i) Currency gains/losses | Remeasurement gain/loss is included in the income statement for the period. | Translation gain/loss (the plug) is posted to Accumulated Translation Adjustment in OCI |

In a similar manner to the U.S. GAAP, IFRS stipulates that the functional currency is the dominant currency in which the entity generates and spends cash. Identification of the currency of revenues and expenditures are the primary criteria. Secondary criteria can be followed if the primary criteria fail to identify the functional currency. These secondary factors include (a) the currency in which the entity's operations are funded; (b) the currency in which the receipts from operating activities are usually retained. (See Exhibit 10.3.)

## An Example

*Antiques-U.S.* is a multinational corporation based in the USA. It owns 100% of a U.K. subsidiary which is located in London but is named *Antiques-France*. The functional and the reporting currency of *Antiques-U.S.* is the U.S. dollar and the functional currency of *Antiques-France* is the euro. *Antiques-France* is a leading provider of replicas of British heritage wood furniture. The main outlets for the products of *Antiques-France* are shops throughout France. More recently, *Antiques-France* has expanded its operations into a U.S. market after discovering American interest in British antiques. In 20x1, about 10% of the sales of *Antiques-France* consisted of exports to the USA.

From this information, it is clear that the euro is the primary currency of the economic environment in which *Antiques-France* operates. It generates most of its cash flows in euros, most of its sales are transacted in euros and are influenced by local forces, and its goods and services are acquired in France. Therefore, the euro would be the functional currency under U.S. GAAP. IFRS would produce the same conclusion because the euro mainly influences the revenues generated and the expenses incurred for labor, materials, and other costs required for providing goods.

Under both U.S. GAAP and IFRS, determining the euro as the functional currency of *Antiques-France* leads to interesting accounting implications. In particular, the part of the U.S. foreign operations carried out within the USA by *Antiques-France* are considered to be foreign-currency transactions for *Antiques-France* because a "foreign-currency transaction" is a transaction carried out in a currency other than the functional currency. The gain or loss on foreign-currency transactions, updated as of the balance sheet date, should be posted to the Profit & Loss (Income) account.

### 11.7.3 Risk Exposure of Net Investment

Like any other entity, the balance sheet of a semi-autonomous foreign operation that has a functional currency different from the functional currency of the parent entity has three main components: assets, liabilities, and owners' equity (= net assets). The balance sheet equation of this foreign operation is expressed in units of the functional currency of the foreign operations (*fCFO*) as follows:

Assets in *fCFO* – Liabilities in *fCFO* = Net Assets in *fCFO*

Therefore, a component of the assets invested in the foreign operations has a natural hedge to the extent of the amount of the liabilities or obligations of these foreign operations. But this leaves the net assets in *fCFO* exposed to volatility of currency exchange rates.

If all three components of the balance *were* to be converted to the functional currency of the parent entity at the current currency exchange rate, the converted balance sheet would also balance because this conversion simply multiplies all the components by a constant scalar. In the currency converted balance sheet when the conversion is in units of the reporting (functional) currency of the parent entity (*RCP*), the balance sheet of these foreign operations would be as follows:

Assets in *RCP* – Liabilities in *RCP* = Net Assets in *RCP*

The parent entity would be interested in *RCP/fCFO*, and the ratio of net assets would be measured in different units of currency as time passes. The management of the parent entity wants to avoid changes in currency exchange rate that would move this ratio below unity and present a risk of loss. This move can be caused (in this construction) only by adverse movement of currency exchange rates, which the management may wish to hedge.

However, *RCP* is not the amount of net investments shown on the translated balance sheet under current accounting standards. Instead, both U.S. GAAP and IFRS require translating the assets and liabilities at the current rate, but translating net assets at the historical rates of its different components (capital stock, additional paid-in capital, beginning balance of retained earnings, net income added to retained earnings and ending balance of retained earnings). *This departure from the current rate method applies only to net assets and only to the translation from a functional currency other than the functional currency of the parent entity.* [26]

When all assets and liabilities are translated using one scalar (the currency spot exchange rate at the time of consolidation) and equity accounts are translated at different scalars (a mixture of historical rates), a difference or a gap is created between translated assets on one side of the balance sheet and translated liabilities and equity accounts on the other side. This gap is a translation adjustment and would be roughly equal to the difference in rates (current exchange rate – average historical rates) times net assets in units of the functional currency of the foreign operations. This process results in two concepts of "net assets":

1. The "net assets" that represent equity accounts translated at historical rates of currency exchange.
2. The "net assets" that represent the investment in foreign operations that is actually exposed to risk of loss due to changes in currency exchange rates.

The relationship between these two concepts could be expressed as follows:

*Net Assets Converted at Historical Rates ± Translation Adjustment = Net Assets at the Current Rate.*

The two concepts are different representations of the same investment and they differ only by difference in the measurement basis. The first measure is used for purposes of consolidation, while the latter measure is used to assess exposure to currency risk. Figure 11.5 provides a picture of the relationship between the two concepts.

For hedging net investment in foreign operations, accounting standards have made an exception to the general rule of not allowing the hedge of a net position. Although net investment in foreign operations is the net of foreign-currency-denominated assets minus foreign-currency-denominated liabilities, accounting standards have allowed hedging net investment in foreign operations as if it were a single asset. Because hedging currency risk results in gains or losses related to the currency position of net investment in foreign operations, these gains and losses are reported and treated as a modification of the currency translation adjustment account on the balance sheet.

### 11.7.4 An Illustration of the Translation Adjustment Account and Hedging

*Pharma-R-US*, a U.S.-based wholesale distributor of medicine and pharmacy products, established a subsidiary *Pharma-R-IN* in Delhi, India as of 1/1/20x1. The company owns 100% of the subsidiary,

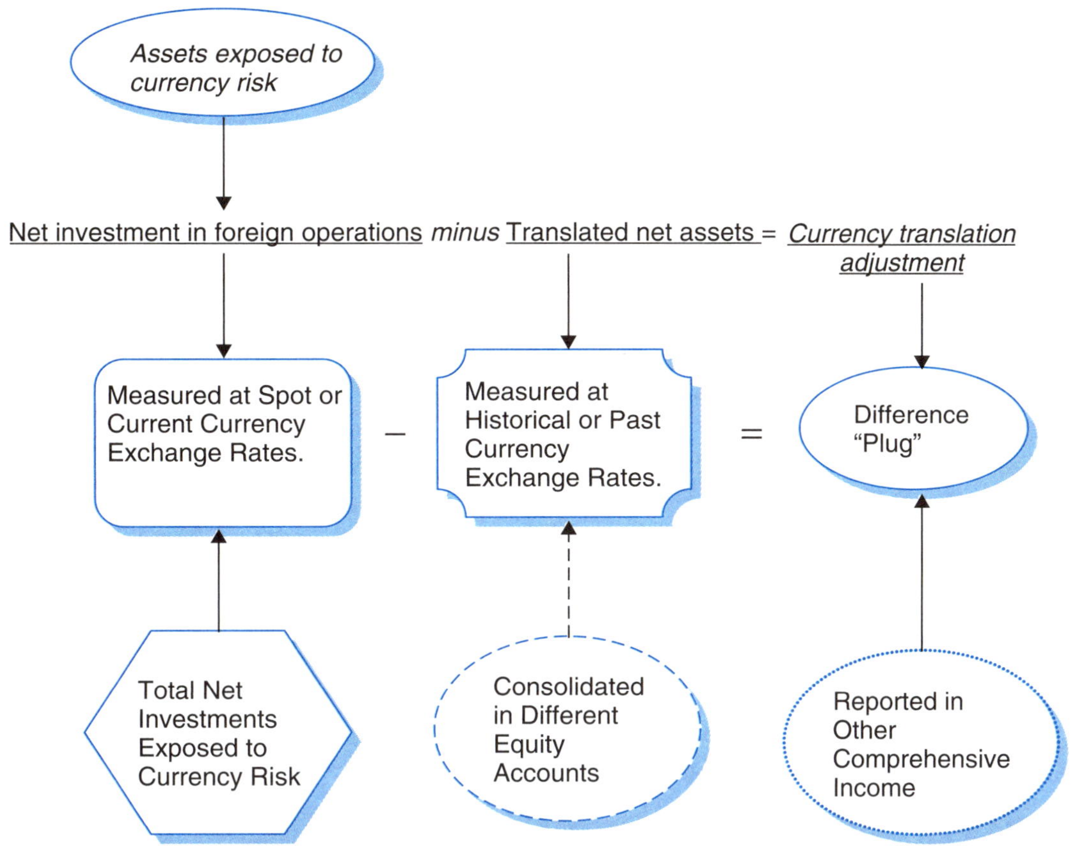


**Figure 11.5** An Interpretation of the Relationship between Net Assets as Investment at Risk and as Translated for Consolidation

but the subsidiary operates in a semi-autonomous fashion because its activities cover India and Pakistan which have cultures and modes of operations different from that of the company's headquarters in the USA. The functional currency of the subsidiary is the Indian rupee.[27] On 1/1/20x1, the exchange rate USD/INR was ₹54 for US$1.00. The cost of acquiring and establishing the Indian subsidiary was $3.00 million, or ₹162 million. During the fiscal year 20x1, *Pharma-R-IN* reported net income of ₹8.50 million.

The currency exchange rate of USD/INR changed during 20x1 from ₹54.0 at the beginning of the year to ₹57.5 on December 31, 20x1 (which was the same rate on January 1, 20x2). The average exchange rate during the year was ₹55.2 for US$1.00.

Table 11.5 presents the following five components for the year ended on 12/31/20x1.

Column C1: The financial statements of the parent entity in U.S. dollars.
C2: The financial statements of the foreign operation in Indian rupees.
C3: The exchange rates of Indian rupees for one U.S. dollar.
C4: The financial statements of the foreign operation in U.S. dollars (C2 times C3).
C5: The consolidated financial statements of *Pharma-R-US*, including the operations in India.

Column C5 also shows the account that absorbs the translation gain or loss of the financial statements of foreign operations. This is the *translation adjustment account*, a component of OCI. This account consists of the imbalance between translated investments in assets at the current rate net of the translated financing sources: translated liabilities at current rate and translated equity at historical rates.

**Table 11.5** The Balance Sheets of *Pharma-R-US* and *Pharma-R-IN* on December 31, 20x1

| | *Financial Statements in 1,000 Units of Currency* | | | | |
|---|---|---|---|---|---|
| | *C1* | *C2* | *C3* | *C4* | *C5* |
| | *Pharma-R-US* Parent (All are in 1,000 U.S. Dollar) $ | *Pharma-R-IN* India (All in 1,000 Indian Rupee) ₹ | Currency Exchange Rate ₹ for $1.00 | *Pharma-R-IN* Converted in 1,000 U.S. Dollar) $ | *Pharma-R-US* Consolidated (All are in 1,000 U.S. Dollar) $ |
| **Assets** | | | | | |
| Cash | 550 | 12,000 | ₹ 57.50 | 208.70 | 758.70 |
| Accounts Receivable | 1,040 | 80, 640 | 57.50 | 1,402.43 | 2,442.43 |
| Marketable Securities | 500 | 7,000 | 57.50 | 121.74 | 621.74 |
| Investment in India | 3,000 | | 57.50 | | |
| Inventory | 3,200 | 88,100 | 57.50 | 1,532.17 | 4,732.17 |
| Building Plant & Eq. | 4,070 | 138,000 | 57.50 | 2,400.00 | 6,470.00 |
| Patents & Trademarks | 810 | | | | 810.00 |
| | 13,170 | 325,740 | | 5665.04 | 15,835.04 |
| **Liabilities** | | | | | |
| Notes Payable | 2,840 | 45,316 | 57.50 | 788.10 | 3,628.10 |
| Bank Loans | 1,200 | 67,700 | 57.50 | 1,177.40 | 2,377.4 |
| Bonds | 3,500 | | 57.50 | | 3,500.00 |
| Deferred Taxes | 200 | | 57.50 | | 200.00 |
| **Equity** | | | | | |
| | | 162,000 | 54.00 | 3000 | — |
| Common Stock | 1,000 | | | | 1,000.00 |
| Additional Paid-in Capital | 2,300 | | | | 2,300.00 |
| Retained Earnings | 2,130 | 50,724 | 55.0 | 922.25 | 3052.25 |
| Other Comp. Income (Accumulated Currency Translation Adjustment) | 0 | | | (222.71) | (222.71) |
| | | 8,430 | | | |
| | 13,170 | 325,740 | | 5,665.04 | 15,835.04 |

The financial statements in Table 11.5 are for the first year that ended December 31, 20x1.

### *11.7.4.1 Second Year: 20x2*

At the beginning of the year, the management at the headquarters of *Pharma-R-US* in Chicago decided to lock in the currency exchange rate of the rupee to U.S. dollar for its net investment in the Indian operations. Table 11.5 is a report on the end of 20x1 and the beginning of 20x2. As of January 1, 20x2, the company's net investment in India (that is exposed to currency risk) is as follows:

Net investment in India = Assets at current rate – Liabilities at current rate
= \$5,665,040.00 – \$1,965,500.00 = \$3,699,540.00
Or (in rupees) = ₹325,740,000.00 – ₹113,016,000.00 = ₹212,724,000.00 at the current exchange rate of ₹57.5 for \$1.00 on 1/1/20x2.

Given that the U.S. dollar is appreciating against the Indian rupee, the management decided to hedge the currency risk of that investment by entering into a currency forward contract with the dealer *Sukarno Ltd*. The terms of the contract are as follows:

1. The notional amount is ₹212,724,000.
2. *Pharma-R-US* will sell to *Sukarno Ltd*. Indian rupees at the forward price of \$1.00 for 59 (or \$0.0172414 for 1.00), which would be paying 212,724,000 and receiving \$3,605,492.
3. Delivery date is December 31, 20x2.
4. The contract can be settled net.
5. There is no premium paid.

## Information Note

Estimating the interest rate implicit in a forward contract follows the same process as discussed in the Information Note above. For this case we estimate the cost of carry as follows:

At continuous compounding, the rate is 0.02608695
At simple compounding the rate is ≈ 0.02575

### *11.7.4.2 Hedge Accounting at* Pharma-R-US

## Exhibit 11.6 *Pharma-R-US* Incorporated Hedge Documentation (For *FX Forward Contract FX44-INR*)

| | |
|---|---|
| *Date* | *January 1, 20x2* |
| Risk being hedged | Exposure to loss due to unexpected variability of the exchange rate between the U.S. dollar and the Indian rupee (INR). |
| Hedge objective | Eliminating exposure of net investment in *Pharma-R-IN* to future volatility of currency exchange rate. |
| Risk management | Because of the recent currency movements, the management estimates that the company's net investment in *Pharma-R-IN* is exposed to currency risk and that the hedge instrument *FX Forward Contract FX44-INR* would be effective in hedging this exposure. This hedging relationship is consistent with the risk-management philosophy described by the adopted *Pharma-R-US* system-wide risk management. |
| Hedged item | The hedged item in this case is net investment in *Pharma-R-IN* of ₹212,724,000. |
| Hedge instrument | • *FX Forward Contract FX44-INR*<br>• Counterparties are *Pharma-R-US* and FX dealer *Sukarno, Ltd.*<br>• *Pharma-R-US* is to deliver (sell) Indian rupees for U.S. dollars at the forward rate of ₹58 for $1.00.<br>• Notional amount is ₹212,724,000.<br>• Delivery date is December 31, 20x2.<br>• No premium is paid for the contract.<br>• The contract may be net settled. |
| Hedge effectiveness | Effectiveness will be measured by the dollar offset ratio (DOR). The company will use the spot-to-spot currency exchange rate to measure the change in the value of the net investment and change in the fair value of the *Forward Contract FX44-INR*. |

**Table 11.6** Measurement of the Fair Value of the Forward Contract & Change in Net Investment in *Pharma-R-IN*

| | | | | | |
|---|---|---|---|---|---|
| Panel 1 | | | | | |
| | | 1/1/20x1 | 3/15/20x1 | 8/20/20x1 | 12/31/20x1 |
| A | Currency Spot Rate in ₹ (INR) for US$1.00 | 57.50 | 58.60 | 59.69 | 61.25 |
| B | Currency Spot Rate in US$ for ₹1.00 (INR) | 0.017391 | 0.0170648 | 0.016753 | 0.0163265 |
| C | Δ Net Investment in *Pharma-R-IN* in US$ | 0 | (69,391) | (66,327) | (90,727) |
| D | | | | (135,718) | (226,445) |
| Panel 2: Forward Contract | | | | | |
| E | Forward Exchange Rate for Dec. 31 Delivery in ₹(INR) for US$1.00 | 58.00 | 58.90 | 59.95 | 61.25 |
| F | Forward Exchange Rate for Dec. 31 Delivery in US$ for ₹1.00 (INR) | 0.0172414 | 0.016978 | 0.0166806 | 0.0163265 |
| G | Forward Contract Nominal Value in US$. | 0 | 56,032 | 63,264 | 75,326 |
| H | | | | 119,296 | 194,622 |
| I | Discount Factor | | 0.97969 | 0.9901 | 1.0 |
| J | P. V. of Cum. Δ Forward Contract in *Pharma-R-IN* in US$ (Hx I) | | 54,894 | 118,115 | 194,625 |
| K | Change in P. V. of Forward Contract in US$ | | 54,894 | 63,221 | 76,510 |
| Panel 3: Effectiveness Test | | | | | |
| L | Hedge Effectiveness (K/C) | | 54,894/ 69,391 ≈0.80 | 63,221/ 66,327 ≈0.95 | 76,510/ 90,727 ≈0.84 |

| Panel 4: Calculations | |
|---|---|
| *Row C*<br>The Dollar-denominated value of Net Investment | Calculated as the Notional amount times the change in currency spot rate<br>• For March 15: ₹212,724,000 × ($0.0170648 – $0.017391) = (69,391)<br>• For August 10: [₹212,724,000 × ($0.016753 – $0.017391) – (69,391)<br>= $135,719 – $69,391 = $135,718 – $69,391<br>• ($0.016753 – $0.0170648) = ($66,327)<br>• For December 31: ₹212,724,000 × ($0.0163265 – 0.016753) = (90,727) |
| *Row G* | Calculated as the changes in the value of the forward contract = notional amount times the change in Forward Rate of Currency Exchange<br>₹212,724,000 × ($0.016978 – $0.0172414) = $56,032 (gain)<br>₹212,724,000 × ($0.0166806 – $0.016978) = $63,264 (gain)<br>₹212,724,000 × ($0.0163,265 – $0.0166806) = $75,326 (gain) |
| *Row I* | Row F times the Present Value Discount Factor using the interest rate implicit in the Forward Contract, which is computed above as 0.02609, assuming simple interest compounding.<br>PV Discount Factors:<br>○ For 3/15/20x1: 1/[1+ (0.02609 × 290/365)] = 0.97969<br>○ For 8/10/20x1: 1/[1+ (0.02609 × 140/365)] = 0.9901 |

** All numbers have rounding errors

## Journal Entries

These transactions may be recorded in the Journal in a manner similar to the following entries.

| No. | | Journal Entries | Debit In US Dollars | Credit In US Dollars) |
|---|---|---|---|---|
| 1. | 1/1/20x1 | *Memorandum*<br>*To protect the value of our Net Investment in Pharma-R-IN, Pharma-R-US entered today into a Forward Contract with FX Dealer Sukarno for a notional amount of $3,667,655,000. Pharma-R-US to pay ₹58 (Indian rupees) for US$1.00 or ₹1.00 for $0.0172414 for delivery on December 31, 20x1. The contract may be net settled. No premium was paid to Sukarno.* | | |

| | | | | |
|---|---|---|---|---|
| 2. | 3/15/20x1 | Cumulative Translation Adjustment<br>Net Investment in *Pharma-R-IN*<br><br>*To record translation loss on Net Investment in Pharma-R-IN*<br><br>as currency exchange rate changed from ₹57.50 for $1.00 to ₹58.60 for $1.00 (or, from $0.017391 for ₹1.00 to $0.0170648). | $69,391 | <br>69,391 |
| 3. | 3/15/20x1 | FX Forward Contract Receivable—Dealer Sukarno<br>Cumulative Translation Adjustment<br><br>*To record change in P. V. of currency exchange gain on the Forward Contract*<br><br>The currency exchange forward rate between the US Dollar and the Indian Rupee has changed from ₹58 for $1.00 to ₹58.9 (or, from $0.0172414 for ₹1.00 to $0.016978). | $54,894 | <br>$54,894 |
| 4. | 8/20/20x1 | Cumulative Translation Adjustment<br>Net Investment in *Pharma-R-IN*<br><br>*To record translation loss on Net Investment in Pharma-R-IN*<br><br>Currency exchange rate changed from ₹58.60 for $1.00 to ₹59.69 for $1.00 (or, from 0.0170648 for ₹1.00 to 0.016753). | $67,327 | <br>$67,327 |
| 5. | 12/31/20x1 | FX Forward Contract Receivable—Dealer Sukarno<br>Cumulative Translation Adjustment<br><br>*To record change in P.V. currency exchange gain on the Forward Contract*<br><br>The currency exchange forward rate between the US Dollar and the Indian Rupee has changed from ₹58.90 for $1.00 to ₹59.95 (or, from 0.016978 for ₹1.00 to 0.0166806). | 26,714 | <br>26,714 |

| | | | | |
|---|---|---|---|---|
| 6. | 12/31/20x1 | Cumulative Translation Adjustment<br>  Net Investment in *Pharma-R-IN*<br><br>*To record translation loss on our Net Investment in Pharma-R-IN*<br><br>The currency exchange rate changed from ₹59.69 for \$1.00 to ₹61.25 for \$1.00 (or, from \$0.016753 for ₹1.00 to \$0.0163265). | \$90,727 | <br>\$90,727 |
| 7. | 12/31/20x1 | FX Forward Contract Receivable—Dealer Sukarno<br>  Cumulative Translation Adjustment<br><br>*To record change in P. V. of currency exchange gain on the Forward Contract*<br><br>The currency exchange forward rate between the US Dollar and the Indian Rupee has changed from ₹59.95 for \$1.00 to ₹61.25 (or, from 0.0166806 for ₹1.00 to \$0.0163265). | 55,482 | <br>55,482 |
| 8. | 12/31/20x1 | Cash<br>  FX Forward Contract Receivable—Dealer Sukarno<br><br>*To record collection of the balance of FX Forward Contract Receivable—Dealer Sukarno.* | \$194,625 | <br>\$194,625 |

### Analysis

Total gain on the Forward Contract is what *Pharma-R-US* has collected from Dealer Sukarno, which is \$194,625. Total currency loss on translation of Net Investment is 226,445. The difference is \$31,820. This is the ineffective component or the net loss on the hedge of Net Investment in Foreign Operations and has been charged to Cumulative Translation Adjustment, which will appear as part of Other Comprehensive Income. The effects of other activities aside, this cost increases the balance of OTC at the end of year 20x2 to be 253,990 (or 222,710 + 31,280). Notice that Net Investment in Foreign Operations was revalued simply because it was hedged and the hedge was effective.

## 11.8 Summary of Key Points

- In Chapter Ten, definitions of different currency concepts led to examination of transaction-settlement risk and how enterprises account for that risk exposure.
- In this chapter, the focus is on accounting for currency operating risk and translation (accounting) risk.

- Because currency operating risk relates to future consequences of adverse movements in currency exchange rates, hedging forecasted (foreign-currency-denominated) sales or forecasted purchase is treated in this chapter as hedging currency operating risk. However, hedging forecasted sales will require hedging strategies different from that of hedging forecasted purchase. Additionally, this chapter provides an outline of the necessary conditions required for a hedge of a forecasted transaction to qualify for the application of hedge accounting.

  - An illustration of hedging forecasted purchase of products on contracts denominated in foreign currency (in this case, the Brazilian real) included a presentation of the hedge documentation, evaluation of hedge effectiveness, in addition to the measurement and reporting of gains and losses caused by currency exchange rate movements.
  - This illustration used options as a hedge instrument and included a discussion of treating the time value of options and the hedge in cases when options are out-of-the-money.

- The second illustration of hedging currency operating risk is hedging a purchase commitment that is denominated in a foreign currency (in this case, it is the Chinese renminbi). This illustration uses a currency forward contract as the hedge instrument and includes: (a) details of how the fair value of the forward contract is estimated at different points in time using the interest rate implicit in the forward agreement; (b) an evaluation of hedge effectiveness using the DOR; and (c) recording of the effects of different currency exchange rate movements.
- The third component of the chapter is the accounting for cash flow hedge of a currency swap contract. A discussion of currency swap contracts is followed by an illustration of hedging a forecasted purchase using (privately written) options. The illustration details the measurement of the present value of the swap contract at different points in time and how the change in the present value is treated in offsetting the risk being hedged. The analysis shows the impact of the currency swap on both interest rate hedge and currency hedge.
- The last segment of this chapter introduces currency translation risk by the way of review to show the difference between the net investment in foreign operations that is subject to currency risk and the translated net assets that is measured for the purpose of consolidation. The difference between the two amounts is a function of the difference between current spot currency exchange rate (on the date of consolidation) and historical rates of exchange. This difference is referred to as *currency translation adjustment* which is an equity account reported as part of OCI.

  - Hedging the risk of net investment in foreign operations is allowed for hedging the "net" of assets minus liabilities measured at the spot (current) rate. The gains or losses on this hedge are treated as an adjustment of the currency translation adjustment account.
  - An illustration is provided for hedging net investment in foreign operations using a currency swap contract. The fair value of the swap contract is estimated at different times (of reporting period end or when currency exchange rates change). The illustration concludes with the journal entries for the entire cycle of the hedging relationship up to the point of posting to the cumulative translation adjustment account and final hedge settlement.

## Notes

1 In a simple random walk model, the change from one period to the next takes random steps. The expected value (mean) of those steps is zero. Alternatively stated, a simple random walk model implies that the current price is the best predictor of the next period's price.
2 Banks in the USA provide summaries of their own transactions in the Call Report.
3 www.isda.org. See the graph in Chapter Six for the volume of transactions as reported by the surveys undertaken by ISDA.
4 It is noted that Table 11.1 is obtained from the website of the Federal Reserve Bank of New York. That is to say, even the Fed obtains information about over-the-counter markets from survey data.
5 Accounting standards require full specification of the commodity or product being exchanged. For this purchase of Brazilian wood flooring materials, it would be adequate to note "specs,—33bd.Ft." It would also be important to note who would be paying the cost of shipping. In this illustration, we assume the seller will pay all the costs of shipping and delivery, which is designated as "Free on Board (destination)."
6 As noted in Chapter Ten, the Brazilian currency since 1994 is the Brazilian real (plural is reais), each real consists of 100 centavos. The currency exchange trading code is BRL and the symbol is written as R$.
7 The debate continues about the nature of option time value: is it a financing cost or is it a cost of the hedging transaction? Both the FASB and IASB are currently debating whether it should be charged to earnings directly or deferred in OCI and charged to earnings when the hedged transaction affects earnings. It is likely that both boards will come to a common agreement on the choice of the accounting approach.
8 The formal retrospective test is not reported here,
9 Current U.S. GAAP and IFRS permit the management to de-designate and re-designate a hedge any time at will without reference to any criteria other than management intent. Because of the unlimited discretion granted to management, this particular treatment is under discussion between IASB and the FASB in order to come up with a compromise.
10 To facilitate the presentation, let the party whose accounting records are under consideration be called "the domestic party" and the counterparty be called "the foreign party."
11 ¥ is the currency symbol for both the Japanese yen and the Chinese renminbi.
12 This dual accounting treatment of hedging firm commitment is allowed only in foreign-currency-denominated contracts. See, ASC 815-20-55-136; and ASC 815-20-55-137.
13 This particular designation is made only to simplify the presentation under the assumption that the transaction and the accounting are viewed from the perspective of the party who has the "domestic" currency.
14 Recall that in an efficient market without frictions, the forward rate at inception is the best (unbiased) predictor of the spot rate at termination.
15 It is noted that in a single (same) currency swap, the principal or notional amounts are not exchanged.
16 Currency swaps with positive values are called "off market."
17 Forward rates are sometimes referred to as "swap rates." The reader should not confuse "swap rates" with "swap spreads."
18 Settlement in reality is much more frequent but the annual frequency is used here for simplification in order to understand the main issues.
19 The counterparties are free to agree on any amount for the terminal settlement.
20 Subject to rounding errors.
21 Recall from Chapter Six that the short-cut method does not require quantitative test of hedge effectiveness. The method is permitted in U.S. GAAP only.
22 Arguably, this is not a real loss unless the enterprise intends to liquidate foreign operations. It is a translation, or a currency conversion loss, which financial analysts call "paper loss." However, we will know below that the management does not believe that currency translation loss is a paper loss. In general,

however, managements of international enterprises enter into hedging relationships that could end up costing economic resources.

23 I use the term "conversion" on purpose because, as will be presented later, accounting standards both in the USA and internationally distinguish between currency translation and currency remeasurement.

24 ASC 830-10-55-5(f)(2) states that the parent's currency would generally be the functional currency if the foreign entity is a device or shell corporation for holding investments or obligations, that could readily be carried on the parent's or an affiliate's books.

25 The dictionary's definition of the word temporal is "related to time." Because of the connection of exchange rate used here to time—time of acquisition for non-monetary items and time of consolidation for monetary items—this currency conversion process is called the "temporal method."

26 Investments on the balance sheet of the parent are carried at cost (or rather equity method). Historical rates of currency exchange are used for the equity or net assets reported by foreign operations to be offset in consolidation by the investment in foreign operations reported on the parent's financial statements.

27 The currency of India is called the Indian rupee; since 2010, it has the new symbol "₹" and is traded on FX exchanges under the currency code INR.

# CHAPTER 12

# RISK DISCLOSURE IN FINANCIAL STATEMENTS

## 12.1 Disclosure and Geography

Disclosure means that one party reveals to another what was hitherto private (secret) information. In this sense, all financial statements, measurements, and the related components fall under the umbrella of disclosure. However, in the context of accounting, we use the term "disclosure" to describe everything other than the balance sheet, income statement, and cash flow statement. Furthermore, the location where any particular financial information is disclosed, especially concerning the impact of various derivatives transactions, has increased in importance and frequency in accounting pronouncements as contracts become more complex to understand. This reference to the location of disclosure has become referred to as the "geography" of financial reporting. The disclosure might be qualitative, descriptive in the form of narrative statements, or quantitative within the text or in a separate tabular or graphic format.

Since 1933, regulators and accounting standard setters in the USA have operated under the assumption that reducing information asymmetry between preparers and users of financial statements cannot be completely left up to management's discretion. Under a completely voluntary disclosure regime, managers are very likely to disclose the information that reflects well on them and, perhaps, little else. For this reason, the Securities Act of 1933 and the Securities and Exchange Commission Act of 1934 took the lead in mandating disclosure of information for public enterprises.[1] Over the years, numerous amendments to these laws and regulations have been made in an attempt to operationalize the intent of these laws. In total, the present environment of disclosures about risk identification and discussion is an amalgamation of all these regulations and amendments.

Different legal mechanisms require companies to comply with certain disclosure laws in Western countries. For instance, The Company Law in the U.K. can be traced back to colonial times but has undergone extensive reviews in 1998 and 2006.[2]

The remainder of this chapter concerns different forms of disclosures, whether required by laws and regulations, by accounting standards, or voluntarily.

## 12.2 General Disclosures

Regulation S-K (§229.503(c) requires disclosure of *risk factors* in *plain English* in accordance with the Securities Act of 1933. Reporting risk factors could be instructive and informative. For example, in compliance with this requirement, in stating some aspects of its risk factors, The Boeing

Corporation reports critical concerns such as: "We enter into fixed-price contracts which could subject us to losses if we have cost overruns."

Similarly, while JPMorgan Chase report risks that are consequential: market risk, credit risk, liquidity risk, and several other significant and important types of risk, the disclosure also includes some risk factors that are common sense and totally uninformative such as:[3] "JPMorgan Chase's international growth strategy may be hindered by local political, social and economic factors, and will be subject to additional compliance costs and risks" (p. 14).

Other enterprises are not much different. Google, Inc., for example, presented 30 different risks in the list of risk factors. These include generic statements such as the following:[4]

- Web spam and content farms could decrease our search quality, which could damage our reputation and deter our current and potential users from using products or services (p.15).

&

- If we were to lose the services of Larry, Sergey, Eric or other key personnel, we may not be able to execute our business strategy (p. 17).

These cases are cited here only to show that corporate practices in adopting the regulation to disclose risk factors seem to reflect compliance with "the letter of the law," resulting in reporting a "laundry list" of risks to which almost all enterprises are exposed. This practice has failed to distinguish between the risks that could have material consequences to the reporting enterprise and all other hypothetical generic factors. Fear of litigation appears to subsume the desire to inform investors and drives this type of disclosure in compliance with the letter, not the intent, of regulation.

## 12.3 Disclosure Related to Strategic Risk

Reporting Management's Discussion & Analysis (MD&A) is perhaps one of the most significant vehicles toward communicating to investors the large picture of what is facing the enterprise. The Securities and Exchange Commission (SEC) identifies the basic and overriding objective of MD&A as to "provide such other information that the registrant believes to be necessary to an understanding of its financial condition, changes in financial condition and results of operations." More specifically, the SEC's *Financial Reporting Manual* states that the nature of the MD&A requirement is "principles-based" and is intended to provide management with flexibility to describe the financial matters impacting the registrant with the following objectives:[5]

a. To provide a narrative explanation of a company's financial statements that enables investors to see the company through the eyes of management.
b. To enhance the overall financial disclosure and provide the context within which financial information should be analyzed.
c. To provide information about the quality of, and potential variability of, a company's earnings and cash flow so that investors can ascertain the likelihood that past performance is indicative of future performance.

Although it is not written with that specific description, MD&A is essentially a requirement to provide information about the enterprise's strategic risk as described earlier in Chapter Two. The SEC has repeatedly asserted that:

> [W]e believe that management's most important responsibilities include communicating with investors in a clear and straightforward manner. MD&A is a critical component of that communication. The Commission has long sought through its rules, enforcement actions and interpretive processes to elicit MD&A that not only meets technical disclosure requirements but generally is informative and transparent.
>
> (SEC, 2003)

In numerous releases the commission emphasizes the role of MD&A as presenting information to investors from the management's perspective with focus on materiality, trends and uncertainties, significant accounting treatments and analysis.

MD&A must include information about liquidity, capital resources, results of operations, off-balance sheet arrangements, tabular disclosure of contractual arrangements, critical accounting estimates and stock-based compensation in IPOs, forward-looking information (with the attendant safe harbor provisions),[6] and any other acts or events with the potential of having a material impact on the enterprise's future operations.

The next two exhibits provide illustrations of the nature of MD&A disclosures. The first, Exhibit 12.1, is an excerpt from the general description of Intel Corporation MD&A in Form 10-K of 2011, while Exhibit 12.2, reported in DuPont's Form 10-K of 2011, is a specific and rather explicit cautionary disclosure about reliance on the forward-looking information in the MD&A.

As noted above, the SEC has issued safe harbor provisions to protect preparers of financial statements from liability in connection with providing forward-looking information so long as it is based on *reasonably possible* assumptions and is provided in good faith.[7]

## Exhibit 12.1 An Illustration of the Scope of MD&A (Intel Corporation)

MANAGEMENT'S DISCUSSION AND ANALYSIS OF FINANCIAL CONDITION AND RESULTS OF OPERATIONS

Our Management's Discussion and Analysis of Financial Condition and Results of Operations (MD&A) is provided in addition to the accompanying consolidated financial statements and notes to assist readers in understanding our results of operations, financial condition, and cash flows. MD&A is organized as follows:

- *Overview.* Discussion of our business and overall analysis of financial and other highlights affecting the company in order to provide context for the remainder of MD&A.
- *Strategy.* Overall strategy and the strategy for our major market segments.
- *Critical Accounting Estimates.* Accounting estimates that we believe are most important to understanding the assumptions and judgments incorporated in our reported financial results and forecasts.
- *Results of Operations.* Analysis of our financial results comparing 2009 to 2008 and comparing 2008 to 2007. At the end of 2009, we reorganized our business to better align our major product groups around the core competencies of Intel architecture and our manufacturing operations. The analysis of our major operating segments' financial results reflects this reorganization and prior-period analysis, and amounts have been adjusted retrospectively.

- *Business Outlook.* Our expectations for selected financial items for 2010.
- *Liquidity and Capital Resources.* An analysis of changes in our balance sheets and cash flows, and discussion of our financial condition and potential sources of liquidity.
- *Fair Value of Financial Instruments.* Discussion of the methodologies used in the valuation of our financial instruments.
- *Contractual Obligations and Off-Balance-Sheet Arrangements.* Overview of contractual obligations and contingent liabilities and commitments outstanding as of December 26, 2009, including expected payment schedule, and explanation of off-balance-sheet arrangements.

The various sections of this MD&A contain a number of forward-looking statements. Words such as "expects," "goals," "plans," "believes," "continues," "may," "will," and variations of such words and similar expressions are intended to identify such forward-looking statements. In addition, any statements that refer to projections of our future financial performance, our anticipated growth and trends in our businesses, and other characterizations of future events or circumstances are forward-looking statements. Such statements are based on our current expectations and could be affected by the uncertainties and risk factors described throughout this filing and particularly in the "Business Outlook" section (see also "Risk Factors" in Part I, Item 1A of this Form 10-K). Our actual results may differ materially, and these forward-looking statements do not reflect the potential impact of any divestitures, mergers, acquisitions, or other business combinations that had not been completed as of February 22, 2010.

(Source: Form 10-K, 2011; http://www.sec.gov/Archives/edgar/data/50863/000095012310015237/f54119e10vk.htm#111)

## Exhibit 12.2 MD&A Qualification about Forward-Looking Information (E. I. Du Pont De Nemours and Company)

CAUTIONARY STATEMENTS ABOUT FORWARD-LOOKING STATEMENTS

This report contains forward-looking statements which may be identified by their use of words like "plans," "expects," "will," "anticipates," "believes," "intends," "projects," "estimates" or other words of similar meaning. All statements that address expectations or projections about the future, including statements about the company's strategy for growth, product development, regulatory approval, market position, anticipated benefits of recent acquisitions, outcome of contingencies, such as litigation and environmental matters, expenditures and financial results, are forward-looking statements.

Forward-looking statements are based on certain assumptions and expectations of future events which may not be accurate or realized. Forward-looking statements also involve risks and uncertainties, many of which are beyond the company's control. Some of the important factors that could cause the company's actual results to differ materially from those projected in any such forward-looking statements are:

- Fluctuations in energy and raw material prices;
- Failure to develop and market new products and optimally manage product life cycles;

- Outcome of significant litigation and environmental matters, including those related to divested businesses;
- Failure to appropriately manage process safety and product stewardship issues;
- Effect of changes in tax, environmental and other laws and regulations or political conditions in the U.S. and other countries in which the company operates;
- Conditions in the global economy and global capital markets, including economic factors, such as inflation, deflation and fluctuations in currency exchange rates, interest rates and commodity prices, as well as regulatory requirements;
- Impact of business disruptions, including supply disruptions, and security threats, regardless of cause, including acts of sabotage, terrorism or war, weather events and natural disasters;
- Inability to protect and enforce the company's intellectual property rights; and
- Successful integration of acquired businesses and completion of divestitures of underperforming or non-strategic assets or businesses.

For some of the important factors that could cause the company's actual results to differ materially from those projected in any such forward-looking statements, see the Risk Factors discussion set forth under Part I, Item 1A beginning on page 8.

(Source: 10-K Form, 2011, p. 16 at http://www.sec.gov/Archives/edgar/data/30554/000003055412000005/dd-12312011x10k.htm#s6CE33D84ABB40CA4444DAAD246B0DA62)

## 12.4 Market Risk Disclosures

Regulation S-K (§ 229.303) requires quantitative and qualitative disclosures about *market risk*. By market risk, the regulation means the "risks arising from changes in interest rates, foreign currency exchange rates, commodity prices, equity prices, and other market changes that affect market risk sensitive instruments." These regulations are complemented by the requirements of ASC 815 and 825 discussed below.

ASC 815-10-50-1 states that the objectives of this subtopic are to assist users in achieving several goals by requiring comprehensive disclosure of derivative instruments. (In international accounting, these disclosures are required by IFRS 7, IFRS 9, and IAS 39):

- To understand how and why an entity uses derivative instruments.
- To describe for every reporting period the (geographical) location of presentation on the balance sheet and income statement and the strategies and objectives of holding financial derivatives. This requirement applies to all financial derivatives whether they are or are not designated in accounting as hedging instruments.
- To report the volume of derivative instruments (such as notional amounts and fair values).
- To explain the accounting for derivative instruments and related hedging items.
- To disclose how derivative instruments and related hedging activities affect an entity's financial position, financial performance, and cash flows.

Market risk encompasses external factors that adversely impact the enterprise's cash flow and present value. External factors with the potential of reducing the value of assets or increasing the value of liabilities can arise in connection with any activity or function of the enterprise. One way of evaluating exposure to market risk is to measure the value at risk for the enterprise's net assets. However, in practice, market risk encompasses the macro uncontrollable factors defined by the SEC and accounting standards: it is the exposure to loss due to adverse movement in commodity prices, interest rate, currency exchange rates, or equity price indexes.

### 12.4.1 Disclosure of Financial Instruments and Hedging

The required disclosure about financial instruments consists of narrative (qualitative) and quantitative information, which are quite extensive. A brief summary of this requirement is provided below in two ways: (1) categorization of types of information required, and (2) an all-in-one exhibit.

Categorization of required disclosures is presented in the form of responding to a hypothetical investor's queries:

1. *Reasons*:
   Why did the enterprise enter into these financial contracts?
   a. To hedge.
   b. As investment.
   c. To speculate.
2. *Object*:
   What activity or function?
   a. Interest rate risk.
   b. Currency risk.
   c. Commodity price risk.
   d. Equity price risk
   e. Other types of risk
3. *Volume*:
   What is the amount of financial instruments that these enterprise have?
   a. Notional amounts.
   b. Fair values.
4. *Success*:
   How well does the company manage these derivatives?
   Disclosure of gains and losses partitioned by
   a. Financial instruments used for hedging versus others.
   b. Flow to earnings versus Other Comprehensive Income in the current reporting period.
   c. Amounts of gains and losses reclassified from Other Comprehensive Income to earnings.
   d. Amounts of gains and losses based on effectiveness or ineffectiveness of the hedging relationship.
5. *Measurement*:
   What basis is used for measurement of values, gains and losses?
   a. The fair value levels (Level 1, 2, and 3) adopted for valuation.
   b. The method used to assess hedging effectiveness.

6. *Type*:

   What types of contracts are in the financial instruments portfolio?

All the information disclosed in response to the above questions must be partitioned by type of contracts such as swaps, options, futures, forwards.

## Exhibit 12.3 All-in-One Required Quantitative Disclosures about *All* Financial Instruments[a]

(ASC 815-10-50-4A – through 4F)

| *Instrument* | *Activity* | *Amounts* | | *Geography* |
|---|---|---|---|---|
| *Designated as hedge instrument whether derivatives or non-derivatives* | *Fair values* | On the balance sheet | Identify the line item | On the balance sheet |
| | *Disaggregation* | By type of contract[b] | Fair values of designated hedge instruments & of the hedged item in FVH | By line item |
| | *Gain or loss* | Income statement | The ineffective portion of CFH and NIH[c]<br>The amount excluded from assessment of effectiveness | Income statement Or the balance sheet |
| | | OCI[d] (Cash flow & net investment hedges) | Effective portion during current period | |
| | | | Effective portion during the term of the hedge | |
| | *Netting* | Not allowed either for master agreement or cash collateral<br>No netting of gains and losses | | |
| | *Frequency* | Quarterly | | |
| | *Mode of presentation* | Hedge instrument | Tabular form | |
| | | Hedged item | Tabular or non-tabular form | |
| *Not designated as hedge instrument* | | • Management choice to disclose gains and losses<br>• The derivatives included in the Trade Portfolio by type. | | |

*Notes*:

(a) *All* financial instruments include derivatives, non-derivatives, designated for hedging, or undesignated for hedging.

(b) Types of contract such as interest rate swaps; currency swaps; forwards, futures …

(c) CFH = cash flow hedge; NIH = net investment hedge

(d) OCI = Other Comprehensive Income

## 12.4.2 Illustrations

### *12.4.2.1 Financial Institutions*

JPMorgan Chase is selected as an illustration of disclosures by a financial institution. The disclosures in Form 10-K filed with the SEC are extensive. The extent to which an enterprise is exposed to loss of value is an overall measure of market risk independent of the cause of value changes. One such measure is value at risk (*VaR*) presented in Chapter Three. *VaR* measures the maximum expected loss in fair value specified in a short time horizon (a day or a week, for example) under normal operating conditions with a probability level of confidence.[8] *VaR* could be evaluated for individual assets, portfolio of assets, or net assets of a segment. The more assets are added to the portfolio, the narrower the dispersion, the higher the diversification benefits and the smaller the measured *VaR* (as shown in Chapter Three).

JPMorgan Chase discloses *VaR* for several types of portfolios.[9] JPMorgan Chase presents *VaR* for the trade and loan portfolios of the Investment Banking operations and shows the reduction in *VaR* due to diversification. The management goes on to note the following:

> IB [Investment Banking] trading *VaR* includes substantially all market-making and client-driven activities as well as certain risk management activities in IB. This includes the credit spread sensitivities of certain mortgage products and syndicated lending facilities that the Firm intends to distribute. The Firm uses proxies to estimate the VaR for these and other products when daily time series are not available.[10]

Exhibit 12.4 presents one of JPMorgan Chase's tables reporting comparative *VaR* information reported in the 2011 Form 10-K for Investment Bank trade and credit portfolios with a 95% confidence. All measures are the result of simulation of *as if* scenarios based on the preceding 12 months' transactions. In this Exhibit, the bank reports on the benefits of diversification in the measurement of the sum of (average) *VaR* for the four portfolios in Investment Banking for (a) one-day horizon, and (b) 95% confidence, and has a total *VaR* of about $100 million before applying the diversification effect. However, taking into account the diversification effect reduced the Investment Banking *VaR* from about $100 million to about $58 million—the diversification benefit is 42% of total *VaR*. It should be noted that *VaR* for the Fixed Income portfolio alone is $50 million, but when three other portfolios (Foreign exchange, Equities, and Commodities and other) are added, the combined *VaR* increases by only $8 million after taking diversification into account.

The histogram in Figure 12.1 presents the daily market risk-related revenue, which is also based on simulated data from historical records. The chart shows that the bank could post market risk-related gains on 233 of the 260 days in this period, with seven days exceeding $200 million. The inset graph looks at those days on which the Firm would experience losses and depicts the amount by which *VaR* exceeded the actual loss on each of those days.

Exhibit 12.5 presents the volume of financial derivatives at JPMorgan Chase in terms of fair values. The two segments of this exhibit present different information about the notional volume of derivatives and it is not clear how to reconcile the differences (2011 Form 10-K, Note 6, p. 202).[11] For example, the gross notional amount of derivatives receivable impact on the balance sheet is noted as $1,868,677 million, the so-called "gross amount of net receivable is $92,477 million. But that is the amount later presented as the receivable (i.e., present value), not the notional. In short, it is not feasible to use these publicly reported data to reconcile the numbers presented in different tables. A brief review of this difficulty should suffice for our purposes.

## Exhibit 12.4 Value at Risk for Investment Banking and Credit Portfolios

**Total IB trading VaR by risk type, Credit portfolio VaR and other VaR**

| As of or for the year ended December 31, | **2011** | | | 2010 | | | At December 31, | |
|---|---|---|---|---|---|---|---|---|
| (in millions) | Avg. | Min | Max | Avg. | Min | Max | **2011** | 2010 |
| **IB VaR by risk type** | | | | | | | | |
| Fixed income | **$50** | **$31** | **$68** | $65 | $33 | $95 | **$49** | $52 |
| Foreign exchange | **11** | **6** | **19** | 11 | 6 | 20 | **19** | 16 |
| Equities | **23** | **15** | **42** | 22 | 10 | 52 | **19** | 30 |
| Commodities and other | **16** | **8** | **24** | 16 | 11 | 32 | **22** | 13 |
| Diversification benefit to IB trading VaR | **(42)**[a] | **NM**[b] | **NM**[b] | (43)[a] | NM[b] | NM[b] | **(55)**[a] | (34)[a] |
| **IB trading VaR** | **58** | **34** | **80** | 71 | 40 | 107 | **54** | 77 |
| Credit portfolio VaR | **33** | **19** | **55** | 26 | 15 | 40 | **42** | 27 |
| **Diversification benefit to IB trading and credit portfolio VaR** | **(15)**[a] | **NM**[b] | **NM**[b] | (10)[a] | NM[b] | NM[b] | **(20)**[a] | (5)[a] |
| **Total IB trading and credit portfolio VaR** | **76** | **42** | **102** | 87 | 50 | 128 | **76** | 99 |
| **Other VaR** | | | | | | | | |
| Mortgage Production and Servicing VaR | **30** | **6** | **98** | 23 | 8 | 47 | **16** | 9 |
| Chief Investment Office ("CIO") VaR | **57** | **30** | **80** | 61 | 44 | 80 | **77** | 56 |
| Diversification benefit to total other VaR | **(17)**[a] | **NM**[b] | **NM**[b] | (13)[a] | NM[b] | NM[b] | **(10)**[a] | (10)[a] |
| **Total other VaR** | **70** | **46** | **110** | 71 | 48 | 100 | **83** | 55 |
| Diversification benefit to total IB and other VaR | **(45)**[a] | **NM**[b] | **NM**[b] | (59)[a] | NM[b] | NM[b] | **(46)**[a] | (65)[a] |
| Total IB and other VaR | $101 | $67 | $147 | $99 | $66 | $142 | $113 | $89 |

(a) Average VaR and period-end VaR were less than the sum of the VaR of the components described above, which is due to portfolio diversification. The diversification effect reflects the fact that the risks were not perfectly correlated. The risk of a portfolio of positions is therefore usually less than the sum of the risks of the positions themselves

(b) Designated as not meaningful ("NM"), because the minimum and maximum may occur on different days for different risk components, and hence it is not meaningful to compute a portfolio-diversification effect.

Source: JPMorgan Chase Annual Report filed with Form 10-K, 2011, p. 160.

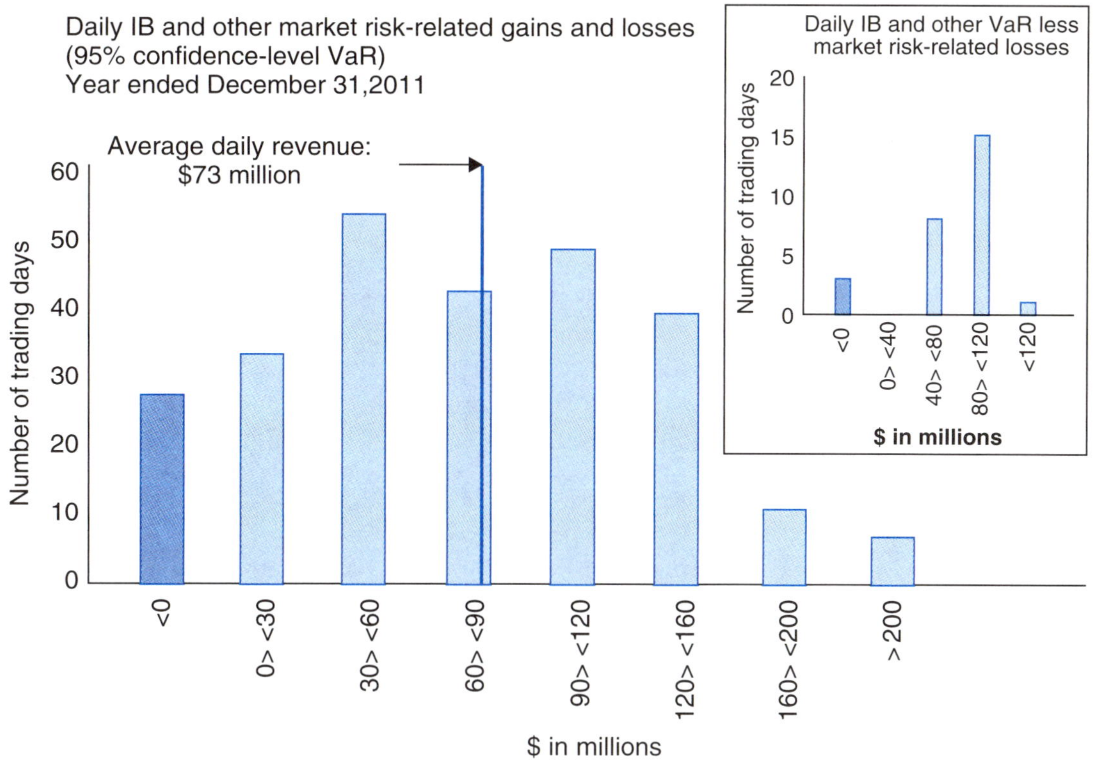


**Figure 12.1** Daily Revenues at Risk with 95% Confidence

The first table (from 10-K page 204) reports total notional derivative amounts to be $71,156 million in 2011 and $78,905 million in 2006. The next table (p. 205) shows the following for 2011:

- Total *gross notional amounts* of all (receivable) financial derivatives (excluding structured notes for which the fair value accounting option is adopted) are $1,884,499,000,000, which is partitioned as follows:
  - $1,868,677,000,000 is not designated as hedges (for accounting purposes).
  - $15,822,000,000 is designated as hedges (for accounting purposes).
- Gross amount of net derivative receivables is $92,477,000,000.
- This amount is the net derivatives receivables balance net of credit valuation adjustment (CVA) as repeated on page 196 of the 2011 Form 10-K.
- Total *gross notional amounts* of all liability in financial derivatives (other than structured notes for which the accounting fair value option is adopted) are $1,837,256,000,000, which is partitioned as follows:
  - $1,833,301,000,000 is not designated as hedges (for accounting purposes).
  - $3,955,000,000 is designated as hedge (for accounting purposes).
- The amount of net derivative payable is $74,977,000,000.
  - This amount is the net derivatives liabilities balance net of debt valuation allowance (DVA) as repeated on page 196 of the 2011 Form 10-K.[12]

A table showing the impact of derivatives on income follows on page 205. The net derivatives impact on net income was $1,391 million, which was the net impact of $8,026 million gains after deducting $6,635 million of hedging losses. The $1,391 million is also presented as $94 million from hedge ineffectiveness and $1,297 million from excluded components such as forward points on forward contracts (2011 Form 10-K, Note 6, p. 204).

This disclosure is preceded by reporting the basic features of financial derivative instruments consistent with disclosures required in ASC 815:

1. The bank uses financial derivatives to hedge interest rate risk, foreign currency exchange rate risk, and commodity price risk.
2. Hedge accounting is not applied to all derivative instruments, such as credit default swaps and derivatives intended for risk management (other than hedging).
3. Showing the following elements of documentation:
   a. A statement of management risk objectives and strategy.
   b. Identification of the derivative hedging instrument.
   c. Identification of the hedged item.
   d. Statement of how effectiveness is measured.
   e. Effectiveness is measured by statistical and nonstatistical techniques, including the dollar offset method.
   f. The ineffective hedge is reported in current period's earnings.
   g. Discontinuation of ineffective hedging relationships.
4. Fair value accounting treatment is used to hedge fixed-rate long-term debt, available-for-sale securities, and certain commodity derivatives.
5. Cash flow hedge accounting treatment is used to hedge cash flow volatility of floating interest rate debt, rollover of short-term assets and liabilities, and foreign-currency-denominated revenue and expense.
6. Foreign currency hedges are used to protect the value of the firm's net investment in certain foreign subsidiaries and branches where the functional currency is not the U.S. dollar.

## Exhibit 12.5 The Volume of Financial Derivatives at JPMorgan Chase

*Notional amount of derivative contracts*

The following table summarizes the notional amount of derivative contracts outstanding as of December 31, 2011 and 2010.

| | Notional amounts[a] | |
|---|---|---|
| December 31, (in billions) | **2011** | 2010 |
| **Interest rate contracts** | | |
| Swaps | **$38,704** | $46,299 |
| Futures and forwards | **7,888** | 9,298 |
| Written options | **3,842** | 4,075 |
| Purchased options | **4,026** | 3,968 |
| **Total interest rate contracts** | **54,460** | 63,640 |

| | | |
|---|---|---|
| **Credit derivatives** | **5,774** | 5,472 |
| **Foreign exchange contracts** | | |
| Cross-currency swaps | **2,931** | 2,568 |
| Spot, futures and forwards | **4,512** | 3,893 |
| Written options | **674** | 674 |
| Purchased options | **670** | 649 |
| **Total foreign exchange contracts** | **8,787** | 7,784 |
| **Equity contracts** | | |
| Swaps | **119** | 116 |
| Futures and forwards | **38** | 49 |
| Written options | **460** | 430 |
| Purchased options | **405** | 377 |
| **Total equity contracts** | **1,022** | 972 |
| **Commodity contracts** | | |
| Swaps | **341** | 349 |
| Spot, futures and forwards | **188** | 170 |
| Written options | **310** | 264 |
| Purchased options | **274** | 254 |
| **Total commodity contracts** | **1,113** | 1,037 |
| **Total derivative notional amounts** | **$71,156** | $78,905 |

(a) Represents the sum of gross long and gross short third-party notional derivative contracts.

While the notional amounts disclosed above give an indication of the volume of the Firm's derivatives activity, the notional amounts significantly exceed, in the Firm's view, the possible losses that could arise from such transactions. For most derivative transactions, the notional amount is not exchanged; it is used simply as a reference to calculate payments.

*Impact of derivatives on the Consolidated Balance Sheets*

The following table summarizes information on derivative receivables and payables (before and after netting adjustments) that are reflected on the Firm's Consolidated Balance Sheets as of December 31, 2011 and 2010, by accounting designation (e.g., whether the derivatives were designated as hedges or not) and contract type.

**Free-standing derivative receivables and payables**[a]

| | Gross derivative receivables | | | | Gross derivative payables | | | |
|---|---|---|---|---|---|---|---|---|
| **December 31, 2011 (in millions)** | Not designated as hedges | Designated as hedges | Total derivative receivables | Net derivative receivables | Not designated as hedges | Designated as hedges | Total derivative payables | Net derivative payables |
| **Trading assets and liabilities** | | | | | | | | |
| Interest rate | **$1,433,900** | **$7,621** | **$1,441,521** | **$46,369** | **$1,397,625** | **$2,192** | **$1,399,817** | **$28,010** |
| Credit | **169,650** | **—** | **169,650** | **6,684** | **165,121** | **—** | **165,121** | **5,610** |

| | | | | | | | | |
|---|---|---|---|---|---|---|---|---|
| Foreign exchange(b) | 163,497 | 4,666 | 168,163 | 17,890 | 165,353 | 655 | 166,008 | 17,435 |
| Equity | 47,736 | — | 47,736 | 6,793 | 46,366 | — | 46,366 | 9,655 |
| Commodity | 53,894 | 3,535 | 57,429 | 14,741 | 58,836 | 1,108 | 59,944 | 14,267 |
| **Total fair value of trading assets and liabilities** | **$1,868,677** | **$15,822** | **$1,884,499** | **$92,477** | **$1,833,301** | **$3,955** | **$1,837,256** | **$74,977** |

Source: Annual Report filed as part of Form10-K, 2011, pp. 203 -204.

### *12.4.2.2 Non-Financial Enterprises*

Interest rate- and currency-related risks are essential to the features of core business of a financial institution, but less so for enterprises in other industries. Nevertheless, engaging in hedging is also a factor in these industries. For illustration, below is a summary of disclosures by three non-financial companies.

#### Wal-Mart Stores, Inc.

*Derivative Uses*: hedging and non-trading.
*Objectives*: Two goals of risk reduction:

a. To manage exposure to changes in interest rate and currency exchange rates.
b. To maintain an appropriate mix of fixed- and floating-rate debt.

*Added Risks*:

a. Use of derivative financial instruments in hedging programs subjects the company to certain risks, such as market and credit risks.
b. Market risk represents the possibility that the value of the derivative instrument will change. In a hedging relationship, the change in the value of the derivative is offset greatly by the change in the value of the underlying hedged item.

*Accounting:*

a. Contracts that are effective at meeting the risk reduction and correlation criteria are recorded using hedge accounting.
b. The ineffective portion of an instrument's change in fair value is immediately recognized in earnings during the period.
c. Instruments that do not meet the criteria for hedge accounting, or contracts for which the company has not elected hedge accounting, are valued at fair value with unrealized gains or losses reported in earnings during the period of change.

The company provided a breakdown of the types of interest rate swaps and currency swaps as follows:[13]

The majority of the Company's derivative instruments relate to interest rate swaps. The fair values of these interest rate swaps have been measured in accordance with Level 2 inputs of the fair value hierarchy, using the income approach. These inputs include the relevant interest rate and foreign currency forward curves. As of January 31, 2012 and 2011, the notional amounts and fair values of these interest rate swaps are as follows (asset/(liability)):

| | *January 31, 2012* | | *January 31, 2011* | |
|---|---|---|---|---|
| *(Amounts in millions)* | *Notional Amount* | *Fair Value* | *Notional Amount* | *Fair Value* |
| Receive fixed-rate, pay floating-rate interest rate swaps designated as fair value hedges | $3,945 | $183 | $4,445 | $267 |
| Receive fixed-rate, pay fixed-rate cross-currency interest rate swaps designated as net investment hedges | 1,250 | 316 | 1,250 | 233 |
| Receive floating-rate, pay fixed-rate interest rate swaps designated as cash flow hedges | 1,270 | (16) | 1,182 | (18) |
| Receive fixed-rate, pay fixed-rate cross-currency interest rate swaps designated as cash flow hedges | 2,884 | (3) | 2,902 | 238 |
| Total | $9,349 | $480 | $9,779 | $720 |

The fair values above are the estimated amounts the Company would receive or pay upon a termination of the agreements relating to such instruments as of the reporting dates.

## 12.5 Liquidity Risk

Liquidity risk relates to several dimensions of business operations, including:

1. The fluctuations in anticipated cash inflows are greater than the fluctuations in anticipated cash outflows;
2. The extent to which funds available from all reliable sources are adequate to cover the enterprise's obligations;
3. The necessity of liquidating assets at high cost to meet due obligations; and
4. The extent to which cash balance and funds available are adequate to finance normal operations.

The earliest regulations about disclosure of liquidity risk were spelled out in the Securities Act Release No. 33-6711 in 1987, in which the SEC issued a ruling to require inclusion of the following in MD&A:[14]

(1) Liquidity. Identify any known trends or any known demands, commitments, events or uncertainties that will result in or that are reasonably likely to result in the registrant's liquidity increasing or decreasing in any material way.

[...]

(2) Capital Resources. Describe any known material trends, favorable or unfavorable, in the registrant's capital resources. Indicate any expected material changes in the mix and

> relative cost of such resources. The discussion shall consider changes between equity, debt and any off-balance sheet financing arrangements.

In December 2001, the Big Six audit firms filed a petition with the SEC requesting additional guidance regarding disclosure of liquidity and capital resources including off-balance sheet arrangements in MD&A.[15] MD&A disclosures should include any

> known events, trends, or uncertainties that are reasonably likely to impact the registrant materially. If a known market risk affected reported trends or financial condition in the period presented, or is reasonably likely to affect materially future reported results or liquidity, discussion of the market risk and its effects is necessary in MD&A.

Following the financial crisis of 2007, investors demanded more information about an enterprise's exposure to liquidity risk. In response, although lagging the issuance of IFRS 7, on June 27, 2012, the FASB issued an Exposure Draft calling for more disclosure of liquidity, liquidity risk, and interest rate risk, thereby formalizing the SEC's long-held 1987 requirement. Like IFRS 7, the Accounting Standards Update distinguishes between financial institutions and other types of firms.

## 12.5.1 Basic Definitions Related to Financial Instruments

Before presenting this outline, a brief review of the related concepts presented in Chapter Three will be useful:

- *Gap*: the difference between interest-rate-sensitive assets and interest-rate-sensitive liabilities.
- *Maturity*: the contractual settlement date.
- *Duration*: is either *Macaulay's Duration* or *Modified Macaulay's Duration*. *Macaulay's Duration* (for a fixed-rate instrument) is a ratio of (a) the present value of time-weighted cash flow (inflow for a fixed-rate financial asset and outflow for a fixed-rate financial liability) divided by (b) the present value of the financial instrument. For floating-rate instruments, it is the time to reset interest rate. For a zero-coupon bond, duration is equal to the term of the contract.
- *Gap Analysis*: the extent to which a change in interest rate affects income for different durations (or maturities).
- *Stress Testing*: the sensitivity of cash flow and income to different levels of adverse changes in interest rate at different durations (or maturities).
- *Repricing*: Resetting of the financing cost of floating-rate instruments at the reset dates.
- *Yield Curve*: The curve structure tracking the relationship between interest rates and maturities. If no qualification is offered, the yield curve is assumed to be for U.S. Treasury securities, otherwise every type or risk class has its own yield curve. The slope, the relationship between short-term and long-term shapes, and level of yield curves may vary over time and with changes in interest rates.

## 12.5.2 A Summary of the Proposed ASU Disclosures[16]

The objective of the proposed disclosure is to "provide information about the risks and uncertainties that a reporting entity might encounter in meeting its financial obligations." An outline of the proposed standard is presented below and a comparison with IFRS 7 is presented in Exhibit 12.6.

Essential to this disclosure is disaggregating financial assets and liabilities into classes. While identifying classes requires judgment, the proposed standard provides guidance in stating that

> [T]he entity shall determine the appropriate level of disaggregation on the basis of the nature, characteristics, or risks of the financial instruments. In this context, risks can refer to the underlying risks associated with the financial asset or financial liability or how the financial instruments contribute to the risk conveyed in the disclosure.[17]

### 12.5.2.1 Financial Institutions

These establishments should disclose the following information by classes of the financial items:[18]

- Gap for interest-rate-sensitive assets, interest-rate-sensitive liabilities on or off the balance sheet and for each expected maturity (expected settlement date). For this requirement, financial instruments include leases and insurance contracts.
- Weighted average of contractual yield for each class of financial assets and financial liabilities.
- Stress testing to show the cash flow and income effect of adverse movements in interest rate by class of item for different maturities under three different *as if* scenarios:

  i. *Parallel* shifts up and down by 100 Basis Points and 200 Basis Points;
  ii. *Tilt* shift: flattening shifts by increasing the short-end by 100 Basis Points and decreasing the long-end by 100 Basis Points; and
  iii. *Bend* shift: steepening shifts by decreasing the short-end by 100 Basis Points and increasing the long-end by 100 Basis Points.
  iv. *Constraint*: no forward-looking assumptions or strategies of any kind should be incorporated in the hypothetical *as if* shifts in the yield curve.

- Various Macaulay's durations by class of item for different maturities.
- Impact of *repricing* financial assets and financial liabilities at the reset dates for floating-rate instruments, and at maturity for fixed-rate instruments.
- Information for the following four years must be provided in tabular form with the first year's data presented for each quarter.
- Available cash which includes all liquid assets of high quality and available unsecured lines of credit that could generate cash as needed.
- Whether the financial institution is also a deposit institution.

### 12.5.2.2 Non-Financial Institutions

These enterprises should show:

- Available Cash—same as financial institutions.
- Undiscounted cash flow obligations by expected maturity with an explanation of any differences between maturity at the settlement date and expected maturity.

## Exhibit 12.6 Disclosure of Liquidity Risk and Interest Rate Risk (FASB June 2012 Exposure Draft of ASU and IFRS 7)

| | | *FASB Exposure Draft* | | *IFRS 7* |
|---|---|---|---|---|
| | | *Financial institutions* | *Non-financial institutions* | |
| Liquidity risk | Interest-rate-gap analysis | ✓ | × | ✓ |
| | Available liquid funds | ✓ | ✓ | × |
| | Expected financial cash flow obligations | × | ✓ | ✓ |
| Interest-rate risk | Repricing gap analysis | ✓ | × | × |
| | Interest rate sensitivity analysis | ✓ | × | Similar disclosures All entities |

## Information Log: Implications of the Proposed Standard Update about Liquidity

What are the likely implications of adopting this proposed standard about disclosure of liquidity for financial institutions' reports?

The possible effects might include: (1) providing quantitative instead of descriptive and qualitative information; (2) including the liquidity disclosure as a supplementary footnote to financial statements, but not as a substitute for MD&A liquidity disclosures required by the SEC; and (3) subjecting the liquidity disclosure to actual audit.

With respect to the first implication, consider, for example, the following disclosure by JPMorgan Chase.

> LIQUIDITY RISK MANAGEMENT
>
> Liquidity is essential to the ability to operate financial services businesses and, therefore, the ability to maintain surplus levels of liquidity through economic cycles is crucial to financial services companies, particularly during periods of adverse conditions. The Firm relies on external sources to finance a significant portion of its operations, and the Firm's funding strategy is intended to ensure that it will have sufficient liquidity and a diversity of funding sources necessary to enable it to meet actual and contingent liabilities during both normal and stress periods. JPMorgan Chase's primary sources of liquidity include a diversified deposit base, which was $1,127.8 billion at December 31, 2011, and access to the equity capital markets and to long-term unsecured and secured funding sources, including through asset securitizations and borrowings from FHLBs. Additionally, JPMorgan Chase maintains

significant amounts of highly-liquid unencumbered assets. The Firm actively monitors the availability of funding in the wholesale markets across various geographic regions and in various currencies. The Firm's ability to generate funding from a broad range of sources in a variety of geographic locations and in a range of tenors is intended to enhance financial flexibility and limit funding concentration risk.

(Source: JPMorgan Chase, Form 10-K, 2011, p. 127. http://www.sec.gov/Archives/edgar/data/19617/000001961712000163/corp10k2011.htm)

In this disclosure, the bank reports: (a) the objective of maintaining liquidity, (b) reference to external sources of funds, (c) a quantitative number for internal resources, (d) the bank has ample borrowing capacity from domestic and international sources, and (e) the bank has a significant amount of unencumbered assets.

Of these five components, the only quantitative measure provided is the size of the bank's deposits, which is available elsewhere in the financial statements. The qualitative statements about other elements of the disclosure are nebulous because each one of these elements could be any point in a wide distribution of time.

If the proposed accounting standard is adopted, that type of qualitative disclosure will be accompanied by quantitative information to assist users in understanding where the bank falls on the range of all possible scenarios.

## 12.5.3 Related Disclosures

Not all enterprises are affected by any given risk and, if they are affected by the same type of risk, these effects would not be in the same way or magnitude as other enterprises. For example, "liquidity risk" is of relevance to public utilities such as Dominion Resources, Inc. partly because of the divergence between durations of sources of cash inflows and cash outflows. The cost structure of inputs reveals long-term cash flow commitments, but by providing electric service to retail customers, cash inflows are sensitive to the collectability of short-term receivables. "Liquidity risk" for this type of industry has a different character and scope than it does for a bank, for example. However, in addition, Dominion Resources also discloses exposure to credit risk, interest-rate risk, and commodity price risk, all of which have implications to liquidity risk.

For another example, IBM discloses exposure to "Other Risk" in connection with warrants as follows: "The company is exposed to a potential loss if a client fails to pay amounts due under contractual terms. The company utilizes credit default swaps to economically hedge its credit exposures." (2011 Form10-K, p. 98). While the company is concerned about default risk of warrant holders, the default itself will affect liquidity because it negatively impacts cash inflows.

In addition, IBM makes the following disclosure with respect to certain derivative instruments:

> These instruments, designated as net investment hedges, expose the company to liquidity risk as the derivatives have an immediate cash flow impact upon maturity which is not offset by a cash flow from the translation of the underlying hedged equity. The company monitors this cash loss potential on an ongoing basis, and may discontinue some of these hedging relationships by de-designating the derivative instrument in order to manage the liquidity risk.
>
> (Source: Form 10-K, 2011, p. 97)

It is therefore critical to realize that liquidity risk is a function of all activities having cash flow implications.

## 12.6 Credit Risk

Credit risk is defined as exposure to loss due to debtors' probable default. Under this broad definition, credit risk also includes counterparty risk: the possibility that each party to a contract might lose due to the counterparty's nonperformance of contractual agreement. Counterparty risk arises in any financial arrangements of loans, mortgages, derivatives, and contracts of structured finance, but it has more significance in derivative contracts because the economic obligations of each party to derivative contracts (other than options) are not completely fulfilled until settlement and the holders of assets and liabilities flip as external determinants of fair values change.

The enterprise can manage these exposures in different ways such as purchasing protection through credit default swap, setting authorization limits, evaluation of customers' credit ratings, requiring collateral, diversifying the portfolio of debtors and counterparties, or selling (factoring) the loans that have high exposure.

### Information Log: Counterparty Risk (CVA & DVA)

As the term "counterparty risk" implies, each party to a contract is exposed to some type of credit risk. For the purpose of this introduction we consider two main types: (1) risk causing loss due to the probability of not fully collecting claims from the counterparty, and (2) risk causing gain due to the probability that an enterprise may not be able to fulfill its obligations in full. The second type could be viewed as the impact of liquidity risk of the entity on its own ability to pay its obligations.

The measurement of counterparty risk could be quite complex, but for our purposes we need to know the difference between two values:

1. The value of a financial derivative is generally measured based on prospective cash flows discounted at the risk-free rate.
2. The fair or market value of a financial derivative in a liquid-efficient market embodies the impact of credit risk.

Credit risk could then be approximated as the difference between fair market value in a liquid and efficient market and the value measured at the risk-free rate. Because discounting a given series of cash flows at the risk-free rate will result in higher valuation than discounting the same series of cash flows at a rate equal to the risk-free rate plus a risk premium, the market-determined fair market value of a derivative instrument will normally be equal to or less than its risk-free value. This difference is either:

a. a credit risk valuation adjustment (CVA), or
b. a debt risk valuation adjustment (DVA), which is effectively an adjustment for liquidity risk exposure.

Measurement difficulty, however, is encountered when the valuation of derivative instruments is based on Level 3 or Level 2 of the fair value hierarchy in which the management invokes numerous assumptions and might not adjust for credit risk.

In its 10-K, JPMorgan Chase provides useful descriptions for both CVA and DVA (p. 185).

- Credit valuation adjustments ("CVA") are necessary when the market price (or parameter) is not indicative of the credit quality of the counterparty. As few classes of derivative contracts are listed on an exchange, derivative positions are predominantly valued using internally developed models that use as their basis observable market parameters. An adjustment is necessary in order to reflect the credit quality of each derivative's counterparty and arrive at fair value. The adjustment also takes into account contractual factors designed to reduce the Firm's credit exposure to each counterparty, such as collateral and legal rights of offset.
- Debt valuation adjustments ("DVA") are taken to reflect the credit quality of the Firm in the valuation of liabilities measured at fair value. The methodology to determine the adjustment is consistent with CVA and incorporates JPMorgan Chase's credit spread as observed through the credit default swap market.

JPMorgan Chase also explains how DVA is used as an estimated gain to offset CVA (an estimated loss).

- Net revenue was $26.3 billion, compared with $26.2 billion in the prior year. Investment banking fees were $5.9 billion, down 5% from the prior year; these consisted of debt underwriting fees of $2.9 billion (down 8%), advisory fees of $1.8 billion (up 22%) and equity underwriting fees of $1.2 billion (down 26%). Fixed Income Markets revenue was $15.3 billion, compared with $15.0 billion in the prior year, with continued solid client revenue. The increase also reflects DVA gains of $553 million, compared with DVA gains of $287 million in the prior year. Equity Markets revenue was $4.8 billion, approximately flat compared with the prior year, as slightly lower performance was more than offset by DVA gains of $356 million, compared with DVA Annual Report gains of $181 million in the prior year. Credit Portfolio revenue was $246 million as net interest income and fees on retained loans, as well as DVA gains of $528 million were predominantly offset by a $769 million loss, net of hedges, from CVA on derivative assets. (pp. 81–82).

**The Dilemma:**

It should be emphasized that exposure to liquidity risk by one enterprise is an indicator of the credit risk faced by external parties that have extended credit to this enterprise. I, therefore, remain not persuaded by the proposition that a firm not facing financial distress could, with no known restrictions, estimate the probability of its own default on the debt it carries and then use this estimation as the basis for recognition of gains.

Recently, the FASB issued ASU 2010-20 to make significant changes (similar to IFRS 7) in disclosure requirements (Topic ASC 310). The main objective in developing this update is to:

> provide financial statement users with greater transparency about an entity's allowance for credit losses and the credit quality of its financing receivables. The objective of the amendments in this update is for an entity to provide disclosures that facilitate financial statement users' evaluation of the following:
>
> 1. The nature of credit risk inherent in the entity's portfolio of financing receivables
> 2. How that risk is analyzed and assessed in arriving at the allowance for credit losses
> 3. The changes and reasons for those changes in the allowance for credit losses.[19]

This proposed standard update provided several important features:

- Requiring inclusion of further disaggregation of the information presented to assist investors and external users in understanding the credit risk associated with receivable contracts.
- Changes to the methodology the enterprise uses to estimate loss allowances.
- Reporting credit quality indicator (such as externally determined credit ratings).
- Disaggregating the allowances information by "portfolio segment" and "class." A portfolio segment can be the type, the industry, or the risk category of the debtors.

Enterprises make efforts to tell investors how they measure and manage credit risk. Four companies provide useful examples.

## 12.6.1 Measurement and Management of Credit Risk: Illustrations

### *12.6.1.1 Dominion Resources, Inc.*

Exhibit 12.7 shows how Dominion Resources, Inc., a utility company in Virginia and the East Coast, discloses its exposure to credit risk.

**Exhibit 12.7 An Illustration of Disclosing Exposure to Credit Risk (Dominion Resources, Inc.)**

CREDIT RISK

Dominion's exposure to potential concentrations of credit risk results primarily from its energy marketing and price risk management activities. Presented below is a summary of Dominion's credit exposure as of December 31, 2011 for these activities. Gross credit exposure for each counterparty is calculated as outstanding receivables plus any unrealized on- or off-balance sheet exposure, taking into account contractual netting rights.

| | *Gross Credit Exposure* | *Credit Collateral* | *Net Credit Exposure* |
|---|---|---|---|
| (millions) | | | |
| Investment grade[1] | $349 | $30 | $319 |
| Non-investment grade[2] | 4 | — | 4 |
| No external ratings: | | | |
| Internally rated-investment grade[3] | 84 | — | 84 |
| Internally rated-non-investment grade[4] | 97 | — | 97 |
| Total | $534 | $30 | $504 |

1. Designations as investment grade are based upon minimum credit ratings assigned by Moody's and Standard & Poor's. The five largest counterparty exposures, combined for this category represented approximately 33% of the total net credit exposure.
2. The five largest counterparty exposures, combined, for this category represented approximately 1% of the total net credit exposure.
3. The five largest counterparty exposures, combined, for this category represented approximately 8% of the total net credit exposure.
4. The five largest counterparty exposures, combined, for this category represented approximately 12% of the total net credit exposure.

Virginia Power's exposure to potential concentration of credit risk results primarily from sales to wholesale customers and was not considered material at December 31, 2011.

(Source: Form 10-K, 2011, http://services.corporate-ir.net/SEC.Enhanced/SecCapsule.aspx?c=110481&fid=8037786)

### *12.6.1.2 The Boeing Corporation*

Because of the nature of the industry and the indivisibility of the products it produces, Boeing appears to have both clientele and credit concentration. To inform investors, the company identified the commercial customer with largest financing receivable and additionally provided the ranking of its own internal credit ratings of the customers for whom the company financed purchases. Exhibit 12.8 is an excerpt from the 2011 Form 10-K filed by the company with the SEC.

## Exhibit 12.8 The Boeing Corporation's Disclosure of Exposure to Credit Risk

*A significant portion of our and Boeing Capital Corporation's customer financing portfolio is concentrated among certain customers based in the United States, and in certain types of Boeing aircraft, which exposes us to concentration risks.* (p. 12).

[...]

We assign internal credit ratings for all customers and determine the creditworthiness of each customer based upon public information and information obtained directly from our customers. We utilize these credit ratings as one of the factors in assessing the adequacy of our allowance for losses on receivables. Our rating categories are comparable to those used by the major credit rating agencies. The customer financing valuation benefit recorded in 2011 was primarily driven by changes in the internal credit rating categories assigned to our receivable balances from AirTran Holdings, LLC (AirTran).

The following table details our financing receivable balances at December 31, by the internal credit rating category which was used as a factor in determining our allowance for losses on receivables. [*Dollar numbers are in millions*]

| Rating categories | 2011 | 2010 |
|---|---|---|
| BBB | $1,316 | |
| BB | 67 | |
| B | 103 | $207 |
| CCC | 512 | 2,432 |
| D | 653 | |
| Other | 200 | 113 |
| Total carrying value of financing receivables | $2,851 | $2,752 |

At December 31, 2011, our allowance primarily related to receivables with ratings of BBB and CCC and we applied default rates that averaged 4% and 48% to exposure associated with those receivables. On May 2, 2011, Southwest Airlines Co. (Southwest) completed its acquisition of AirTran Holdings, Inc. and AirTran Holdings, Inc. became a wholly owned subsidiary of Southwest. AirTran.

[...]

In the fourth quarter of 2011, American Airlines filed for Chapter 11 bankruptcy protection. We believe that our customer financing receivables from American Airlines of $653 are sufficiently collateralized such that we do not expect to incur losses related to those receivables as a result of the bankruptcy.

Declines in collateral values are also a significant driver of our allowance for losses. Generally, out-of-production aircraft have had greater percentages of collateral value declines than in-production aircraft. Our portfolio consists primarily of financing receivables for out-of-production aircraft.

(Source: Form 10-K, 2011, p. 74; http://services.corporate-ir.net/SEC.Enhanced/SecCapsule.aspx?c=85482&fid=7984582)

### *12.6.1.3 Caterpillar Company's Concentration of Credit Risk*[20]

Credit risk concentration arises when a relatively small number of debtors constitute a relatively large proportion of borrowed assets. Similarly, credit risk would be considered concentrated if a relatively large number of customers or borrowers reside in one region or country.

Disclosure of any credit risk concentration would be informative to investors in assessing the risk of collectability. The case of The Boeing Corporation noted above serves as an illustration of these conditions.

Many organizations face the risk of default due to credit risk concentration and often disclose the policies they have in place to manage this risk. For example, Caterpillar Co. discloses the various methods of reducing that risk exposure. These methods are:

a. Financial instruments with potential credit risk consist primarily of trade and finance receivables, investments, and counterparties to derivative contracts.

b. The company performs regular credit evaluations of dealers and customers.
c. Trade receivables are unsecured and collateral is generally not required.
d. Using letters of credit and security agreements to reduce exposure to credit losses.
e. No single dealer or customer represents a significant concentration of credit risk.
f. The company maintains master netting agreements with ISDA and thereby limits loss exposure to net gains in derivative instruments.

#### *12.6.1.4 JPMorgan Chase Rating Credit Risk of Derivatives*

Financial derivatives are unique instruments in that about 90% of outstanding notional amount is traded in dark markets over the counter without any transparency. An enterprise having financial derivatives in its asset portfolio is exposed to credit risk, but unless this enterprise volunteers disclosures related to this risk, investors would not have any type of information.

JPMorgan Chase provides an example of disclosing the credit ratings of derivative counterparties in a manner similar to the credit rating disclosure of debtors. The management of JPMorgan Chase's self-reported ratings of credit risk of derivative receivables are presented in Form 10-K and show a positive skewed distribution of fair values (10-K Form, 2011, p. 142) as follows:

| | *Million* | *Percentage* |
|---|---|---|
| AAA/Aaa to AA–/Aa3 | $25,100 | 35% |
| A+/A1 to A–/A3 | $22,942 | 32% |
| BBB+/Baa1 to BBB–/Baa3 | $9,595 | 14% |
| BB+/Ba1 to B–/B3 | $10,545 | 15% |
| CCC+/Caa1 and below | $2,488 | 4% |
| Total | $70,670 | 100% |

While this rating provides summary information, it is useful in showing the extent to which JPMorgan Chase is exposed to counterparty default risk of derivative receivables.

## **12.7** Disclosures about Operational Risk

The Basel Accord defines operational risk as the risk of loss due to people or systems.[21] This is the definition adopted in Chapter Two, which includes internal controls and information and regulation risk.

### 12.7.1 Disclosures about Internal Control and Information System

Following the collapse of Enron and WorldCom in early 2000, it became clear that the "risk of loss due to people and systems" is not limited to banking institutions. The Sarbanes-Oxley Act (SOX) was enacted in 2002 in which the law entrusted the SEC to make a ruling that requires registered companies to report on (a) the effectiveness and efficiency of operations; (b) reliability of financial reporting; and (c) compliance with applicable laws and regulations. As a result of the Act and the regulations that followed, a public company's *quarterly* financial reporting must include a report by the management containing:[22]

- A statement of management's responsibility for establishing and maintaining adequate internal controls and procedures for financial reporting.
- The evaluation and conclusions of management about the effectiveness of the company's internal controls and procedures for financial reporting.
- A certification by the CEO and the CFO that the design and operations of internal controls are effective.
- A certification by the external auditor attesting to the certification of the management and on that management's evaluation of the company's internal controls and procedures for financial reporting.

The Sarbanes-Oxley Act (SOX) of 2002 required the SEC to establish a process by which registrants file at least two reports in addition to the conventional audit opinion report. These reports are (1) a certification by each of the CEO and the CFO individually on the quality of the design and effectiveness of internal controls; and (2) a certification by the auditor concerning the efficacy of the management's report (See Exhibit 12.9 for an example).

## Exhibit 12.9 DineEquity CEO Certification about Internal Controls

**Certification Pursuant to**
**Rule 13a-14(a) of the**
**Securities Exchange Act of 1934, As Amended**
I, Julia A. Stewart, certify that:

1. I have reviewed this Annual Report on Form 10-K of DineEquity, Inc.;
2. Based on my knowledge, this report does not contain any untrue statement of a material fact or omit to state a material fact necessary to make the statements made, in light of the circumstances under which such statements were made, not misleading with respect to the period covered by this report;
3. Based on my knowledge, the financial statements, and other financial information included in this report, fairly present in all material respects the financial condition, results of operations and cash flows of the registrant as of, and for, the periods presented in this report;
4. The registrant's other certifying officer and I are responsible for establishing and maintaining disclosure controls and procedures (as defined in Exchange Act Rules 13a-15(e) and 15d-15(e)) and internal control over financial reporting (as defined in Exchange Act Rules 13a-15(f) and 15d-15(f)) for the registrant and have:

   (a) Designed such disclosure controls and procedures, or caused such disclosure controls and procedures to be designed under our supervision, to ensure that material information relating to the registrant, including its consolidated subsidiaries, is made known to us by others within those entities, particularly during the period in which this report is being prepared;
   (b) Designed such internal control over financial reporting, or caused such internal control over financial reporting to be designed under our supervision, to provide reasonable assurance regarding the reliability of financial reporting and the preparation of financial

statements for external purposes in accordance with generally accepted accounting principles;

(c) Evaluated the effectiveness of the registrant's disclosure controls and procedures and presented in this report our conclusions about the effectiveness of the disclosure controls and procedures, as of the end of the period covered by this report based on such evaluation; and

(d) Disclosed in this report any change in the registrant's internal control over financial reporting that occurred during the registrant's most recent fiscal quarter (the registrant's fourth fiscal quarter in the case of an annual report) that has materially affected, or is reasonably likely to materially affect, the registrant's internal control over financial reporting; and

5. The registrant's other certifying officer and I have disclosed, based on our most recent evaluation of internal control over financial reporting, to the registrant's auditors and the audit committee of the registrant's board of directors (or persons performing the equivalent functions):

(a) All significant deficiencies and material weaknesses in the design or operation of internal control over financial reporting which are reasonably likely to adversely affect the registrant's ability to record, process, summarize and report financial information; and

(b) Any fraud, whether or not material, that involves management or other employees who have a significant role in the registrant's internal control over financial reporting.

Date: March 1, 2012 /s/ JULIA A. STEWART
Julia A. Stewart
*Chairman and Chief Executive Officer*

(Source: Form 10-K, 2011, Exhibit 31.1; https://materials.proxyvote.com/Approved/254423/20120326/AR_122616/HTML2/dineequity-ar2011_0136.htm)

Implementing the requirements of SOX was the last in a series of attempts to reform and ascertain the quality of internal controls to reduce the company's exposure to operational risk. The first major regulatory effort came as a result of the Foreign Corrupt Practices Act (FCPA) of 1977 based on a Congressional committee report chaired by Representative Moss. The FCPA required registered public companies to devise and maintain a system of internal accounting controls sufficient to provide reasonable assurances that the enterprise's assets are safeguarded and ascertaining that transactions are based on proper authorization and recorded in accordance with GAAP. The FCPA's concern was with the accounting side of internal controls to ensure that U.S. enterprises no longer bribe foreign officials to procure business contracts. In the interim between FCPA and SOX, the Treadway Committee came up with the COSO report in 1985 discussed in Chapter Four. The COSO report highlighted the important role of internal controls and internal auditing.

The culmination of these efforts and the collapse of Enron and WorldCom in early 2000 have elevated the role of internal control systems from a subset of accounting to additionally provide a platform for audit planning. Added to the accounting perspective, the auditing perspective of internal controls heightened its significance in reducing the enterprise's exposure to operational risk—i.e., safeguarding assets and permitting auditors to plan the audits to increase their confidence in their diagnosis of the enterprise's viability.

To comply with the SEC rulings concerning the implementation of SOX, management could be held liable for negligence in maintaining effective internal controls. Furthermore, the external auditor is held responsible for providing the required assurance of the authenticity of the management's certification.[23]

Early efforts at implementing the SEC rulings have led the Public Company Accounting Oversight Board (PCAOB) to issue Auditing Standard No. 2, which required extensive and intensive redesign and evaluation of internal control, including identifying every control point in the organization. A major U.S. corporation claimed that applying the standard has led to identifying 177,000 control points within the consolidated entity. The excessive demands of AS No. 2 led to the adoption of AS No. 5 with more realistic expectations. However, AS No. 2 succeeded in sensitizing the management and the external auditor to the immense significance of internal control systems in: (a) safeguarding the enterprise's assets, (b) reducing information system risk, (c) reducing fraud and theft by employees, and (d) ensuring that transactions are duly authorized.

In some cases, the management's report on internal control is critical of the management. Consider the report by the management of General Motors in its 2006 Form 10-K in Exhibit 12.10.

### Exhibit 12.10 An Excerpt from the Management Report on Internal Control at General Motors

> The Corporation in certain instances lacked the technical expertise and did not maintain adequate procedures to ensure that the accounting for derivative financial instruments under SFAS No. 133, *Accounting for Derivative Instruments and Hedging Activities*, was appropriate. Procedures relating to hedging transactions in certain instances did not operate effectively to (a) properly evaluate hedge accounting treatment (b) meet the documentation requirements of SFAS No. 133, (c) adequately assess and measure hedge effectiveness on a quarterly basis, and (d) establish the appropriate communication and coordination between relevant GM departments involved in complex financial transactions. This material weakness resulted in a restatement of prior financial statements, as described in Note 2 to the Consolidated Financial Statements and, if not remediated, has the potential to cause a material misstatement in the future.
>
> Source: General Motors Form 10-K, 2006, p. 196; http://www.sec.gov/Archives/edgar/data/40730/000095012407001502/k11916e10vk.htm

## 12.7.2 Disclosure about Employees' Compensation and Risk Governance

The second important disclosure about managing operational risk relates to the role of the board of directors in risk oversight and the impact of compensation on enterprise risk. In 2009, the SEC issued a ruling to enhance disclosures in the Proxy Statement about the leadership of the management of registered enterprises in managing risk and about the extent to which employees' (not only the executives') compensation exposes the enterprise to undue risk.[24] This ruling was effective as of February 28, 2010. In particular, the ruling requires narrative disclosure about:

- The board's role in risk oversight, which may include plans to improve the Enterprise Risk Management, reviews and enhancement of internal audits and internal controls.

- The extent to which risks arising from a company's compensation policies and practices for *all* employees are *reasonably likely* to have a material adverse effect on the company.
- The extent to which these compensation policies and practices relate to the company's risk management and risk governance.

This ruling is recent and, to my knowledge, it still needs to be tested.

## 12.8 Concentration Risk

Concentration risk is often discussed in terms of functional diversification (non-concentration). For example, the online *Business Dictionary* defines concentration risk in terms of credit risk as "the probability of loss arising from heavily lopsided exposure to a particular group of counterparties."[25]

While they may not be labeled as such, there are clientele concentration risks, country concentration risks, supply chain concentration risks, and the like. Accounting standards deal with some of these risk exposures but not others. The primary standards addressing this issue are ASC 310 which address credit concentration risk and ASC 280 (the corresponding international standards are IFRS 7 and IFRS 8). The literature refers to ASC 280 (and IFRS 8) as Segment Reporting but it can best be described as *Concentration Risk Reporting*. ASC 280-10-05-3 sets the scope of the standard as follows:

> A public entity could provide complete sets of financial statements that are disaggregated in several different ways, for example, by *products* and *services*, by *geography*, by *legal entity*, or by *type of customer*. However, it is not feasible to provide all of that information in every set of financial statements. The guidance in this Subtopic requires that general-purpose financial statements include selected information reported on a *single* basis of segmentation. The method for determining what information to report is referred to as the management approach. The management approach is based on the way that management organizes the segments within the public entity for making operating decisions and assessing performance. Consequently, the segments are evident from the structure of the public entity's internal organization, and financial statement preparers should be able to provide the required information in a cost-effective and timely manner. [Emphasis added.]

In spite of proclaiming ASC 280 as devoted to a single basis of segmentation, the standard addresses more than a "single" basis of concentration risk.

### 12.8.1 Categories of Concentration Risk

#### *12.8.1.1 Clientele Concentration*

ASC 280-10-50-42 requires disclosing information about clientele concentration.

> [I]f revenues from transactions with a single external customer amount to 10 percent or more of a public entity's revenues, the public entity shall disclose that fact, the total amount of

revenues from each such customer, and the identity of the segment or segments reporting the revenues.

As an example of disclosing clientele concentration, The Boeing Corporation reported the following:

> We derive a significant portion of our revenues from a limited number of commercial airlines. We can make no assurance that any customer will exercise purchase options, fulfill existing purchase commitments or purchase additional products or services from us after our contract with the customer ends. In addition, fleet decisions, airline consolidations or financial challenges involving any of our major commercial airline customers could significantly reduce our revenues and limit our opportunity to generate profits from those customers (p. 6).[26]

IFRS 8 adopted the same criteria, which were absent from its predecessor IAS 14.[27]

### *12.8.1.2 Concentration of Credit Risk*

Concentration of credit risk can arise for many reasons. We have seen the nature of industry of The Boeing Corporation as one of these reasons: a substantial portion of its revenues are sales to a limited number of customers.

However, Intel, Inc. provides a clear disclosure of both clientele risk and concentration of credit risk—two customers have 32% of sales and 44% of accounts receivable. Default of either one of these two customers would be highly costly. Nike, Inc. also has an issue with concentration of credit risk. Excerpts from Form 10-K filings of these two companies are reproduced in this section.

#### Clientele and Credit Risk Concentration at Intel, Inc.

> A substantial majority of our trade receivables are derived from sales to original equipment manufacturers and original design manufacturers. We also have accounts receivable derived from sales to industrial and retail distributors. Our two largest customers accounted for 34% of net revenue for 2011 and 38% of net revenue for 2010 and 2009. Additionally, these two largest customers accounted for 32% of our accounts receivable as of December 31, 2011 and 44% of our accounts receivable as of December 25, 2010. We believe that the receivable balances from these largest customers do not represent a significant credit risk based on cash flow forecasts, balance sheet analysis, and past collection experience (p. 63).
>
> (Source: Intel, Inc. 2011 Form 10-K http://www.intc.com/intelAR2011/common/pdfs/Intel_2011_Form_10-K.pdf)

#### Concentration of Credit Risk at Nike, Inc.

> *Consolidation of retailers or concentration of retail market share among a few retailers may increase and concentrate our credit risk, and impair our ability to sell our products.*
>
> The athletic footwear, apparel, and equipment retail markets in some countries are dominated by a few large athletic footwear, apparel, and equipment retailers with many stores. These retailers have in the past increased their market share and may continue to do so in the future by expanding through acquisitions and construction of additional stores. These situations concen-

trate our credit risk with a relatively small number of retailers, and, if any of these retailers were to experience a shortage of liquidity, it would increase the risk that their outstanding payables to us may not be paid. In addition, increasing market share concentration among one or a few retailers in a particular country or region increases the risk that if any one of them substantially reduces their purchases of our products, we may be unable to find a sufficient number of other retail outlets for our products to sustain the same level of sales and revenues (p. 14).

(Source, 2011 Form 10-K, Nike, Inc. at http://www.sec.gov/Archives/edgar/data/320187/000119312511194791/d10k.htm)

### *12.8.1.3 Country Concentration Risk*

Country risk is the exposure to loss due to idiosyncratic domestic, economic or political problems in foreign regions in which the enterprise operates. If the enterprise's foreign operations are concentrated in a single region, the enterprise will be affected by adverse economic events in that region. For example, the collapse of MF Global, the eighth largest bankruptcy in U.S. history, was caused by exposure to liquidity risk in relationship to its investment in sovereign European bonds of Ireland, Italy, Greece, and Portugal. At a more specific level, difference in cultures and the way of doing business between countries could give risk to risk of loss. For example, Xerox Corporation had problems arising from different cultural habits in collecting receivables in its operation in Mexico.[28]

Accounting standards recognize the risk of loss due to concentration of transactions in one country or one geographic location. ASC 280 requires that an enterprise disclose geographic information to allow users to assess the extent to which the enterprise is exposed to country risk.

## Information Log: The standard on country concentration

ASC 280-1-50-41 A public entity shall report the following geographic information …

a. Revenues from external customers attributed to the public entity's country of domicile and attributed to all foreign countries in total from which the public entity derives revenues. If revenues from external customers attributed to an individual foreign country are material, those revenues shall be disclosed separately. A public entity shall disclose the basis for attributing revenues from external customers to individual countries.
b. Long-lived assets other than financial instruments, long-term customer relationships of a financial institution, mortgage and other servicing rights, deferred policy acquisition costs, and deferred tax assets located in the public entity's country of domicile and located in all foreign countries in total in which the public entity holds assets. If assets in an individual foreign country are material, those assets shall be disclosed separately.

### *12.8.1.4 Product Market Concentration Risk*

Under ASC 280 and IFRS 8, enterprises are required to disclose financial information about operating segments.[29] ASC 280-10-10-1 states the objectives of reporting disaggregate information about operating segments as follows:[30]

The objective of requiring disclosures about segments of a public entity and related information is to provide information about the different types of business activities in which a public entity engages and the different economic environments in which it operates to help users of financial statements do all of the following:

a. Better understand the public entity's performance
b. Better assess its prospects for future net cash flows
c. Make more informed judgments about the public entity as a whole.

The FASB elected to use the "management approach" by reporting segment information to show how the company is managed "through the eyes of the management." ASC 280-1050-27 states that "[T]he amount of each segment item reported shall be the measure reported to the chief operating decision maker for purposes of making decisions about allocating resources to the segment and assessing its performance." Therefore, the cornerstone of segment disclosure is the identification of the Chief Operating Decision Maker (CODM) and all information to be reported is, theoretically, expected to be what the management actually uses internally for evaluating segment performance and deciding how to allocate resources to operating segments, but there is no such requirement or verification. As a result, segment reports do not conform to GAAP standards used to prepare the income statement and balance sheet and the entity is required to provide reconciliation between segment reports and GAAP financial statements.

### Operating (and Reportable) Segments

An operating segment is a component of a business activities that can be identified based on one of the following criteria:

1. *Functional*: An operating segment is a decision-making unit having three characteristics:

    - The component engages in business activities that earn revenues and incur expenses.
    - The operating results of the component are regularly reviewed by the entity's CODM in assessing performance and making decisions about resource allocation.
    - The component has discrete financial information.

2. *Volumetric*: A segment with material operating characteristics: at least 10% of sales, assets, or profits.

Operating segments (that are not material) may be combined if *all* of them meet *all* of the following requirements: similarity of products or services, closeness of production processes, similar clientele, and similar (presence or absence) regulatory environment. Under all conditions, however, the sum of individually reported segments should not fall below 75 percent of the consolidated revenues.

### The Problem with Segment Reporting

The FASB and IASB have elected to use the "management approach." ASC 280-1050-27 states that "[T]he amount of each segment item reported shall be the measure reported to the chief operating decision maker for purposes of making decisions about allocating resources to the segment and assessing its performance." Although there is no verification of this relationship between what is reported and what the management uses internally, identification of the CODM is critical. The wide ranging latitude given to the CODM leads to several consequences:

- The definition of operating segments may not in practice conform to the above criteria and or be consistent with the way in which CODM manages the enterprise.
- Allocations of assets, of shared costs, and of overheads are to be determined by the CODM as he or she sees to be consistent with the internal management reporting and uses.
- Because of the discretion and allocations allowed, the CODM does not conform to GAAP, and the end result of reported segments would *not* be consistent with consolidated financial statements that are normally prepared under GAAP. Therefore, reconciliation is required.
- While reporting of product market segments does not follow GAAP, geographic reporting does.

In the final analysis, segment reporting is given plenty of chances to be corrupted by arbitrary allocations and reflect management wishes rather than management internal reporting. Under these conditions, there can be no consistency across segments or across companies and the enhancement of comparability attributable to ASC 280 remains an unattained goal. An illustration of this problem is provided in Exhibit 12.11.

### Exhibit 12.11 An Illustration Regarding Allocations Made for Segment Reporting

To ensure the efficient use of the company's space and equipment, several segments may share plant, property and equipment assets. Where assets are shared, landlord ownership of the assets is assigned to one segment and is not allocated to each user segment. This is consistent with the company's management system and is reflected accordingly in the table on page 138. In those cases, there will not be a precise correlation between segment pre-tax income and segment assets. Similarly, the depreciation amounts reported by each segment are based on the assigned landlord ownership and may not be consistent with the amounts that are included in the segments' pre-tax income. The amounts that are included in pre-tax income reflect occupancy charges from the landlord segment and are not specifically identified by the management reporting system. Capital expenditures that are reported by each segment also are consistent with the landlord ownership basis of asset assignment.

(Source: IBM Form 10-K of 2011, p. 137; www.ibm.com/annualreport/2011/bin/assets/2011_ibm_sec10k.pdf)

## 12.9 Summary of Key Points

Over the years, the SEC has championed requiring risk disclosure through the vehicle of Management's Discussion and Analysis.

- The SEC requires disclosure of risk factors facing the enterprise. While the ruling is valuable, the implementation has failed to discriminate between the risks that matter and all other risks. As a result, implementation of this requirement turned out to be uninformative.
- The SEC required disclosure of liquidity risk information as far back as 1987, long before IFRS 7 (2008) and before the outstanding FASB proposed Accounting Standards Update (June 27, 2012).
- Disclosure of concentration risk (diversification) comes in several forms:

    - Diversification of product lines (segment reporting).
    - Disclosure of credit concentration.
    - Disclosure of clientele concentration.
    - Regional and geographic disclosure.

- Publishing the certification of the quality and effectiveness of internal control system by both the management and the auditor is required as part of the annual report and Form 10-K.
- Recent ruling requires disclosure of the extent to which employees' compensation plans expose the enterprise to undue risk.
- Disclosure is required of liquidity and interest rate risks as part of MD&A, which is the foundation for the detailed disclosures of IFRS 7 and the proposed FASB Standards Update of June 27, 2012. These standards require disclosure of (a) detailed breakdown of expected contractual cash inflow and outflow over different time horizons, (b) interest-rate-gap and sensitivity measures, and (3) Macaulay's Duration measure.
- Disclosure of hedging activities: volume of financial instruments, fair values of financial instruments and the extent to which hedging activities are effective.
- Disclosure of hedge contracts by type and size.

## Notes

1 As of the time of writing this manuscript, there is no single law or enforcement agency in the European Union corresponding to the SEC. However, individual Western countries have organizations and structures with similar goals. In the United Kingdom, for example, there is the Companies Law and recently, the Financial Services Administration, and in Canada many of these disclosure requirements reside within the Ontario Stock Exchange.

2 http://www.bis.gov.uk/assets/biscore/business-law/docs/c/12-560-company-law-flexible-framework-discussion-paper.pdf

3 http://files.shareholder.com/downloads/ONE/1968659076x0xS19617-12-163/19617/filing.pdf

4 http://www.sec.gov/Archives/edgar/data/1288776/000119312512025336/d260164d10k.htm

5 Securities and Exchange Commission. Division of Corporation Finance: Financial Reporting Manual, March 2012. Item No. 9110, p. 288; http://www.sec.gov/divisions/corpfin/cffinancialreportingmanual.pdf

6 Safe harbor provisions are intended to protect issuers with respect to required disclosures other than statements of historical facts.

7 There are qualitative differences between "likely," "probable," "more likely than not," and "reasonably possible." The SEC rulings show preference for the expression of "reasonably possible" although none of this expression is well defined in the literature.

8 Typical *VaR* disclosures are based on the assumption of normal distribution, which may provide an approximation of the true distribution. Extreme Value Statistics are not used in making this evaluation.
9 The comprehensive nature of this annual report is the reason I have selected it for analysis in different sections of the book.
10 The 2011 Form 10-K, page 159.
11 2011 Form 10-K at http://files.shareholder.com/downloads/ONE/1968659076x0xS19617-12-163/19617/filing.pdf
12 DVA stands for Debt Valuation Allowance (also called Debit Valuation Adjustment), which is essentially similar to CVA.
13 Wal-Mart Stores, Inc. Form 10-K, 2011, p. 39 (of Annual Report embedded in Form 10-K); http://www.sec.gov/Archives/edgar/data/104169/000119312506066792/d10k.htm
14 Securities Act Release No. 6711 (April 17, 1987), Concept Release on Management's Discussion and Analysis of Financial Condition and Results of Operations, 52 FR 13715.
15 Paragraph (a) of Item 303 of Regulation S-K as amended several times over the past 40 years. See, for example, http://www.sec.gov/rules/other/33-8056.htm
16 *An afterthought*: The current standards (825-10-50-23) state that "[a]n entity is encouraged, but not required to disclose quantitative information about the market risks of financial instruments that is consistent with the way it manages or adjusts those risks. *Gap* analysis of interest rate repricing or maturity dates the duration of the financial instruments among other market risk indicators." In June 2012, the FASB is proposing that financial institutions disclose gap analysis, repricing, and duration of financial institutions only. The incremental approach to standard setting will probably eventually lead to requiring other essential market risk disclosures.
17 This would be revised ASC 825-10-50-23E.
18 Defined in ASU as (a) entities or (b) reportable segments that (i) provide insurance, or (ii) primary source of earnings is the spread between earned interest income and interest paid on borrowed funds. Exempted from the disaggregation are institutions that value assets and liabilities at fair value through earnings (e.g., brokerage houses and hedge funds).
19 FASB, Accounting Standards Update No. 2020-20, "Disclosures about the Credit Quality of Financing Receivables and the Allowance for Credit Losses" July 2010.
20 Form 10-K, 2011, p. A61; http://www.caterpillar.com/cda/files/3342293/7/2011+10K.pdf
21 http://www.bis.org/publ/bcbsca.htm
22 http://www.sec.gov/rules/final/33-8238.htm#ia
23 Securities and Exchange Commission. RELEASE NOS. 33-8238; 34-47986; IC-26068; File Nos. S7-40-02; S7-06-03] at http://www.sec.gov/rules/final/33-8238.htm
24 Securities and Exchange Commission [Release No. 33-9089; 34-61175; IC-29092; File No. S7-13-09] http://www.sec.gov/rules/final/2009/33-9089.pdf
25 http://www.businessdictionary.com/definition/concentration-risk.html#ixzz20WGkevzx
26 http://www.sec.gov/Archives/edgar/data/12927/000119312512048565/d255574d10k.htm
27 IFRS 8 converged more to ASC 280 than did IAS 14.
28 Xerox found that over a period of years, several senior managers in Mexico had collaborated to circumvent certain of Xerox's accounting policies and administrative procedures. The charge-offs related to provisions for uncollectible long-term receivables, the recording of liabilities for amounts due to concessionaires and, to a lesser extent, for contracts that did not fully meet the requirements to be recorded as sales-type leases (p. 225). General Accountability Office (GAO). October 2002. Financial Restatements Trends, Market Impacts, Regulatory Responses, and Remaining Challenges, GAO-03-138; http://www.gao.gov/new.items/d03138.pdf
29 IFRS 8 was issued in 2006 and basically converges to the SFAS 131 (ASC 280), which is a significant departure from IAS 14, which did not take the management approach.
30 It is interesting that the concepts of "risk" and "diversification" remain in the background, although the very fact of requiring segment reporting is an acknowledgment of their relevance.

# APPENDIX TO CHAPTER ONE

## The Gambler Who Does Not Lose

### Information Log

This appendix provides an allegory for some of the transactions in Chapter Seven and Chapter Eight. It is set in an environment to which people could relate. It is recommended that one reads this allegory before reading Chapter Seven.

The University of Illinois is located in central Illinois and straddles the two small towns of Champaign and Urbana that are separated by a yellow traffic line on Wright Street that goes North and South. As close as these two towns are, there are those who claim that the two towns have their distinctive characteristics. It is claimed, although I have no empirical evidence, that more of the Urbana folks are into meditation and freelance artistic activities, while more of the Champaign inhabitants are known to have more interest in traditional commerce. There in Urbana lives the free spirited Franklin Edwards (FE) who steadfastly refuses to take a regular job where he would receive orders from a boss. Instead, he started his own business to provide farmers in the area with what he calls "crop insurance" against adverse weather and crop failure. Since FE is not a licensed insurer, his service is actually betting against the weather. To the west of FE, there in Champaign is a locally grown transportation company, The Lincoln Coach (TLC) that provides a shuttle service between Champaign-Urbana and O'Hare Airport outside Chicago. Both the owner and the manager (Adam Lincoln) of TLC take pride in offering customers a unique pricing scheme. The scheme consists of several elements:

1. The shuttle ticket price is indexed to the price of gasoline; i.e., it goes up and down with gasoline price movements. The indexing is based on a simple formula that TLC does not mind disclosing.
2. Prices are formulated for immediate travel or for future travel on a specific date.
3. Prices for immediate travel can be purchased on the spot (this is why they are called spot prices), while tickets for future travel can be purchased in advance. With non-cancellable commitment, TLC would guarantee the future travel prices for anyone making an advance reservation irrespective of future changes in gasoline prices. This is why the advance reservation price is called forward's or future's price.

FE in Urbana is aware of the pricing system of TLC. To diversify his activities, he developed an interest in forecasting gasoline price movements and, for years, he has had a modest success in his predictions. Thinking of new business, FE went to Adam Lincoln, the manager of TLC, and negotiated an agreement having the following terms:

1. FE commits to purchasing advance reservation tickets from TLC (but not more than 10 tickets per week).
2. FE has no intention of traveling to O'Hare, but the purpose of this agreement is to assure TLC the sale of some future tickets at a guaranteed price, known in advance. The contract price on which they agree is called $P_{Fd}$ where the subscript "F" is for "future" indicating that it is an advance reservation and the subscript "d" would be the first letter of the day of the week on which the travel would be made (M for Monday, T for Tuesday and so on).
3. At 5:00 p.m. every day, FE and Adam Lincoln apply the pricing formula using the price of gasoline as of 5:00 p.m. to see what future travel prices would be for the dates FE has purchased. The new price estimated for the specified travel day is referred to as $RP_{Fd}$ where R stands for revised and other symbols are as before.
4. On any given day, d,

   a. If $RP_{Fd} > P_{Fd}$ → TLC pays FE the difference.
   b. If $RP_{Fd} = P_{Fd}$ → no payments exchange hands.
   c. If $RP_{Fd} < P_{Fd}$ → FE pays TLC the difference.

5. Price differences would be settled every day after the above comparison is made.
6. Settlement of price differences is done by electronic transfer to the account of the party who has the claim on price difference.

On Wednesday April 4, gasoline prices were such that the prices of taking the shuttle to Chicago are $25.71 for spot price (same day travel) and $27.00 for tickets reserved for travel on Tuesday April 10. The energetic FE knows that his predictions of gasoline price movements are often more correct than wrong and using this information will, on average, make him some small profits, although he is not so much concerned about the size of profits since he also has the other business dealings with farmers.

In the following few days, the price of gasoline changed and the prices of the tickets (both for same day travel and for future travel reservation) for the shuttle to Chicago also changed in response. The movement of ticket prices is shown in Exhibit A1.1.

## Exhibit A1.1 Reservation Price for Travel on Tuesday April 10

| | *Tickets for immediate travel* | *Reservation of tickets for travel on Tuesday April 10* |
|---|---|---|
| Wednesday, April 4 | $25.71 | $27.00 |
| Thursday, April 5 | $25.71 | $27.00 |
| Friday, April 6 | $25.71 | $27.00 |
| Saturday April 7 | $26.77 | $27.85 |
| Sunday April 8 | $26.77 | $27.85 |
| Monday April 9 | $28.08 | $28.90 |
| Tuesday April 10 | $32.20 | $32.20 |

Notice that the cost of travel on Tuesday April 10, the terminal day of the agreement, is *the same* whether the passenger purchases the ticket on the spot or makes a reservation.

FE and TLC execute the contract as agreed upon, but Adam Lincoln still has to include these settlements in a daily report to the owner. The accountant at TLC advises him to choose one of two methods, which he calls reporting strategies.

*Reporting Strategy 1*: Adam Lincoln could report what TLC paid FE, which is the loss on betting on the price of the shuttle ticket, or what TLC collected from FE. Adam Lincoln understood the accountant to say that this reporting strategy does not link the collection or payment to spot prices and the actual shuttle service itself. In the last day, April 10, TLC will, in principle, collect $32.20 from other travelers and pay FE $5.20 for each advance ticket he reserved. The net profit of ST is equal to $1.29, which is calculated as $32.20 (spot and forward price for this day) less $25.71 (the cost to TLC which is the opportunity cost indicating as if TLC purchased the ticket from someone else on April 4 to make it available to FE for travel on April 10) less $5.20 (the excess of terminal day spot price over the agreement future's price guaranteed by FE). This $1.29 is exactly equal to $27.00, future's price on April 4, less the opportunity cost of $25.71. The result of using this Reporting Strategy will be as follows:

## Exhibit A1.2 Reporting Strategy 1 (Adam Lincoln reports only the numbers in italics)

| | *Tickets for cost of same day travel* | *Reservation of tickets for travel on Tuesday April 10* | *(TLC Paying FE) or receiving from FE* |
|---|---|---|---|
| Wednesday, April 4 | $25.71 | $27.00 | 0 |
| Thursday, April 5 | $25.71 | $27.00 | 0 |
| Friday, April 6 | $25.71 | $27.00 | 0 |
| Saturday April 7 | $26.77 | $27.85 | (***0.85***) |
| Sunday April 8 | $26.77 | $27.85 | 0 |
| Monday April 9 | $28.08 | $28.90 | (***1.05***) |
| Tuesday April 10 | $32.20 | $32.20 | (***3.30***) |
| Net changes as of Tuesday April 10 | **$ 6.49** | $ 5.20 | (***$5.20***) |
| | (32.20 –25.71 = $6.49) | | (=0.85 + 1.05 + 3.30 = $5.20) |

*Reporting Strategy 2*: Alternatively, Adam Lincoln could link the results of the agreement with FE to the travel activity and prices. For example, on April 7, the spot price of the ticket for same day travel increased by $1.06 from $25.71 to $26.77 ST. Therefore, in the "spot" market, TLC makes an additional $1.06 profit. In the meantime, TLC could have sold on April 7 an advance reservation for travel on April 10 for the price of $27.85. But by agreeing with FE to settle for $27.00 only, TLC is sacrificing) $0.85 (for the purpose of this illustration, I am ignoring the time value of money).

However, the net position of TLC is an opportunity gain of $0.21 which is $1.06 – 0.85. Adam Lincoln could then report to the owner only the net of what TLC has gained (or lost) on the agreement made with FE if the entire travel picture is considered.

Other periods could be accounted for in the same way. A summary of Reporting Strategy 2 is in Exhibit A1.3.

## Exhibit A1.3 TLC Reporting Strategy 2

| | *Price of tickets for same day travel* | *Increases (decreases) in shuttle prices* | *Reservation price of tickets for travel on Tuesday April 10* | *Funds (*Paid to FE*) of funds collected from FE* | *Net gain (*loss*) to be reported to Owner* |
|---|---|---|---|---|---|
| Wednesday, 4/4 | $25.71 | 0 | $27.00 | 0 | 0 |
| Thursday, 4/5 | $25.71 | 0 | $27.00 | 0 | 0 |
| Friday, 4/6 | $25.71 | 0 | $27.00 | 0 | 0 |
| Saturday 4/7 | $26.77 | $1.06 | $27.85 | (*0.85*) | **0.21** |
| Sunday 4/8 | $26.77 | 0 | $27.85 | 0 | 0 |
| Monday 4/9 | $28.08 | $1.31 | $28.90 | (*1.05*) | **0.26** |
| Tuesday 4/10 | $32.20 | $4.12 | $32.20 | (*3.30*) | **0.92** |
| Net | | | | | **$1.29** |

Comparing the two reporting strategies, the accountant pointed out the following to Adam Lincoln:

- In Reporting Strategy 1, the owner of TLC will only see losses day after day until the end when the net effect is known and the owner knows that the agreement with FE netted TLC what the company wanted; $27.00 – $25.71 = $1.29.
- In Reporting Strategy 2, the owner only sees a gain or no loss situation. This strategy, the accountant points out, reflects well on Adam Lincoln, although in the end, the net profit is still $1.29 as the case is with Strategy 1.

*The Lesson:* Understanding the basic role of Futures Exchange (FE). Please return to this illustration as you begin studying Chapter Seven.

# APPENDIX TO CHAPTER SEVEN

Proposed Changes in the Classification of Financial Instruments*

## Introduction

Today the FASB released for public comment a proposed ASU[1] on the recognition, classification, measurement, and presentation of financial instruments.[2] Comments are due by May 15, 2013. Under the proposal, which affects all entities that hold financial assets or owe financial liabilities, a mixed measurement attribute approach would be applied to classification and measurement. This Heads Up provides an overview of the proposed ASU, and the appendix discusses key issues in a question-and-answer format.

Editor's Note: In light of the global financial crisis and a desire to improve and converge financial reporting standards, the FASB added a project on the accounting for financial instruments to its agenda in December 2008. In May 2010, the FASB issued a proposed ASU that would have expanded the scope of fair value accounting to encompass most financial assets and financial liabilities (see Deloitte's May 28,2010, Heads Up). However, most respondents favored a mixed measurement attribute model (see Deloitte's November 5, 2010, Heads Up). In response, the FASB substantially revised its original proposal to incorporate greater use of amortized cost measurement and, in January 2012, began joint deliberations with the IASB to converge key aspects of their respective approaches to classifying and measuring financial instruments (see Deloitte's September 24, 2012, Heads Up). Although important differences between U.S. GAAP and IFRSs remain, today's proposed ASU would result in greater convergence between the two models for classifying and measuring financial instruments.[3] See Q&A 7 in the appendix of this Heads Up for a comparison of key aspects of the two models.

## Proposed Classification and Measurement Approach

### Scope

The proposal applies to all entities and to most financial instruments (e.g., receivables, payables, loans, debt securities, and equity investments). Financial instruments that are exempted from the scope of the proposed ASU include instruments classified in stockholders' equity, stock compensation arrangements, pension plan assets and obligations, lease receivables and payables, financial guarantee contracts, and derivative instruments under ASC 815.[4]

* This appendix is authored by Magnus Orrell and Jason Nye, February 14, 2013 and is reproduced with permission from Deloitte & Touche, LLP.

## Classification of Financial Assets

The classification and measurement of financial assets depends on their contractual cash flow characteristics and the business model in which they are managed. Under the proposal, there are three principal classification and measurement categories:

- Fair value for which all changes in fair value are recognized in net income (FV-NI).
- Fair value with qualifying changes in fair value recognized in other comprehensive income (FV-OCI).[5]
- Amortized cost.

The proposed ASU eliminates the guidance on embedded derivatives in hybrid financial assets and instead requires the entire instrument to be classified on the basis of the contractual cash flow characteristics criterion and the entity's business model for managing the asset. The existence of an embedded feature in a financial asset may affect the outcome of the cash flow characteristics assessment.

## Contractual Cash Flow Characteristics Assessment

Under the contractual cash flow characteristics criterion, an entity assesses whether the contractual terms of a financial asset "give rise on specified dates to cash flows that are solely payments of principal and interest on the principal amount outstanding [('SPPI')]."[6] In the proposed ASU, principal is defined as "the amount transferred by the holder at initial recognition," while interest is defined as "consideration for the time value of money and for the credit risk associated with the principal amount outstanding during a particular period of time, which may include a premium for liquidity risk."

| *Examples of Assets That Fail to Meet the SPPI Criterion* | *Examples of Assets That Generally Meet the SPPI Criterion* |
|---|---|
| • Investments in convertible bonds.<br>• Investments in bonds indexed to the debtor's net income or an equity index.<br>• Investments in inverse floaters.<br>• Investments in equity securities or other ownership interests. | • Investments in unleveraged inflation-linked bonds indexed to inflation of the currency in which the bond is denominated.<br>• Investments in variable-rate debt instruments with a choose-your-rate option where the reset period always matches the period covered by the interest rate.<br>• Investments in variable-rate bonds with a cap on the interest rate.<br>• Collateralized full recourse loan receivables. |

## Financial Assets That Fail to Meet the SPPI Criterion

Generally, financial assets that fail to meet the SPPI criterion are classified and measured at FV-NI. Examples include investments in equity securities and debt instruments with commodity-indexed payments. There is a practicability exception for equity investments that do not have a readily determinable fair value.[7] An entity is permitted to measure an equity investment without a readily determinable fair value at its cost minus impairment, if any, plus or minus changes resulting from observable price changes in orderly transactions for identical or similar investments of the same issuer ("adjusted cost"). Such an investment is considered impaired if it is more likely than not that the fair value is less than its carrying amount. If an impairment exists, the investment is written down to its fair value.

The proposed ASU retains the equity method of accounting for equity investees over which the entity has significant influence but limits its scope. If an investor holds an equity investment that otherwise would have qualified for the equity method for sale when it first qualified for the equity method, that investment must be accounted for at FV-NI or, if the practicability exception is available and applied, at adjusted cost rather than using the equity method. An equity method investment is considered to be held for sale if the investor has identified potential exit strategies and defined the time at which it expects to exit the investment when it first recognized the investment. An entity is not permitted to account for an equity method investment that is not held for sale at FV-NI. The impairment requirements for equity method investments are similar to those applicable to equity investments for which the entity has applied the practicability exception to account for the investment at adjusted cost.

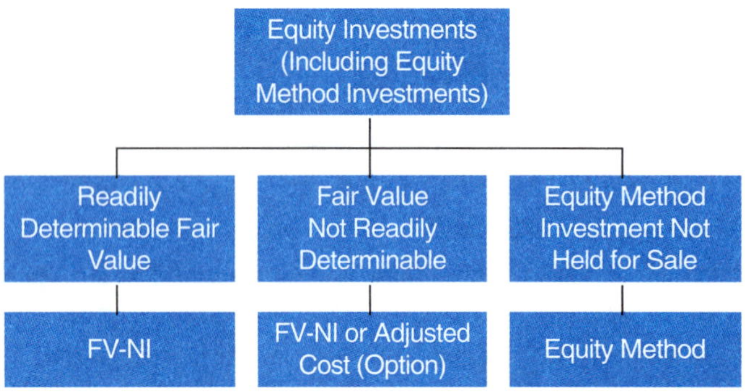


## Financial Assets That Meet the SPPI Criterion

### *Business Model Assessment*

To determine the appropriate accounting for financial assets that meet the SPPI criterion (many loans, receivables, and debt securities), an entity assesses the business model in which they are managed. The entity considers factors such as how performance is evaluated by key management personnel and the frequency and volume of sales and the reason for those sales. The proposed ASU identifies three distinct business models in which an asset may be held and managed:

1. A business model that has the objective of holding the assets to collect contractual cash flows ("hold to collect").

2. A business model that has the objective of both holding financial assets to collect contractual cash flows and selling financial assets ("hold and sell"). In other words, the entity has not determined whether it expects to hold or sell the assets.
3. A business model with an objective that is not consistent with (1) or (2) above.

Financial assets that meet the SPPI criterion and are held in a hold-to-collect business model are accounted for at amortized cost. Managing assets to generate interest income is an example of a business activity that is consistent with the hold-to-collect businessmodel.[8] Other than to manage credit risk, sales under such a business model should be very infrequent.

Financial assets that meet the SPPI criterion and are held in a hold-and-sell business model are accounted for at FV-OCI or, optionally, at FV-NI. An example is an entity's portfolio of financial assets that is rebalanced frequently to match the duration of its liabilities.[9]

Financial assets that are held in a business model that is neither hold to collect nor hold and sell are accounted for at FV-NI. Thus, a portfolio of financial assets that are held for sale would be classified in this category.

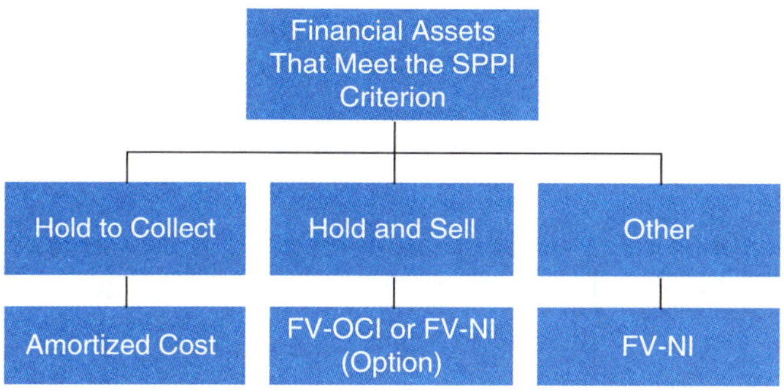


## *Reclassifications*

If an entity changes its business model (e.g., it shuts down a held-to-collect business and actively markets it for sale), the entity is required to prospectively reclassify related financial assets as of the last day of the reporting period during which the change occurs. The proposed ASU does not permit reclassifications for reasons other than a change in business model. Thus, a financial asset that an entity decides to sell would not be reclassified as long as the decision was not accompanied by a change in business-model.[10] The proposed ASU notes that reclassifications are expected to occur very infrequently.

## Financial Liabilities

Financial liabilities are measured at amortized cost, with the following exceptions:

- Short sale obligations are accounted for at FV-NI.
- Financial liabilities for which the entity has a business strategy to subsequently transact at fair value (e.g., transfer the liability to a third party) are accounted for at FV-NI.
- Nonrecourse financial liabilities that are contractually required to be settled with only the cash flows from related financial assets are accounted for on the same basis as the related financial asset (i.e., amortized cost, FV-OCI, or FV-NI).

Unlike financial assets, embedded derivatives in financial liabilities are separately accounted for at FV-NI if they are required to be separated under ASC 815-15 unless an entity elects to account for the hybrid financial liability in its entirety at FV-NI.

The issuer of a loan commitment, revolving line of credit, or commercial letter of credit would account for the commitment in the same manner as the underlying loan to be made under the commitment (i.e., amortized cost, FV-OCI, or FV-NI) provided the probability of exercise is not remote.[11]

## Fair Value Option

On initial recognition of a financial asset or financial liability, an entity may elect to account for certain financial assets and financial liabilities at FV-NI even if they would otherwise have been accounted for at amortized cost or FV-OCI. This option is available when:[12]

- Financial assets are held and managed in a hold-and-sell business model.
- An entity manages the net exposure for a group of financial assets and financial liabilities on a fair value basis and provides net exposure information to its management.
- A hybrid financial liability contains an embedded derivative that significantly modifies its cash flows provided it is clear with little or no analysis that separation of the embedded derivative is not precluded.

If an entity has elected the fair value option for a financial liability, any changes in fair value attributable to instrument-specific credit risk are recognized in OCI rather than in net income.

## Presentation

On the face of the statement of financial position, an entity is required to present the following:

- Financial assets and financial liabilities separately, grouped by measurement category.
- A separate line item for hold-to-collect financial assets that have been identified for sale.
- Parenthetical fair value information for all financial assets and financial liabilities accounted for at amortized cost except for receivables and payables due in less than a year and demand deposit liabilities. This requirement does not apply to nonpublic entities.
- Parenthetical amortized cost information for its own outstanding debt instruments accounted for at FV-NI.

## Effective Date and Transition

The FASB has not yet determined an effective date for the final guidance. An entity would make a cumulative-effect adjustment to the statement of financial position as of the beginning of the first reporting period for which the guidance is effective. The amendments cannot be early adopted, except for the presentation in OCI of fair value changes attributable to instrument-specific credit risk for hybrid financial liabilities for which the fair value option is available and applied.

**Editor's Note:** Watch for upcoming Deloitte *Heads Up* newsletters with additional analysis and insights related to the proposal. Also, join us on February 20, 2013, for a *Dbriefs* webcast on the status of the financial instruments project.

## Appendix—Q&As

### 1. The FASB's Objectives

#### *Question 1.1*

What are the FASB's objectives in this project?

#### *Answer*

The FASB intends for the proposal to result in "more decision-useful information about an entity's involvement in financial instruments, while reducing the complexity in accounting for those instruments." The guidance is intended to link "the measurement of financial assets to the way in which an entity expects to benefit from the cash flows embedded in those assets." That is, the proposed ASU would link measurement of a financial instrument to both the cash flow characteristics of the instrument and the entity's business model for managing financial instruments. In contrast, current U.S. GAAP emphasizes an instrument's legal form (e.g., whether the instrument is a debt security or a loan receivable) and management's intentions.

The FASB also seeks to improve the clarity and organization of the guidance on classification and *measurement* to make it easier to understand and apply. The proposal reduces complexity by (1) aligning the classification of investments in debt securities and loan receivables, (2) limiting the scope of the fair value option,[13] and (3) eliminating the bifurcation of hybrid financial assets.

In addition, to increase convergence between the FASB's guidance and IFRS 9, the FASB and IASB jointly deliberated key aspects of their respective models.

### 2. Impact of the Proposed ASU

#### *Question 2.1*

What types of entities and industries will be affected by the FASB's proposal?

#### *Answer*

Virtually all entities hold financial assets or owe financial liabilities and, thus, would be affected by the proposal. Entities in the financial services industry, such as banks and insurance companies, are expected to be affected the most, since typically the majority of their assets and liabilities are financial assets and liabilities. Entities in industries for which the FASB is proposing to retain specialized industry guidance will not necessarily have to change all aspects of their accounting for financial instruments (e.g., investment companies will continue to apply the specialized industry guidance in ASC 946).

## Question 2.2

What types of financial instruments will be affected, and in what category would an entity generally classify these instruments under the FASB's proposal?

## Answer

The proposal addresses the accounting for a broad range of financial assets and financial liabilities, including investments in debt and equity securities, loans, trade receivables, trade payables, and issued debt financing.

The table below illustrates likely classifications of common types of financial instruments under current U.S. GAAP and the FASB's proposed guidance. Note that an entity's classifications may differ on the basis of facts and circumstances (such as an entity's business model).

| *Instrument*[14] | *Current U.S. GAAP* | *FASB's Proposed ASU* |
|---|---|---|
| Investments in marketable[15] equity securities that are held for trading and for which the investor does not have significant influence over the investee | FV-NI | FV-NI |
| Investments in marketable equity securities that are not held for trading and for which the investor does not have significant influence over the investee | FV-OCI or, optionally, FV-NI | FV-NI |
| Nonmarketable equity investments for which the investor does not have significant influence over the investee | Cost or, optionally, FV-NI | FV-NI or, optionally, adjusted cost[16] |
| Equity investments that are not held for sale at inception and for which the investor has significant influence over the investee | Equity method (i.e., at cost with adjustments for proportionate earnings or losses) or, optionally, FV-NI | Equity method |
| Equity investments that are held for sale at inception and for which the investor has significant influence over the investee | Equity method or, optionally, FV-NI | FV-NI or, optionally, adjusted cost[16] |
| Investments in debt securities held for trading | FV-NI | FV-NI |
| Investments in debt securities that are neither held for trading nor held to maturity | FV-OCI or, optionally, FV-NI | FV-OCI or, optionally, FV-NI |
| Investments in debt securities for which the investor has the intention and ability to hold to maturity | Amortized cost or, optionally, FV-NI | Amortized cost |
| Loans and receivables held for sale | Lower of cost or fair value or, optionally, FV-NI | FV-NI |

| | | |
|---|---|---|
| Loans and receivables held for investment in a held-to-collect business model | Amortized cost or, optionally, FV-NI | Amortized cost |
| Issued debt securities | Amortized cost or, optionally, FV-NI | Amortized cost |
| Hybrid financial assets | Bifurcate embedded derivative if certain conditions are met or, optionally, FV-NI for the hybrid in its entirety | FV-NI (i.e., without bifurcation), provided that the feature results in cash flows that are not solely principal and interest |
| Hybrid financial liabilities | Bifurcate embedded derivative if certain conditions are met or, optionally, FV-NI for the hybrid in its entirety | Bifurcate embedded derivative if certain conditions are met; FV-NI option generally available for hybrid in its entirety |

## 3. Classification and Measurement of Financial Assets

Under the proposed ASU, an entity classifies a financial asset by assessing the contractual cash flows of the instrument and the business model in which the instrument is managed. Both assessments are performed at initial recognition. Hybrid financial assets would be classified in their entirety and would not be bifurcated.

**Editor's Note:** In its Basis for Conclusions for the proposed ASU, the FASB notes that an entity would first assess the contractual cash flow characteristics of the instrument and then assess the business model in which the asset is managed. Although the sequence of assessing the criteria is not expected to result in different outcomes, assessing the cash flow characteristics criterion before the business model may result in unnecessary work if, for example, an entity knows that the business model in which an asset will be managed would not permit a classification other than FV-NI.

### *Question 3.1*

Does the proposed ASU require entities to account for all financial assets at FV-NI?

### *Answer*

No. The FASB proposes a mixed-attribute model under which financial assets are accounted for at FV-NI, FV-OCI, or amortized cost on the basis of their cash flow characteristics and the business model in which they are managed. Equity investments are accounted for at FV-NI unless (1) they result in consolidation, (2) the equity method of accounting applies, or (3) the investment does not have a readily determinable fair value and the entity has elected to apply a practicability exception.

## Question 3.2

When is a financial asset accounted for at something other than FV-NI?

### Answer

The proposed ASU states that a "financial asset is classified at something other than [FV-NI] if it meets the contractual cash flow characteristics criterion and is managed within a business model" for which related objectives are consistent with subsequent measurement at amortized cost or FV-OCI. See Q&As 4.1, 4.2, and 5.1 through 5.5 for more information.

## Question 3.3

Does the level of market activity for an asset (i.e., the liquidity of the market for the asset and the extent to which market transactions in the asset are occurring) affect its classification?

### Answer

In classifying financial assets other than equity investments, an entity would not necessarily consider the level of market activity. From a practical perspective, however, the level of market activity may influence the frequency and volume of the entity's sales. An entity must consider whether its business activities for managing financial instruments are consistent with the "hold-to-collect" or "hold-and-sell" business model assessments (i.e., amortized cost or FV-OCI classifications, respectively). An entity should consider, among other things, the "frequency and volume of sales in prior periods, why sales have occurred in the past, and expectations about the sales activity in the future."

The proposal contains an elective practicability exception from FV-NI for equity investments that do not have a readily determinable fair value (e.g., because price quotations on a securities exchange are not available).

## Question 3.4

Does the FASB propose any changes to the fair value option for financial instruments that is available under existing U.S. GAAP?

### Answer

Yes. The existing unconditional fair value option for financial instruments within the proposal's scope would be replaced with a conditional option. The proposal states that under this option, an entity may irrevocably elect to account for the following instruments at FV-NI:

- [A]group of financial assets and financial liabilities for which both of the following conditions are met:
    a. The entity manages the net exposure relating to the financial assets and financial liabilities (which may be derivative instruments subject to Topic 815) on a fair value basis.
    b. The entity provides information on a net exposure basis to its management.

- [A] hybrid financial liability provided that neither of the following conditions exists:
    a. The embedded derivative or derivatives do not significantly modify the cash flows that otherwise would be required by the contract
    b. It is clear with little or no analysis when a similar hybrid instrument is first considered that separation of the embedded derivative or derivatives is prohibited.

In addition, an entity may irrevocably elect to account for an instrument that qualifies for the FV-OCI classification at FV-NI.

Changes in the fair value of a financial liability for which the fair value option has been elected are presented separately in OCI rather than in net income to the extent that they result from a change in instrument-specific credit risk. Cumulative gains and losses recognized in OCI that are associated with changes in instrument-specific credit risk are recognized in net income upon the settlement of the liability.

## *Question 3.5*

How would an entity classify and measure investments in equity instruments?

## *Answer*

The proposed ASU notes that an "entity shall subsequently measure an equity investment [(e.g., investments in ownership interests in an entity, including equity securities)] at [FV-NI] unless":

1. The investment must be accounted for under the equity method of accounting.
2. The investment results in consolidation of the investee.
3. The investment does not have a readily determinable fair value and is accounted for under a practicability exception.

### Practicability Exception

The exception noted in (3) above only applies to equity investments without a readily determinable fair value that do not qualify for the practical expedient to estimate fair value by using net asset value per share (or its equivalent) under ASC 820. Under the exception, an entity may measure its equity investment at cost less impairment, plus or minus changes resulting from observable price changes in orderly transactions for the identical investment or a similar investment of the same issuer.

An equity investment that is accounted for under the exception described above "is impaired if it is more likely than not that the fair value of the investment is less than its carrying value." An entity must perform this assessment each reporting period by qualitatively considering certain impairment indicators, including:

a. A significant deterioration in the earnings performance, credit rating, asset quality, or business prospects of the investee
b. A significant adverse change in the regulatory, economic, or technological environment of the investee

c. A significant adverse change in the general market condition of either the geographic area or the industry in which the investee operates
d. A bona fide offer to purchase, an offer by the investee to sell, or a completed auction process for the same or similar investment for an amount less than the cost of that investment
e. Factors that raise significant concerns about the investee's ability to continue as a going concern, such as negative cash flows from operations, working capital deficiencies, or non-compliance with statutory capital requirements or debt covenants.

### *Equity Method of Accounting*

Equity investments that give the investor significant influence over the investee are accounted for under the equity method of accounting unless the investment is held for sale at the moment significant influence is established. The proposed ASU states that an equity investment is held for sale if both of the following indicators are present:

- The investor has identified potential exit strategies even though it may not yet have determined the specific method of exiting the investment.
- The investor has defined the time at which it expects to exit the investment, which may be either an expected date or range of dates or a time defined by specified facts or circumstances, such as achieving specified milestones or the stated investment objectives of the investor.

If an equity investment that otherwise would qualify for the equity method of accounting is held for sale, it is accounted for at FV-NI or by using the practicability exception.

## 4. Assessing the Cash Flow Characteristics of Financial Assets

A financial asset satisfies the contractual cash flow characteristics criterion if the contractual terms "give rise on specified dates to cash flows that are solely payments of principal and interest on the principal amount outstanding [SPPI]." Principal is defined as the "amount transferred by the holder at initial recognition," while interest is defined as "consideration for the time value of money and for the credit risk associated with the principal amount outstanding during a particular period of time, which may include a premium for liquidity risk."

Further, if "the contractual cash flows include payments that are unrelated to principal, the time value of money, and the credit risk, the contractual cash flows do not represent [SPPI]." In such case, the instrument must be accounted for at FV-NI.

**Editor's Note:** The principal amount is defined as the amount transferred at initial recognition rather than the principal amount defined in the contract or the amount originally funded to the debtor. These definitions of principal and interest potentially could disqualify many purchased prepayable debt instruments from meeting the SPPI criterion. For example, if a loan is prepayable at its contractual principal amount by the borrower and is purchased at a significant discount to par (e.g., because it is credit impaired), it may be argued that the lender potentially could realize a return that is significantly higher than the compensation would be for the time value of money and the credit risk on the principal amount outstanding.

## Question 4.1

How does an entity assess contractual terms that change the timing or amount of cash flows, including changes in cash flows contingent upon the occurrence of a particular event or change in circumstances?

## Answer

A contractual term may give rise to contingent cash flows (i.e., changes in the timing or amount of cash flows) that are SPPI. A contingent term that results in cash flows that are not SPPI would cause an asset to fail to meet the SPPI criterion regardless of the probability of the contingent event occurring unless the contingent event is extremely rare, highly abnormal, and very unlikely to occur.

Prepayment and extension options may change the timing or amount of cash flows. The proposed ASU provides implementation guidance on prepayment terms or extension options.

- Prepayment provisions give rise to cash flows that are SPPI if both of the following conditions are met:
  a. The provision is not contingent on future events, other than to protect …
     1. The holder against the credit deterioration of the issuer (for example, defaults, credit downgrades, or loan covenant violations)or a change in control of the issuer [or]
     2. The holder or issuer against changes in relevant taxation or law.
  b. The prepayment amount substantially represents unpaid amounts of principal and interest on the principal amount outstanding, which may include reasonable additional compensation for the early termination of the contract.
- Extension options give rise to cash flows that are SPPI if both of the following conditions are met:
  a. The provision is not contingent on future events, other than to protect …
     1. The holder against the credit deterioration of the issuer (for example, defaults, credit downgrades, or loan covenant violations)or a change in control of the issuer [or]
     2. The holder or issuer against changes in relevant taxation or law.
  b. The terms of the contractual provision result in contractual cash flows during the extension period that are [SPPI].

## Question 4.2

### Background

The proposed ASU states that "[c]ash flows that are interest always have a close relation to the amount advanced to the debtor (that is, the funded amount) because interest is consideration for the time value of money and for the credit risk associated with the issuer of the instrument and with the instrument itself." Contractual terms that create leverage or that require interest rates to reset for a period that does not match the period covered by the interest rate would "modify" the relationship between principal and the time value of money and credit risk associated with the principal amount outstanding.

### *Question*

Under the proposed ASU, how does an entity assess terms that "modify" the relationship between principal and interest (i.e., leveraged interest and interest mismatch features)?

### *Answer*

The general principle is that a contractual term that modifies the economic relationship between principal and interest causes an asset to fail to meet the SPPI criterion if it could result in cash flows that are more than insignificantly different from the cash flows of a comparable financial asset (i.e., a benchmark instrument) that excludes the modifying term.

## Terms That Create Leverage

The proposal notes that "[m]ore than insignificant leverage increases the variability of the contractual cash flows so that they do not have the economic characteristics of interest." An example of a term that creates leverage is an interest rate equal to LIBOR multiplied by two.

## Interest Rate Reset

Some variable-rate debt instruments have an interest rate reset period that is different from the time period covered by the rate (e.g., a constant maturity bond or a loan that pays one-month LIBOR reset only every third month). Because of the mismatch between the tenor of the interest rate and the reset period, such terms are considered to modify the economic relationship between principal and interest.

## Assessing the Modifying Term

An "entity is required to assess the modification to the economic relationship to determine whether the contractual cash flows represent [SPPI]." An entity assesses the modification by comparing the cash flows of the instrument in question to the cash flows of a benchmark instrument. The benchmark instrument is a "contract of the same credit quality and with the same contractual terms, except for the contractual [provision] under evaluation." If the cash flows are more than insignificantly different, the instrument fails to meet the SPPI criterion.

### *Question 4.3*

What conditions must be met for a beneficial interest in a securitized financial asset to meet the contractual cash flows characteristics criterion?

## *Answer*

As stated in the proposed ASU,

> A beneficial interest in a securitized financial asset gives rise to contractual cash flows that are solely payments of principal and interest on the principal amount outstanding if all of the following conditions are met:
>
> a. The contractual terms of the beneficial interest being assessed for classification (without looking through to the underlying pool of financial instruments) give rise to cash flows that are [SPPI] (for example, the interest rate on the beneficial interest is not linked to a commodity index). A tranche is deemed to satisfy this condition if it otherwise would have payments that are solely principal and interest but is prevented from meeting this requirement solely because it is prepayable if a prepayment occurs in the underlying pool.
> b. The underlying pool of financial instruments has the following cash flow characteristics:
>
>    1. The underlying pool is required to contain one or more instruments that have contractual cash flows that are solely payments of principal and interest on the principal amount outstanding.
>    2. The underlying pool also may include instruments that do either of the following:
>
>       i. Reduce the cash flow variability of the instruments in (b)(1) and, when combined with the instruments in (b)(1), result in cash flows that are solely payments of principal and interest on the principal amount outstanding (for example, an interest rate cap or floor or a contract that reduces the credit risk on some or all of the instruments in (b)(1))
>       ii. Align the cash flows of the tranches of beneficial interests with the cash flows of the pool of underlying instruments in (b)(1) to address differences in and only in any of the following:
>
>          01. Whether the interest rate is fixed or floating
>          02. The currency in which the cash flows are denominated including inflation in that currency
>          03. The timing of the cash flows.
>
>       An entity must look through until it can identify the underlying pool of instruments that are creating, rather than passing through, the cash flows. This is the underlying pool of financial instruments that (b) refers to.
>
> c. The exposure to credit risk in the underlying pool of financial instruments that are inherent in the tranche of beneficial interest is equal to or lower than the exposure to credit risk of the underlying pool of financial instruments. For example, this condition would be met if the underlying pool of instruments were to lose 50 percent as a result of credit losses and under all circumstances the tranche would lose 50 percent or less.

## 5. Business Model Assessment

Financial assets that meet the SPPI criterion and that are "managed together with other financial assets within a distinct business model ... that has the objective of holding the assets to collect contractual cash flows" are accounted for at amortized cost. If an "asset is held and managed within a business model that has the ... objective of both holding financial assets to collect contractual cash flows and selling financial assets," it is accounted for at FV-OCI. A financial asset that does meet the SPPI criterion but is not managed in a business model consistent with amortized cost or FV-OCI is accounted for at FV-NI. Further, the proposed ASU states:

> The entity's business model for managing financial assets is evidenced by the way the business is managed, including how its performance is evaluated by the entity's key management personnel. ... The determination of the business model for managing financial assets is not driven by a single factor; rather all objective evidence that is relevant to assessing the entity's business model should be considered, including the following:
>
> a. How the performance of the business is reported to the entity's key management personnel
> b. How management is compensated, for example, whether the compensation is based on fair value of the assets managed
> c. The frequency and volume of sales in prior periods, why sales have occurred in the past, and expectations about the sales activity in the future.

### *Question 5.1*

Does management intent affect the business model assessment?

### *Answer*

No, not in the same way management's intentions drive the classification and measurement of investments in debt and equity securities under current U.S. GAAP. Today, a security is classified as trading, and therefore accounted for at FV-NI, if management acquires it with the **intent** of selling it within hours or days, or longer in certain cases. A security is classified as held to maturity, and therefore accounted for at amortized cost, if management has the positive **intent** and ability to hold the security to maturity.

In contrast, management's intentions do not directly affect classification under the proposed ASU. Instead, an entity classifies and measures a financial instrument by considering the instrument's cash flow characteristics and how that asset is managed along with other financial assets in a distinct business model. However, management's intentions with respect to a particular type of financial asset may be incorporated into its policies and procedures, and therefore inform the business model's performance and activities, including the frequency and volume of sales. That is, management's intentions with respect to a single instrument will not directly affect classification under the proposed ASU. However, management's intentions may influence or be incorporated into the objective evidence relevant to assessing an entity's business model.

## Question 5.2

What are examples of business activities that are consistent with a hold-to-collect business model?

### Answer

Examples of activities that may be consistent with a hold-to-collect business model include:

- "A business activity that entails managing financial assets to generate interest income via collection of interest and principal over the life of the instrument."
- A "focus on managing the credit risk of the assets to maximize the collection of contractual cash flows."

However, sales of financial assets "that result from managing the credit exposure" may not be consistent with the hold-to-collect business model (see Q&A 5.3).

## Question 5.3

What types of sales could be consistent with a hold-to-collect business model?

### Answer

Under the proposed ASU, "[s]ales of financial assets as a result of a significant deterioration in the issuer's creditworthiness" could be consistent with a hold-to-collect business model. In addition, sales that result from the following events or circumstances could be consistent with a hold-to-collect business model:

a. A change in tax law that eliminates or reduces the tax-exempt status of interest on debt instruments
b. A major business combination or major disposition that results in an entity's reassessment of its business model and subsequent realignment of the assets managed within that business model
c. A change in statutory or regulatory requirements that significantly modifies either what constitutes a permissible investment or the maximum level of investments in certain kinds of debt instruments
d. A significant increase by a regulator in the industry's capital requirements that causes the entity to sell financial assets to meet regulatory requirements
e. A significant increase in the risk weights of debt instruments used for regulatory risk-based capital purposes.

Sales that result from events other than a significant deterioration in the issuer's creditworthiness that are isolated, nonrecurring, unusual for the entity, and result from events that could not have been reasonably anticipated would not be inconsistent with the objective of amortized cost classification.

Also, sales that occur close to maturity and for which proceeds approximate the remaining contractual cash flows may be consistent with the hold-to-collect business model.

> **Editor's Note:** A change in statutory or regulatory requirements, an increase in regulated capital requirements, or an increase in risk weights used for regulatory risk-based capital purposes should apply to all entities subject to the regulator in question for the resultant sales to be consistent with the amortized cost business model.

Sales of financial assets "that result from managing the credit exposure because of concentrations of credit risk would not be consistent with the objective of amortized cost classification." In addition, "sales in response to changes in market interest rates, prepayment risk, or foreign exchange risk is inconsistent with the objective of an amortized cost business model."

## *Question 5.4*

What are examples of business activities that are consistent with a hold-and-sell business model?

### *Answer*

Examples of such activities include:

- A "business activity that entails managing exposure to interest rate risk or maintaining a certain yield profile by holding and selling financial assets in accordance with a stated risk management policy. ... [Such] activity may entail less frequent buying and selling or rebalancing activities in stable interest rate, liquidity, and economic environments, whereas rapid or unexpected changes in market conditions may necessitate more frequent buying or selling or more significant rebalancing activities."
- Liquidity management under which an "entity may hold and sell financial assets (or rebalance the asset mix in the portfolio to achieve a better asset-liability profile) to meet an entity's liquidity needs."

## *Question 5.5*

When would a financial asset that meets the SPPI criterion be accounted for at FV-NI?

### *Answer*

The proposed ASU states that "[f]inancial assets [that meet the SPPI criterion but] that do not meet the business model for either amortized cost or [FV-OCI] classification would be [accounted for at FV-NI]. Holding financial assets for sale would not be consistent with the primary objective of amortized cost or [FV-OCI]."

## 6. Subsequent Sales and Reclassifications

An entity should "prospectively reclassify financial assets if, and only if, the business model within which the assets are held and managed changes. A change in the business model that requires reclassification of financial assets must be determined by an entity's senior management as a result of external or internal change, must be significant to the entity's operations, and must be demonstrable to external parties."

An entity should "reclassify the financial assets that are subject to a change in the business model as of the last day of the reporting period in which the change in the business model occurs."

### *Question 6.1*

Should an entity reclassify an instrument accounted for at amortized cost when it decides to sell the instrument?

### *Answer*

Generally, no. When an entity subsequently identifies a financial asset for sale that at recognition was classified in the amortized cost category,

> [T]he entity shall continue to classify and measure the financial asset at amortized cost (less allowance for expected credit losses) and shall recognize a related gain, if any, only when the sale is complete. If the fair value of the financial asset subsequently identified for sale is below the net carrying amount (including allowance for expected credit losses), an entity shall measure impairment ... as the entire amount of the difference between the asset's net carrying amount and its fair value and include that impairment loss in net income.

Further, an entity is required to disclose detailed information about financial assets carried at amortized cost that it subsequently sold.

> **Editor's Note:** If an entity subsequently identifies financial assets for sale that at recognition were classified in the amortized cost category, the entity's business model may have changed. If available evidence indicates that a change in business model has occurred, an entity should reclassify affected financial assets regardless of whether they are identified for sale.

### *Question 6.2*

How should an entity classify and measure a pool of financial assets (e.g., a pool of originated loans) when management has not identified which instruments in the pool will be sold and which will be held for the collection of contractual cash flows?

### *Answer*

As stated in the proposed ASU, the "entity should use its best estimates to determine the appropriate business model for the financial assets by classifying a percentage of the pool into one of the classification categories." An entity may manage "identical or similar financial assets through different business models."

> **Editor's Note:** The proposed ASU notes that if, "at recognition, the entity has not yet determined whether it will hold the individual asset to collect contractual cash flows or sell the asset," the asset's business model is consistent with an FV-OCI classification. It is unclear how this guidance interacts with the guidance that requires an entity to allocate assets between the three classification categories when management has not identified which instruments in a pool will be sold and which will be held.

## 7. Comparison to IFRSs

### *Question 7*

Will this project result in convergence with IFRSs?

### *Answer*

In 2012, the boards deliberated key components of their respective approaches and decided to converge many aspects of their models. Nevertheless, differences between the two models remain. The table below outlines key similarities and differences between the FASB's proposed ASU and IFRS 9 (2010) as it would be amended by the IASB's November 2012 exposure draft (ED).[17]

| *Subject* | *IFRS 9 (2010) as Amended by the ED*[18] | *FASB's Proposed ASU* |
|---|---|---|
| Classification and measurement categories for financial assets other than equity investments | • Amortized cost.<br>• Fair value through other comprehensive income (FVTOCI).<br>• Fair value through profit or loss (FVTPL). | • Amortized cost.<br>• FV-OCI.<br>• FV-NI. |
| Classification and measurement categories for financial liabilities | • Amortized cost.<br>• FVTPL if the liability is a derivative, is acquired or incurred principally for the purpose of repurchasing it in the near term, or is part of a portfolio of financial instruments that are managed together and for which there is evidence of a recent actual pattern of profit taking.<br>• Special guidance applies to a secured borrowing that results from an asset transfer that does not qualify for derecognition, a financial guarantee contract, or a commitment to provide a below market loan. | • Amortized cost.<br>• FV-NI if the liability is a derivative, a short sale, or will be subsequently transacted at fair value.<br>• FV-NI or FV-OCI if the liability represents a nonrecourse liability settled with cash flows only from related financial assets that are accounted for at FV-NI or FV-OCI, respectively. |
| Classification and measurement categories for equity investments | • FVTPL with an option to irrevocably designate equity investments that are not held for trading at FVTOCI at initial recognition.<br>Note that IFRS 9 (2010) indicates that in limited circumstances, "cost may be an appropriate estimate of fair value."<br>• In accordance with IAS 28,[19] the equity method of accounting applies to equity investments that give the investor significant influence over the investee.[20] | • FV-NI.<br>• Cost, adjusted for impairment, plus or minus changes resulting from observable price changes in orderly transactions for an identical or similar investment of the same issuer for equity investments that do not have a readily determinable fair value and do not qualify for the practical expedient in ASC 820 permitting investors to measure certain investments at net asset value per share.<br>• Equity method of accounting applies to equity investments that give the investor significant influence over the investee except that such investments must be accounted for at FV-NI or at adjusted cost under the practicability exception if they are held for sale upon qualification for the equity method of accounting. |

| | | |
|---|---|---|
| Method of classifying financial assets | Based on both the entity's business model for managing the financial assets and the contractual cash flow characteristics of the financial asset. | Based on (1) the contractual cash flow characteristics of the financial asset and (2) the business model in which the financial asset is managed. |
| Contractual cash flow characteristics assessment | A financial asset may be classified at something other than FVTPL if the contractual terms of the financial asset give rise on specified dates to cash flows that are solely payments of principal and interest on the principal amount outstanding. Interest is consideration for the time value of money and for the credit risk associated with the principal amount outstanding during a particular period of time (SPPI criterion).<br><br>Note that principal is not explicitly defined. | A financial asset may be classified at something other than FV-NI if the contractual terms of the financial asset give rise on specified dates to cash flows that are solely payments of principal and interest on the principal amount outstanding. Interest is consideration for the time value of money and for the credit risk associated with the principal amount outstanding during a particular period of time (SPPI criterion).<br><br>Note that principal is defined as the amount transferred by the holder at initial recognition. |
| Amortized cost classification criteria for financial assets | • The asset meets the SPPI criterion.<br>• The asset is held in a business model whose objective is to hold assets for the collection of contractual cash flows. | • The asset meets the SPPI criterion.<br>• The asset is held and managed in a business model whose objective is to hold the assets for the collection of contractual cash flows.<br><br>Note that the implementation guidance on the amortized cost classification in the FASB's proposed ASU differs from the guidance proposed under the amendments to IFRS 9(2010). |
| Classification criteria for financial assets other than equity investments to be accounted for at FV-OCI | • The asset meets the SPPI criterion.<br>• The asset is held in a business model in which assets are managed both in order to collect contractual cash flows and for sale. | • The asset meets the SPPI criterion.<br>• The asset is held and managed in a business model that has the objective of both holding financial assets to collect contractual cash flows and selling financial assets. That is, at recognition, the entity has not yet determined whether it expects to hold the asset to collect contractual cash flows or sell the asset. |

| | | |
|---|---|---|
| | | Note that the implementation guidance on the FV-OCI classification in the FASB's proposed ASU differs from the guidance proposed under the amendments to IFRS 9 (2010). |
| Classification of financial assets other than equity investments at FV-NI (or FVTPL) | Any financial asset that is not measured at amortized cost or at FVTOCI. | A financial asset that fails to qualify for either amortized cost or FV-OCI. |
| Hybrid financial instruments | • An entity measures and classifies a hybrid financial asset in its entirety, taking into consideration the instrument's contractual cash flow characteristics and the business model in which the instrument is managed.<br>• Embedded derivatives in hybrid financial liabilities are bifurcated and accounted for separately at FVTPL when certain conditions are met. | • An entity measures and classifies a hybrid financial asset in its entirety, taking into consideration the instrument's contractual cash flow characteristics and the business model in which the instrument is managed.<br>• Embedded derivatives in hybrid financial liabilities are bifurcated and accounted for separately at FV-NI when certain conditions are met.<br><br>Note that the conditions under which embedded derivatives in hybrid financial liabilities are bifurcated differ from those under IFRSs. |
| Fair value option | • An entity may account for financial assets at FVTPL that would otherwise be required to be accounted for at amortized cost or FVTOCI by using an irrevocable election at initial recognition if exercising such an option eliminates or significantly reduces an accounting mismatch.<br>• An entity may account for financial liabilities at FVTPL that would otherwise be accounted for at amortized cost by using an irrevocable election at initial recognition if (1) exercising such an option eliminates or significantly reduces an accounting | • An entity may account for a group of financial assets and financial liabilities at FV-NI by using an irrevocable fair value option at initial recognition if both (1) the entity manages the net exposure related to the financial assets and financial liabilities (which may be derivative instruments) on a fair value basis, and (2) the entity provides information on a net exposure basis to key management personnel.<br>• An entity may account for hybrid financial liabilities at FV-NI in their entirety by using an |

| | | |
|---|---|---|
| | mismatch or (2) a group of financial liabilities or a group of financial assets and liabilities is managed and its performance is evaluated on a fair value basis in accordance with a documented management or investment strategy and information on that basis is provided to the entity's key management personnel.<br><br>Note that this option is not available for financial assets.<br><br>• An entity may account for hybrid financial liabilities at FVTPL in their entirety by using an irrevocable fair value option at initial recognition unless (1) the embedded derivative or derivatives do not significantly modify the cash flows that otherwise would be required by the contractor (2) it is clear with little or no analysis when a similar hybrid instrument is first considered that separation of the embedded derivative or derivatives is prohibited.<br><br>• An entity may account for an equity investment at FVTOCI that is not held for trading by using an irrevocable election at initial recognition. | irrevocable fair value option at initial recognition unless (1) the embedded derivative or derivatives do not significantly modify the cash flows that otherwise would be required by the contractor (2) it is clear with little or no analysis when a similar hybrid instrument is first considered that separation of the embedded derivative or derivatives is prohibited.<br><br>• An entity may account for a financial asset that meets the contractual cash flow characteristics criterion and is managed in a FV-OCI business model at FV-NI by using an irrevocable fair value option at initial recognition.<br>• An entity may account for a nonfinancial hybrid liability at FV-NI in its entirety by using a fair value option if the entity determines that the hybrid liability contains an embedded derivative subject to bifurcation and separate accounting in accordance with ASC 815-15. |
| Reclassifications of financial assets other than equity investments | • Required if the business model changes.<br>• Recorded as of the first day of the period after the period in which the business model changes. | • Required if the business model changes.<br>• Recorded as of the last day of the period in which the business model changes. |

## Subscriptions

If you wish to receive Heads Up and other accounting publications issued by Deloitte's Accounting Standards and Communications Group, please register at www.deloitte.com/us/subscriptions.

### Dbriefs for Financial Executives

We invite you to participate in Dbriefs, Deloitte's webcast series that delivers practical strategies you need to stay on top of important issues. Gain access to valuable ideas and critical information from webcasts in the "Financial Executives" series on the following topics:

- Business strategy & tax.
- Corporate governance.
- Driving enterprise value.
- Financial reporting.
- Financial reporting for taxes.
- Risk intelligence.
- Sustainability.
- Technology.
- Transactions & business events.

Dbriefs also provides a convenient and flexible way to earn CPE credit—right at your desk. Subscribe to Dbriefs to receive notifications about future webcasts at www.deloitte.com/us/dbriefs.

Registration is available for this upcoming Dbriefs webcast. Use the link below to register:

- Accounting for Financial Instruments: A Comprehensive Update on the Joint Project (February 20, 2 p.m. (EST)).

## Technical Library: The Deloitte Accounting Research Tool

Deloitte makes available, on a subscription basis, access to its online library of accounting and financial disclosure literature. Called Technical Library: The Deloitte Accounting Research Tool, the library includes material from the FASB, the EITF, the AICPA, the PCAOB, the IASB, and the SEC, in addition to Deloitte's own accounting and SEC manuals and other interpretive accounting and SEC guidance.

Updated every business day, Technical Library has an intuitive design and navigation system that, together with its powerful search features, enable users to quickly locate information anytime, from any computer. Technical Library subscribers also receive Technically Speaking, the weekly publication that highlights recent additions to the library.

In addition, Technical Library subscribers have access to Deloitte Accounting Journal entries, which briefly summarize the newest developments in accounting standard setting.

For more information, including subscription details and an online demonstration, visit www.deloitte.com/us/techlibrary.

## Notes

1 FASB Proposed Accounting Standards Update, *Recognition and Measurement of Financial Assets and Financial Liabilities*.

2 Separately, the FASB recently released a proposed ASU on the accounting for credit losses on financial assets (see Deloitte's December 21, 2012, *Heads Up*).

3 In November 2012, the IASB released an exposure draft proposing limited amendments to its requirements for classifying and measuring financial instruments under IFRS 9 (2010), *Financial Instruments*. Comments are due by March 28, 2013.

4 For titles of *FASB Accounting Standards Codification* (ASC) references, see Deloitte's "Titles of Topics and Subtopics in the *FASB Accounting Standards Codification*."

5 For the FV-OCI category, the following are recognized in net income rather than OCI: interest income or expense, credit losses, changes in fair value attributable to foreign currency exchange rates, fair value hedging adjustments, and realized gains or losses from sales or settlements.

6 The proposed ASU contains guidance on how to apply the SPPI test to financial instruments with more complex features, such as contractually linked interests and instruments with contingent cash flows or prepayment, term extension, put, call, leverage, or interest mismatch features. See Q&As 4.1 through 4.3 in the appendix for more information.

7 This practicability exception is not available for equity investments that qualify for the net asset value practical expedient under ASC 820-10-35-59. The exception is also not available to broker-dealers or investment companies.

8 See Q&As 5.2 and 5.3 in the appendix for examples of other activities that are consistent with the hold-to-collect business model.

9 When FV-OCI financial assets have unrealized losses, a valuation allowance on deferred tax assets is evaluated separately from other deferred tax assets (rather than being combined and analyzed together).

10 If an entity identifies an amortized-cost-classified financial asset as held for sale, the asset continues to be accounted for as amortized cost (less an allowance for expected credit losses) but is presented as a separate line item on the statement of financial position. However, if the instrument's fair value is less than its amortized cost (less an allowance for expected credit losses), impairment is measured as the entire difference between the asset's fair value and its net carrying amount.

11 If the probability of exercise is remote, any commitment fee received is recognized over the commitment period under ASC310-20.

12 This option is also available for a nonfinancial hybrid liability that contains an embedded derivative that otherwise would require separate accounting under ASC 815-15.

13 Replacing the unconditional fair value option with one that can be applied only in limited circumstances reduces the number of accounting choices entities can use to account for similar instruments. This is expected to improve comparability.

14 The terminology in this column is based on current U.S. GAAP (e.g., equity securities may be classified as "trading securities" under ASC 320, but the proposed ASU does not contain a similar designation).

15 A marketable security is one that has a readily determinable fair value whereas a nonmarketable security does not have a readily determinable fair value.

16 Entities holding nonmarketable equity interests may measure such investments at cost adjusted for impairment and observable price changes in identical or similar instruments from the same issuer.

17 IASB ED/2012/4, *Classification and Measurement: Limited Amendments to IFRS 9*.

18 Including amendments in ED/2012/4.

19 IAS 28 (Revised 2011), *Investments in Associates and Joint Ventures*.

20 Venture capital organizations, or mutual funds, unit trusts and similar entities including investment-linked insurance funds may apply a fair value option when accounting for equity investments that are otherwise required to be accounted for under the equity method of accounting.

# APPENDIX TO CHAPTER NINE

## The Significance of Embedded Derivatives (The Case of Landsvirkjun, Iceland)

Landsvirkjun is a state-owned Icelandic electric power producer and distributor producing about 74% of the electricity used in Iceland. As of April 2012, the company was also studying the cost of laying a submarine cable to export electricity to Europe. The company's hallmark is producing electric power from a renewable natural resource by using the island's abundant geothermal steam and hydroelectric generation.

Although the company is state-owned it operates as a publicly held company. Icelandic GAAP was the basis for financial reporting until 2007 when the company switched to IFRS as adopted by the European Union.[1] In the meantime, a decision was made to identify and account for embedded derivatives. The company relies heavily on supplying electric power to aluminum companies and the management entered into long-term take-or-pay contracts with these clients, especially Alcoa and Alcan.

In anticipation of adopting IFRS, the company began in 2006 to prepare for the valuation and recognition of embedded derivatives. The 2006 Annual Report (pp. 19–20) states:[2]

> The company is in the process of valuing the embedded derivatives contained in sales contracts with aluminium smelters. The indications are that they have a significant net positive value for the company, but these derivatives will be recorded in the Financial Statements for 2007 as the company adopts IFRS as of January 1, 2007.

In 2007, Landsvirkjun began the recognition and reporting of the fair value of the embedded features and recognized them as assets (gain) or liabilities (losses). The management acknowledges that the valuation of these derivatives is based on models the company has adopted—a level three type of fair value estimation.

The management of Landsvirkjun realizes the significance of embedded derivatives on the company's earnings as specifically stated in its annual reports. The quote below from 2009 Annual Report (p. 18) is representative of management disclosure:[3]

> Financial income in excess of financial expenses totalled USD 95.1 million in 2009, while financial expenses in excess of financial income amounted to approximately USD 660.6 million the year before. *The difference* of USD 755.7 million can largely be attributed to fair-value changes in embedded derivatives relating to the company's electric power sales contracts with aluminium smelters, which move in line with world market prices for aluminium. Other derivatives and foreign exchange differences also have an effect. In 2009, the exchange rate difference was negative by USD 48.8 million, while it was negative by USD 128.6 million in 2008.

Fair-value changes in embedded derivatives were positive by USD 253.3 million in 2009, while they were negative by USD 497.2 million in 2008. [Emphasis added]

Two results are gleaned from the annual reports from 2007 through 2010. The first impact is presented in Figure A9.1, which shows the high degree of volatility the estimated fair value of embedded derivative assets have ranged between $195 million (about 4% of total assets) and $686 million (about 14% of total assets). The second impact is the rather significant impact on reported profits as presented in Table A9.1. In 2007, net profit before tax has more than doubled with the recognition of the estimated gain on embedded derivatives, and in 2009 the gain on embedded derivatives resulted in reporting net profit instead of reporting a loss. The reverse effect took place in 2008 where estimated recognized losses on embedded derivatives resulted in reporting net loss instead of profit, and in 2010 the losses on embedded derivatives amounted to 40% of net profit before tax.

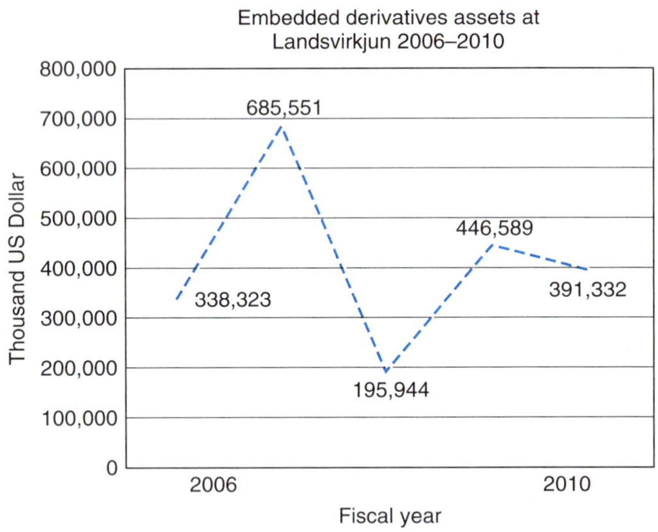


**Figure A9.1** Hedging Fixed-Rate Debt Using Interest Rate Swap

**Table A9.1** Impact of Embedded Derivatives on Reported Profits (The Case of Landsvirkjun)

| | *2007* | *2008* | *2009* | *2010* |
|---|---|---|---|---|
| Reported net profit before tax | 626,702 | (414,580) | 209,940 | 82,569 |
| Gain (Loss) on Embedded Derivatives | 326,835 | (497,167) | 253,304 | (55,583) |
| *As If* net profit before tax and embedded derivatives | 299,867 | 82,587 | (43,364) | 138,152 |

## Notes

1 This means the company follows the EU Directive, which includes any carve outs or delays in implementation of standards by EU.
2 http://www.landsvirkjun.com/media/enska/about-us/AnnualReport_EN_2006.pdf
3 Source: http://www.landsvirkjun.com/media/enska/finances/Annual_report_2009.pdf

# BIBLIOGRAPHY

## Main Sources


Abdel-khalik, A. R. and T. F. Keller. (1979). *Earnings or Cash Flows: An Experiment on Functional Fixation and the Valuation of the Firm*. Accounting Research Studies #16, American Accounting Association, Sarasota, FL.

Acharya, V. V., S. M. Schaefer, and Y. Zhang. (2007). *Liquidity Risk and Correlation Risk: A Clinical Study of the General Motors and Ford Downgrade of May 2005*. Centre for Economic and Policy Research, Washington, DC.

Allais, M. (1953). Le comportement de l'homme rationnel devant le xioms: Critique des postulats et xioms de l'école américaine. *Econometrica*, 21: 503–546.

Altman, E. I. (1968). Financial Ratios, Discriminant Analysis and the Prediction of Corporate Bankruptcy, *Journal of Finance*, Vol. 23, No. 4: 589–609.

American Institute of Certified Public Accountants (1973). *Objectives of Financial Statements: Report of the Group on the Objectives of Financial Statements*. New York.

Ammann, Manuel and Ralf Seiz. (2006). Pricing and Hedging Mandatory Convertible Bonds. *Journal of Derivatives*, Vol. 13: 30–46.

Apte, P. G. (2009). *International Finance*, Second Edition. McGraw-Hill, New York.

Arrow, K. J. (1951). Alternative approaches to the theory of choice in risk-taking situations, *Econometrica*, 19: 404–437.

Arzac, E. R. (1997). PERCS, DECS, and Other Mandatory Convertibles. *Journal of Applied Corporate Finance*, Vol. 10, No. 1. Spring: 54–63.

Balassa, B. (1964). "The Purchasing Power Parity Doctrine: A Reappraisal", *Journal of Political* Economy, Vol. 72, No. 6: 584–596.

Bank of England. (2005). *Report of the Board of Banking Supervision Inquiry into the Collapse of Barings*. Her Majesty's Stationary Office, The House of Commons. http://www.numa.com/ref/barings/bar00.htm

Bank for International Settlements. (2003). Sound Practices for the Management and Supervision of Operational Risk. February. Basel, Switzerland.

Bank for International Settlements. (2008). Principles for Sound Liquidity Risk Management and Supervision. June. Basel, Switzerland.

Bank for International Settlements. (2009). Proposed Enhancements to Basel II Framework. January. Basel, Switzerland.

Barsky, R. B., F. Thomas Juster, M. S. Kimball, and M. D. Shapiro. (1997). Preference Parameters and Behavioral Heterogeneity: An Experimental Approach in the Health and Retirement Study, *The Quarterly Journal of Economics*, 112: 537–579.

Basel Committee on Banking Supervision. (1998). *Framework for Internal Control Systems in Banking Organizations*. Bank for International Settlements, Basel, Switzerland.

Basel Committee on Banking Supervision. (December 2010). *International Framework for Liquidity Risk Measurement, Standards and Monitoring. Consultative Document*. Bank for International Settlements, Basel, Switzerland.www.bis.org/publ/bcbs165.pdf

Basel Committee on Banking Supervision. (2011). *Operational Risk—Supervisory Guidelines for the Advanced Measurement Approaches*. Bank for International Settlements, Basel, Switzerland.

Basel Committee on Banking Supervision. (June 2011). *Principles for the Sound Management of Operational Risk*. Bank for International Settlements. Basel, Switzerland. http://www.bis.org/publ/bcbs195.pdf

Basu, A. (April 29, 2010) "Eicher Motors leans on vendors to ease supply" *Live Mint & The Wall Street Journal* http://www.livemint.com/Companies/NhuMfM7HAspl1Pc3HGjgtL/Eicher-Motors-leans-on-vendors-to-ease-supply.html

Beaver, W. H. (1966). Financial Ratios as Predictors of Failure, *Journal of Accounting Research: Empirical Research Studies*, Vol. 4: 71–111.

Bemmann, M. (2005). Improving the Comparability of Insolvency Predictions, (*Verbesserung der Vergleichbarkeit von Schaetzgueteergebnissen von Insolvenzprognosestudien*) German version, Dresden Economics Discussion Paper Series No. 08/05. SSRN: http://ssrn.com/abstract=738648

Bergman, J. (April 7, 2011). "Airline CFO: Hedging Saved Us $400 Million." http://www.cnbc.com/id/42463121/Airline_CFO_Hedging_Saved_Us_400_Million

Berinato, S. (August 1, 2001). "What Went Wrong at Cisco in 2001." CIO: http://www.cio.com/article/30413/What_Went_Wrong_at_Cisco_in_2001

Bernstein, P. L. (1966). *Against the Gods: The Remarkable Story of Risk*, Wiley, New York.

Black, F. and M. Scholes. (1973). The Pricing of Options and Corporate Liabilities, *Journal of Political Economy*, Vol. 81, No. 3: 637–654.

Booth, R. A. (1999). The Suitability Rule, Investor Diversification, and Using Spread to Measure Risk, *Business Lawyer*, Vol. 54: 1599–1627.http://papers.ssrn.com/sol3/papers.cfm?abstract_id=200388

Bowman, E. H. (1982). Risk Seeking by Troubled Firms, *Sloan Management Review*, Vol. 23, No. 4: 33–42.

Braddock, John. (2010). "A Very Brief History of Financial Risk Management: Marco Polo to the New Millennium." http://www.jcbraddock.com/other/CMCAS_Speech_June04.pdf

Brighton Webs Ltd: Statistics for Energy and the Environment, "Beta Distribution." http://www.brighton-webs.co.uk/distributions/beta.htm

*Business Times* (October 2, 2012). "Fuel hedges prove costly gamble for Asian airlines." http://www.btimes.com.my/Current_News/BTIMES/articles/20080807175702/Article/#ixzz286DIt3wJ

California Debt and Investment Commission. (2007). *Duration Basics*. CDIC #6–10. Sacramento, CA. http://www.treasurer.ca.gov/cdiac/publications/duration.pdf

Cohn, R. A., W. G. Lewellen, R. C. Lease and G. G. Schlarbaum. (1975). Individual Investor Risk Aversion and Investment Portfolio Composition. *The Journal of Finance*, No. 30: 605–620.

Committee on Risk Assessment of Hazardous Air Pollutants. (1994). *Science and Judgment in Risk Assessment*. National Academy Press, Washington, DC.

Committee of Sponsoring Organizations of the Treadway Commission (COSO). (2004). *Enterprise Risk Management—Integrated Framework*. http://www.coso.org/documents/COSO_ERM_ExecutiveSummary.pdf

Cox, J. C., S. A. Ross, and M. Rubinstein. (September 1979). Option Pricing: A Simplified Approach, *Journal of Financial Economics*, Vol. 7: 229–263.

Cox, S. and Y. Lin. (2007). "Natural Hedging of Life Annuity and Mortality Risk", *North American Actuarial Journal*, Vol. 11, No. 3: 1–15.

Criteria of Control Committee (COCO). (1995). *Guidance on Internal Control*. Canadian Institute of Chartered Accountants, Toronto, Ontario, Canada.

Deloitte Development, LLC. (2005). Disarming the Value Killers: A Risk Management Study.http://www.corpgov.deloitte.com/binary/com.epicentric.contentmanagement.servlet.ContentDeliveryServlet/CanEng/Documents/Risk%20Oversight/DisarmingTheValueKillers.pdf

Dohmen, T., A. Falk, D. Huffman, and U. Sunde. (2007). "Are risk aversion and impatience related to cognitive ability?" Discussion Paper No. 2735. The Institute for the Study of Labor, IZA, University of Bonn and CEPR, Bonn, Germany. http://ftp.iza.org/dp2735.pdf

Donkers, B. and A. Van Söest. (1999). Subjective Measures of Household Preferences and Financial Decisions, *Journal of Economic Psychology*, Vol. 20: 613–642.

Donkers, B., B. Melenberg, and A. Van Söest. (2001). Estimating Risk Attitudes Using Lotteries: A Large Sample Approach, *The Journal of Risk and Uncertainty*, Vol. 22: 165–195.

Dwyer, D. W. and J. Zhao. (15 April, 2009). MOODY'S KMV RISKCALC™ V3.1: North America Large Firm Model Modeling Methodology. http://www.moodysqra.com/us/research/docs/Americas/RiskCalc_v3_1_LargeFirm.pdf

Ernst & Young (2011). *Derivative Instruments and Hedging Activities*. Financial Reporting Development.

Fama, E. F. and K. R. French. (1993). Common Risk Factors in the Returns on Stocks and Bonds, *Journal of Financial Economics*, Vol. 33, No. 1: 3–56. (The Three Factors are updated at http://mba.tuck.dartmouth.edu/pages/faculty/ken.french/data_library.html)

FASB. (July 17, 2013). Inclusion of the Fed Funds Effective Swap Rate (or Overnight Index Swap Rate) as a Benchmark Interest Rate for Hedge Accounting Purposes a Consensus of the FASB Emerging Issues Task Force *Accounting Standards Update No. 2013-10*, Derivatives and Hedging (Topic 815). Norwalk, CT.

FDIC. (2009). "2009 Annual Report, IV Financial Statements and Notes." http://www.fdic.gov/about/strategic/report/2009annualreport/statements_dif_2.html

Federal Bureau of Investigation. (2012). "Facts and Figures, 2010–2011, Investigative Programs." Available at http://www.fbi.gov/stats-services/publications/facts-and-figures-2010–2011/investigative-programs

Financial Accounting Standards Board (August 9, 2012). "Accounting for Financial Instruments Summary of Decisions Reached to Date During Redeliberations as of August 9, 2012." http://www.fasb.org/cs/ContentServer?site=FASB&c=Document_C&pagename=FASB%2FDocument_C%2FDocumentPage&cid=1176156422130

Fitch Ratings. (August, 2011). "Fitch Revises Rating Outlook on Colonial Properties Trust to Positive; Affirms IDR at 'BB+'." http://muslimdiscount.com/fitch-revises-rating-outlook-on-colonial-properties-trust-to-positive-affirms-idr-at-bb/

Florida Department of Agriculture and Consumer Services. (March 2011). "Florida Citrus Statistics 2009–2010." http://www.nass.usda.gov/Statistics_by_State/orang rus/fcs/2009–10/fcs0910.pdf

Friend, I. and M. E. Blume. (1975). The Demand for Risky Assets. *The American Economic Review*, No. 65: 900–922.

Fuerbringer, J. with P. T. Kilborn. (February 7, 2002). "Bank Trader Losses Total $750 Million." *The New York Times*. Available at: http://www.nytimes.com/2002/02/07/business/bank-trader-s-losses-total-750-million.html?pagewanted=all&src=pm

Graham, B. (1973). *The Intelligent Investor*, Harper & Row, New York.

Graham, B. (1986). *The Intelligent Investor* (with a Foreword by Warren Buffett). Fourth Edition. Harper & Row, New York.

Graham, B. and D. Dodd. (2008). *Security Analysis* (with a Foreword by Warren Buffett). Sixth Edition. Foreword by Warren Buffett, McGraw-Hill, New York.

Gregory, J. (2012). *Counterparty Credit Risk and Credit Value Adjustment: A Continuing Challenge for Global Financial Markets*. Wiley, New York.

Guiso, L. and M. Paiella. (2005). "The role of risk aversion in predicting individual behavior," University of Sassari and Banca Italia, Discussion Paper, No. 546.

Hayes, J. L. (July 2011). Mind-Boggling Numbers. Jack Hayes International, Inc. http://hayesinternational.com/2012/07/mind-boggling-numbers/

Henry, D. (August 4, 2009). "SEC fines GE $50 million for accounting misdeeds." *Bloomberg Business Week*. http://www.businessweek.com/bwdaily/dnflash/content/aug2009/db2009084_567813.htm

Hinton, C. (October 16, 2008)."Southwest swings to quarterly loss on hedging: Continental swings to quarterly loss on fuel costs, Hurricane Ike". *MarketWatch*: *The Wall Street* Journal. http://articles.marketwatch.com/2008-10-16/news/30770099_1_quarterly-loss-southwest-airlines-fuel

Holton, G. A. (2002). "History of Value-at-Risk: 1922–1998." Working Paper, Contingency Analysis, Boston. http://www-stat.wharton.upenn.edu/~steele/Courses/434/434Context/RiskManagement/VaRHistlory.pdf

Holton, G. A. (2004). Defining Risk, *Financial Analysts Journal*, Vol. 60, No. 6: 19–25.

Hull, J. C. (2011). *Options, Futures and Other Derivatives*. Eighth Edition. Pearson Education, Boston, MA.

Jaynes, E. T. (2003). *Probability Theory: The Logic of Science*. Cambridge University Press, Cambridge, United Kingdom.

Jensen, R. E. (2012). "History of Fraud in America," http://www.trinity.edu/rjensen/FraudAmericanHistory.htm

Kahneman, D. and A. Tversky. (1979). Prospect Theory: An Analysis of Decision under Risk, *Econometrica*, Vol. 47, No. 2: 263–291.

Kahneman, D. and A. Tversky, Editors. (2000). *Choices, Values and Frames*. Russell Sage Foundation, Cambridge University Press, Cambridge, United Kingdom.

Katona, G. (1951). *Psychological Analysis of Economic Behavior*. McGraw Hill, New York.

Katz, D. and R. L. Kahn. (1966). *The Social Psychology of Organizations*. Wiley, New York.

Kealhofer, S. (2003a). Quantifying Credit Risk I: Debt Prediction. *Financial Analysts Journal* (May/Jun), Vol. 59, No. 1: 30–44.

Kealhofer, S. (2003b). Quantifying Credit Risk II: Debt Valuation. *Financial Analysts Journal* (May/Jun), Vol. 59, No. 3: 77–92.

Kelly, S. (April 1, 2011). "The SEC frowns on Black-Scholes. Risk: Treasury & the Future of Finance Today." http://www.treasuryandrisk.com/2011/04/01/sec-frowns-on-blackscholes

Klett, T. R., R. R. Charpentier, and J. W. Schmoker. (2000). Assessment of Operations Procedures, Chapter OP, *US Geological Survey World Petroleum Assessment*. U.S. Geological Survey Digital Data Series 60. http://energy.cr.usgs.gov/WEcont/chaps/OP.pdf

Knight, F. (1921). *Risk, Uncertainty and Profit*. Harper & Row, New York. http://www.rmartin.com/risk_defined.html.

Kogan, N. and M. A. Wallach. (1967). Risk taking as a function of the situation, the person, and the group, in G. Mandler, *New Directions in Psychology III*. Holt, Rinehart and Winston, New York.

Lopez, J. A. (2002). What is Operational Risk? *Western Banking Quarterly*. Federal Reserve Bank of San Francisco, 2002–02. http://www.frbsf.org/publications/economics/letter/2002/el2002–02.html

Lopez, J. A. (2008). What Is Liquidity Risk? *Economic Letters*. Federal Reserve Bank of San Francisco, http://www.frbsf.org/publications/economics/letter/2008/el2008–33.html

M24digital.com. (September 1, 2011). "The credit rating agencies will have to report on their methodology." http://m24digital.com/en/2011/09/01/the-credit-rating-agencies-will-have-to-report-on-their-methodology/

Markowitz, H. M. (March 1952). Portfolio Selection, *The Journal of Finance*, Vol. 7, No. 1: 77–91.

McDermott Will & Emery (February 2009). "SEC Focuses its Reforms on Credit Rating Methodologies and Disclosure." http://www.mwe.com/index.cfm/fuseaction/publications.nldetail/object_id/e3261ae1–1b87–4bdd-9d69-d3f1d4355153.cfm

Merton, R. C. (1974). On the Pricing of Corporate Debt: The Risk Structure of Interest Rates. *Journal of Finance*, Vol. 29, No. 2 (May): 449–470.

Miller, W. (July 2009). "Comparing Models of Corporate Bankruptcy Prediction: Distance to Default vs. Z-Scores." *Research Report*. Morningstar®, Inc. Chicago, IL

Montante, D. (2000). Financial Risk Management: An Earnings-at-Risk Approach. E. I. du Pont de Nemours & Company. http://www.slideworld.com/slideshows.aspx/Financial-Risk-Management-An-EarningsatRisk-A-ppt-804160

Morningstar® (2009). "Credit Rating Methodology." http://news.morningstar.com/pdfs/corp_credit_rating.pdf

National Research Council (NRC). (1994). *Science and Judgment in Risk Assessment*. The National Academies Press, Washington, DC.

Nini, G., D. C. Smith, and A. Sufi. (December 2011). Creditor Control Rights, Corporate Governance, and Firm Value. Working Paper.http://ssrn.com/abstract=1428880

Office of Comptroller of the Currency. (2012). OCC's Quarterly Report on Bank Trading and Derivatives Activities First Quarter 2012. Washington, DC, p. 10. http://www.occ.treas.gov/news-issuances/news-releases/2012/2012–96a.pdf

Orrell, M. and Nye, J. (February 14, 2013). "A Proposal on Valentine's Day FASB Issues Proposed ASU on Classifying and Measuring Financial Instruments." *Heads Up*, Vol. 20, No. 7. Deloitte & Touche, LLP, New York.

OFHEO (Office of Federal Housing Enterprise Oversight). *Report of the Special Examination of Freddie Mac* (2003). Office of Federal Housing Enterprise Oversight, Washington, DC, December, pp. 178.

OFHEO (Office of Federal Housing Enterprise Oversight). *Report of the Special Examination of Fannie Mae*, 2006. Washington, DC, May, pp. 338.

Page, M. and L. F. Spira. (2004). *The Turnbull Report, Internal Control and Management: The Developing Role of Internal Control*. The Institute of Chartered Accountants of Scotland. Great Britain. http://www.icas.org.uk/res_page_spira_report.pdf

Partnoy, F. (2003). *Infectious Greed: How Deceit and Risk Corrupted the Financial Markets*. Henry Holt & Company, Inc., New York.

Paton, W. A. and A. C. Littleton (1940). *An Introduction to Corporate Accounting Standards*. American Accounting Association, Sarasota, FL.

Pricewaterhouse Coopers. (2010). *Guide to Accounting for Derivative Instruments and Hedging Activities*. PwC, National Professional Services Group, New York.

Pricewaterhouse Coopers. (2012). *Manual of Accounting: Financial Instruments*. Great Britain.

Punmia, B. C. and K. Khandelwal. (2006). *Project Planning and Control P.E.R.T. and C.P.M.: For Degree Classes*. Laxmi Publications, New Delhi, India.

RiskMetrics Group (1999) CorporateMetrics™ Technical Document. http://www.riskmetrics.com.

Roggi, O., M. Garvey, and A. Damodaran (2012). *Risk Taking: A Corporate Governance Perspective*. International Finance Corporation, World Bank, Washington, DC.

Samuelson, P. A. (1964). "Theoretical Notes on Trade Problems", *Review of Economics and* Statistics, Vol. 46, No. 2: 145–154.

Santomero, A. M. and D. F. Babbel. (2001). *Financial Markets, Instruments, and Institutions*. Second Edition. McGraw-Hill, New York.

Securities and Exchange Commission (January 31, 1997). *Disclosure of Accounting Policies For Derivative Financial Instruments and Derivative Commodity Instruments and Disclosure of Quantitative and Qualitative Information about Market Risk Inherent in Derivative Financial Instruments, Other Financial Instruments, and Derivative Commodity Instruments; final Rule (Amendment to Section 210.4-08(n) of Regulation S-X and to Item 310 of*

*Regulation S-B)*. Release Nos. 33-7386; 34-38223; IC-22487; FR-48; International Series No. 1047; File No. S7-35-95.
Securities and Exchange Commission (December 19, 2003). *Interpretation: Commission Guidance Regarding Management's Discussion and Analysis of Financial Condition and Results of Operations*. 17 CFR Parts 211, 231 and 241 Release Nos. 33-8350; 34-48960; FR-72]. http://www.sec.gov/rules/interp/33-8350.htm
Securities and Exchange Commission (March 2012). *Financial Reporting Manual*. Washington, DC. http://www.sec.gov/divisions/corpfin/cffinancialreportingmanual.pdf
Sharpe, W. F. (1964). Capital Asset Prices: A Theory of Market Equilibrium under Conditions of Risk, *Journal of Finance*, Vol. 19, No. 3: 425–442.
Simon, H. A. (1959). Theories of Decision-Making in Economics and Behavioral Science, *American Economic Review*, Vol. 49: 253–283.
Simon, H. A. (1979). Rational Decision-Making in Business Organizations [The 1978 Nobel Memorial Prize in Economics lecture], *American Economic Review*, Vol. 69: 493–513.
Sitkin, S. B. and L. R. Pablo. (1992). Reconceptualizing the Determinants of Risk Behaviour, *Academy of Management Review*: 9–38.
Smithson, C. W. (1998). *Managing Financial Risk: A Guide to Derivative Products, Financial Engineering and Value Maximization*. McGraw-Hill, New York.
Standard & Poor's "Rating Criteria." (2012). http://www2.standardandpoor.com/spf/pdf/fixedincome/corporateratings_052007.pdf
Stymiest, B. and M. D. Mackinlay (1999) "Five years to the *Dey*." Report on Corporate Governance, Institute of Corporate Directors, Toronto Stock Exchange. Toronto, Canada. http://www.ecgi.org/codes/documents/5years.pdf
Taleb, N. N. (2007). *The Black Swan: The Impact of the Highly Improbable*. Random House, New York.
Terzi, C. and I. Posta (2010). Review of Enterprise Risk Management in the United Nations System Benchmarking Framework. Document No. JIU/REP/2010/4, Geneva, p. 4. http://www.unjiu.org/data/reports/2010/en2010_4.pdf
The US Geological Survey uses Triangular Distribution in the Analysis of Undiscovered Petroleum Resources. Page 12 of the following source: http://energy.cr.usgs.gov/WEcont/chaps/OP.pdf
Tversky, A. and D. Kahneman. (1991). Loss Aversion in Riskless Choice: A Reference-Dependent Model, *The Quarterly Journal of Economics*, MIT Press, Vol. 106, No. 4: 1039–1061.
United States Government Accountability Office. (October 2002). *Financial Statement Restatements: Trends, Market Impacts, Regulatory Responses, and Remaining Challenges*. Report to the Chairman, Committee on Banking, Housing, and Urban Affairs, U.S. Senate, GAO-03-138, p. 125. http://www.gao.gov/new.items/d03138.pdf
United States Government Accountability Office (July 2006) *Financial Statement Restatements: Update of Public Company Trends, Market Impacts, and Regulatory Enforcement Activities*. GAO-06678, Financial Restatements, p. 5. http://www.gao.gov/new.items/d06678.pdf
van Drop, J. Ren's, and S. Kotz. (2002). A Novel Extension of the Triangular Distribution and its Parameter Estimation. *The Statistician* 51, Part 1, pp. 63–79.
von Bertalanffy, K. L. (1950a). An Outline of General System Theory, *The British Journal for the Philosophy of Science*, Vol. 1: 134–165.
von Bertalanffy, K. L. (1950b). The Theory of Open Systems in Physics and Biology, *Science*, 111: 23–29.
Whaley, R. E. (2006). *Derivatives: Markets, Valuation, and Risk Management*. Wiley, New Jersey.
Zuckerman, M. and M. Kuhlman. (2000). Personality and Risk-Taking: Common Biosocial Factors, *Journal of Personality*, 68: 999–1029.
Zyphur, M. J., J. Narayanan, R. D. Arvey, and G. J. Alexander. (2009). Genetics of Economic Risk Preferences, *Journal of Behavioral Decision Making*, 22: 367–377.

## Further Reading

Allen, L., J. Boudoukh, and A. Saunders. (2004). *Understanding Market, Credit, and Operational Risk: The Value at Risk Approach*. Blackwell Publishers, Boston.
Altman, E. I. and V. M. Kishore. (1996). Almost Everything You Wanted to Know about Recoveries on Defaulted Bonds, *Financial Analysts Journal*, Vol. 52, No. 6 (November/December): 57–64.
Bierwag, G. O., G. G. Kaufman, and A. L. Toevs. (July/August, 1983). Duration: Its Development and Use in Bond Portfolio Management: *Financial Analysts Journal*, July–August: 15–35.

Bodie, Z., A. Kane, and A. Marcus. (2009). *Investments*. Eighth Edition. McGraw-Hill, New York.
Boyle, P. and F. Boyle. (2001). *Derivatives: The Tools that Changed Finance*. Risk Books, London.
Cormac, B. (2009). *Accounting for Financial Instruments*. Wiley, West Sussex, England.
Crosbie, P. and J. Bohn. (2003). *Modeling Default Risk: Modeling Methodology*. Moody's KMV™, New York.
Crouhy, M., D. Galai, and R. Mark. (2006). *The Essentials of Risk Management*. McGraw-Hill, New York.
Doherty, N. A. (2000). *Integrated Risk Management: Techniques and Strategies for Reducing Risk*. McGraw-Hill, New York.
Dwyer, D. W., A. E. Kocagil, and R. M. Stein. (5 April 2004). MOODY'S KMV RISKCALC™ v3.1 Model: Next-Generation Technology for Predictin9 Private Firm Credit Risk; http://www.moodyskmv.com/products/files/RiskCalc_v3_1_Model.pdf
Eitman, D. K., A. I. Stonehill, and M. H. Moffett. (2010). *Multinational Business Finance*. Twelfth Edition, Pearson Education, Inc., Boston.
Fabozzi, F. J. and S. V. Mann. (2010). *Introduction to Fixed Income Analytics: Relative Value Analysis, Risk Measures, and Valuation*. Second Edition. Wiley, New York.
Gregory, J. (2010). *Counterparty Credit Risk: The New Challenge for Global Financial Markets*. Wiley, New York.
Hull, J. C. (2010). *Risk Management and Financial Institutions*. Second Edition. Pearson Education, Inc., Boston.
Jarion, P. (2001). *Value at Risk*. Second Edition. McGraw-Hill, New York.
Katona, G. (1953). Rational Behavior and Economic Behavior, *Psychology Review*, Vol. 60 (July): 307–318.
Linsmeier, T. J. and N. D. Pearson. (1997). Risk Measurement: An Introduction to Value at Risk, *Accounting Horizons*, Vol. 11, No. 1: 107–135.
Markowitz, H. M. (1959). *Portfolio Selection: Efficient Diversification of Investments*. Wiley, New York.
McDonald, R. L. (2009). *Fundamentals of Derivatives Markets*. Pearson Educational, Inc., Boston.
Mishkin, F. (1999). *The Economics of Money, Banking and Financial Markets*. Fifth Edition. Addison-Wesley Publishing Co., Boston.
Officer, L. H. (1976). Purchasing Power-Parity Theory of Exchange Rates: A Review Article. *Staff Papers, International Monetary Fund*, Vol. 23, No. 1 (Mar., 1976), pp. 1–60.
Pearson, N. and C. Smithson (2002). VAR—The State of Play, *Review of Financial Economics*, Vol. 11: 175–189.
Pratt, J. W. (1964). Risk Aversion in the Small and in the Large. *Econometrica*, Vol. 32, Nos. 1&2: 122–136.
Ramirez, J. (2007). *Accounting for Derivatives: Advanced Hedging Under IFRS*. Wiley, West Sussex, England.
Rayan, S. G. (2007). *Financial Instruments and Institutions: Accounting and Disclosure Rules*. Wiley, New York.
Rejda, G. E. (2008). *Principles of Risk Management and Insurance*. Tenth Edition. Pearson Education, Inc., Boston.
Sadr, A. (2009). *Interest Rate Swaps and Their Derivatives: A Practitioner's Guide*. Wiley, New Jersey.
Saunders, A. and M. M. Cornett. (2008). *Financial Institutions Management: A Risk Management Approach*. Sixth Edition. McGraw-Hill, New York.
Shubert, S. and T. C. Miller (December 20, 2008). "At Siemens, Bribery Was Just a Line Item." *The New York Times*. http://www.nytimes.com/2008/12/21/business/worldbusiness/21siemens.html?_r=0
Simon, H. A. (1957). *Models of Man*. Wiley, New York.
Stoll, H. and R. Whaley. (1988). Futures and Options on Stock Indexes: Economic Purpose, Arbitrage and Market Structure, *Review of Futures Markets*, Vol. 7: 224–248.
Trieschmann, J. S. and S. G. Gustavson. (1998). *Risk Management and Insurance*. Tenth Edition. South-Western, Cincinnati.
Trombley, M. A. (2003). *Accounting for Derivatives and Hedging*. McGraw-Hill, New York.
von Winterfeldt, D. and W. Edwards (1986). *Decision Analysis and Behavioral Research*. Cambridge University Press, Cambridge, United Kingdom.
Wilmott, P. (2007). *Paul Wilmott Introduces Quantitative Finance*. Wiley, New York.

## Other Information Sources

### Regulators

Accounting Standards Codification (ASC): www.fasb.org. (All U.S. GAAP references are under Accounting Standards Codification since 2000)
Alder Financial: Glossary: http://alderfinancial.com/Financial%20Glossary.htm

International Financial Reporting Standards (IFRS): www.ifrs.org
Securities and Exchange Commission (SEC): www.sec.gov (all rulings of the SEC are under this government website)
Financial Service Authority (FSA); the United Kingdom regulatory body: www.fsa.gov.uk

## Websites Relating to Specific Topics

"Aegon N. V., Floating Rate Perpetual Capital Securities." http://www.quantumonline.com/search.cfm?tickersymbol=AEB&sopt=symbol
Convertibles: SEC educational note on: http://www.sec.gov/answers/convertibles.htm
Chicago Board of Options Exchange: https://www.cboe.com/Institutional/IndexFlex.aspx
Definitions of four different benchmarks for LIBOR and EURIBOR can be found at http://www.euribor-ebf.eu/.
Dictionary http://dictionary.reference.com/browse/risk http://www.rmartin.com/risk_defined.html.
FASB Derivatives Implementation Group. (2001). Statement 133 Implementation Issue C10: http://www.fasb.org/derivatives/issuec10.shtml
FASB Derivatives Implementation Group. (2006). Statement 133 Implementation Issue No. A1: http://www.fasb.org/derivatives/issuea1.shtml
FLEX® Options: https://www.cboe.com/Institutional/IndexFlex.aspx
Forms of privately written option and swap contracts:

- http://www.commbank.com.au/business/agribusiness/commodities-risk-management/cotton/consumer-options.aspx
- http://www.commbank.com.au/business/agribusiness/commodities-risk-management/wool/consumer-swaps.aspx

Futures contract specification: An example from CME-NYMEX: http://www.cmegroup.com/trading/metals/ferrous/hrc-steel_contract_specifications.html
Warrant subscription example: London Stock Exchange announcement on warrant subscription: http://www.londonstockexchange.com/exchange/news/market-news/market-news-detail.html?announcementId=11039365
On the history of Chicago Mercantile Exchange since 1989: http://en.wikipedia.org/wiki/Chicago_Mercantile_Exchange
Natural Gas trading: www.naturalgas.org
RiskMetrics products: http://www.msci.com/products/riskmetrics.html
Shaughnessy Financial. Glossary: http://www.shaughnessyfinancial.com/glossary.php?show=y
Soybean: Information source: http://entnemdept.ufl.edu/creatures/veg/bean/brown_marmorated_stink_bug.htm
SEC case of Joseph Jett: http://www.sec.gov/litigation/aljdec/id127cff.htm
US Bancorp 6.5% Fixed to Floating Perpetual Preferred Stock (Non-Cumulative): http://www.dividendyield-hunter.com/USBM.html
US Treasury Zero-Coupon Curve: http://www.bloomberg.com/apps/quote?ticker=F08203M:IND
Variable step-up bonds: An example of: http://www.one-financial.com/en_investment_solutions_variable_step_up_bonds_series_1.asp
Volume of trade and other information: www.isda.org
Warrant Subscription: Example: http://www.londonstockexchange.com/exchange/news/market-news/market-news-detail.html?announcementId=11039365

## Annual Reports and Filings with Regulators

American Airlines, Form 10-K, 2006: http://sec.edgar-online.com/american-airlines-inc/10-k-annual-report/2006/02/24/section13.aspx
Bank of America, 2009: http://www.sec.gov/Archives/edgar/data/70858/000119312509041126/d10k.htm
Barclays plc Annual Report 2010: http://group.barclays.com/about-barclays/investor-relations/financial-results-and-publications/annual-reports
Coca-Cola, Form 10-K, 2009: http://investing.businessweek.com/research/stocks/financials/drawFiling.asp?docKey=136–0001047469100014 76–1PFCKABMTRA5RALS1H2O2MV0O9&docFormat=HTM&formType=10-K

ConnMed, Form 10-K, 2010: http://www.faqs.org/sec-filings/100225/CONMED-CORP_10-K/

Dell, Form 10-K, 2010: http://i.dell.com/sites/content/corporate/financials/en/Documents/fy10-year-in-review/FY10_Form10K_Final.pdf

Deutsche Telekom AG, Bonn, Federal Republic of Germany as Guarantor for the Bonds issued by Deutsche Telekom International Finance B.V.: www.telekom.com/static/-/54298/3/mandatory-convertible-bond-2006-si

E. I. Du Ponte de Nemours: http://www.sec.gov/Archives/edgar/data/30554/000003055412000005/dd-12312011x10k.htm#s6CE33D84ABB40CA4444DAAD246B0DA62

EADS (European Aeronautic Defence and Space Company) 2010 Annual Report:

- http://www.eads.com/eads/int/en/investor-relations/events-reports/annual-report/2010.html
- http://applications.eads.com/eads/investor-relations/int/annual-report2010/data/FS_EV_050511_PDFi.pdf

FDIC (Federal Deposit Insurance Corporation) 2009 Annual Report, IV Financial Statements and Notes: http://www.fdic.gov/about/strategic/report/2009annualreport/statements_dif_2.html

Google, Inc., Form 10-K, 2011: http://www.sec.gov/Archives/edgar/data/1288776/000119312512025336/d260164d10k.htm

HealthSouth, Form 10-Q, March 31, 2011: http://investor.healthsouth.com/secfiling.cfm?filingID= 785161– 11–32

Intel, Form 10-K, 2011; Item 7, p. 25: http://www.sec.gov/Archives/edgar/data/50863/000095012310015237/f54119e10vk.htm#111

Landsvirkjun (Iceland) Annual Reports: http://www.landsvirkjun.com/about-us/reports/

London Stock Exchange: http://www.londonstockexchange.com/exchange/news/market-news/market-news-detail.html?announcementId=11039365

MidSouth Bank, Form 10-K, 2012: http://www.midsouthbanking.com/pdf/MSB2011–10K.pdf

JPMorgan Chase, Form 10-K, 2010: http://www.sec.gov/Archives/edgar/data/19617/000095012311019773/y86143e10vk.htm

Seagate Technology Holdings, Form 10-Q, May 2009, pp. 96–97: http://files.shareholder.com/downloads/SEA/2068719678x0xS1193125–09–100353/1137789/filing.pdf

Xerox Corporation (p. 97 of the Annual Report and p. 185 of Form 10-K for 2010): http://services.corporate-ir.net/SEC.Enhanced/SecCapsule.aspx?c=104414&fid=73989

# INDEX

Page numbers in italics refer to tables and figures.